Lecture Notes in Computer Science   8620

Commenced Publication in 1973
Founding and Former Series Editors:
Gerhard Goos, Juris Hartmanis, and Jan van Leeuwen

T0212730

Antonis Bikakis   Paul Fodor
Dumitru Roman (Eds.)

Rules on the Web

From Theory to Applications

8th International Symposium, RuleML 2014
Co-located with the 21st European Conference
on Artificial Intelligence, ECAI 2014
Prague, Czech Republic, August 18-20, 2014
Proceedings

 Springer

Volume Editors

Antonis Bikakis
University College London
Department of Information Studies
Gower Street, London WC1E 6BT, UK
E-mail: a.bikakis@ucl.ac.uk

Paul Fodor
Stony Brook University
Department of Computer Science
Stony Brook, NY 11794, USA
E-mail: pfodor@cs.stonybrook.edu

Dumitru Roman
SINTEF, University of Oslo
Forskningsveien 1, 0314 Oslo, Norway
E-mail: dumitru.roman@sintef.no

ISSN 0302-9743   e-ISSN 1611-3349
ISBN 978-3-319-09869-2   e-ISBN 978-3-319-09870-8
DOI 10.1007/978-3-319-09870-8
Springer Cham Heidelberg New York Dordrecht London

Library of Congress Control Number: 2014945231

LNCS Sublibrary: SL 2 – Programming and Software Engineering

Typesetting: Camera-ready by author, data conversion by Scientific Publishing Services, Chennai, India

Printed on acid-free paper

Springer is part of Springer Science+Business Media (www.springer.com)

Volume Editors

Antonis Bikakis
University College London
Department of Information Studies
Gower Street, London WC1E 6BT, UK
E-mail: a.bikakis@ucl.ac.uk

Paul Fodor
Stony Brook University
Department of Computer Science
Stony Brook, NY 11794, USA
E-mail: pfodor@cs.stonybrook.edu

Dumitru Roman
SINTEF, University of Oslo
Forskningsveien 1, 0314 Oslo, Norway
E-mail: dumitru.roman@sintef.no

ISSN 0302-9743   e-ISSN 1611-3349
ISBN 978-3-319-09869-2   e-ISBN 978-3-319-09870-8
DOI 10.1007/978-3-319-09870-8
Springer Cham Heidelberg New York Dordrecht London

Library of Congress Control Number: 2014945231

LNCS Sublibrary: SL 2 – Programming and Software Engineering

Typesetting: Camera-ready by author, data conversion by Scientific Publishing Services, Chennai, India

Printed on acid-free paper

Springer is part of Springer Science+Business Media (www.springer.com)

Antonis Bikakis   Paul Fodor
Dumitru Roman (Eds.)

Rules on the Web
From Theory to Applications

8th International Symposium, RuleML 2014
Co-located with the 21st European Conference
on Artificial Intelligence, ECAI 2014
Prague, Czech Republic, August 18-20, 2014
Proceedings

 Springer

Preface

The International Web Rule Symposium, RuleML, has evolved from an annual series of international workshops since 2002, international conferences in 2005 and 2006, and international symposia since 2007. RuleML 2014, the eighth symposium of this series, collocated in Prague, Czech Republic, with the 21st European Conference on Artificial Intelligence (ECAI-2014), brought together researchers and practitioners from industry, academia, and the broader AI community, and presented new research results and applications in the field of rules. It was a premier place to meet and to exchange ideas from all fields of rules and reasoning technology, and created an important bridge between academia and industry in the field of rules, logics, and semantic technology, stimulating the cooperation and interoperability between business and research.

This annual symposium is the flagship event of the Rule Markup and Modeling Initiative (RuleML). RuleML (http://ruleml.org) is a non-profit umbrella organization. It consists of several technical groups organized by representatives from academia, industry, and public sectors working on rule technologies and applications. Its aim is to promote the study, research, and application of rules in heterogeneous, distributed environments, such as the Web. RuleML acts as an intermediary between various "specialized" rule vendors, industrial and academic research groups, as well as standardization bodies such as W3C, OMG, OASIS, and ISO. One of its major contributions is the Rule Markup Language, a unifying family of XML-serialized rule languages spanning across all industrially relevant kinds of Web rules.

The technical program of RuleML 2014 included presentations of novel rule-based technologies, such as Semantic Web rule languages and standards, rule engines, formal and operational semantics, and rule-based systems. Besides the regular track, RuleML 2014 included three special tracks: Rules and Human Language Technology, Learning (Business) Rules from Data, and Legal Rules and Norms. These tracks reflect the significant role of rules in several research and application areas, which include: the relation between natural language and rules, automation of business rules generation from existing data, and aspects related to legal rules and norms for Web and corporate environments.

Special highlights of this year's RuleML Symposium included two keynote talks, two invited talks, and one tutorial:

- Prof. Luc De Raedt (Katholieke Universiteit Leuven, Belgium): "On Probability, Rules and Learning" (Keynote talk)
- Prof. Adrian Paschke (Freie Universität Berlin, Germany): "Rules, Events and Actions in Semantic Complex Event Processing" (Keynote talk)
- Prof. Arild Waaler (University of Oslo, Norway): "Efficient Mapping Rules in OBDA" (Invited talk)

– Prof. Jürgen Angele (Procitec GmbH and Semedy AG, Zug, Switzerland): "Rule-Based Clinical Decision Support" (Invited talk)
– Prof. Johannes Fürnkranz (TU Darmstadt, Germany): "Rule Learning" (Tutorial)

In addition, the program included the 8th International Rule Challenge, dedicated to practical experiences with rule-based applications, and the RuleML 2014 Doctoral Consortium, which focused on PhD research in the area of rules and markup languages.

This volume includes 17 full papers and six short papers, which were presented during the technical program of RuleML 2014, as well as one paper and two abstracts for the keynote and invited talks. The papers were selected from 48 submissions through a peer-review process. Each paper was reviewed by at least two members of the Program Committee and the Program Committee chairs.

A special thanks is due to the excellent Program Committee for their hard work in reviewing the submitted papers. Their criticism and very useful comments and suggestions were instrumental in achieving a high-quality publication. We also thank the symposium authors for submitting high-quality papers, responding to the reviewers comments, and abiding by our production schedule. We further wish to thank the keynote and invited speakers for contributing their inspiring talks. We are very grateful to the organizers of the 21st European Conference on Artificial Intelligence (ECAI-2014) for enabling this fruitful collocation with RuleML 2014. RuleML 2014 was financially supported by industrial companies, research institutes, and universities and was technically supported by several professional societies. We wish to thank our sponsors, whose financial support helped us to offer this event, and whose technical support allowed us to attract many high-quality submissions. Last, but not least, we would like to thank the development team of the EasyChair conference management system and our publisher, Springer, for their support in the preparation of this volume and the publication of the proceedings.

August 2014

Antonis Bikakis
Paul Fodor
Dumitru Roman

Organization

General Chair

Leora Morgenstern   Leidos Corporation, USA

Program Chairs

Antonis Bikakis   University College London, UK
Paul Fodor   Stony Brook University, USA
Dumitru Roman   SINTEF/University of Oslo, Norway

Local Chairs

Jan Rauch   University of Economics, Prague,
                                     Czech Republic
Tomáš Kliegr   University of Economics, Prague,
                                     Czech Republic
Stanislav Vojíř   University of Economics, Prague,
                                     Czech Republic

Track Chairs

Rules and Human Language Technology

Francois Levy   LIPN, University of Paris, France
Adam Wyner   University of Aberdeen, UK

Learning (Business) Rules from Data

Tomáš Kliegr   University of Economics, Prague,
                                     Czech Republic
Davide Sottara   Arizona State University, USA

Legal Rules and Norms

Monica Palmirani   Universitá di Bologna, Italy
Guido Governatori   NICTA, Australia

International Rule Challenge Chairs

Theodore Patkos	FORTH-ICS, Greece
Adam Wyner	University of Aberdeen, UK
Adrian Giurca	BTU Cottbus-Senftenberg, Germany

Dotoral Consortium Chairs

Petros Stefaneas	National Technical University of Athens, Greece
Monica Palmirani	Universitá di Bologna, Italy

Publicity Chair

John Hall	Model Systems, UK

Social Media Chair

Adrian Giurca	BTU Cottbus-Senftenberg, Germany

Rule Responder Chairs

Adam Wyner	University of Aberdeen, UK
Zhili Zhao	Freie Universität Berlin, Germany

Program Committee

Darko Anicic
Grigoris Antoniou
Tara Athan
Martin Atzmueller
Ebrahim Bagheri
Nick Bassiliades
Bernhard Bauer
Guido Boella
Johan Bos
Jerome Boyer
Lars Braubach
Christoph Bussler
Federico Chesani
Abdelghani Chibani
Horatiu Cirstea
Jack G. Conrad

Bruno Cremilleux
Claudia D'Amato
Agnieszka Dardzinska
Christian De Sainte Marie
Juergen Dix
Schahram Dustdar
Vadim Ermolayev
Riguzzi Fabrizio
Jacob Feldman
Michael Fink
Giorgos Flouris
Enrico Francesconi
Fred Freitas
Norbert E. Fuchs
Johannes Fürnkranz
Aldo Gangemi

Dragan Gasevic
Martin Giese
Adrian Giurca
Guido Governatori
Matthias Grabmair
Brigitte Grau
Christophe Gravier
Alex Guazzelli
Giancarlo Guizzardi
Ioannis Hatzilygeroudis
Stijn Heymans
Martin Holena
Yuh-Jong Hu
Jiří Ivánek
Tomas Kliegr
Stratos Kontopoulos
Tobias Kuhn
Brian Lam
Evelina Lamma
Florian Lemmerich
Francois Levy
Senlin Liang
Francesca Lisi
Emiliano Lorini
Yue Ma
Michael Maher
Petr Masa
Angelo Montanari
Grzegorz Nalepa
Jose Ignacio Panach Navarrete
Adeline Nazarenko

Monica Palmirani
Jeffrey Parsons
Adrian Paschke
Theodore Patkos
Célia Da Costa Pereira
Wim Peters
Luis Ferreira Pires
Mark Proctor
Zbyszek Ras
Antonino Rotolo
Luiz Olavo Bonino Da Silva Santos
Giovanni Sartor
Rolf Schwitter
Guy Sharon
Milan Simunek
Davide Sottara
Ahmet Soylu
Petros Stefaneas
Umberto Straccia
Terrance Swift
Daniela Tiscornia
Ioan Toma
Leon van der Torre
Wamberto Vasconcelos
Giulia Venturi
George Vouros
Renata Wassermann
Radboud Winkels
Adam Wyner
Amal Zouaq

External Reviewers

Harald Beck
Krzysztof Kluza
Benjamin Jailly
Konstantinos Kotis

Antonis Koukourikos
Christoph Redl
Kia Teymourian

RuleML 2014 Sponsors

Model Systems

ShareLaTeX

Partner Organizations

Invited Talks

On Probability, Rules and Learning (Abstract)

Luc De Raedt

Department of Computer Science, Katholieke Universiteit Leuven
Celestijnenlaan 200A, POBox 2402, 3001 Heverlee, Belgium
{firstname.lastname}@cs.kuleuven.be

Abstract. Rules represent knowledge about the world that can be used for reasoning. However, the world is inherently uncertain, which may affect both rules and data. Indeed, rules capturing expert knowledge are only an approximation of a complex reality, and data may be uncertain due to missing values, noisy measurents, or ambiguities.

While a wide variety of formalisms and techniques exist to cope with uncertainty, the approach taken will be based on probabilistic (logic) programming [3]. More specifically, it shall be centered around the probabilistic Prolog, ProbLog [2] (see also http://dtai.cs.kuleuven.be/problog/), which extends the programming language Prolog with probabilistic facts and is based on Sato's distribution semantics [7]. It combines the deductive power of Prolog with the ability to state the belief that certain facts are true, very much as in probabilistic databases. As such it is a natural rule-based representation for dealing with uncertainty. ProbLog supports probabilistic inference, that is, it can compute the probability $P(Q|E)$ of a query Q given some evidence E [5].

It also supports learning. To learn parameters, it starts from examples that are partial interpretations (that is, partial descriptions of a possible world), and employs an Expectation-Maximisation approach [5]. ProbLog rules can be learned using a generalization of traditional rule-learning algorithms [4]. These rules are learned form uncertain data.

ProbLog has been applied to a number of applications in domains such as bioinformatics [1], action- and activity recognition [8] and robotics [6].

References

1. De Maeyer, D., Renkens, J., Cloots, L., De Raedt, L., Marchal, K.: Phenetic: network-based interpretation of unstructured gene lists in e. coli. Molecular BioSystems 9(7), 1594–1603 (2013)
2. De Raedt, L., Kimmig, A., Toivonen, H.: ProbLog: A probabilistic Prolog and its application in link discovery. In: Proceedings of the 20th International Joint Conference on Artificial Intelligence, IJCAI-2007 (2007)
3. De Raedt, L., Kimmig, A.: Probabilistic programming concepts. CoRR abs/1312.4328 (2013)
4. De Raedt, L., Thon, I.: Probabilistic rule learning. In: Frasconi, P., Lisi, F.A. (eds.) ILP 2010. LNCS, vol. 6489, pp. 47–58. Springer, Heidelberg (2011)

5. Fierens, D., Van den Broeck, G., Renkens, J., Shterionov, D., Gutmann, B., Thon, I., Janssens, G., De Raedt, L.: Inference and learning in probabilistic logic programs using weighted Boolean formulas. Theory and Practice of Logic Programming (TPLP) FirstView (2014)
6. Nitti, D., De Laet, T., De Raedt, L.: A particle filter for hybrid relational domains. In: 2013 IEEE/RSJ International Conference on Intelligent Robots and Systems (IROS), pp. 2764–2771. IEEE (2013)
7. Sato, T.: A statistical learning method for logic programs with distribution semantics. In: Proceedings of the 12th International Conference on Logic Programming, ICLP-1995 (1995)
8. Skarlatidis, A., Paliouras, G., Artikis, A., Vouros, G.A.: Probabilistic event calculus for event recognition. CoRR abs/1207.3270 (2012)

Reaction RuleML 1.0 for Rules, Events and Actions in Semantic Complex Event Processing

Adrian Paschke

Freie Universitaet Berlin, Germany
paschke@inf.fu-berlin.de

Abstract. Reaction RuleML is a standardized rule markup language for the representation and interchange of reaction rules. This paper gives an introduction to the core knowledge representation mechanisms of Reaction RuleML 1.0 such as multi-sorted signatures and their interpretation, action primitives for knowledge updates, interchange and testing, order-sorted external type systems and the Reaction RuleML metamodel, scopes and mode declarations, semantic profiles, imports of documents, modules and messages. These mechanisms form the basis for an adequate treatment of rules, events and actions, as needed in semantic complex event processing (SCEP), such as, interchange, translation and testing based on the intended semantics defined in semantic profiles; modularization and distribution of knowledge interfaces with their signatures defining, e.g., complex event detection patterns; closed scoped reasoning on top of scoped modules with dynamic constructive views on meta knowledge; transactional complex actions; conversation based message interchange for question answering (Q&A) and rule-based agent architectures such as RuleResponder, etc.

Efficient Mapping Rules in OBDA

Arild Waaler, Dag Hovland, Martin G. Skjæveland,
and Evgenij Thorstensen

Department of Informatics, University of Oslo, Norway
{arild, hovland, martige, evgenit}@ifi.uio.no

Ontology-based information systems (IS) need to combine reasoning and query answering over ontologies with building and maintain collections of mappings between ontologies and data sources. In its most general form, a mapping is a rule $\phi \rightsquigarrow \psi$ stating that a query ϕ (the body) over the data sources corresponds to a query ψ (the head) over the ontology. To answer the query ψ, an IS has to find the mappings related to ψ, execute the queries they specify over the data sources, then use the mappings to map the answers back to the ontological vocabulary. The choice of mappings is therefore tightly connected to the complexity of query answering, both over ontologies and databases.

A well-studied type of mappings are global-as-view (GAV) mappings, common in Ontology-based data access (OBDA) settings. A GAV mapping has the form $Q_{DB}(\boldsymbol{x}) \rightsquigarrow A(\boldsymbol{x})$, and associates the answers to a query Q over the data sources to a single atomic concept or role A from the ontology. Such mappings enjoy some nice computational properties. In particular, the lack of existential variables in the right-hand side allows for the efficient unfolding of an ontology query into queries over the data sources, as well as efficient checking of properties such as redundancy and inconsistency.

Another example of a useful type of mappings are GAV mappings where each variable on the right-hand side occurs once, and constants do not occur. Such a mapping $Q_{DB}(\boldsymbol{x}) \rightsquigarrow A(\boldsymbol{x})$ can always be applied to a query containing A, and unification between the right-hand side of this mapping and the query is simply a matching. The resulting substitution is thus a homomorphism from the mapping head to a subquery. As a consequence, with these types of mappings, given two queries Q and Q' over the ontology with $Q \subseteq Q'$, an unfolding ϕ' of Q' can be transformed into an unfolding of Q by applying the homomorphism σ that witnesses the query containment to ϕ'.

More broadly we will demonstrate the role that mapping rules play in the development, use and inner workings of an OBDA IS and illustrate how queries over an ontology is rewritten to SQL queries over a large corporate data store. We will also illustrate the problem of exponential blow-up of rewritten queries caused by the complex relationship between the ontology, mappings, and databases. The example material that we will use are queries collected from geologists with a real need to be able to efficiently formulate complex queries over multiple databases, and ontology and mappings developed in an effort to solve the problem; developed the context of the Optique project.[1]

---

[1] optique-project.eu.

Table of Contents

Rules and Human Language Technology

Learning (Business) Rules from Data

Legal Rules and Norms

Reaction RuleML 1.0 for Rules, Events and Actions in Semantic Complex Event Processing

Adrian Paschke

Freie Universitaet Berlin, Germany
paschke@inf.fu-berlin.de

Abstract. Reaction RuleML is a standardized rule markup language for the representation and interchange of reaction rules. This paper gives an introduction to the core knowledge representation mechanisms of Reaction RuleML 1.0 such as multi-sorted signatures and their interpretation, action primitives for knowledge updates, interchange and testing, order-sorted external type systems and the Reaction RuleML metamodel, scopes and mode declarations, semantic profiles, imports of documents, modules and messages. These mechanisms form the basis for an adequate treatment of rules, events and actions, as needed in Semantic Complex Event Processing (SCEP), such as, interchange, translation and testing based on the intended semantics defined in semantic profiles; modularization and distribution of knowledge interfaces with their signatures defining, e.g., complex event detection patterns; closed scoped reasoning on top of scoped modules with dynamic constructive views on meta knowledge; transactional complex actions; conversation based message interchange for Question Answering (Q&A) and rule-based agent architectures such as RuleResponder, etc.

1 Reaction RuleML for Reaction Rules

RuleML is a knowledge representation language designed for the interchange of the major kinds of Web rules in an XML format that is uniform across various rule logics and platforms. It has broad coverage and is defined as an extensible family of sublanguages, whose modular system of schemas permits rule interchange with high precision. RuleML 1.0 encompasses both Deliberation RuleML 1.0 and Reaction RuleML 1.0[1].

Reaction RuleML is a standardized rule markup language and semantic interchange format for reaction rules and rule-based event processing. Reaction rules include distributed Complex Event Processing (CEP), Knowledge Representation (KR) calculi, as well as Event-Condition-Action (ECA) rules, Production (CA) rules, and Trigger (EA) rules. [17] Reaction RuleML 1.0 incorporates this reactive spectrum of rules into RuleML 1.0 employing a system of step-wise extensions of the Deliberation RuleML 1.0 foundation starting with an extension of Derivation Rules (DR) for spatio-temporal-interval reasoning. [2,20]

---

[1] http://reaction.ruleml.org

A. Bikakis et al. (Eds.): RuleML 2014, LNCS 8620, pp. 1–21, 2014.

Reaction RuleML defines a generic rule syntax distinguishing between metadata, interface and implementation enabling distributed and modularized (scoped) rulebases and rules. The syntax comes with predefined algebra operators and an ontological RuleML metamodel for the definition of general concepts such as events, actions, time, intervals, space, processes, agents and messages. It supports extensible generic syntax elements and sorted/typed extensions with external ontologies and procedural attachments. Semantic Profiles attach semantics to Reaction RuleML rulebases and messages and enable the semantic interpretation and interchange, e.g., in distributed rule-based agent system such as RuleResponder[2], and rule-based Complex Event Processing (CEP) architectures [23].

This paper is an introduction to the core mechanism of Reaction RuleML as representation language and interchange format for reaction rules, events and actions. The survey is organizes as follows: Section 2 gives a compact overview of the terms, formulas and primitives in the Reaction RuleML language. Section 3 describes the approach towards multi-sorted signature definitions and section 4 defines the multi-sorted semantics for such signatures. Section 5 explains how external type systems and the Reaction RuleML metamodel can be used for external sorts (types). The mechanism of dialects and semantic profiles, defining the intended semantics for the evaluation of Reaction RuleML knowledge bases, is described in section 6. The mechanisms for modularization with scopes and scoped reasoning is introduced in section 7 and the conclusion in section 8 highlights how this core mechanism described in this paper can be used for expressive and efficient rule-based Semantic Complex Event Processing (SCEP).

2   Introduction to the Reaction RuleML Language

This section introduces some of the main language elements of Reaction RuleML. The XML element (tag) names and their "@" attributes names are given in brackets. Their full content models and definition can be found in the Reaction RuleML 1.0 specification[3]. For better understanding, we sometimes also present them in a non-normative formal notation in this paper. The language of Reaction RuleML includes different types of terms, formulas and performatives:

Definition 1. *Terms*

- *constants, which are distinguished into **individual terms** (Ind) (built from the constant symbols) and **datatype terms** (Data) (typically from an external data type system), and **variables** (Var) (using variable symbols).*
- *positional **complex terms** (Expr) of the form $t(t_1...t_n)$, where t_1, ..., t_n are terms themselves, and **list terms** (Plex) of the form $[t_1...t_n]^4$ including empty lists [].*

---

[2] http://responder.ruleml.org [18]

[3] http://wiki.ruleml.org/index.php/Content_Models_of_Reaction_RuleML_1.0

[4] Special interpretations of lists can be introduced in semantic profiles, e.g. $[p\ t_1...t_n] \equiv p(t_1...t_n)$.

- **uniterms** *(as in SWSL [7]) are HiLog [6]) terms, which are generalizations of (first-order logic) complex terms, where the expression symbols can be used as individuals, functions and predicates and where variables are allowed to occur anywhere in the term including the function name, predicate name and object identifier name of an individual.*
- *unpositional* **slotted terms** *(slot) (as in POSL [3]) $t(slot_1 - > t_1...slot_n - > t_n)$, with order of the slots (named arguments) being immaterial.*
- **frame terms** *(as in SWSL [7], PSOA RuleML [4] and RIF [5,1]), which are based on F-Logic [8], of the form $t_{oid}[slot_1 - > t_1...slot_n - > t_n]$, where t_{oid} (frame object identifier, oid), $slot_1$, ..., $slot_n$ (slot attributes of the frame object), $t_1,...,t_n$ (attribute values) are terms themselves and the order of the frame slots is immaterial.*
- **psoa terms** *(positional-slotted, object-applicative) (as in PSOA RuleML [4]) which apply a function or predicate symbol, possibly instantiated by an object, to zero or more positional or slotted arguments, $o\#f([t_{1,1}...t_{1,n_1}] ... [t_{m,1}...t_{m,n_m}]p_1 - > v_1 ... p_k - > v_k)$ is a psoa term if $f \in Const$ and $o, t_{1,1}, ..., t_{1,n_1} , ..., t_{m,1}, ..., t_{m,n_m} , p_1, ..., p_k, v_1, ..., v_k, m \geq 0, k \geq 0$ are base terms.*
- **equality terms** *(Equal) $t = s$, where t and s are terms and equation $=$ being unoriented (symmetric) or oriented (directed).*
- **typed terms** *(@type) (as in Rule Responder [15,18] and RBSLA [10,12]) of the form $t\#s$, where t is a term of type s, i.e. all individuals of t are members of s.[5]*
- **reified terms** *(Reify) (as in SWSL [7]) treat any RuleML content as a term.*
- **metadata terms** *(meta) (as in RBSLA's metadata annotated labelled logic and used in Reaction RuleML's scoped reasoning) are any Reaction RuleML terms t used in metadata formulas to define meta knowledge.*
- **external terms** *(@iri) (as in Rule Responder [15,18] and RBSLA [10,12]) t_{iri}, where iri is a resource identifier referencing or querying external data (from external data sources / knowledge bases) or externally defined built-in functions or predicate invocations (such as libraries from RuleML, SWRL [24], RIF DTB [24])), as well as procedural attachments (as implemented e.g. in Prova [21]).*
- **remote messaging terms** *(Send, Receive) (as in Rule Responder [15,18] and implemented e.g. in Prova [21]) of the form $t@a$ where t is a RuleML term which is remote from @a.*

With uniterms Reaction RuleML provides the ability to reify certain formulas, so that they can be used as terms, and vice versa to represent these uniterms as formulas, which are then interpreted as truth or modal statements. This form of uniterm reification in Reaction RuleML is restricted to objects (which are treated as "first-class" citizens in the Reaction RuleML language) of different sorts such as *events* (**Event**), *actions* (**Action**), *times/spatials/intervals* (**Time**,

---

[5] Subclass relationship in Reaction RuleML is represented by a rule $s_1(t\#s_1) \rightarrow s_2(t\#s_2)$.

Spatial, Interval), *operators* (Operator), *fluents* (Fluent), *states* and *situations* (Situation). This gives Reaction RuleML dialects the expressiveness of HiLog [6], enabling them to treat such uniterms as objects and as statements about objects at the same time, which is necessary, e.g., for active processing of object operations and functions as well as the model-theoretic truth interpretation of their effects. Reaction RuleML dialects and their semantic profiles by defining the signatures can introduce restrictions on the use of uniterms, e.g., permitting using them only as predicates (**non-reified dialects**) or as individual objects and functions (**reified dialects**). While the default interpretation in non-reified dialects is by means of (truth) value interpretation, in reified active dialects their interpretation is as terms or as effect-full active functions in active dialects. In dialects where there might be ambiguity (e.g., uniterms are used both as formulas and as terms), the intended interpretation can be made explicit by the attribute @per with fillers "copy" (uninterpreted complex term), "value" ((truth) value interpretation), "modal" (modal interpretation) and "effect" (active effect-full function), as the following examples in Reaction RuleML XML syntax illustrate:

```
<!-- action execution -->     <!-- complex term -->     <!-- (truth) value interpretation -->
<Action>                      <Action>                   <Action>
    <Expr per="effect">           <Expr per="copy">          <Expr per="value">
        <Fun>book</Fun>               <Fun>book</Fun>            <Fun>book</Fun>
        <Var>Flight</Var>             <Var>Flight</Var>          <Var>Flight</Var>
    </Expr>                       </Expr>                    </Expr>
</Action>                     </Action>                  </Action>
```

This attribute is also applied to equality terms and external terms which can be used as predicates and as functions. External terms reference or query (using the @iri attribute with XPath/Xpointer queries) an external resource. Furthermore, typed terms (@type) can refer to internal types defined by the local vocabulary term name of a type signature, as well as external types defined in an external type systems (see section 5). Note, the different sorts of Reaction RuleML terms are not necessarily distinct, e.g., a uniterm can be defined by an external term and can be given a type, making it an external typed uniterm.

A more general form of **reification** is supported by reified terms (Reify) which allow any RuleML formula or term available within the current dialect as content, treating it as a term for making statements about statements on which meta reasoning can be preformed.

While simple terms and uninterpreted complex terms are not formulas, the other Reaction RuleML terms, such as uniterms, equality terms, etc., can be used to represent atomic formulas. More general formulas are built from atomic formulas via logical connectives and operators (e.g., modal operators).

Definition 2. *(Formulas) A* **formula** *can have the following forms:*

- **Atoms**: *An atomic formula (Atom) is a formula.*
- **Connectives/Operators**: *conjunction (And), disjunction (Or), negation (classical negation (Neg), default negation (Naf) and polymorphic negation (Negation), which can be given a specific interpretation by a semantic profile*

(Profile) and/or an assigned type (@type), e.g., inflationary negation as in production rules, explicit negation as weaker form of true classical negation in extended logic programs, etc.), modal operators (Operator), where the modal operator is given as an operator type (using @type), e.g. temporal, alethic, deontic modal operators), algebra operators (various predefined operators from the temporal, spatial, interval, event, action algebras of Reaction RuleML, as well as the generic (Operator), which can reuse operator types defined in external vocabularies).

- **Quantifiers**: *universal (guarded) quantification ("Forall declare variables such that guard formula"), existential (guarded) quantification ("Exists declare variables such that guard formula") and a generic (guarded) quantifier ("Quantifier declare variables such that guard formula"), which can be given a specific interpretation by a semantic profile and/or an assigned type).*
- **Signatures**: *a signature formula (signature) defines the signature of a knowledge formula, e.g., a rule interface signature, event pattern signature, frame type signature, etc.*
- **Constraints**: *a constraint formula is either a **guard** constraint / pre constraint (guard) or a post constraint (after), an entailment constraint (Entails), an constraint rule (e.g., a integrity constraint of the form "if [constraints] then false", a weight / cardinality rule, a choice rules, etc.), or a **test** (with pre-defined expected entailed **answers**).*
- **Rules**: *a rule (Rule) is a formula made up of internal formulas (rule parts) which vary depending on the type of rule. In its most general form in Reaction RuleML it consists of the following rule parts:*
  - **on**: *the on formula (on(ϕ)), where ϕ is an **event** formula (Event) defining possibly quantified event pattern signatures (signature) for atomic events or complex events described by event algebra operators.*
  - **if**: *the if formula (if(ϕ)), where ϕ is a **condition** formula (also called **pre-constraint** condition) consisting of atoms (Atom), connectives (And, Or, negations), operators (modal operators), constraints and quantifiers.*
  - **then**: *the then formula (then(ϕ)), where ϕ is a (logical) **conclusion** formula consisting of quantifiers, atoms, negation connectives and a generic operator (which can be typed with logical connectives such as a conjunction and modal operators).*
  - **do**: *the do formula (do(ϕ)), where ϕ is an **action** formula (Action) consisting of quantifiers, atomic actions, complex actions defined by action algebra operators and action performatives (see performatives).*
  - **after**: *the after formula (after(ϕ)), where ϕ is a (**post constraint**) condition formula.*
  - **else**: *the else formula (else(ϕ)), where ϕ is an (else) conclusion formula.*
  - **elseDo**: *the elseDo formula (elseDo(ϕ)), where ϕ is an (alternative) action formula.*
- **Entailments**: *Entailment formulas (Entails) of the form $\phi \vdash \varphi$, where ϕ and φ are rulebase formulas. Entailment formulas are used to assert or*

query that a sequence of formulas in the first rulebase ϕ entails the sequence of formulas in the second rulebase φ.

- **Equivalences**: *An equivalence formula (Equivalence) of the form $\phi \equiv \varphi$ is "syntactic sugar" for a pair of conjoined converse rule formulas.*
- **Facts**: *a fact is an atomic formula (including facts made of uniterms representing events, times, spatial, intervals, etc).*
- **Modals**: *A modal formula is a formula whose main logical operator is a modal operator (Operator(ϕ)). An atomic modal formula is a modal formula which contains one and the only modal operator.*
- **Meta Knowledge**: *meta knowledge formula (@ϕ), where ϕ is a meta knowledge formula represented by an atomic, negation, modal, rule, equivalence, equality, rule or entailment formula using metadata terms.*[6]
- **Queries**: *a query formula (Query) is either an atomic formula, a connective / operator formula (e.g., modal formulas), or a signature formula (e.g., an event pattern signature).*
- **Answers**: *an answer formula (Answer) is the result of a query represented in terms of "solved" formulas (ground atoms, oriented equations with the variable bindings, or entailments).*
- **Messages**: *are structural formulas (Message) used to interchange knowledge.*
- **Rulebases**: *are structural formulas (Rulebase) introducing a static structuring of groups of Reaction RuleML formulas as **modules**.*
- **Document**: *a structural document formula (RuleML) is an (ordered) transactions of **performatives** (knowledge actions) on the **knowledge base (KB)**.*
- **Test Suites**: *Test suites are special structural formulas representing test knowledge bases (TestSuite), consisting of a **Test Assertions** base (Assert) (typically a set of facts, events or actions) and multiple **Test Cases** (TestItem). [9]*

Meta knowledge formulas represent the metadata and the knowledge interface of knowledge implementations / representations.

Definition 3. *(**Metadata and the Knowledge Interface**) The optional explicit meta knowledge comprises descriptive **metadata** (meta) and the **knowledge interface**, which contains information about the knowledge scope (scope), guard constraints (guard), intended semantics (evaluation), explicit signature (signature), qualifying metadata (qualification) and quantifiers (quantification).*

*The **knowledge implementation** is a knowledge instance (a representational knowledge object) of the knowledge interface. Furthermore, several knowledge formulas can have further specialized meta knowledge, such as*

---

[6] Reaction RuleML dialects and semantic profiles might impose further restrictions on the meta knowledge formulas such as permitting only unary formulas consisting of simple name-value pairs (@*name*(*value*) or *name* = *value*).

a truth/uncertainty degree *(degree)* for atomic formulas *(Atom)* and equations *(Equal)*, message information *(Message)* such as conversation identifier *(cid)*, protocol *(protocol)*, sender/recevier agent *(sender, receiver)*, etc. Several meta knowledge attributes specify additional information, e.g. about, sort *(@type)*, arity *(@arity)*, cardinality of set values *(@card, @maxCard, @minCard)*, relative weight *(@weight)*, default quantification closure *(@closure)*, inference/execution direction *(@direction)*, ordering *(@index)*, remote resource locator *(@iri)*, global node identifier *(@node)*, internal key and key reference *(@key, @keyref)*, input-output mode declaration *(@mode)*, material implication *(@material)*, equality orientation *(@oriented)*, interpretation semantics of relations and functions *(@per)*, prefix and vocabulary definition for "webized" IRI mappings *(@prefix, @vocab)*, processing/execution safety *(@safety)*, reasoning and execution style *(@style)*, and indeterminism/determinisms of functions and operators *(@val)*.

Rule base formulas *(Rulebase)* introduce a (possibly nested) structuring of groups of knowledge formulas, called **modules** (see section 7). Queries *(Query)* and answers *(Answer)* interpret rule bases as queries and answers from the KB. Tests are special knowledge bases *(TestSuite)* with a test assertion base (ground knowledge formulas) and test items *(TestItem)* consisting of a test query and expected answer. [9] Messages *(Message)* transport RuleML documents as their payload. RuleML documents and messages can be included *(XInclude)* and imported *(Consult)*. A RuleML document is a **RuleML knowledge base** which permits (ordered) transactions of **performatives**, which are (complex) knowledge update actions.

Definition 4. *Performatives* *are (complex) action formulas which perform actions on the knowledge of a Reaction RuleML KB. Reaction RuleML defines performative actions for asserting (Assert), retracting (Retract), updating/modifying (Update), importing/consulting (Consult), querying (Query), answering (Answer), testing (Test), sending (Send), receiving (Receive) and general acting (Action) on knowledge.*

3 Signature Definitions

To determine which terms and formulas are well-formed Reaction RuleML uses signature definitions (**signature**). [13] Signatures are syntactic patterns which define the language structures in which symbols are allowed to occur so that matching instantiations of such signatures are considered to be well-formed.

Definition 5. *(Signature)* *A   signature T is   a   tuple $\langle \overline{T}, \overline{SC}, \overline{MOD}, \overline{C}, arity, sort, scope,   mode \rangle$,   where $\overline{T} = \{T_1, .., T_n\}$ is   the* **signature pattern / signature declaration***, with each T_i and T being symbols denoting signature names, called **sorts**, $\overline{C}$ is the set of constant symbols, called the **universe**, which might be possibly further partitioned into*

- *different non-overlapping domains of discourse, called **scopes**, where $\overline{SC} = \{Sc_1, .., Sc_m\}$ with each $Sc_j \in \overline{(SC)}$ being symbols denoting the scope name of a subset domain of the set of all constants.*
- *pairwise disjoint sets of input-output symbols, called **modes**, where $\overline{MOD} = \{Mod_1, .., Mod_o\}$ with each $Mod_k \in \overline{MOD}$ being symbols denoting the mode of these subsets of all constants*

*The function arity gives the number n of sorts in the signature pattern of a sort T, called the **arity**. The function scope associates with each symbol c in the universe its scope $SC_j \in \overline{SC}$. The function mode associates with each symbol c in the universe its mode $Mod_k \in \overline{MOD}$. The function sort associates with each symbol c in the universe its sort.*

More about scopes and modes can be found in section 7. To support polymorphism Reaction RuleML, in general, allows defining multiple (to countably infinite) signatures with the same signature name, which only differ in their inner definition. However, Reaction RuleML dialects, such as **classical Reaction RuleML dialects**, can restrict this to only allow one signature definition with a unique name per sort.

Reaction RuleML needs to represent knowledge formulas and terms / individual objects of different sorts such as events, actions, time and intervals, states, situations, etc. Reaction RuleML dialects therefore support two possible ways to model different sorts of individuals in a structure. The first one is for **unsorted Reaction RuleML dialects**, which need to be compliant to standard FOL. These dialects assume that there is a single universe of discourse, containing unsorted individuals which are only distinguished by different predicates and functions. The second approach, for **sorted Reaction RuleML dialects**, is to use a multi-sorted signature, which defines several sort domains instead of just one universe of discourse. In the following we define the multi-sorted base signature, which introduces predicates and functions. This signature can be further extended by sorted dialects in Reaction RuleML.

Definition 6. (Multi-sorted Base Signature for Sorted Dialects) *The multi-sorted base signature S_b is defined as a tuple $\langle \overline{T}, \overline{P}, \overline{F}, \overline{C}, \overline{SC}, \overline{MOD}, arity, sort, scope, mode \rangle$ where $\overline{T} = \{T_1, .., T_n\}$ is a set of symbols called **sorts**, $\overline{P}$ is a sequence of predicate symbols $\langle P_1, .., P_n \rangle$, called **predicates**, $\overline{F}$ is a finite sequence of function symbols $\langle F_1, .., F_m \rangle$, called **functions**, and the rest is a signature as defined before. The function sort associates with each predicate, function or constant its sort as follows:*

- *if c is a constant, then $sort(c)$ returns the signature sort T of c.*
- *if p is a predicate of arity k, then $sort(p)$ is a $k+1$-tuple of sorts, $sort(p) = (T_1, .., T_k, T_{k+1})$, where each term t_i of p is of some sort T_j (repetitions are allowed) and T_{k+1} is of sort predicate.*
- *if f is a function of arity k, then $sort(f)$ is a $k+1$-tuple of sorts, $sort(f) = (T1; ::; T_k; T_{k+1})$, where $(T_1; ::; T_k)$ (repititions allowed) defines the sorts of the domain of f and T_{k+1} defines the sort of the range of f.*

Additional meta knowledge can be attached to the knowledge formulas and terms. Reaction RuleML therefore supports a **labelled logic** extension[7], which allows to label knowledge terms and formulas with additional **meta knowledge annotations**. The extended signature with additional meta knowledge is the combined signature of the base signature and the meta knowledge signature.

Definition 7. *(Multi-Sorted Base Signature with Meta Knowledge) The base multi-sorted signature $\overline{S_b}$ extended with meta knowledge is defined as the union of the base knowledge signatures and the meta knowledge signatures: $S_{b_{meta}} = \langle S_b \cup S_{meta}, @ \rangle$. The additional function @ is a meta function which associates with each symbol in S_b its set of meta knowledge from S_{meta}.*

To explicitly annotate knowledge formulas or terms with a set of additional meta knowledge labels (meta knowledge formulas) the function @ is introduced.

Definition 8. *(Meta Annotations / Labels) The function @ is a partial injective labelling function that assigns a set of meta knowledge formulas $@(L_1), .., @(L_n)$ to a knowledge formula or term ϕ.*

The implicit form $@(L_1), .., @(L_n)\ \phi$, where ϕ is a knowledge formula or term and L_i is a meta knowledge formula, expresses that $@(\phi) = L_1, .., L_n$. The Reaction RuleML XML syntax distinguished different meta knowledge formulas, as listed in section 2.

Each Reaction RuleML dialect can further partition the base sorts of the multi-sorted base signature into further sorts and restrict or extend them in the **dialects' signatures**, which are used to specify which formulas and terms are well-formed. Reaction RuleML dialects define signatures for required subsets of the sorts of terms and formulas, as they have been introduced in the previous section 2. For instance, signatures for `Time` and `Interval` in the temporal reasoning dialects, restrictions of the `rule` formula signatures to only `if` and `then` parts (in DR-RRML), or, e.g., `Action` signatures with predefined primitive action sorts for asserting, retracting and updating knowledge in production rule dialects (PR-RRML), or `Event` sorts in event processing dialects (ECA-RRML, CEP-RRML). Further restrictions or extension can be introduced in **semantic profiles** (see section 6). For instance, a semantic profile for Datalog reasoning imposes the restriction of a function free signature, i.e., $\overline{F} = \emptyset$. Furthermore, with **signature formulas** (`signature`) further domain signatures can be also directly defined in the knowledge interface declarations in a Reaction RuleML document.

4   Multi-sorted Semantic Interpretation

For attributing meaning (or truth values) to sentences (well-formed formulas) in Reaction RuleML multi-sorted semantic structures are used.

---

[7] As pioneered in the RBSLA project `http://rbsla.ruleml.org` [12].

Definition 9. *(Multi-sorted Semantic Structure) An interpretation (semantic structure) I for a multi-sorted base signature S_b consists of the following.*

- *A non-empty set U, called the universe of I, and for every sort T_i the set of members of I of sort T_i is $T_i^I \subseteq I$. The universe of I is the union of its sorts: $U = T_1^I \cup ... \cup T_n^I$.*
- *the structure interprets predicate, function and constant symbols in accordance with their sorts as follows:*
  - *if c is a constant symbol and $sort(c) = T$ then $c^I \subseteq T^I$.*
  - *if p is a n-place predicate relation symbol and $sort(p) = \langle T_1, ..., T_n, T_{n+1} \rangle$ then $p^I \subseteq T_1^I \times ... \times T_n^I - > T_{n+1}^I$.*
  - *if f is a n-place function symbol and $sort(f) = \langle T_1, ..., T_n, T_{n+1} \rangle$ then $p^I \subseteq T_1^I \times ... \times T_n^I - > T_{n+1}^I$.*

Reaction RuleML permits the union of its sort to be not necessarily disjoint and sorts can be subsets of other sorts including order-sorted hierarchies (see section 5). The variable **assignment** and **satisfaction** for any Reaction RuleML (dialect) language Φ are defined in the usual way.

Definition 10. *(Variable Assignment) The assignment function σ from the set of variables $\overline{X}$ (or a subset) of Φ into the universe $U(\Phi)$ must respect the sorts of the variables (in order-sorted type systems also subtypes). That is, if X_i is a variable of type T, then $\sigma(X) \in T^I$. In general, if ϕ is a typed predicate or function in Φ and σ an assignment to the interpretation I, then $I \models \phi[\sigma]$, i.e., ϕ is true in I when each variable X_i of ϕ is substituted by the values $\sigma(X)$ wrt to its sort.*

Reaction RuleML dialects are restricted to finite assignments where ϕ is defined on all free variables of ϕ. Furthermore, for typical logic programming dialects, since the assignment to constant and function symbols is fixed and the domain of discourse corresponds one-to-one with the constants $\overline{c}$ in the signature, it is possible to identify an interpretation I with a subset of the (extended) Herbrand base.

Reaction RuleML permits different sets of partially or totally ordered **truth values** $\overline{TV}$ which are defined in its dialects and semantic profile signatures. Classical semantic profiles typically use two Boolean values $T = true$ and $F = false$, i.e. $\overline{TV} = \{T, F\}$. Other logic programming profiles e.g., equilibrium logics (answer set programming) and partial equilibrium logics (well-founded semantics) are three-valued logics with an additional $U = undefined$ value and a truth order such as $true > undefined > false$. In (order) sorted dialects also a special object value $\bot$ for terms which are meaningless or empty with respect to the sort signatures can be allowed in the valuation function. Further constraints can be imposed in a profile, e.g., for negation operators, such as the widely adopted reverse truth ordering that negation operator must be anti-monotonic or double negation law for default negation (`Naf`) and explicit negation (`Neg`) in extended logic programs with extended well-founded semantics, etc. In general, Reaction RuleML uses a multi-valued uncertainty degree between $[0..1]$ with the typical assignment to truth values of 0 for F, 1 for T and 0.5 for U in three-valued logics. A general **truth valuation function** $Val(\varphi, \sigma)$ gives to every sentence φ and assignment σ a truth value $Val(\varphi, \sigma) \in \overline{TV}$ for φ in the model σ.

If a semantic structure I assigns the value true to a well-formed formula ϕ, with σ being an assignment to the semantic structure, then ϕ is said to be a **model** of that formula, written with Tarski's satisfaction relation as $I \models \phi[\sigma]$. Accordingly, we say a formula ϕ is **satisfied** by an interpretation I (ϕ is true in $I: I \models \phi$) iff $I \models_\sigma \phi$ for all variable assignments σ. ϕ is **valid** iff $I \models \phi$ for every interpretation I.

Definition 11. *(Model) Let I be an interpretation of a Reaction RuleML dialect language Σ. Then I is a model of a closed formula ϕ, if ϕ is true wrt I. Further, I is a model of a set $\overline{\phi}$ of closed formulas, if I is a model of each formula of $\overline{\phi}$. I is a model of a Reaction RuleML knowledge base Φ, $I \models \Phi$, iff $I \models \phi$ for every formula $\phi \in \Phi$.*

Reaction RuleML dialects and their semantic profiles refine their **intended models** and the set of allowed semantic structures, which are used for the **entailment** definitions. For instance dialects and their profiles for classical first-order logic interpretation consider the set of all semantic structures and the intended models are all models, modal logics instead typically deal with possible world models, whereas logic programming profiles typically use Herbrand semantic structures and minimal models, stable models or well-founded models.

For proofs, if $\overline{I}$ is a set of structures of Σ, then $\Phi \Rightarrow \Psi$ means that for every structure $I \in \overline{I}$ which is a model of Φ, I is also a model of Ψ. Logical **entailment** in Reaction RuleML is defined with respect to the set of intended models.

Definition 12. *(Entailment) If $\overline{I}$ is a set of semantic structures then a formula ϕ entails a formula φ, written as $\phi \vdash \varphi$, iff for every semantic structure $I_i \in \overline{I}$, if it is an intended model of ϕ then it is also an intended model for φ.*

After this general introduction of the basic mechanisms of multi-sorted signatures and their multi-sorted interpretations in Reaction RuleML, the following sections now highlight further syntactic and semantic extension mechanism of Reaction RuleML.

5   Metamodel and External Type Systems

The design of the (Reaction) RuleML language follows widely accepted design principles for good language design such as minimality, referential transparency, orthogonality and it is designed to be **extensible**. [16,2,20] For common elements which occur in most typical rule languages, Reaction RuleML introduces generic XML elements. These generic XML elements can be given a specific sort using the **typing mechanism** (@type) of RuleML. [2] For instance, a generic operator (Operator) can be typed as, e.g., logical connective, modal operator, and algebra operator. A polymorphic negation (Negation) can be typed as, e.g. negation-as-failure or classical negation. A generic quantifier (Quantifier), can be typed as

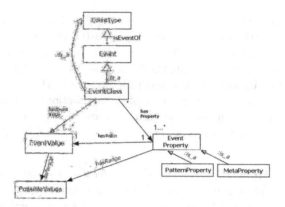

Fig. 1. Defining Event Types as Metamodel Event Class

universal or existential quantifier. Variables (**Var**) and terms (**Ind, Data, Expr**) can be typed. Any of the typical objects in reaction rules such as times (**Time**), intervals (**Interval**), events (**Event**), actions (**Action**), fluents (**Fluent**), situations (**Situation**), semantic profiles (**Profile**), messages (**Message**), agents (**Agent**), protocols (**Protocol**), etc., are introduced as generic XML elements which can be given a specific type. All these generic XML elements are sort extension points in the Reaction RuleML language which can be given a specific type.

Their types can come from the **Semantic Metamodel** of Reaction RuleML which defines typical sorts of the Reaction RuleML vocabulary in an ontological metamodelling approach (using OWL as representation language). A type is defined as a class definition which has properties and values. The properties are distinguished into meta properties and normal class properties. Their range is defined by possible values (data or object type values). The class gives the definition of a type (a sort). Figure 1 illustrates the approach.

Using this metamodelling approach top level ontology types are defined in the Reaction RuleML metamodel. Other ontologies can further specialize one of these top-level types. For ease of use and efficient XML processing, syntactic short cuts are introduced as specific XML elements in Reaction RuleML. For instance, `<Forall>` is the short cut XML element used for the generic typed `<Quantifier type="ruleml:Forall">`, instead of `<Negation type="ruleml:InflationaryNegation">` the short cut element `<Naf>` can be used as the typical sort of negation in production rules, etc.

The metamodel and other **external type systems** are introduced in the signature of Reaction RuleML as externally defined sorts.

Definition 13. *(**External Type Alphabet**) An external type alphabet $\overline{T}$ is a finite set of monomorphic sort symbols built over the distinct set of terminological class concepts of an (external type) language.*

Definition 14. *(**Combined Type Signature**) A combined type signature $\overline{ST}$ is the union of all its constituent signatures including the external type signatures:* $\overline{ST} = \langle S_1 \cup .. \cup S_n \cup T_1 \cup .. \cup T_k \rangle.$

A semantic structure with external types is a multi-sorted interpretations of the combined signature $\overline{ST}$, where the constants, predicates and function symbols in the combined signature are interpreted in accordance with their (external) sorts. For variables the assignment function of variables into the combined universe must respect the sorts of the variables. The type systems typically considered in Reaction RuleML are built-in and data type vocabularies (a set of external datatype symbols that have a fixed interpretation in any semantic structure) and order-sorted type systems (i.e., with sub-type relations such as object-oriented class hierarchies, e.g., Java classes or ontologies).

Definition 15. *(Order-sorted Type System) A finite order-sorted type system OTS comes with a partial order $\leq$, i.e., TS under $\leq$ has a greatest lower bound $glb(T_1, T_2)$ for any two types T_1 and T_2 having a lower bound at all. Since TS is finite also a least upper bound $lub(T_1, T_2)$ exists for any two types T_1 and T_2 having an upper bound at all.*

For order sorted logics and reasoning with, e.g., hybrid polymorphic order-sorted unification, we refer to [11] and for an implementation in Prova [18,21] and OO-jDrew. The external types and their "real" objects, such as events, actions, processes, etc., that Reaction RuleML models and uses for reasoning may have rather complex composite structures. To make clear that the inner composition of the representation elements of the universe of a Reaction RuleML structure and their inherent meanings, where it is not for interpretation of sorts, functions and predicates, is not relevant, we use isomorphic structures for the interpretation in Reaction RuleML.

Definition 16. *(Isomorphism) Let I_1, I_2 be two interpretations of a signature with sorts $T_1, .., T_n$ and let, then $f : U_1 \to U_2$ is an isomorphism of I_1 and I_2 if f is a one-to-one mapping from the universe of I_1 onto the universe of I_2 such that:*

1. *For every sort T_i, $t \in T_i^{I_1}$, iff $f(t) \in T_i^{I_2}$*
2. *For every constant c, $f(c^{I_1}) = c^{I_2}$*
3. *For every n-ary predicate symbol p with n-tuple $t_1, .., t_n \in U_1$, $\langle t_1, .., t_n \rangle \in p^{I_1}$ iff $\langle f(t_1), .., f(t_n) \rangle \in p^{I_2}$*
4. *For every n-ary function symbol f with n-tuple $t_1, .., t_n, \in U_1$, $f(f^{I_1}(t_1, .., t_n)) = f^{I_2}(f(t_1), .., f(t_n))$*

This isomorphism ensures that any conclusion must hold in all isomorphic structures.

6   Dialects and Semantic Profiles

Dialects in Reaction RuleML provide a certain layer of general representation expressiveness by defining the dialects language, typically for a particular sort of reaction rules or a combination of different sorts. **Semantic profiles** in Reaction RuleML are used to define the *intended semantics* for knowledge interpretation (typically a model-theoretic semantics), reasoning (typically entailment regimes and proof-theoretic semantics), and for execution (e.g., operational semantics such as selection and consumption policies and windowing techniques in complex event event processing). That is, they further detail the syntax and semantics of a dialect and provide necessary information about the intended semantics for Reaction RuleML knowledge representations as required for interchange, translation, inference, and verification and validation. A dialect has a default semantic profile defining the *default semantics*, i.e., the semantics which by default is used for interpretation. Deviating semantic profiles (`Profile`) can be specified (`evaluation`) on all formulas and terms in Reaction RuleML giving them a different interpretation and execution from the default semantics. Multiple alternative semantic profiles are allowed with or without a priority ordering and their scope can be specified (see section 7).

Semantic profiles might define specialized or deviating structures (e.g., defining certain truth valuations for negation), intended models (e.g., in terms entailment regimes) and axioms and propositions (e.g., domain independent meta axioms of a theory, e.g., for calculi such as event calculus, situation calculus), as well as proof-theories and properties of operational semantics (e.g., process semantics and protocols, windowing techniques, selection and consumption policies in complex event processing and actions), etc. And, they might specialize the language of a dialect, e.g., by limiting the dialect's signature to subsignatures.

Definition 17. *(**Subsignature**) A signature S_1 is a subsignature of S_2, i.e., $S_1 \subseteq S_2$ iff S_1 is a signature which consists only of symbols from S_2 without changing their sort and arity.*

Semantic Profiles can be defined internally within a Reaction RuleML document (`Profile`) or externally. External semantic profiles can be referenced by their profile name (`@type`) and imported by their resource identifier (`@iri`). Their specification can be given in any XML format (`content`), including RuleML formulas (`formula`), as well as other formal and textual languages (which are not directly machine processable). For non-Reaction RuleML profiles a semantics-preserving translation function τ needs be defined in order to allow interpretations of Reaction RuleML knowledge bases with the profile's semantics.

Definition 18. *(**Semantic Profile**) A semantic profile, $SP = \langle S_{SP}, \Sigma_{SP}, I_{SP}, \Phi_{SP}, \tau_{SP} \rangle$, (partially) defines a profile signature S_{SP}, a language Σ_{SP}, an interpretation I_{SP}, a domain-independent theory Φ_{SP}, and a semantics-preserving translation function $\tau_{SP}(\cdot)$ which translates from Reaction RuleML to the profile's language / signature (and vice versa with the inverse function τ_{SP}^{-1}).*

Note, a semantic profile does not need to provide a full definition, since a semantic profile is interpreted as a substructure of the expanded profile semantic multi-structure of a Reaction RuleML dialect, i.e., the partial definitions in a profile are completed with the default semantic profile of the dialect by expanding the profile multi-structure, which is used for interpretation.

Definition 19. *(Expanded Profile Semantic Multi-Structure)* *A profile semantic multi-structure* $\overline{I} = \langle I_R, I_D, \overline{I}_{SP} \rangle$ *is a set of semantic structures such that* I_R *is the basic structure of Reaction RuleML,* I_D *is the default structure of the dialect, and* $\overline{I}_{SP}$ *is itself a semantic multi-structure consisting of the structures of the used semantic profiles* I_{SP_i}. *For the interpretation the modifying* **expansion** *of* $\overline{I}$ *is used, which is obtained as follows:*

1. I_R *is modified and expanded with* I_D *and the expansion is used as default interpretation.*
2. I_D *is modified and expanded with* $\overline{I}_{SP}$ *and the expansion is used as profile interpretation. In case "n" alternative substructures are define in* $\overline{I}_{SP}$, *there are also n alternative expansions and one of the n expansions is used for interpretation. It is up to the interpreter to decide which one to use, e.g., by priority ordering of the profiles).*

That is, the expanded interpretation of a semantic multi-structure first selects one of the (expanded) profile semantics and if there is no profile semantics defined, then it will use the default semantics of the dialect.

Definition 20. *(Substructure)* *Given two semantic structures* I_1 *and* I_2, I_1 *is a substructure of* I_2 *iff:*

- $U_1 \subseteq U_2$, *i.e., the universe of* I_1 *is a subset of the universe of* I_2 *(with the universe of a multi-sorted structure being the union of its sorts).*
- I_1 *is obtained by restricting the interpretation of* I_2 *to the universe* U_1 *of* I_1, *i.e.,*
  - *for every sort* T *and individual* a *from* U_1, $a \in T^{I_1}$ *iff* $a \in T^{I_2}$.
  - *if* c *is a constant then* $c^{I_1} = c^{I_2}$.
  - *for every predicate symbol* p *of arity* n *and for every n-tuple of individuals from* U_1, $\langle a_1, .., a_n \rangle \in p^{I_1}$ *iff* $\langle a_1, .., a_n \rangle \in p^{I_2}$.
  - *for every function symbol* f, f^{I_1} *is the restriction of* f^{I_2} *to* U_1, *i.e., the restriction of a function* $f : A \to B$ *to a subset of its domain* $A' \subseteq A$ *is the function* $f' : A' \to B$ *written as* $f' = f \upharpoonright A$.

Definition 21. *(Reduct and Expansion)* *Given two signatures* S_1 *and* S_2, *if* $S_1 \subseteq S_2$ *and* I_2 *is a structure for* S_2, *then the reduct, written as* $I_1 = I_2 \upharpoonright S_1$, *of* I_2 *to* S_1 *is a structure* I_1 *without the symbols which are not in* S_1. *Conversely,* I_2 *is the expansion of* I_1 *to* S_2. *The universe* U_1 *of* I_1 *is the union of sorts of* $I_2 \in S_1$, *i.e.,* $U_1 \subseteq U_2$, *with the same interpretation in* I_1 *and* I_2.

As we will see in the next section, interpretations might differ in modules for knowledge defined with local and private scopes.

7 Modularization and Scoped Reasoning

Reaction RuleML supports knowledge modularization and distribution. A syntactic way to distribute knowledge locally within a KB is by separating the representation of a knowledge formula into several syntactic parts and connecting and conjoining them syntactically by key-keyref pairs (@key, @keyref). The key is a local ("webized") identifier, with a unique name assumption, which can be defined as meta knowledge on any Reaction RuleML language element. A key reference is a local reference (within a KB) using the key as locator to connect and conjoin the key element with the key reference element. Multiple references to a key element are possible (1 : m as well as n : m by defining both key and keyref on pairwise conjoint elements). The resulting combined syntax elements need to be well-formed to allow meaningful interpretations, i.e., key-keyref pairs need to be on similar syntactic elements and for each key reference a matching unique key needs to be defined in a KB. A typical application of the key-keyref mechanism is the separation of the knowledge interface with signatures from the knowledge implementation, so that both can be represented and reused independently. This enables, e.g., template definitions (e.g., abstracted signature patterns, knowledge templates), modularization and information hiding, e.g., by publishing the interface in a document distributed from the document with the (possibly private) implementation. With XML Inclusion (XInclude) such distributed documents can be syntactically included into one KB enabling local key intra-references within it. Furthermore, with the @iri attribute remote resources can be referenced as external terms and external (RuleML) documents and messages (Message) can be consulted/imported (Consult) or received (Receive) as modules to the KB.

Definition 22. *(**Module and Submodule**) A module Φ is a tuple $\langle \overline{@\phi}, \overline{\phi} \rangle$, where $\overline{\phi}$ is an ordered or unordered finite set of knowledge formulas $\phi_i \in \overline{\phi}$ (without or with duplicates) and $\overline{@\phi}$ is an ordered or unordered finite set of meta knowledge formulas $@\phi_i \in \overline{@\phi}$, called the **module interface**. A module Ψ is a submodule of Φ if $\Psi \subseteq \Phi$.*

The importing Reaction RuleML KB is the super module of all modules. All asserted, imported and received rule bases are submodules of this KB module. The module's knowledge interface might explicitly declare the meta knowledge of the module. This includes, e.g., the module's descriptive metadata such as the module's name and source, the declaration of the module's signature patterns, the intended semantic profiles, scopes, modes and further quantifications and qualifications such as validity times, prioritization for conflict handling, etc. As described in section 6 the semantic profile predefines the intended semantics, including, e.g., the semantic properties and assumptions such as closed world, open world, etc. As described in section 3 modes partition the universe into subsets having a different mode. Reaction RuleML predefines the modes (@mode) "+" (input mode), "−" (output mode) and "?" (open mode, i.e., input and output). Scopes define subsets of the universe as domain of discourse which are used for interpretation. Reaction RuleML predefines the scopes (@scope) "*global*" (globally visible), "*local*" (visible with local interpretation) and "*private*" (hidden and not visible outside of the module). Dialects might introduce further scopes such as, e.g. "*supremum*" and "*infima*" which expand the scope of nested submodules to its least upper bound or greatest lower bound. Further, named **metadata scopes** (scope) can be defined and used as scoped domain of discourse.

Definition 23. *(Metadata Scope) Let KB be a KB. A metadata scope $KB_@$ (aka constructive view on KB), which is defined by one or more closed metadata (constraint) formulas $\{@(L_1), .., @(L_n)\}$ on the KB, is a submodule $KB_@ \subseteq KB$, where for every formula ϕ in $KB_@$ their metadata $@(\phi)$ satisfies the metadata constraints defined by the metadata scope. The scope's sub-signature $S_@$ is said to be the* **scoped domain of discourse***.*

Scoped reasoning can be performed on such metadata scopes (aka **constructive views** on the KB) by defining closed scoped literals in conditions, queries, event patterns. Scope literals are interpreted in the the scoped domain of discourse and by default have the scopes' closure. The scope definition of a scope literal might contain variables. In addition to scopes Reaction RuleML supports **guards** which act as additional pre-conditional constraints on the literal. To illustrate this interaction between scopes, guards, and the knowledge base in scoped reasoning, the following rule program (in Prova syntax to avoid the long XML syntax of Reaction RuleML) makes decisions on the basis of rules which have been authored by different persons and only applies those rules from trusted authors.

```
%simplified decision rules of an agent
@author(developer1) r(X):-q(X).
@author(developer2) r(X):-s(X).
q(2).
s(-2).
% for simplicity this is a fact, but could be also a complex rule which computes the trust
% value from the reputation value of developer1
trusted(developer1).
% the rule defines a scope @author(A) on the goal r(X) and a guard pre-constraint that all
% found authors (bound to variable A) must be trusted.
p(X):-  @author(A) r(X) [trusted(A)].
% query results only in the solution X=2, because developer1 is trusted but developer2 is not
:-solve(p(X)).
```

By default a Reaction RuleML KB and its (sub-)modules are contextually annotated by metadata about their source ($@src([Locator])$) and their name ($@label([OID])$), with *Locator* being the KB's source location (location of Reaction RuleML document) and *OID* being the implicitly or explicitly defined object identifer. By default, the scope of relations and functions is global and their arguments' scope is local. A global scope corresponds to a metadata scope defined over all knowledge qualified with the source of the KB ($@source([Locator])$) and the local scope corresponds to the metadata scope defined over all knowledge qualified with the name of the module ($@label([OID])$). The mode of formulas when used as conditions, constraints, queries and event patterns is "$+$" (input) and the mode of conclusions, answers and active actions is "$-$" (output); with a corresponding mode for their constant arguments and by default for variables the mode is "?" (open). The default quantification scope is universal (Forall). There is a nested submodule inheritance, i.e., meta knowledge defined on outer modules is automatically inherited to the inner modules.

The set of input formulas In and the set of output formulas Out are visible and can be imported and accessed by other modules. Accordingly their scope must be either *global* or *local*. The set of formulas with *private* scope consists of internal formulas $Priv$ and hence not accessible by other modules. This is used for defining the semantics of imports (`Consult`, `XInclude`) and the composition semantics of modules.

Definition 24. *(Import) A document KB' is said to be an import to a document KB, if it is directly imported into KB (or it is imported into another document, which is directly imported into KB). An imported document KB' becomes a module of the KB.*

Semantic profiles might specify an additional translation and renaming mapping, e.g., to consistently map all imported local symbols into the local symbols of the importing KB. Furthermore, they can define the concrete module composition semantics, e.g., as a conservative composition using renaming output transformations on the output formulas and outer join operator for the composition, and a mechanism to avoid cyclic imports.

The interpretation of such a multi-module KB is defined as a modular extension of the semantic multi-structure, which was already used for importing semantic profiles.

Definition 25. *(**Modular Semantic Multi-Structure**) A modular semantic multi-structure $\overline{M} = \langle M_{KB_0}, M_{KB_1}, M_{KB_2}, .. \rangle$ is a set of semantic structures such that M_{KB} is the semantic structure of the importing KB and M_{KB_k} is a set of semantic structures of the imported modules. The semantic structures M_{KB} and all structures M_{KB_k} are required to coincide in the mappings of global symbols in all semantic structures. But, they might differ for local and private symbols in their interpretation using the module scope to constrain the domain of discourse to allow deviating local interpretations in each M_{KB_k}.*

The module composition semantics defined in a semantic profile can specify how to do the expansion of the modular semantic multi-structure. The default is that the semantics of imported modules expands to the semantics of the importing KB. But, other composition semantics can be defined in the semantic profile of the importing KB.

Reaction RuleML supports actions for sending (`Send`) and receiving (`Receive`) knowledge via messages (`Message`) in **messaging reaction rules** (`@style="messaging"`). Messages interchange Reaction RuleML documents as their payload between agents (`Agent`), which are rule-based agents (aka inference services). The sent RuleML documents are imported to the KB of the receiving agent using the primitive(s) defined in the received document to actively process the knowledge in the receiver's KB. An important difference to "standard" imports, as described before, is, that these knowledge updates are local to the **conversation scope** of the message interaction which takes place in the **execution scope** of messaging reaction rules. A typical application of this conversation-based interactions is distributed Question-Answering (Q&A)

between distributed KBs (i.e., agents providing query interfaces to their KBs), where the send and receive actions in messaging reaction rules act as queries and answers to external KBs. They can be given a truth-valued interpretation in the model-theoretic semantics and can be interpreted as goals which are proven by the external knowledge. An important aspect in this distributed interaction is the interface declaration of knowledge, in particular the signatures and their scope visibility. The agent conversations might follow certain protocols (`Protocol`) and might be given an additional pragmatic interpretation (`directive`). For further information we refer to the RuleResponder project. [15,18,19]

8 Conclusion - Reaction RuleML for Reaction Rules

In this paper we have introduced the core mechanisms of Reaction RuleML as XML-based representation and interchange language for reaction rules. Multi-sorted **signature definitions** and **multi-sorted interpretations** allow events, actions, times, etc., as "first-class citizens" in the language, with their sorts possibly defined in **external (order-sorted) type systems** such as ontologies and object class hierarchies. Syntactic and semantic **modularization** enables knowledge **imports** as modules and distribution of knowledge interface definitions from knowledge implementations/representations, referenced locally (`@key`, `@keyref`) or globally (`@node`, `@iri`). **Scopes** define visibility properties and local closed interpretation of terms and formulas in modularized KBs. **Metadata scopes** act as constructive views on the KB by dynamically selecting knowledge from the KB by their descriptive and qualifying metadata annotations, enabling **scoped reasoning**. **Semantic profiles** define possible intended semantics for the evaluation of Reaction RuleML KBs. For instance, profiles defining certain calculi such as situation calculus or event calculus can be used for the logical interpretation of the domain-dependent theories represented in the KR-RRML dialect. Profiles for temporal reasoning (including temporal modal logic profiles) can be used for representations in the temporal DR-RRML. Active dialects such as PR-RRML, ECA-RRML and CEP-RRML support active reaction rules (`@style="active"`) with implicit or explicit (complex) events and with active actions such as knowledge update actions defined in terms of primitives. Various logics have been proposed for such active rules reaching from event/action logics, temporal action languages, evolving logic programs to other non-monotonic logics such as transaction logic.

With extensible algebra operators, complex event patterns (event signatures), complex actions, as well as pre- and post-conditions Reaction RuleML provides the required representational expressiveness for such kind of active reaction rules. We highlight some of the features for efficient SCEP in Reaction RuleML 1.0, which become possible with the described core mechanism in this paper.

- **Knowledge update actions** and other effect full **(complex) actions** transit the knowledge base from one state to the next. Reaction RuleML makes an implicit rule base assumption for such update primitives, which means the knowledge update is interpreted as a (sub)module in the KB. The module is annotated with various metadata such as the rule base's module name, the source and a state time stamp. This metadata can be used for efficient life cycle management. For instance, a module can be simply retracted by retracting all knowledge which is in the metadata scope of this module. A transition of transactional updates (@safety=transaction), which leads to a set of modules in the KB, can be easily rolled-back by reverting the transition on the metadata scopes of these modules.

- **Complex event patterns** can be defined by signature definitions using **event algebra operators** which are interpreted by semantics profiles (such as the interval-based event calculus event algebra [22]).
- Various **selection an consumption policies** for event instance sequences can be defined in terms of scopes and guard constraints. For instance, using the metadata time stamp of event instances in the KB, a guarded metadata scope can define a time window in the guard constraint selecting only events with a meta data time stamp within the defined window.
- Typical **functionalities of event processing** as described in the Reference Architecture of the Event Processing Technial Society [23], such as event preparation functions with selection and filtering, event analysis functions for transformations and ratings, detection functions with complex event patterns, and event reactions with routing by sending and receiving messages, can be represented in terms of (messaging) reaction rules in CEP-RRML [14].
- With **messaging reaction rules** conversation based **pragmatic interactions** between knowledge processing agents (e.g. distributed **event processing agents** - EPAs - or rule-based **Q&A inference services**) are possible following **agent based coordination** and negation protocols as well as (possibly **concurrent**) **event-action workflows**.

References

1. Hallmark, G., Paschke, A., de SainteMarie, C.: RIF Production Rule Dialect, W3C Recommendation, 2nd edn. (February 2013), http://www.w3.org/TR/rif-prd/
2. Boley, H., Paschke, A., Shafiq, O.: RuleML 1.0: The Overarching Specification of Web Rules. In: Dean, M., Hall, J., Rotolo, A., Tabet, S. (eds.) RuleML 2010. LNCS, vol. 6403, pp. 162–178. Springer, Heidelberg (2010)
3. Boley, H.: Integrating Positional and Slotted Knowledge on the Semantic Web. Journal of Emerging Technologies in Web Intelligence 4(2), 343–353 (2010)
4. Boley, H.: A RIF-Style Semantics for RuleML-Integrated Positional-Slotted, Object-Applicative Rules. In: Bassiliades, N., Governatori, G., Paschke, A. (eds.) RuleML 2011 - Europe. LNCS, vol. 6826, pp. 194–211. Springer, Heidelberg (2011)
5. Boley, H., Kifer, M.: RIF Framework for Logic Dialects, W3C Recommendation, 2nd edn. (February 2013), http://www.w3.org/TR/rif-fld
6. Chen, W., Kifer, M., Warren, D.S.: HiLog: A foundation for higher-order logic programming. Journal of Logic Programming 15(3), 187–230 (1993)
7. Battle, S., et al.: Semantic Web Services Language (SWSL), W3C Member Submission (September 2005), http://www.w3.org/Submission/SWSF-SWSL/
8. Kifer, M., Lausen, G., Wu, J.: Logical Foundations of Object-oriented and Frame-based Languages. J. ACM 42(4), 741–843 (1995)

9. Paschke, A.: The ContractLog Approach Towards Test-driven Verification and Validation of Rule Bases - A Homogeneous Integration of Test Cases and Integrity Constraints into Evolving Logic Programs and Rule Markup Languages (RuleML). International Journal of Interoperability in Business Information Systems (2005)

10. Paschke, A.: Rule Based Service Level Agreements (RBSLA), RuleML project (December 2006), http://rbsla.ruleml.org/

11. Paschke, A.: A typed hybrid description logic programming language with polymorphic order-sorted dl-typed unification for semantic web type systems. In: OWLED (2006)

12. Paschke, A.: Rule based service level agreements: RBSLA; knowledge representation for automated e-contract, SLA and policy management. Idea Verlag GmbH (2007)

13. Paschke, A.: Rules and logic programming for the web. In: Polleres, A., d'Amato, C., Arenas, M., Handschuh, S., Kroner, P., Ossowski, S., Patel-Schneider, P. (eds.) Reasoning Web 2011. LNCS, vol. 6848, pp. 326–381. Springer, Heidelberg (2011)

14. Paschke, A.: Semantic Complex Event Processing. Tutorial at Dem@Care Summer School on Ambient Assisted Living, Chania, Crete, Greece, September 16-20 (May 2013), http://www.slideshare.net/swadpasc/dem-aal-semanticceppaschke

15. Paschke, A., Boley, H.: Rule Responder, RuleML project (October 2007), http://responder.ruleml.org/

16. Paschke, A., Boley, H.: Rule Markup Languages and Semantic Web Rule Languages. In: Giurca, A., Gasevic, D., Taveter, K. (eds.) Handbook of Research on Emerging Rule-Based Languages and Technologies: Open Solutions and Approaches, pp. 1–24. IGI Publishing (May 2009)

17. Paschke, A., Boley, H.: Rules Capturing Events and Reactivity. In: Giurca, A., Gasevic, D., Taveter, K. (eds.) Handbook of Research on Emerging Rule-Based Languages and Technologies: Open Solutions and Approaches, pp. 215–252. IGI Publishing (May 2009)

18. Paschke, A., Boley, H.: Rule Responder: Rule-Based Agents for the Semantic-Pragmatic Web. International Journal on Artificial Intelligence Tools 20(6), 1043–1081 (2011)

19. Paschke, A., Boley, H., Kozlenkov, A., Craig, B.L.: Rule responder: Ruleml-based agents for distributed collaboration on the pragmatic web. In: Proceedings of the 2nd International Conference on Pragmatic Web, ICPW 2007, Tilburg, The Netherlands, October 22-23. ACM International Conference Proceeding Series, vol. 280, pp. 17–28. ACM (2007)

20. Paschke, A., Boley, H., Zhao, Z., Teymourian, K., Athan, T.: Reaction RuleML 1.0: Standardized Semantic Reaction Rules. In: Bikakis, A., Giurca, A. (eds.) RuleML 2012. LNCS, vol. 7438, pp. 100–119. Springer, Heidelberg (2012)

21. Paschke, A., Kozlenkov, A.: Prova - Prolog + Java Rule Language, Open Source project (October 2006), https://prova.ws/

22. Paschke, A., Kozlenkov, A.: Rule-based event processing and reaction rules. In: Governatori, G., Hall, J., Paschke, A. (eds.) RuleML 2009. LNCS, vol. 5858, pp. 53–66. Springer, Heidelberg (2009)

23. Paschke, A., Vincent, P., Alves, A., Moxey, C.: Tutorial on advanced design patterns in event processing. In: Proceedings of the Sixth ACM International Conference on Distributed Event-Based Systems, DEBS 2012, Berlin, Germany, July 16-20, pp. 324–334. ACM (2012)

24. Polleres, A., Boley, H., Kifer, M.: RIF Datatypes and Built-ins 1.0, W3C Recommendation (June 2010), http://www.w3.org/TR/rif-dtb

A Logical Characterization
of a Reactive System Language

Robert Kowalski and Fariba Sadri

Department of Computing,
Imperial College, London, UK
{rak,fs}@doc.ic.ac.uk

Abstract. Typical reactive system languages are programmed by means of rules of the form *if antecedent then consequent*. However, despite their seemingly logical character, hardly any reactive system languages give such rules a logical interpretation. In this paper, we investigate a simplified reactive system language KELPS, in which rules are universally quantified material implications, and computation attempts to generate a model that makes the rules *true*.

The operational semantics of KELPS is similar to that of other reactive system languages, and is similarly incomplete. It cannot make a *rule* true by making its antecedent *false*, or by making its consequent *true* whether or not its antecedent becomes *true*. In this paper, we characterize the *reactive models* computed by the operational semantics. Informally speaking, a model is *reactive* if every action in the model is an instance of an action in the consequent of a rule whose earlier conditions are *true*.

Keywords: reactive systems, model generation, completeness, LPS, KELPS.

1   Introduction

State transition systems play an important role in many areas of Computing. They underpin the operational semantics of imperative programming languages, the dynamic behavior of database management systems, and many aspects of knowledge representation in artificial intelligence. In many of these systems, state transitions are performed by executing reactive rules, which describe relationships between earlier and later states. Reactive rules occur explicitly as condition-action rules in production systems, event-condition-action rules in active databases, and transition rules in Abstract State Machines [4]. They are implicit in Statecharts [5] and BDI agents plans. They are the core of Reaction RuleML [16].

Simple state transition systems have an operational semantics in which computation consists in generating a finite sequence $act_1, \dots , act_n$ of actions to transform an initial state S_0 into a goal state S_n. In this paper, we investigate the logical semantics of a state transition system, KELPS, which generates actions by using reactive rules. Given an initial state S_0 and a potentially non-terminating sequence of external events $ext_1,\dots, ext_i,\dots$, computation in KELPS consists in generating associated sequences

A. Bikakis et al. (Eds.): RuleML 2014, LNCS 8620, pp. 22–36, 2014.
© Springer International Publishing Switzerland 2014

$act_1, \dots , act_i, \dots$ of actions and states $S_1, \dots , S_i, \dots$, with the purpose of making the reactive rules *true*.

In previous papers [11, 12, 14], we presented a Logic-based agent and Production System language LPS, which combines reactive rules with logic programs. KELPS [13] is a simplified Kernel of LPS without logic programs. Its operational semantics is similar to that of imperative reactive rule languages, which generate sequences of actions and states, but maintain only a single current state, using destructive state transformations. However, the reactive rules in KELPS are represented in first-order logic (FOL), as sentences of the form $\forall X$ [*antecedent* $\rightarrow \exists Y$ [*consequent*]], where all the time-stamps in *consequent* are constrained to be later than or equal to the latest time-stamp in *antecedent*.

KELPS is not intended to be a practical computer language, but has been simplified to focus on the main issues concerning the logical semantics of reactive system languages more generally. It can be regarded as a compiled form of LPS, in which relations defined intensionally by logic programs are compiled into extensionally defined predicates, defined by atomic sentences. The resulting kernel language is not as expressive and well-structured as LPS, but is still very expressive compared with many other reactive system languages. In particular, antecedents of rules in KELPS can recognize a large class of complex events, and consequents of rules can generate complex alternative, conditional plans of actions.

In [11, 12, 14] we showed that the operational semantics (OS) of LPS (and therefore of KELPS) is *sound*: Any sequence of states and events that the OS recognizes as solving the computational task is indeed a model that makes the reactive rules *true*. However, the OS is *incomplete*, because it generates only *reactive models*, in which the consequents of reactive rules are made *true* after their antecedents become *true*. It does not generate models that *proactively* make consequents *true* whether or not their antecedents become *true*; that make antecedents *false*, to prevent making their consequents *true*; or that unnecessarily make their antecedents *true*, and are then forced to make their consequents *true*. Moreover, it does not generate models that contain actions that are irrelevant to the computational task.[1]

Fig. 1 presents an informal illustration of the different kinds of models. In addition to a single reactive rule, the example also includes a causal theory, used to update states destructively, and a definition of the temporal constraint predicates, defined extensionally by means of atomic sentences. All of the models include both the set of all external events and the set of all actions motivated by the reactive rule and triggered by the external events. The non-reactive models also contain additional, unmotivated or unnecessary actions.

In this paper, we characterize the reactive models I generated by the KELPS OS. These models all have the property that every action in I is motivated by being an instance of an action that occurs explicitly in the consequent of a reactive rule whose earlier conditions are already *true*. For example, in the reactive model of Fig. 1, the action *dispatch(bob, book, tuesday)*, is an instance of *dispatch(C, Item, T2)* in the consequent of the rule, and all earlier conditions, *orders(bob, book, monday)* and

---

[1] In section 6.1, we discuss the relationship between these different kinds of models and the models that are generated using abductive logic programming [7] and the frame axioms of the event calculus [15]. We will see that reactive models need not be minimal.

reliable(bob, monday), of the associated instance of the rule are *true* before the time of the action. However, in the proactive model, although the action *dispatch(mary, book, tuesday)* is also an instance of *dispatch(C, Item, T2)*, the earlier instance *reliable(mary, monday)* of the condition *reliable(C, T1)* is not *true*. Moreover, in the irrelevant model, the action *send-voucher(mary, wednesday)* has no relationship with any of the actions in the rule at all.

In the remainder of the paper, we present the KELPS language (section 2), its model-theoretic (section 3) and operational semantics (section 4), the relationship between the two semantics (section 5), the relationship with Abductive Logic Programming [8], MetateM [1] and Transaction Logic [2] (section 6), and future work (section 7).

If a customer orders an item and the customer is reliable,
then dispatch the item and send an invoice to the customer for the item.

Reactive rule: $orders(C, Item, T1) \wedge reliable(C, T1)$
                    $\rightarrow dispatch(C, Item, T2) \wedge send\text{-}invoice(C, Item, T3) \wedge$
                    $T1 < T2 \leq T3 \leq T1 + 3$

Auxiliary predicate definitions: *monday < tuesday,   tuesday < wednesday, etc.*

Causal theory: *initiates(send-invoice(C, Item), payment-due(C, Item))*
                  terminates(pays-invoice(C, Item), payment-due(C, Item))

Initial state at sunday: *reliable(bob)*

External events: *orders(bob, book, monday), orders(mary, book, monday)*

A reactive model: *orders(bob, book, monday), orders(mary, book, monday)*
reliable(bob, sunday), reliable(bob, monday), reliable(bob, tuesday), etc.
send-invoice(bob, book, tuesday), dispatch(bob, book, tuesday),
payment-due(bob, book, tuesday), payment-due(bob, book, wednesday), etc.
sunday < monday,   monday < tuesday,   tuesday < wednesday, etc.

A proactive model: The reactive model with the addition of:
send-invoice(mary, book, tuesday), dispatch(mary, book, tuesday),
payment-due(mary, book, tuesday), payment-due(mary, book, wednesday), etc.

An irrelevant model: The reactive model with the addition of:
send-voucher(mary, wednesday).

Here the models are all Herbrand models, represented by the set of *all* atomic sentences that are *true* in the model. In particular, the models contain all the atomic sentences needed to define the temporal relations.

Fig. 1. Examples of Models of Reactive Rules in KELPS

2 The KELPS Language

The operational semantics of KELPS maintains a single current state S_i at time i. It reasons with the reactive rules, to generate a set of actions $acts_{i+1}$, which it combines with external events ext_{i+1}, to produce a consistent set of concurrent events $ev_{i+1} = ext_{i+1} \cup acts_{i+1}$. The events ev_{i+1} are used to update the current state S_i, generating the successor state $S_{i+1} = succ(S_i, ev_{i+1})$.

In KELPS, states are represented by sets of ground atoms[2], also called *facts* or *fluents*. Events are also represented by ground atoms. Such sets of ground atoms can be understood in two ways: They can be understood literally as theories or as Herbrand interpretations, which are model-theoretic structures. It is this second interpretation that underpins the logical semantics of KELPS.

States and events can be represented with or without timestamps. The representation without timestamps facilitates destructive updates, because if a fact is not terminated by a set of events, then the fact without timestamps simply persists from one state to the next. However, the representation with timestamps makes it possible to combine all the states and events into a single Herbrand interpretation.

2.1 Vocabulary

KELPS is a first-order, sorted language, including a special sort for time. In the version of KELPS presented in this paper, we assume that time is linear and discrete, and that the succession of time points is represented by the ticks of a logical clock, where 1, 2, ... stand for $s(0)$, $s(s(0))$, ..., $t+1$ stands for $s(t)$ and $t+n$ stands for $s^n(t)$. Thus S_i represents the state at time i, and ev_{i+1} represents the set of events taking place in the transition from state S_i to S_{i+1}. Other representations of time are also possible, as illustrated informally in Fig. 1.

Predicates: The predicate symbols of the language are partitioned into sets representing fluents, events, auxiliary predicates and meta-predicates:

Fluent predicates represent facts in the states S_i. The last argument i of a timestamped fluent atom $p(t_1, ..., t_n, i)$ is a time parameter, representing the time i of the state S_i to which the fluent belongs. The unstamped fluent atom $p(t_1, ..., t_n)$ is the same atom without this timestamp. Fluents can also have other time parameters, called *reference times*, for example *friday* in *payment-due(friday, i)*, which expresses that at time i payment is due on *friday*.

Event predicates represent events contributing to the transition from one state to the next. The last argument of a timestamped event atom $e(t_1, ..., t_n, i)$ is a time parameter, representing the time of the successor state S_i. The unstamped event atom $e(t_1, ..., t_n)$ is the same atom without this time parameter. Event predicates are partitioned into *external event predicates* and *action predicates*.

Auxiliary predicates are of two kinds: *time-independent predicates*, such as *isa(book, product)*, and *temporal constraint predicates*, which express *temporal constraints*, including inequalities of the form $i < j$ or $i \leq j$ between time points, other

---

[2] By *atom* we mean an atomic formula possibly containing variables. By *atomic sentence* or *ground atom*, we mean an atomic formula not containing variables.

relationships between time points, such as *max(T1, T2, T)* and *min(T1, T2, T)*, and arithmetic relationships involving time points, such as *plus(T1, 3, T2)*.

In LPS, auxiliary predicates are defined by logic programs. In KELPS, they are defined more simply by a (possibly infinite) set *Aux* of atomic sentences. This assumption that the temporal constraint predicates are defined by sets of ground atoms is the same as the assumption made in the semantics of constraint predicates in constraint logic programming (CLP) [6]. The KELPS OS exploits this relationship with CLP by using a constraint solver to check temporal constraints for satisfiability. As is common in the theory of CLP, it is sufficient to ensure that constraints are satisfiable. However, in practice, it is useful also to simplify the constraints.

The *meta-predicates* consist of the two predictates *initiates(events, fluent)* and *terminates(events, fluent)*, which are used to specify the postconditions of events and to perform state transitions, as illustrated in Fig. 1. The first argument is a set of events, to cater for the case where two events together have different effects from the individual events on their own (such as buying two books and getting the cheaper one for half price). In LPS, these meta-predicates are defined by a logic program. In KELPS, they are defined by a set of atomic sentences[3] in a *causal theory C*, which also contains constraints on the preconditions and co-occurrence of events.[4]

2.2   KELPS Framework

Definition. A KELPS framework (or program) is a triple *<R, Aux, C>*, where *R* is a set of reactive rules, *Aux* is a set of ground atoms defining auxiliary predicates, and *C* is a causal theory.

Rules in *R* are constructed from formulas that represent complex events or plans, expressed as conjunctions of state conditions, event atoms, and temporal constraints. Operationally, state conditions are queries to the current state, treated as a database. Like relational database queries, state conditions can be formulas of FOL. For example, the state condition ∀*It* ∀*D* [*manages(M, D, T)* ∧ *item(It, D)* → *instock(It, T)*] behaves as a query that returns managers *M* all of whose departments *D* have all of their items *It* in stock at time *T*.

Definition. A *state condition* is an FOL formula whose atoms are either time-independent predicates or fluent atoms having the same timestamp, which is unbound in the condition.

Rules can have disjunctive consequents. For example:

orders(C, Item, T1)
→ [*dispatch(C, Item, T2)* ∧ *send-invoice(C, Item, T3)* ∧ *T1 < T2 ≤ T3 ≤ T1 + 3*]
∨ [*send-apology(C, Item, T4)* ∧ *T1 < T4 ≤ T1 + 5*]]

---

[3] In the examples, in Fig. 1 and elsewhere in the paper, we use universally quantified sentences as a shorthand for the set of all their well-sorted ground instances.

[4] In earlier papers, this causal theory was called a "domain theory".

Different alternatives in the consequent can have different deadlines. If the antecedent becomes true, then the plan with the earliest deadline can be attempted first. If it fails to be achieved within the deadline, then an alternative plan with a later deadline can be attempted. However, any actions performed in the earlier, partially executed plan cannot be directly undone. Any "backtracking" to try an alternative plan must be performed in the context of the state updated by the successful actions in the failed plan.

Definition. A *reactive rule* is a sentence of the form:

$$\forall X \ [antecedent \rightarrow \exists Y \ [consequent]] \ \text{where:}$$

- *consequent* is a disjunction $consequent_1 \lor ... \lor consequent_n$.
- X is the set of all variables, including time variables, that occur in *antecedent* and are not bound in state conditions. Y is the set of all variables, including time variables, that occur only in *consequent* and are not bound in state conditions.
- *antecedent* and each $consequent_i$ is a conjunction of state conditions, event atoms and temporal constraints.
- The only variables occurring in temporal constraints are those that occur in state conditions and event atoms of the rule, or ones that are functionally dependent on such variables.
- All the timestamps in Y are constrained in the *consequent* to be later than or equal to the timestamps in X.[5]

Because of the restrictions on the quantification of variables, and the logical equivalence $\exists Y[p \lor q] \Leftrightarrow \exists Y \ p \lor \exists Z \ q$, we can omit the quantifiers $\forall X$ and $\exists Y$, and simply write *antecedent* $\rightarrow$ *consequent* or *antecedent* $\rightarrow$ $consequent_1 \lor ... \lor consequent_n$.

Definition. A *causal theory*, $C = C_{post} \cup C_{pre}$, consists of two parts: C_{post} is a set of atomic sentences defining the predicates *initiates* and *terminates*. C_{pre} is a set of sentences of the form $\forall X \ [antecedent \rightarrow false]$, where *antecedent* is a conjunction consisting of a single state condition with timestamp T and event atoms with timestamp $T+1$, where T is included in X.

For example, the preconditions for *dispatch(C, Item, T)* in Fig. 1 might include:

$$dispatch(C1, Item, T) \land dispatch(C2, Item, T) \land C1 \neq C2 \rightarrow false$$
$$dispatch(C, Item, T+1) \land \neg \ instock(Item, T) \rightarrow false$$

where *instock(Item)* is a fluent, initiated and terminated by the actions *stock(Item)* and *dispatch(C, Item)*, respectively.

The definitions of the predicates *initiates* and *terminates* by means of atomic sentences is similar to the use of add-lists and delete-lists in STRIPS [19]. However, it is more general, because the first argument is a *set* of events. Stating explicitly the fluents initiated and terminated by every possible set of concurrent events is not very

---

[5] More precisely, for every substitution σ that replaces the time variables in X and Y by ground times and such that the temporal constraints in *consequent* σ are *true* in **Aux**, the all timestamps in *consequent* σ are later than or equal to the latest timestamp in *antecedent* σ.

practical, but it clarifies the model-theoretic semantics and simplifies the operational semantics. Moreover, it paves the way for the more practical representation in which the *initiates* and *terminates* predicates are defined by logic programs in LPS.

Reactive rules R and preconditions C_{pre} have the same semantics. Moreover, they both have a deontic (but non-modal) character. The reactive rules specify obligations that must be fulfilled, typically by performing actions, whereas the preconditions specify combinations of state conditions and events that are prohibited.

3   The KELPS Model-Theoretic Semantics

In the model-theoretic semantics of KELPS, the reactive rules R and preconditions C_{pre} are interpreted according to the standard, non-modal semantics of classical first-order logic. This contrasts with the semantics of modal logics, in which states are represented by possible worlds, linked by accessibility relations. In KELPS, states and events are timestamped and included in a single model-theoretic structure.

Definition. If $<R, Aux, C>$ is a KELPS framework, S is a set of unstamped fluents, representing a single state, and ev is a set of unstamped events, representing concurrent events, then the associated *successor state* is:

$$succ(S, ev) = (S - \{p \mid terminates(ev, p) \in C_{post} \}) \cup \{p \mid initiates(ev, p) \in C_{post}\}.$$

Notation. If S_i is a set of fluents without timestamps, then $S_i{}^*$ represents the same set of fluents with the timestamp i. If $events_i$ is a set of concurrent events without timestamps, all taking place in the transition from state S_{i-1} to state S_i, then $events_i{}^*$ represents the same set of events with the timestamp i.

If S_0 is an initial state, $ext_1, \ldots, ext_i, \ldots$, is a sequence of sets of external events and $acts_1, \ldots, acts_i, \ldots$ is a sequence of sets of actions, then:

$$S^* = S_0{}^* \cup S_1{}^* \cup \ldots \cup S_i{}^* \cup \ldots \quad \text{where } S_{i+1} = succ(S_i, ev_{i+1})$$
$$ev^* = ev_1{}^* \cup ev_2{}^* \cup \ldots \cup ev_i{}^* \cup \ldots \quad \text{where } ev_i = ext_i \cup acts_i, \text{ for } i \geq 1.$$

Computation in conventional reactive systems consists in generating a stream $act_1, \ldots, act_i, \ldots$ of actions in response to a stream of external events $ext_1, \ldots ext_i, \ldots$. Computation in KELPS is similar, but it has a purpose, which conventional reactive systems lack, namely to make rules and the preconditions of actions *true*:

Definition. Given a KELPS framework $<R, Aux, C>$, an initial state S_0 and a sequence $ext_1, \ldots, ext_i$ of sets of external events, the *computational task* is to generate sets $acts_{i+1}$ of actions for every $i \geq 0$, such that $R \cup C_{pre}$ is *true* in the Herbrand interpretation $M = Aux \cup S^* \cup ev^*$.

The definition of truth is the classical definition for FOL. It allows the generation of actions that make the rules *true* by making their antecedents *false*, or by making their consequents *true* whether their antecedents are *true* or *false*. It also allows actions that are irrelevant to the task. In this paper, we identify the reactive models that can be generated by the OS.

Note that the generated actions $acts_{i+1}$ in KELPS need not be a direct reaction to the current situation $S_i^* \cup ev_i^*$, but can be a partial response to some subsequence of earlier states and events. Nor need the choice of actions be deterministic. There can be several different sets of actions $acts_{i+1}$ that can be chosen for execution in the transition from a given state S_i to the next state S_{i+1} and there can be many different models M that satisfy a given computational task. However, once an action has been chosen and successfully executed, it cannot be directly undone. At best, it may be possible only to choose and execute other actions to reverse its effects.

3.1   Herbrand Interpretations

The semantics of Herbrand interpretations is a simplified version of the standard semantics of first-order logic.

Definition. Given the vocabulary of a sorted first-order language, the *Herbrand universe* is the set of all well-sorted *ground* (i.e variable-free) terms that can be constructed from the constants and function symbols of the vocabulary. The *Herbrand base* is the set of all well-sorted ground atoms that can be constructed from the predicate symbols and the ground terms of the vocabulary. A *Herbrand interpretation* is a subset of the Herbrand base. A *Herbrand model M* of a set S of sentences is a Herbrand interpretation such that every sentence s in S is *true* in M.

The main difference from the standard definition of truth is the base case: If I is a Herbrand interpretation, then a ground atom A is *true* in I if and only if $A \in I$. Thus, a rule $\forall X [antecedent \rightarrow \exists Y [consequent_1 \vee ... \vee consequent_n]]$ is *true* in I if and only if, for every ground instance *antecedent* σ that is *true* in I, there exists a ground instance *consequent_i* $\sigma \theta$ that is also *true* in I. Here the substitutions σ and θ replace the variables X and Y, respectively, by terms of the appropriate sort in the Herbrand universe U of I. For simplicity, we assume that, except for time parameters, all fluents have the same ground instances over U in all states.

3.2   The Temporal Structure of KELPS Interpretations

The timestamping of fluents and events, and the restrictions on the syntax of KELPS provide KELPS interpretations with a rich structure of sub-interpretations. This structure is captured by the following theorem, which is an immediate consequence of the definition of truth for sentences in Herbrand interpretations.

Theorem 1
1. If s is a conjunction of temporal constraints whose time parameters are all ground, then s is *true* in $\mathbf{Aux} \cup \mathbf{S^*} \cup ev^*$ if and only if s is *true* in $\mathbf{Aux}$.
2. If s is an FOL sentence containing only state conditions, event atoms and temporal constraints whose time parameters are all ground, then:
    a. If all the timestamps in s are the same time i,
        then s is *true* in $\mathbf{Aux} \cup \mathbf{S^*} \cup ev^*$ if and only if s is *true* in $\mathbf{Aux} \cup S_i^* \cup ev_i^*$.

b. If i is the latest timestamp in s, then s is *true* in $Aux \cup S^* \cup ev^*$
if and only if s is *true* in $Aux \cup S_0^* \cup ... S_i^* \cup ev_1^* \cup ... ev_i^*$.

There is an obvious similarity with the possible world semantics of modal logic. Each sub-interpretation $Aux \cup S_i^* \cup ev_i^*$ is analogous to a possible world, and the single interpretation $Aux \cup S^* \cup ev^*$ is analogous to a complete frame of possible worlds and accessibility relations. However, in KELPS, timestamped fluents and events are all contained in a single Herbrand interpretation; but in the possible world semantics, fluents belong to possible worlds, and events belong to accessibility relations.

3.3   Sequential Notation

The antecedents and alternative consequents of reactive rules are both partially ordered state conditions and event atoms. Antecedents represent complex (or composite) events, and alternative consequents represent conditional plans of actions. Although these state conditions and event atoms are partially ordered, they are used to recognize or generate linearly ordered sequences of states and events.

It is useful to have a notation that distinguishes between the different sequences represented by the same conjunction of partially ordered state conditions and event atoms:

Notation. Let *condition1* ∧ *condition2* be a conjunction of state conditions and event atoms, *constraints* a conjunction of temporal constraints, and C the conjunction *condition1* ∧ *condition2* ∧ *constraints*. If there exists a substitution σ that grounds all the time parameters of C, and if *constraints* σ is true in Aux, then:

1. *condition1* < *condition2* ∧ *constraints* denotes that for every timestamp t_1 in *condition1* σ and every timestamp t_2 in *condition2* σ, $t_1 < t_2$.
2. *condition1* ≤ *condition2* ∧ *constraints* denotes that for every timestamp t_1 in *condition1* σ and every timestamp t_2 in *condition2* σ, $t_1 \leq t_2$.

We refer both to *condition1* < *condition2* ∧ *constraints* and to *condition1* ≤ *condition2* ∧ *constraints* as *sequencings* of C. Note that *condition1* < *condition2* and *condition1* ≤ *condition2* hold when *condition1* or *condition2* are empty (equivalent to *true*).

3.4   Reactive Interpretations

Fig. 1 gives examples of different kinds of models of a KELPS program. The following definition characterizes reactive interpretations, which include reactive models as a special case. Loosely speaking, an action occurs in a reactive interpretation if and only if it occurs in the consequent of an instance of a reactive rule, and all earlier state conditions and event atoms in the instance are already *true*.

Definition. Given a KELPS framework $<R, Aux, C>$, initial state S_0 and set ev^* of timestamped events, let C_{pre} be *true* in $I = Aux \cup S^* \cup ev^*$, and let $ev^* = ext^* \cup acts^*$ be a partitioning of ev^* into external events ext^* and actions $acts^*$. Then I is *reactive* if and only if, for every action *act* in I, there exists a rule $r \in R$ of the form:

   antecedent → [*other* ∨ [*earlier* ∧ *action* ∧ *remainder* ∧ *temp*]] where:

1) *temp* consists of all the temporal constraints in *earlier*∧*action*∧*remainder*∧ *temp*
2) all the non-timestamp variables in *action* occur in *antecedent* or *earlier*[6] and
3) there exists an instance $r\ \sigma$ of r such that:
    a) *act* is *action* σ
    b) *antecedent* σ ∧ *earlier* σ ∧ *action* σ ∧ *temp* σ is *true* in I and
    c) *earlier* σ < *action* σ ≤ *remainder* σ ∧ *temp* σ.

I is a *reactive model* of <R, Aux, C>, if and only if I is a *reactive interpretation* and R is *true* in I.

4   The KELPS Operational Semantics

The operational semantics exploits the internal structure of KELPS interpretations $Aux \cup S* \cup ev*$ to generate them by *progressively* extending a partial interpretation $Aux \cup S_0* \cup ... S_i* \cup ev_1* \cup ... ev_i*$ one step at a time. Moreover, it does so by maintaining only the current state S_i and the events ev_i that gave rise to S_i, without remembering earlier states and events. For this purpose, it maintains a current set of partially evaluated rules R_i, which need to be monitored in the future, and a current goal state G_i, which needs to be made *true* in the future.

To deal with complex events in the *antecedents* of rules without remembering past states and events, the OS maintains a current set of rules R_i, starting with $R_0 = R$. Each rule in R_i is the instantiated remainder *later* σ ∧ *temp* σ → *consequent* σ of a rule *earlier* ∧ *later* ∧ *temp* → *consequent* in R whose earlier part *earlier* σ is already *true*.

Logically, the goal state G_i is a conjunction of disjunctions. Each disjunct of a disjunction is the instantiated remainder *later* σ ∧ *temp* σ of a rule *antecedent* → [*other* ∨ [*earlier* ∧ *later* ∧ *temp*]] in R whose earlier part *antecedent* σ ∧ *earlier* σ is already *true*. Because of their similarity to goal clauses in logic programming, such disjuncts are also called *goal clauses* in KELPS.

Operationally, the goal state is a set (conjunction) of independent threads, and each thread is a goal tree, whose non-root nodes are goal clauses. The goal tree representation helps to structure the search space of alternative plans, and to guide the search strategy for trying different alternatives. If the goal trees are searched in a depth-first fashion, then they can be implemented by stacks, as in Prolog. Backtracking is possible, but previously generated actions and states cannot be undone.

The following specification of the OS is very abstract and ignores many optimizations that can improve efficiency. These are described in earlier papers [12, 13, 14, 15]. Some of these optimizations restrict the models that can be generated, and hence affect the relationship between the interpretations generated by the OS and the interpretations sanctioned by the model-theoretic semantics.

In the following definition, the OS is presented as an agent cycle. At the end of the cycle, external events are input and combined with selected actions. The resulting combined set of events is used to update the current state. In other versions of the OS, these updates were performed at the beginning of the cycle.

---

[6] This is a form of range restriction, which ensures that when an action is selected for execution, all its non-timestamped variables are grounded.

Definition. The OS Cycle. Initially S_0 is given, $R_0 = \mathbf{R}$, $G_0 = \{\}$ and $ev_0 = \{\}$.
For $i \geq 0$, given S_i, R_i, G_i, and ev_i, the i-th cycle consists of the following steps:

Step 1. Evaluate antecedents of rules. For every sequencing *current* θ $<$ *rest* $\theta \wedge$ *constraints* θ of the antecedent of an instance $r\theta$ of a rule r

$$\text{current} \;\wedge\; \text{rest} \;\wedge \text{constraints} \;\rightarrow \text{consequent}$$

in R_i, where *current* θ is *true* in $\mathbf{Aux} \cup S_i^* \cup ev_i^*$ and θ instantiates only the variables in *current* and any evaluable time variables in *constraints* that are functionally dependent on the timestamp of *current*, add *rest* $\theta \wedge$ *constraints* $\theta \rightarrow$ *consequent* θ as a new reactive rule to R_i.

If *rest* θ is empty (equivalent to *true*) and *constraints* θ is *true* in $\mathbf{Aux}$ then transfer *consequent* θ from R_i to G_i, starting a new thread, which is a goal tree with *consequent* θ at the root. Add each disjunct of *consequent* θ whose constraints are satisfiable as a child of the root.

Step 2. Evaluate state conditions and simple event atoms in goal clauses. Choose a set of sequencings:

$$\text{current} \;\; \theta \;\; < \text{rest} \; \theta \;\; \wedge \text{constraints} \; \theta$$

of instances $C\theta$ of goal clauses C from one or more threads in G_i, where *current* θ is *true* in $\mathbf{Aux} \cup S_i^* \cup ev_i^*$ and θ instantiates only the variables in *current* and any evaluable time variables in *constraints* that are functionally dependent on the timestamp of *current*. For each such choice, add *rest* $\theta \wedge$ *constraints* θ to G_i, as a child of C.

Step 3. Choose a conjunction of actions for attempted execution. Choose a set of sequencings:

$$\text{actions} \; \tau \leq \text{rest} \; \tau \wedge \text{constraints} \; \tau$$

of instances $C \tau$ of goal clauses C from one or more threads in G_i, where τ instantiates only the timestamp variables in *actions*, and *actions* τ is the conjunction of *all* the ground action atoms in $C \tau$ that have the same timestamp $i+1$. Let *candidate-acts$_{i+1}$* be the set of all the action atoms in all such *actions* τ.

Step 4. Update S_i, G_i, R_i. Choose a subset *acts$_{i+1}$*$^* \subseteq$ *candidate-acts$_{i+1}$* such that C_{pre} is *true* in $\mathbf{Aux} \cup S_i^* \cup ev_{i+1}^*$, where $ev_{i+1}^* = ext_{i+1}^* \cup acts_{i+1}^*$ and the set of external events ext_{i+1}^* is given. Let $S_{i+1} = succ(S_i, ev_{i+1})$. Let $G_{i+1} = G_i$ and $R_{i+1} = R_i$.

Note that the OS allows attempting to make an instance of a consequent of a reactive rule true even though the same instance of the consequent has already been made true. This can be avoided easily in the OS, but would make the corresponding definition of reactive interpretations substantially more complex. However, there are other optimisations that can also be made easily in the OS, without affecting the definition of reactive interpretation. These optimisations include removing from R_i rules whose antecedents are timed out, and removing from G_i leaf node goal clauses containing a conjunct that is timed out.

5   Relationships between the Model-Theoretic Semantics and the Operational Semantics

The proof of soundness for the OS of LPS [11, 12, 14] also applies to KELPS:

Theorem 2. Soundness. Given a KELPS framework *<R, Aux, C>*, initial state S_0 and sequence $ext_1,\ldots, ext_i,\ldots$ of sets of external events, suppose that the OS generates the sequences $acts_1*,\ldots, acts_i*,\ldots$ of actions and $S_1*,\ldots, S_i*,\ldots$ of states. Then $R \cup C_{pre}$ is true in $I = Aux \cup S* \cup ev*$ if, for every goal tree that is added to a goal state G_i, $i \geq 0$, the goal clause *true* is added to the same goal tree in some goal state $G_j, j \geq i$.

The following theorems characterise the interpretations generated by the OS.

Theorem 3. The OS generates only reactive interpretations. Given a KELPS framework *<R, Aux, C>*, initial state S_0 and set of external events *ext**, let *acts** be the set of actions generated by the OS, and *ev** = *ext** $\cup$ *acts**. Then $I = Aux \cup S*$ $\cup ev*$ is a reactive interpretation.

Theorem 4. The OS can generate any reactive interpretation. Given a KELPS framework *<R, Aux, C>*, initial state S_0 and set of external events *ext**, let *acts** be a set of actions such that $I = Aux \cup S* \cup ev*$ is a reactive interpretation. Then there exist choices in steps 2, 3 and 4 such that the OS generates *acts** (and therefore generates *I*).

6   Related Work

In terms of expressive power, KELPS is similar to Reaction RuleML [16], and much of the comparison with other systems presented in [16] also holds for KELPS. Moreover, our earlier papers [11, 12, 13, 14] also include extensive discussions of the relationships between LPS and production systems, BDI agents, event-condition action rules in active databases, action languages in AI and other models of computation. For lack of space and to avoid repeating these comparisons, in this paper we will focus instead on pointing out only the most important relationships, which are with abductive logic programming, MetateM and Transaction Logic.

6.1   Abductive Logic Programming (ALP)

Despite the fact that logic programming plays only a supporting role in LPS, and no role at all in KELPS, ALP played an important role in the development of LPS, and therefore of KELPS. More importantly, the origin [9, 10] of LPS [11, 12, 14] in ALP

[8] helps to explain the semantics of KELPS and the issues concerning completeness, which are the focus of this paper.

An ALP framework is a triple $<L, I, A>$, where L is a logic program, I is a set of integrity constraints, and A is a set of atomic sentences, which are candidate assumptions. KELPS is closely related to the special case of ALP in which L is a set of atomic sentences including S_0, *ext** and *Aux*, I consists of reactive rules R and preconditions C_{pre}, and A is the set of all possible actions. The biggest difference is the way in which KELPS generates $S*$.

In applications of ALP to planning problems [3, 18], it has been common to include the event calculus [15] in the logic program L. Although this use of the event calculus has been interpreted as a solution to the frame problem [17], we believe that it cannot compete for efficiency with destructive change of state. However, destructive change of state does not have an obvious logical semantics. In particular, if states are regarded as syntactic objects, defined by axioms, then it is not possible to change the axioms during the course of trying to prove a theorem.

In KELPS, we solve this problem by regarding states and events as belonging to model-theoretic structures. This corresponds to a semantics for ALP in which, given an ALP framework $<L, I, A>$, an *abductive solution* is a subset Δ of A, such that I is *true* in a canonical model of $L \cup \Delta$. This is very close to the semantics of KELPS.

The issues concerning the completeness of KELPS are of two different kinds. The first is inherited from the semantics of abduction, namely that the semantics allows models in which Δ contains irrelevant actions. The second results from replacing the event calculus by destructive updates.

In the case of abduction, the first issue is dealt with by imposing further restrictions on the solutions Δ - for example, requiring that Δ be minimal, in the sense that no $\Delta' \subset \Delta$ (properly contained in Δ) is also a solution. But guaranteeing minimality is computationally expensive, and in practice some weaker, often informally specified requirement, such as relevance, is imposed. In the case of KELPS, the analogous relevance requirement is that generated actions be instances of action atoms that occur explicitly in the consequent of a reactive rule.

The second issue does not arise in ALP when the event calculus is included in the program L, because then the event calculus can be used to make facts *true* by generating events that initiate them, and to make facts *false* by generating events that terminate them. In the case of KELPS, the more restricted causal theory C_{post} is used only to update states with given sets of events.

6.2   MetateM

MetateM [1] is a temporal modal logic language in which a program consists of sentences of the logical form:

'past and present formula' **implies** 'present or future formula'

Computation consists in generating a model in which all such sentences are *true*. These programs are similar in spirit to the reactive rules of KELP and have a similar model-theoretic semantics. The main differences are that, in KELPS, time is represented explicitly, models are classical rather than modal, and models are constructed by means of destructive updates. Completeness has been shown [1] for propositional MetateM, without external events, maintaining the entire history of past states, backtracking from the future into the past in the search for a model, and encoding frame axioms in the reactive rules.

6.3   Transaction Logic

Transaction Logic [2] is a declarative, logic-based language for defining complex transactions, which update states of a logic program or database. Transactions in Transaction Logic have a logical, model-theoretic semantics defined in terms of paths between states, generated by means of destructive updates. Although there is no direct analogue of reactive rules, they can be simulated by means of transactions.

KELPS shares with Transaction Logic the view of computation as generating sequences of destructively updated states that can be viewed as databases, in contrast with conventional programming languages, in which states are simply collections of variable-value assignments. KELPS also shares with Transaction Logic the view that transactions are sequences of sets of actions and database queries expressed in full FOL.[7] The main differences are that in KELPS, transactions are the consequents of reactive rules that are triggered when the antecedents become *true*, time is represented explicitly, and all states, actions and events are combined into one model-theoretic structure.

7   Conclusions and Future Work

This paper does not exhaust all of the theoretical issues concerning the semantics of KELPS and LPS. However, there are also important practical issues concerning knowledge representation and implementation that need further work. In particular, there are two extensions of KELPS and LPS that would significantly improve their expressive power. One is to allow the consequents of reactive rules to contain conditions that also have antecedent-consequent form. This can be implemented simply by allowing the remainder generated in step 2 of the OS to have the form of a reactive rule. The other extension is to allow reactive rules to contain more complex event conditions. This extension also does not affect the semantics, and can be implemented, for example, by storing a history of past events.

There are a number of implementations of LPS. Focusing on a single implementation and making it available for wider use are the main priority for future work.

Acknowledgements. Many thanks to Howard Boley for encouraging us with this work, and to the referees for their helpful comments on the paper.

---

[7] Transaction Logic also uses logic programs both to define intentional database predicates and to define sequences of state conditions and events. This capability is also available in LPS, but has been eliminated from KELPS for simplicity.

References

1. Barringer, H., Fisher, M., Gabbay, D., Owens, R., Reynolds, M.: The imperative future: Principles of executable temporal logic. John Wiley & Sons, Inc. (1996)
2. Bonner, A., Kifer, M.: Transaction logic programming. In: Warren, D.S. (ed.) Logic Programming: Proc. of the 10th International Conf., pp. 257–279 (1993)
3. Eshghi, K.: Abductive Planning with Event Calculus. In: ICLP/SLP, pp. 562–579 (1988)
4. Gurevich, Y.: Evolving algebras 1993: Lipari guide. In: Specification and validation Methods, pp. 9–36 (1995)
5. Harel, D.: Statecharts: A Visual Formalism for Complex Systems. Sci. Comput. Programming 8, 231–274 (1987)
6. Jaffar, J., Lassez, J.L.: Constraint logic programming. In: Proceedings of the 14th ACM SIGACT-SIGPLAN Symposium on Principles of programming languages, pp. 111–119. ACM (1987)
7. Kakas, A.C., Kowalski, R., Toni, F.: The Role of Logic Programming in Abduction. In: Handbook of Logic in Artificial Intelligence and Programming, vol. 5, pp. 235–324. Oxford Univerpsity Press (1998)
8. Kakas, A.C., Mancarella, P., Sadri, F., Stathis, K., Toni, F.: The KGP model of agency. In: Proc. ECAI 2004 (2004)
9. Kowalski, R., Sadri, F.: From Logic Programming Towards Multi-agent Systems. Annals of Mathematics and Artificial Intelligence 25, 391–419 (1999)
10. Kowalski, R., Sadri, F.: Integrating Logic Programming and Production Systems in Abductive Logic Programming Agents. In: Polleres, A., Swift, T. (eds.) RR 2009. LNCS, vol. 5837, pp. 1–23. Springer, Heidelberg (2009)
11. Kowalski, R., Sadri, F.: An Agent Language with Destructive Assignment and Model-Theoretic Semantics. In: Dix, J., Leite, J., Governatori, G., Jamroga, W. (eds.) CLIMA XI. LNCS (LNAI), vol. 6245, pp. 200–218. Springer, Heidelberg (2010)
12. Kowalski, R., Sadri, F.: Abductive Logic Programming Agents with Destructive Databases. Annals of Mathematics and Artificial Intelligence 62(1), 129–158 (2011)
13. Kowalski, R., Sadri, F.: A Logic-Based Framework for Reactive Systems. In: Bikakis, A., Giurca, A. (eds.) RuleML 2012. LNCS, vol. 7438, pp. 1–15. Springer, Heidelberg (2012)
14. Kowalski, R., Sadri, F.: Model-theoretic and operational semantics for Reactive Computing. To Appear in New Generation Computing (2014)
15. Kowalski, R., Sergot, M.: A Logic-based Calculus of Events. New Generation Computing 4(1), 67–95 (1986)
16. Paschke, A., Boley, H., Zhao, Z., Teymourian, K., Athan, T.: Reaction RuleML 1.0: standardized semantic reaction rules. In: Bikakis, A., Giurca, A. (eds.) RuleML 2012. LNCS, vol. 7438, pp. 100–119. Springer, Heidelberg (2012)
17. Shanahan, M.: Solving the frame problem: A mathematical investigation of the common sense law of inertia. MIT press (1997)
18. Shanahan, M.: An abductive event calculus planner. The Journal of Logic Programming 44(1), 207–240 (2000)
19. Fikes, R.E., Nilsson, N.J.: STRIPS: A new approach to the application of theorem proving to problem solving. Artificial Intelligence 2(3), 189–208 (1972)

On Using Semantically-Aware Rules
for Efficient Online Communication

Zaenal Akbar, José María García, Ioan Toma, and Dieter Fensel

Semantic Technology Institute, University of Innsbruck, Austria
`firstname.lastname@sti2.at`

Abstract. The ever growing number of communication channels not only enables a broader outreach for organizations, but also makes it more difficult for them to manage a very large number of channels and adapted content efficiently. Thus, finding the right channels to disseminate some content and adapting this content to specific channel requirements are real challenges for sharing information both efficiently and effectively. In this work, we present a rule-based system that addresses these challenges by decoupling the information to be shared from the actual channels where it is published. We propose semantic models to characterize and integrate various information sources and channels. A set of independent rules then interrelates these models, specifying the concrete publication workflow and content adaptation required. Furthermore, we evaluate our rule-based system using two different use cases, discussing the added value that the defined rules provide to this scenario and how they contribute to overcoming the identified challenges effectively.

Keywords: online communication, rule-based systems, knowledge modelling, social media.

1 Introduction

In order to be able to disseminate the information about their products or services, each organization needs to reach the widest possible audience. During the era of Internet, the number and kind of dissemination channels have been increasing: websites, e-mails, and social media have become mainstream means of communication.

For the organizations, being present on several channels is not enough, since they also have to make sure that their content is suitable for each channel. In this case, information dissemination is not only about finding suitable channels, but also fitting the content to the available channels dynamically. These are the main challenges for effective and efficient information dissemination, and for online communication in general.

Our solution to overcoming these challenges is to decouple information from channels, defining separate models for each of them, and then interlinking them with an intermediary component [1]. Semantic technologies play four important

A. Bikakis et al. (Eds.): RuleML 2014, LNCS 8620, pp. 37–51, 2014.

roles in the solution [2]: semantic analysis, semantic channels as sharing data with reusable vocabularies, semantic content modeling, and semantic matchmaking.

In this paper, we discuss in detail the intermediary component to interlink content and channel, whose main objective is to align both components. Although this interlinking process is comprised of several elements, in this work we focus on the processing rules called *publication rules*. We first show the formalization of our solution, followed by rules construction accompanied by motivating examples. Furthermore, we discuss current implementation of this solution and two different use cases that validate our proposal.

The remainder of this paper is organized as follows: Section 2 describes our conceptual solution to overcoming the identified challenges of online communication. Section 3 introduces the publication rules as the main element of our online communication platform. Section 4 describes the technologies to implement our publication rules. Section 5 shows the application of our proposal to two different use cases. Finally, we discuss some related works in Section 6 and our conclusions and future work in Section 7.

2   Conceptual Approach

In this section, we describe our proposed conceptual solution to enable effective and efficient online communication. The proposed solution separates the content and channel to enable various dimensions of reuse in transactional communication [1]. This solution requires the development of information models, channel models and an intermediary component to align both models.

Our conceptual solution is shown in Fig. 1 where various information models and channel models were devised in order to represent the available information and targeted channels respectively. A component called *Weaver* corresponds to the intermediary component. Each component is described as follows:

Information Model. An information model is an ontology that describes the information items that are used in typical acts of communication in a certain domain. As a formal, explicit specification of a shared conceptualisation [3], an ontology represents the concepts, the relations between concepts, and their constraints. In the information models, the relevant concepts for information dissemination are determined and shared among the content sources (i.e. documents, databases) which might have different data formats/representations.

Channel Model. In online communication, a channel can be described as a means of exchanging information through the online space, which can be referred to (but not necessarily) with an Uniform Resource Identifier (URI) [4]. More than just as a place to spread or access information, a channel is also considered as a way to express or refer to the information. Each channel may have its own particularities including which types of information items can be read from or written to and access methods, among other particularities.

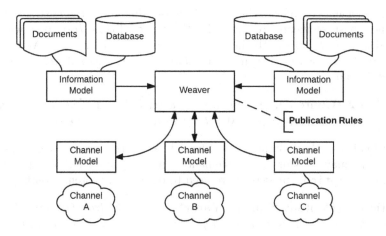

Fig. 1. Our conceptual solution for effective and efficient Online Communication

Weaver. The Weaver is the component responsible for aligning the information and channel models. Formally, it has nine elements [1]: *a)* an information item, *b)* an editor, *c)* an editor interaction protocol, *d)* an information type, *e)* a processing rule, *f)* a channel, *g)* an executor, *h)* an executor interaction protocol. This paper is focused on the definition of processing rules called publication rules that govern how the information and channel models fit together.

Rules. A rule is a form of representing knowledge specifying a certain conclusion whenever a certain premise is satisfied, represented as `IF Premise THEN Conclusion`. Generally, rules can be divided into three categories: deduction (derivation) rules, normative (integrity) rules, and reactive (active) rules [5]. Reactive rules are usually further divided into the form of Event-Condition-Action (ECA) rules and Condition-Action (CA) rules also known as production rules. We use production rules (in the form `IF Conditions DO Actions`) as the foundations to define our publication rules, where the `Actions` part will be executed whenever a change makes `Conditions` true.

3 Publication Rules

In this section, we describe the publication rules in detail, starting with the essential definitions, followed by the rule constructors, and finishing with a few examples of rule usage for complex online communication scenarios.

3.1 Definitions

Definition 1 (Information Item). *An information item I is the basic element of information in the domain of interest. Each element is identified by a name and the expected type of its value.*

The basic elements of information differ from one domain to the next. An example of these basic elements are `name` with the expected type *Text*, `date` with the expected type *Date*, `url` with the expected type *URL*, and so on. An element `name` might be divided further into `firstName` and `lastName`, depending on the modeled domain.

Definition 2 (Content). *A content C is described as a tuple of information items $I = (i_1, \cdots, i_n)$ where $|I| > 0$ is the number of items covered by C.*

The cardinality of the contents shows the richness of the information items represented, and may vary for each implementation. For example, information items (`title`, `description`, `location`) are used to describe a content `Event`.

Definition 3 (Content Transformator). *A content transformator T is an operator which transforms an input content C to produce a transformed content C^T.*

A content transformator operates on the information items of an input content, for example selecting a subset of the available items, shortening the value of an item, and so on.

Definition 4 (Channel). *A channel H is a place to publish contents C where each channel supports at least one content transformator T.*

Definition 5 (Transformation Specification). *A transformation specification S is a tuple of (H, T) where H is a channel and T is a content transformator that specifies that T is supported by H.*

Typically, an expert who is familiar with the channel specificities determines whether a content transformator is supported by a channel.

Definition 6 (Mapping). *A mapping M is a tuple of (C, H) where C is the content to be published and H is the targeted channel.*

The mapping is determined by experts who understand which content will be published to which channel including which content transformation is required. A content could be mapped to one or more channels and a channel could be mapped with one or more contents.

Definition 7 (Publication). *A publication P is a tuple of (C^T, H) where C^T is the transformed content of C and H is the selected publication channel.*

Based on the previously explained definitions, we define the publication rules as follows:

Definition 8 (Publication Rules). *A publication rule R for a content C to a channel H is a mapping of C and H and a content transformator T supported by the channel H to produce a publication P. Given a transformation specification $S(H, T)$, a publication rule can be represented as $\{M(C, H) \wedge T(C) \rightarrow P(C^T, H)\}$*

With this definition, a publication rule is interlinking the information model (content) and channel model trough a mapping and a content transformation. The interlinking intention is to fit a content to a particular channel or to find the proper channels for a content. Therefore, a publication rule serves as: *a*) a mapping between a content and a channel, and *b*) a transformation of the content according to the mapped channels' specificities.

The publication rules are also controllable through a workflow or scheduling specification. For this case, we introduce the following definitions:

Definition 9 (Publication Workflow). *A publication workflow is a coordinated publication where a publication P_1 will be performed only after a publication P_0 has been successfully executed. Given a transformation specification $S(H, T)$, a publication rule with a workflow can be represented as $\{M(C, H) \wedge T(C) \wedge P_0 \rightarrow P_1(C^T, H)\}$.*

A workflow is useful to specify the publication order for a certain channels, one after another. For example, when we need a reference to a specific channel, the workflow can be used to ensure that the content will be published in the right order.

3.2 Rule Construction

Based on the definitions previously discussed, we define three different types of actions that could be fired by the rules as follows:

1. `Mapping` – an action to align a content to a channel
2. `Transform` – an action to transform a content using a content transformation operator associated with a channel
3. `Publish` – an action to publish a content to a channel

Each action will assert a new fact and together with predefined facts they form a collection of facts to be used to identify if a specific condition is fulfilled. We define four different types of facts as follows:

1. `hasTransformation` – a predefined fact to specify if a channel has a content transformation operator
2. `hasMapping` – a fact, will be inserted by the action `Mapping` to specify if a content is mapped to a channel
3. `isTransformedBy` – a fact, will be inserted by the action `Transform` to specify if a content has been transformed using a specific content transformation operator
4. `hasPublished` – a fact, will be inserted by the action `Publish` to specify if a content has been published to a channel

Based on those defined actions and facts, we constitute the publication rules with one basic fact and three basic rules as follows:

1. `Mapping(C,H)`
   This is a fact to mapping a content and a channel.

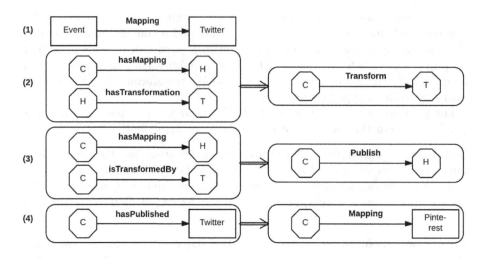

Fig. 2. An example of fact and rules construction

2. IF hasMapping(C,H) THEN Transform(C)
   This rule performs a content transformation operation using a transformation operator associated to a channel.
3. IF hasMapping(C,H) ∧ isTransformedBy(C,T) THEN Publish(C,H)
   This rule performs a publishing action on a content to a channel whenever a mapping and a transformation have applied successfully.
4. IF hasPublished(C,H1) THEN Mapping(C,H2)
   This rule is to define a workflow, where a content will be published to the second channel whenever it has been published to the first channel.

Fig. 2 shows an example of the fact and publication rules construction using Grailog representation [6]. The octagon shapes represent variables (C for contents, H for channels, T for transformation operators), the rectangle shapes represent instances of content or channel or transformation operator, the single-line arrows represent the relationships, the double-lines arrows imply the rule consequences. The rounded boxes with solid-lines imply conjunctions. Given two transformation operators $t_1, t_2 \in T$, an information model Event $\in C$ contains information items (name, description, location, url, startDate, endDate) $\in I$, two channel models Twitter, Pinterest $\in H$ to represent Twitter (https://twitter.com) and Pinterest (https://pinterest.com) respectively. Two predefined content transformation specification are (Twitter, t_1), (Pinterest, t_2) $\in S$.

Fact and rules in Fig. 2 are constructed to publish information about an event to social media channels Twitter and Pinterest. Fact (1) is mapping an event to Twitter,rule (2) defines a content transformation action whenever a content is mapping to a channel using a transformation operator associated with the channel, rule (3) defines a publishing action whenever the content transformation has successfully applied, rule (4) defines a mapping between some content to

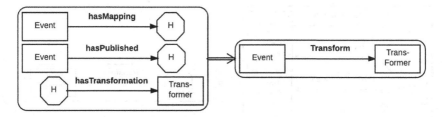

Fig. 3. A rule to define an implicit content transformation

channel Pinterest whenever the content has been already published to channel Twitter successfully. In this example, each instance of Event will be mapped to Twitter, then transformed by a transformation operator associated with Twitter and finally will be published to Twitter. After being successfully published, a second mapping is triggered to channel Pinterest, consequently repeating the content transformation and publish actions with this second mapping.

3.3   Rule Usage on Complex Online Communication

In addition to the typical publication rules (`Mapping - Transform - Publish`) as shown in previous section, our publication rules are also capable of handling various complex scenarios of online communication.

Implicit Content Transformation. A typical publication rule contains a mapping and a content transformation. However, a publication rule can also be constructed by defining the content transformation implicitly. As shown in Fig. 3, a more flexible rule can be devised by defining a rule to match a transformation operator from previous publication activities. In this example, the rule does not specify the content transformation explicitly. The rule will be matched to a transformation (`Transformer`) from previously published similar content (`Event`) to a similar channel (variable H).

Diverse Content Transformation. A channel may have more than one content transformation operator. Applying a different transformation to the same content will produce a different output. In the rule shown in Fig. 4, to publish a content C which has been published before (in this case to channel `Twitter`), the rule will be matched to a different transformation operator from that previously used. The box with dashed-lines indicates a negation, such that only the `Transformer`, which is not used by the previous publication, will be satisfied.

Rule Overwriting. A rule can also be used to overwrite another rule permanently or temporarily (depending on certain conditions). As shown in Fig. 5, we can overwrite a mapping fact by using rules. Fact (1) defines a mapping between the content Event to channel Twitter, rule (2) will be to overwrite the

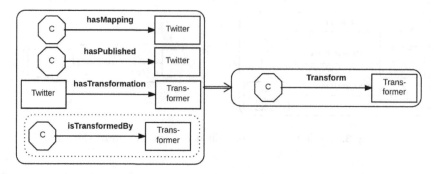

Fig. 4. A rule to use a different transformation implicitly

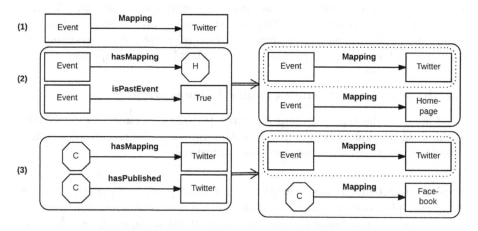

Fig. 5. A fact and two rules to overwrite the mapping

mapping whenever the event is identified as a past event, rule (3) will overwrite
the mapping if the content has been published on Twitter. Each rule will retract
the old mapping fact and insert a new one.

4   Implementation

In this section we explain the implementation of the publication rules in our
online communication platform. Fig. 6 shows the platform which consists of various components that are grouped based on their functionality in the conceptual
solution explained in Section 2.

Documents. The online data sources hold the related information to be disseminated. There are two types of data sources currently supported:

1. Annotated sources. An additional information (metadata) can be attached
   to the existing piece of data with the intention to describe the data. More

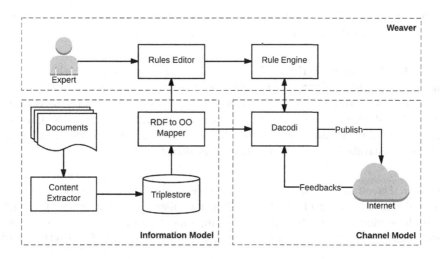

Fig. 6. The Online Communication platform architecture

annotated sources are available on the internet with a specific vocabulary to enable machines to interpret and use the data.

2. Un-annotated sources. The information is available without a common format/representation, existing in various database systems.

Content Extractor. This component is responsible for obtaining the content from data sources and representing them into the common vocabularies. The Linked Open Vocabularies (`http://lov.okfn.org/dataset/lov/`) are used primarily to achieve a reusable and interoperable information model: *a*) Dublin Core, a specification of all metadata terms to support of resource description (`http://dublincore.org/`), *b*) Friend of a Friend, a vocabulary to describe people, the links between them, the things they create and do (`http://www.foaf-project.org/`), *c*) Good Relations, a vocabulary to describe e-commerce products and services (`http://purl.org/goodrelations/`), *d*) Schema.org, a collection of tags to markup a page in ways recognized by major search engines (`http://schema.org/`). We use Apache Any23 (`https://any23.apache.org/`) to extract content (in the format of triples/RDF) from the annotated sources, and for un-annotated sources a manual mapping is required to relate the database items into the desired vocabularies.

Triplestore. A triplestore is a database repository to store triples/RDF statements extracted from data sources. We use OWLIM (`http://www.ontotext.com/owlim`) for a persistent storage and Apache Jena's (`https://jena.apache.org/`) In-Memory model for a non-persistent storage.

RDF to OO Mapper. This component maps the RDF models (instances of classes including their properties) from the triplestore into object-oriented models to be used by other components. In our current implementation we are using RDFBeans (`http://rdfbeans.sourceforge.net/`).

Rule Engine and Editor. To matching the facts against the defined rules, we use Drools (`http://drools.jboss.org/`) as rule engine, which implements and extends the Rete Algorithm [7] as its matching algorithm. To enable domain experts to maintain the rules, we use Drools Guvnor (`http://guvnor.jboss.org/`) as rule editor, it has rich web-based interface as well as a controllable access to the rules repository.

Dacodi. Dacodi is the component responsible for distributing the content to the selected communication channels, as well as for collecting and analyzing feedback from those channels [8]. In our current implementation, Dacodi offers various functionalities such as: role management, publication, feedback collection, and front-end.

After the information models are defined and targeted dissemination channels are selected, the publication rules can be specified and constructed by an expert through the rules editor. Then, the stored rules will be consumed by the rule engine to construct a knowledge base to be employed by the Dacodi to make a publication decision. For each new content successfully extracted by the content extractor, a new fact is inserted into the knowledge base by the Dacodi, triggering the rule engine to match the fact against the existing rules. Whenever a match is found, the associated publication actions will be executed, followed by a scheduling monitoring to all feedbacks for each published content on each channel.

5   Use Cases

In order to validate our proposal, in this section, we show two use cases where the publication rules have been applied. First we discuss how the rules are implemented in PlanetData (`http://www.planet-data.eu`) and Tourismusverband Innsbruck (`http://www.innsbruck.info`), followed by a discussion on the contributions of the publication rules to both use cases.

PlanetData. PlanetData is an European project funded by the EU Seventh Framework Programme between 2007 - 2013. For its dissemination activities, various information models have been defined, such as Project, Activity, Partners, WorkPackage, Event, Deliverable, FactSheet, Presentation, and others, as well as numerous dissemination channels: such as News, HomepageNews, RSS, PlanetData Mailing List, PlanetData Wiki, FacebookWall, and Semantics [9].

A subset of the publication rules for the PlanetData use case is shown in Fig. 7. The rules are intended to publish information about events to relevant channels. An object `Event` is used to represent all information items of event, including

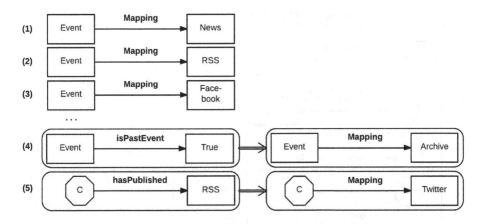

Fig. 7. A subset of the facts and publication rules for PlanetData

an item `pastEvent` as the representation of its dueness. The objects `News`, `RSS`, `Facebook`, `Archive` and `Twitter` are used to represent channels: the news section of the project website, the website RSS output, the project Facebook account, the archive section of the website and the project Twitter account, respectively.

As shown in Fig. 7, there are three methods to perform a mapping between a content to its selected dissemination channels. First, by using explicit mapping through facts (1-3); second by using a conditional mapping where a mapping will hold only if a certain condition is satisfied as shown in the rule (4) (the mapping between event to a channel Archive will hold only if the event has happened some time ago); third by using a publication workflow as shown in rule (5) (the mapping to the channel Twitter will hold only after the event has been published to the channel RSS). The rules for content transformation and publication are identical to the rules shown in Fig. 2.

Tourismusverband Innsbruck. The relevant information for dissemination found in Tourismusverband Innsbruck (TVb)'s website have been categorized as Hotels, Food and Drink Establishment, Events, Trips, Place of Interest and News. Those categories are then modeled as concepts in TVb's ontology where the main concepts are Place, Event, Organization, Trip (Action), Creative Work, and Person [10].

As dissemination channels, TVb is using Facebook, Twitter, YouTube, and a Blog, and has been planning to use other channels such as Google+, Pinterest, tumblr [11]. A subset of the current publication rules for TVb is shown in Fig. 8. The objects `Hotel`, `Trip`, `Event`, `PoI`, `News` are used to represent the information concepts for hotel, trip, event, place of interest and news respectively. On the other hand, the objects `Facebook`, `YouTube`, and `Twitter` are used to represent the TVb's Facebook account, TVb's YouTube account and TVb's Twitter account respectively.

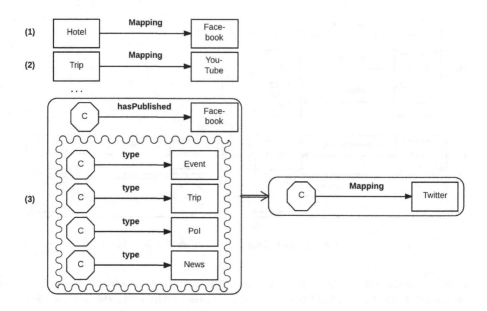

Fig. 8. A subset of the facts and publication rules for Tourismusverband Innsbruck

Fig. 8 shows a subset of facts and rules implementation where a box with a solid-wavy-line implies a disjunction. There are two methods to do a mapping; first by using explicit mapping through facts (1-2); second through a workflow definition as shown in rule (3) where a mapping to the channel Twitter for a content (event or trip or place of interest or news) will hold only after the content has been published to the channel Facebook. The rules for content transformation and publication are identical to the rules shown in Fig. 2.

Discussion

From both use cases, once the content types and targeted channels have been selected, the publication rules can be easily constructed. Given predefined content transformation operators for each channel, the mapping between content and channel can be defined explicitly and implicitly through rules. A publication workflow can be specified by adding referenced publication to the condition part of the relevant rules. In PlanetData, a content which needs to be published to Twitter must have a reference link to RSS, therefore the publication to RSS is included as criteria in condition of the Twitter's publication rule. TVb introduced a blog as a new input source where its contents are annotated with the Schema.org vocabulary. Since this vocabulary is supported by our information model, there is no need to modify the rule. A change is required only in the Dacodi to add the blog's URL as an input source to be included in the next content extraction cycle.

In both use cases, the publication rules have shown numerous ways of inter-linking the information models and channel models in the context of content dissemination. While the interlinking is determined by the experts, their representations might be specified explicitly through facts or implicitly through rules. These rich representations validate our solution to have various dimensions of reusing the content and channel in transactional communication.

6 Related Work

As the web is becoming more dynamic, reactive capability becomes more important in a variety of web applications [12,13]. Reactive rules as a form to represent knowledge can be used to realize this reactivity. The reaction rules have been standarized to include reaction rules and rule-based event processing in Reaction RuleML [14,15]. The publication rules presented in this paper are reactive rules derived from production (Condition-Action) rules which are capable of reacting to any changes in the input models. As our main usage is for online communication applications, the input models are ontologies (information models) which are domain specific. Our work is related to at least three relevant topics, described in the following paragraphs.

The first relevant topic is the channel to channel interlinking of online publishing. In this case, there are two prominent existing services: IFTTT (`http://ifttt.com`) and Zapier (`http://zapier.com`). Both services offer a solution to connect a channel to other channels including publishing content between channels through an automatic tool which is represented in a simple form `IF Trigger THEN Action`. Compared to these services, the main difference to our approach is in the creation of `Trigger`. In our approach, a knowledge-model is built, independent of any input channels. Instead of specifying a channel (i.e Facebook, Twitter) directly in Trigger, we use an information concept (i.e `Event`) instead, where the source of this concept could be a Facebook, a Twitter, or any other channels. We argue that using an information model as Trigger is highly suitable for integrating various input channels and offers high scalability. Whenever a new input channel is introduced where its content type is already included in the information model, then there is no need to create a new rule ("recipe" in IFTTT or "Zap" in Zapier).

The second relevant topic is to schema/ontology matching. The aim of the publication rules is to match two semantically represented models (information and channel). In this sense, the rules can be seen a matching mechanism. But in contrast to schema/ontology matching (such as [16,17]), the matching is determined by the experts where each implementation has a different matching mechanism, such as different information models and/or targeted channels. Moreover, our rule framework enables the selection of content transformation operator dynamically by using rules (as shown at Subsection 3.3) as a contrary to a static selection by defining the operator explicitly in a fact. A publication workflow can be defined by adding a reference to a publication as criteria to the condition of the rule as shown in rule (5) in Fig. 7 and rule (3) in Fig. 8.

The third relevant topic refers to workflow control. Controlling a workflow with a rule-based system has been investigated in a few works such as in [18,19]. From the three most commonly used workflow frameworks (control-flow graph, triggers, and temporal constraints), our workflow representation is an implementation of the triggers framework, where a workflow defines which publication activity needs to be executed first before the other activity.

7   Conclusions and Future Work

In this work we presented our rule-based solution for providing efficient and effective online communication, based on the separation of information and channel models. The publication rules introduced in this paper are reactive rules that are constructed to match the semantically represented domain specific information models to the channel models. This matching determines which information has to be disseminated to which channel, which content transformation and which publication workflow (if any) is required.

We have applied this type of rule to an online communication platform, which has been validated with two different use cases. In addition to reactiveness to changes in the information models, our rule-based solution also introduces new capabilities to dynamically adapt the content transformations and publication workflows if necessary. In conclusion, in order to achieve an effective and efficient online communication, publication rules devote a significant role to enable various dimensions of interlinking the information and channel models.

As future work, considering that in online communication the information is becoming more specific and targeted to a specific audience, we plan to extend the publication rules and associated channel models to reflect those specificities, such as enabling the definition of specific transformations for a certain channel. Furthermore we are going to incorporate more contextual dimensions into the publication rules, such as publication time, and location of target audience, among others.

Acknowledgements. We would like to thank all the members of the Online Communication working group (http://oc.sti2.at) for their valuable feedback and suggestions. This work was partly funded by the European Union's Seventh Framework Programme (FP7) under grant agreements no. 284860 (MSEE) and 257641 (PlanetData).

References

1. Fensel, D., Leiter, B., Thaler, S., Thalhammer, A., Toma, I.: Effective and efficient on-line communication. In: 23rd International Workshop on Database and Expert Systems Applications (DEXA), pp. 294–298 (2012)
2. Toma, I., Fensel, D., Gagiu, A.E., Stavrakantonakis, I., Fensel, A., Leiter, B., Thalhammer, A., Larizgoitia, I., Garcia, J.M.: Enabling scalable multi-channel communication through semantic technologies. In: International Conference on Web Intelligence, vol. 1, pp. 591–596 (2013)

3. Studer, R., Benjamins, V., Fensel, D.: Knowledge engineering: Principles and methods. Data & Knowledge Engineering 25(1-2), 161–197 (1998)
4. Fensel, A., Fensel, D., Leiter, B., Thalhammer, A.: Effective and efficient online communication: The channel model. In: International Conference on Data Technologies and Applications, pp. 209–215 (2012)
5. Boley, H., Kifer, M., Pătrânjan, P.-L., Polleres, A.: Rule interchange on the web. In: Antoniou, G., Aßmann, U., Baroglio, C., Decker, S., Henze, N., Patranjan, P.-L., Tolksdorf, R. (eds.) Reasoning Web. LNCS, vol. 4636, pp. 269–309. Springer, Heidelberg (2007)
6. Boley, H.: Grailog 1.0: Graph-Logic Visualization of Ontologies and Rules. In: Morgenstern, L., Stefaneas, P., Lévy, F., Wyner, A., Paschke, A. (eds.) RuleML 2013. LNCS, vol. 8035, pp. 52–67. Springer, Heidelberg (2013)
7. Forgy, C.L.: Rete: A fast algorithm for the many pattern/many object pattern match problem. Artificial Intelligence 19(1), 17–37 (1982)
8. Toma, I., Fensel, D., Oberhauser, A., Fuchs, C., Stanciu, C., Larizgoitia, I.: Sesa: A scalable multi-channel communication and booking solution for e-commerce in the tourism domain. In: 2013 IEEE 10th International Conference on e-Business Engineering (ICEBE), pp. 288–293 (September 2013)
9. Fensel, D., Leiter, B., Brenner, C.: Planetdata on-line communication handbook. White paper, Semantic Technology Institute, University of Innsbruck (April 2012), http://oc.sti2.at/results/white-papers/planetdata-line-communication-handbook
10. Akbar, Z., Lasierra, N., Tymaniuk, S.: Tourismusverband ontology. Technical report, Semantic Technology Institute, University of Innsbruck (January 2014), http://oc.sti2.at/results/white-papers/tourismusverband-ontology
11. Akbar, Z., Garcia, J.M.: Tourismusverband publication rules. Technical report, Semantic Technology Institute, University of Innsbruck (March 2014), http://oc.sti2.at/results/white-papers/tourismusverband-publication-rules
12. Bry, F., Eckert, M.: Twelve theses on reactive rules for the web. In: Grust, T., et al. (eds.) EDBT 2006 Workshops. LNCS, vol. 4254, pp. 842–854. Springer, Heidelberg (2006)
13. Berstel, B., Bonnard, P., Bry, F., Eckert, M., Pătrânjan, P.-L.: Reactive rules on the web. In: Antoniou, G., Aßmann, U., Baroglio, C., Decker, S., Henze, N., Patranjan, P.-L., Tolksdorf, R. (eds.) Reasoning Web. LNCS, vol. 4636, pp. 183–239. Springer, Heidelberg (2007)
14. Paschke, A., Kozlenkov, A.: Rule-based event processing and reaction rules. In: Governatori, G., Hall, J., Paschke, A. (eds.) RuleML 2009. LNCS, vol. 5858, pp. 53–66. Springer, Heidelberg (2009)
15. Paschke, A., Boley, H., Zhao, Z., Teymourian, K., Athan, T.: Reaction ruleml 1.0: Standardized semantic reaction rules. In: Bikakis, A., Giurca, A. (eds.) RuleML 2012. LNCS, vol. 7438, pp. 100–119. Springer, Heidelberg (2012)
16. Rahm, E., Bernstein, P.A.: A survey of approaches to automatic schema matching. The VLDB Journal 10(4), 334–350 (2001)
17. Saake, G., Sattler, K.U., Conrad, S.: Rule-based schema matching for ontology-based mediators. Journal of Applied Logic 3(2), 253–270 (2005)
18. Davulcu, H., Kifer, M., Ramakrishnan, C.R., Ramakrishnan, I.V.: Logic based modeling and analysis of workflows. In: Proceedings of the 7th Symposium on Principles of Database Systems, pp. 25–33 (1998)
19. Mukherjee, S., Davulcu, H., Kifer, M., Senkul, P., Yang, G.: Logic-based approaches to workflow modeling and verification. In: Chomicki, J., Meyden, R., Saake, G. (eds.) Logics for Emerging Applications of Databases, pp. 167–202. Springer (2004)

Conceptual Model Interoperability:
A Metamodel-driven Approach

Pablo Rubén Fillottrani[1,2] and C. Maria Keet[3]

[1] Departamento de Ciencias e Ingeniería de la Computación,
Universidad Nacional del Sur, Bahía Blanca, Argentina
prf@cs.uns.edu.ar
[2] Comisión de Investigaciones Científicas, Provincia de Buenos Aires, Argentina
[3] Department of Computer Science, University of Cape Town, South Africa
mkeet@cs.uct.ac.za

Abstract. Linking, integrating, or converting conceptual data models represented in different modelling languages is a common aspect in the design and maintenance of complex information systems. While such languages seem similar, they are known to be distinct and no unifying framework exists that respects all of their language features in either model transformations or inter-model assertions to relate them. We aim to address this issue using an approach where the rules are enhanced with a logic-based metamodel. We present the main approach and some essential metamodel-driven rules for the static, structural, components of ER, EER, UML v2.4.1, ORM, and ORM2. The transformations for model elements and patterns are used with the metamodel to verify correctness of inter-model assertions across models in different languages.

1 Introduction

The volume and the need to share existing data sources becomes increasingly important, like in enterprise information integration [11], company mergers and acquisitions [4], scientific collaborations in several fields [1,20,18], e-government initiatives [14,19,21], and in general the broader adoption of the Semantic Web. Interoperability at the level of conceptual models is a key in this goal, in order to maximize the extent to which data can be exchanged while preserving its original meaning. This involves linking, converting, and integrating conceptual models represented in different modelling languages; e.g., when a database back-end is designed with EER, the application layer that uses the database is specified in UML, and the business rules were extracted from the experts using ORM.

Results have been obtained to address this issue. Besides one-off unidirectional algorithms to transform a language, e.g., from ORM to UML [5], several multi-language approaches exist, ranging from linking each model to a graph [7] or description logic language [15] to transformations mediated by a dictionary of common terms [3]. However, these solutions are only partial, for they, among others, omit several constructs (e.g., weak entity types, roles) or modify the language (e.g., by removing datatypes from UML), and therewith have imprecise

A. Bikakis et al. (Eds.): RuleML 2014, LNCS 8620, pp. 52–66, 2014.

'equivalence' mappings or the algorithms are not available. Overall, there is very limited interoperability of conceptual data models in praxis.

To address these issues we have developed an approach that uses a formalised metamodel with a set of modular rules to mediate the linking and transformation of elements in the conceptual models represented in different languages, which simplifies the verification of inter-model assertions and model conversion. The previously developed metamodel [16,17] with all static structural entities (including constraints) of the main conceptual modelling languages—UML v2.4.1, EER, and ORM2—has been formalised and has a table with mappings between terms used in the different languages (e.g., UML association and EER relationship). This is used with a newly specified set of rules from/to the metamodel and within-metamodel conversions to convert model elements and check the validity of inter-model assertions. A major advantage of using a formalised metamodel is that it also can induce a series of transformations/link checks, thanks to the constraints specified in the metamodel. For instance, relating a relationship induces the checking of its roles, of the object types that participate in it, and their identifiers, due to the chain of mandatory participations in the metamodel.

We discuss related works in Section 2 and introduce the metamodel-driven approach in Section 3. Section 4 contains a selection of the rules for the main elements, which is elaborated in Section 5 concerning mapping validations in a broader context. We discuss and conclude in Section 6.

2   Related Works

Several papers mainly have proposed transformations from one conceptual modelling language to another, without considering the case of validating inter-model assertions. Nevertheless, it is useful to consider also their approaches, for transformations could be used to check inter-model assertions (out of scope are transformations other than between conceptual models, such as QVT for MOF and ATL for the Eclipse platform).

Venable and Grundy's work [22,10,23] uses a metamodel in the CoCoA graphical language that covers a part of ER and a part of NIAM (a precursor to ORM), and it was implemented in MView and Ponamu. Their metamodel omits, mainly, value types, nested entity types, and composite attributes, and NIAM is forced to have attributes as in ER in the 'integrated' metamodel. Their "dynamic" ad hoc mappings are thus limited, and they have not been made public.

Boyd and McBrien [7] use the Hypergraph Data Model to relate ER, relational, UML, and ORM schemas, and include transformation rules between them through mapping each schema into the graph. The advantage is that it provides a simple irreducible form for schemas that can be used to prove schema equivalence, but it does not consider inter-model assertions and the specification omits roles, aggregation, weak entity types, several constraints, and it removes the data type specification from UML to match EER's partial attribute.

Atzeni et al [2,3] devised a comprehensive approach with extensible automatic schema translations, which has been implemented. Unlike [22], they have a term dictionary that aids with the transformation, and the translations are produced in Datalog. However, it does not include ORM, the dictionary has only 9 constructs, it lacks metamodel relations and constraints between them, and the system considers model transformations only.

Bowers and Delcambre's framework [6] is a flat representation of schema and data. Its representational language ULD covers only ordinal, set and union class constructs, and cardinality constraints, and it operates at the implementation-level, providing examples for the relational model, XML, RDF, and RDF Schema only. The transformations are handled by Datalog.

Two principal works to relate ORM to UML or ER are [12,5]. Halpin provides diagram element to diagram element mappings and approximations [12] and some conversions from ORM to ER are implemented with undisclosed algorithms. Bollen does provide comprehensive rules for transforming ORM's object types, nested object types, fact types and some constraints into UML diagrams [5]. Those rules are then combined in a sequence of algorithms to transform a ORM conceptual schema into a UML class diagram. While the rules are sound, some of the algorithms exhibit steps and iterations which are not clearly defined leading to ambiguous results.

Fill and Burzynski [9] outline three metamodel-mediated approaches to integrate conceptual models and ontologies, being integration on the level of meta models, by using references in the meta model of the existing conceptual models, and a hybrid of the two, but no details. The tool it is said to be implemented in, ADONIS, now focuses entirely on BPMN.

A different strand of research on unification that does not use a metamodel, is to use one logic formalism for several conceptual modelling languages, notably a Description Logic language [8,13,15]. Different logics are used, however, and they do not cover all features of the language due to the complexity trade-offs made. For instance, in [8] identifiers are absent, and the $\mathcal{DLR}_{ifd}$ used in [15] does not consider the ORM's relationship constraints or UML's aggregation. Also, approximate transformations are not represented.

3 The Metamodel-driven Approaches

The focus is interoperability and integration of conceptual data models represented in different languages, but to be able to assert a link between two entities in different models and *evaluate automatically* whether it is a valid assertion and what it does entail, one has to know what type of entities they are, whether they are the same, and if not, whether one can be transformed into the other for that particular selection. That is, we first need an approach for transforming a model (or a selection thereof) in one language into another. This is depicted in Fig. 1 and illustrated with some sample data. There are three input items at the top, the algorithms on the right, and the two output items at the bottom. In this paper we focus on the rules and algorithms, but they avail of the formalised metamodel and term mapping table to function well. For instance, it needs to recognise that a UML class in the diagram can be mapped 1:1 to a ORM entity type, and transform a UML attribute to an ORM value type.

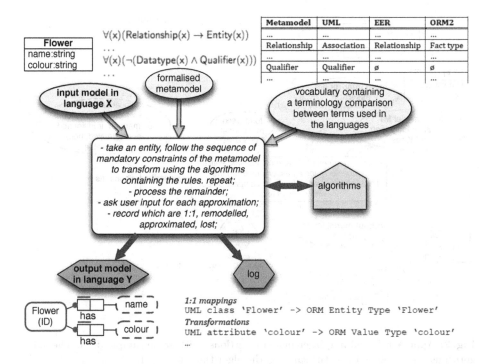

Fig. 1. Approach for transforming a model in one language into another, with some sample data

This knowledge is then used for the inter-model assertions, whose approach is illustrated in Fig. 2. It uses both the formalised metamodel and the algorithms; a structured version of this approach is included as Algorithm 1 in the Appendix. In addition, compared to transformation, it can be run in both directions from one fragment to the other, where one direction is chosen arbitrarily. The next two subsections provide some detail on the formalised metamodel and transformation lists, before we proceed to the rules in Section 4.

3.1 Formalised Metamodel and Term Mappings

The metamodel, described in [16,17] and represented as a set of UML v.2.4 diagrams with annotations, is a consistent conceptual model about the entities and constraints in the selected modelling languages, covering almost all their native features. It aims at representing in a unified way whatever is present in the languages, and several notions from Ontology (philosophy) and ontologies (Artificial intelligence) were used in its development so as to increase understanding of the language features, to reconcile or unify perceived differences, and to improve the quality of the metamodel; e.g., on attributes and the positionalist nature of relationships [17].

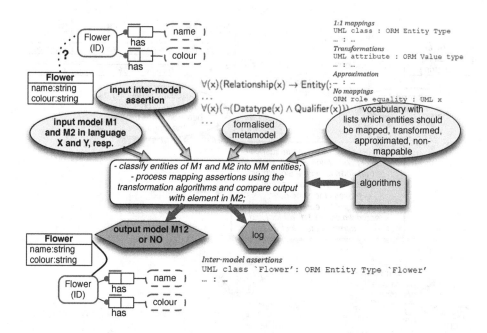

Fig. 2. Approach for adding inter-model assertions, with some sample data. The "algorithms" box is essentially the same as the algorithms in Fig. 1.

It is formalized in two versions, both available at http://www.meteck.org/ SAAR.html . The first is a set of function-free first order logic set of formula with equality. Fig. 3 shows a fragment relating relationship, role, and object type with identification constraints. The second is a subset of the first that is representable and approximated in OWL 2 for easy computational use, represented in $\mathcal{SHIQ}(D)$, with some 100 classes, 70 object properties (partially due to encodings of ternaries), and 663 axioms.

The metamodel is complemented with a vocabulary in the form of a list of terminology comparison and conventions of the entities in UML Class Diagrams, EER, and ORM, and their corresponding names in the metamodel (see [17]).

3.2   Categorisation of Rules

As the model features are more or less similar across the languages, we have divided them into four groups: 1:1 mappings, transformations, approximations, and those for which there are no alternatives. The four lists largely follow from the metamodel of the static, structural components and constraints [17], although in some cases there is a conceptual equivalence, but not exactly in the representation; e.g., UML and EER both have attributes, but EER does not record the datatype, so they are not 1:1 from an algorithmic viewpoint.

$\forall(x,y)(\texttt{Contains}(x,y) \rightarrow \texttt{Relationship}(x) \land \texttt{Role}(y))$
$\forall(x)\exists^{\leq 2}y(\texttt{Contains}(x,y))$
$\forall(x)(\texttt{Role}(x) \rightarrow \exists(y)(\texttt{Contains}(y,x)))$
$\forall(x,y,z)(\texttt{Contains}(x,y) \land \texttt{Contains}(z,y) \rightarrow (x=z))$
$\forall(x,y,z)(\texttt{RolePlaying}(x,y,z) \rightarrow \texttt{Role}(x) \land \texttt{CardinalityConstraint}(y) \land \texttt{EntityType}(z))$
$\forall(x)(\texttt{Role}(x) \rightarrow \exists(y,z)(\texttt{RolePlaying}(x,y,z)))$
$\forall(x,y,z,v,w)(\texttt{RolePlaying}(x,y,z) \land \texttt{RolePlaying}(x,v,w) \rightarrow (y=v) \land (z=w))$
$\forall(x,y,z,v,w)(\texttt{RolePlaying}(x,y,z) \land \texttt{RolePlaying}(v,y,w) \rightarrow (x=v) \land (z=w))$
$\forall(x)(\texttt{CardinalityConstraint}(x) \rightarrow \exists(y)(\texttt{MinimumCardinality}(x,y) \land \texttt{Integer}(y)))$
$\forall(x)(\texttt{CardinalityConstraint}(x) \rightarrow \exists(y)(\texttt{MaximumCardinality}(x,y) \land \texttt{Integer}(y)))$
$\forall(x,y)(\texttt{ReifiedAs}(x,y) \rightarrow \texttt{Relationship}(x) \land \texttt{NestedObjectType}(y))$
$\forall(x)(\texttt{NestedObjectType}(x) \rightarrow \exists(y)(\texttt{ReifiedAs}(x,y)))$
$\forall(x,y,z)(\texttt{ReifiedAs}(x,y) \land \texttt{ReifiedAs}(z,y) \rightarrow (x=z))$
$\forall(x,y,z)(\texttt{ReifiedAs}(x,y) \land \texttt{ReifiedAs}(x,z) \rightarrow (y=z))$
$\forall(x,y)(\texttt{ReifiedAs}(x,y) \rightarrow \forall(z,w)(\texttt{Contains}(x,z) \leftrightarrow \texttt{RolePlaying}(z,w,y)))$
$\forall(x,y)(\texttt{Identifies}(x,y) \rightarrow (\texttt{IdentificationConstraint}(x) \land \texttt{ObjectType}(y))$
$\forall(x)(\texttt{IdentificationConstraint}(x) \rightarrow \exists(y)(\texttt{Identifies}(x,y)))$
$\forall(x,y,z)((\texttt{Identifies}(x,y) \land \texttt{Identifies}(x,z)) \rightarrow (y=z))$
$\forall(x)(\texttt{ObjectType}(x) \rightarrow \exists(y)(\texttt{Identifies}(y,x)))$
$\forall(x,y,z)((\texttt{DeclaredOn}(x,y) \land \texttt{DeclaredOn}(x,z) \land \texttt{IdentificationConstraint}(x) \land (\neg(y=z))) \rightarrow$
$\qquad\qquad (\texttt{ValueProperty}(y) \leftrightarrow \neg\texttt{AttributiveProperty}(z)))$
$\forall(x)(\texttt{IdentificationConstraint}(x) \rightarrow \exists(y)(\texttt{DeclaredOn}(x,y)))$
$\forall(x,y)((\texttt{DeclaredOn}(x,y) \land \texttt{SingleIdentification}(x)) \rightarrow (\texttt{Attribute}(y) \lor \texttt{ValueType}(y)))$
$\forall(x)(\texttt{SingleIdentification}(x) \rightarrow \exists(y)(\texttt{DeclaredOn}(x,y)))$
$\forall(x,y,z)((\texttt{SingleIdentification}(x) \land \texttt{DeclaredOn}(x,y) \land \texttt{DeclaredOn}(x,z)) \rightarrow (y=z))$

Fig. 3. A fragment of the metamodel FOL formalization

1:1 Mappings. The mappings are those where the elements are the same, and the conversion are straightforward single steps. They are: Relationships (n-ary, with $n \geq 2$), Role, Object type and Associative object type, Subsumption (class and relationship), Disjoint roles, Disjoint entity types, Subset constraint, Object type cardinality, Completeness (classes), Mandatory.

Transformations. Transformations are those where the elements are essentially the same, but not from a syntax viewpoint and therefore require a set of steps that should be treated as one atomic rule. They are: UML (dimensional) Attribute from/to ORM (dimensional) Value Type, UML attribute/ORM value type to and EER (dimensional) Attribute, EER Weak entity type to its ORM version, EER Multivalued Attribute to separate object types in UML and ORM, ORM Value Type to UML and ER attribute, Internal Identifier, Attributive property cardinality, Single identification.

Approximations. The core distinction between transformations and approximations, is that the latter includes a choice point with input from the user or some arbitrary (modifiable) default value may be used; hence, firing the same rule in the same situation twice does not necessarily lead to the same outcome. It is up to the modeller to accept approximations or not. They are: patterns for UML qualified association, EER Weak entity (type with additional relationship), and ORM external identifier when it suits, as depicted in Fig. 4; Role value constraints (with subclasses); UML's composite and shared aggregate with named relationship/fact type; composite attribute; EER (dimensional) Attribute to UML attribute/ORM value type;

Entities for which there are no alternatives. The three families of languages do not have the same expressiveness even at the ontological level, and some of those features cannot be represented or approximated in the other language. They are:

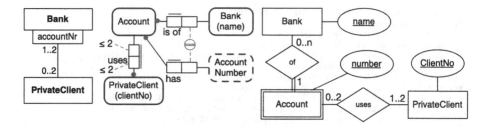

Fig. 4. Patterns for approximations between UML's qualified association, EER weak entity type, and ORM's external identifier

UML to ORM: missing inclusive mandatory; EER to ORM: inclusive mandatory; UML to EER: disjunctive mandatory, qualified Identifier, value constraints; ORM to UML: compound cardinality, value comparison, role equality, disjoint relationships, relationship equality, join subset, join disjointness, join equality, all relationship constraints; ORM to EER: disjunctive mandatory, compound cardinality, value comparison, value type constraints, role equality, disjoint relationships, relationship equality, join subset, join disjointness, join equality, all relationship constraints. We do not consider them further in this paper.

4 Interoperability Rules

In principle, there are two choices for specifying the interoperability rules: create a mesh between the languages, or do it via the metamodel. If we have n conceptual data modeling languages and assuming there were only simple 1:1 mappings or when one glosses over some details, then the former option will require $n!$ rules while the later only $2n$ rules. We already know there are not only simple mappings, so the lower bound of $2n$ will increase due to the intra-metamodel rules to transform entities, such as an attribute into a value type and vice versa. Overall, while the difference in rules might not be large when considering only three languages, one must note that they come in different flavours and versions. The use of the intermediate metamodel helps to reuse rules while focusing on the real changes. For example, a UML v2.0 attribute to an ORM value type mapping can use the same intra-metamodel transformation, but with mesh-transformations, a new one would have to be added. Therefore, we will use the metamodel-mediated rules. This does require annotations to the entities in the metamodel, to the effect that the algorithm checks the annotation what to do: map straight to the entity in the other language, or perform a transformation or approximation first within the metamodel.

1:1 Mapping Rules and the Metamodel. For the 1:1 mappings, this amounts to straightforward rules, and only a few are shown; the rest follows the same pattern. We abbreviate the metamodel as MM in the following rules.

(OT) Object Type

   (O1) Class $\xrightarrow{\text{UML to MM}}$ Object Type

     in: `Class`

       out: `Class` $\rightarrow$ Object Type

   (1O) Object Type $\xrightarrow{\text{MM to UML}}$ Class

     in: Object Type

       out: Object Type $\rightarrow$ `Class`

   (xOx) Likewise for the other 1:1 mappings between Class, Entity type and Entity type, with (O2) $\xrightarrow{\text{ORM to MM}}$; (2O) $\xrightarrow{\text{MM to ORM}}$; (O3) $\xrightarrow{\text{EER to MM}}$; (3O) $\xrightarrow{\text{MM to EER}}$.

(Rol) Role

   (Ro1) Association end $\xrightarrow{\text{UML to MM}}$ Role

     in: `AssociationEnd`

       out: `AssociationEnd` $\rightarrow$ Role

   (1Ro) Role $\xrightarrow{\text{MM to UML}}$ `AssociationEnd`

     in: Role

       out: Role $\rightarrow$ `AssociationEnd`

   (xRox) Likewise for the other 1:1 mappings of Role and Relationship component, with (Ro2) $\xrightarrow{\text{ORM to MM}}$; (2Ro) $\xrightarrow{\text{MM to ORM}}$; (Ro3) $\xrightarrow{\text{EER to MM}}$; (3Ro) $\xrightarrow{\text{MM to EER}}$.

(Rel) Relationship

   (R1) Association $\xrightarrow{\text{UML to MM}}$ Relationship

     in: `Association(AssociationEnd : Class, AssociationEnd : Class)`

       out: `AssociationEnd` $\rightarrow$ Role   *// i.e., using (Ro1)*

       out: `Association` $\rightarrow$ Relationship

       out: `Class` $\rightarrow$ Object Type   *// i.e., using (O1)*

       out: Relationship(Role:Object type, Role:Object Type)

   (1R) Relationship $\xrightarrow{\text{MM to UML}}$ `Association`

     in: Relationship(Role:Object type, Role:Object Type)

       out: Role $\rightarrow$ `AssociationEnd`   *// i.e., using (1Ro)*

       out: Relationship $\rightarrow$ `Association`

       out: Object Type $\rightarrow$ `Class`   *// i.e., using (1O)*

       out: `Association(AssociationEnd : Class, AssociationEnd : Class)`

   (xRx) Likewise for the other 1:1 mappings of Fact type and Relationship, with (1R) $\xrightarrow{\text{MM o UML}}$; (R2) $\xrightarrow{\text{ORM to MM}}$; (2R) $\xrightarrow{\text{MM to ORM}}$; (R3) $\xrightarrow{\text{EER to MM}}$; (3R) $\xrightarrow{\text{MM to EER}}$.

A mapping $\xrightarrow{\text{UML to ORM}}$ for a class `C` in UML model M_1 and generating an entity type for model transformation to ORM model M_2 then is simply composed of the component-rules. For instance, for an inter-model assertion:

GenOT Class $\xrightarrow{\text{UML to ORM}}$ Entity type

  in: `C`

    out: (O1)

out: (2O)   // i.e., an ORM `EntityType` named C

For a relationship mapping $\xrightarrow{\text{UML to EER}}$, with A the association in the UML model asserted to be equivalent to some relationship R in an EER model, the following set of rules apply when verifying the mapping is correct:

(MapR) Association $\xrightarrow{\text{UML to ER}}$ Relationship
  in: $A(ae_1 : C_1, ae_2 : C_2)$
    out: (R1)
    out: (3R)
    out: match pattern out(3R) with $R(rc_1 : E_1, rc_2 : E_2)$

To check the validity of the mapping, one also could have started with the EER $R(rc_1 : E_1, rc_2 : E_2)$ and work towards $A(ae_1 : C_1, ae_2 : C_2)$ using (R3) and (1R). The generation of a new model in another language and checking of an asserted inter-model relation for the other 1:1 mappings listed in the previous section follow a similar pattern and is omitted for brevity.

Transformations. We describe two transformations, which are arguably the most important for they are used most widely. It follows the same approach as with the 1:1 mappings, but the rules become increasingly more elaborate, and for ease of comprehension, we have changed the type of arrow.

To handle a model generation or mapping for a UML attribute and ORM value type, we first need to declare their respective mappings into the metamodel, and then the transformation at the level of the metamodel. This is described in the next set of rules, where the (xDx) rules for datatypes are specified alike those for object types, with the same naming scheme.

(Att) Attributive property
    (A1) Attribute $\xmapsto{\text{UML to MM}}$ Attribute
    in: `Attribute(Class, DataType)`
      out: (O1)
      out: (D1)
      out: `Attribute` $\to$ Attribute
      out: Attribute(Object type, Data type)
    (1A) Attribute $\xmapsto{\text{MM to UML}}$ Attribute
    ....   // steps in (A1) in reverse order
(VT) Value type
    (V1) Value type $\xmapsto{\text{ORM to MM}}$ Value type
    in: `ValueType` $\wedge$ `mapped_to(ValueType, DataType)`
      out: (D1)
      out: `mapped_to` $\to$ mapped_to
      out: `ValueType` $\to$ Value type
      out: ValueType $\wedge$ mapped_to(Value type, Data type)
    (1V) Value type $\xmapsto{\text{ORM to MM}}$ Value type
    ....   // steps in (V1) in reverse order

(Att-VT) Attribute and Value type conversions
  (Att-to-VT) Attribute $\xmapsto{MM}$ Value type
  in: Attribute(Object type, Data type)
    out: (D1)
    out: Role
    out: Relationship
    out: mapped_to
    out: Attribute $\rightarrow$ Value type
    out: Relationship(Role:Object type, Role:Value type)
    out: mapped_to(Value type, Data type)
  (VT-to-Att) Value type $\xmapsto{MM}$ Attribute
  in: Value type $\wedge$ mapped_to(Value type, Data type)
    out: (D1)
    out: Object type
    out: ValueType $\rightarrow$ Attribute
    out: Attribute(Object type, Data type)

It is now possible to generate an ORM value type from an attribute in a UML diagram, and vv., and, in a similar fashion, to verify whether an inter-model assertion between a particular UML attribute and ORM value type is correct (at least structurally). This is specified in the following two rules.

GenVT Attribute $\xmapsto{UML\ to\ ORM}$ Value type
  in: $A(C, D)$
    out: (A1)
    out: (Att-to-VT)
    out: (2R)
    out: (1V)   *// i.e., an ORM model with* $F(r_c : C, r_v : V)$,
                                  V *and* mapped_to(V, D)

MapVTAtt Value type $\xmapsto{ORM\ to\ UML}$ Attribute
  in: $V \wedge$ mapped_to(V, D)
    out: (V1)
    out: (VT-to-Att)
    out: (1A)   *// i.e., a UML Class Diagram with* $A(C, D)$
    out: match pattern out(1A) with attribute declaration in the UML diagram

These basic pieces can, in turn, be used for more complex transformations and approximations (illustrated below).

Approximations. As mentioned above, approximates contain a 'choice' step that requires input from the user to complete the transformation. Such choice points in the rules are indicated in italics. We select the rules for identifiers in EER and ORM, as they are important in a model, and illustrate it with the case of simple (single attribute) identifier. To be able to do so, the attribute mapping from EER is introduced first; the mandatory and cardinality constraint (a 1:1) are straight-forward mappings into and from the metamodel and have the same naming pattern, i.e., M1, 1M etc, and C1, 1C etc, with MinimumCardinality abbreviated as mic and MaximumCardinality as mac.

(Att) Attribute
 (Ae1) Attribute $\leadsto_{\text{EER to MM}}$ Attribute
  in: `Attribute(Class, __)`
   out: (O1)
   out: `__` → *choose* a DataType
   out: Attribute → `Attribute`
   out: Attribute(Object type, Data type)
 (1Ae) Attribute $\leadsto_{\text{MM to EER}}$ Attribute
  in: Attribute(Object type, Data type)
   out: (O1)
   out: Attribute → `Attribute`
   out: DataType → `__`
   out: `Attribute(Class, __)`

With these rules, one can generate, e.g., an EER single attribute identifier from an ORM reference scheme, and vv., and confirm a mapping between the two; one of the four options are declared in the following rule set.

MapSID ORM reference scheme $\leadsto_{\text{ORM to EER}}$ EER single attribute identifier
 in: $\text{FT}(r_e : E_1, r_v : V) \wedge \text{mapped\_to}(V, D) \wedge M \wedge C(\text{mic} = 1, \text{mac} = 1)$
  out: (O2)   *// ORM entity type into MM object type*
  out: (V1)   *// ORM value type into MM value type*
  out: (M2)   *// ORM mandatory into MM mandatory*
  out: (C2)   *// ORM cardinality into MM cardinality*
  out: (VT-to-Att)   *// MM conversion value type to attribute*
  out: (3O)   *// MM object type into entity type E of EER*
  out: (1Ae)   *// generate EER Diagram attribute: A(E, __)*
  out: (3M)   *// MM mandatory into mandatory of EER*
  out: (3C)   *// MM cardinality into cardinality of EER*
  out: match pattern out(1Ae,3M,3C) with single identifier declaration in the EER diagram

Arguably, it looks like one might be able to do this more succinctly by defining the notion of identifier-using-an-attribute and identifier-using-a-value-type and to use that in the transformation and create different versions of (Atto-to-VT) and (VT-to-Att) that include the mandatory 1:1 constraints. However, this also requires duplications that cannot be isolated, and the above option is then the more transparent one.

5   Validating Mappings with the Metamodel and Rules

The metamodel is useful for creating less, and more efficient, mapping and transformation rules, but this is not its only advantage. It can drive the validation of mappings and the generation of model transformations thanks to the constraints declared in the metamodel. Consider again the centre-part of Fig. 2 with its "process mapping assertions using the transformation algorithms". The approach takes as input two models (M_1 and M_2), an inter-model assertion (e.g., a UML binary association R_1 and an ORM fact type R_2, the look-up list with the mappings, transformation, approximations, and the non-mappable elements (see Section 3.2), and the formalised metamodel (see Fig. 3). Once the model elements of M_1 and M_2 are classified in terms of the metamodel, the mapping validation process start, which goes through several steps, depending on what is asserted to be a mapping. This is illustrated for a R_1 to R_2 mapping.

Step 1. It can be seen from the vocabulary that association and fact type correspond to Relationship in the metamodel, and thus enjoy a 1:1 mapping. The ruleset that will be commenced with are R1 from UML to the metamodel and 2R to OMR's fact type.

Step 2. R1 and 2R refer to Role and Object type of the metamodel. The metamodel states that there must be at least 2 contains relations from Relationship to Role (Fig. 3, line 2). There are 2, which each cause the role-rules to be evaluated, with Ro1 of R_1's two association ends and 2Ro for ORM's roles.

Step 3. The metamodel states that Role must participate in the relationship rolePlaying (Fig. 3, lines 5 and 6), and it has a participating Object type (possibly a subtype thereof) and optionally a Cardinality constraint. They also have 1:1 mappings, which is straight-forward for cardinality (1C and C2).

Step 4. The class participating in R_1 causes its rules to be evaluated, being an O1 to Object type and 2O to ORM's entity type.

Step 5. Each Object type must have at least one Identification constraint (Fig. 3, last 9 lines), be this an internal one or an external one, and involving one or more attributes or value types (which one it is has been determined by the original classification). If it is a Single identification, then a rule similar to MapSID (see previous section) is called and executed (which, in turn, calls the Att-to-VT rule and the use of Data type).

There are no further mandatory constraints from the 'chain' from Relationship to Role to Object type to Single identification (that, in turn, consults Attribute and Data type for the 'UML to ORM' example here). The sequence readily becomes longer if the participating object type is actually one of its subtypes: e.g., Nested object type has a mandatory constraint such that it must be related to the Relationship it objectifies, which causes the verification to go through a new sequence of steps following the chain of mandatory constraints. If the relationship would have been a subtype of Relationship, then the four stages above will have been specified more precisely correspondingly (e.g., adding attributes). Because an object type need not to have non-identifier attributes, a check for the presence of this entity has to be added.

Consider again Fig. 2 and the possible mapping between the UML class Flower and ORM's entity type Flower, which can be validated from UML to ORM or ORM to UML. If the former then, like Step 4, above, 1O and O2 is called and, like in Step 5, the identifier. The mapping can work, provided one admits to using the UML internal identifier as candidate for single identifier (reference scheme) in ORM. Executing it in the other direction from ORM to UML, one could include a choice point and add ORM's reference scheme as a UML user-defined identifier (indicated with a {id} after the name of the attribute).

6   Discussion and Conclusions

We have presented a metamodel-driven approach for model transformations and inter-model assertions where the models are represented in different languages. Besides the input model and a mapping table, it uses a formalised metamodel to direct a sequence of the language transformations, and it uses a set of mapping, transformation, and approximation rules to carry it out. We presented a selection of the rules, in particular considering the static structural, components of ER, EER, UML v2.4.1, ORM, and ORM2. The transformations for model elements and patterns, in turn, are used with the metamodel to verify correctness of inter-model assertions across models in different languages. An next step is to implement them and evaluate them with actual conceptual models.

The metamodel-driven approach requires quite an investment upfront, first and foremost in terms of designing the metamodel. Its formalization ironed out some duplications and enabled the capturing also of the textual constraints. While one could have chosen to remain at the term dictionary level for the entities in the conceptual data modelling languages, alike [3], this extra work pays off in increased coverage of features, higher precision of mappings, as well as explicit approximations where asked for by the user. In addition, it makes the whole procedure more transparent, and the rules are usable essentially for both transformations and for validations of inter-model mapping assertions.

The overall fine-grained granular and modular approach with the rules for the transformation and mappings also increase the reusability of the rules across the various larger-sized mappings, and can be used to construct a set of transformation steps or larger 'chunks' of the model, alike for the qualified associations, external uniqueness, and weak entity types in Fig. 4. It does not, however, readily offer a single procedure for testing schema equivalence, which is not only out of scope of the current work, but also extremely unlikely in the case of inter-model assertions, for the simple reasons that that is typically not the aim, and the intersection of entities that are truly the same across the three conceptual modelling language families (UML, EER, and ORM) is small (see also figures 1 and 2 in [17]).

These sets of rules not only contributes to the comprehension of differences between heterogenous conceptual models, they also serve as the formal framework for a tool supporting the design, management and integration of conceptual schemas and ontologies in different modelling languages. Even though it is not always possible to find exact matches between entities in the different models, the approximations rules will help users to find corresponding alternatives.

Acknowledgements. This work is based upon research supported by the National Research Foundation of South Africa (Project UID: 90041) and the Argentinian Ministry of Science and Technology.

References

1. See the list of collaborations (2014), http://www.tipharma.com/
2. Atzeni, P., Cappellari, P., Torlone, R., Bernstein, P.A., Gianforme, G.: Model-independent schema translation. VLDB Journal 17(6), 1347–1370 (2008)
3. Atzeni, P., Gianforme, G., Cappellari, P.: Data model descriptions and translation signatures in a multi-model framework. AMAI Mathematics and Artificial Intelligence 63, 1–29 (2012)
4. Banal-Estanol, A.: Information-sharing implications of horizontal mergers. International Journal of Industrial Organization 25(1), 31–49 (2007)
5. Bollen, P.W.L.: A formal ORM-to-UML mapping algorithm research memo RM 02/016, Faculty of Economics and Business Administration. University of Maastricht (2002), http://arno.unimaas.nl/show.cgi?fid=46
6. Bowers, S., Delcambre, L.M.L.: Using the uni-level description (ULD) to support data-model interoperability. Data & Knowledge Engineering 59(3), 511–533 (2006)
7. Boyd, M., McBrien, P.: Comparing and transforming between data models via an intermediate hypergraph data model. J. on Data Semantics IV, 69–109 (2005)
8. Calvanese, D., Lenzerini, M., Nardi, D.: Unifying class-based representation formalisms. Journal of Artificial Intelligence Research 11, 199–240 (1999)
9. Fill, H.G., Burzynski, P.: Integrating ontology models and conceptual models using a meta modeling approach. In: Proc. of 11th Int. Protégé Conference (2009); amsterdam 2009
10. Grundy, J., Venable, J.: Towards an integrated environment for method engineering. In: Proceedings of the IFIP TC8, WG8.1/8.2 Method Engineering, ME 1996, vol. 1, pp. 45–62 (1996)
11. Halevy, A.Y., Ashish, N., Bitton, D., Carey, M.J., Draper, D., Pollock, J., Rosenthal, A., Sikka, V.: Enterprise information integration: successes, challenges and controversies. In: Özcan, F. (ed.) SIGMOD Conference, pp. 778–787. ACM (2005)
12. Halpin, T.: Information Modeling and Relational Databases. Morgan Kaufmann Publishers, San Francisco (2001)
13. Hofstede, A.H.M.T., Proper, H.A.: How to formalize it? formalization principles for information systems development methods. Information and Software Technology 40(10), 519–540 (1998)
14. Hovy, E.: Data and knowledge integration for e-government. In: Digital Government, pp. 219–231. Springer (2008)
15. Keet, C.M.: Ontology-driven formal conceptual data modeling for biological data analysis. In: Elloumi, M., Zomaya, A.Y. (eds.) Biological Knowledge Discovery Handbook: Preprocessing, Mining and Postprocessing of Biological Data, ch. 6, pp. 129–154. Wiley (2013)
16. Keet, C.M., Fillottrani, P.R.: Structural entities of an ontology-driven unifying metamodel for UML, EER, and ORM2. In: Cuzzocrea, A., Maabout, S. (eds.) MEDI 2013. LNCS, vol. 8216, pp. 188–199. Springer, Heidelberg (2013)
17. Keet, C.M., Fillottrani, P.R.: Toward an ontology-driven unifying metamodel for UML class diagrams, EER, and ORM2. In: Ng, W., Storey, V.C., Trujillo, J.C. (eds.) ER 2013. LNCS, vol. 8217, pp. 313–326. Springer, Heidelberg (2013)
18. Louie, B., Mork, P., Martin-Sanchez, F., Halevy, A., Tarczy-Hornoch, P.: Data integration and genomic medicine. J. of Biomedical Informatics 40(1), 5–16 (2007)
19. Calo, K.M., Cenci, K.M., Fillottrani, P.R., Estevez, E.C.: Information sharing – benefits. Journal of Computer Science & Technology 12(2), 49–55 (2012)

20. Nelson, E.K., Piehler, B., Eckels, J., et al.: Labkey server: An open source platform for scientific data integration, analysis and collaboration. BMC Bioinformatics 12(1), 71 (2011)
21. United Nations Department of Economic and Social Affairs: United Nations E-Government Survey 2010 – Leveraging e-government at a time of financial and economic crisis. Tech. Rep. ST/ESA/PAD/SER.E/131, United Nations (2010), http://unpan3.un.org/egovkb/global_reports/10report.htm
22. Venable, J., Grundy, J.: Integrating and supporting Entity Relationship and Object Role Models. In: Papazoglou, M.P. (ed.) ER 1995 and OOER 1995. LNCS, vol. 1021, pp. 318–328. Springer, Heidelberg (1995)
23. Zhu, N., Grundy, J., Hosking, J.: Pounamu: A metatool for multi-view visual language environment construction. IEEE Conf. on Visual Languages and Human-Centric Computing (2004)

Appendix

Algorithm 1. Overview checking inter-model assertions.

---

input: model M_1 and model M_2, represented in languages L_1 and L_2; intermodel equivalence assertions

1 **for** *each entity* $e \in M_1, M_2$ **do**
2 | classify e according to metamodel entities in the vocabulary
3 **end**
4 **for** *each equivalence assertion* $e_1 \equiv e_2, e_1 \in M_1, e_2 \in M_2$ **do**
5 | **if** $type(e_1) \xrightarrow{L_1 \ to \ MM \ to \ L_2} type(e_2) \in 1:1Mappings$ **then**
6 | // there is a corresponding 1:1 mapping
7 | call relevant Algorithm (set of mapping rules);
8 | **else**
9 | // then lookup transformations
10 | **if** $type(e_1) \xmapsto{L_1 \ to \ MM \ to \ L_2} type(e_2) \in Transformations$ **then**
11 | call relevant Algorithm;
12 | **else**
13 | // offer user approximation
14 | **if** $type(e_1) \rightsquigarrow_{L_1 \ to \ L_2} type(e_2) \in Approximations$ **then**
          Data: Ask whether the user would accept an approximation; $a \leftarrow$ answer
15 | **if** $a == yes$ **then**
16 | call relevant Algorithm;
17 | **else**
18 | **output**: *"There is no accepted approximations from e_1 to e_2. Your asserted link will be removed. "*
19 | **end**
20 | **else**
21 | **output**: *"There is no transformation nor approximation for e_1 and e_2. Your asserted link is invalid, and will be removed."*
22 | **end**
23 | **end**
24 | **end**
25 **end**
26 run reasoner on combined model;
27 **if** $reasoner == ok$ **then**
28 | **return** "The assertions are logically correct."
29 **else**
30 | **return** "The models together with the assertions resulted in an inconsistency. You must revise and run the procedure again."
31 **end**

On Verifying Reactive Rules
Using Rewriting Logic

Katerina Ksystra, Nikos Triantafyllou, and Petros Stefaneas

National Technical University of Athens,
Iroon Polytexneiou 9, 15780 Zografou, Athens, Greece
{katksy,nitriant}@central.ntua.gr,
petros@math.ntua.gr

Abstract. Rule-based programming has been gaining a lot of interest in the industry lately, through the growing use of rules to model the behavior of software systems. A demand for verifying and analyzing rule based systems has thus emerged. In this paper we propose a methodology, based on rewriting logic specifications written in CafeOBJ, for reasoning about structural errors of systems whose behavior is expressed in terms of reactive rules and verifying safety properties within the same framework. We present our approach through a simple but illustrative example of an e-commerce web site.

Keywords: Reactive Rules, Verification, Rewrite Theory Specification, Theorem Proving, Model Checking, Structure Errors, Safety properties.

1 Introduction

Reactive rule-based systems are an attractive paradigm to software engineering since they enable systems to react to events, or combinations of events, occurring in an arbitrary order. Additional characteristics supported by rules, like flexibility and expressivity, are highly desired especially when modeling industrial systems.

However, analyzing the behavior of reactive rule based systems presents many difficulties because rules can interact with each other during execution. Thus, changing, introducing or removing a single rule from a rule base can have undesirable side effects. For these reasons, their extensive and formal analysis is required. This need becomes stronger when the rule based system is complex and/or used in critical domains. Also, the existing tool support for reasoning about rules is limited. To this end, in this paper we present a formal framework that can support the specification of reactive rule based systems and the verification of their behavior. More precisely:

- We express Production and Event Condition Action rules as rewrite theory specifications of Observational Transition Systems written in CafeOBJ (section 2).

A. Bikakis et al. (Eds.): RuleML 2014, LNCS 8620, pp. 67–81, 2014.
© Springer International Publishing Switzerland 2014

- We propose a methodology to detect structural errors, like confluence and termination, and to verify safety properties for reactive rule-based systems (section 3).
- We illustrate the proposed approach through a running example (sections 2, 3).

1.1   Overview of Reactive Rules and Motivation

Reactivity on the Web, the ability to detect events and respond to them automatically in a timely manner, is needed for bridging the gap between the existing, passive Web, where data sources can only be accessed to obtain information, and the dynamic Semantic Web, where data sources are enriched with reactive behavior [1]. The two main categories of reactive rules are Production and Event Condition Action (ECA) rules. The former have the syntax *If condition do action* and are at the basis of Business Rules Management Systems. They specify the execution of an action in case some conditions are satisfied, i.e. define reaction to states changes. The latter have the syntax *On event if condition do action*, specify a system's response to events and are used to describe more complex systems. More precisely, the ECA paradigm states that a rule autonomously reacts to actively or passively detected simple or complex events by evaluating a condition or a set of conditions and by executing a reaction whenever the event happens and the condition(s) is true [2].

The properties of interest to rule systems verification include both safety properties and structure properties, such as confluence and termination of the rules. These properties are briefly described below;

A safety property is an assertion that a desirable property holds in all reachable states (i.e. is an invariant) of the rule-based system and is specific to the purpose of the specified application. Confluence concerns whether the result of executing a set of triggered rules depends on the execution order of the rules or not. A rule program is considered confluent in other words when from any initial state, all program executions lead to the same final state. Termination analysis aims to ensure that a set of rules will eventually terminate (i.e. reach a final state) and will not continue to trigger each other infinitely. A system may never terminate due to circular triggering of rules for example.

The behavior of rule based systems depends on their operational semantics. These are determined through the semantics of a rule execution procedure, which is usually called rule engine. A simple rule engine that executes production rules, consists of the following steps [3]:

1. Set the working memory to the initial state.
2. Build the set of all applicable and eligible rules. This set is called the agenda of the rule engine.
3. If the agenda is empty, the execution ends.
4. Otherwise, use a conflict set resolution strategy and choose a rule r in the agenda.
5. Update the working memory by executing the action of r. If the rule action contains several assignments, execute them in sequence.
6. Go to step 2.

The purpose of the rule eligibility strategy (step 2) is to avoid trivial infinite loops caused by applying again and again the same rule. It defines what a trivial loop is, and avoids them by making some rules ineligible. The purpose of the conflict set resolution strategy (step 3) is to pick the next rule to execute from the agenda. Again, several such strategies exist. Assigning a priority to each rule is a commonly used strategy.

Commercial engines employ such strategies to support logging execution traces, to provide simulation capabilities, and finally test and debug a rule set. For example, the problem of confluence can be solved by using priorities. It has been argued however that using this approach can be iterative since after prioritizing rules, say $r1$ and $r2$, a new pair of rules causing non-confluence may be identified [4]. The problem of termination can be solved by not allowing rules to trigger each other. However, this can reduce the usefulness of the language [4]. Even though most engines provide the support described above, they also present the discussed downsides and in addition they do not permit reasoning about the rule based system. We believe that formal methods can provide a feasible solution to this problem complementing the existing tools.

2   Formal Specification of Reactive Rules

Some first steps to use algebraic specification techniques in this research area were presented in [5] and [6], where we proposed the use of OTS/CafeOBJ method to prove safety properties about reactive rule-based systems. In particular we gave an Observational Transition System (OTS) semantics to Production and Event Condition Action rules so that verification of reactive rules can be supported. OTSs are state transition systems (or state machines) that have emerged as a subclass of behavioral specifications [7] and are used to model the behavior of distributed concurrent systems. OTSs are described as equational theory specifications in CafeOBJ and the OTS/CafeOBJ method ([8], [9]) is then used to theorem prove that systems (formalized as OTSs) have desired properties. This approach has been effectively used for the specification of various complex systems [10] and the verification of invariant and liveness [11] properties of them.

The framework proposed in [6] however cannot express naturally structure properties about reactive rules, such as confluence and termination. To this end, in this paper we extend the previous approach by adopting a different logical formalism, so that the behavior of reactive rules can be formally analyzed in a seamless manner. The extended framework and its theoretical foundations are presented in the sections below;

2.1   CafeOBJ Rewriting Logic Specification

CafeOBJ [12] is an algebraic specification language which is a modern successor of OBJ [13]. The basic building blocks of a CafeOBJ specification are modules. In the body of a module we can declare sorts, operators, variables and equations. A sort is a name given to a set of values. Sorts can be partially ordered, interpreted as subset relations among the sets corresponding to the sorts [14]. Operators are declared over sorts. Terms are inductively defined with operators and variables. Equations are used to define (standard) equivalence relations over terms. Operators may be (data) constructors [14]. Examples of constructors are as follows; `op true : -> Bool {constr}`, `op s : Nat -> Nat {constr}`. Bool is the sort given to the set of Boolean values. Operators with no arguments such as true are called constants. Given a natural number n, s(n) denotes the successor of n [14]. Finally, as with OBJ, CafeOBJ is executable by term rewriting [15] and uses equations as left to right rewrite rules.

Rewriting logic in CafeOBJ is based on a simplified version of Meseguer's rewriting logic [16] for concurrent systems which gives an extension of traditional algebraic specification towards concurrency. RWL incorporates many different models of concurrency in a natural, simple, and elegant way, thus giving CafeOBJ a wide range of applications. Unlike Maude [17], CafeOBJ design does not fully support labeled RWL which permits full reasoning about multiple transitions between states, but supports reasoning about the existence of transitions between states (or configurations) of concurrent systems via a built-in predicate (denoted `==>`) with dynamic definition encoding both the proof theory of RWL and the user defined transitions [15]. This predicate evaluates to true whenever there exists a transition from the left hand side argument to the right hand side argument [15].

For a ground term t, a pattern p and an optional condition c, CafeOBJ can traverse all the terms reachable from t wrt transitions in a breadth-first manner and find terms (called solutions) such that they are matched with p and c holds for them. This can be done using the command `red t =(k,d)=>* p [suchThat c]`, where k is the maximum number of solutions and d is the maximum depth of search. Also, a natural number (id) is assigned to each term visited by a search and then by using the command `show path id` a transition path to the term identified by id is displayed. Typically, the command is used to display a transition path to a solution found by a search from t [14].

CafeOBJ supports both equational theory and rewrite theory specification. State transitions are described in equations in the former and in rewriting rules in the latter. Equational theory specification is used for interactive theorem proving whereas for rewrite theory specification CafeOBJ can conduct exhaustive searches. In [14] an attempt to combine the above is presented. They describe a way to theorem prove that rewrite theory specifications of OTSs have invariant properties by proof score writing.

2.2   Reactive Rules and CafeOBJ

We present here how reactive rules can be formally defined as a set of rewrite theory specifications in CafeOBJ. In a rewrite theory, states can be expressed as tuples of values `< a1, a2, b1, b2 >` or as collections of observable values `(o1[p1]: a1) (o1[p2]: a2) (o2[p1]: b1) (o2[p2]: b2)` (soups), where observable values are pairs of (parameterized) names and values. The main difference between the two expressions is the following; when the states are expressed as tuples, the state expressions must be explicitly described on both sides of each transition. But when expressing states as soups, only the observable values that are involved in the transitions need to be described on both sides of each transition. By adapting the definition presented in [6], here we define a set of reactive rules as rewrite theory specifications of OTSs expressed as collections of observable values as follows;

Definition 1. *A production rule is expressed as a term of the form* R_i = *On* C_i *do* A_i *where* A_i *can either denote a variable assignment, or an assertion, retraction, update of the knowledge base (add/remove/update facts from the KB respectively) or some other generic action with side effects. In the case where* A_i *denotes a variable assignment this is expressed by a transition rule of the form:* ctrans [Ri] (V: v0) D => (V: v1) D if Ci = true .

Ri is the label of the transition rule and v_0, v_1 *are variables. Also, the keyword* ctrans *is used because the rule is conditional. The above rule states that the observable value* V *will become* v_1 *if the condition of the rule is true. Also,* D *denotes an arbitrary data type needed for the definition of the transition. When the result of action* A_i *is the assertion of the fact* k_i *to the knowledge base, its definition is the following;* ctrans [assert ki] (knowledge: K) D => (knowledge : (ki U K) D if Ci /in K .

In the above rewrite rule knowledge is the observable value corresponding to the knowledge base and it is defined as a set of boolean elements. U is an operator for adding elements in a set and /in is an operator that returns true when an element belongs to a set, here the knowledge base. When the result of action A_i *is the retraction of the fact* k_i *from the knowledge base, its definition is;* ctrans [retract ki] (knowledge: K) D => (knowledge: K / ki) D if Ci /in K .

Operator / denotes that an element is removed from a set. When action A_i *is an update action, its definition is the following;* ctrans [retract ki] (knowledge: K) => (knowledge: (K / ki) U kj) if Ci /in K .

Finally, if A_i *is a generic action and extra observable values* (o_i) *need to be used for its definition, we have;* ctrans [ai] (oi: vi) D => (oi: vj) D if Ci = true .

In order to express ECA rules as rewrite rules we need an observable value that will "remember" the occurred events. For this reason, in each event we assign a natural number and when an event is detected its number is stored the observable value event-memory. Using event-memory we can map events to transitions/rewrite rules [6].

Definition 2. *An Event Condition Action rule of the form* R_i := *On* E_i *if* C_i *do* A_i *is defined in CafeOBJ terms as two transitions.*

- The first one specifies the event E_i *and in particular the fact that the system after the detection of the event it stores its identification number in the observable value event-memory . This is defined as;* ctrans [Ei] (event-memory: null) => (event-memory: i) if c-ei = true .

In the above rewrite rule, the value null of event-memory, denotes that no other event is detected at the pre state and c-ei is a boolean CafeOBJ term denoting the detection conditions for E_i.

- The second transition rule specifies the action A_i. More precisely it defines that the system must respond to the detected event by performing the corresponding action, where A_i is again either a generic action or a predefined action of the rule language. The triggering of the action as a response to the event is simply defined by adding the condition that in the pre state the event memory will contain the index of the occurred event, i.e. ctrans [ai] (event-memory: m) (oi: vi) => (event-memory: null) (oi: vj) if Ci = true and (m = i) .

This ensures that only the guard of this transition rule will hold at the pre state and thus this will be the only applicable transition for that state of the system. Also after the occurrence of the action, event-memory will become null again denoting that the system is ready to detect another event.

Let us note here that in cases where the action of the rule may activate an internal event (say E_j), the observable value stores the id of the event, j, and becomes null again when the corresponding to the internal event action is applied (if it does not activate another internal event).

Running Example. To illustrate the definitions presented in this paper, we will use as a running example, a company's e-commerce web site [3]. This company has customers with registered profiles on the site, which contain information about the customers' age and their category (Silver, Gold, or Platinum). When a customer puts items in his/her shopping cart a discount is computed based on the pricing policy of the company, i.e. on the customer's profile and the value of the cart. The behavior of this system is defined by the following three production rules; (R1) The gold-discount rule implements a policy that increments the discount granted to Gold customers by 10 points, if their shopping cart is worth 2,000 or more. (R2) The platinum-discount rule implements a policy that increments the discount granted to Platinum customers by 15 points, if their shopping cart is worth 1,000 or more. (R3) The upgrade rule implements a policy that promotes Gold customers to the Platinum category, if they are aged 60 or more. These rules can be written as a set of rewrite transition rules in CafeOBJ according to definition 1. First, the state of our system is formally described in the module below;

```
mod! STATE { pr(TYPE + NAT)
[Obs < State]
-- configuration
op void : -> State {constr}
op _ _ : State State -> State {constr assoc comm id: void}
-- observable values
op category:_ : type -> Obs {constr}
op value:_ : Nat -> Obs {constr}
op age:_ : Nat -> Obs {constr}
op discount:_ : Nat -> Obs {constr} }
```

As we can see a state is defined as a set of the following observable values (category:) (value:) (age:) (discount:). The three last values are represented by natural numbers and for this reason the module imports the predefined module NAT. Also pr(TYPE) imports a previously defined CafeOBJ theory which specifies the various customer types, i.e. gold, platinum and silver. Next, the rules R1-R3 are defined in the module RULES as a rewrite theory.

```
mod! RULES { pr(STATE + EQL)
var G : type
vars V N M  : Nat

ctrans [gold] : (category: G) (value: V) (age: N) (discount: M)
=> (category: G) (value: V) (age: N) (discount: (M + 10)) if
((V >= 2000) and (G = gold)) .
ctrans [platinum] : (category: G) (value: V) (age: N) (discount: M)
=> (category: G) (value: V) (age: N) (discount: (M + 15)) if
((V >= 1000) and (G = platinum)) .
ctrans [upgrade] : (category: G) (value: V) (age: N) (discount: M)
=> (category: platinum) (value: V) (age: N) (discount: M) if
(G = gold) and (N >= 60) . }
```

The gold rewrite rule, states that if the observable value `category` is gold and the `value` is equal or greater than 2000 then the value `discount` will be increased by 10 points. The platinum rewrite rule, states that if the observable value `category` is platinum and the `value` is equal or greater than 1000 then the value `discount` will be increased by 15 points. The upgrade rewrite rule states that if the observable value `category` is gold and the `age` is 60 or more then the value `category` will become platinum.

3   Formal Verification of Reactive Rules

As discussed in [3], there is an ambiguity between the upgrade and discount rule. If a gold customer is eligible to both being granted the gold discount and being upgraded to the platinum category, then this customer may end up with either a 15 or 25 per cent discount, depending on the execution order of the rules. This can be a hazard for the business application implementing this set of rules. We will present how such structural errors can be detected using our approach.

In particular, in this section we define some CafeOBJ operators which allow us to reason about confluence and termination properties of reactive rule based systems specified as rewrite logic theories. Also we demonstrate how existing operators can be used together with the proposed formalization of reactive rules to verify invariant properties about them.

3.1   Proving Termination Properties

Termination in a rule based system concerns with the existence of a state of that system where no more rules are applicable. More precisely;

Theorem (Termination). A rule program's state s is terminating if and only if there is no infinite sequence $s \to s1 \to s2 \to \ldots$ In other words a state s is terminating if it leads to a state where no rules can be applied. That is, there exist two states such that; $s \to s'$ and $\neg(s = s')$ where s' is a final state. Based on this, we can check if a state terminates by defining the following predicate in CafeOBJ terms;

```
op terminates? : State -> Bool
terminates?(s) = s =(1,*)=>! (event-memory: M1) (value: V1) (o: N)
red notConfluent?(s) .
```

The expression `t1=(1,*)=>!` t2 indicates that the term matching to t2 should be a different term from t1 to which no transition rules are applicable. Also, the term `(event-memory: M1) (value: V1) (o: N)` represents an arbitrary state and it depends on the observable values of the specified system. By reducing the above predicate, we ask CafeOBJ to find a *a final state* reachable from the state s. If true is returned (together with a final state) it means that the state s is terminating; if false is returned it means that in the state s, no transition can be applied. Finally, the CafeOBJ reduction may not terminate, indicating that s is not terminating. Using the above predicate, we can check if the whole rule based system terminates or not, by defining the search to be performed for the initial state of the system; `op init : -> State, red terminates?(init) .`

When the number of reachable states reachable from init is small enough, the whole reachable state space can be checked by, `init =(1,*)=>`, where $*$ denotes infinity. Otherwise, the bounded reachable state space whose depth is d may be checked by, `init =(1,d)=> .`

Running Example. Here we test the set of rules of the running example for termination. We must mention that in most real life applications the initial state of the system is explicitly defined during the design of the system. An e-shop site for example before the implementation could have the following characteristics; initially, no customer is registered at the site, when someone registers for the first time his/her category is silver, the discount is zero and so on.

It is possible however, for a system to be defined without explicitly defining its initial state. In such cases, we can still check the desired properties (confluence and termination) by defining an arbitrary initial state and then discriminate the cases based on the conditions of the transition rules. In our example these cases are; (age < 60 or age >= 60), (discount = gold or platinum), (value < 1000 or value >= 1000) and (value < 2000 or value >= 2000). For the last two only the following (value < 1000 or 1000 <= value < 2000 or value >= 2000) need to be checked. Here we present the most indicative cases;

```
(a) open RULES .
op s : -> State .
eq s = (category: gold) (value: 500) (age: 50) (discount: 0)
red terminates?(s) .
```

In this case CafeOBJ returns false and the following message, which is reasonable since no transition can be applied.

```
** No more possible transitions.
(false): Bool
```

(b) eq s = (category: gold) (value: 500) (age: 60) (discount: 0)
red terminates?(s) .

In this case where upgrade is the only applicable rule the CafeOBJ system returns true and the final state (category: platinum) (value: 500) (age: 50) (discount: 0) .

(c) eq s = (category: gold) (value: 2000) (age: 50) (discount: 0)
red terminates?(s) .

In this case the gold rule can be applied to s and to all reachable states from s. Thus in CafeOBJ the above reduction does not halt indicating that this initial state is not terminating. The same conclusion holds for the platinum rule as well. Having detected this issue we can correct the rule base by adding constraints to the application of these rules, for example (discount: (M1 + 10) <= 100) and (discount: (M1 + 10) <= 100) respectively, since the discount cannot surpass this value. In this way the rules will stop triggering when the discount reaches the maximum value. When the same case is tested after adding the above constraints CafeOBJ finds the final state; (category: gold) (value: 2000) (age: 50) (discount: 100) .

3.2 Proving Confluence Properties

After checking that a rule based system is terminating, it is important to be able to determine if it is confluent or not (if the rules do not terminate they will not be confluent either).

Theorem (Non-Confluence). A rule program's state s is non-confluent if there exist two traces $trace_1$ and $trace_2$ from this state that lead to distinct states. That is, there exist two traces and three states such that; $s \xrightarrow{trace_1} s1$ and $s \xrightarrow{trace_2} s2$ and $\neg(s1 = s2)$, where $s1$ and $s2$ are final states. Based on this, we can check a state for non-confluence by defining the following predicate in CafeOBJ terms;

```
op notConfulent? : State -> Bool
notConfluent?(s) =(2,*)=>! (event-memory: M1) (value: V1) (o: N) .
red notConfluent?(s) .
```

The above reduction i.e. asks CafeOBJ to search if it can find starting from an arbitrary state s two *different final states* of the system. For this reason we use again the predicate with the exclamation mark at the end (final state) but in the number indicating the number of solutions we assign the value two (two different states). If two such solutions are found it means that the state s is not confluent. Otherwise if false is returned and one solution is found, the state is confluent. To check a rule based system for confluence we perform the search for the initial state of the system, as before, using the command `red notConfluent?(init)`.

Running Example. Here we test the set of rules of the running example for confluence. Again we can discriminate the cases for an arbitrary initial state. For example:

```
(a) open RULES .
op s : -> State .
eq s = (category: gold) (value: 500) (age: 60) (discount: 0)
red notConfluent?(s) .
```

In this case where upgrade is the only applicable rule CafeOBJ returns false, as it finds one final state meaning that the state s is confluent. Now let us consider the state which is defined by the following observable values; the value of the items of the cart is equal to 2000 dollars, the age of the customer is 60 years old and her/his category is gold. This is the state we mentioned at the beginning of the section, in which the customer is eligible to both being granted the gold discount and being upgraded to the platinum category.

```
(b) eq s = (category: gold) (value: 2000) (age: 60) (discount: 0)
red notConfluent?(s) .
```

CafeOBJ returns true as it finds two solutions, denoting that s is not confluent as we expected. In particular it returns;

```
** Found [state 25] (category: platinum) (value: 2000) (age: 60)
(discount: 90)
** Found [state 27] (category: platinum) (value: 2000) (age: 60)
(discount: 95)
```

Using the command `show path id` we can see the two transition paths that cause the problem (and then we can add constraints in the conditions of the rules as before to solve this issue by letting for example the upgrade rule to be applied first). Even though the presented example is quite simple it demonstrates that detecting such errors before the implementation of a rule based system can prove really helpful especially when designing complex critical systems.

3.3 Proving Safety Properties

The built-in CafeOBJ search predicate can also be used to prove safety properties for a system specified in rewriting logic (RWL). In this work, we are interested in invariant properties.

Definition (Invariant property). A desirable safety property p is an invariant for a rule based system if it holds in each reachable state (R_s) of the system, i.e. $\forall s \in R_s . p(s)$.

For the verification of such properties model checking and/or theorem proving can be used; An invariant property can be model checked by searching if there is a state reachable from the initial state such that the desirable property does not hold [14]. This can be achieved using the following expression: `red init =(1,*)=>* p [suchThat c]` .

In the above term c is a CafeOBJ term denoting the negation of the desired safety property. Thus, CafeOBJ will return true for this reduction if it discovers (within the given depth) a state which violates the safety property. This methodology is very effective for discovering (shallow) counterexamples. However, model checking does not constitute a formal proof and is complementary to theorem proving. Formal proofs are required when we are dealing with critical systems. In [14] a methodology to (theorem) prove safety properties of OTS specifications written in RWL is presented. This methodology can be used to reason about rule based systems expressed in our framework as we will demonstrate throughout the running example.

Running Example. For our rule based system an invariant safety property could be the following; *a customer cannot belong to the platinum category if his/her age is less than 60 years.* This is expressed in CafeOBJ terms as;

```
op isSafe : State -> Bool .
eq isSafe((category: G) (value: V) (age: N) (discount: M)) =
not ((G == platinum) and (N < 60)) .
```

The proof is done by induction on the number of transition rules of the system. First, the following operator is used [14];

```
vars pre con : Bool
op check : Bool Bool -> Bool
eq check(pre, con) = if (pre implies con) == true then true
else false fi .
```

This operator takes as input a conjunction of lemmas and/or induction hypotheses and a formula to prove and returns true if the proof is successful and false if *pre implies con* does not reduce to true (this is why the built in `==` CafeOBJ operation is used, which is reduced to false iff the left and right hand side arguments are not reduced to the same term). Using this predicate the base case of the proof is successfully discharged using the following CafeOBJ code:

```
eq init = (category: gold) (value: 2000) (age: 50) (discount: 0) .
red check(true, isSafe(init)) .
```

The inductive step consists of checking whether from an arbitrary state, say s, we can reach in one step a state, say s', where the desired property does not hold. This can be verified using the following reduction [14]: `red s =(*, 1)=>+ s' suchThat (not check(isSafe(s),isSafe(s')))` .

When false is returned it means that CafeOBJ was unable to find a state s' such that the safety property holds in s and it does not hold i s'[1]. If a solution is found, i.e. the above term is reduced to true, then either the safety property is not preserved by the inductive step or we must provide additional input to the CafeOBJ machine. In the second case this input may be either in the form of extra equations defining case analysis or by asserting a lemma (in which case the new lemma has to be verified separately). Consider the inductive step where the *gold* transition rule is applied to s.

```
eq s = (category: gold) (value: 2000) (age: N) (discount: 0) .
red s =(*, 1)=>+ s' suchThat (not check(isSafe(s),isSafe(s'))) .
```

In the above equation (category: gold) (value: 2000) (age: N) (discount: 0) is an arbitrary state of the rule based system to which gold rule can be applied. CafeOBJ returns false, and thus the induction case is discharged. Consider the case where the *platinum* rule is applied;

```
eq s = (category: platinum) (value: 2000) (age: N) (discount: 0) .
red s =(*, 1)=>+ s' suchThat (not check(isSafe(s),isSafe(s'))) .
```

CafeOBJ returns false for this case, thus the induction case is discharged. Following the same methodology the induction case for the upgrade rule was discharged as well, and thus the proof concludes. The full specification of the e-commerce site, the reasoning about the structure properties and proof of the invariant can be found at [18].

4   Related Work and Discussion

In the area of active databases, a lot of research concerning analysis of rule-based systems exists [19]. A survey on the different approaches of reaction rules can be found in [20]. For example, ECA-LP [21] supports state based knowledge updates including a test case/integrity constraint based verification and validation for transactional updates. Previous attempts, e.g. [22] and [23], propose the visualization of the execution of rules to study their behavior where rules can be shown in different levels of abstraction.

More recent approaches related to the application of formal methods for analyzing rule based systems and relevant to ours, include the following; In [24] authors propose a constraint-based approach to the verification of rule programs. They present a simple rule language, describe how to express rule programs and verification properties into constraint satisfiability problems and discuss some challenges of verifying rule programs using a CP Solver that derive from the fact that the domains of the input variables are commonly very large. Finally, they present how to detect structure properties of a simple rule based system. In [3] authors analyze the behavior of Event Condition Action rules by translating

---

[1] To modularly verify each transition rule separately we usually, define for each such transition a new module which only contains one transition rule at a time.

them into an extended Petri net and verify termination and confluence properties of a light control system expressed in terms of ECA rules. [4] presents an approach to verify the behavior of Event Condition Action rules where a tool that transforms such rules to timed automata is developed. Then the Uppaal tool is used to prove desired safety properties for an industrial rule-based application.

Our approach for the verification of rule programs is based on a different formalism; in particular it uses the OTS/CafeOBJ method and rewriting logic. To the best of our knowledge this is the first time it is used in the area of reactive rules. One motivation for this work was a recent advancement in the field, and in particular the methodology to theorem prove rewrite theories [14]. Compared to existing similar approaches, it has the following contributions.

First, compared to [3] where structure errors are formally analyzed, our methodology can be used for the verification of both structure (confluence and termination) and safety properties for the specified rule system. This extends our previous work [6] where only safety properties could be proved. Second, when proving safety properties both model checking and theorem proving techniques can be applied, in contrast to [4] and [24] where only model checking support is provided. The combination of these two proving methods provides strong verification power. Model checking can be used to search the system for a state when the desired invariant property is violated (counter example) and next if no such state is discovered, theorem proving techniques can be applied to ensure that the system preserves the property in any reachable state. In this way infinite state systems can be specified. Also, CafeOBJ and Maude allow inductive data structures in state machines to be model checked and few model checkers exist with this feature. Finally our approach can be used for the specification and verification of complex systems due to the simplicity of the CafeOBJ language and its natural affinity for abstraction [25].

However the proposed methodology does not come without limitations. When a proof is constructed by humans, they might forget cases to consider or proofs of some lemmas in the proof [10]. To solve this issue, some tools have been developed such as Creme [26] and Gateau [27]. We are also working towards developing a tool that will automate the OTS/CafeOBJ verification method using the Athena proof system [28]. Another possible limitation could be the fact that researchers should be familiar with the CafeOBJ formalism in order to use the proposed approach. However, we believe that the mapping from reactive to rewrite rules is natural enough and the verification method has a clear structure, thus allowing non-expert users to adopt our methodology with minimum effort.

5   Conclusion

We have argued that even though most commercial rule engines provide some support to rule testing, the use of formal methods can be beneficial, even required at some cases, for ensuring the proper behavior of complex and critical rule based systems. For this reason we proposed a methodology for expressing a set of reactive rules into rewrite theories in CafeOBJ that can be used to; (1) formally specify reactive rules, (2) detect structure errors, like confluence and termination, and (3) prove invariant safety properties of the specified reactive rule based system, via theorem proving and model checking techniques. This diversity of options to verification (techniques and properties) offered by the resulted form of the reactive rules and the underlying logic, consists the main contribution of our work.

To conclude, this methodology allows the verification of the knowledge base against the specification of the reactive rule based system and thus formal proofs about its consistency can be obtained. As a future work we intend to conduct more case studies using the proposed methodology so that it can be extended to support most rule-based systems and apply it to a real world application. Another future direction is to develop a tool to automate (part of) the mapping from reactive rules to a rewrite specification written in CafeOBJ. Finally, we intend to use similar formal techniques in order to verify an open-source rule engine implementation. Thus together with the proposed framework, end-to-end validation will be enabled.

Acknowledgments. This research has been co-financed by the European Union (European Social Fund ESF) and Greek national funds through the Operational Program "Education and Lifelong Learning" of the National Strategic Reference Framework (NSRF) - Research Funding Program: THALIS.

References

1. Berstel, B., Bonnard, P., Bry, F., Eckert, M., Pătrânjan, P.-L.: Reactive rules on the web. In: Antoniou, G., Aßmann, U., Baroglio, C., Decker, S., Henze, N., Patranjan, P.-L., Tolksdorf, R. (eds.) Reasoning Web 2007. LNCS, vol. 4636, pp. 183–239. Springer, Heidelberg (2007)
2. Paschke, A.: ECA-RuleML: An Approach combining ECA Rules with temporal interval-based KR Event/Action Logics and Transactional Update Logics. ECA-RuleML Proposal for RuleML Reaction Rules Technical Goup (2005)
3. Jin, X., Lembachar, Y., Ciardo, G.: Symbolic verication of ECA rules. In: International Workshop on Petri Nets and Software Engineering (PNSE 2013) and International Workshop on Modeling and Business Environments (ModBE 2013), pp. 41–59 (2013)
4. Ericsson, A., Berndtsson, M., Pettersson, P.: Verification of an industrial rule-based manufacturing system using REX. In: 1st International Workshop on Complex Event Processing for Future Internet, iCEP-FIS (2008)
5. Ksystra, K., Triantafyllou, N., Stefaneas, P.: On the Algebraic Semantics of Reactive Rules. In: Bikakis, A., Giurca, A. (eds.) RuleML 2012. LNCS, vol. 7438, pp. 136–150. Springer, Heidelberg (2012)
6. Ksystra, K., Stefaneas, P., Frangos, P.: An Algebraic Framework for Modeling of Reactive Rule-Based Intelligent Agents. In: Geffert, V., Preneel, B., Rovan, B., Štuller, J., Tjoa, A.M. (eds.) SOFSEM 2014. LNCS, vol. 8327, pp. 407–418. Springer, Heidelberg (2014)
7. Goguen, J., Malcolm, G.: A hidden agenda. Theoretical Computer Science 245(1), 55–101 (2000)

8. Ogata, K., Futatsugi, K.: Proof scores in the OTS/CafeOBJ method. In: Najm, E., Nestmann, U., Stevens, P. (eds.) FMOODS 2003. LNCS, vol. 2884, pp. 170–184. Springer, Heidelberg (2003)

9. Ogata, K., Futatsugi, K.: Some Tips on Writing Proof Scores in the OTS/CafeOBJ method. In: Futatsugi, K., Jouannaud, J.-P., Meseguer, J. (eds.) Goguen Festschrift. LNCS, vol. 4060, pp. 596–615. Springer, Heidelberg (2006)

10. Ogata, K., Futatsugi, K.: Proof Score Approach to Analysis of Electronic Commerce Protocols. Int. J. Soft. Eng. Knowl. Eng. 20(253), 253–287 (2010)

11. Ogata, K., Futatsugi, K.: Proof score approach to verification of liveness properties. IEICE Transactions E91-D, 2804–2817 (2008)

12. Diaconescu, R., Futatsugi, K.: CafeOBJ report: The language, proof techniques, and methodologies for object-oriented algebraic specification. AMAST Series in Computing. World Scientific, Singapore (1998)

13. Goguen, J., Winkler, T., Meseguer, J., Futatsugi, K., Jouannaud, J.P.: Introducing OBJ. In: Software Engineering with OBJ: Algebraic Specification in Action. Kluwer (2000)

14. Ogata, K., Futatsugi, K.: Theorem Proving Based on Proof Scores for Rewrite Theory Specifications of OTSs. In: Iida, S., Meseguer, J., Ogata, K. (eds.) Futatsugi Festschrift. LNCS, vol. 8373, pp. 630–656. Springer, Heidelberg (2014)

15. Diaconescu, R., Futatsugi, K., Iida, S.: CafeOBJ Jewels. In: Futatsugi, K., Nakagawa, A.T., Tamai, T. (eds.) CAFE: An Industiral-Strength Algebraic Formal Method, pp. 33–60. Elsevier (2000)

16. Meseguer, J.: Conditional rewriting logic as a unified model of concurrency. Theoretical Computer Science 96(1), 73–155 (1992)

17. http://maude.cs.uiuc.edu/

18. http://cafeobjntua.blogspot.com/

19. Vlahavas, I., Bassiliades, N.: Parallel, object-oriented, and active knowledge base systems. Kluwer Academic Publishers, Norwell (1998)

20. Paschke, A., Kozlenkov, A.: Rule-Based Event Processing and Reaction Rules. In: Governatori, G., Hall, J., Paschke, A. (eds.) RuleML 2009. LNCS, vol. 5858, pp. 53–66. Springer, Heidelberg (2009)

21. Paschke, A.: ECA-LP / ECA-RuleML: A Homogeneous Event-Condition-Action Logic Programming Language. In: Int. Conf. on Rules and Rule Markup Languages for the Semantic Web, Athens, Georgia, USA (2006)

22. Fors, T.: Visualization of rule behaviour in active databases. In: VDB, pp. 215–231 (1995)

23. Benazet, E., Guehl, H., Bouzeghoub, M.: A visual tool for analysis of rules behaviour in active databases. In: Sellis, T. (ed.) RIDS 1995. LNCS, vol. 985, pp. 182–196. Springer, Heidelberg (1995)

24. Berstel, B., Leconte, M.: Using Constraints to Verify Properties of Rule Programs. In: ICST Third International Conference on Software Testing, Verification and Validation, Paris, France (2010)

25. Diaconescu, R., Futatsugi, K., Ogata, K.: CafeOBJ: Logical Foundations and Methodologies. Computing and Informatics 22, 257–283 (2003)

26. Nakano, M., Ogata, K., Nakamura, M., Futatsugi, K.: Creme: An Automatic Invariant Prover of Behavioral Specifications. Int. J. Soft. Eng. Knowl. Eng. 17(6), 783–804 (2007)

27. Seino, T., Ogata, K., Futatsugi, K.: A toolkit for generating and displaying proof scores in the OTS/CafeOBJ method. ENTCS 147(1), 57–72 (2006)

28. http://www.proofcentral.org/athena/

Using Rules to Develop a Personalized and Social Location Information System for the Semantic Web

Iosif Viktoratos[1], Athanasios K. Tsadiras[1], and Nick Bassiliades[2]

[1] Department of Economics,
[2] Department of Informatics,
Aristotle University of Thessaloniki, 54124 Thessaloniki, Greece
{viktorat,tsadiras,nbassili}@auth.gr

Abstract. In this work, the design and implementation of an innovative context-aware location based social networking service is presented. The proposed system, called "Geosocial SPLIS", utilizes Semantic Web technologies to deliver personalized information to the end user. It addresses some drawbacks of knowledge-based personalization systems and aims to provide a collaborative knowledge creation platform for other systems. To achieve this, it a) collects data from external sources such as Google Places API and Google+ b) adopts the schema.org ontology to represent people and places profiles, c) provides a web editor for adding rules (modeling user preferences and group-targeted place offers) at run time, d) uses RuleML and Jess rules to represent these rules, e) combines at run-time the above to match user context with up to date information, presented on Google Maps and f) matches user's preferences with those of his/her nearby friends to present POI's that are suitable to all of them. All data and rules are stored in the Sesame RDF triple store in order to be shared among various systems.

Keywords: Semantic Web, Ontologies, Rules, Context, Location Based Services, Points of Interest, Preferences, Group-Targeted Offers.

1 Introduction

Nowadays, a sector of Location Based Services (LBS) [1, 2], used daily by millions of people, is Location Based Social Networking Services (LBSNS) [3,4]. LBSNS are applications that provide users with the capability to locate each other and interact with one another depending on their physical distance. Two of the most popular examples are Facebook Places (https://www.facebook.com/about/location) and Foursquare (https://foursquare.com/).

Successful LBSNS should fulfill user requirements and provide them with rich and personalized information according to their profile (e.g. preferences etc.) and their environment (location, day, etc.), usually referred as context [5]. Consequently, researchers focus on enhancing contextual knowledge collection and perception process by developing a) hardware structures (e.g. GPS, sensors) and b) software technologies such as ontologies and rules [6-8]. Concerning the second domain, ontologies

A. Bikakis et al. (Eds.): RuleML 2014, LNCS 8620, pp. 82–96, 2014.

(e.g. RDF/S, OWL) enhanced contextual knowledge because they a) offer the ability to represent physical entities and the associations between them, b) enable knowledge sharing and interoperability among heterogeneous systems and c) they can be reused and extended easily [6-8]. Ontologies are often combined with rules for increased expressiveness because rule-based systems are more autonomous and proactive, being able to conceive context changes and respond accordingly without user intervention [7, 8].

In this work, an innovative location based social networking service called "Geosocial SPLIS[1]" will be presented in order to demonstrate how semantic web technologies can enhance LBSNS and offer high level personalized information. Geosocial SPLIS is an extension of a system called "SPLIS" described in [9]. SPLIS provided a web editor for POI owners to assert their own properties and group targeted offers, which were represented as rules (e.g. "If a person is a student and day is Sunday then coffee price has discount 20%"). SPLIS evaluated such kind of rules on the fly depending on regular user's context and delivered personalized offers to them. Geosocial SPLIS, apart from POI owners, provides regular users with the capability to add their own contextualized rule based preferences through a web editor (e.g. "If day is Sunday then I would like to visit a Coffee shop") in order to match these preferences with POI owners' personalized offers. Data from editor are being transformed into RuleML and then into Jess so as to be machine understandable. After that, all data[2] and rules are stored in the Sesame RDF triple store being fully compatible with the popular schema.org (http://schema.org/) ontology (adopted by Google, Bing and Yahoo). Using the above, the system evaluates data and rules on the fly and presents contextualized information on Google Maps (https://maps.google.gr/).

1.1   Related Work on Knowledge-Based Personalization in LBS

To begin with, Ciaramella et al. [10] combined predefined rules in SWRL format in order to determine the user's respective situation and, after that, a set of available services is proposed proactively to him/her. Another rule based LBS is Sem-Fit [11], which uses fuzzy rules to recommend hotels to a user. A user is able to provide an evaluation of the returning results. After that, Sem-Fit updates the rules so as to provide better results. Moreover, Niforatos et al. [12] proposed a service which informs user about nearby offers while he/she is on the move. Additionally, Armenatzoglou et al. [13] developed a flexible conference assistant that integrates Semantic Web technologies to support personalized, context-aware notifications to conference attendees.

Multiple services use social media data to achieve better personalization. An example is PhotoMap [14], which exploits rules in SWRL format to attach physical and social context to photo shots (for example where the photo was taken and who was there). Serrano et al. [15] proposed a tourist information service which combines RDF

---

[1]   Can be accessed at http://tinyurl.com/GeoSPLIS

[2]   Server can be accessed at http://platon.econ.auth.gr:8080/ openrdf-sesame and data can be accessed at http://platon.econ.auth.gr:8080/openrdf-workbench/ repositories/3

data taken from sources such as foaf profile with predefined rules in SWRL format to recommend places of interest related to user profile. Last but not least, Li et al. [16] proposed a semantic-based mobile ad hoc social network that uses a semantics-aware discovery mechanism to locate users with similar interests.

1.2   Geosocial SPLIS Relation to Other Works and Overall Contribution

With respect to the related works that were described above, apart from the advantages they possess, they have some disadvantages such as [15-18]:

- They use a predefined set of rules. Rule based systems are useful when enough amounts of web usage data are available and a limited set of rules cover a narrow range of knowledge.
- Designing, implementing and maintaining new rules is a time consuming process which requires a lot of effort and cost.
- Developers' rules are not always efficient for every situation or for every user.

Geososial SPLIS deals with these problems by offering users the capability to add rules dynamically at runtime through an intuitive user-oriented interface. Instead of having problems and becoming obsolete the system becomes more and more intelligent as soon as more rules are inserted into the system. By exploiting social intelligence and letting users to take part in the knowledge construction process, the system's knowledge base becomes richer and richer. Moreover, user defined rules are more consistent, qualitative and efficient than those of the developers and can provide customized information of higher quality [10].

In the following section, the design and the implementation details of Geosocial SPLIS are described, while in Section 3 the system's processes are discussed. In Section 4 some use case scenarios are demonstrated. Section 5 presents some evaluation results and, finally, section 6 discusses the conclusions of our work and indicates future directions.

2   Design and Implementation

Human mobility behavior in everyday life is not completely random and presents strong daily patterns (e.g. a user visits a bar at night) [19]. People have preferences such as "if it is morning and weather is sunny I would like to go for a coffee", which depend on his/her current situation. Geosocial SPLIS general idea is to model and evaluate such kind of preferences and provide customized context-aware information, attractive to each user. In detail, Geosocial SPLIS provides users the capability to expose their preferences by authoring rules that represent them, through a user-friendly web editor. After that, every time a user is logged into the system, it gets his/her context, evaluates his/her rule-based preferences and POI owners' rules and delivers personalized information (figure 1). Geosocial SPLIS is able to handle rules that involve a) every existing property of a POI, b) user's location (e.g. I want a coffee shop which is are less than 600 meters away), c) weather and d) time-day (e.g. I would like restaurants which serve Chinese cuisine, if it is Sunday 13:00-16:00).

A variety of software technologies combined for system implementation. To begin with, Sesame [20] is used for RDF data manipulation. Moreover, RuleML (and more specific Reaction RuleML) was chosen as a rule representation language, because a) it is a powerful markup language (XML with a predefined schema) which supports various types of rules such as deductive, reactive and normative and b) it provides interoperability among various systems by allowing rules to be represented in a formal way [21]. It was selected instead of SWRL because of the fact that SWRL employs open world reasoning without default negation, while our approach needs close world reasoning (e.g. checking the context of a user, in order to decide whether a preference is in effect). RIF-PRD (http://www.w3.org/TR/rif-prd/) could have been used, but at this time is not supported by tools as much as RuleML. Furthermore, Jess was chosen a machine executable language because it is a lightweight rule engine that matches well with web technologies [22]. Also Drools [22] could have been used instead of Jess, giving similar results. To transform RuleML rules to Jess, XSLT files [23] are used. Furthermore, common web technologies such Java Server Pages (JSP), html, JavaScript and AJAX are used for visualization [24].

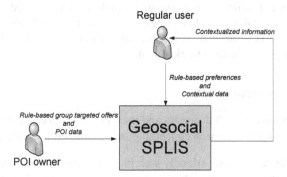

Fig. 1. Geosocial SPLIS general design

3   Geosocial SPLIS Operation Process

In this section an overview about system processes is included.

3.1   Presentation of Information Process

Presentation of information process includes the following steps:

1. **Data collection.** A detailed reference concerning POI data collection from Google Places API can be found in [9]. Concerning Geosocial SPLIS users, they can either fill in a registration form or login via Google+ (https://plus.google.com/) and the relevant data are stored in RDF. If they chose the second option, system collects profile data from their Google+ account (name, age etc.). A data mapping is directly done as Google+ property names are compatible with schema.org. Every time a user logs in using Google+ account, the system updates existing data to keep track of changes.

2. **Data retrieval.** After a user's login, data concerning user's context (profile properties, relationships, rules, time, day, weather[3]) and data concerning nearby POIs (properties, owner, rules) are retrieved from the repository.
3. **Rule evaluation.** Data mentioned above are asserted to the Jess rule engine, which evaluates both user's rules (preferences) and POIs' rules (POI owner's group targeted offers) using the asserted facts. Concerning user's rules, Jess checks the if-part of these rules (they involve user contextual properties and place data) and concludes whether a POI is interesting or not for the user.
4. **Presentation of personalized information.** Finally, data are being transferred to the client for visualization. Similarly to [9], different colour of markers on the presented map assists users to find POI's that possess valid for them offers while a star over a marker on the map indicates that the current user is the owner of the specific POI. Additionally, Geosocial SPLIS combines POI offers with user preferences. According to this, if a user's preference is satisfied for a POI, that is a user's rule is fired for that POI, then the POI is represented with a bigger marker. By clicking on a marker, apart from viewing place data, a user can also write a review, rate them, make a "like" or a "check in". The user can also obtain additional information explaining which rules were fired and why, concerning his/her rules and POI rules. In order to avoid confusion, a user rule/preference is illustrated with a person icon in front of the message and a POI rule is represented by a marker icon.

3.2   Processes Concerning Rules

A detailed description about POI owners and their processes concerning rules can be found in [9]. A thorough discussion concerning user defined rules, follows.

Rule Insertion Process. A user-friendly web interface has been designed so that users can easily add their rules through completing specific forms. A demonstration of rule creation in Geosocial SPLIS is given in figure 2, where a user asserts the rule "*If day is Sunday and weather is Sunny, then I would like an IceCreamShop*". The web interface provides fields for entering the title and the priority of the rule. After that, by clicking on the four buttons "Add...Condition" he/she is able to customize the contextual condition. The condition customization consists of a) the property field (weather, day, time, distance) b) the operator field ("is" for day or weather and "<",">" for time or distance) and c) the value. Elements concerning properties and operators are represented by read-only texts and value elements by drop down menus. This approach is adopted to resolve user data heterogeneity and avoid any mistakes. By clicking on the relevant red button, users can delete a condition. By repeating this process, they can add as many conditions as they like; a logical "AND" is implied among them.

After that, by clicking on a drop down menu they can choose the type of POI that they prefer. It is worth mentioning that schema.org hierarchy is adopted. For example if a user chose the place type "Store" all its subcategories are included (e.g. GroceryStrore etc.). In addition by clicking on the "Add Where Condition" button they are

---

[3] http://www.worldweatheronline.com/

able to make their rule more specific by customizing the POI properties. A property drop down menu, an operator drop down menu ("is" and "contains" for text and "<",">" for numbers and dates) and a value field are included.

A user is also able to add a textual explanation of the rule, so that the meaning of the rule can become clear both to him/her and also to other users. Additionally the editor provides a preview button to check the rule before submitting it and a clear button to reset the process. User can also click on one of the most popular rules, or on one of his/her friends' rules in the left side of the screen and the forms concerning this rule are automatically filled.

The rule that is authored in the forms, is transformed to RuleML syntax (for inter-operability with other systems on the web) and afterward, via xslt, is transformed to the Jess rule language, in order to become machine executable. For example, Table 1 illustrates the rule of Figure 2, in RuleML and Jess. Concerning Jess representation, a) the JESS salience operator is used for resolving rule conflict issues (it is used only in POI owners' case if two rules concern the same slot e.g. "If it is Saturday Coffee costs 2 €", "If a person is a student coffee costs 1,5 €"), b) "recommendation" is called the template that stores relative places that match the rule in case it is fired and c) "EXPLANATION" is a variable for storing the rule explanation that is afterwards presented to the end user. Finally, rule data are stored in RDF triples format. Some of them are illustrated in Table 1. An extension has been made to the RDF/S ontology, by adding the corresponding class and its properties e.g. title, priority, explanation, description, ruleml_link etc. Notice that "policy_description" property is a text that is automatically created from the data the user entered into the rule forms and it is used for helping other users to understand the rule in case the rule's creator inputs either a non-comprehensible explanation message or no explanation text at all.

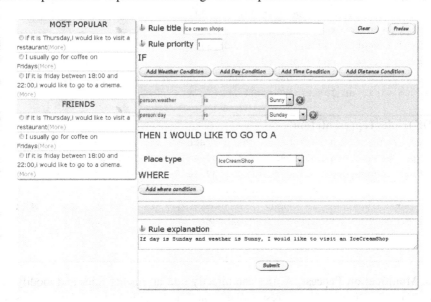

Fig. 2. Rule editor usage example

Table 1. Rule representations in RuleML,Jess and RDF format

RuleML representation

```
<?xml version="1.0" encoding="UTF-8"?>
<RuleML …">
        <Assert> <Rule style="active"> <label>drzgjtgt </label>
<explanation> If day is Sunday and weather is Sunny, I would like to
visit an IceCreamShop </explanation>
              <if> <And>
<Atom> <Rel>place</Rel>
<slot> <Ind>type</Ind> <Ind> IceCreamShop </Ind> </slot>
<slot><Ind>uri</Ind><Var>id</Var></slot>
</Atom>
    <Atom> <Rel>person</Rel>
              <slot> <Ind>day</Ind> <Ind>sunday</Ind> </slot>
              <slot><Ind>weather</Ind> <Ind>sunny</Ind> </slot>
      </Atom>
            </And> </if>
            <then> <Assert>
          <Atom> <Rel>recommendation</Rel>
              <slot><Ind>id</Ind><Var>id</Var></slot>
          </Atom>
               </Assert></then>
    </Rule></Assert></RuleML>
```

Jess representation

```
(defrule kctysfvn (declare (salience 1))
(place( type IceCreamShop) ( uri ?id))
(person ( weather sunny) ( day sunday))
=>(assert (recommendation( id ?id)))
(store EXPLANATION "If day is Sunday and weather is Sunny, I would
like to visit an IceCreamShop"))
```

RDF triples representation

```
<http://schema.org/Person#16> <http://schema.org/policy>
<http://schema.org/policy9fc1d8e4-1c39-4e36-8a35-56223cb98811>.
<http://schema.org/policy9fc1d8e4-1c39-4e36-8a35-56223cb98811>
<http://schema.org/policy_description>
"IF person:weather is Sunny AND person:day is Sunday THEN I WOULD
LIKE TO GO TO A place:type IceCreamShop".
                        ......
```

Rule Modification Process. A user can directly find all his/her rules and modify or delete them by choosing the corresponding icon. The same form-based interface as in rule insertion process is provided for updating existing rules.

"Get a Rule" Process. In order to simplify the overall process and engage users as much as possible, except from creating their own rules they are encouraged to get rules from other users. First of all, they are able to search among existing rules. Additionally, in Geosocial SPLIS starting page, a) the 3 most popular rules from all users and b) the 3 most popular rules from user's friends are displayed, in order the users to acquire some of them if they are suitable. Furthermore, as soon as a user "check in" into a POI or "like" it, a list of the 5 most popular rules concerning the POI category is also displayed in a pop up window (e.g. if they "like" a cinema, the 5 most popular rules concerning cinemas will be displayed). Moreover, by clicking on their friends profile they are able to view and get their rules. In order to avoid confusion in rule update process (for example in cases where user A gets a rule which was created by user B and then modifies it), as soon as a user modifies a rule, a new rule is created. If a user deletes a rule, the user is simply "unlinked" from the rule so as not to affect other users that have this rule. The rule is deleted if no one else use it.

3.3   Processes Exploiting Social Ties

Common Social Interaction Processes. Geosocial SPLIS provides to the users the capability to search for new people and become friends with each other as in other location-based social networking services. After they select a person, they can view his/her profile data (name, age etc.) and friends. They can also, as usual send a request message to him/her, asking to become friend. After two users become friends, additionally, they are able to view each other rules.

Nearby Friends. A user is also able to spot his/her friends which are nearby and find common places and offers. In this mode Geosocial SPLIS:

a) Collects i) user's rules, ii) his nearby (logged in) friends' rules and iii) contextual information.

b) Evaluates all the above rules and fetches the nearby POIs which are recommended by the fired rules.

c)   For these POIs, it gets their group targeted offers (POIs' rules), and evaluates them concerning all users contexts (the user and his/her friends).

d) Provides personalized information by displaying:
- With a red marker a POI that does not have any offer at all.
- With a yellow marker a POI that has at least one offer, but none of them is valid for any of the friends or the user at that moment.
- With a half yellow-half green marker a POI which has a valid offer for at least one of the friends or the user.
- With a green marker a POI which has an offer for all of the friends and the user.
- With a bigger marker a POI that is recommended by a user rule and at least one of his/her friends' rules.

This process is illustrated with a use case scenario in the following section.

4   Use Case Scenarios

A use case scenario concerning two different user profiles is presented in this section, to demonstrate Geosocial SPLIS capabilities. The scenario considers two different users, being friends with each other, having the following profiles.

    a)   User A ("John") is a 20-year old male student, his current profile snapshot is taken on Saturday, at 13:45 in a location A where the weather is sunny".

    b)   User B ("Mary") is a 21-year old female student, which is logged in the system at the same time with John in a location B, close to a location A".

After that, we assume that John and Mary have used the web editor described in Section 3 and possess the rules which are presented in Table 2.

Table 2. Users' rules

	John's rules	Mary's rules
Rule 1	"If it is Saturday between 13:00 and 16:00, I would like to go for coffee "	"If it is Friday between 19:00 and 22:00, find me some Restaurants which serve Italian cuisine"
Rule 2	"If it is Wednesday and time is after 18:00, find me cinemas which are closer than 1000 m"	"I would like to go for coffee, if weather is Sunny and time is before 18:00 o'clock"
Rule 3	"On Saturday afternoons (12:00-15:00), recommend me a Museum"	–

4.1   Scenario Concerning Individuals

As it was discussed above, after a user is inserted into Geosocial SPLIS, it evaluates his/her rules/preferences and nearby POIs' rules/group targeted offers. Considering John, rules 1 and 3 are fired because it is Saturday and time is 13:45. Consequently, available coffee shops and museums are represented with a bigger marker and are recommended to him (figure 3 below). In order to help user find easier a POI category, the marker contains the first letter of the category it belongs (e.g. "M" if it is a Museum). By clicking on the nearby POIs, John can get personalized info. As discussed above, a big green marker represents a place he would like to go regarding his context, which has also an offer for him. Taking for example the POI "Friends Cafe" which is represented with a big green marker, he is able to view a) its data b) the POI owner's message for the group targeted offer that matches his profile and c) his rule which was fired and recommended this place (figure 4a). John can also add a "like", a review or a rating to the POI. He can also view the reviews and ratings which have been submitted by other users. On the other hand, concerning Mary, the second rule is fired for her. As a result, coffee shops are represented with bigger marker and similarly, if she clicks on "Friends Café" she can get the personalized info illustrated in figure 4b. Notice that in the left side of the screen, by checking the corresponding explanations, they can directly get some of the three most popular rules a) of all users or b) of their friends.

Fig. 3. Starting screen for John

a) Personalized info for John   b) Personalized info for Mary regard-
regarding "Friends Café"   ing Friends Café

Fig. 4. Personalized info concerning the two users and the place "Friends Cafe"

4.2   Scenario Concerning Nearby Friends

By choosing "Friends"→"Nearby friends" from the menu, John and Mary are able to spot their nearby friends. Taking for example John, we assume that Mary is his only nearby friend which is logged in at this time. When he visits this page the system:

a) Gets his and Mary's context and rules.
b) Evaluates all the above rules, and then fetches the nearby POIs which are recommended by the fired rules. In our scenario John's rule 1 and 3 are fired and as a result museums and coffee shops are recommended. Additionally, Mary's rule 2 is fired, which recommends coffee shops.
c) For the POIs that result by their rules, the system gets their offers (POIs' rules), and evaluates them based on John and Mary's contexts.
d) After that, it displays personalized information as discussed in 3.3.

According the above, John's personalized info is illustrated in figure 5. All coffee shops (markers containing the letter "C") are displayed with a bigger marker because of the fact that Mary would like to visit a coffee shop at this time too. Museums are represented with a small marker for the opposite reason (they concern only John). Also on the left side of the screen there is a description of the icon colours and, below them, there is a table displaying the rules which are fired and their possessor.

By clicking on the related markers he can directly find common places with his nearby friends (big markers), places with offers for all of them etc. For example, he can directly find a POI where both of them would like to go, which has also an offer for him and Mary (a big green marker). After clicking on a marker he is able to view the POI rules (if any) and the user defined rules which are fired for this place, in order to understand a) who has an offer and why, b) who would like to visit this POI at the moment. Taking for example the POI "MOJO cafe bar" which is represented with a half green-half yellow marker, he is able to view a) that the offer is valid only for Mary (she is a female student) and b) that both of them would like to go there (figure 6a). Similarly concerning the POI "Friends Cafe", John can directly understand that both of them have an offer and both of them would like to go there now (figure 6b).

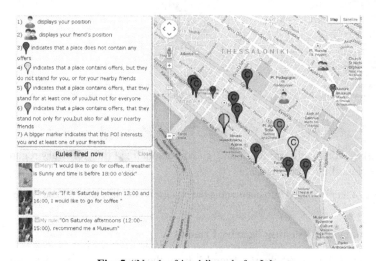

Fig. 5. "Nearby friends" mode for John

a)   b)

Fig. 6. Personalized info for John regarding a) "MOJO cafe bar" and b) "Friends Cafe"

5   Evaluation

A survey was conducted to evaluate the implementation of Geosocial SPLIS. An electronic questionnaire was developed and 83 university students of a department of economics were asked to use Geosocial SPLIS and answer the questions. The survey consisted of three parts: a) processes concerning rules and the personalization of information, b) social processes and c) the system in general.

5.1   Operations Concerning Rules and Presentation of Information

After a short introductory presentation to the system's general idea, participants made an account and logged in. Initially, they added the rule "If day is Wednesday, then I would like Restaurants" and then modified it. After that, they got a random rule from another user and searched for nearby POIs concerning their rules. Finally, they answered the following questions:

Q1. How easy was to add a rule?
Q2. How easy was to modify a rule?
Q3. Are you satisfied with the provided interface?
Q4. How easy was to find and get a rule from another user?
Q5. How easy was to understand why a place was recommended?
Q6. How easy was to find a place that resulted by your rules and had an offer for you?

The results of the questions above are presented in figure 7. For every question, over 80% of the answers were "sufficiently satisfied" or "very much satisfied". Additionally, Cronbach's alpha indicator value was calculated to provide a measure of reliability. This indicator gets values between 0 and 1 and the closer it is to 1, the higher the reliability [25]. This indicator was calculated to 0.82 for our survey, showing a high internal consistency.

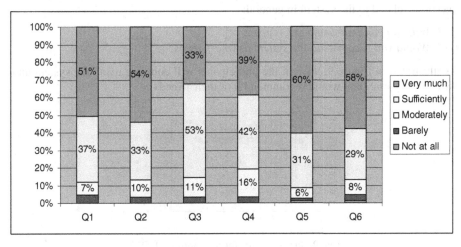

Fig. 7. Survey results for questions Q1-Q6

5.2   Social Processes

Afterwards, the participants made groups of three persons, became friends with each other and tested "nearby friends' mode". Finally, they answered the following questions:

Q7.   How easy was to send a friend request?
Q8.   How easy was to understand which of your friends recommend a place and why?
Q9.   How easy was to find common places for you and your friends?
Q10. How easy was to find places that resulted by your friends' rules and had an offer for you?

The results of the questions above are presented in figure 8. Once again, in every question, over 80% of the answers were "sufficiently satisfied" or "very much satisfied". Cronbach's alpha indicator value was calculated to 0.84 which is very satisfactory.

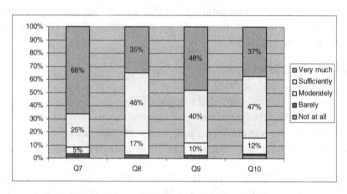

Fig. 8. Survey results for questions Q7-Q10

5.3   System in General

After completing the above tasks, participants were asked to answer the following questions related to the system in general:

Q11. Will you continue using the system?
Q12. Would you recommend the system to your friends?

As illustrated in Figure 9, 94% of the participants will continue using the system and 98% of the participant would recommend it to their friends.

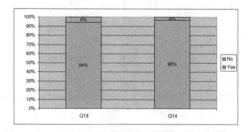

Fig. 9. Survey results for questions Q11-Q12

6   Conclusions and Future Work

In this work, an innovative knowledge-based LBSNS, called Geosocial SPLIS, was designed and implemented to offer semantic based contextualized information. On the one hand, regular users enjoy proactively POIs and offers depending on their preferences and their contextual situation, and on the other, POI owners (by being able to specify their offering policy rules) can exhibit a highly targeted marketing strategy by reaching their potential customers right on time. In order to achieve all the above, Geosocial SPLIS a) collects data from sources such as Google Places API and Google+ b) adopts an innovative, widely accepted ontology such as schema.org c) offers users the capability to create rules at run time by providing a web based editor d) transforms these rules into RuleML and Jess format and e) displays personalized information on Google Maps.

Geosocial SPLIS experimental testing made clear that the capability of having a dynamic knowledge base (by enabling non technical run time users to add data and rules) can provide qualitative contextualized information by addressing some of the disadvantages of rule based systems. As soon as more and more rules are being added to the system, the more interesting and intelligent it becomes because of the fact that there are rules (user preferences and group targeted offers in our case) for multiple contextual situations. High level personalized information is also achieved, since users are able to add or modify their rules according to their needs and they do not depend on the developer. Engaging non technical users to generate content is a great challenge but previous Web 2.0 examples (e.g. Wikipedia) demonstrate that this is feasible.

Geosocial SPLIS implementation can evolve in the future in various ways. The system could be enhanced by collecting data for multiple web sources (e.g. other social media such as Facebook, Twitter etc. or other available APIs) or expand the web editor to provide contextualized preferences concerning movies, videos etc. Furthermore, we are currently working on the development of a mobile version of Geosocial SPLIS for smartphones and tablets.

References

1. Baldauf, M., Frohlich, P., Masuch, K., Grechenig, T.: Comparing viewing and filtering techniques for mobile urban exploration. Journal of LBS 5, 38–57 (2011)
2. Michael, K., Michael, M.G.: The social and behavioural implications of location based services. Journal of Location Based Services 5(3-4), 121–137 (2011)
3. Roick, O., Heuser, S.: Location Based Social Networks – Definition, Current State of the Art and Research Agenda. Transactions in GIS 17(5), 763–784 (2013)
4. Zheng, Y., Xie, X., Ma, W.Y.: GeoLife: A Collaborative Social Networking Service among User. IEEE Data Eng. Bull. 33(2), 32–39 (2010)
5. Hosseini-Pozveh, M., Nematbakhsh, M., Movahhedinia, N.: A multidimensional approach for context-aware recommendation in mobile commerce. (IJCSIS) International Journal of Computer Science and Information Security 3(1) (2009)
6. Ilarri, S., Illarramendi, A., Mena, E., Sheth, A.: Semantics in Location-Based Services. IEEE Internet Computing 15(6), 10–14 (2011)

7. Patkos, T., Bikakis, A., Antoniou, G., Papadopouli, M., Plexousakis, D.: A semantics-based framework for context-aware services: lessons learned and challenges. In: Indulska, J., Ma, J., Yang, L.T., Ungerer, T., Cao, J. (eds.) UIC 2007. LNCS, vol. 4611, pp. 839–848. Springer, Heidelberg (2007)

8. Giurca, A., Tylkowski, M., Muller, M.: RuleTheWeb!: Rule-based Adaptive User Experience. In: Proceedings of the RuleML2012@ECAI Challenge, at the 6th International Symposium on Rules, Montpellier, France, August 27-29. CEUR Workshop Proceedings, vol. 874 (2012)

9. Viktoratos, I., Tsadiras, A., Bassiliades, N.: A Rule Based Personalized Location Information System for the Semantic Web. In: Knuth, E., Neuhold, E.J. (eds.) Operating Systems 1982. LNCS, vol. 152, pp. 27–38. Springer, Heidelberg (1985)

10. Ciaramella, A., Cimino, M.G., Lazzerini, B., Marcelloni, F.: Situation-Aware Mobile Service Recommendation with Fuzzy Logic and Semantic Web. In: Ninth Int. Conference on Intelligent Systems Design and Applications. IEEE (2009)

11. García-Crespo, Á., López-Cuadrado, J.L., Colomo-Palacios, R., González Carrasco, I., Ruiz-Mezcua, B.: Sem-Fit: A semantic based expert system to provide recommendations in the tourism domain. Expert Systems with Applications 38 (2011)

12. Niforatos, E., Karapanos, E., Sioutas, S.: PLBSD: A platform for proactive location-based service discovery. Location Based Services Journal 6 (2012)

13. Armenatzoglou, N., et al.: FleXConf: A flexible conference assistant using context-aware notification services. In: Meersman, R., Herrero, P., Dillon, T. (eds.) OTM 2009 Workshops. LNCS, vol. 5872, pp. 108–117. Springer, Heidelberg (2009)

14. Viana, W., Filho, J.B., Gensel, J., Villanova-Oliver, M., Martin, H.: PhotoMap: From location and time to context-aware photo annotations. Journal of Location Based Services 2(3), 211–235 (2008)

15. Serrano, D., Hervás, R., Bravo, J.: Telemaco: Context-aware System for Tourism Guiding based on Web 3.0 Technology. In: International Workshop on Contextual Computing and Ambient Intelligence in Tourism (2011)

16. Li, J., Wang, H., Khan, S.U.: A Semantics-based Approach to Large-Scale Mobile Social Networking. Mobile Networks and Applications 17(2), 192–205 (2012)

17. Dell'Aglio, D., Celino, I., Cerizza, D.: Anatomy of a Semantic Web-enabled Recommender System. In: 9th Int. Semantic Web Conference on Proceedings of the 4th Int. Workshop Semantic Matchmaking and Resource Retrieval in the Semantic Web, Shanghai (2010)

18. Felfernig, A., Friedrich, G., Jannach, D., Zanker, M.: An Integrated Environment for the Development of Knowledge-Based Recommender Applications. Int. J. Electron. Commerce 11(2), 11–34 (2006)

19. Ye, M., et al.: On the semantic annotation of places in location-based social networks. In: Proc.17th Int.Conf. ACM SIGKDD Knowledge Discovery& Data Mining, pp. 520–528 (2011)

20. Broekstra, J., Kampman, A., van Harmelen, F.: Sesame: An architecture for storing and querying RDF data and schema information. In: Lieberman, H., Fensel, D., Hendler, J., Wahlster, W. (eds.) Semantics for the WWW. MIT Press (2011)

21. Kontopoulos, E., Bassiliades, N., Antoniou, G.: Deploying Defeasible Logic Rule Bases for the Semantic Web. Data and Knowledge, Engineering 66(1), 116–146 (2008)

22. Liang, S., Fodor, P., Wan, H., Kifer, M.: OpenRuleBench: An Analysis of the Performance of Rule Engines. In: WWW 2009(2009)

23. Sherman, G.: A Critical Analysis of XSLT Technology for XML Transformation. Senior Technical Report (2009)

24. Fields, D.K., Kolb, M.A., Bayern, S.: Web Development with Java Server Pages. Manning Publications (2001) ISBN:193011012X

25. Tavakol, M., Dennick, R.: Making sense of Cronbach's alpha. International Journal of Medical Education 2, 53–55 (2011)

Checking Termination of Logic Programs with Function Symbols through Linear Constraints

Marco Calautti, Sergio Greco, Cristian Molinaro, and Irina Trubitsyna

DIMES, Università della Calabria, 87036 Rende (CS), Italy
{calautti,greco,molinaro,trubitsyna}@dimes.unical.it

Abstract. Enriching answer set programming with function symbols makes modeling easier, increases the expressive power, and allows us to deal with infinite domains. However, this comes at a cost: common inference tasks become undecidable. To cope with this issue, recent research has focused on finding trade-offs between expressivity and decidability by identifying classes of logic programs that impose limitations on the use of function symbols but guarantee decidability of common inference tasks. Despite the significant body of work in this area, current approaches do not include many simple practical programs whose evaluation terminates. In this paper, we present the novel class of *rule-bounded programs*. While current techniques perform a limited analysis of how terms are propagated from an individual argument to another, our technique is able to perform a more global analysis, thereby overcoming several limitations of current approaches. We also present a further class of *cycle-bounded programs* where groups of rules are analyzed together. We show different results on the correctness and the expressivity of the proposed techniques.

Keywords: Logic programming with function symbols, bottom-up evaluation, program evaluation termination, stable models.

1 Introduction

Enriching answer set programming with function symbols has recently seen a surge in interest. Function symbols make modeling easier, increase the expressive power, and allow us to deal with infinite domains. At the same time, this comes at a cost: common inference tasks (e.g., cautious and brave reasoning) become undecidable.

Recent research has focused on identifying classes of logic programs that impose some limitations on the use of function symbols but guarantee decidability of common inference tasks. Efforts in this direction are the class of *finitely-ground* programs [7] and the more general class of *bounded term-size* programs [26]. Finitely-ground programs have a finite number of stable models, each of finite size, whereas bounded term-size (normal) programs have a finite well-founded model. Unfortunately, checking if a logic program is bounded term-size or even finitely-ground is semi-decidable.

A. Bikakis et al. (Eds.): RuleML 2014, LNCS 8620, pp. 97–111, 2014.

Considering the stable model semantics, decidable subclasses of finitely-ground programs have been proposed. These include the classes of *ω-restricted programs* [33], *λ-restricted programs* [14], *finite domain programs* [7], *argument-restricted programs* [21], *safe programs* [19], *Γ-acyclic programs* [19], *mapping-restricted programs* [6], and *bounded programs* [17]. The above techniques, that we call *termination criteria*, provide (decidable) sufficient conditions for a program to be finitely-ground.

Despite the significant body of work in this area, there are still many simple practical programs which are finitely-ground but are not detected by any of the current termination criteria. Below is an example.

Example 1. Consider the following program $\mathcal{P}_1$ implementing the bubble sort algorithm:

$$r_0 : \text{bub}(\text{L}, [\,], [\,]) \leftarrow \text{input}(\text{L}).$$
$$r_1 : \text{bub}([\text{Y}|\text{T}], [\text{X}|\text{Cur}], \text{Sol}) \leftarrow \text{bub}([\text{X}|[\text{Y}|\text{T}]], \text{Cur}, \text{Sol}), \text{X} \leq \text{Y}.$$
$$r_2 : \text{bub}([\text{X}|\text{T}], [\text{Y}|\text{Cur}], \text{Sol}) \leftarrow \text{bub}([\text{X}|[\text{Y}|\text{T}]], \text{Cur}, \text{Sol}), \text{Y} < \text{X}.$$
$$r_3 : \text{bub}(\text{Cur}, [\,], [\text{X}|\text{Sol}]) \leftarrow \text{bub}([\text{X}|[\,]], \text{Cur}, \text{Sol}).$$

Here **input** is a base predicate symbol whose extension is a fact containing the list we would like to sort. The bottom-up evaluation of this program always terminates for any input list. The ordered list **Sol** can be obtained from the atom **bub**$([\,], [\,], \text{Sol})$ in the program's minimal model.   □

None of the termination criteria in the literature is able to realize that $\mathcal{P}_1$ is finitely-ground. One problem with them is that when they analyze how terms are propagated from the body to the head of rules, they look at arguments *individually*. For instance, in rule r_1 above, the simple fact that the second argument of **bub** has a size in the head greater than the one in the body prevents several techniques from realizing termination of the bottom-up evaluation of $\mathcal{P}_1$. More general classes such as mapping-restricted and bounded programs are able to do a more complex (yet limited) analysis of how some groups of arguments affect each other. Still, all current termination criteria are not able to realize that in every rule of $\mathcal{P}_1$ the *overall* size of the terms in the head does not increase w.r.t. the *overall* size of the terms in the body. One of the novelties of the technique proposed in this paper is the capability of doing this kind of analysis, thereby identifying finitely-ground programs that none of the current techniques include.

The technique proposed in this paper easily realizes that the bottom-up evaluation of $\mathcal{P}_1$ always terminates for any input list. In fact, our technique can understand that, in every rule, the overall size of the terms in the body does not increase during their propagation to the head, as there is only a simple re-distribution of terms. Many practical programs dealing with lists and tree-like structures satisfy this property—below are two examples. However, our technique is not limited only to this kind of programs.

Example 2. Consider the following program $\mathcal{P}_2$ performing a depth-first traversal of an input tree:

r_0 : visit(Tree, [ ], [ ]) ← input(Tree).
r_1 : visit(Left, [Root|Visited], [Right|ToVisit]) ←
$\qquad\qquad\qquad\qquad\qquad$ visit(tree(Root, Left, Right), Visited, ToVisit).
r_2 : visit(Next, Visited, ToVisit) ← visit(null, Visited, [Next|ToVisit]).

Here **input** is a base predicate symbol whose extension contains a tree-like structure represented by means of the ternary function symbol **tree**. The program visits the nodes of the tree and puts them in a list following a depth-first search. The list L of visited elements can be obtained from the atom visit(null, L, [ ]) in the program's minimal model. For instance, if the input tree is

$\qquad$ input(tree(a, tree(c, null, tree(d, null, null)), tree(b, null, null))).

the program produces the list [b, d, c, a] containing the nodes of the tree in opposite order w.r.t. the traversal. □

Also in the case above, even if the program evaluation terminates for every input tree, none of the currently known techniques is able to detect it, while the technique proposed in this paper does.

Example 3. Consider the following program $\mathcal{P}_3$ computing the concatenation of two lists:

$\qquad\qquad r_0$: reverse(L_1, [ ])   ← input1(L_1).
$\qquad\qquad r_1$: reverse(L_1, [X|L_2]) ← reverse([X|L_1], L_2).
$\qquad\qquad r_2$: append(L_1, L_2)   ← reverse([ ], L_1), input2(L_2).
$\qquad\qquad r_3$: append(L_1, [X|L_2]) ← append([X|L_1], L_2).

Here **input1** and **input2** are base predicate symbols whose extensions contain two lists L_1 and L_2 to be concatenated. The result list L can be retrieved from the atom append([ ], L) in the minimal model of $\mathcal{P}_3$. It is easy to see that the bottom-up evaluation of the program always terminates. □

Contribution. We propose novel techniques for checking if a logic program is finitely-ground. Our techniques overcome several limitations of current approaches being able to perform a more global analysis of how terms are propagated from the body to the head of rules. To this end, we use linear constraints to measure and relate the size of head and body atoms. We first introduce the class of *rule-bounded* programs, which looks at individual rules, and then propose the class of *cycle-bounded* programs, which relies on the analysis of groups of rules. We study the relationship between the proposed classes and current termination criteria.

Organization. Section 2 reports preliminaries on logic programs with function symbols. Section 3 introduces the class of rule-bounded programs. Section 4 presents the class of cycle-bounded programs. Related work and conclusions are reported in Sections 5 and 6, respectively.

2   Preliminaries

This section recalls syntax and the stable model semantics of logic programs with function symbols [15,16,13].

Syntax. We assume to have (pairwise disjoint) infinite sets of *constants, logical variables*[1], *predicate symbols*, and *function symbols*. Each predicate and function symbol g is associated with an *arity*, denoted $arity(g)$, which is a non-negative integer for predicate symbols and a positive integer for function symbols.

A *term* is either a constant, a logical variable, or an expression of the form $f(t_1, ..., t_m)$, where f is a function symbol of arity m and $t_1, ..., t_m$ are terms.

An *atom* is of the form $p(t_1, ..., t_n)$, where p is a predicate symbol of arity n and $t_1, ..., t_n$ are terms. A *literal* is an atom A (*positive* literal) or its negation $\neg A$ (*negative* literal).

A *rule* r is of the form $A_1 \vee ... \vee A_m \leftarrow B_1, ..., B_k, \neg C_1, ..., \neg C_n$, where $m > 0$, $k \geq 0$, $n \geq 0$, and $A_1, ..., A_m, B_1, ..., B_k, C_1, ..., C_n$ are atoms. The disjunction $A_1 \vee ... \vee A_m$ is called the *head* of r and is denoted by $head(r)$. The conjunction $B_1, ..., B_k, \neg C_1, ..., \neg C_n$ is called the *body* of r and is denoted by $body(r)$. With a slight abuse of notation, we sometimes use $body(r)$ (resp. $head(r)$) to also denote the *set* of literals appearing in the body (resp. head) of r. If $m = 1$, then r is *normal*; in this case, $head(r)$ denotes the head atom. If $n = 0$, then r is *positive*.

A *program* is a finite set of rules. A program is *normal* (resp. *positive*) if every rule in it is normal (resp. positive). We assume that programs are *range restricted*, i.e., for every rule, every logical variable appears in some positive body literal. W.l.o.g., we also assume that different rules do not share logical variables.

A term (resp. atom, literal, rule, program) is *ground* if no logical variables occur in it. A ground normal rule with an empty body is also called a *fact*.

A predicate symbol p is *defined by* a rule r if p appears in the head of r. Predicate symbols are partitioned into two different classes: *base* predicate symbols, which are defined by facts only, and *derived* predicate symbols, which can be defined by any rule. Facts defining base predicate symbols are called *database facts*.[2]

A *substitution* θ is of the form $\{X_1/t_1, ..., X_n/t_n\}$, where $X_1, ..., X_n$ are distinct logical variables and $t_1, ..., t_n$ are terms. The result of applying θ to an atom (or term) A, denoted $A\theta$, is the atom (or term) obtained from A by simultaneously replacing each occurrence of a logical variable X_i in A with t_i if X_i/t_i belongs to θ. Two atoms A_1 and A_2 *unify* if there exists a substitution θ, called a *unifier* of A_1 and A_2, such that $A_1\theta = A_2\theta$. The *composition* of two substitutions $\theta = \{X_1/t_1, ..., X_n/t_n\}$ and $\vartheta = \{Y_1/u_1, ..., Y_m/u_m\}$, denoted $\theta \circ \vartheta$, is the substitution obtained from the set $\{X_1/t_1\vartheta, ..., X_n/t_n\vartheta, Y_1/u_1, ..., Y_m/u_m\}$ by

---

[1] Variables appearing in logic programs are called "logical variables" and will be denoted by upper-case letters in order to distinguish them from variables appearing in linear constraints, which are called "integer variables" and will be denoted by lower-case letters.

[2] Database facts are not shown in our examples as they are not relevant for the proposed techniques.

removing every $X_i/t_i\vartheta$ such that $X_i = t_i\vartheta$ and every Y_j/u_j such that $Y_j \in \{X_1, ..., X_n\}$. A substitution θ is *more general* than a substitution ϑ if there exists a substitution η such that $\vartheta = \theta \circ \eta$. A unifier θ of A_1 and A_2 is called a *most general unifier* (mgu) of A_1 and A_2 if it is more general than any other unifier of A_1 and A_2 (indeed, the mgu is unique modulo renaming of logical variables).

Semantics. Consider a program $\mathcal{P}$. The *Herbrand universe* $H_\mathcal{P}$ of $\mathcal{P}$ is the possibly infinite set of ground terms which can be built using constants and function symbols appearing in $\mathcal{P}$. The *Herbrand base* $B_\mathcal{P}$ of $\mathcal{P}$ is the set of ground atoms which can be built using predicate symbols appearing in $\mathcal{P}$ and ground terms of $H_\mathcal{P}$.

A rule r' is a *ground instance* of a rule r in $\mathcal{P}$ if r' can be obtained from r by substituting every logical variable in r with some ground term in $H_\mathcal{P}$. We use $ground(r)$ to denote the set of all ground instances of r and $ground(\mathcal{P})$ to denote the set of all ground instances of the rules in $\mathcal{P}$, i.e., $ground(\mathcal{P}) = \cup_{r \in \mathcal{P}} ground(r)$.

An *interpretation* of $\mathcal{P}$ is any subset I of $B_\mathcal{P}$. The truth value of a ground atom A w.r.t. I, denoted $value_I(A)$, is *true* if $A \in I$, *false* otherwise. The truth value of $\neg A$ w.r.t. I, denoted $value_I(\neg A)$, is *true* if $A \notin I$, *false* otherwise. A ground rule r is *satisfied* by I, denoted $I \models r$, if there is a ground literal L in $body(r)$ s.t. $value_I(L) = false$ or there is a ground atom A in $head(r)$ s.t. $value_I(A) = true$. Thus, if the body of r is empty, r is satisfied by I if there is an atom A in $head(r)$ s.t. $value_I(A) = true$. An interpretation of $\mathcal{P}$ is a *model* of $\mathcal{P}$ if it satisfies every ground rule in $ground(\mathcal{P})$. A model M of $\mathcal{P}$ is minimal if no proper subset of M is a model of $\mathcal{P}$. The set of minimal models of $\mathcal{P}$ is denoted by $\mathcal{MM}(\mathcal{P})$.

Given an interpretation I of $\mathcal{P}$, let $\mathcal{P}^I$ denote the ground positive program derived from $ground(\mathcal{P})$ by *(i)* removing every rule containing a negative literal $\neg A$ in the body with $A \in I$, and *(ii)* removing all negative literals from the remaining rules. An interpretation I is a *stable model* of $\mathcal{P}$ if $I \in \mathcal{MM}(\mathcal{P}^I)$. The set of stable models of $\mathcal{P}$ is denoted by $\mathcal{SM}(\mathcal{P})$. It is well known that stable models are minimal models (i.e., $\mathcal{SM}(\mathcal{P}) \subseteq \mathcal{MM}(\mathcal{P})$), and $\mathcal{SM}(\mathcal{P}) = \mathcal{MM}(\mathcal{P})$ for positive programs. A positive normal program has a unique minimal model.

3 Rule-Bounded Programs

In this section, we present *rule-bounded programs*, a class of finitely-ground programs for which checking membership in the class is decidable. Their definition relies on a novel technique which uses linear inequalities to measure terms and atoms' sizes and checks if the size of the head of a rule is always bounded by the size of a mutually recursive body atom (we will formally define what "mutually recursive" means in Definition 2 below).

For ease of presentation, we restrict our attention to positive normal programs. However, our technique can be applied to an arbitrary program $\mathcal{P}$ with disjunction in the head and negation in the body by considering a positive normal program $st(\mathcal{P})$ derived from $\mathcal{P}$ as follows. Every rule $A_1 \vee ... \vee A_m \leftarrow body$ in

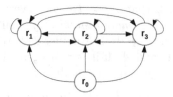

Fig. 1. Firing graph of $\mathcal{P}_1$

$\mathcal{P}$ is replaced with m positive normal rules of the form $A_i \leftarrow body^+$ $(1 \leq i \leq m)$ where $body^+$ is obtained from $body$ by deleting all negative literals. In fact, as already stated in [19], the minimal model of $st(\mathcal{P})$ contains every stable model of $\mathcal{P}$—whence, finiteness and computability of the minimal model of $st(\mathcal{P})$ implies that $\mathcal{P}$ has a finite number of stable models, each of finite size, which can be computed. In the rest of the paper, a program is understood to be a positive normal program. We start by introducing some preliminary notions.

Definition 1 (Firing graph). *The firing graph of a program $\mathcal{P}$, denoted $\Omega(\mathcal{P})$, is a directed graph whose nodes are the rules in $\mathcal{P}$ and such that there is an edge $\langle r, r' \rangle$ if there exist two (not necessarily distinct) rules $r, r' \in \mathcal{P}$ s.t. head(r) and an atom in body(r') unify.* □

Intuitively, an edge $\langle r, r' \rangle$ of $\Omega(\mathcal{P})$ means that rule r may cause rule r' to "fire". The firing graph of program $\mathcal{P}_1$ of Example 1 is depicted in Figure 1. In the definition above, when $r = r'$ we assume that r and r' are two "copies" that do not share any logical variable.

A *strongly connected component* (SCC) of an arbitrary directed graph G is a maximal set $\mathcal{C}$ of nodes of G s.t. every node of $\mathcal{C}$ can be reached from every node of $\mathcal{C}$ (through the edges in G). We say that an SCC $\mathcal{C}$ is *non-trivial* if there exists at least one edge in G between two not necessarily distinct nodes of $\mathcal{C}$. For instance, the firing graph in Figure 1 has two SCCs, $\mathcal{C}_1 = \{r_0\}$ and $\mathcal{C}_2 = \{r_1, r_2, r_3\}$, but only $\mathcal{C}_2$ is non-trivial.

Given a program $\mathcal{P}$ and an SCC $\mathcal{C}$ of $\Omega(\mathcal{P})$, $pred(\mathcal{C})$ denotes the set of predicate symbols defined by the rules in $\mathcal{C}$. We now define when the head atom and a body atom of a rule are mutually recursive.

Definition 2 (Mutually recursive atoms). *Let $\mathcal{P}$ be a program and r a rule in $\mathcal{P}$. The head atom $A = head(r)$ and an atom $B \in body(r)$ are mutually recursive if there is a non-trivial SSC $\mathcal{C}$ of $\Omega(\mathcal{P})$ s.t.:*

1. *$\mathcal{C}$ contains r, and*
2. *$\mathcal{C}$ contains a rule r' (not necessarily distinct from r) s.t. $\langle r', r \rangle$ is an edge of $\Omega(\mathcal{P})$ and head(r') unifies with B.* □

In the previous definition, when $r = r'$ we assume that r and r' are two "copies" that do not share any logical variable. Intuitively, the head atom A of a rule r and an atom B in the body of r are mutually recursive when there might be an actual propagation of terms from B to A (through the application of a sequence of rules). As a very simple example, in the rule $p(f(X)) \leftarrow p(X), p(g(X))$, the first body atom is mutually recursive with the head, while the second one is not as it does not unify with the head atom.

Given a rule r, we use $rbody(r)$ to denote the set of atoms in $body(r)$ which are mutually recursive with $head(r)$. Moreover, we define $srbody(r)$ as the set consisting of every atom in $rbody(r)$ that contains all logical variables appearing in $head(r)$. We say that r is *linear* if $|rbody(r)| \leq 1$. A program $\mathcal{P}$ is *linear* if every rule in $\mathcal{P}$ is linear.

We say that a rule r in an SCC $\mathcal{C}$ of the firing graph is *relevant* if the set of atoms $body(r) \setminus rbody(r)$ does not contain all logical variables in $head(r)$. Roughly speaking, a non-relevant rule will be ignored because its head size is bounded by body atoms which are not mutually recursive with the head (i.e., atoms that do not unify with any rule head or atoms whose predicate symbols are defined by rules in other SCCs). We illustrate the notions introduced so far in the following example.

Example 4. Consider the following program $\mathcal{P}_4$:

$$r_1 : \underbrace{s(f(X), Y)}_{A} \leftarrow \underbrace{q(X, f(Y))}_{B}, \underbrace{s(Z, f(Y))}_{C}.$$

$$r_2 : \underbrace{q(f(U), V)}_{D} \leftarrow \underbrace{s(U, f(V))}_{E}.$$

The firing graph consists of the edges $\langle r_1, r_1 \rangle, \langle r_1, r_2 \rangle, \langle r_2, r_1 \rangle$. Thus, there is only one SCC $\mathcal{C} = \{r_1, r_2\}$, which is non-trivial, and $pred(\mathcal{C}) = \{q, s\}$. Atoms A and B (resp. A and C, D and E) are mutually recursive. Moreover, $rbody(r_1) = \{B, C\}$, $srbody(r_1) = \{B\}$, $rbody(r_2) = srbody(r_2) = \{E\}$. Both r_1 and r_2 are relevant. $\square$

We use $\mathbb{N}$ to denote the set of natural numbers $\{1, 2, 3, ...\}$ and $\mathbb{N}_0$ to denote the set of natural numbers including the zero. Moreover, $\mathbb{N}^k = \{(v_1, ..., v_k) \mid v_i \in \mathbb{N} \text{ for } 1 \leq i \leq k\}$ and $\mathbb{N}_0^k = \{(v_1, ..., v_k) \mid v_i \in \mathbb{N}_0 \text{ for } 1 \leq i \leq k\}$. Given two k-vectors $\overline{v} = (v_1, ..., v_k)$ and $\overline{w} = (w_1, ..., w_k)$ in $\mathbb{N}_0^k$, we use $\overline{v} \cdot \overline{w}$ to denote the classical scalar product, i.e., $\overline{v} \cdot \overline{w} = \sum_{i=1}^{k} v_i \cdot w_i$.

As mentioned earlier, the basic idea of the proposed technique is to measure the size of terms and atoms in order to check if the rules' head sizes are bounded when propagation occurs. Thus, we introduce the notions of term and atom size.

Definition 3. *Given a rule r and a term t occurring in r, the* size *of t w.r.t. r is recursively defined as follows:*

$$size(t, r) = \begin{cases} 0 & \text{if } t \text{ is either a logical variable not occurring in } head(r) \text{ or a constant;} \\ x & \text{if } t \text{ is a logical variable } X \text{ occurring in } head(r); \\ \sum_{1 \leq i \leq m \wedge size(t_i, r) \neq 0} (1 + size(t_i, r)) & \text{if } t = f(t_1, ..., t_m). \end{cases}$$

where x is an integer variable. Given an atom $A = p(t_1, ..., t_n)$ in r, the size *of A w.r.t. r, denoted $size(A, r)$, is the n-vector $(size(t_1, r), ..., size(t_n, r))$.* $\square$

In the definition above, every integer variable x intuitively represents the possible sizes that the logical variable X can have during the bottom-up evaluation. Notice that if t is a constant or a logical variable X occurring only in the body, then $size(t, r) = 0$ (in both cases, t does not contribute to the growth of the head). The size of a term of the form $f(t_1, ..., t_m)$ is defined by summing up the size of each t_i having non-zero size, plus 1 (to account for the number of terms of non-zero size which are arguments of f).

Example 5. Consider rule r_1 of program $\mathcal{P}_1$ (see Example 1). Using lc to denote the list constructor operator "|", the rule can be rewritten as follows:

$$\texttt{bub}(\texttt{lc}(Y, T), \texttt{lc}(X, Cur), Sol) \leftarrow \texttt{bub}(\texttt{lc}(X, \texttt{lc}(Y, T)), Cur, Sol), X \le Y.$$

Let A (resp. B) be the atom in the head (resp. the first atom in the body). Then,

$$size(A, r_1) = ((1 + y) + (1 + t), \quad (1 + x) + (1 + cur), \quad sol)$$
$$size(B, r_1) = ((1 + x) + [1 + (1 + y) + (1 + t)], \quad cur, \quad sol) \qquad \square$$

We are now ready to define rule-bounded programs.

Definition 4 (Rule-bounded programs). *Let $\mathcal{P}$ be a program, $\mathcal{C}$ a nontrivial SCC of $\Omega(\mathcal{P})$, and $pred(\mathcal{C}) = \{p_1, ..., p_k\}$. We say that $\mathcal{C}$ is rule-bounded if there exist k vectors $\overline{\alpha}_h \in \mathbb{N}^{arity(p_h)}$, $1 \le h \le k$, such that for every relevant rule $r \in \mathcal{C}$ with $A = head(r) = p_i(t_1, ..., t_n)$ there exists an atom $B = p_j(u_1, ..., u_m)$ in $srbody(r)$ s.t. the following inequality is satisfied*

$$\overline{\alpha}_j \cdot size(B, r) - \overline{\alpha}_i \cdot size(A, r) \ge 0$$

for every non-negative value of the integer variables in $size(B, r)$ and $size(A, r)$.

We say that $\mathcal{P}$ is rule-bounded if every non-trivial SCC of $\Omega(\mathcal{P})$ is rule-bounded. $\qquad \square$

Intuitively, for every relevant rule of a non-trivial SCC of $\Omega(\mathcal{P})$, Definition 4 checks if the size of the head atom is bounded by the size of a mutually recursive body atom for all possible sizes the terms can assume. Below is an example of rule-bounded program.

Example 6. Consider again program $\mathcal{P}_4$ of Example 4. Recall that the only nontrivial SCC of $\Omega(\mathcal{P}_4)$ is $\mathcal{C} = \{r_1, r_2\}$, and both r_1 and r_2 are relevant. To determine if the program is rule-bounded we need to check if $\mathcal{C}$ is rule-bounded. Thus, we need to find $\overline{\alpha}_q, \overline{\alpha}_s \in \mathbb{N}^2$ such that there is an atom in $srbody(r_1)$ and an atom in $srbody(r_2)$ which satisfy the two inequalities derived from r_1 and r_2 for all non-negative values of the integer variables therein. Since both $srbody(r_1)$ and $srbody(r_2)$ contain only one element, we have only one choice, namely the one where B is selected for r_1 and E is selected for r_2.

Thus, we need to check if there exist $\overline{\alpha}_q, \overline{\alpha}_s \in \mathbb{N}^2$ s.t. the following linear constraints are satisfied for all non-negative values of the integer variables appearing in them

$$\begin{cases} \overline{\alpha}_q \cdot size(B, r_1) - \overline{\alpha}_s \cdot size(A, r_1) \ge 0 \\ \overline{\alpha}_s \cdot size(E, r_2) - \overline{\alpha}_q \cdot size(D, r_2) \ge 0 \end{cases} \Rightarrow \begin{cases} \overline{\alpha}_q \cdot (x, 1 + y) - \overline{\alpha}_s \cdot (1 + x, y) \ge 0 \\ \overline{\alpha}_s \cdot (u, 1 + v) - \overline{\alpha}_q \cdot (1 + u, v) \ge 0 \end{cases}$$

By expanding the scalar products and isolating every integer variable we obtain:

$$\begin{cases} (\alpha_{q_1} - \alpha_{s_1}) \cdot x + (\alpha_{q_2} - \alpha_{s_2}) \cdot y + (\alpha_{q_2} - \alpha_{s_1}) \geq 0 \\ (\alpha_{s_1} - \alpha_{q_1}) \cdot u + (\alpha_{s_2} - \alpha_{q_2}) \cdot v + (\alpha_{s_2} - \alpha_{q_1}) \geq 0 \end{cases}$$

The previous inequalities must hold for all $x, y, u, v \in \mathbb{N}_0$; it is easy to see that this is the case iff the following system admits a solution:

$$\begin{cases} \alpha_{q_1} - \alpha_{s_1} \geq 0, & \alpha_{q_2} - \alpha_{s_2} \geq 0, & \alpha_{q_2} - \alpha_{s_1} \geq 0, \\ \alpha_{s_1} - \alpha_{q_1} \geq 0, & \alpha_{s_2} - \alpha_{q_2} \geq 0, & \alpha_{s_2} - \alpha_{q_1} \geq 0 \end{cases}$$

Since a solution does exist, e.g. $\alpha_{s_1} = \alpha_{s_2} = \alpha_{q_1} = \alpha_{q_2} = 1$ (recall that every α_i must be greater than 0), the SCC $\mathcal{C}$ is rule-bounded, and thus the program is rule-bounded. $\square$

The method to find vectors $\overline{\alpha}_p$ for all $p \in pred(\mathcal{C})$ shown in the previous example can always be applied. That is, we can always isolate the integer variables in the original inequalities and then derive one inequality for each expression that multiplies an integer variable plus the one for the constant term, imposing that all such expressions must be greater than or equal to 0.

It is worth noting that the proposed technique can easily recognize many (finitely-ground) practical programs where terms are simply exchanged from the body to the head of rules (e.g., see Examples 1, 2, and 3).

Example 7. Consider program $\mathcal{P}_1$ of Example 1. Recall that the only non-trivial SCC of $\Omega(\mathcal{P}_1)$ is $\{r_1, r_2, r_3\}$ (see Figure 1) and all rules in it are relevant. Since $|srbody(r_i)| = 1$ for every r_i in the SCC, we have only one set of inequalities, which is the following one (after isolating integer variables):

$$\begin{cases} (\alpha_{b_1} - \alpha_{b_2}) \cdot x_1 + (2\alpha_{b_1} - 2\alpha_{b_2}) \geq 0 \\ (\alpha_{b_1} - \alpha_{b_2}) \cdot y_2 + (2\alpha_{b_1} - 2\alpha_{b_2}) \geq 0 \\ (\alpha_{b_1} - \alpha_{b_3}) \cdot x_3 + (\alpha_{b_2} - \alpha_{b_1}) \cdot cur_3 + (\alpha_{b_1} - 2\alpha_{b_3}) \geq 0 \end{cases}$$

where subscript b stands for predicate symbol **bub**, whereas subscripts associated with integer variables are used to refer to the occurrences of logical variables in different rules (e.g., y_2 is the integer variable associated to the logical variable Y in rule r_2). A possible solution is $\overline{\alpha}_b = (2, 2, 1)$ and thus $\mathcal{P}_1$ is rule-bounded.

Considering program $\mathcal{P}_2$ of Example 2, we obtain the following constraints:

$$\begin{cases} (\alpha_{v_1} - \alpha_{v_2}) \cdot root_1 + (\alpha_{v_1} - \alpha_{v_3}) \cdot right_1 + (3\alpha_{v_1} - 2\alpha_{v_2} - 2\alpha_{v_3}) \geq 0 \\ (\alpha_{v_3} - \alpha_{v_1}) \cdot next_2 + 2\alpha_{v_3} \geq 0 \end{cases}$$

where subscript v stands for predicate symbol **visit**. By setting $\overline{\alpha}_v = (2, 1, 2)$, we get positive integer values of $\alpha_{v_1}, \alpha_{v_2}, \alpha_{v_3}$ s.t. the inequalities above are satisfied for all $root_1, right_1, next_2 \in \mathbb{N}_0$. Thus, $\mathcal{P}_2$ is rule-bounded.

The firing graph of program $\mathcal{P}_3$ of Example 3 has two non-trivial SCCs $\mathcal{C}_1 = \{r_1\}$ and $\mathcal{C}_2 = \{r_3\}$. The constraints for $\mathcal{C}_1$ are:

$$\left\{ (\alpha_{r_1} - \alpha_{r_2}) \cdot x_1 + (2\alpha_{r_1} - 2\alpha_{r_2}) \geq 0 \right.$$

where subscript r stands for predicate symbol `reverse`. It is easy to see that by choosing any (positive integer) values of α_{r_1} and α_{r_2} such that $\alpha_{r_1} \geq \alpha_{r_2}$, the inequality above holds for all $x_1 \in \mathbb{N}_0$. Likewise, the constraints for $\mathcal{C}_2$ are

$$\left\{ (\alpha_{a_1} - \alpha_{a_2}) \cdot x_3 + (2\alpha_{a_1} - 2\alpha_{a_2}) \geq 0 \right.$$

where subscript a stands for predicate symbol `append`. By choosing any (positive integer) values of α_{a_1} and α_{a_2} such that $\alpha_{a_1} \geq \alpha_{a_2}$, the inequality above holds for all $x_3 \in \mathbb{N}_0$. Thus, $\mathcal{P}_3$ is rule-bounded.   □

Notice that when checking if an SCC $\mathcal{C}$ is rule-bounded we need to check, for every relevant rule $r \in \mathcal{C}$, if there exists an atom in $srbody(r)$ which satisfies the condition stated in Definition 4. Thus, in the worst case, there are $\prod_{r \in \mathcal{C}} |srbody(r)|$ sets of inequalities for which the condition must be verified. In order to obtain a single set of inequalities for $\mathcal{C}$, the definition might be modified by requiring an inequality *for every* atom in $srbody(r)$. While this variant of Definition 4 would lead to a lower complexity of checking if a program is rule-bounded, the obtained class of rule-bounded programs would be smaller. Clearly, one may also look only at a subset of the $\prod_{r \in \mathcal{C}} |srbody(r)|$ sets of inequalities (e.g., a fixed or polynomial number of them). It is worth noting that in practical cases most of the rules are linear (and thus $|srbody(r)| \leq 1$).

Two key properties of rule-bounded programs are: they are finitely-ground and it is decidable to check whether a given program is rule-bounded.

Theorem 1. *Every rule-bounded program is finitely-ground.*   □

Theorem 2. *Checking whether a program is rule-bounded is in NP.*   □

It is worth noting that the analysis of the structure of programs is a compile-time operation and the complexity depends on the size of the SCCs, which are usually small.

Theorem 3. *Rule-bounded programs are incomparable with mapping-restricted and bounded programs.*   □

Observe that in the previous theorem we have considered only the most general subclasses of finitely-ground programs proposed so far, which generalize previous classes such as argument-restricted programs [21].

4   Cycle-Bounded Programs

As saw in the previous section, to determine if a program is rule-bounded we check through linear constraints if the size of the head atom is bounded by the size of a body atom for every relevant rule in a non-trivial SCC of the firing graph (cf. Definition 4). Looking at each rule individually has its limitations, as shown by the following example.

Example 8. Consider the following simple program $\mathcal{P}_8$:

$$r_1 : \; \mathsf{p}(\mathsf{X},\mathsf{Y}) \quad \leftarrow \mathsf{q}(\mathsf{f}(\mathsf{X}),\mathsf{Y}).$$
$$r_2 : \; \mathsf{q}(\mathsf{W},\mathsf{f}(\mathsf{Z})) \leftarrow \mathsf{p}(\mathsf{W},\mathsf{Z}).$$

It is easy to see that the bottom-up evaluation always terminates, but the program is not rule-bounded. The linear inequalities for the program are (cf. Definition 4):

$$\begin{cases} (\alpha_{q_1} - \alpha_{p_1}) \cdot x + (\alpha_{q_2} - \alpha_{p_2}) \cdot y + \alpha_{q_1} \geq 0 \\ (\alpha_{p_1} - \alpha_{q_1}) \cdot w + (\alpha_{p_2} - \alpha_{q_2}) \cdot z - \alpha_{q_2} \geq 0 \end{cases}$$

It can be easily verified that there are no positive integer values for α_{p_1}, α_{p_2}, α_{q_1}, α_{q_2} such that the inequalities hold for all $x, y, w, z \in \mathbb{N}_0$. The reason is the presence of the expression $-\alpha_{q_2}$ in the second inequality. Intuitively, this is because the size of the head atom increases w.r.t. the size of the body atom in r_2. However, notice that the cycle involving r_1 and r_2 does not increase the overall size of propagated terms. This suggests we can check if an *entire cycle* (rather than each individual rule) propagates terms of bounded size. □

To deal with programs like the one shown in the previous example, we introduce the class of *cycle-bounded programs*, which is able to perform an analysis of how terms propagate through a *group* of rules, rather than looking at rules *individually* as done by the rule-bounded criterion.

Given a program $\mathcal{P}$, a cycle $\pi = \langle r_1, r_2 \rangle, \langle r_2, r_3 \rangle, ..., \langle r_n, r_1 \rangle$ of $\Omega(\mathcal{P})$ is *basic* if every edge does not occur more than once. We say that π is *relevant* if every r_i is relevant, for $1 \leq i \leq n$.

In the following, we first present the cycle-bounded criterion for linear programs and then show how it can be applied to non-linear ones.

Dealing with linear programs. Notice that $rbody(r)$ contains exactly one atom B for every linear rule r in a non-trivial SCC of the firing graph; thus, with a slight abuse of notation, we use $rbody(r)$ to refer to B.

Definition 5 (Linear cycle-bounded programs). *Let $\mathcal{P}$ be a linear program, $\pi = \langle r_1, r_2 \rangle, ..., \langle r_n, r_1 \rangle$ a basic cycle of $\Omega(\mathcal{P})$, p the predicate symbol defined by r_n, and k the arity of p. Also, let θ_i be an mgu of $head(r_i)$ and $rbody(r_{i+1})$, for $1 \leq i \leq n-1$.[3] Given an mgu θ_i ($1 \leq i \leq n-1$) and a pair X/t in θ_i, we define the equality*

$$eq(X/t) = \begin{cases} size(X, r_i) = size(t, r_{i+1}) & \textit{if } X \textit{ appears in } head(r_i); \\ size(X, r_{i+1}) = size(t, r_i) & \textit{if } X \textit{ appears in } rbody(r_{i+1}); \end{cases}$$

and define $eq(\theta_i) = \{eq(X/t) \mid X/t \in \theta_i\}$. We say that π is cycle-bounded if there exists a vector $\overline{\alpha} \in \mathbb{N}^k$ such that the following constraints are satisfied

$$\{\overline{\alpha} \cdot size(rbody(r_1), r_1) - \overline{\alpha} \cdot size(head(r_n), r_n) \geq 0\} \cup eq(\theta_1) \cup ... \cup eq(\theta_{n-1})$$

---

[3] Note that such θ_i's always exist by definition of firing graph.

for every non-negative value of the integer variables occurring in the constraints. We say that $\mathcal{P}$ is cycle-bounded *if every relevant basic cycle of $\Omega(\mathcal{P})$ is cycle-bounded.*   □

Example 9. Consider again program $\mathcal{P}_8$ of Example 8. The program is clearly linear and $\Omega(\mathcal{P}_8)$ has two relevant basic cycles $\pi_1 = \langle r_1, r_2 \rangle, \langle r_2, r_1 \rangle$ and $\pi_2 = \langle r_2, r_1 \rangle, \langle r_1, r_2 \rangle$. To check if π_1 is cycle-bounded we need to check if there exist $\alpha_{q_1}, \alpha_{q_2} \in \mathbb{N}$ s.t. the following constraints are satisfied for all $x, y, w, z \in \mathbb{N}_0$:

$$\begin{cases} \alpha_{q_1} \cdot (x+1) + \alpha_{q_2} \cdot y - \alpha_{q_1} \cdot w - \alpha_{q_2} \cdot (z+1) \geq 0 \\ x = w \\ y = z \end{cases}$$

Notice that the last two equalities above are derived from the mgu $\{X/W, Y/Z\}$ used to unify $head(r_1)$ and $rbody(r_2)$. To check the above condition, we can replace x with w and y with z in the first constraint, thereby obtaining $\alpha_{q_1} - \alpha_{q_2} \geq 0$, which is satisfied for $\alpha_{q_1} \geq \alpha_{q_2}$. Thus, π_1 is cycle-bounded. Likewise, it can be verified that π_2 is cycle-bounded too and thus $\mathcal{P}_8$ is cycle-bounded. Program $\mathcal{P}_3$ (cf. Example 3) is another linear program that is cycle-bounded.   □

Dealing with Non-linear Programs. The application of the cycle-bounded criterion to arbitrary programs consists in applying the technique to a set of linear programs derived from the original one. Given a rule r, the set of *linear versions* of r is defined as the set of rules $\ell(r) = \{head(r) \leftarrow B \mid B \in rbody(r)\}$. Given a program $\mathcal{P} = \{r_1, ..., r_n\}$, the set of *linear versions* of $\mathcal{P}$ is defined as the set of linear programs $\ell(\mathcal{P}) = \{\{r'_1, ..., r'_n\} \mid r'_i \in \ell(r_i) \text{ for } 1 \leq i \leq n\}$.

Definition 6 (Cycle-bounded programs). *A (possibly non-linear) program $\mathcal{P}$ is* cycle-bounded *if every (linear) program in $\ell(\mathcal{P})$ is cycle-bounded.*   □

Like rule-bounded programs, cycle-bounded programs are finitely-ground.

Theorem 4. *Every cycle-bounded program is finitely-ground.*   □

Theorem 5. *Checking if a program is cycle-bounded is decidable.*   □

Theorem 6. *Cycle-bounded programs are incomparable with rule-bounded, mapping-restricted, and bounded programs.*   □

While Theorem 5 establishes decidability of checking if a program is cycle-bounded, we conjecture that the problem is in Π_2^p. Moreover, we point out that cycle-bounded programs are also incomparable with criteria less general than the mapping-restricted and the bounded ones (e.g., argument-restrictedness).

5   Related Work

A significant body of work has been done on termination of logic programs under top-down evaluation [9,36,22,25,8,30,24,28,29,23,5,4,3] and in the area of term rewriting [37,32,2,11,12]. Termination properties of query evaluation for normal programs under tabling have been studied in [26,27,34].

In this paper, we consider logic programs with function symbols *under the stable model semantics* [15,16] (recall that, as discussed in Section 3, our approach can be applied to programs with disjunction and negation by transforming them into positive normal programs), and thus all the excellent works above cannot be straightforwardly applied to our setting—for a discussion on this see, e.g., [7,1]. In our context, [7] introduced the class of *finitely-ground programs*, guaranteeing the existence of a finite set of stable models, each of finite size, for programs in the class. Since membership in the class is not decidable, decidable subclasses have been proposed: *ω-restricted programs*, *λ-restricted programs*, *finite domain programs*, *argument-restricted programs*, *safe programs*, *Γ-acyclic programs*, *mapping-restricted programs*, and *bounded programs*. An adornment-based approach that can be used in conjunction with the techniques above to detect more programs as finitely-ground has been proposed in [18].

Compared with the aforementioned classes, rule- and cycle-bounded programs allow us to perform a more global analysis and identify many practical programs as finitely-ground, such as those where terms in the body are rearranged in the head, which are not included in any of the classes above. We observe that there are also programs which are not rule- or cycle-bounded but are recognized as finitely-ground by some of the aforementioned techniques (see Theorems 3 and 6).

Similar concepts of "term size" have been considered to check termination of logic programs evaluated in a top-down fashion [31], in the context of partial evaluation to provide conditions for strong termination and quasi-termination [35,20], and in the context of tabled resolution [26,27]. These approaches are geared to work under top-down evaluation, looking at how terms are propagated from the head to the body, while our approach is developed to work under bottom-up evaluation, looking at how terms are propagated from the body to the head. This gives rise to significant differences in how the program analysis is carried out, making one approach not applicable in the setting of the other. As a simple example, the rule $p(X) \leftarrow p(X)$ leads to a non-terminating top-down evaluation, while it is completely harmless under bottom-up evaluation.

6   Conclusions

Recently, there has been a great deal of interest in enhancing answer set programming with function symbols. Research has focused on identifying classes of logic programs allowing only a limited use of function symbols but guaranteeing decidability of common inference tasks. Despite many excellent techniques that have been proposed in recent years, there are still many terminating practical programs which are not captured by any of the approaches in the literature.

In this paper, we have introduced the novel class of rule-bounded programs, which overcomes different limitations of current approaches by performing a more global analysis of programs, thereby identifying many programs commonly arising in practice as finitely-ground. We have also introduced the class of cycle-bounded programs where groups of rules are analyzed.

As a direction for future work, we plan to investigate how our techniques can be combined with current termination criteria. Since they look at programs from different standpoints, an interesting issue is to study how they can be integrated so that they can benefit from each other. To this end, an interesting approach would be to plug termination criteria in the generic framework proposed in [10] and study their combination in such a framework. Another intriguing issue would be to analyze the relationships between the notions of safety of [10] and the notions of boundedness used by termination criteria.

References

1. Alviano, M., Faber, W., Leone, N.: Disjunctive ASP with functions: Decidable queries and effective computation. TPLP 10(4-6), 497–512 (2010)
2. Arts, T., Giesl, J.: Termination of term rewriting using dependency pairs. Theoretical Computer Science 236(1-2), 133–178 (2000)
3. Baselice, S., Bonatti, P.A., Criscuolo, G.: On finitely recursive programs. TPLP 9(2), 213–238 (2009)
4. Bonatti, P.A.: Reasoning with infinite stable models. Artificial Intelligence 156(1), 75–111 (2004)
5. Bruynooghe, M., Codish, M., Gallagher, J.P., Genaim, S., Vanhoof, W.: Termination analysis of logic programs through combination of type-based norms. ACM Trans. Program. Lang. Syst. 29(2) (2007)
6. Calautti, M., Greco, S., Trubitsyna, I.: Detecting decidable classes of finitely ground logic programs with function symbols. In: PPDP, pp. 239–250 (2013)
7. Calimeri, F., Cozza, S., Ianni, G., Leone, N.: Computable functions in ASP: Theory and implementation. In: Garcia de la Banda, M., Pontelli, E. (eds.) ICLP 2008. LNCS, vol. 5366, pp. 407–424. Springer, Heidelberg (2008)
8. Codish, M., Lagoon, V., Stuckey, P.J.: Testing for termination with monotonicity constraints. In: Gabbrielli, M., Gupta, G. (eds.) ICLP 2005. LNCS, vol. 3668, pp. 326–340. Springer, Heidelberg (2005)
9. De Schreye, D., Decorte, S.: Termination of logic programs: The never-ending story. Journal of Logic Programming 19/20, 199–260 (1994)
10. Eiter, T., Fink, M., Krennwallner, T., Redl, C.: Liberal safety for answer set programs with external sources. In: AAAI (2013)
11. Endrullis, J., Waldmann, J., Zantema, H.: Matrix interpretations for proving termination of term rewriting. J. Autom. Reas. 40(2-3), 195–220 (2008)
12. Ferreira, M.C.F., Zantema, H.: andH. Zantema. Total termination of term rewriting. Appl. Algebra Eng. Commun. Comput. 7(2), 133–162 (1996)
13. Gebser, M., Kaminski, R., Kaufmann, B., Schaub, T.: Answer Set Solving in Practice. In: Synthesis Lectures on Artificial Intelligence and Machine Learning. Morgan & Claypool Publishers (2012)
14. Gebser, M., Schaub, T., Thiele, S.: Gringo: A new grounder for answer set programming. In: Baral, C., Brewka, G., Schlipf, J. (eds.) LPNMR 2007. LNCS (LNAI), vol. 4483, pp. 266–271. Springer, Heidelberg (2007)
15. Gelfond, M., Lifschitz, V.: The stable model semantics for logic programming. In: ICLP/SLP, pp. 1070–1080 (1988)

16. Gelfond, M., Lifschitz, V.: Classical negation in logic programs and disjunctive databases. New Generation Computing 9(3/4), 365–386 (1991)
17. Greco, S., Molinaro, C., Trubitsyna, I.: Bounded programs: A new decidable class of logic programs with function symbols. In: IJCAI, pp. 926–932 (2013)
18. Greco, S., Molinaro, C., Trubitsyna, I.: Logic programming with function symbols: Checking Termination of bottom-up Evaluation Through Program Adornments. TPLP 13(4-5), 737–752 (2013)
19. Greco, S., Spezzano, F., Trubitsyna, I.: On the termination of logic programs with function symbols. In: ICLP (Technical Communications), pp. 323–333 (2012)
20. Leuschel, M., Vidal, G.: Fast offline partial evaluation of logic programs. Information and Computation 235(0), 70–97 (2014)
21. Lierler, Y., Lifschitz, V.: One more decidable class of finitely ground programs. In: Hill, P.M., Warren, D.S. (eds.) ICLP 2009. LNCS, vol. 5649, pp. 489–493. Springer, Heidelberg (2009)
22. Marchiori, M.: Proving existential termination of normal logic programs. In: Nivat, M., Wirsing, M. (eds.) AMAST 1996. LNCS, vol. 1101, pp. 375–390. Springer, Heidelberg (1996)
23. Nguyen, M.T., Giesl, J., Schneider-Kamp, P., De Schreye, D.: Termination analysis of logic programs based on dependency graphs. In: King, A. (ed.) LOPSTR 2007. LNCS, vol. 4915, pp. 8–22. Springer, Heidelberg (2008)
24. Nishida, N., Vidal, G.: Termination of narrowing via termination of rewriting. Appl. Algebra Eng. Commun. Comput 21(3), 177–225 (2010)
25. Ohlebusch, E.: Termination of logic programs: Transformational methods revisited. Appl. Algebra Eng. Commun. Comput. 12(1/2), 73–116 (2001)
26. Riguzzi, F., Swift, T.: Well-definedness and efficient inference for probabilistic logic programming under the distribution semantics. TPLP 13(2), 279–302 (2013)
27. Riguzzi, F., Swift, T.: Terminating evaluation of logic programs with finite three-valued models. ACM Transactions on Computational Logic (2014)
28. Schneider-Kamp, P., Giesl, J., Serebrenik, A., Thiemann, R.: Automated termination proofs for logic programs by term rewriting. ACM Trans. Comput. Log. 11(1) (2009)
29. Schneider-Kamp, P., Giesl, J., Ströder, T., Serebrenik, A., Thiemann, R.: Automated termination analysis for logic programs with cut. TPLP 10(4-6), 365–381 (2010)
30. Serebrenik, A., De Schreye, D.: On termination of meta-programs. TPLP 5(3), 355–390 (2005)
31. Sohn, K., Van Gelder, A.: Termination detection in logic programs using argument sizes. In: PODS, pp. 216–226 (1991)
32. Sternagel, C., Middeldorp, A.: Root-labeling. In: Voronkov, A. (ed.) RTA 2008. LNCS, vol. 5117, pp. 336–350. Springer, Heidelberg (2008)
33. Syrjänen, T.: Omega-restricted logic programs. In: Eiter, T., Faber, W., Truszczyński, M. (eds.) LPNMR 2001. LNCS (LNAI), vol. 2173, pp. 267–280. Springer, Heidelberg (2001)
34. Verbaeten, S., De Schreye, D., Sagonas, K.F.: Termination proofs for logic programs with tabling. ACM Trans. Comput. Log. 2(1), 57–92 (2001)
35. Vidal, G.: Quasi-terminating logic programs for ensuring the termination of partial evaluation. In: PEPM, pp. 51–60 (2007)
36. Voets, D., De Schreye, D.: Non-termination analysis of logic programs with integer arithmetics. TPLP 11(4-5), 521–536 (2011)
37. Zantema, H.: Termination of term rewriting by semantic labelling. Fundamenta Informaticae 24(1/2), 89–105 (1995)

A Datalog$^+$ RuleML 1.01 Architecture for Rule-Based Data Access in Ecosystem Research

Harold Boley[1], Rolf Grütter[2], Gen Zou[1], Tara Athan[3], and Sophia Etzold[2]

[1] Faculty of Computer Science, University of New Brunswick, Fredericton, Canada
{harold.boley,gen.zou}@unb.ca
[2] Swiss Federal Research Institute WSL, Birmensdorf, Switzerland
{rolf.gruetter,sophia.etzold}@wsl.ch
[3] Athan Services (athant.com), West Lafayette, Indiana, USA
taraathan@gmail.com

Abstract. Rule-Based Data Access (RBDA) enables automated reasoning over a knowledge base (KB) as a generalized global schema for the data in local (e.g., relational or graph) databases reachable through mappings. RBDA can semantically validate, enrich, and integrate heterogeneous data sources. This paper proposes an RBDA architecture layered on Datalog$^+$ RuleML, and uses it for the ΔForest case study on the susceptibility of forests to climate change. Deliberation RuleML 1.01 was mostly motivated by Datalog customization requirements for RBDA. It includes Datalog$^+$ RuleML 1.01 as a standard XML serialization of Datalog$^+$, a superlanguage of the decidable Datalog$^\pm$. Datalog$^+$ RuleML is customized into the three Datalog extensions Datalog[$\exists$], Datalog[$=$], and Datalog[$\perp$] through MYNG, the RuleML Modular sYNtax confiGurator generating (Relax NG and XSD) schemas from language-feature selections. The ΔForest case study on climate change employs data derived from three main forest monitoring networks in Switzerland. The KB includes background knowledge about the study sites and design, e.g., abundant tree species groups, pure tree stands, and statistical independence among forest plots. The KB is used to rewrite queries about, e.g., the eligible plots for studying a particular species group. The mapping rules unfold our newly designed global schema to the three given local schemas, e.g. for the grade of forest management. The RBDA/ΔForest case study has shown the usefulness of our approach to Ecosystem Research for global schema design and demonstrated how automated reasoning can become key to knowledge modeling and consolidation for complex statistical data analysis.

1 Introduction

Ontology-Based Data Access (OBDA) has emerged as a major application area of Semantic Technologies for validating, enriching, and integrating heterogeneous databases (e.g., [1]). Complementary systems for Rule-Based Data Access

A. Bikakis et al. (Eds.): RuleML 2014, LNCS 8620, pp. 112–126, 2014.

(RBDA) have been developed as well (e.g., [2]). For ontology-rule synergy, OBDA and RBDA have been generalized to Knowledge-Based Data Access (KBDA).[1]

While the earlier logic-database combinations, e.g. procedural Prolog-SQL interfaces, interleaved knowledge-based reasoning with data access, KBDA keeps these layers separate, using declarative mappings to bridge between the two. This way, the (higher-level) ontology and rule technologies can be advanced independently from, yet be combined with, the (lower-level) optimizations progressing for DB engines. KBDA can thus provide the urgently needed knowledge level for the growing number of data sources (e.g., about climate change) of big volume, variety, and velocity in a cost-effective manner.

KBDA builds on earlier work in knowledge-based information/data/schema integration (e.g., [3–5]). It *integrates* data complying to local (heterogeneous) schemas into data complying to a global (homogeneous) schema, usually employing Global-As-View (GAV) mappings. It also *validates* and *enriches* local-schema data with global-schema knowledge represented as ontologies or rulebases.

Some KBDA approaches use a *mediator* architecture for **query rewriting** [2,6, 7] – corresponding to *top-down* processing and *backward* reasoning – while others use a *warehouse* architecture for **database materialization** [8] – corresponding to *bottom-up* processing and *forward* reasoning. Given that both have their advantages, we will propose a unified mediator/warehouse architecture.

KBDA KBs usually encompass rule knowledge to enrich the factual data mapped – again via rules – from the local (heterogeneous) schemas of one or more databases to a global (homogeneous) schema. Given these and other roles of rules, we will focus on RBDA in the following.

RuleML provides a family of rule (including fact) languages of customizable expressivity, a family-uniform XML format, and a suite of tools for rule processing, including the MYNG tool for generating serialization schemas in RNC and XSD. Deliberation RuleML 1.01 introduces a standard XML serialization of Datalog$^+$, a superlanguage of the decidable Datalog$^\pm$, which is being increasingly used for RBDA. Section 2 will present a unified architecture for KBDA, examine KBs and Mappings in Datalog$^+$ RuleML, and discuss relational-graph transformations for the global schema.

WSL creates knowledge and publishes data about Swiss forests, giving an integrated federal perspective on heterogeneous databases of various (e.g., geographically and thematically) specialized sources. In particular, the WSL project addressed in this work is about the susceptibility of forests to climate change [9]. Section 3 will show how this RuleML-WSL collaboration, termed ΔForest, is bringing the RBDA technologies of Section 2 to bear on WSL knowledge and databases.

2   RBDA Technology

We will now examine RBDA technology, starting with 'the rules of OBDA' from a mediator perspective, continuing with a unification of mediator and warehouse

---

[1] An overview is at http://www.cs.unb.ca/~boley/talks/RulesOBDA.pdf

architectures for KBDA, and then expanding on Datalog$^+$ RuleML and PSOA RuleML for our focus area of RBDA.

2.1 Kinds of Rules in KBDA

Motivated by rule-ontology synergies, we will discuss key mediator concepts of KBDA and their foundation in three kinds of (Datalog$^+$) rules, to be exemplified through the ΔForest case study in Section 3.

(1) A **conjunctive query** is a special Datalog rule whose conjunctive body can be rewritten as in (2) and unfolded as in (3), and whose n-ary head predicate instantiates the distinguished answer variables of the body predicates. OBDA ontologies beyond RDF Schema (RDFS) expressivity usually permit **negative constraints** for data validation, which are represented as Boolean conjunctive queries corresponding to RBDA integrity rules, e.g. in the extension Datalog[$\perp$] of Datalog$^+$ [10].
(2) OBDA ontologies support **query rewriting** through global-schema-level reasoning. They usually include the expressivity of RDFS, whose class and property subsumptions can be seen as single-premise Datalog rules with, respectively, unary and binary predicates, and whose remaining axioms are also definable by rules. Such ontologies often extend RDFS to the description logic DL-Lite [11] (as in OWL 2 QL [12]), including subsumption axioms that correspond to (head-)existential rules. RBDA rulebases are also being used for rewriting, e.g. via Description Logic Programs [13] (as in OWL 2 RL [12], definable in RIF-Core [14]), Datalog$^\pm$ [10], and Disjunctive Datalog [15]. We will refer to the store containing ontologies or rulebases for rewriting as the KB.
(3) KBDA data integration is centered on GAV mappings, which are safe Datalog rules for **query unfolding** of each global head predicate into a conjunction of local body predicates. These (heterogeneous) conjunctive queries can be further mapped to the database languages of the sources (e.g., to SQL or SPARQL). The store containing mappings for unfolding always is a rulebase.

2.2 A Unified Architecture for KBDA

Mediator and warehouse architectures for KBDA have often been considered in isolation. An architectural unification is achievable by using parts of the KB disjointly for mediator-style Query Rewriting [16–18] and warehouse-style DB Materialization [8], and using the Mappings reversely for mediator-style Query Unfolding and warehouse-style DB Folding. The unified architecture can thus be employed for a mediator, warehouse, and bidirectional strategy of KBDA (cf. Fig. 1), allowing for 'pluggable' domain refinements (cf. Fig. 2).

The architecture shows queries (as decorated Qs) and databases (as decorated DBs) explicitly while indicating answers (via solid triangular or diamond-shaped arrow heads) implicitly. Each query Q_i'' targeting the local source DB_i abstracts from the relational/graph/... database level, but becomes grounded to, e.g., SQL/SPARQL^2/... at the DB_i interface (indicated by a diamond head).

---

^{2} Unlike the relational SQL for local data, the graph-oriented SPARQL plays an ambiguous role as a query language for local-schema data and global-schema knowledge.

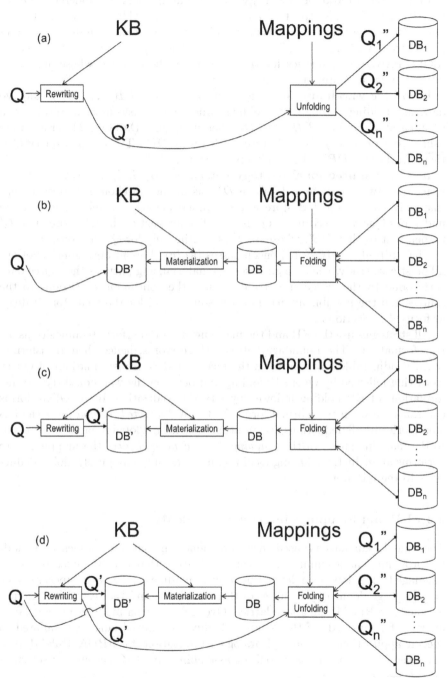

Fig. 1. From (a) mediator, (b) warehouse, and (c) bidirectional to (d) unified architecture

In (a), the **mediator strategy**, an incoming query Q undergoes Query Rewriting to Q' using (part or all of) the KB store. This Q' then undergoes Query Unfolding through the Folding/Unfolding transformation using the Mappings store, with results Q_1'', Q_2'', ..., Q_n''. The Q_i'' are finally grounded to (SQL/SPARQL/...) queries for the original databases DB_i, whose answers – ultimately for Q – are returned.

In (b), the **warehouse strategy**, databases DB_1, DB_2, ..., DB_n undergo database Folding through the Folding/Unfolding transformation, resulting in an integrated database DB. This DB then undergoes Database Materialization using (part or all of) the KB store, with result DB'. The original query Q is then sent to this DB', whose answers are returned.

In (c), the **bidirectional strategy**, databases DB_1, DB_2, ..., DB_n are transformed (in two steps) to a database DB' as in the warehouse strategy except that only part of the KB store is used. Independently, an incoming query Q undergoes Query Rewriting to Q' using a disjoint part of the KB store. This Q' is then sent to that DB', whose answers – ultimately for Q – are returned.[3]

The **unified strategy** (d) encompasses (a)-(c). This meets the needs of our ΔForest case study, where, e.g., R scripts materializing parts of the source data correspond to the warehouse strategy while the continuing extensions to the sources and the possible addition of new sources call for the mediator strategy, as focused in Section 3.

All strategies use the KB and the mapping store to perform (compositions of) transformations. The boundary between these stores, hence their transformations, is adjustable, both between the mediator-style transformations of Query Rewriting followed by Query Unfolding and between the warehouse-style transformations of DB Folding followed by DB Materialization. Intermediate forms can range between two normal forms. In the *KB-directed normal form* the KB store performs all deductions except atom-level local/global renamings, reserved to the mapping store. In the *mapping-directed normal form* the mapping store performs all deductions having local premises, leaving only purely global deductions to the KB store.

2.3   KB and Mappings in Datalog$^+$ RuleML

The RuleML language is based on a set of monotonic schema modules, each module providing the grammar of a syntactic feature that can be mixed-in to the language [19]. A language defined by a set of modules is always a superlanguage of a language defined by a subset of those modules, and the resulting structure is called the RuleML language lattice. Over fifty schema modules are available, allowing for hundreds of thousands of highly customized languages tailored to specific applications, including Datalog customizations for RBDA. RuleML provides the MYNG GUI[4] as a tool for assembling an RNC schema by selecting

---

[3] The two directions of the bidirectional strategy thus enable parallel processing with DB' acting as the synchronization point.

[4] http://deliberation.ruleml.org/1.01/myng

syntactic features, as well as determining the closest lenient XSD schema for the desired sublanguage.

XML processing instructions of type "xml-model" refer to a schema that the document should validate against. This processing instruction can be used to provide an indication of the smallest RuleML sublanguage containing a RuleML document. Engines may take advantage of this information to optimize algorithms such as for rulebase transformation, query answering, and query rewriting.

Deliberation RuleML 1.01^5 introduces several new options for obtaining a more fine-grained customization of sublanguages. A small set of extensions of Datalog yields a major payoff: a standard XML serialization of Datalog$^+$, a superlanguage of the decidable Datalog$^\pm$ [10]. The highlight of Deliberation RuleML 1.01 is the ability to combine one or more of the following Datalog extensions which together define Datalog$^+$:

- Existential Rules, where the "then" part of a rule has existentially quantified variables,
- Equality Rules, where the "then" part of a rule is the "Equal" predicate, (this was already allowed in RuleML 1.0)
- Integrity Rules, where the "then" part of a rule is falsity, as a convenient way to express negative integrity constraints.

2.4 Relations and Graphs in PSOA RuleML

The two modeling paradigms of relational and graph languages can be used simultaneously in the global and local schemas of KBDA architectures.

Relational languages are used, e.g., for modeling knowledge in classical logic and data from relational databases. In these languages, a relationship among n entities becomes an n-ary predicate applied to n positional arguments. Some KBDA engines, e.g. Nyaya [7], use Datalog$^\pm$ for global relational querying. Graph languages are used, e.g., in frame logic and Semantic Web applications. In these languages, an object consists of a globally unique Object IDentifier (OID) typed by a class and described by an unordered collection of n attribute-value slots, where the value can identify an object. Other KBDA engines, e.g. Ontop [20], use SPARQL for global graph querying.

Mapping rules between the global and local schemas of the form $paradigm_1 :\text{-} paradigm_2$ in KBDA can be within the same modeling paradigm or across the two paradigms, yielding four combinations of transformations: relational :- relational, relational :- graph, graph :- relational, and graph :- graph. Similarly, KB rules, which describe transformations within the global schema, can also be of the four forms. Hence, a language like PSOA RuleML [21], capable of knowledge and data modeling in both paradigms, can support the specification of these transformations. PSOA RuleML introduces positional-slotted, object-applicative (psoa) terms, which permit a relation application to have an OID – typed by the relation – and, orthogonally, its arguments to be positional or

---

^{5} http://deliberation.ruleml.org/1.01

slotted. Psoa terms can be used as classical atoms without OIDs for relational modeling, and as frame atoms for graph modeling. Thus, all four kinds of transformations can be described in PSOA RuleML. In particular, graph :- relational transformations, which permit graph querying over relational databases, can be described by rules with frames in the conclusion and relations in the premise. Here, the positional argument that acts as the simple key in the relation becomes the OID of a frame, and the other positional arguments become slot values whose slot names correspond to relational column headings.

3   ΔForest Case Study

The WSL project [9] aims for an assessment of the susceptibility of forest ecosystems to the expected changing environmental conditions going along with climate change, such as temperature or precipitation. The susceptibility of a forest stand to climate change depends particularly on the change of the mortality rate. The death of single trees without a distinguishable reason and mortality of suppressed trees due to competition for nutrients or water are natural processes within the forest stand development, since only a limited number of trees can survive at one location depending on site properties, climate conditions, and tree species.

The higher the growth rate of a forest the higher is also the mortality. Accordingly, the absolute mortality is not a useful indicator to express the stand vitality. For dense forests a log-log linear relationship, called *self-thinning line*, exists for the density as number of trees per ha and the quadratic-mean tree diameter with slope and intercept (corresponding to maximum stand density) depending on tree species [22–24]. The relative mortality in a given period is defined as a shift in the self-thinning line. A change in relative mortality can then be attributed to changing environmental conditions.

The following working hypotheses are tested: (i) The relative mortality is a useful indicator for the susceptibility of forest stands to changing climatic conditions. (ii) At temperature-limited sites, increasing temperatures will increase the maximum stand density and relative mortality will decrease. (iii) At moisture-limited sites, increasing temperatures and frequency of drought events will reduce maximum stand density and relative mortality will increase.

Analysis is conducted for 285 pure and mixed forest stands in Switzerland, covering the five tree species groups of interest: beech (*Fagus sylvatica*), oak (*Quercus petraea* and *Quercus robur*), spruce (*Picea abies*), pine (*Pinus sylvestris*), fir (*Abies alba*), and several climatic regions. Data are derived from three main monitoring networks in Switzerland: yield plots (EKF) [25], monitoring of nature reserves (NWR) [26], and the Swiss Long-Term Forest Ecosystem Research (LWF) network [27]. Data cover a time period from 1933 to 2010.

During the WSL project [9], a number of conditions have to be controlled which otherwise might impair the validity of the results. To achieve this, the following questions need to be answered, formalizations of which will be developed as queries in our ΔForest case study:

1. Are there sufficiently many eligible plots in order to perform an analysis per tree species group of interest?
2. Which eligible plots represent pure tree stands and which eligible plots represent mixed tree stands?

Re 1. To make a significant statement about how two or more variables are related, the sample size (i.e., the number of plots) must exceed a certain lower bound.

Re 2. The calculation of the self-thinning line assumes pure tree stands. Plots that represent mixed tree stands require a more complex analysis than those representing pure tree stands.

In what follows, the schema and rules for answering Questions 1 and 2 will be formalized, by ultimately mapping them to the forestry data sources.

3.1   Global Schema and KB Rules

Based on *local schemas* for the three data sources, the ΔForest *global schema* describes two kinds of predicates (cf. Fig. 2):

- External predicates of high arity (for knowledge consolidation): no dot prefix
- Internal predicates of low arity (for knowledge modeling): dot prefix

In order to construct relational global queries asking for eligible plots that represent tree stands, where a given tree species group is abundant (Question 1) or dominant (Question 2), we require the global schema to include the following external predicates (two tables of DB' in Fig. 2):

```
PlotsStatic(plot source x y altitude class)
SGAbundance(plot species-group percentage)
```

The external predicate `PlotsStatic`, which has a simple key, `plot`, can be directly transformed to frames using graph :- relation rules discussed in Section 2.4, hence allowing also graph querying over the global schema.

In order to model the knowledge domain of the study, we require the global schema to also contain the following internal predicates:

```
.EligiblePlot(plot)              .TreeStandAbundance(component percentage)
.IndependentPlot(plot)           .TreeStandKey(component plot species-group)
.PreEligiblePlot(plot)           .TreeStandMerged(plot species-group percentage)
.PossiblyDependentPlot(plot)     .TreeStandClass(stand class)
.LightlyManagedPlot(plot)        .PlotDistance(plot1 plot2 distance)
.ForestManagement(plot grade)    .Location(plot x y)
.PureTreeStand(component)        .Source(plot source)
.MixedTreeStand(component)       .Altitude(plot altitude)
.SpeciesGroupOfInterest(species-group)
```

The internal predicates are transformed to the external predicates with the following consolidation (external :- internal) rules:[6]

---

[6] In the study a number of lower bounds ranging around 15 percent are explored. Thus the global view may be considered to be parameterized by this quantity.

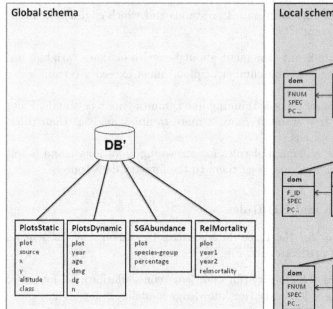
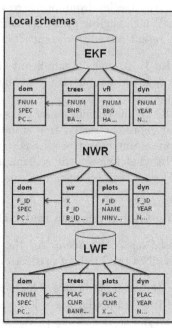

Fig. 2. Schemas of ΔForest, 'plugging' into DB', DB_1=EKF, DB_2=NWR, and DB_3=LWF of Fig. 1 (with n=3), where the KB partitioning in (c) and (d) becomes a split, e.g., between external :- internal vs. internal :- internal rules (the keys of the global schema – three being composite – are shown in bold red)

```
PlotsStatic(?plot ?src ?x ?y ?alt ?class) :- .EligiblePlot(?plot)
                                             .Source(?plot ?src)
                                             .Location(?plot ?x ?y)
                                             .Altitude(?plot ?alt)
                                             .TreeStandClass(?plot ?class).
SGAbundance(?plot ?sg ?pct) :- .EligiblePlot(?plot)
                               .TreeStandKey(?id ?plot ?sg)
                               .TreeStandAbundance(?id ?pct)
                               ?pct>=lower.

lower = 15.
```

The external predicates have the following equality-rule key constraints.

```
?src1=?src2 ?x1=?x2 ?y1=?y2 ?alt1=?alt2 ?class1=?class2 :-
                PlotsStatic(?plot ?src1 ?x1 ?y1 ?alt1 ?class1)
                PlotsStatic(?plot ?src2 ?x2 ?y2 ?alt2 ?class2).
?pct1=?pct2 :-  SGAbundance(?plot ?sg ?pct1)
                SGAbundance(?plot ?sg ?pct2).
```

Any violation of these key constraints indicates a key constraint violation in the source data.

The eligibility criteria take into account the following factors:

- The study assumes that the impact of forest management on tree mortality is negligible at the investigated sites. Nature reserves by definition prohibit all grades of forest management. Accordingly, none of the NWR plots need to be excluded from the study because of forest management. In the EKF data, forest management is graded as A, B, C, D, H, and P, where A has the lowest impact, D, H, and P the highest. In order for the study assumption to hold, forest management must not be of grade C, D, H, or P. Forest management is not recorded for LWF plots. This information must be obtained interactively by asking the respective forestry experts.
- Plots in the study must be statistically independent of each other. Plots that are located within a distance of 500 meters from each other are possibly dependent, because there is a high probability that stand characteristics are the same.
- Plots are ineligible for the study if they do not contain a time-averaged abundance greater than a threshold value of at least one of the following species groups of interest: oak, beech, spruce, pine, or fir.

The eligibility criteria are captured in the following concept-inclusion (internal : - internal) rules:

```
.EligiblePlot(?plot)    :-  .IndependentPlot(?plot)
                            .PreEligiblePlot(?plot).
.PreEligiblePlot(?plot) :-  .LightlyManagedPlot(?plot)
                            .TreeStandKey(?id ?plot ?sg)
                            .PureTreeStand(?id).
.PreEligiblePlot(?plot) :-  .LightlyManagedPlot(?plot)
                            .TreeStandKey(?id ?plot ?sg)
                            .MixedTreeStand(?id).
```

Additional rules among internal predicates assist in determining if the eligibility criteria are satisfied[7], and are related to each other in the following way (negative-constraint rules employ Or() conclusions to represent falsity – "⊥" of Datalog[⊥] – in a queryable manner):

```
.IndependentPlot(?plot)       :- .Source(?plot "nwr").
.IndependentPlot(?plot)       :- .Source(?plot "lwf").
.PossiblyDependentPlot(?plot1) :- .PlotDistance(?plot1 ?plot2 ?d)
                                  .PreEligiblePlot(?plot2)
                                  ?d < 500.
.IndependentPlot(?plot)       :- .Source(?plot "ekf")
                                  Naf(.PossiblyDependentPlot(?plot)).
```

---

[7] In our study, a stand whose dominant species group is not a group of interest may be treated as a mixed stand, while in the general ecological domain it would be considered a pure stand. We distinguish between these general and study-specific concepts of the same name through an implicit namespace.

```
.PlotDistance(?plot1 ?plot2 ?d) :- .Source(?plot1 "ekf")
                                   .Source(?plot2 "ekf")
                                   .Location(?plot1 ?x1 ?y1)
                                   .Location(?plot2 ?x2 ?y2)
                                   ?d = func:sqrt(func:pow(?x1-?x2,2) +
                                                 func:pow(?y1-?y2,2))
                                   ?d > 0.
Or() :- .PlotDistance(?plot ?plot ?distance).
.LightlyManagedPlot(?plot) :- .ForestManagement(?plot "B").
.LightlyManagedPlot(?plot) :- .ForestManagement(?plot "A").
.LightlyManagedPlot(?plot) :- .ForestManagement(?plot "O").
.ForestManagement(?plot "O") :- .Source(?plot "nwr").
.PureTreeStand(?id) :- .TreeStandAbundance(?id ?pct)
                       .TreeStandKey(?id ?plot ?sg)
                       .SpeciesGroupOfInterest(?sg)
                       ?pct >= pure.
.pure = 70.
.MixedTreeStand(?id) :- .TreeStandAbundance(?id ?pct)
                        .TreeStandKey(?id ?plot ?sg)
                        .SpeciesGroupOfInterest(?sg)
                        Naf(.PureTreeStand(?id))
                        ?pct >= lower.
.TreeStandClass(?plot "pure") :- .PureTreeStand(?id)
                                 .TreeStandKey(?id ?plot ?sg).
.TreeStandClass(?plot "mixed") :- .MixedTreeStand(?id)
                                  .TreeStandKey(?id ?plot ?sg).

.SpeciesGroupOfInterest("oak").  .SpeciesGroupOfInterest("beech").
.SpeciesGroupOfInterest("fir").  .SpeciesGroupOfInterest("spruce").
.SpeciesGroupOfInterest("pine").
```

The following existential rule is employed to introduce a simple key, ?id, for the predicate .TreeStandMerged, which has a composite key, ⟨?plot, ?sg⟩. The existential variable ?id is used in predicates .PureTreeStand and .MixedTreeStand to uniquely identify a single-species-group vegetative component on a plot. It can act as an object identifier in graph representations. In the existential rule conclusion, the predicate .TreeStandKey associates the original composite key ⟨?plot, ?sg⟩ with the introduced key ?id, and the predicate .TreeStandAbundance replaces the composite key of .TreeStandMerged with the new key ?id.

```
Exists ?id (.TreeStandKey(?id ?plot ?sg) .TreeStandAbundance(?id ?pct)) :-
  .TreeStandMerged(?plot ?sg ?pct).
```

3.2   Query Processing and Mappings

Question 1. In order to answer the first question, the **trees** tables of EKF, NWR, and LWF (not shown) are preprocessed using the statistical package R.[8] Preprocessing results in three instances of the table dom(?plot ?sg ?pct), where

---

[8] http://www.r-project.org/

?pct is the percentage, based on the basal area, of a tree species group (argument ?sg) on a plot (argument ?plot).

The following rules map the *local schemas* of EKF, NWR, and LWF to the *internal global predicates*, employing the KB-directed normal form except for merging oak species into a single species group and adding their percentages:

```
.TreeStandMerged(?plot "beech" ?pct) :- EKF.dom(?plot "Fagus sylvatica" ?pct).
.TreeStandMerged(?plot "beech" ?pct) :- NWR.dom(?plot "Fagus sylvatica" ?pct).
.TreeStandMerged(?plot "beech" ?pct) :- LWF.dom(?plot "Fagus sylvatica" ?pct).
.TreeStandMerged(?plot "oak" ?pct) :- EKF.dom(?plot "Quercus petraea" ?pct1)
                                      EKF.dom(?plot "Quercus robur" ?pct2)
                                      ?pct = ?pct1 + ?pct2.
.TreeStandMerged(?plot "oak" ?pct) :- NWR.dom(?plot "Quercus petraea" ?pct1)
                                      NWR.dom(?plot "Quercus robur" ?pct2)
                                      ?pct = ?pct1 + ?pct2.
.TreeStandMerged(?plot "oak" ?pct) :- LWF.dom(?plot "Quercus petraea" ?pct1)
                                      LWF.dom(?plot "Quercus robur" ?pct2)
                                      ?pct = ?pct1+?pct2.
```

The rules for spruce, pine and fir, not shown, are similar to those for beech. Additional plot characteristics are mapped as follows (.Location :- NWR mapping not shown):

```
.Location(?plot ?X ?Y) :- EKF.vfl(?plot ?BBG ?area ?Z ?X ?Y ?ORT ?GDE ?KT).
.Location(?plot ?X ?Y) :- LWF.Plots(?PLAC ?plot ?X ?Y ?Z ?LAT ?LON ?area).
.ForestManagement(?plot ?grade) :-
  EKF.trees(?plot ?BNR ?BA ?AJ ?grade ?AHC ?D1 ?D2 ?V7 ?SOZ ?HGEM ?HBER).
```

Question 1 for oaks is rephrased in terms of eligible plots representing tree stands where oaks are abundant, i.e., above the lower bound for the kinds of tree stand considered. This is formalized as a query using the external predicate SGAbundance:

```
q(?plot) :- SGAbundance(?plot "oak" ?pct).
```

In order to expand the query, the SGAbundance-headed KB rule and the fact regarding the value of lower are used to rewrite q as follows:

```
q(?plot) :- .EligiblePlot(?plot)
            .TreeStandKey(?id ?plot "oak")
            .TreeStandAbundance(?id ?pct)
            ?pct >= 15.
```

and then, using the existential rule, we obtain:

```
q(?plot) :- .EligiblePlot(?plot)
            .TreeStandMerged(?plot "oak" ?pct)
            ?pct >= 15.
```

This conjunctive query may be split as follows:

```
q(?plot)  :- q1(?plot) q2(?plot).
q1(?plot) :- .EligiblePlot(?plot).
q2(?plot) :- .TreeStandMerged(?plot "oak" ?pct)
             ?pct >= 15.
```

The query q2 is *unfolded* using the mapping rules introduced above.

```
q2(?plot) :- EKF.dom(?plot "Quercus petraea" ?pct1)
             EKF.dom(?plot "Quercus robur" ?pct2)
             ?pct1+?pct2 >= 15.
q2(?plot) :- NWR.dom(?plot "Quercus petraea" ?pct1)
             NWR.dom(?plot "Quercus robur" ?pct2)
             ?pct1+?pct2 >= 15.
q2(?plot) :- LWF.dom(?plot "Quercus petraea" ?pct1)
             LWF.dom(?plot "Quercus robur" ?pct2)
             ?pct1+?pct2 >= 15.
```

The full rewriting of q1 is not detailed here for space reasons. Partial database materialization, e.g. for .PlotDistance, would improve the efficiency of the query processing. On the other hand, full materialization of .EligiblePlot is not reasonable because the extension of this class is dependent on the value of the lower parameter, so a different materialization would be needed for each parameter value. Hence, the unified RBDA strategy explained in Section 2.2, which combines rewriting and materialization, fits the needs of the study.

Question 2. The second question is formalized with two queries using the external predicate PlotsStatic:

```
qPure(?plot) :- PlotsStatic(?plot ?src ?x1 ?y1 ?alt1 "pure" ).
qMixed(?plot) :- PlotsStatic(?plot ?src ?x2 ?y2 ?alt2 "mixed").
```

Query rewriting and unfolding work in a way similar to Question 1 except that abundance is compared to a bound of 70 (percent) using constant .pure. Eligible plots with abundance of a species group of interest above this value represent pure tree stands; the remaining eligible plots represent mixed tree stands.

4   Conclusions

In this paper, OBDA is complemented by Rule-Based Data Access (RBDA) and generalized to Knowledge-Based Data Access (KBDA). RBDA is founded on three kinds of rules: Query rules (including integrity rules), KB rules (for query rewriting and DB materialization), as well as mapping rules (for query unfolding and DB folding). A unified KBDA architecture is presented with mediator, warehouse, and bidirectional data-access strategies. Datalog[+] RuleML 1.01 is used for customizing rule expressivity, XML-based rule serialization, and platform-independent rule processing.

The ΔForest study applies RuleML techniques to real-world RBDA by formalizing two questions of a WSL project on ecosystems facing climate change. This case study has already shown the usefulness of our approach to Ecosystem Research, e.g. for the project's global schema design, and demonstrated how automated reasoning can become key to knowledge modeling and consolidation for complex statistical data analysis.

In the context of the open RBDA/ΔForest collaboration between RuleML and WSL, various avenues for future work are being explored, described as part of the RBDA wiki page.[9] Implementations of the specified architecture can reuse the (open source) KBDA technology referenced in this paper and the wiki page. In particular, relevant KBDA efficiency techniques [28] could be adapted to ΔForest. Moreover, our RBDA architecture could be applied to other areas of Ecosystem Research such as oceanography (ΔOcean). Finally, while our current RBDA focus is on Data Querying (RBDQ), Reaction RuleML 1.0[10] can also express updates as needed for Data Management (RBDM).

The RuleML blog[11] can contribute to bringing together the communities in Datalog$^\pm$, RuleML 1.x, RBDA, and Ecosystem Research.

References

1. Calvanese, D., et al.: Optique: OBDA solution for big data. In: Cimiano, P., Fernández, M., Lopez, V., Schlobach, S., Völker, J. (eds.) ESWC 2013. LNCS, vol. 7955, pp. 293–295. Springer, Heidelberg (2013)
2. Baget, J.-F., Croitoru, M., da Silva, B.P.L.: ALASKA for ontology based data access. In: Cimiano, P., Fernández, M., Lopez, V., Schlobach, S., Völker, J. (eds.) ESWC 2013. LNCS, vol. 7955, pp. 157–161. Springer, Heidelberg (2013)
3. Kühn, E., Puntigam, F., Elmagarmid, A.K.: Multidatabase transaction and query processing in logic. In: Elmagarmid, A.K. (ed.) Database Transaction Models for Advanced Applications. Morgan Kaufmann Publishers (1991)
4. Lakshmanan, L.V.S., Sadri, F., Subramanian, I.N.: On the logical foundations of schema integration and evolution in heterogeneous database systems. In: Ceri, S., Tsur, S., Tanaka, K. (eds.) DOOD 1993. LNCS, vol. 760, pp. 81–100. Springer, Heidelberg (1993)
5. Bassiliades, N., Vlahavas, L., Elmagarmid, A.K., Houstis, E.N.: InterBase-KB: Integrating a knowledge base system with a multidatabase system for data warehousing. IEEE Transactions on Knowledge and Data Engineering 15(5), 1188–1205 (2003)
6. Calvanese, D., Giacomo, G.D., Lembo, D., Lenzerini, M., Poggi, A., Rodriguez-Muro, M., Rosati, R., Ruzzi, M., Savo, D.F.: The MASTRO system for ontology-based data access. Semantic Web Journal 2(1), 43–53 (2011)
7. De Virgilio, R., Orsi, G., Tanca, L., Torlone, R.: NYAYA: A system supporting the uniform management of large sets of semantic data. In: IEEE 28th International Conference on Data Engineering, pp. 1309–1312 (April 2012)
8. Motik, B., Nenov, Y., Piro, R., Horrocks, I.: Parallel materialisation of Datalog programs in centralised, main-memory RDF systems. To appear in AAAI (2014)
9. Rigling, A., Zingg, A.: Relative Mortalität als Indikator für die Sensitivität von Waldbeständen. WSL Projekt, Bew-Pin 201104N0134
10. Calì, A., Gottlob, G., Lukasiewicz, T.: A general Datalog-based framework for tractable query answering over ontologies. Journal of Web Semantics 14, 57–83 (2012)
11. Calvanese, D., Giacomo, G., Lembo, D., Lenzerini, M., Rosati, R.: Tractable reasoning and efficient query answering in description logics: The DL-Lite family. Journal of Automated Reasoning 39(3), 385–429 (2007)

---

[9] http://wiki.ruleml.org/index.php/Rule-Based_Data_Access
[10] http://wiki.ruleml.org/index.php/Specification_of_Reaction_RuleML_1.0
[11] http://blog.ruleml.org/

12. Motik, B., Cuenca Grau, B., Horrocks, I., Wu, Z., Fokoue, A., Lutz, C.: OWL 2 Web Ontology Language Profiles, W3C Recommendation, 2nd edn. (October 2009), http://www.w3.org/TR/owl2-profiles/
13. Grosof, B.N., Horrocks, I., Volz, R., Decker, S.: Description logic programs: Combining logic programs with description logic. In: Proceedings of the 12th International Conference on World Wide Web, WWW 2003, pp. 48–57 (2003)
14. Boley, H., Hallmark, G., Kifer, M., Paschke, A., Polleres, A., Reynolds, D.: RIF Core Dialect, W3C Recommendation, 2nd edn. (February 2013), http://www.w3.org/TR/rif-core/
15. Eiter, T., Gottlob, G., Mannila, H.: Disjunctive Datalog. ACM Trans. Database Syst. 22(3), 364–418 (1997)
16. Gottlob, G., Orsi, G., Pieris, A.: Ontological queries: Rewriting and optimization. In: Abiteboul, S., Böhm, K., Koch, C., Tan, K.L. (eds.) Proceedings of the 27th International Conference on Data Engineering, ICDE 2011, pp. 2–13. IEEE Computer Society, Hannover (2011)
17. Calvanese, D., De Giacomo, G., Lenzerini, M., Vardi, M.Y.: Query processing under GLAV mappings for relational and graph databases. Proc. of the VLDB Endowment 6(2), 61–72 (2012)
18. Cuenca Grau, B., Motik, B., Stoilos, G., Horrocks, I.: Computing Datalog rewritings beyond Horn ontologies. In: Proc. of the 23rd Int. Joint Conf. on Artificial Intelligence, IJCAI 2013 (2013)
19. Athan, T., Boley, H.: Design and implementation of highly modular schemas for XML: Customization of RuleML. In: Palmirani, M., Sottara, D., Olken, F. (eds.) RuleML - America 2011. LNCS, vol. 7018, pp. 17–32. Springer, Heidelberg (2011)
20. Rodríguez-Muro, M., Kontchakov, R., Zakharyaschev, M.: Ontology-based data access: Ontop of databases. In: Alani, H., et al. (eds.) ISWC 2013, Part I. LNCS, vol. 8218, pp. 558–573. Springer, Heidelberg (2013)
21. Boley, H.: A RIF-Style Semantics for RuleML-Integrated Positional-Slotted, Object-Applicative Rules. In: Bassiliades, N., Governatori, G., Paschke, A. (eds.) RuleML 2011 - Europe. LNCS, vol. 6826, pp. 194–211. Springer, Heidelberg (2011)
22. Pretzsch, H., Biber, P.: A Re-evaluation of Reineke's rule and stand density index. For. Sci. 51, 304–320 (2005)
23. Reineke, L.: Perfecting a stand density index for even-aged forests. J. Agric. Res. 46, 627–638 (1933)
24. Schütz, J.P., Zingg, A.: Improving estimations of maximal stand density by combining Reineke's size-density rule and yield level, using the example of spruce (Picea abies (L.) Karst.) and European Beech (Fagus sylvatica L.). Ann. For. Sci. 67 (2010)
25. Zingg, A., Bachofen, H.: Wachstumsforschung an der WSL. Schweizer Wald 134(9), 15–23 (1998)
26. Brang, P., Commarmot, B., Rohrer, L., Bugmann, H.: Monitoringkonzept für Naturwaldreservate in der Schweiz. Eidg. Forschungsanstalt für Wald, Schnee und Landschaft WSL; ETH Zürich, Professur für Waldökologie, Birmensdorf, Zürich (February 2008), http://www.wsl.ch/publikationen/pdf/8555.pdf
27. Dobbertin, M., Kindermann, G., Neumann, M.: Analysis of forest growth data on intensive monitoring plots. In: Fischer, R., Lortenz, M. (eds.) Forest Condition in Europe: Technical Report of ICP Forests and FutMon, pp. 115–127. Institute for World Forestry, Hamburg (2011)
28. Bak, J., Brzykcy, G.z., Jedrzejek, C.: Extended rules in knowledge-based data access. In: Palmirani, M., Sottara, D., Olken, F. (eds.) RuleML - America 2011. LNCS, vol. 7018, pp. 112–127. Springer, Heidelberg (2011)

A Hybrid Diagnosis Approach Combining Black-Box and White-Box Reasoning

Mingmin Chen[1], Shizhuo Yu[1], Nico Franz[2], Shawn Bowers[3], and Bertram Ludäscher[1]

[1] Dept. of Computer Science, University of California, Davis, CA, USA
{michen,szyu,ludaesch}@ucdavis.edu
[2] School of Life Sciences, Arizona State University, AZ, USA
nico.franz@asu.edu
[3] Dept. of Computer Science, Gonzaga University, WA, USA
bowers@gonzaga.edu

Abstract. We study model-based diagnosis and propose a new approach of hybrid diagnosis combining black-box and white-box reasoning. We implemented and compared different diagnosis approaches including the standard hitting set algorithm and new approaches using answer set programming engines (DLV, Potassco) in the application of EULER/X toolkit, a logic-based toolkit for alignment of multiple biological taxonomies. Our benchmarks show that the new hybrid diagnosis approach runs about twice fast as the black-box diagnosis approach of the hitting set algorithm.

1 Motivation and Related Work

Model-based diagnosis was studied extensively in many areas, such as type error debugging, circuit diagnosis, OWL debugging, etc. Various approaches [17,7,3,15,2,14] have been proposed to diagnose or debug errors. Most of these diagnosis approaches compute *minimal inconsistent subsets* (a.k.a. diagnoses) and/or *maximal consistent subsets*. A common element of all these approaches is that they use a routine isInconsistent as a "black-box" to determine if a set of constraints is *unsatisfiable*. The best black-box approach we know of is [14] which is a hybrid of the Logarithmic Extraction Algorithm [2] and the Hitting Set (HST) Algorithm in [15].

The downside of these black-box approaches is that they do not look into the proof itself that the reasoner may provide in the isInconsistent routine, which may potentially lose some reusable information to reduce the number of invocations of reasoners. On the other hand, various provenance approaches have been studied to provide derivations and proof trees, such as [13] which proposes an approach by adding annotations to predicates to generate a *provenance semiring* of a derivation, Datalog debugging [16] which proposes a provenance-enriched rewriting for debugging and profiling declarative rules. Inspired by these provenance approaches, we introduce our own white-box provenance approach to generate diagnosis proof trees for model-based diagnosis problem. Both approaches in [13] and [16] are not good at generating derivations of rules with negations, whereas our white-box provenance approach works for rules with negations too. White-box and black-box approaches output different products. The idea of inferring one from the other or combining both approaches is proposed in [18,4,10].

A. Bikakis et al. (Eds.): RuleML 2014, LNCS 8620, pp. 127–141, 2014.

We also propose a new hybrid approach which combines the black-box and white-box approaches to obtain diagnoses.

Our white-box provenance approach and hybrid approach can be applied to general model-based diagnosis problems which can be encoded in Datalog rules with negations and aggregates. One interesting application of the new approaches is the inconsistency analysis feature of EULER/X toolkit [6], a toolkit for logic-based taxonomy integration. In EULER/X we use answer set programming (ASP) systems (DLV and Potassco) as underlying reasoners. We implemented the existing black-box approach, our white-box approach, and hybrid approach in EULER/X toolkit and compared them in the benchmarks.

EULER/X. The problem of aligning multiple related biological taxonomies was studied and modeled in monadic first-order logic in the CLEANTAX project [20,19]. A *taxonomy* is a containment (or *isa*) hierarchy with additional taxonomic constraints. The EULER/X toolkit [6], a toolkit for logic-based taxonomy integration, builds on this effort while utilizing additional and more time-efficient logic approaches such as answer set programming [5]. EULER/X further more provides diversified and interactive workflow features leading to the identification and visualization of consistent merged taxonomies. Under this approach an expert initiates the process of aligning two related but different taxonomies (T_1, T_2) by providing a set of articulations A and a set of taxonomic constraints TC.

Jointly these input conditions – T_1, T_2, A, and TC – can generate various and potentially inter-dependent instances of inconsistency; and thus a failure to yield consistent alignments and visualizations. When asserting the initial articulations experts will frequently make mistakes for various reasons; including (1) human error in information entry or transcription, (2) a failure to understand transitive interdependencies among input articulations, (3) incorrect accounting for low-level (child) concepts in relation to parent concepts, (4) unwarranted violations of one or more taxonomy constraints, and (5) other forms of logically inconsistent input. Each kind of error will yield a logically inconsistent alignment, where one input condition is somehow in contradiction with one or more additional conditions. Repair of such errors is needed, however the native ASP reasoner output is virtually unreadable by humans, offering little comprehension why the inputs are inconsistent and what cause the inconsistency. In order to identify and remedy these problems, it is critical to "isolate" local sources of inconsistency that are particularly relevant to facilitating the desired repair action from the global inconsistency phenomenon. To this end the EULER/X toolkit provides a novel *Inconsistency Analysis* feature which motivates the investigation of different diagnosis approaches.

Contributions. This paper proposes a new hybrid diagnosis approach combining black-box and white-box reasoning. Our white-box provenance approach records the provenance of rules with or without aggregates. We have implemented different black-box, white-box, and mixed approaches for generating diagnoses, and diagnosis proof trees in the application of EULER/X toolkit using ASP systems for constraint solving and reasoning. We also show in the benchmarks that our hybrid approach runs much faster comparing to the existing best black-box approach of hitting set algorithm for generating all diagnoses.

2 Background

A *system* is a pair (SD, C) where the *system description* SD is a set of fixed sentences (assumed to be true), and C is a set of *constraints* (which the user wants to be true, but which might be inconsistent with SD). $C_0 \subseteq C$ is called a *Minimal Inconsistent Subset (MIS)* of (SD, C) if (i) $SD \cup C_0$ is inconsistent and $SD \cup C'$ is consistent for any proper subset $C' \subsetneq C_0$. Conversely, $C_0 \subseteq C$ is called a *Maximal Consistent Subset (MCS)* of C if $SD \cup C_0$ is consistent and there is no other consistent C_1 with $C_0 \subsetneq C_1 \subseteq C$. We denote by $\mathcal{MIS}$ and $\mathcal{MCS}$ the set of all *MIS* and all *MCS*, respectively.[1]

Given a set C with n constraints, one can use "brute force" and find all diagnoses by checking the consistency of all 2^n subsets and prune the non-minimal ones. Often it is unnecessary to check *all* combinations. For example, if we know a combination S is inconsistent, then any superset of S is inconsistent as well, so we don't need to check those supersets. One the other hand, any subset of a consistent set is also consistent:

Fact 1. *If a set of constraints is unsatisfiable in the system, any of its superset is unsatisfiable.*

Fact 2. *If a set of constraints is satisfiable in the system, all its subsets are satisfiable.*

Actually, most of the existing black-box diagnosis approaches use these two facts. In the next section, we will recap the best black-box approach [14] we know of which is a hybrid of Logarithmic Extraction Algorithm [2] and combined with Hitting Set (HST) Algorithm in [15].

3 Black-Box Approaches

We will first look at a black-box approach for generating all diagnoses – Horridge's approach [14] which uses Logarithmic Extraction Algorithm [2] as a subroutine in the HST algorithm. Logarithmic Extraction Algorithm is to compute one single *MIS* which is shown in Algorithm 1.

In Algorithm 1, depending on how we split F in line 3 of Function-1R, the time complexity of this algorithm is different. In general, we split F by half and half. As the name of this algorithm suggests, it calls isInconsistent $log\ n$ times on average. In the worst case (we always go to line 8 and 9 in Function-1R), it invokes isInconsistent $O(n)$ times. We have Lemma 1 which originates from [17] and is crucial for the idea of computing all *MIS*.

Lemma 1. *Denote by $\mathcal{MIS}(SD, C)$ all the MIS, and assume $S = \{s_1, s_2, \ldots, s_t\}$ is a MIS, we have $\mathcal{MIS}(SD, C) = \bigcup_{1 \leq i \leq t} \mathcal{MIS}(SD, C \backslash \{s_i\})$.*

By this lemma, we get an algorithm to compute all *MIS*. However, it is inefficient if we don't remember what has been computed and what has not since we are

---

[1] *MIS* are also known as *diagnosis* [17], *justification* [14], *minimal conflict sets* [8], and *minimal unsatisfiable set* [3]; *MCS* are a.k.a. *maximal satisfiable set* [3].

Algorithm 1. Logarithmic Extraction

Input: System description SD, a set of constraints C
Output: One single diagnosis (MIS)

Function-1 ComputeSingleMIS(SD, C)
1: **return** *ComputeSingleMIS(SD, $\emptyset$, C)*

Function-1R ComputeSingleMIS(SD, S, F)
1: **if** $|F| = 1$ **then**
2:     **return** F
3: $S_L, S_R \leftarrow$ *split(F)*
4: **if** isInconsistent($S \cup S_L$) **then**
5:     **return** *ComputeSingleMIS(SD, S, S_L)*
6: **if** isInconsistent($S \cup S_R$) **then**
7:     **return** *ComputeSingleMIS(SD, S, S_R)*
8: $S'_L \leftarrow$ *ComputeSingleMIS(SD, S $\cup$ S_R, S_L)*
9: $S'_R \leftarrow$ *ComputeSingleMIS(SD, S $\cup$ S'_L, S_R)*
10: **return** $S'_L \cup S'_R$

---

likely to recompute something. For instance, to get $MIS(SD, C \backslash \{c_1\})$, we may compute $MIS(SD, C \backslash \{c_1, c_2\})$ which may be already computed when getting $MIS(SD, C \backslash \{c_2\})$. We definitely need some caching optimization to avoid such a case. $\{c_1, c_2\}$ is called *path* when we compute $MIS(SD, C \backslash \{c_1, c_2\})$. HST algorithm [15] which we show in Algorithm 2 records all the *paths* it has already visited (i.e. argument *allpaths* in ComputeAllMISHST), and will not visit them again.

In the worst case, ComputeAllMIS calls ComputeSingleMIS for $\Theta(2^n)$ times. Horridge et al. [14] proposed a mixed algorithm of HST algorithm [17] and Logrithmic extractraction algorithm [2] to generate MIS, i.e., Algorithm 1 is a subroutine used in the Algorithm 2 to compute one single MIS. This gives us the worst case time complexity of $O(2^n) * O(n) * R(n) = O(n * 2^n) * R(n)$ where $R(n)$ is the time complexity of isInconsistent. We implement isInconsistent using Answer Set Programming, so $R(n)$ is as hard as Σ_2^P by [9]. Eiter and Gottlob [8] have pointed out the time complexity of computing all diagnoses (i.e. MIS) is *TRANS-ENUM*-complete, which means there is no efficient (polynomial time) algorithm to get MIS unless *TRANS-ENUM* had (but is believed not) a polynomial time algorithm.

4   White-Box Provenance Approach

As mentioned in the last section, the best black-box approach calls isInconsistent a (large) number of times to generate MIS, which seems not quite efficient. isInconsistent routine is usually implemented using the underlying reasoner. Can we get from the reasoner not only the yes/no answer? Can we call the reasoner once to obtain all desired diagnoses?

We consider the diagnosis problem whose isInconsistent is implemented using answer set programming system, and either a system description sentence or a constraint is encoded as Datalog rules (with/without negation/aggregate). Inspired by the ideas of

---

Algorithm 2. ComputeAllMIS (HST Algorithm)

Input: System description SD, a set of constraints C
Output: All diagnoses ($\mathcal{MIS}$)

Function ComputeAllMIS(SD, C)
1: S, curpath, allpaths $\leftarrow \emptyset$
2: $S \leftarrow$ *ComputeAllMISHST(SD, C, S, curpath, allpaths)*
3: **return** S

Function ComputeAllMISHST($SD,C,S,curpath,allpaths$)
1: **for** $path \in allpaths$ **do**
2:     **if** $curpath \supseteq path$ **then**
3:         // Path termination without consistency check
4:         **return** S
5: **if** not isInconsistent(SD, C) **then**
6:     allpaths $\leftarrow$ allpaths $\cup$ {curpath}
7:     **return** S
8: $J \leftarrow \emptyset$
9: **for** $s \in S$ **do**
10:     **if** $s \cap$ curpath $= \emptyset$ **then**
11:         // MIS reuse (saves recomputing a MIS)
12:         $J \leftarrow s$
13: **if** $J = \emptyset$ **then**
14:     $J \leftarrow$ *ComputeSingleMIS(SD, S)*
15: $S \leftarrow S \cup \{J\}$
16: **for** $ax \in J$ **do**
17:     curpath $\leftarrow$ curpath $\cup \{ax\}$
18:     **return** *ComputeAllMISHST(SD, C\\{ax}, S, curpath, allpaths)*

---

provenance semiring [13] and Datalog debugging [16], we propose a white-box provenance approach which rewrites all the Datalog rules, records the derivation of inconsistency which is a boolean expression, and generates an inconsistency proof tree using the boolean expression. The basic idea of recording the derivation of inconsistency is to first rewrite all the rules by adding annotations. For a rule without head (or false is the head), NOK is added as the head which stands for "Not OK", i.e., inconsistency. We show the detailed Datalog rule rewritings as follows.

4.1 Non-aggregate Rule Rewriting

A rule r is *safe* if every variable in r must also occur positively in the body.

1. For any constraint rule with head predicate:

$$r_1 : H_1(\bar{Y}) :- B_1(\bar{X}_1), B_2(\bar{X}_2), \ldots, B_n(\bar{X}_n).$$

We rewrite it by adding annotations for each predicate (including head and body predicates) where P_i is the provenance of $B_i(\bar{X}_i)$ for $1 \leq i \leq n$, and we use $\otimes$ to represent logical and[2]:

$$H_1(\bar{Y}, r_1 \otimes (P_1 \otimes \ldots \otimes P_n)) :- B_1(\bar{X}_1, P_1), B_2(\bar{X}_2, P_2), \ldots, B_n(\bar{X}_n, P_n).$$

2. For any constraint rule without head predicate (i.e., **false** is the head):

$$r_2 : \mathsf{false} :- B_1(\bar{X}_1), B_2(\bar{X}_2), \ldots, B_n(\bar{X}_n).$$

We rewrite it to a constraint with head predicate **NOK** where P_i is the provenance of $B_i(\bar{X}_i)$ for $1 \leq i \leq n$ and **NOK** stands for "Not OK", i.e. inconsistency:

$$\mathsf{NOK}(r_2 \otimes (P_1 \otimes \ldots \otimes P_n)) :- B_1(\bar{X}_1, P_1), B_2(\bar{X}_2, P_2), \ldots, B_n(\bar{X}_n, P_n).$$

We use a trick to get rid of non-safe rules: For any predicate V that has negation in some rules, we add a complement predicate $\tilde{V}$ for V, and add choice rules of "$V(\bar{X}):-$ not $\tilde{V}(\bar{X}), domain(\bar{X})$" and "$\tilde{V}(\bar{X}) :-$ not $V(\bar{X}), domain(\bar{X})$".

4.2   Aggregate Rule Rewriting

Datalog rules in answer set programming could also have aggregates. For example, in DLV, we may have aggregates such as #count. We show the rewriting for constraints with #count.

For a constraint:

$$r_3 : \mathsf{false} :- \#count\{X : V(X), B_1(X, \bar{Y}_2), \ldots, B_n(X, \bar{Y}_n)\} = 0.$$

First we have the complement rule $\tilde{V}$ for V, and add choice rules of "$V(X) :-$ not $\tilde{V}(X), domain(X)$" and "$\tilde{V}(X):-$ not $V(X), domain(X)$". Then we rewrite the constraint to a soft constraint where P_i is the provenance of $B_i(X, \overline{Y_i})$ for $1 \leq i \leq n$ and add two predicates **POK** and **OK** which stand for Possibly OK and OK (i.e. consistency), respectively:

$$\mathsf{POK}(r_3, P_{\tilde{V}} \otimes P_1 \otimes \ldots \otimes P_n) :- \tilde{V}(X, P_{\tilde{V}}),$$
$$B_1(X, \bar{Y}_1, P_1), B_2(X, \bar{Y}_2, P_2), \ldots, B_n(X, \bar{Y}_n, P_n).$$
$$\mathsf{OK}(r_3) :- V(X),$$
$$B_1(X, \bar{Y}_1), B_2(X, \bar{Y}_2), \ldots, B_n(X, \bar{Y}_n).$$
$$\mathsf{NOK}(r_3 \otimes P) :- \mathsf{POK}(r_3, P), \mathsf{not\ OK}(r_3).$$

We only show the rewriting for rules with aggregates of such a format because in this is the only format with aggregate we encounter in our real world application of EULER/X toolkit. Rules of other format can also be rewritten similarly.

---

[2] It is the same as times operator as in provenance semiring [13].

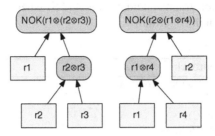

Fig. 1. Example diagnosis proof trees

4.3   Generation of Diagnosis Proof Tree

With the rewritten rules enriched with annotations, one can query answer set programming system all the possible answers for **NOK** and obtain a boolean expression for each possible answer. For instance, suppose the possible answers for **NOK** is

$$\{\mathsf{NOK}(r_1 \otimes (r_2 \otimes r_3)), \mathsf{NOK}(r_2 \otimes (r_1 \otimes r_4))\}$$

The boolean expressions for **NOK** are $r_1 \otimes (r_2 \otimes r_3)$ and $r_2 \otimes (r_1 \otimes r_4)$). For each boolean expression, we construct its boolean expression tree [1] which is a diagnosis proof tree for the inconsistency. We have the two diagnosis proof trees shown in Fig. 1.

A diagnosis proof tree shows how different constraints together lead to the inconsistency. The rule-rewriting based white-box approach is shown in Algorithm 3. We will show an example of diagnosis proof tree in the Application section (Section 6).

Algorithm 3. White-Box Approach

Input: System description *SD*, a set of constraints *C*

Output: All diagnosis proof trees

ComputeAllProofTrees(SD, C):

1: Encode *SD* and *C* in Datalog rules
2: Rewrite Datalog rules to ones with provenance
3: Run ASP reasoner to get boolean expressions for **NOK**
4: Construct diagnosis proof trees using the boolean expressions

---

5   Mixed Black-Box / White-Box Approach

It is hard to compare black-box approaches and white-box provenance approach in the sense that they generate different outputs for model-based diagnosis problem. Black-box approaches generate $\mathcal{MIS}$ whereas white-box approach generates proof trees. Note that the leaf nodes of a proof tree together forms a set of constraints which is either a $\mathcal{MIS}$ or a superset of a $\mathcal{MIS}$. Starting from these constraints, a $\mathcal{MIS}$ may be obtained by running HST algorithm.

We propose the hybrid approach, in which white-box approach serves as a filter to shrink the universe (constraint candidates for $\mathcal{MIS}$) when generating $\mathcal{MIS}$. This hybrid approach is shown in Algorithm 4.

Algorithm 4. Hybrid Approach

Input: System description SD, a set of constraints C
Output: All diagnoses ($\mathcal{MIS}$)

ComputeAllMISHybrid(SD, C):
1:    $Ts \leftarrow$ *ComputeAllProofTrees(SD, C)*
2:    $C' \leftarrow$ set of leaf nodes of the proof trees Ts
3:    **return** *ComputeAllMIS(SD,C')*

If the size of the input constraint set C is large, white-box approach could potentially shrink the constraint set to a much smaller one C' for HST Algorithm and thus reduce the running time of the HST algorithm. In the following sections, we will show the application of different diagnosis algorithms in EULER/Xtoolkit and compare the performance between black-box approach and hybrid approach for generating $\mathcal{MIS}$ in the benchmarks.

Relation Between All These Approaches. We show the relation between different approaches in Fig. 2. A system (SD, C) is the initial input for different diagnosis approaches. We will also show how to compute $\mathcal{MIS}$ / $\mathcal{MCS}$ from each other in Section 6.2.

6   Real World Application – EULER/X

EULER/X [6] is a logic-based toolkit for aligning multiple biological taxonomies. A *taxonomy* is an *isa* hierarchy made up of taxonomic concepts. An *articulation* defines a relation between taxonomic concepts using union ($\cup$) and Region Connection Calculus (RCC-5) relations. RCC-5 includes five basic relationships that compare the extensions of taxonomic concepts: viz. (1) congruence (==), $E_1 == E_2$ meaning that two taxonomic concepts E_1 and E_2 are equivalent; (2) proper inclusion (>), $E_1 > E_2$ meaning that E_1 properly includes E_2; (3) inverse proper inclusion (<), $E_1 < E_2$ meaning that E_1 is properly included in E_2; (4) overlap (><), $E_1 >< E_2$ meaning that E_1 is overlapping with E_2; (5) exclusion (!), $E_1 ! E_2$ meaning that E_1 and E_2 have an empty intersection. Ambiguity can be asserted using the disjunction 'or'. *isa* in the taxonomy can be treated as < or ==. The toolkit ingests the taxonomies (T_1, T_2), a set of articulations [12,11] (A), and takes into account three additional constraints (TC): (1) nonemptiness - a given concept has minimally one representing instance; (2) sibling disjointness - two given child concepts of a parent concept are exclusive of each other; and (3) coverage - a given parent concept is completely circumscribed by the union of its children concepts. The toolkit then generates merged taxonomies.

A taxonomy alignment can be treated as a system (SD, C) where two input taxonomies and taxonomic constraints together are the system description, i.e., $SD =$

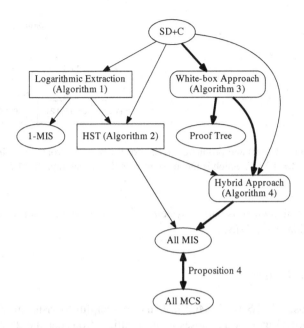

Fig. 2. Relations between different approaches (boxes: existing approaches; rounded boxes: new approaches; bold edges: how our hybrid approach works from end to end)

$T_1 \cup T_2 \cup TC$, and input articulations are the constraints C. As mentioned in Section 1, a taxonomy alignment may yield inconsistent results because articulations may be wrongly asserted by domain experts due to various reasons. To analyze the inconsistency of a taxonomy alignment, EULER/X toolkit applies different diagnosis approaches including black-box approach, white-box approach, and hybrid approach.

6.1 Example

Example 1. Suppose we have two minimal taxonomies as shown on the left in Fig. 3. Taxonomy 1 has three concepts 1.A, 1.B, and 1.C. The concept hierarchy is modeled by the two "is-a" constraints: c_0: "1.B isa 1.A", and c_1: "1.C isa 1.A". We also have a *coverage* constraint c_2: "1.A = 1.B + 1.C"; and a *sibling disjointness* constraint c_3: "1.B disjoint 1.C". Taxonomy 2 has a single concept 2.D. There are three articulations between the taxonomies: c_4: "1.A > 2.D", c_5: "1.B ! 2.D", and c_6: "1.C ! 2.D". By running EULER/X, we find that this alignment is inconsistent.

With HST algorithm, we find that there is only one diagnosis (*MIS*) which is "c_4 : 1.A > 2.D, c_5 : 1.B ! 2.D, c_6 : 1.C ! 2.D". White-box provenance approach generates one proof tree, which is shown as Fig. 3. Domain expert may interpret the proof tree though not that obvious that $c_2 \otimes c_5 \otimes c_6$ means "1.A ! 2.D", and NOK(c_4) means that c_2, c_5, c_6 and c_4 together introduce the inconsistency, i.e., "1.A ! 2.D" and "1.A > 2.D" cannot both hold. The set of leaf nodes of the proof tree is $\{c_2, c_4, c_5, c_6\}$. Since c_2 is a

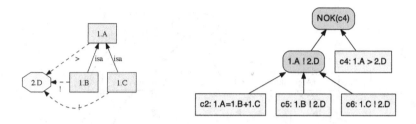

Fig. 3. Input alignment (left) and proof tree (right) for Example 1. From constraints c_2, c_5, and c_6 it follows that "1.A ! 2.D", which is inconsistent with the articulation c4: "1.A > 2.D"

taxonomic constraint which is part of system description, we get a set of $\{c_4, c_5, c_6\}$ as constraint candidates for $\mathcal{MIS}$.

6.2   Diagnostic Lattice

With all diagnoses $\mathcal{MIS}$ (and $\mathcal{MCS}$), it may be helpful to visualize all diagnoses. EULER/X toolkit visualizes diagnoses as in a lattice. Consider the 2^n combinations of n articulations, we can build a lattice where an edge means there is a direct subset relation between the two sets, i.e., there is an edge (A, B) iff $A \subsetneq B$ and $|B - A| = 1$. We call it *Diagnostic Lattice*. For example, the lattices with articulation set size of 2, 3, 4 are shown in Fig. 4.

In the diagnostic lattice, we color a node red if the set of articulations it represents is inconsistent; otherwise, color it green. Recall Fact 1 and 2, which we could call *Inconsistency Propagation* (red edges) and *Consistency Propagation* (green edges), respectively: Any ancestor (superset) of an inconsistent (red) node is also inconsistent; similarly, any descendent (subset) of a consistent (green) node is also consistent. *MIS* is essentially a red node whose parents are green; *MCS* is a green node whose children are red. We color *MIS*, *MCS* solid red, solid green, respectively. We color an edge as dashed red if it applies Red Propagation Rule; color it as dashed green if it applies Green Propagation Rule; color it solid blue if it applies neither of the two rules. For example, we have four articulations $\{a, b, c, d\}$, among which $\{a, b\}$, $\{a, c\}$, and $\{d\}$ are *MIS*, we have the colored lattice in Fig. 5.

Actually we can represent both *MIS* and *MCS* with boolean functions. Using the solid red nodes, we get $\mathsf{NOK}(\{a, b, c, d\}) = (a \wedge b) \vee (a \wedge c) \vee d$. Using the solid green nodes, we get $\mathsf{OK}(\{a, b, c, d\}) = a \vee (b \wedge c)$. We found that $\mathsf{NOK}(\{a, b, c, d\}) = \neg\mathsf{OK}(\{a, b, c, d\})$.

Example 2. Fig. 6 shows a more complex example with 12 articulations, so the number of combinations of articulations (the number of the nodes in lattice) is 2^{12}, which is 4096. By using our lattice approach, we get 5 *MIS* and 7 *MCS* among all 4096 combinations, together with the clusters of other inconsistent or consistent nodes, shown in Fig. 7.

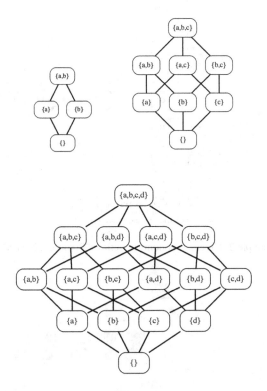

Fig. 4. Lattices with articulation set size of 2, 3, and 4

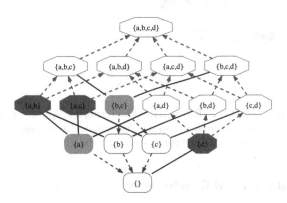

Fig. 5. Diagnostic lattice. (solid red octagon: MIS, solid green rounded box: MCS)

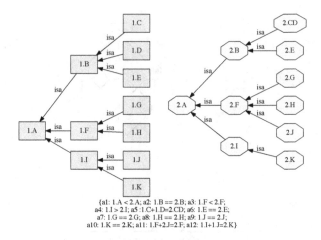

{a1: 1.A < 2.A; a2: 1.B == 2.B; a3: 1.F < 2.F;
a4: 1.I > 2.I; a5 :1.C+1.D=2.CD; a6: 1.E == 2.E;
a7: 1.G == 2.G; a8: 1.H == 2.H; a9: 1.J == 2.J;
a10: 1.K == 2.K; a11: 1.F+2.J=2.F; a12: 1.I+1.J=2.K}

Fig. 6. Input for Example 2 (Green: Taxonomy1, Yellow: Taxonomy2, a1-a12: Articulations)

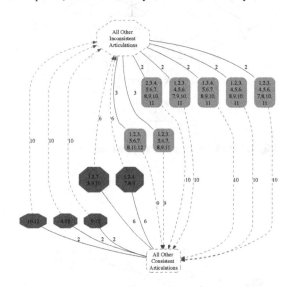

Fig. 7. $\mathcal{MIS}$ (Octagon) and $\mathcal{MCS}$ (Rounded Box) for Example 2. All other non-minimal inconsistent subsets and non-maximal consistent subsets are collapsed as "clouds", the labels of edges show the path length from MIS/MCS to the top/bottom of the lattice.

7   Implementation and Benchmarks

We implemented black-box, white-box, and hybrid approach combining black-box / white-box approaches in EULER/X toolkit[3]. We use different answer set programming engine in our implementation, such as DLV, Potassco. We do benchmarks using both

---

[3] It is an open-source toolkit which can be downloaded in
http://bitbucket.org/eulerx/euler-project

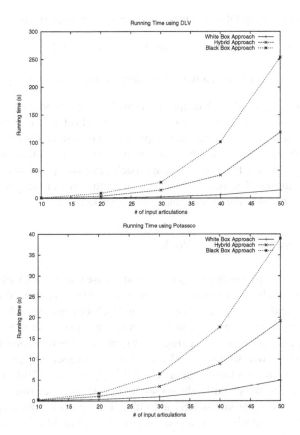

Fig. 8. Average running time using DLV (top) and Potassco (down) as underlying reasoners

real-world and artificial examples on all three approaches, of which white-box approach generates proof trees, the other two generate all diagnoses ($\mathcal{MIS}$). The two approaches we benchmarked to generate $\mathcal{MIS}$ are the Horridge's black-box approach [14] (HST Algorithm with Logarithmic Extraction Algorithm as its subroutine) and the hybrid approach.

We measure in our benchmarks average running time of different approaches using increasingly larger input datasets generated by an artificial inconsistent dataset generator. An artificial dataset includes two isomorphic taxonomies T_1 and T_2 each with n taxonomic concepts and a set of n articulations. Assuming φ is the isomorphism mapping[4] from T_1 to T_2, such that for two taxonomic concepts $T_1.A$ and $T_1.B$ such that $T_1.A$ isa $T_1.B$, we have $\varphi(T_1.A)$ isa $\varphi(T_1.B)$. We say that $T_1.C$ and $\varphi(T_1.C)$ is a *pair*, and these n articulations are between the n pairs. We keep the ratio of problematic articulations to be 10% in the artificial examples. All tests run on an 8-core, 32GB-memory Linux server. The average running time is shown as in Fig. 8.

---

[4] There could be many of such isomorphism mappings, but we only consider one of them.

Fig. 8 shows that using DLV and Potassco as underlying reasoners:

1. White-box approach runs much faster than either hybrid approach or black-box approach;
2. Hybrid approach runs around twice fast compared to black-box approach;

The reason is simple, white-box approach invokes the reasoner only once whereas the other two invokes reasoner multiple times. Also, hybrid approach runs faster than black-box approach because white-box approach significantly shrinks the candidate constraints for inconsistency, which results in the number invocations to reasoner decreases. However, notice that white-box approach generates proof trees and does not generate all diagnoses. The new hybrid approach improves the diagnosis generation significantly compared to the existing black-box approach.

8   Conclusion and Future Work

We discuss different approaches for general model-based diagnosis, including existing black-box approach [14], and new approaches proposed in this paper, white-box provenance approach, and hybrid approach combining black-box and white-box provenance. white-box provenance is a new approach which rewrite answer set programming rules (including safe, non-safe and with aggregates) to generate diagnosis proof trees. Hybrid approach combines both black-box and white-box provenance and generates all diagnoses. We implemented all these approaches in the application of EULER/X toolkit for taxonomy alignment. Benchmarks show that our hybrid approach runs twice as fast as the existing black-box approach of HST algorithm. Future work includes understanding the relation between the white-box diagnosis proof trees and $\mathcal{MIS}$ and optimizing the generation of $\mathcal{MIS}$.

Acknowledgements. We would like to thank the anonymous reviewers for their helpful comments on this paper. This work was supported in part by NSF awards IIS-1118088 and DBI-1147273.

References

1. Andersen, H.R., Hulgaard, H.: Boolean expression diagrams. In: Proceedings of the 12th Annual IEEE Symposium on Logic in Computer Science, LICS 1997, pp. 88–98. IEEE (1997)
2. Baader, F., Suntisrivaraporn, B.: Debugging snomed ct using axiom pinpointing in the description logic $\mathcal{EL}^+$. In: Proceedings of the International Conference on Representing and Sharing Knowledge Using SNOMED (KR-MED 2008). Citeseer, Phoenix (2008)
3. Bailey, J., Stuckey, P.J.: Discovery of minimal unsatisfiable subsets of constraints using hitting set dualization. In: Hermenegildo, M.V., Cabeza, D. (eds.) PADL 2004. LNCS, vol. 3350, pp. 174–186. Springer, Heidelberg (2005)
4. Beckert, B., Gladisch, C.: White-box testing by combining deduction-based specification extraction and black-box testing. In: Gurevich, Y., Meyer, B. (eds.) TAP 2007. LNCS, vol. 4454, pp. 207–216. Springer, Heidelberg (2007)

5. Bonatti, P., Calimeri, F., Leone, N., Ricca, F.: Answer set programming. In: Dovier, A., Pontelli, E. (eds.) 25 Years of Logic Programming. LNCS, vol. 6125, pp. 159–182. Springer, Heidelberg (2010)
6. Chen, M., Yu, S., Franz, N., Bowers, S., Ludäscher, B.: Euler/x: A toolkit for logic-based taxonomy integration. In: 22nd Intl. Workshop on Functional and (Constraint) Logic Programming (WFLP), Kiel, Germany (2013)
7. de la Banda, M.G., Stuckey, P.J., Wazny, J.: Finding all minimal unsatisfiable subsets. In: Proceedings of the 5th ACM SIGPLAN International Conference on Principles and Practice of Declaritive Programming, pp. 32–43. ACM (2003)
8. Eiter, T., Gottlob, G.: Hypergraph transversal computation and related problems in logic and AI. In: Flesca, S., Greco, S., Leone, N., Ianni, G. (eds.) JELIA 2002. LNCS (LNAI), vol. 2424, pp. 549–564. Springer, Heidelberg (2002)
9. Eiter, T., Ianni, G., Krennwallner, T.: Answer set programming: A primer. In: Tessaris, S., Franconi, E., Eiter, T., Gutierrez, C., Handschuh, S., Rousset, M.-C., Schmidt, R.A. (eds.) Reasoning Web. LNCS, vol. 5689, pp. 40–110. Springer, Heidelberg (2009)
10. Engel, C., Hähnle, R.: Generating unit tests from formal proofs. In: Gurevich, Y., Meyer, B. (eds.) TAP 2007. LNCS, vol. 4454, pp. 169–188. Springer, Heidelberg (2007)
11. Franz, N., Chen, M., Yu, S., Bowers, S., Ludäscher, B.: Names are not good enough: reasoning over taxonomic change in the andropogon complex. submitted for publication (2014)
12. Franz, N., Peet, R.: Perspectives: Towards a language for mapping relationships among taxonomic concepts. Systematics and Biodiversity 7(1), 5–20 (2009)
13. Green, T.J., Karvounarakis, G., Tannen, V.: Provenance semirings. In: Proceedings of the Twenty-sixth ACM SIGMOD-SIGACT-SIGART Symposium on Principles of Database Systems, pp. 31–40. ACM (2007)
14. Horridge, M., Parsia, B., Sattler, U.: Explaining inconsistencies in owl ontologies. In: Godo, L., Pugliese, A. (eds.) SUM 2009. LNCS (LNAI), vol. 5785, pp. 124–137. Springer, Heidelberg (2009)
15. Kalyanpur, A., Parsia, B., Horridge, M., Sirin, E.: Finding all justifications of owl dl entailments. In: Aberer, K., et al. (eds.) ASWC 2007 and ISWC 2007. LNCS, vol. 4825, pp. 267–280. Springer, Heidelberg (2007)
16. Köhler, S., Ludäscher, B., Smaragdakis, Y.: Declarative datalog debugging for mere mortals. In: Barceló, P., Pichler, R. (eds.) Datalog 2.0 2012. LNCS, vol. 7494, pp. 111–122. Springer, Heidelberg (2012)
17. Reiter, R.: A theory of diagnosis from first principles. Artificial Intelligence 32(1), 57–95 (1987)
18. Tan, J., Narasimhan, P.: Rams and blacksheep: Inferring white-box application behavior using black-box techniques. Technical report, Technical Report CMU-PDL-08-103. Carnegie Mellon University Parallel Data Laboratory (2008)
19. Thau, D., Bowers, S., Ludäscher, B.: Merging taxonomies under rcc-5 algebraic articulations. In: 2nd International Workshop on Ontologies and Information Systems for the Semantic Web, pp. 47–54. ACM (2008)
20. Thau, D., Ludäscher, B.: Reasoning about taxonomies in first-order logic. Ecological Informatics 2(3), 195–209 (2007)

Multi-valued Argumentation Frameworks

Pierpaolo Dondio

School of Computing, Dublin Institute of Technology,
Kevin Street 2, Dublin 8, Ireland
Pierpaolo.dondio@dit.ie

Abstract. In this paper we explore how the seminal Dung's abstract argumentation framework can be extended to handle arguments containing gradual concepts. We allow arguments to have a degree of truth associated with them and we investigate the degree of truth to which each argument can be considered accepted, rejected and undecided by an abstract argumentation semantics. We propose a truth-compositional recursive computation, and we discuss examples using the major multi-valued logics such as Godel's, Zadeh's and Łukasiewicz's logic. The findings are a contribution in the field of non-monotonic approximate reasoning and they also represent a well-grounded proposal towards the introduction of gradualism in argumentation systems.

Keywords: Abstract Argumentation, multi-valued Logic, Possibility Theory.

1   Introduction

The aim of this paper is to extend the well-studied abstract argumentation framework by Dung [2] to handle arguments containing graded and vague concepts. An abstract argumentation framework is a direct graph where nodes represent arguments and arrows represent the attack relation. These frameworks were introduced to analyse defeasible arguments and study conflict resolution strategies among them. To this end, various semantics have been proposed to identify the set of acceptable arguments. In this work we deal with grounded semantics and we follow the labelling approach proposed in [6], where a semantics assigns to each argument a label in, out or undec, meaning that the argument is considered consistently acceptable, non-acceptable or undecided.

In Dung's original work, arguments are either fully asserted or not asserted at all, and as a consequence abstract argumentation results are often too strict and coarse to support a decision making process.

In quest for an argumentation system able to handle *numbers*, few approaches have been proposed to handle various degree of strengths (such as [7]), or gradualism [1].

Recent approaches [4,5] have tried to marry abstract argumentation and probability calculus. Following a similar conceptual framework, here we investigate how to marry abstract argumentation and multi-valued logic to handle vague arguments. In our framework each argument has a degree of truth associated with it, quantifying to which degree it holds. Our last statement - *arguments hold to a degree of truth* - is at

A. Bikakis et al. (Eds.): RuleML 2014, LNCS 8620, pp. 142–156, 2014.

least problematic. However, there are cases where the structure of arguments is defined in a way that makes it reasonable. In general, an argument can be defined as a construct used in discussions with a support and a claim that is derived from the support. An argument could be an inference rule from a premise (support) to a conclusion (claim). Premises and conclusions could be multi-valued propositions containing graded concepts or fuzzy terms that satisfy a certain state of affairs to a degree. For instance, the rule *"if the tomato is rotten, do not eat it"* can be used as an argument to avoid eating a specific tomato, it has a premise containing the fuzzy term *rotten* and therefore different tomatoes can satisfy the premise of the rule to a different degree.

Arguments containing vague or graded concepts are involved in conflicts, even if the nature of the conflict is not as well defined as in the case of Boolean propositions. As an example of conflict, let us presume that during a legal trial witness A said that *"the murderer was thin"* and witness B said that *"the murderer was tall"*. Suspect S_1 is skinny and suspect S_2 is about 1.9 metres tall.

Two arguments can be put forward based on the available evidence. One, based on witness A's testimony, is against S_1 and the other, based on B's testimony, is against S_2. Each of them is satisfied to a degree. Since both are satisfied, there is an undecided situation to some degree x. However, if S_2 is taller than S_1 is thinner, it could be argued – to a different degree y – that there is an undefeated argument against S_2 only. However, since S_2 is not *completely* tall, we might argue – to another degree z probably less than y and potentially null – that there is a consistent argument against S_1 only. How the degrees x, y, z can be quantified is the aim of this work.

The paper is organized as follows. The next section provides the background definitions for abstract argumentation and multi-valued logic. Sections 3 and 4 describe our computational framework with the required examples, followed by a description of related works in section 6. A conclusion summarises the paper and highlight future works.

2   Abstract Argumentation

2.1   Background Definitions

Definition 1. *An argumentation framework AF is a pair (Ar, R), where Ar is a non-empty finite set whose elements are called arguments and $R \subseteq Ar \times Ar$ a binary relation, called the attack relation. If $(a, b) \in R$ we say that a attacks b in* . Two arguments a, b are **rebuttals** *iff $(a, b) \in R \wedge (b, a) \in R$.*

Definition 2. *(conflict-free). Args is conflict-free iff $\nexists a, b \in Args \mid (a, b) \in R$.*

Definition 3. *(admissible set). Args defends an argument $a \subseteq Ar$ iff $\forall b \in Ar$ such that $(b, a) \in R$, $\exists c \in Args$ such that $(c, b) \in R$.*

The set of arguments defended by $Args$ is denoted $F(Args)$. A set $Args$ is *admissible* if $Args \subseteq F(Args)$ and it is complete if $Args = F(Args)$

An abstract argumentation semantics identifies a set of arguments that can survive the conflicts encoded by the attack relation R. We follow the labelling approach of [6], where a semantics assigns to each argument a label in, out or undec.

Definition 4. *(labelling). Let* $AF = (Ar, R)$. *A labelling is a total function* $L : Ar \rightarrow \{in, out, undec\}$. *We write in(L) for* $\{a \in Ar | L(a) = in\}$, *out(L) for* $\{a \in Ar | L(a) = out\}$, *and undec(L) for* $\{a \in Ar | L(a) = undec\}$.

Definition 5. *(complete labelling, from definition 5 in [6]). Let* (Ar, R) *be an argumentation framework. A complete labelling is a labelling that for every* $a \in Ar$ *holds that:1. if a is labeled in then all attackers of a are labeled out; 2. if all attackers of a are labeled out then a is labeled in; 3. if a is labeled out then a has an attacker labeled in; 4. if a has an attacker labeled in then a is labeled out*

Theorem 1. *(from [6]) Let L be a labelling of argumentation framework* (Ar, R). *It holds that L is a complete labelling iff for each argument* $a \in Ar$ *it holds that: 1. if a is labeled in then all its attackers are labeled out; 2. if a is labeled out then it has at least one attacker that is labeled in; 3. if a is labeled undec then it has at least one attacker that is labeled undec and it does not have an attacker that is labeled in.*

Theorem 2. *(from theorem 6 and 7 in [7]) Given* $AF = (Ar, R)$, *L is the grounded labelling iff L is a complete labelling where undec(L) is maximal (w.r.t. set inclusion) among all complete labellings of AF.*

In figure 1 two argumentation graphs are depicted. Grounded semantics assigns the status of *undec* to all the arguments of the argumentation framework on the left, since it represents the complete labelling with the maximal set, while in the argumentation framework on the right, according to theorem 1, there is only one complete labelling (thus grounded), where argument a is *in* (no attackers), b is *out* and c is *in*. Note how a reinstates c.

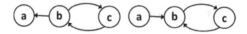

Fig. 1. Two Argumentation Graphs (A) and (B)

2.2   Subgraph Notation and Labelling of Subgraphs of an AF

As explained in section 3, when uncertainty or gradualism is added to arguments it is important to study the behaviour of a semantics over the subgraphs of the starting argumentation graph. Given an argumentation framework $AF = (Ar, R)$ with $|Ar| = n$, and the graph g identified by Ar and R, we consider the set $\mathcal{H}$ of all the subgraphs of g. We focus on particular sets of subgraphs, i.e. elements of $2^{\mathcal{H}}$.

Given $a \in Ar$, we define:

$$A = \{h \in \mathcal{H} \mid a \text{ is a node of } h\} \quad ; \quad \bar{A} = \{h \in \mathcal{H} \mid a \text{ is not a node of } h\}$$

A and $\bar{A}$ are respectively the set of subgraphs where argument a is present and the complementary set of subgraphs where a is not present. If $Ar = \{a_1, .., a_n\}$, a single subgraph g can be expressed by an intersection of n sets A_i or $\overline{A}_i$ ($i \le n$) depending on whether the ith argument a_i is or is not contained in g. A set of subgraphs can be expressed by combining some of the sets $A_1, .., A_n, \overline{A}_1, .., \overline{A}_n$. with the connectives $\{\cup, \cap\}$. We write AB to denote $A \cap B$ and $A + B$ for $A \cup B$. For instance, in figure 1 left the single subgraph with only b and c present is denoted with $\overline{A}BC$, while the expression AB denotes a set of two subgraphs (ABC and $AB\overline{C}$) where arguments a and b are present and the status of c (not in the expression AB) is indifferent.

Given a subgraph $h \in \mathcal{H}$, the labelling of h follows the rules of the chosen semantics. We therefore define a *subgraph labelling* $\mathcal{L}$ as a total function over the Cartesian product of arguments in Ar and subgraphs in $\mathcal{H}$, therefore $\mathcal{L}: Ar \times \mathcal{H} \rightarrow \{in, out, undec\}$. When labelling a subgraph, we follow this choice: an argument a is automatically labelled *out* in all the subgraphs where a is not present (since it does not promote any claim) *or* when it is present but it is labelled *out* by the semantics, representing the effect on a of the other arguments. This is the only sensible choice: if an argument a is not present in a subgraph this means that a does not hold even *isolated*, since in that situation some of its premises are not satisfied. Note how, when an argument is not in the subgraph, it is a situation of perfect knowledge (we know that some of its premises are not satisfied), so it would be incorrect to assign the label *undec* or an *unknown* status to the argument. In order to be labelled *undec*, an argument has to exist and promote a claim first!

In the case of grounded semantics there is only one labelling per subgraph h, that we call $\mathcal{L}(h)$ (we omit Ar). We call $in(\mathcal{L}(h))$, $out(\mathcal{L}(h))$, $undec(\mathcal{L}(h))$ the sets of arguments labelled *in, out, undec* in the labelling $\mathcal{L}(h)$. In order to study how an argument behaves across subgraphs in H, we define these sets of subgraphs:

$$\forall a \in Ar \, (A_{IN} = \{h \in \mathcal{H}: a \in in(\mathcal{L}(h))\}, A_{OUT} = \{h \in \mathcal{H}: a \in out(\mathcal{L}(h))\},$$
$$A_U = \{h \in \mathcal{H}: a \in undec(\mathcal{L}(h))\})$$

i.e. the sets of subgraphs where a is labelled *in, out, undec*.

Example 1. In the graph of figure 1 left, there are 3 arguments and 2^3 subgraphs; argument a is labelled *in* in all the subgraphs where a is present and b is not present (and c becomes irrelevant), i.e. $A_{IN} = A\overline{B}$. It is *undec* when all the arguments are present (the single subgraph $A_U = ABC$) while a is *out* when it is not present or when b is present and c is not present, i.e. $A_{OUT} = \overline{A} + AB\overline{C}$.

2.3   Computing A_{IN}

A brute force algorithm to find A_{IN} (or A_{OUT}) simply computes the grounded semantics in all the subgraphs of Ar and select the subgraphs where the required label of a holds. In [18] we proposed a recursive algorithm to compute A_{IN} under grounded labelling that here we modify[1] to make it suitable to our problem.

---

[1] The original algorithm in [18] generates non-overlapping sets of subgraphs containing *indifferent* arguments, as explained in section 3.

Algorithm 1. A is a node, L a label, P is the list of parent nodes of A.

```
FindSet(A,L,P):
if A in P:
    return empty_set //cycle found
if L = IN:
    if A terminal:
        return a //terminal condition
    else:
        add A to P
        for each child C of A
            Cset = Cset AND FindSet(C,OUT,P)
return (a AND Cset)   // condition 1
if L = OUT:
    if A terminal:
        return NOT(a) //terminal condition
    else
        add A to P
        for each child C of A
    Cset = Cset OR FindSet(C,IN,P)
        return (NOT(a) OR Cset)      // condition 2
```

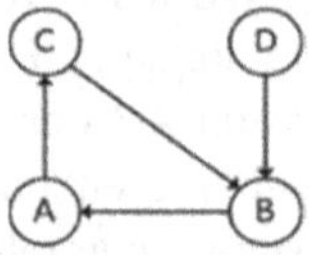

Fig. 2. An argumentation graph

Given a starting argument a and a label $l \in \{in, out\}$, the algorithm traverses the transpose graph (a graph with reversed arrows) from a down to its attackers, propagating the constraints of the grounded labelling. The constraints needed are listed in definition 5 and theorem 1. If argument a – attacked by n arguments x_n – is required to be labeled in, we impose the set A_{IN} to be:

$$A_{IN} = A \left(X_{1_{OUT}} + X_{2_{OUT}} + \cdots + X_{n_{OUT}} \right) \quad \text{(c. 1)}$$

i.e. argument a can be labeled in in the subgraphs where:

1. a is present in the subgraph (i.e. the set A) and
2. all the attacking arguments x_i are out (sets $X_{i_{OUT}}$).

If a is required to be labeled out, the set of subgraphs is:

$$A_{OUT} = \bar{A} + X_{1_{IN}} X_{2_{IN}} \cdots X_{n_{IN}} \quad \text{(c. 2)}$$

i.e. a is labeled out in all the subgraphs where it is not present or at least one of the attackers is labeled in. Thus we recursively traverse the graph, finding the subgraphs that are compatible with the starting label of a. The sets $X_{n_{OUT}}, X_{n_{IN}}$ are found when terminal nodes are reached. When a terminal node x_T is reached the following conditions are applied:

1. if x_T is required to be in then $X_{T_{IN}} = X_T$
2. if node x_T is required to be out then $X_{T_{OUT}} = \overline{X_T}$

The way algorithm 1 treats cycles guarantees that only grounded labellings are identified. If a cycle is detected, the recursion path terminates, returning an empty set that also has the effect of discarding all the sets of subgraphs linked by a logical *AND* (in condition 1) to the cyclic path.

Example 2. Referring to figure 2, *a* is labelled *in* when:

$$A_{IN} = AB_{OUT} = A(\bar{B} + D_{IN} + C_{IN}) = A(\bar{B} + D + CA_{OUT}) = A(\bar{B} + D).$$

Note how CA_{OUT} identifies a cycle and returns the empty set.

2.4   Multi-valued Logic

In the setting of multi-valued logics, the convention prescribing that a proposition is either true or false is changed. A sentence is now not true or false only, but may have a truth degree taken from an ordered scale, called truth space S, such as [0,1]. Multi-valued logic can model situations affected by vagueness, where a statement is satisfied to a certain extend and the concepts discussed are graded. This is usual in natural language when words are modeled by fuzzy sets, such as *tall, young, fast*. We identify a proposition with a fuzzy set and the degree of membership of a state of affairs to this fuzzy set evaluates the degree of fit between the proposition and the state of facts it refers to. This degree of fit is called *degree of truth* of a proposition ϕ. Semantically, a many-valued interpretation I maps each basic proposition ϕ, ψ into [0,1] and is then extended inductively as follows:

$$I(\phi \wedge \psi) = I(\phi) \otimes I(\psi) \quad ; \quad I(\phi \vee \psi) = I(\phi) \oplus I(\psi)$$
$$I(\phi \rightarrow \psi) = I(\phi) \rhd I(\psi) \quad ; \quad I(\bar{\phi}) = \ominus I(\psi)$$

where $\otimes, \oplus, \rhd$ and $\ominus$ are called triangular norms, triangular co-norms, implication functions, and negation functions, which extend the classical Boolean conjunction, disjunction, implication, and negation to the many-valued case. These functions have all to satisfy the following properties: tautology, contradiction, commutativity, associativity and monotonicity, but not all of them satisfy excluded middle ($x \otimes \ominus x = 0$) or double negation ($\ominus\ominus x = x$). We usually distinguish two main logics: Łukasiewicz's and Gödel's logic; the Zadeh's logic is a sublogic of Łukasiewicz's logic. Their operators are shown in table 1. For a comprehensive analysis see [16].

Table 1. Combination functions of various fuzzy logics

	Łukasiewicz's L.	**Gödel's logic**	**Zadeh's logic**
$a \otimes b$	*max* $(a+b-1,0)$	*min* (a,b)	*min* (a,b)
$a \oplus b$	*min* $(a+b,1)$	*max* (a,b)	*max* (a,b)
$a \rhd b$	*min* $(1-a+b,1)$	$\begin{cases} 1 \text{ if } a \leq b \\ b \text{ otherwise} \end{cases}$	*max* $(1-a,b)$
$\ominus a$	$1-a$	$\begin{cases} 1 \text{ if } a = 0 \\ 0 \text{ otherwise} \end{cases}$	$1-a$

3   Gradualism, Vagueness and Abstract Argumentation

Let us presume our argumentation framework includes n arguments and that each argument is an inference rules between propositions of a language. If these propositions are affected by uncertainty or/and vagueness, we are not sure if the claim of the argument can be used in the argumentation process. If the proposition ϕ representing a claim is probabilistic, it can hold or not; if ϕ is vague, it partially holds (and partially not). The consequence is that multiple scenarios of the same argumentation process are possible or should be taken into account, each scenario described by a subset of the original argumentation framework.

The case of probabilistic uncertainty has been recently analyzed in [5] and [4]. In a probabilistic argumentation framework arguments have a probability attached to them, indicating the likelihood of the argument to hold (based on the probability to which its premises are true, or are believed to be true). Since the premises are affected by probabilistic uncertainty, the premises are satisfied (and the claim follows) in a subset of situations with likelihood x, and they are not satisfied in the complementary set of situations (with likelihood $1 - x$). Given an argumentation graph with n arguments, there are 2^n possible situations, each of them identifying a subgraph of the original argumentation graph. Li [4] calls these situations *induced argumentation frameworks*. Each induced framework behaves as an abstract Dung-style framework and it has a probability of existing attached to it, computed using the (joint) probability distribution P defined over the arguments. Given a semantics, the probability of an argument a to be labelled *in* (or *out* or *undec*) is the sum of the probabilities of all the induced frameworks where the chosen semantics produces the required label for a. This computation is referred to in [5] as the *constellation approach*.

In a multi-valued argumentation setting, arguments have a degree of truth attached to them, indicating to which extent their claims are compatible with a state of affair. We therefore assume an underlying model of arguments as inference rules between multi-valued propositions, each proposition with a degree of truth in [0,1]. A support and/or claim of an argument might contain vague or graded terms, and they can therefore have a degree of truth when applied to a specific state of affairs. For instance, I can argue that *"if a tomato is rotten, do not eat it"*. The support and therefore the claim of the argument assumes different degrees of truth when applied to different tomatoes.

If a claim has a degree of truth μ attached to it, this means that the current *state of affairs* satisfies the claim to a certain degree μ but at the same time it also satisfies the negation of the claim with a degree quantified by the negation operator $\ominus$. These values are not referring to two distinct situations – as in the case of probabilistic uncertainty - but they represent degrees of truth attached to two co-existing situations both compatible with the same state of affairs. In a multi-valued setting, an argument always holds partially, *always* because there is no probabilistic uncertainty involved and *partially* because it can be experienced at different degrees. However, at the same time this is also true for the negation of the claim. Going back to the tomato, the tomato is rotten, but maybe *not so rotten* to avoid eating parts of it.

Given n arguments with vague claims, there are again 2^n ways to which the set of arguments can partially satisfy the same state of affairs, each situation with a degree of truth associated. In each situation we consider the degree to which some arguments satisfy the state of affairs and the others do not satisfy it. We start by defining a multi-valued argumentation framework as follows:

Definition 6. *A multi-valued argumentation framework (MVAF) is a tuple $((Ar, R), \mu)$ where (Ar, R) is an abstract argumentation framework and $\mu: Ar \to [0,1]$ assigns a degree of truth to each argument in Ar.*

We write μ_A as a shortcut for $\mu(a)$. Our aim is to find the degree to which an argument a is labelled *in* (or *out* or *undec*), called $\mu_{A_{IN}}$ ($\mu_{A_{OUT}}, \mu_{A_U}$). We stress the crucial difference between μ_A and $\mu_{A_{IN}}$. μ_A is the degree of truth to which the isolated argument a holds, *before* the argumentation process; $\mu_{A_{IN}}$ is the resulting degree of truth of a after having accounted for the effect of the other attacking arguments

3.1   Computing $\mu_{A_{IN}}$

A starting idea simply translates the approach of probabilistic argumentation (the *constellation approach*) to the case of vagueness. This implies to first find all the subgraphs where a is labelled *in*, and then quantify the degree of truth of the resulting disjunction of subgraphs. Each subgraph is a conjunction of vague claims (or their negation) and its degree of truth is the degree to which this conjunction is satisfied by the state of affairs. As an example, let's consider a simple argumentation graph where argument a is attacked by b, and b is attacked by c. The constellation approach finds the following three subgraphs: $A_{IN} = ABC + A\bar{B}C + A\bar{B}\bar{C}$. The recursive algorithm 1 returns the following set: $A_{IN} = AB_{OUT} = A(\bar{B} + C_{IN}) = A(\bar{B} + C) = A\bar{B} + AC$. Note how we could also express the set A_{IN} as $A\bar{B} + ABC$ using disjoint sets. In the probabilistic case all the above expressions are equivalent, but this is not the case for vague arguments and multi-valued logic. For instance, if $\mu_A = 0.8, \mu_B = 0.3, \mu_C = 0.9$, using Zadeh's *max* and *min* operators the *constellation approach* gives a value of 0.3, the recursive algorithm 0.7 and the disjoint set notation 0.8. Which computation should be preferred? Our answer is two-fold.

First, we note how the above expressions of A_{IN} are computed using classical sets operators, that are adequate if a probabilistic measure is used over arguments. However, we are not allowed to further simplify the expression of A_{IN} in case of vague arguments. The claims of the arguments are now multi-valued propositions associated to fuzzy sets, whose operators do not behave as the classical counterparts. Therefore, while the *constellation approach* implicitly assumes the classical set theory and cannot be extended to the multi-valued case, the recursive algorithm 1 could still generate a correct expression for A_{IN} if we do not simplify its output but we stop at $A_{IN} = A(\bar{B} + C)$. For instance, Łukasiewicz strong operators do not satisfy the distributive property and therefore the expression cannot be simplified further.

Second, it is the role of the arguments *indifferent* to the labelling of a. We set this reasonable principle: if an argument status is indifferent to the label of a, why bother considering its degree of truth? If in the probabilistic case the above question is irrelevant (since $p(a) + p(\bar{a}) = 1$), it is not when dealing with vague arguments. Let's consider the *constellation approach* first. Its expression is $A_{IN} = ABC + A\bar{B}C + A\overline{BC}$. In the last two terms, ($A\bar{B}C$ and $A\overline{BC}$), b is not in the subgraphs, c becomes disconnected from a and therefore irrelevant for the labelling of a. Therefore, c's degree of truth should not alter the degree of truth of a. The same happens with the recursive approach using disjoint sets. In the term ABC, why should I consider b? b is labelled *out* and therefore irrelevant for the labelling of a.

We claim that, in order to assess the degree of truth of A_{IN}, the correct expression is the one generated by algorithm 1, i.e. $A_{IN} = A(C + \bar{B})$, where all the arguments indifferent to the labelling of a are removed and multi-valued logic properties are not violated. Algorithm 1 directly maps the definition of complete grounded labelling as found in Caminada [6], its output is independent from the logic employed, and therefore it is correct both for the uncertain case (probabilistic or possibilistic) and the vague one.

We now show that the output of algorithm 1 does not contain *indifferent* arguments. The reasons for an argument b to be indifferent to the grounded labelling of a are the following:

1. b is disconnected from a.
2. b is in the subgraph but labeled *out* (Boella 2009).
3. If n *in*-labeled nodes are attacking an *out* node, only one attacking argument at a time is needed to label a, while the others are indifferent.

Points 1 and 3 are respected by algorithm 1. Disconnected arguments are never considered by algorithm 1 since they are simply not visited by the recursive algorithm, while the disjunction in condition 2 of algorithm 1 guarantees that only one of the attackers is considered in each term. This allows us to stress a key advantage of algorithm 1 compared to the *constellation approach*. While the constellation approach computation fragments the structure of the argumentation graphs in a collection of subgraphs, Algorithm 1 is a path-based traversal of the graph and it preserves the topology of the graph.

Point 2 is also verified by algorithm 1, since the last line of the algorithm (*return NOT(a) OR Cset*) is not considering argument a in its second term (since a is always labelled *out* in that case). Algorithm 1 guarantees to find a set of set subgraphs that is complete [18], i.e. its union covers all the possible subgraphs where a certain labelling of a holds.

We then exploit the fully truth-compositional nature of multi-valued logic operators. Unlike probability or possibility calculus the three multi-valued logic proposed have truth-functional operators, i.e. the degree of truth of an expression is fully determined by the degree of truth of its components. As stressed by Dubois [20], we are allowed to use truth-functional operators as long as we are dealing with gradual properties with no uncertainty involved, otherwise possibility theory has to be applied and the truth-compositional property is lost.

Therefore degrees of truth can be computed during the recursive visit of algorithm1. Degrees of truth of arguments are found when terminal conditions are reached and the values are propagated back to the recursive step and combined with the truth-functional multi-valued logic operators. We use as conjunction, disjunction and negation the operators $\oplus, \otimes, \ominus$ of the multi-valued logic employed, and replacing arguments with their degrees of truth when terminal conditions are met. The truth-compositional property of multi-valued operators makes computing degrees of truth under grounded semantics having the same complexity class as a recursive tree traversal, i.e. a linear complexity proportional to the number of nodes and links, while the constellation approach is obviously of above-polynomial complexity.

Example 3. Let us continue example 2. $\mu_{A_{IN}}$ is:

$$\mu_{A_{IN}} = \mu(A \otimes B_{OUT} \otimes C_{OUT}) = \mu(A \otimes (\overline{B} \oplus E_{IN}) \otimes (\overline{C} \oplus E_{IN})) = \mu(A \otimes (\overline{B} \oplus E) \otimes (\overline{C} \oplus E))$$

Degrees of truth are computed during the recursion exploiting the truth-functionality as follows:

$$\mu_{A_{IN}} = \mu(A \otimes B_{OUT} \otimes C_{OUT}) = \max(\mu_A + \mu((\overline{B} \oplus E_{IN}) \otimes (\overline{C} \oplus E_{IN})) - 1,0) =$$
$$= \max(\mu_A + \max(\mu(\overline{B} \oplus E_{IN}) + \mu(\overline{C} \oplus E_{IN}) - 1,0) - 1,0)) =$$
$$= \max(\mu_A + \max(\min(\mu_{\ominus B} + \mu_E, 1) + \min(\mu_{\ominus C} + \mu_E, 1) - 1,0) - 1,0) =$$
$$= \max(\mu_A + \max(\min(1 - \mu_B + \mu_E, 1) + \min(1 - \mu_C + \mu_E, 1) - 1,0) - 1,0)$$

Using the values of example 3 it is $\mu_{A_{IN}} = 0.3$. The computation seems to consistently use both argumentation semantics and multi-valued logic.

4   Attack, Reinstatement, Accrual and Rebuttals

The following examples illustrate, for all the three logics considered, the behavior of our frameworks w.r.t. fundamental situations that any argumentation framework has to handle, namely attack, reinstatement, accrual of arguments and reinstatement.

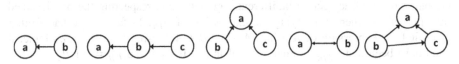

Fig. 3. Argumentation graphs for the examples 4, 5, 6, 7, 8

Example 4 Attack. If argument a is attacked by b, how is the degree of a modified? It is $A_{IN} = A\overline{B}$. Using Zadeh's operators, it is $\mu_{A_{IN}} = \min(\mu_A, 1 - \mu_B)$. In general with Zadeh's operators $\mu_{A_{IN}} < \mu_A$ (degree of truth is diminished), but it remains the same when $\mu_A < 1 - \mu_B$. Therefore, the degree of truth of a could remain unchanged and the attack from b neglected if $\mu_A + \mu_B < 1$. This imposes a minimum degree of truth on the attacker to activate the attack. Note how this finding seems to justify the notion of a threshold for *attack activation* present in [1]. Using Łukasiewicz's logic it is:

$$\mu_{A_{IN}} = \min(\mu_A + 1 - \mu_B - 1,0) = \min(\mu_A - \mu_B, 0) = \begin{cases} \mu_A - \mu_B \ if \ \mu_A > \mu_A \\ 0 \ if \ \mu_A \le \mu_B \end{cases}$$

Therefore a is always diminished, and totally defeated if the degree of the attacker is greater than μ_A. Interestingly, this is the exact behaviour proposed by Pollock [7], whose proposal was not grounded in any multi-valued logic system.

Note how, using Zadeh's *min* operator, an argument can be totally defeated only if $\mu_B = 1$, while using Łukasiewicz's logic it is totally defeated every time $\mu_A \leq \mu_B$.

Finally, Godel's logic negation operator always assigns a null degree of truth to $\mu_{\ominus A}$ if $\mu_A > 0$. In practical terms, this implies removing the negated terms from the output of algorithm 1. This means that, using grounded semantic only one out of the three quantities $\mu_{A_{IN}}, \mu_{A_{OUT}}, \mu_{A_U}$ has a not null value. In the case of b attacking a, it is obviously $\mu_{A_{IN}} = 0$.

Regarding $\mu_{A_{OUT}}$, it is $A_{OUT} = \bar{A} + B$. For Godel's logic the resulting degree is the degree of the attacker B, for Zadeh's logic $\mu_{A_{OUT}}$ remains equal to μ_A iff $1 - \mu_A < \mu_B$ and under Łukasiewicz's logic $\mu_{A_{OUT}} = 1$ (a totally defeated) when $\mu_B \geq \mu_A$.

Example 5. Reinstatement Chain. A chain of 3 arguments helps to reason about reinstatement. It is $A_{IN} = A(\bar{B} + C)$.

Under Godel's logic, only AC has a not null degree of truth and $\mu_{A_{IN}} = \min(\mu_A, \mu_C)$. Thus the argument is fully reinstated if $\mu_C > \mu_A$ or it is reinstated to the degree equal to its defender c.

Using Zadeh's logic, $\mu_{A_{IN}}$ is given by the expression $\min(\mu_A, \max(1 - \mu_B, \mu_C))$. We note that, if $1 - \mu_B > \mu_C$, nothing changes from example 4 and no reinsteitment happens, while, when $1 - \mu_B < \mu_C$, $\mu_{A_{IN}}$ could be increased w.r.t. example 4. Both Zadeh's and Godel's logic fully reinstates a if $\mu_C > \mu_A$. Arguably, when $\mu_C > \mu_A$ the two logic systems neglect the degree of truth of the attacker b.

Using Łukasiewicz's logic a is fully reinstated if $1 - \mu_B + \mu_C > 1$, i.e. $\mu_C > \mu_B$, which seems a reasonable result and again it is the same behaviour as Pollock [7].

The reinstatement example provides evidence in favour of our recursive algorithm and our choices of neglecting indifferent arguments and respecting the multi-valued logic properties when simplifying the expression of A_{IN}. In fact, if we had further simplified the expression of A_{IN} into $A_{IN} = A\bar{B} + AC$, using Łukasiewicz's logic, it could have been that $\mu_{A_{IN}}$ resulted more than μ_A! If $\mu_A = 0.5, \mu_B = 0.1, \mu_C = 0.9$, it is $\mu_{A_{IN}} = \min(\max(0.5 + 0.9 - 1,0) + \max(0.5 + 0.9 - 1,0), 1) = 0.8$! We wonder if the reason why $\mu_{A_{IN}} > \mu_A$ is because we neglected the *out*-labelled argument b in the expression $A_{IN} = A\bar{B} + AC$, and the right expression should be $A_{IN} = A\bar{B} + ABC$ or the *constellation approach* expression $A_{IN} = A\bar{B}\bar{C} + A\bar{B}C + ABC$. Both these two expressions guarantee that $\mu_{A_{IN}} \leq \mu_A$, but their behaviour is still counter-intuitive due to the fact that longer conjunctive expressions are harder to satisfy and the resulting degree of truth decreases rapidly[2]. For instance, if $\mu_A = 0.5, \mu_B = 0.5, \mu_C = 1$ we have $\mu_{A_{IN}} = 0$ (even if a is defended by an argument with the maximum degree of truth, there is no reinstatement).

---

[2] A similar remark was done by Pollock [7] against the use of the product rule of probability in defeasible reasoning.

Example 6. Accrual of attacks. The example clarifies the accrual of attacks. It is $A_{IN} = A\bar{B}\bar{C}$ and $A_{OUT} = \bar{A} + C + B$. Considering A_{OUT}, both Godel's and Zadeh's operators do not accrue arguments, since it is the *max* of the two arguments that is considered, as in Pollock [7]. Arguments accrue with Łukasiewicz's logic, since its disjunction operator does.

Example 7. Rebuttal. In case of two rebuttal arguments, grounded semantics gives $A_U = B_U = AB, A_{IN} = A\bar{B}, B_{IN} = B\bar{A}$. Figure 4 shows the behaviour of the three multi-valued logics discussed. Godel and Zadeh always assign a not null value to the *undec* situation equal to $\mu_{A_U} = \mu_{B_U} = \min(\mu_A, \mu_B)$, while with Łukasiewicz's operators it is $\mu_{A_U} = \max(\mu_A + \mu_B - 1, 0)$, and therefore $\mu_{A_U} > 0$ only when $\mu_A + \mu_B > 1$. Intuitively, using Łukasiewicz, two conflicting arguments can coexist if their degrees of truth are small enough to avoid overlapping.

Regarding $\mu_{A_{IN}}$ and $\mu_{B_{IN}}$, Godel's system assigns a null degree of truth to both; while Zadeh's logic always assigns a not null degree, that has an upper bound in the degree to which the other conflicting argument is negated. Łukasiewicz's logic assigns a not null degree equal to $|\mu_A - \mu_B|$ to the argument with the highest degree, and a null degree to the other. Each of this behaviour seems to fit some but not all the situations where gradual arguments conflict and the author seeks to systematically investigate this issue in the next future work.

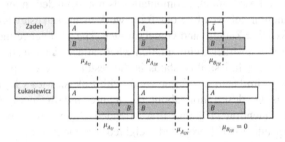

Fig. 4. Rebuttals with different multi-valued logic

Example 8. Multi-valued operators do not always verify the excluded middle principle. This could lead to controversial situations where multi-valued argumentation strongly differs from the classical logic case. Let us consider the argumentation graph in figure 3 (last on the left). If we are using Zadeh's logic, the excluded middle principle is not verified and an argument can be at the same time present and not present in the argumentation process. It is $\mu_{A_{IN}} = \mu(A \otimes B_{OUT} \otimes C_{OUT}) = \mu(A \otimes \bar{B} \otimes (\bar{C} \oplus B))$ $= \mu(A \otimes (\bar{B} \otimes \bar{C} + \bar{B} \otimes B))$ where we applied the distributive property (allowed with Zadeh's logic) to show the presence of the not-null term $\bar{B} \otimes B$.

5   Related Works

Conceptually, our framework is closer to the work done in the context of probabilistic argumentation frameworks. The idea of merging probabilities and abstract argumentation was first presented by Dung [2], and a more detailed formalization was provided by Li [4], along with the works by Hunter [5] and Thimm [12]. [4] introduces the notion of constellation approach. [12] and [5] in his epistemic approach, start from a complementary angle. Both authors assume that there is already an uncertainty measure – potentially not probabilistic – defined on the admissibility set of each argument and they study which properties this uncertainty measure should satisfy in order to be rational. Regarding works that explicitly define fuzzy argumentation systems, we should mention the framework by Janssen [13] where fuzzy labels may be interpreted as fuzzy membership to an extension. However, [13]'s approach differs significantly from ours by the fact that the attack relation that defines the framework is taken to be fuzzy and the conflict-free and admissibility definitions are changed accordingly. In [14] a certitude factor is added to the labels *in*, *out* and *undec* as we do. The work proposes an *equational* approach to abstract argumentation, where arguments degrees have to satisfy a set of properties modelled as equations, properties that might not have any link to a fuzzy logic system. On the contrary, our computation of degrees of truth is a more consistent approach exploiting both argumentation semantics and multi-valued logics.

Regarding other works investigating gradualism in argumentation, we first mention Pollock's work on degrees of justification [7]. Pollock considers the strengths of arguments as cardinal quantities that can be subtracted. The accrual of arguments is denied and it is the argument with the maximum strength that defines the attack. It is interesting to notice how Pollock's computation is not grounded in any logic systems, but his attack function behaves like our framework using Łukasiewicz's logic, while his accrual behaves like Zadeh's and Godel's logics. The vs-defence model, by Cayrol [1], is an extension of abstract argumentation where attacks have a strength associated with them. Argument admissibility status is the result of the comparisons of attack strengths, in a way similar to our frameworks with Łukasiewicz's logic (example 1). However, there is no description about the nature and the computation of such strength. We also mention [10] that first extended Dung's framework introducing different levels of attacks. [9] proposed weighted argument systems, where attacks can have weights, and such weights might have different interpretations: an agent-based priority voting, or a measure of how many premises of the attacked argument are compromised.

6   Conclusions

In this paper we explored how Dung's abstract argumentation framework can be extended to handle arguments affected by vagueness. We studied some basic properties and provided examples using Godel's, Łukasiewicz's and Zadeh's multi-valued logic. The findings are a contribution in the field of approximate reasoning and they also represent a well-grounded proposal towards the introduction of gradualism in argumentation systems. We believe to have provided a novel synthesis between argumentation semantics and gradualism, providing the theoretical foundation of a framework for reasoning under uncertainty that has both the soundness of argumentation semantics w.r.t. the identification of a consistent set of arguments, and the ability to handle gradual and vague properties proper of multi-valued logics.

The present work represents the first theoretical foundation of our framework and it opens numerous opportunities and open issues for future studies.

First, we aim to extend our frameworks to other semantics, starting from *complete* semantics such as *stable* and *preferred*.

Second, this paper presents a limited investigation and discussion on the meaning of gradual arguments and it focuses on theoretical aspects of the frameworks. What does the notion of attack with gradual arguments really mean?

A comprehensive answer requires a more structured definition of arguments and types of attacks. Further studies have to be done in investigating the various multi-value logics proposed here. In particular, the meaning of the degrees of truth computed by each multi-valued logic and which kind of vagueness each logic system is more suitable to model. It seems to the author that none of the systems studied here could reasonably handle all the situations involving vague arguments, but rather each of them captures specific situations.

Finally, work has to be done in investigating how to handle situations in which probabilistic and vague arguments coexist in the same argumentative process.

References

1. Cayrol, C., Lagasquie-Schiex, C.D.: Acceptability semantics accounting for strength of attacks in argumentation. In: 19th ECAI, Lisbon, Portugal, pp. 995–996 (2010)
2. Dung, P.: On the acceptability of arguments and its fundamental role in nonmonotonic reasoning, logic programming and n-person games. Artificial Intelligence 77, 321–357 (1995)
3. Dung, P., Thang, P.: Towards (Probabilistic) Argumentation for Jury-based Dispute Resolution. In: COMMA 2010, pp. 171–182. IOS Press (2010)
4. Li, H., Oren, N., Norman, T.J.: Probabilistic Argumentation Frameworks. In: Modgil, S., Oren, N., Toni, F. (eds.) TAFA 2011. LNCS (LNAI), vol. 7132, pp. 1–16. Springer, Heidelberg (2012)
5. Hunter, A.: A probabilistic approach to modelling uncertain logical arguments. International Journal of Approximate Reasoning (2012)
6. Caminada, M.W.A., Gabbay, D.M.: A logical account of formal argumentation. Studia Logica 93(2-3), 109–145 (2009)
7. Pollock, J.: Defeasible reasoning with variable degrees of justification. Artificial Intelligence 133, 233–282 (2001)
8. Gabbay, M.: Equational approach to argumentation networks. Argument & Computation 3(2-3), 87–142 (2012)
9. Dunne, P.E., Hunter, A., McBurney, P., Parsons, S.: Inconsistency tolerance in weighted argument systems. In: Proc. of AAMAS 2009 (2009)
10. Martinez, D.C., Garcia, A.J.: An abstract argumentation framework with varied-strength attacks. In: Proc. of KR 2008, pp. 135–143 (2008)
11. Vreeswijk, G.: Abstract argumentation systems. Artificial Intelligence 90, 225–279 (1997)
12. Thimm, M.: A Probabilistic Semantics for abstract Argumentation. In: ECAI (2012)
13. Janssen, J.: Fuzzy argumentation frameworks. Information. In: Processing and Management of Uncertainty in Knowledge-based Systems (2008)
14. Gratie, C., Florea, A.M.: Fuzzy labelling for argumentation frameworks. In: McBurney, P., Parsons, S., Rahwan, I. (eds.) ArgMAS 2011. LNCS (LNAI), vol. 7543, pp. 1–8. Springer, Heidelberg (2012)

15. Baroni, P., Romano, M., Toni, F., Aurisicchio, M., Bertanza, G.: Argumentation-Based Approach for Automatic Evaluation of Design Debates. In: Leite, J., Son, T.C., Torroni, P., van der Torre, L., Woltran, S. (eds.) CLIMA XIV 2013. LNCS (LNAI), vol. 8143, pp. 340–356. Springer, Heidelberg (2013)
16. Lukasiewicz, T., Straccia, U.: Managing uncertainty and vagueness in description logics for the semantic web. In: Web Semantics: Science, Services and Agents on the World Wide Web, vol. 6(4), pp. 291–308 (2008)
17. Boella, G., Souhila, K., Van Der Torre, L.: Dynamics in argumentation with single extensions: Attack refinement and the grounded extension. In: Proceedings of The 8th AAMAS Conference (2009)
18. Dondio, P.: Computing the Grounded Semantics in all the Subgraphs of an Argumentation Framework: An Empirical Evaluation. In: Leite, J., Son, T.C., Torroni, P., van der Torre, L., Woltran, S. (eds.) CLIMA XIV 2013. LNCS (LNAI), vol. 8143, pp. 119–137. Springer, Heidelberg (2013)
19. Prade, H., Dubois, D.: What are fuzzy rules and how to use them. Fuzzy Sets Syst. 84, 169–185 (1996)
20. Dubois, Prade, Smeths. Gradual properties vs. uncertainty: Fuzzy logic vs. possibilistic logic, Technical report (2000), retrieved from
http://iridia.ulb.ac.be/~psmets/Gradual_vs_Uncert.pdf

Incomplete and Uncertain Data Handling in Context-Aware Rule-Based Systems with Modified Certainty Factors Algebra*

Szymon Bobek and Grzegorz J. Nalepa

AGH University of Science and Technology
al. Mickiewicza 30, 30-059 Krakow, Poland
{szymon.bobek,gjn}@agh.edu.pl

Abstract. Context-aware systems make use of contextual information to adapt their functionality to current environment state, or user needs and habits. One of the major problems concerning them is the fact, that there is no warranty that the contextual information will be available, nor certain at the time when the reasoning should be performed. This may be due to measurement errors, sensor inaccuracy, or semantic ambiguities of modeled concepts. Several approaches were developed to solve uncertainty in context knowledge bases, including probabilistic reasoning, fuzzy logic, or certainty factors. However, handling uncertainties in highly dynamic, mobile environments still requires more consideration. In this paper we perform comparison of application of different uncertainty modeling approaches to mobile context-aware environments. We also present an exemplary solution based on modified certainty factors algebra and logic-based knowledge representation for solving uncertainties caused by the imprecision of context-providers.

Keywords: context-awareness, mobile devices, knowledge management, uncertainty.

1 Introduction

Context-aware systems aim to make use of context information to allow devices or applications to behave in a context-aware, thus "intelligent" way. The variety of sensors available on mobile devices, and almost unbounded access to the Internet, allows for building more advanced reliable context-aware systems. However, many context-aware systems are based on the assumption that the information they require is always available and certain. In mobile environments these assumption almost never hold.

Contextual data can be delivered to the mobile context-aware system in several different ways: directly from the device sensors [13], from other devices sensors, over peer-to-peer communication channels [2,11], from external data sources like contextual servers [6], from reasoning engines that based on the low-level context and a contextual-model, provide higher-lever context [17]. In each of this cases, the system may experience problems caused by the uncertain contextual information.

---

* The paper is supported by the AGH UST Grant.

A. Bikakis et al. (Eds.): RuleML 2014, LNCS 8620, pp. 157–167, 2014.
© Springer International Publishing Switzerland 2014

Although there are many solutions for uncertainty handling in knowledge bases, there is still little research in the field of mobile context-aware systems. The mobile environment is highly dynamic which requires from the uncertainty handling mechanism to adjust to rapidly changing condition. Probabilistic and machine learning approaches cope very well with most common uncertainties types, but they need time to learn an re-learn. What is more, they use a model that is not understandable for the user, and therefore it cannot be modified by him or her. Fuzzy logic approaches can be used to model uncertainty in an understandable form, but they mainly cope with uncertainty caused by the lack of human precision which is not the primary focus in mobile context-aware system. The aforementioned facts were the main factors why we decided to use rule-based solution for context-based modeling and reasoning. Therefore, the primary objective of the research presented in this paper was to find the best uncertainty handling mechanism that will support rule-based knowledge representation and solve most common uncertainties that are present in mobile context-aware systems.

The rest of the paper is organized as follows. Section 2 presents current state of the art and discusses main drawbacks of available solutions with respect to mobile context-aware systems and presents the motivation for our work. Section 3 describes our approach of applying certainty factor algebra to ALSV(FD) logic. It also tackles the issue of modeling dynamics of certainty factors. A simple use case scenario is presented in Section 4 and summary and possible future work was included in Section 5.

2   Related Work and Motivation

Uncertainty of data may be defined in different ways and can be caused by various different factors. However, we can distinguish three general types of uncertainties [19]:

1. Uncertainty due to lack of knowledge – that comes from incomplete information both at the model level or if the information is not provided by the sensors,
2. Uncertainty due to lack of semantic precision – that may appear due to semantic mismatch in the notion of the information,
3. Uncertainty due to or lack of machine precision – which covers machine sensors imprecision and ambiguity. Although the lack of machine precision may also be caused by erroneous sensors readings, this type of uncertainty is beyond the scope of this classification.

Among many proposals of uncertainty handling mechanisms [21] like Hartley Theory, Shannon Theory, Dempster-Shafer Theory, the following have been found the most successful in the area of context-awareness:

- Probabilistic approaches, mostly based on Bayes theorem, that allows for describing uncertainty caused by the lack of machine precision and lack of knowledge [12,5].
- Fuzzy logic, that provides mechanism for handling uncertainty caused by the lack of human precision [8,22]. It ignores law of excluded middle allowing for imprecise, ambiguous and vague descriptions of knowledge.
- Certainty factors (CF), that describe both uncertainties due to lack of knowledge and lack of precision [9,1]. They are mostly used in expert systems that rely on the rule-based knowledge representation.

- Machine learning approaches, that use data driven rather than model driven approach for reasoning [14]. They allow for handling both uncertainties due to lack of knowledge and lack of precision.

Methods presented above provide different capabilities of representing and handling diverse types of uncertainties listed at the begining of the section. They also require different implementation effort. The comparison of uncertainty handling mechanisms with respect to these criteria was presented in Table 1.

Machine learning approaches deal very well with uncertainties caused by the lack of knowledge and imprecise measurements, as they provide high generalization features, which allows them to make correct decisions on previously unseen data. Probabilistic methods provide handling mechanisms that best fits uncertainties caused by the lack of precision and ambiguity, as they can express vague information in terms of probability. It allows to project the uncertainty to the output and value it with respect to the probability. However, implementation effort of both probabilistic and machine learning approaches is rather high. What is more, the model cannot be directly modified by the user, as it requires expert knowledge in probability theory and machine learning.

Fuzzy logic allows for imprecise, ambiguous and vague descriptions of knowledge. This is very often source of uncertainties caused by the lack of human precision as human operates on concepts that semantic notion is vague as "tall", "small", etc. Although this type of uncertainty is also present in context-aware systems, it is beyond the scope of this paper.

Certainty factors are able to describe both uncertainties related to lack of knowledge, and related to lack of machine precision, which are the most common uncertainties in context-aware systems. One of the main advantages of certainty factors over other uncertainty handling mechanisms is that they can be easily incorporated into existing rule-based system without the necessity of redesigning or remodeling knowledge base. They also require a very low implementation effort.

Table 1. Comparison of uncertainty handling mechanisms. Full circles represent full support, whereas empty circles represent low or no support.

	Uncertainty source			
	Lack of knowledge	Semantic imprecision	Machine imprecision	Implementation effort
Probabilistic	◑	○	●	High
Fuzzy Logic	○	◑	◑	Medium
Certainty Factors	◑	○	●	Low
Machine learning	●	○	●	High

From the comparison presented in the Table 1 we choose certainty factors as the best method for modeling most common uncertainty in mobile context-aware systems that are: uncertainty due to lack of knowledge and lack of precision. Certainty factors cope well with these uncertainties and are easy to design and implement. What is more, together with rules they can be easily understood and modified by the user, which is one of the most important features in nowadays user-centric intelligible systems. Therefore the primary motivation for this work was to incorporate modified certainty factor algebra into a logic-based knowledge representation called XTT2 in a way that fits best the mobile environment requirements. These are defined as: ability to adapt to dynamically changing context and ability for handling uncertainties caused by the lack of knowledge and lack of precision. We decided to use XTT2 rule-based knowledge representation [15], as it is used by the HeaRTDroid – a prototype of a lightweight rule inference engine dedicated for mobile devices [16]. These required us to 1) incorporate certainty factors handling in ALSV(FD) logic which is the foundation of rule representation used in XTT2, 2) provide dynamic adaptation of certainty factors, both at the ALSV(FD) formulae level and on the rule representation level, 3) propose inference strategy that will allow for making decisions under uncertainty. The following sections describe in details the results of our research.

3   Applying Certainty Factors to ALSV(FD) Logic

Certainty factors (CF) are one of the most popular methods for handling uncertainty in rule-based expert systems. However, for a long time they were under strong criticism regarding lack of theoretical background and the assumption of independence of conditions for rules of the same conclusion which not always hold [10]. As a response to these, the Stanford Modified Certainty Factors Algebra was proposed [20]. It accommodated two types of rules with the same conclusion: cumulative rules (with independent list of conditions) and disjunctive rules (with dependent list of conditions). As it will be shown in this section, this makes the certainty factors fit ALSV(FD) logic *generalised* and *simple* attributes.

The basic elements of the language of Attribute Logic with Set Values over Finite Domains (ALSV(FD) for short) are attribute names and attribute values. There are two attributes types: *simple* which allows the attribute to take a single value at a time, and *generalized* that allows the attribute to take set values. The values that every attribute can take are limited by their domains. For the purpose of further discussion let's assume that: A_i represents some arbitrarily chosen attribute, D_i is a domain of this attribute, and V_i represents a subset of values from domain D_i, where $d_i \in V_i$. Therefore we can define a valid ALSV(FD) formula as $A_i \propto d_i$ for simple attributes, where $\propto$ is one of the operators from set $=, \neq, \in, \notin$ and $A_i \propto V_i$ for generalized attributes, where $\propto$ is one of the operators from set $=, \neq, \sim, \not\sim, \subset, \supset$.

3.1   Certainty Factors Algebra

Rule in CF algebra is represented according to formula:

$$condition_1 \wedge condition_2 \wedge \ldots \wedge condition_k \rightarrow conclusion \tag{1}$$

Each of the elements of the formulae from equation (1) can have assigned a certainty factor $cf(element) \in [-1; 1]$ where 1 means that the element is absolutely true; 0 denotes element about which nothing can be said with any degree of certainty; -1

denotes an element, which is absolutely false. The CF of the conditional part of a rule is determined by the formulae:

$$cf(condition_1 \wedge \ldots \wedge condition_k) = \min_{i \in 1 \ldots k} cf(condition_i)$$

The CF of conclusion C of a single i-th rule is calculated according to a formula:

$$cf_i(C) = cf(condition_1 \wedge \ldots \wedge condition_k) * cf(rule) \tag{2}$$

The $cf(rule)$ defines a certainty of a rule which is a measure of the extent, to which the rule is considered to be true. It is instantiated by the rule designer, or it comes from a learning algorithm (like for instance an association rule mining algorithms). Major departure from the traditional Stanford Certainty Factor Algebra [4] is an attempt to remove the major objection raised against it concerning conditional dependency of rules with the same conclusions. To address this issue, rules with the same conclusions were divided into two groups: *cumulative* ans *disjunctive*. Cumulative rules have the same conclusions and have independent conditions (i.e. value of any of the conditions does not determine values of other rules conditions). The formula for calculating the certainty factor of the combination of two cumulative rules is given in (3).

$$cf(C) = \begin{cases} cf_i(C) + cf_j(C) - cf_i(C) * cf_j(C) & \text{if } cf_i(C) \geq 0, cf_j(C) \geq 0 \\ cf_i(C) + cf_j(C) + cf_i(C) * cf_j(C) & \text{if } cf_i(C) \leq 0, cf_j(C) \leq 0 \\ \frac{cf_i(C) + cf_j(C)}{1 - \min\{|cf_i(C)|, |cf_j(C)|\}} & \text{if } cf_i(C)cf_j(C) \notin \{-1, 0\} \end{cases} \tag{3}$$

Disjunctive rules have the same conclusions but are conditionally dependent (i.e. value of any of the conditions determine values of other rules conditions).

The equation for calculating certainty factor of a disjunctive rule is presented in (4).

$$cf(C) = \max_{i \in 1 \ldots k} \{cf_i(C)\} \tag{4}$$

The calculation of the CF for the rules are performed incrementally. This means that for instance for a pair of rules $i - th$ and $i - th + 1$, there is calculated certainty factor $cf_k(C)$ that later is taken into the equation (3) or (4) together with rule $i - th + 2$ to calculate $cf_{k+1}(C)$.

3.2 Certainty Factors in ALSV(FD) Formulae

Every ALSV(FD) formula is a logical expression that can be either true or false according to a value of an attribute in consideration. We can therefore translate every ALSV(FD) formula as a conjunction or alternative of equality formulae. In particular the formula $A_i \in V_i$ can be translated into a form:

$$(A_i = V_i^0) \vee (A_i = V_i^1) \vee \ldots \vee (A_i = V_i^k) \tag{5}$$

where the V_i^k is a k-th element from a subset V_i of domain D_i, and A_i is a simple attribute. On the other hand, for the general attributes A_i, the formulae of a form $A_i \sim V_i$ can be translated into:

$$(A_i^0 \in V_i) \vee (A_i^1 \in V_i) \vee \ldots \vee (A_i^k \in V_i) \tag{6}$$

where A_i^k is a k-th element of a set representing by the general attribute A_i. This formula can be further recursively rewritten as a conjunction of formulaes from equation (5).

Similarly we can continue for every formula in the ALSV(FD) logic. Such a notation allows us to use certainty factors algebra for evaluating the formulae for uncertain attributes values, treating these formulae as a set of cumulative or disjunctive rules. In particular, we can represent the alternative of equality formulae from equation (5), as a set of logical rules of a form:

$$(A_i = V_i^0) \rightarrow Satisfied$$
$$(A_i = V_i^1) \rightarrow Satisfied$$
$$\ldots$$
$$(A_i = V_i^k) \rightarrow Satisfied \tag{7}$$

Every rule CF is assigned a value 1 for simplicity, so the certainty of a formula is determined by the certainty of conditional expressions on the left hand side. The rules are disjunctive, as the value of A_i can be only one (as it is simple attribute), hence the equation (4) applies to this. On the other hand, rule interpretation of formulae (6) generates a set of cumulative rules, as the attribute A_i can take multiple values that do not depend on each other, and hence the equation (3) applies to this case. Real-life examples of these transformations were given in Section 4.

What is more, when dealing with logic that operates finite domains, the negative certainty factors may be as valuable as the positive ones. Let us consider the example from equation (7). Assuming that $V_i' = D_i \setminus V_i$, we can add additional rule to the equation, that will cover the *false* cases of the ALSV(FD) fromula $A_i \in V_i$:

$$(A_i \neq V_i'^0) \wedge (A_i \neq V_i'^1) \wedge \ldots \wedge (A_i \neq V_i'^l) \rightarrow Satisfied \tag{8}$$

Supposing that we have no positive certainty on the value of attribute A_i, but we know which of the values the attribute does not take for sure, we can notice the dependence below:

$$\left(cf(A_i = V_i'^l) = -1 \right) \Rightarrow \left(cf(A_i \neq V_i'^l) = 1 \right)$$

The formula above can now be applied together with rule from equation (8) to infer the certainty factor of the ALSV(FD) formulae in consideration.

3.3 Modeling the Dynamics of Certainty Factors

In many context-aware systems that operate in highly dynamic environments, once observed data cannot be treated as certain for unlimited period of time. For instance user activity observed five minutes ago, may not be certain right now. Therefore, adding expiration time to attributes values can improve uncertainty handling in case of lack of data. The expiration time may be assigned to the attribute in a form of a function over time that decreases certainty factor of an attribute value. Let us consider the expiration time for a value of attribute A to be defined as $expiration(A)$. The simplest expiration time function may be defined as a linear function, that decreases certainty factor of an attribute value over time down to a zero:

$$cf(V, \Delta t) = \begin{cases} cf(V) * \frac{expiration(A) - \Delta t}{expiration(A)} & \text{if } \Delta t \leq expiration(A) \\ 0 & \text{otherwise} \end{cases}$$

where Δt is a difference between the current time and the time when the value V of the attribute A was observed. Different attribute types may have different expiration time functions assigned. Expiration time may be assigned arbitrarily by the system designer in cases when the attribute expiration time is not influenced by the environment dynamics. In other cases, the expiration time function should be dynamically adjusted with respect to the environment dynamics.

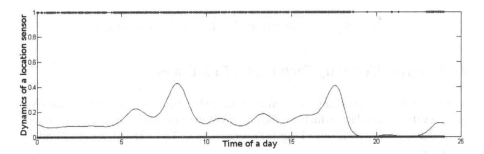

Fig. 1. Dynamics of a location sensor over time [3]

Such a functionality can be achieved with learning middleware approach [3]. Learning middleware is a system that uses linear regression to learn sensors usage patterns from historical data. It automatically generates a model of sensor activity which can be used to dynamically modify the expiration time for the attributes values.

Figure 1 shows the exemplary GPS sensor usage pattern obtained by the learning middleware. The curve describes the probability of the sensor change its reading in particular point of time. We can define this probability as a dynamics of the attribute. Let us consider expiration time for a value of an attribute A to be defined as $expiration(A)$, and the dynamics of an attribute value over time obtained from the learning middleware to be defined as $dynamic(A, t)$, where $dynamic(A, t) \in [0; 1]$. We can now define the dynamic expiration time of an attribute A as

$$expiration(A, t) = expiration(A) * (1 - dynamic(A, t))$$

This will allow to shorten the expiration time in cases where there is a high probability, that the value of the sensor will change, and leave the long expiration time in cases where there is a very low probability that the value of the sensor will change (i.e. location at night).

One of the main disadvantages of the learning middleware is that it needs time and data to learn sensor dynamics. The other approach that allows to discover sensor dynamics is based on the entropy of previous n readings. The entropy is a measure of amount of uncertainty in the data. It can be calculated according to the equation below:

$$entropy(A, n) = -\sum_{x \in X} \frac{x}{n} \log_2 \frac{x}{n}$$

where X is a set of all different readings, and $\frac{x}{n}$ is a proportion of the number of readings such that $A = x$ to total number of readings taken into consideration. Assuming that $n = 4$ and we have following readings from GPS sensor: *still, still, moving, moving*, the entropy of this data equals 1, because we have equal number of *still* and *moving* readings. This is equivalent for high dynamics of data. However, if the readings from the sensor looks as follows *still, still, still, still*, the entropy equals 0, which is an equivalent for low dynamics of data. The expiration dime can be therefore determined according to the equation:

$$expiration(A, n) = expiration(A) * (-log_2 \frac{1}{n} - entropy(A, n))$$

4   Applying Certainty Factors to XTT2 Tables

The certainty factor handling mechanism described in Section 3 operates on the level of ALSV(FD) formulaes, which are foundation of the rule-based knowledge representation called eXtended Tabular Trees [18] version 2 (XTT2 for short). An XTT2 rule is of the form:

$$(condition_1) \wedge (condition_2) \wedge \dots (condition_n) \longrightarrow RHS$$

where $condition_i$ is one of the admissible ALSV(FD) logic formulaes, and RHS is the right-hand side of the rule covering conclusions. In practice the conclusions are restricted to assigning new attribute values, thus changing the system state. Similar rules are grouped within separated tables, and the system is split into such tables linked by arrows representing the control strategy. An example of XTT2 table is presented in Figure 2. It describes a fragment of a context-aware recommendation system, that based on the user activity, weather and user profile suggests nearby points of interests.

(?) weather	(?) {user_profile}	(?) activity	(->) poi
∈ {sunny,cloudy}	~ {eating}	= any	:= outdor-eating
∈ {rainy}	~ {eating}	∈ {walking,running}	:= indoor-eating
∈ {rainy}	~ {eating}	∈ {driving}	:= drivethrough-eating
∈ {rainy,cloudy}	~ {culture,entertainment}	∈ {walking,driving}	:= theatre-cinema
∈ {rainy,cloudy}	= {culture,sighseeing}	∈ {walking,driving}	:= museum
∈ {sunny}	= {sighseeing,culture}	∈ {any}	:= monuments

Table id: tab_2 - Recommendations

Fig. 2. Example of XTT2 table with uncertain data

The system consists of three simple attributes: *weather, activity* and *poi*, and one generalized attribute: *user_profile*. Let consider, that we know that there is going to be *sunny weather* with certainty 0.3, cloudy with 0.1, and rainy with 0.6. The user selected that he is interested in suggestions about places for eating in 60%, culture in 20%, entertainment in 80% and sightseeing in 20%. User may be independently interested in different recommendations, hence the values are trated as disjoint and the sum does not have to be equal 100%. We also have an information from the activity recognition sensor that the user have been recently walking with certainty 0.8, running with 0.1 certainty and driving with certainty 0.1. Having this information we can now calculate certainty factors for every rule conditions. We use equation (4) (disjunctive rules) to simple attributes, and equation (3) (cumulative rules) to generalized attributes.

After calculation we should get the results presented in Table 2. The last column shows the certainty of a conclusion of a rule calculated according to the equation (2). From the calculations we see that we should suggest user either *indoor-eating* places or *theaters and cinemas*, because both have the highest certainty factors. We have no knowledge on which of these two suggestions should have a greater priority, because the certainty factors for all the rules were assigned 1 for simplicity. This however can be changed in the future by taking into consideration user feedback. If the user decides that a better suggestion would be the *theaters and cinema*, the certainty factor of rule producing this conclusion should be increased (if possible) and the certainty factors of remaining rules can be decreased. This will allow the to make better decisions in the future, when the system faces the same or similar situation.

Table 2. The certainty factors for rules presented in figure 2

(?) weather	(?) user_profile	(?) activity	cf(conditions)	cf(rule)	cf(conclusion)
0.3	0.6	0.8	0.3	1	0.3
0.6	0.6	0.8	0.6	1	0.6
0.6	0.6	0.1	0.1	1	0.1
0.6	0.84	0.8	0.6	1	0.6
0.6	0.36	0.8	0.36	1	0.36
0.3	0.36	0.8	0.3	1	0.3

5   Summary and Future Work

In this paper we presented an approach for the uncertainty handling in mobile context-aware environments. We provided comparison of application of different uncertainty modeling approaches to this class of systems and chose one that best fits requirements of such environment. These requirements were defined as ability to adapt to dynamically changing context and ability for handling uncertainties caused by the lack of knowledge and lack of precision. Based on the comparison of capabilities of different uncertainty handling mechanisms we decided to use certainty factors. We provided a solution that allows to bind this formalism with ALSV(FD) logic and XTT2 rule-based representation that are used by the HeaRTDroid inference engine dedicated for mobile platforms. We also described two approaches that allow for automatic adaptation of certainty factors values with respect to dynamically changing context.

As a future work we plan to implement and evaluate the certainty factor based approach described in this paper in HeaRTDroid [1] inference engine. We also plan to use mediation techniques [7] to collect feedback from users and modify certainty factors of XTT2 rules, so they can better fit user preferences. What is more, we would like to compare the approach presented in this paper with a solution that is based on Bayesian networks. Although certainty factors algebra copes very well with uncertainties on the ALSV(FD) level, we believe that it can be successfully replaced by the probabilistic approach on he XTT2 tables level. The XTT2 tables can be interpreted as a tabular conditional probability distributions (CPDs), where the CPDs are learned from statistical analysis of the system performance. The XTT tablesh can be connected to form a graph, which also can be easily translated into Bayesian network without the necessity of redesigning the knowledge base.

References

1. Almeida, A., Lopez-de Ipina, D.: Assessing ambiguity of context data in intelligent environments: Towards a more reliable context managing systems. Sensors 12(4), 4934–4951 (2012)
2. Benerecetti, M., Bouquet, P., Bonifacio, M., Italia, A.A.: Distributed context-aware systems (2001)
3. Bobek, S., Porzycki, K., Nalepa, G.J.: Learning sensors usage patterns in mobile context-aware systems. In: Proceedings of the FedCSIS 2013 Conference, pp. 993–998. IEEE, Krakow (2013)
4. Buchanan, B.G., Shortliffe, E.H.: Rule Based Expert Systems: The Mycin Experiments of the Stanford Heuristic Programming Project. The Addison-Wesley Series in Artificial Intelligence. Addison-Wesley Longman Publishing Co., Inc, Boston (1984)
5. Bui, H.H., Venkatesh, S., West, G.: Tracking and surveillance in wide-area spatial environments using the abstract hidden markov model. Intl. J. of Pattern Rec. and AI 15 (2001)
6. Chen, H., Finin, T.W., Joshi, A.: Semantic web in the context broker architecture. In: PerCom, pp. 277–286. IEEE Computer Society (2004)
7. Dey, A.K., Mankoff, J.: Designing mediation for context-aware applications. ACM Trans. Comput.-Hum. Interact. 12(1), 53–80 (2005)
8. Fenza, G., Furno, D., Loia, V.: Hybrid approach for context-aware service discovery in healthcare domain. J. Comput. Syst. Sci. 78(4), 1232–1247 (2012)
9. Hao, Q., Lu, T.: Context modeling and reasoning based on certainty factor. In: Asia-Pacific Conference on Computational Intelligence and Industrial Applications, PACIIA 2009, vol. 2, pp. 38–41 (November 2009)
10. Heckerman, D.: Probabilistic interpretations for mycin's certainty factors. In: Proceedings of the First Conference Annual Conference on Uncertainty in Artificial Intelligence, UAI 1985, pp. 9–20. AUAI Press, Corvallis (1985)
11. Hu, H.: ContextTorrent: A Context Provisioning Framewrok for Pervasive Applications. University of Hong Kong (2011)
12. van Kasteren, T., Kröse, B.: Bayesian activity recognition in residence for elders. In: 3rd IET International Conference on Intelligent Environments, IE 2007, pp. 209–212 (2007)

---

[1] See http://bitbucket.org/sbobek/heartdroid/overview

13. Kjaer, K.E.: A survey of context-aware middleware. In: Proceedings of the 25th Conference on IASTED International Multi-Conference: Software Engineering, SE 2007, pp. 148–155. ACTA Press (2007)
14. Krause, A., Smailagic, A., Siewiorek, D.P.: Context-aware mobile computing: Learning context-dependent personal preferences from a wearable sensor array. IEEE Transactions on Mobile Computing 5(2), 113–127 (2006)
15. Ligęza, A., Nalepa, G.J.: A study of methodological issues in design and development of rule-based systems: Proposal of a new approach. Wiley Interdisciplinary Reviews: Data Mining and Knowledge Discovery 1(2), 117–137 (2011)
16. Nalepa, G.J., Bobek, S., Ligęza, A., Kaczor, K.: Algorithms for rule inference in modularized rule bases. In: Bassiliades, N., Governatori, G., Paschke, A. (eds.) RuleML 2011 - Europe. LNCS, vol. 6826, pp. 305–312. Springer, Heidelberg (2011)
17. Nalepa, G.J., Bobek, S.: Rule-based solution for context-aware reasoning on mobile devices. Computer Science and Information Systems 11(1), 171–193 (2014)
18. Nalepa, G.J., Ligęza, A., Kaczor, K.: Formalization and modeling of rules using the XTT2 method. International Journal on Artificial Intelligence Tools 20(6), 1107–1125 (2011)
19. Niederliński, A.: rmes, Rule- and Model-Based Expert Systems. Jacek Skalmierski Computer Studio (2008)
20. Parsaye, K., Chignell, M.: Expert systems for experts / Kamran Parsaye, Mark Chignell. Wiley, New York (1988)
21. Parsons, S., Hunter, A.: A review of uncertainty handling formalisms. In: Hunter, A., Parsons, S. (eds.) Applications of Uncertainty Formalisms. LNCS (LNAI), vol. 1455, pp. 8–37. Springer, Heidelberg (1998)
22. Yuan, B., Herbert, J.: Fuzzy cara - a fuzzy-based context reasoning system for pervasive healthcare. Procedia CS 10, 357–365 (2012)

The Hardness of Revising Defeasible Preferences

Guido Governatori[1,3,4], Francesco Olivieri[1,2,3], Simone Scannapieco[1,2,3],
and Matteo Cristani[2]

[1] NICTA, Queensland Research Laboratory, Australia*
[2] Department of Computer Science, University of Verona, Italy
[3] Institute for Integrated and Intelligent Systems, Griffith University, Australia
[4] Queensland University of Technology, Australia

Abstract. Non-monotonic reasoning typically deals with three kinds of knowledge. *Facts* are meant to describe immutable statements of the environment. *Rules* define relationships among elements. Lastly, an ordering among the rules, in the form of a *superiority relation*, establishes the relative strength of rules. To revise a non-monotonic theory, we can change either one of these three elements. We prove that the problem of revising a non-monotonic theory by only changing the superiority relation is a NP-complete problem.

1 Introduction

Preferences are a powerful tool agents use to make decisions. Given a knowledge base, agents are able to set an (partial) ordering among the elements of such a base by stating that they prefer an element better than another.

The number of possible applications of preferences is vast. Given a goal and a set of actions, an agent can choose a particular course of action instead of another in order to achieve the goal. Even in many legal contexts, where the agent typically has neither the power to change the normative system, nor to decide what norms are effective, the agent may argue that one norm applies instead of another. This case is peculiar: we have two norms (rules) stating opposite conclusions, but the apparent conflict can be solved through the preference mechanism.

Through the years, non-monotonic reasoning has been advanced for reasoning with partial, and possibly conflicting information. Settled in the context of logics representing non-monotonic reasoning, we usually deal with three types of knowledge. First, we have *facts*. Facts are meant to describe simple pieces of information which are considered to be always true in the environment the agent acts in. Then we have *rules*. A rule describes how given elements interact with each other in order to obtain some conclusions. Lastly, we have a mechanism to solve conflicts (we assume to work within a skeptical system). Typically, this is presented in the form of a binary relation among pairs of rules. Such a *superiority* (or *preference*) *relation* states a (partial) ordering among the rules: when two rules for opposite conclusions are "applicable" at the same time, the superiority relation solves the conflict in favour of one conclusion upon the other. In fact, the superiority relation expresses more than that; it actually reflects preferences of

---

* NICTA is funded by the Australian Government as represented by the Department of Communications and the Australian Research Council through the ICT Centre of Excellence program.

A. Bikakis et al. (Eds.): RuleML 2014, LNCS 8620, pp. 168–177, 2014.

the agent on the inner structure of the theory, becoming a fundamental mechanism in many real life scenarios. In this paper we use Defeasible Logic, as presented in [4], to formally encode facts, rules and the superiority relation.

Naturally, there is more. The information at hand may change and when this happens, we need to revise our knowledge base or theory. Much work has been done to understand either how to properly change a theory, or which conditions the "new theory" should meet. When updating the knowledge base of a defeasible theory, revising operators may act on either one of the three constitutive elements, being that the facts, the rules [1], the superiority relation, or a combination of those.

Revising facts can be seen as changing the operational environment, or just simply examining a different factual scenario on which rules and the superiority relation are applied to. In a legal proceedings this corresponds to change the evidence of the case. Changing rules expresses the ability in adding and/or removing the dependencies among the atoms of the theory. In a legal setting this means to create, delete or modify some norms. Finally, there are some contexts where the above two approaches are not possible and the only solution left is to change the relative strength between pairs of rules. Always referring to legal systems, this may be the case in situations like that of an average citizen appealing to a court. He has no power to change the Law, and has no power on what norms are effective in the jurisdiction he is situated in. These powers instead are reserved to persons, entities and institutions specifically designated to do so, for example the parliament and, under some given constraints, also by judges (in Common Law juridical system, especially). However, a citizen can argue that one norm takes precedence over another in a specific case. This amounts to saying that one norm is to be preferred to the other in the case.

The main results of the present paper come from a thorough investigation on revising a defeasible theory where only changing the superiority relation is allowed. [2,3] study "patterns", or conditions, on the elements of a defeasible theory that would distinguish situations where a revision is possible, against situations where it is not. Scope of this investigation is to make a step further. We prove that the problem of revising a theory by only changing the superiority relation is NP-complete.

The structure of the paper is as follows. In Section 2 we recall the basics of Defeasible Logic and we introduce the notion of what means for a formula to be "tautological" in the context of revision in Defeasible Logic, where revision operations are limited to the superiority relation. In Section 3 we formally set up the decision problem related to the type of revision we are interested in this paper. We conclude the paper in Section 4 with a summary and a discussion of some related work and possible future work.

2 Defeasible Logic

We shall describe the structure of a defeasible theory, and proceed by reporting definitions of a theory *based on a specific set of rules*, of a theory being *decisive* (along with two preliminary results), and of a literal being *tautological*. Admittedly, this section is dense but such are the necessary means to prove the NP-completeness result of the next section.

A defeasible theory consists of five different kinds of knowledge: facts, strict rules, defeasible rules, defeaters, and a superiority relation [4].

Let PROP be a set of propositional atoms, Lbl be a set of arbitrary labels. The set $Lit = PROP \cup \{\neg p | p \in PROP\}$ denotes the set of *literals*. The *complement* of a literal q is denoted by $\sim q$; if q is a positive literal p, then $\sim q$ is $\neg p$, and if q is a negative literal $\neg p$ then $\sim q$ is p.

Definition 1. *A defeasible theory D is a structure $(F, R, >)$, where*

1. *$F \subseteq Lit$ denote simple pieces of information that are considered always to be true. For example, a fact is that "Sylvester is a cat", formally cat(Sylvester);*
2. *R contains three types of* rules: *strict rules, defeasible rules, and defeaters.*
3. *$> \subseteq R \times R$ is a binary relation whose transitive closure is acyclic.*

A theory is finite *if the set of facts and rules are finite.*

A *rule* is an expression $r : A(r) \hookrightarrow C(r)$ and consists of: (i) A unique name $r \in$ Lbl, (ii) the *antecedent* $A(r)$ which is a finite subset of Lit, (iii) an *arrow* $\hookrightarrow \in \{\rightarrow, \Rightarrow, \leadsto\}$ denoting, respectively, a strict rule, a defeasible rule and a defeater, and (iv) its *consequent* (or *head*) $C(r) \in Lit$, which is a single literal. A *strict rule* is a rule in which whenever the premises are indisputable (e.g., facts), then so is the conclusion. For example,

$$cat(X) \rightarrow mammal(X)$$

means that "every cat is a mammal". On the other hand, a *defeasible rule* is a rule that can be defeated by contrary evidence; for example, "cats typically eat birds":

$$cat(X) \Rightarrow eatBirds(X).$$

The underlying idea is that if we know that something is a cat, then we may conclude that it eats birds, unless there is evidence proving otherwise. *Defeaters* are rules that cannot be used to draw any conclusion. Their only use is to prevent some conclusions, i.e., to defeat defeasible rules by producing evidence to the contrary. An example is "if a cat has just fed itself, then it might not eat birds":

$$justFed(X) \leadsto \neg eatBirds(X).$$

The *superiority relation* $>$ among rules is used to define where one rule may override the (opposite) conclusion of another one, e.g., given the defeasible rules

$$r : cat(X) \Rightarrow eatBirds(X)$$
$$r' : domesticCat(X) \Rightarrow \neg eatBirds(X)$$

which would contradict one another if Sylvester is both a cat and a domestic cat, they do not in fact contradict if we state that r' wins against r, leading to conclude that Sylvester does not to eat birds.

Like in [4], we consider only a propositional version of this logic, and we do not take into account function symbols. Every expression with variables represents the finite set of its variable-free instances.

We use the infix notation $r > s$ to mean that $(r, s) \in >$. The set of strict rules in R is denoted by R_s, and the set of strict and defeasible rules by R_{sd}. We name $R[q]$ the set of rules in R whose head is q. A *conclusion* of D is a tagged literal and can have one of the following forms:

- $+\Delta q$, which means that q is definitely provable in D, i.e., there is a definite proof for q, that is a proof using facts, and strict rules only;
- $-\Delta q$, which means that q is definitely not provable, or refuted, in D (i.e., a definite proof for q does not exist);
- $+\partial q$, which means that q is defeasibly provable in D;
- $-\partial q$, which means that q is not defeasibly provable, or refuted, in D.

Given a defeasible theory D, a proof P of length n in D is a finite sequence $P(1),\dots,P(n)$ of tagged literals of the type $+\Delta q$, $-\Delta q$, $+\partial q$ and $-\partial q$, where the proof conditions defined in the rest of this section hold. $P(1..n)$ denotes the first n steps of proof P.

Given $\# \in \{\Delta, \partial\}$ and a proof P in D, a literal q is #-*provable* in D if there is a line $P(m)$ of P such that $P(m) = +\#q$. A literal q is #-*refuted* in D if there is a line $P(m)$ of P such that $P(m) = -\#q$.

The definition of Δ describes just forward chaining of strict rules.

$$+\Delta\text{: If } P(n+1) = +\Delta q \text{ then}$$
$$(1)\ q \in F \text{ or}$$
$$(2)\ \exists r \in R_s[q] \forall a \in A(r) : +\Delta a \in P(1..n).$$

Literal q is definitely provable if either (1) is a fact, or (2) there is a strict rule for q, whose antecedents have all been definitely proved.

$$-\Delta\text{: If } P(n+1) = -\Delta q \text{ then}$$
$$(1)\ q \notin F \text{ and}$$
$$(2)\ \forall r \in R_s[q] \exists a \in A(r) : -\Delta a \in P(1..n).$$

Literal q cannot be definitely proven ($-\Delta q$) if (1) is not a fact and (2) every strict rule for q has at least one definitely refuted antecedent.

The following definition states notions of being applicable and discarded.

Definition 2. *In the proof condition for* $\pm\partial$, *a rule* $r \in R_{sd}$ *is (i) applicable iff* $\forall a \in A(r)$, $+\partial a \in P(1..n)$; *(ii) discarded iff* $\exists a \in A(r)$ *such that* $-\partial a \in P(1..n)$.

We now introduce the proof conditions to show that a literal is defeasibly provable.

$$+\partial\text{: If } P(n+1) = +\partial q \text{ then}$$
$$(1)\ +\Delta q \in P(1..n) \text{ or}$$
$$(2)\ (2.1)\ -\Delta\sim q \in P(1..n) \text{ and}$$
$$(2.2)\ \exists r \in R_{sd}[q] \text{ s.t. } r \text{ is applicable, and}$$
$$(2.3)\ \forall s \in R[\sim q].\ \text{either } s \text{ is discarded, or}$$
$$(2.3.1)\ \exists t \in R[q] \text{ s.t. } t \text{ is applicable and } t > s.$$

Literal q is defeasibly provable if (1) q is already definitely provable, or (2) we argue using the defeasible part of the theory. For (2), $\sim q$ is not definitely provable (2.1), and there exists an applicable strict or defeasible rule for q (2.2). Every attack s is either discarded (2.3), or defeated by a stronger rule t (2.3.1).

On the other hand, to prove the a literal is defeasibly refuted ($-\partial$) we have to show that all possible ways to prove it fail. This is encoded by the following proof conditions that correspond to a constructive negation of the conditions for $+\partial$.

$-\partial$: If $P(n+1) = -\partial q$ then
(1) $-\Delta q \in P(1..n)$ and either
(2) (2.1) $+\Delta \sim q \in P(1..n)$ or
　　(2.2) $\forall r \in R_{sd}[q]$. either r is discarded, or
　　(2.3) $\exists s \in R[\sim q]$ s.t. s is applicable, and
　　　　(2.3.1) $\forall t \in R[q]$. either t is discarded, or $t \not> s$.

As usual, given $\# \in \{\Delta, \partial\}$, a literal p and a theory D, we use $D \vdash \pm\#p$ to denote that there is a proof P in D where for some line i, $P(i) = \pm\#p$. Alternatively, we say that $\pm\#p$ holds in D, or simply $\pm\#p$ holds when the theory is clear from the context. The set of positive and negative conclusions is called *extension*. Formally,

Definition 3. *Given a defeasible theory D, the* (defeasible) extension *of D is defined as $E(D) = (+\Delta, -\Delta, +\partial, -\partial)$, where $\pm\# = \{l : l$ appears in D and $D \vdash \pm\#l\}, \# \in \{\Delta, \partial\}$.*

The inference mechanism of DL does not allow to derive inconsistencies unless the monotonic part of the logic is inconsistent, as clarified by the following definition.

Definition 4. *A defeasible theory D is inconsistent iff there exists a literal p such that $((D \vdash +\partial p$ and $D \vdash +\partial \sim p)$ iff $(D \vdash +\Delta p$ and $D \vdash +\Delta \sim p))$.*

In the rest of the paper, we shall make use of neither of strict rules, nor defeaters. The restriction does not result in any loss of generality: (1) the superiority relation does not play any role in proving definite conclusions, and (2) for defeasible conclusions [4] proves that it is always possible to remove (a) strict rules from the superiority relation and (b) defeaters from the theory to obtain an equivalent theory without defeaters and where the strict rules are not involved in the superiority relation. A consequence of this assumption is that the theories we work with in this paper are consistent.

Before reporting the transformation used in the proof of NP-completeness, we need to introduce some additional terminology. Definition 5 constructs a defeasible theory starting from a fixed set of rules and an empty set of facts. This formulation limits the revision problem to preference changes, notwithstanding the particular instance of the superiority relation.

Definition 5. *Given a set of defeasible rules R, a defeasible theory D is* based on R *iff*

$$D = (\emptyset, R, >).$$

The aim of Definition 6 is to specify the possible relationships between a literal and all theories based on a set of rules R.

Definition 6. *Given a set of defeasible rules R, a literal p is*

1. *$>$-R-tautological iff for all theories D based on R, $D \vdash +\partial p$.*
2. *$>$-R-non-tautological iff there exists a theory D based on R such that $D \nvdash +\partial p$.*
3. *$>$-R-refutable iff there exists a theory D based on R such that $D \vdash -\partial p$.*
4. *$>$-R-irrefutable iff for all theories D based on R, $D \nvdash -\partial p$.*

The notion of $>$-R-irrefutable represents the negative counterpart of $>$-R-tautological; the same holds for $>$-R-refutable and $>$-R-non-tautological.

If p is $>$-R-*tautological*, then, in every theory based on the set of rules R, an instance of the superiority relation such that p is defeasibly refuted does not exist. Accordingly, if a literal is $>$-R-*tautological*, then we cannot revise it.

On the contrary, if an instance of the superiority relation where p is no longer provable exists, then p is $>$-R-*refutable*.

Definition 7. *A defeasible theory D is* decisive *iff for every literal p in D either $D \vdash +\partial p$, or $D \vdash -\partial p$.*

Proposition 8 ([6]). *Given a defeasible theory D, if the atom dependency graph of D is acyclic, then D is decisive.*

3   Computational Cost Analysis

The processes of revising a defeasible theory by modifying only the superiority relation was first analysed in [2]. The focus of this section is to show that deciding whether such a revision is possible is NP-complete. To this end, we provide a reduction from 3-SAT to the following decision problem.

INSTANCE: A decisive defeasible theory D based on R, i.e., $D = (\emptyset, R, >)$, and a literal p.
QUESTION: Is it possible to change $>$ into $>'$ such that $D' = (\emptyset, R, >')$ and either

1. If $D \vdash +\partial p$, then $D' \vdash -\partial p$?
2. If $D \vdash -\partial p$, then $D' \vdash +\partial p$?

Definition 9 below exhibits a transformation from a 3-SAT formula into a set of defeasible rules.

Definition 9. *Given a 3-SAT formula $\Gamma = \bigwedge_{i=1}^{n} C_i$ such that $C_i = \bigvee_{j=1}^{3} a_j^i$, we define the Γ-transformation as the operation that maps Γ into the following set of defeasible rules*

$$R_\Gamma = \{ r_{ij}^a : \Rightarrow a_j^i$$
$$r_{ij} : a_j^i \Rightarrow c_i$$
$$r_{\sim i} : \Rightarrow \sim c_i$$
$$r_i : \sim c_i \Rightarrow p \}.$$

The above definition clearly shows that the mapping is polynomial in the number of literals appearing in the 3-SAT formula Γ.

The third step of the proof construction is to ensure that the proposed mapping allows the revision problem to give a correct answer (either positive, or negative) for every 3-SAT formula.

Lemma 10. *Any defeasible theory D based on R_Γ of Definition 9 (for any Γ) is decisive.*

Proof. It is easy to verify by case inspection that the atom dependency graph is acyclic.

Proposition 8 and Lemma 10 guarantee that any theory obtained by the Γ-transformation provides an answer. These results are also intended to establish relationships between the notions of tautological and refutable given in Definition 6.

We shall now propose the main result of NP-completeness. First, we shall prove that the revision problem is in NP. Second, we shall demonstrate the NP-hardness by exploiting the formulation of the 3-SAT problem and the transformation proposed in Definition 9.

Theorem 11. *The problem of determining the revision of a defeasible literal by changing the preference relation is* NP-*complete.*

Proof. The proof that the problem is in NP is straightforward. Given a defeasible theory $D = (F, R, >)$ and a literal p to be revised, an oracle guesses a revision (in terms of a new preference relation $>'$ applied to D) and checks if the state of p has changed based on the extensions of D and $D' = (F, R, >')$. The complexity of this check is bound to the calculus of $E(D)$ and $E(D')$, which [7] proves to be linear in the order of the theory.

To prove the NP-hardness, given a 3-SAT formula $\Gamma = \bigwedge_{i=1}^n C_i$ such that $C_i = \bigvee_{j=1}^3 a_j^i$, a defeasible theory D based on the set of defeasible rules R_Γ obtained by Γ-transformation, and a literal p in D, we show that:

1. if p is $>$-R_Γ-tautological, then Γ is not satisfiable;
2. if p is $>$-R_Γ-non-tautological, then Γ is satisfiable.

1. Lemma 10 allows us to reformulate the contrapositive using $>$-R_Γ-refutable. If Γ is satisfiable, then there exists an interpretation I such that

$$I \vDash \Gamma \iff I \vDash \bigwedge_{i=1}^n C_i$$
$$\iff I \vDash C_1 \text{ and } \dots \text{ and } I \vDash C_n$$
$$\iff I \vDash \bigvee_{j=1}^3 a_j^1 \text{ and } \dots \text{ and } I \vDash \bigvee_{j=1}^3 a_j^n.$$

Thus, for each i, there exists j such that $I \vDash a_j^i$.

We build a defeasible theory $D' = (\emptyset, R_\Gamma, >')$ as follows. If there exists a literal b_k^l such that $b_k^l = \sim a_j^i$, then (r_{ij}^a, r_{lk}^b) is in $>'$. It follows that, by construction, D' proves $+\partial a_j^i$. This means that every rule r_{ij} is applicable and it is not weaker than the corresponding rule $r_{\sim i}$. Hence, we have $-\partial \sim c_i$, for all i. Consequently, each rule r_i for p is discarded and we conclude $-\partial p$. Accordingly, p is $>$-R_Γ-refutable.

2. Again, by Lemma 10, every theory based on R_Γ is decisive. Thus, p is $>$-R_Γ-refutable. Accordingly, there exists a theory $D' = (\emptyset, R_\Gamma, >')$ such that $D' \vdash -\partial p$. Given that $R_\Gamma[p] \neq \emptyset$ and $R_\Gamma[\sim p] = \emptyset$ by construction, every rule for p is discarded. Namely, we have $-\partial \sim c_i$, for all i.

Each rule $r_{\sim i}$ is vacuously applicable. To have $-\partial \sim c_i$, there must exist a rule r_{ij} that is applicable. Therefore, for each i there is at least one j such that $+\partial a_j^i$.

We build an interpretation I as follows:

$$I(a^i_j) = 1 \text{ iff } D \vdash +\partial a^i_j.$$

Since for each $1 \leq i \leq n$, we have $I(a^i_j) = 1$ for at least one j, then also $I \vDash C_i$ for all i, and we conclude that $I \vDash \Gamma$.

In addition, Theorem 11 specifies that there are situations where it is not possible to revise a literal by only using the superiority relation. For example, if we take a 3-SAT formula which is a tautology, the Γ-transformation generates a theory that cannot be revised only using the superiority relation.

Corollary 12. *There are theories and literals for which a revision by only modifying the superiority relation is not possible.*

The notion itself of "being a tautology in defeasible logic" may assume unexpected features. [3] provides a thorough characterisation of the problem where this is out of the scope of the present paper, and as such is not reported here. Nonetheless, we give the examples used in [3] to illustrate that finding patterns to determine whether a literal is tautological – in the sense of a literal that is always in the positive extension of theory based on a set of rules – is hard.

We following example shows a theory wherein literal p cannot be contracted by only modifying the superiority relation.

Example 1. Let D be a consistent, defeasible theory based on R where

$$R = \{ \Rightarrow_{r_1} l \Rightarrow_{r_2} \neg a$$
$$\Rightarrow_{r_3} a \Rightarrow_{r_4} p$$
$$\Rightarrow_{r_5} b \Rightarrow_{r_6} p$$
$$\Rightarrow_{r_7} \neg l \Rightarrow_{r_8} \neg b \}.$$

The rules above are depicted in a graphical way, where the subscripts attached to the arrows are the rule labels, and rules are chained. Thus, for example a is the consequent of r_3 as well as the antecedent of r_4.

To contract p, we must block both the chains proving p, those being $r_3 r_4$ and $r_5 r_6$. In order to do so, we should have that $D \vdash +\partial l$ as well as $D \vdash +\partial \neg l$. This is not possible being D consistent.

Unfortunately, recognising patterns as those shown in Example 1 does not guarantee to identify literals that cannot be contracted. In fact, let us consider Example 2.

Example 2. Let $D = (\emptyset, R = \{r_1, \ldots, r_{18}\}, \emptyset)$ be a defeasible theory where

$$R = \{ \qquad \Rightarrow_{r_1} a \Rightarrow_{r_2} p$$
$$\Rightarrow_{r_3} b \Rightarrow_{r_4} p$$
$$\Rightarrow_{r_5} c \Rightarrow_{r_6} p$$
$$\Rightarrow_{r_7} l \Rightarrow_{r_8} \neg a$$
$$\Rightarrow_{r_9} \neg l \Rightarrow_{r_{10}} \neg b$$
$$\Rightarrow_{r_{11}} m \Rightarrow_{r_{12}} \neg b$$
$$\Rightarrow_{r_{13}} \neg m \Rightarrow_{r_{14}} \neg c$$
$$\Rightarrow_{r_{15}} n \Rightarrow_{r_{16}} \neg c$$
$$\Rightarrow_{r_{17}} \neg n \Rightarrow_{r_{18}} \neg a \}.$$

To contract p, we must block derivations of $+\partial a$, $+\partial b$ and $+\partial c$. This can be obtained by adding the following tuples to the superiority relation: (r_7, r_9), (r_{11}, r_{13}) and (r_{15}, r_{17}).

This is a counter-example to the pattern proposed in Example 1 but, once again, there are counter-examples to counter-examples (Example 3), and so on.

Example 3. Let $D = (\emptyset, R = \{r_1, \ldots, r_{25}\}, \emptyset)$ be a defeasible theory where

$$
\begin{array}{ll}
\Rightarrow_{r_{19}} e & \Rightarrow_{r_{20}} p \\
\Rightarrow_{r_{21}} f & \Rightarrow_{r_{22}} p \\
n \Rightarrow_{r_{23}} \neg e & \\
\neg n \Rightarrow_{r_{24}} \neg f & \\
\neg m \Rightarrow_{r_{25}} \neg f. &
\end{array}
$$

To contract p, we must now block derivations also of $+\partial e$, and $+\partial f$. Derivation of e can be blocked only if we prove the antecedent of r_{23}, that is n (the derivation of c is blocked as well). This implies that the derivation of f is blocked only if $+\partial \neg m$ holds (the only antecedent of rule r_{25}). We can now operate only on the provability of either l, or $\neg l$. In both cases, one between a or b cannot be refuted.

4   Summary and Related Works

We started this paper by setting the problem of preference revision within the non-monotonic sceptical formalism of Defeasible Logic. After having introduced the logical mechanism, we proved the main result of NP-completeness for the decisional version of the problem. We have also proved that this type revision is not guaranteed to be successful.

To the best of our knowledge, revision of non-monotonic theories based on modifications of the underlying superiority relation has been neglected so far. Even if preferences have been widely studied in many different application areas (we cite, above others, database management [8,9] and legal reasoning [10]), our analysis is the first formal study to computationally characterise the problem of defeasible preference revision.

As far as we are aware of, the work most closely related to ours is that of [11], where the authors study how to abduct preference relations to support the derivation of a specific conclusion in a given theory. Therefore, the problem they address is conceptually different from what we presented in this paper, given that we focus on modifying an existing superiority relation instead of generating a new one that guarantees the derivation of a specific conclusion.

In [8,9], authors present algorithms for computing minimal and preference-protecting minimal contractions for finite as well as finitely representable preference relations. Nevertheless, also this work has several dissimilarities with ours. First, they focus only on contraction operators, and do not give a complexity analysis of preference revision in general. Second, the analysis carried out is meant for applications where the preference relation is required to be transitive and irreflexive (that is to say, a strict partial order).

As a matter of fact, our work comes full circle and show the computational limits of revision in defeasible contexts. Revision based on change of factual knowledge, which essentially corresponds to an update operation, has been analysed in [12]. Other methods to revise, contract, or expand a defeasible theory were proposed in [1], studying how to revise the belief set of a theory based on the introduction of new rules. It is easy to verify that such revisions operates in polynomial time.

Preference handling in Defeasible Logic can gain much from typisation of preferences themselves. The notion of preference type and its algebraic structure has been studied previously and can be applied directly here [13]. Analogously, one of the possible directions of generalisation for the notion of preference is the notion of partial order, investigated at a combinatorial level by [14] and then studied from a computational viewpoint in [15].

References

1. Billington, D., Antoniou, G., Governatori, G., Maher, M.: Revising nonmonotonic theories: The case of defeasible logic. In: Burgard, W., Christaller, T., Cremers, A.B. (eds.) KI 1999. LNCS (LNAI), vol. 1701, pp. 101–112. Springer, Heidelberg (1999)
2. Governatori, G., Olivieri, F., Scannapieco, S., Cristani, M.: Superiority based revision of defeasible theories. In: Dean, M., Hall, J., Rotolo, A., Tabet, S. (eds.) RuleML 2010. LNCS, vol. 6403, pp. 104–118. Springer, Heidelberg (2010)
3. Governatori, G., Olivieri, F., Scannapieco, S., Cristani, M.: Revision of defeasible logic preferences. CoRR abs/1206.5833 (2012)
4. Antoniou, G., Billington, D., Governatori, G., Maher, M.J.: Representation results for defeasible logic. ACM Transactions on Computational Logic 2, 255–287 (2001)
5. Antoniou, G., Billington, D., Governatori, G., Maher, M.J., Rock, A.: A family of defeasible reasoning logics and its implementation. In: ECAI 2000, pp. 459–463 (2000)
6. Antoniou, G., Billington, D., Governatori, G., Maher, M.J.: Embedding defeasible logic into logic programming. TPLP 6, 703–735 (2006)
7. Maher, M.J.: Propositional defeasible logic has linear complexity. Theory and Practice of Logic Programming 1, 691–711 (2001)
8. Mindolin, D., Chomicki, J.: Minimal contraction of preference relations. In: Fox, D., Gomes, C.P. (eds.) AAAI, pp. 492–497. AAAI Press (2008)
9. Mindolin, D., Chomicki, J.: Contracting preference relations for database applications. Artif. Intell. 175(7-8), 1092–1121 (2011)
10. Governatori, G., Rotolo, A., Olivieri, F., Scannapieco, S.: Legal contractions: a logical analysis. In: Francesconi, E., Verheij, B. (eds.) ICAIL, pp. 63–72. ACM (2013)
11. Inoue, K., Sakama, C.: Abducing priorities to derive intended conclusions. In: Dean, T. (ed.) IJCAI, pp. 44–49. Morgan Kaufmann (1999)
12. Katsuno, H., Mendelzon, A.O.: Propositional knowledge base revision and minimal change. Artificial Intelligence 52, 263–294 (1991)
13. Cristani, M.: Many-sorted preference relations. In: Fensel, D., Giunchiglia, F., McGuinness, D.L., Williams, M.A. (eds.) KR, pp. 265–276. Morgan Kaufmann (2002)
14. Düntsch, I.: A microcomputer based system for small relation algebras. J. Symb. Comput. 18, 83–86 (1994)
15. Cristani, M., Hirsch, R.: The complexity of constraint satisfaction problems for small relation algebras. Artif. Intell. 156, 177–196 (2004)

From Guidelines to Practice: Improving Clinical Care through Rule-Based Clinical Decision Support at the Point of Care

Ayesha Aziz*, Salvador Rodriguez, and Chris Chatwin

School of Engineering and Informatics, University of Sussex, Brighton, UK
{a.aziz,salvador.rodriguez-loya,c.r.chatwin}@sussex.ac.uk

Abstract. Healthcare Information Technology (HIT) is a dynamically evolving industry due to continuous advancements in healthcare technologies. This necessitates the availability of highly dynamic applications that accommodate frequent changes in business logic. The automation of Clinical Decision Support (CDS) in particular is most liable to changes in health business logic or rules. In terms of system's architecture, there is a need to separate business logic and rules from the implementation/functionality of the Electronic Health Record (EHR) application, providing processes and rules as reusable components. We propose an architecture utilizing rule-based technologies to facilitate Decision Support to promptly adapt business logic changes, that are reflected immediately in application behavior. This allows real-time and robust CDS for the physician at point of care. Our rule-based implementation (Business Process Modelling Notation (BPMN)+Rules) was successfully used to emulate Clinical workflows, using as an example, the NICE Lung Cancer Clinical Guideline (CG121) as a test scenario.

Keywords: Rule Based Technology, Clinical Decision Support, Clinical Guidelines, Service Composite Architecture, BPMN.

1 Introduction

The implementation of Evidence based medical (EBM) practices at the point of care confirms the best possible clinical care at low costs [1]. EBM encompasses best practice and standardization for clinical practice. These standards are based on scientific evidence from the Medical literature, clinical trials and the latest research providing the physician with adjudicated data to make informed decisions when formulating patient-specific diagnosis and treatment strategies. A practical implementation of EBM is Clinical Guidelines (CGs). Clinical practice guidelines (also called pathways) assist a healthcare practitioner with managing individual patient conditions. CGs represent a health care procedure as a systematically developed process defining the necessary information in a sequence guided by clinical rules that are appropriate for specific patient needs. Guidelines promote interventions during clinical practice to replace the use of inefficient medical practices with evidence-based practices to improve clinical outcome.

---

* Corresponding author.

A. Bikakis et al. (Eds.): RuleML 2014, LNCS 8620, pp. 178–185, 2014.

Clinical Decision Support (CDS) has been described as one of the key enablers of improved clinical outcomes. A decision support service (DSS) takes as an input the patient data (problems, observations etc.) and yields patient-specific inferences as output enabling a physician to make informed decisions at the point of care. [2] suggest that a computerized CDS service can be beneficial if "decision support is provided automatically as part of clinician workflow". Hence incorporating CDS knowledge within a healthcare workflow can serve as a mechanism to assist a physician to make informed decisions. [3] identify challenges to implementing successful CDS within the healthcare workflow. From an architectural point of view the following two issues are critical, 1)Disseminate best practices in CDS design, development, and implementation and 2) Create an architecture for sharing executable CDS modules and services. To disseminate best clinical practices integrated into a CDSs, clinical guidelines have been incorporated into the CDS functionality of an application used by a physician [4] [5] . Service Oriented Architecture provides a way to manage CDS knowledge as reusable components that can be shared among disparate electronic healthcare environments.

Rule-based systems are by far the most extensively utilized models for decision making in CDSs. We have developed a framework for CDS knowledge representation, processing and execution following a rule-based approach. We propose an architecture that maps clinical knowledge encapsulated in clinical guidelines to a workflow. Traditionally, a number of complex approaches have been adopted to express clinical guidelines, for example, Arden Syntax[1]. The challenge using this approach is that it is tightly coupled with underlying technologies and does not provide a graphical representation of CGs within a workflow. We have used BPMN to model a clinical guideline. All the clinical knowledge embedded in the guideline has been expressed as business processes (in this case, clinical processes and clinical rules). The aim of this research is two-fold. Firstly, separate Clinical knowledge from EHRs. We achieve this by expressing Clinical knowledge as rules. Secondly, enable sharable CDS knowledge. This is achieved by maintaining SCA Composite of the business processes.

2   Methods and Tools

2.1   Methodology: Agile Business Rule Development Methodology

We have followed the Agile Business Rule Development Methodology (ABRD) for this project [6]. This methodology consists of six iterative steps starting from Rule Discovery to Rule Deployment as shown in Fig. 1. The iterative nature of this cycle ensures that CDS knowledge encapsulated in the rules can be updated as needed. Based on ABRD, we apply the following steps:

1. Harvesting: Identify the rules as reusable CDS knowledge components for a clinical guideline.

---

[1] http://www.hl7.org/Special/committees/arden/index.cfm

2. Prototyping: Design a model to represents the rules as part of a clinical process and validate the rules against the business logic they represent.

3. Building: Build executable rules, deploy the rules in a runtime environment, and expose them as web services to be consumed by the requesting application.

4. Enhancing: Follow an iterative approach to modify existing rules and integrate changes as they appear in a clinical scenario

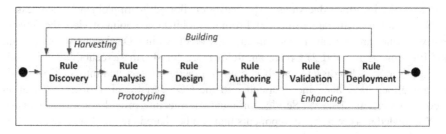

Fig. 1. Agile Business Rules Development Methodology [6]

2.2   Architecture: Technologies and Standards

1. Service Component Architecture:
Service Component Architecture (SCA) is a "set of specifications which describe a model for building applications and systems based upon SOA principles" [7]. In our implementation, we define components representing a particular functionality (in this case medical rules) . A component can either be independently exposed through an external protocol or can be wired together by a process, (a clinical guideline), in a way that is communication protocol neutral (Web Services, Java Messaging Service, Enterprise Java Beans etc). The unit of deployment of SCA is called an SCA Composite. An SCA composite can consist of components, services, references, and wires that connect them together.

2. Tolven eCHR™:
To capture patient information and display CDS alerts, we used the EHR application Tolven eCHR™ [8]. This EHR was selected given its user friendly interface to record and display patient information . Secondly it is an open source platform that allows interoperability with other applications.

3. Tolven Plugin:
In order to receive and send patient medical data, a Java EE based plugin was developed. This plugin interfaces with Tolven eCHR™, allowing it to receive patient data, transform and validate it against vMR format and transfer the vMR as a web service to be utilized for rules processing in the CDS Rules Service. After the rules have been processed the plugin transfers the desired results (in this case, alerts) back to the EHR.

4. CDS Rules Service:

This framework is developed using open source tools and technologies as shown in Fig.2. It includes JBoss jBPM[2] workflow engine, JBoss Drools[3] rules engine, Apache Camel[4] for message routing and Enterprise Service Bus Switchyard[5]. SwitchYard pro-vides the SCA runtime and is the middleware that lies between business applications and routes and transforms messages along the way [9] [10] .

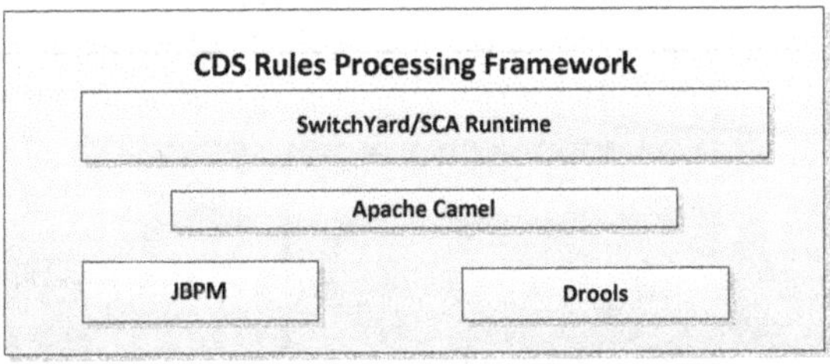

Fig. 2. CDS Rules Processing Framework

5. Eclipse BPMN 2 Modeler:

We modelled the clinical guidelines as workflows using BPMN 2.0 [11], to graphically represent the processes and rules in a medical workflow. The clinical workflow modelled using BPMN is shown in Fig. 3

6. HL7/OMG CDSs:

As a standard for CDS data communication and standard, we use the HL7/OMG standard for clinical decision support. The HL7/OMG Clinical Decision Support Service was designed to enable CDS services to be leveraged using a standard interface [12]. It exposes the CDS functionality as a web service.

7. HL7 Virtual Medical Record (vMR):

The HL7 Virtual Medical Record (vMR)[6] is specifically designed to enable mapping clinical data from EHR technologies for use in CDS. It is based on Health Level Seven Inc. HL7 version 3. The version 3 classes encapsulate patient data in a standardized manner. This data includes Patient demographics, problems, orders, observations, medications and results [13].

2.3   Clinical Scenario for CDS

We have selected NICE UK's Guideline "The diagnosis and treatment of Lung Cancer" (CG121) to test our CDS architecture solution [14]. The guideline provides a

---

[2] http://jbpm.jboss.org/
[3] http://drools.jboss.org/
[4] http://camel.apache.org/
[5] http://switchyard.jboss.org/
[6] http://www.hl7.org/implement/standards/
    product_brief.cfm?product_id=271

sequence of actions that need to be performed by the physician in order to consider a diagnosis for Lung Cancer. We test the initial symptoms of lung cancer by our CDS service, and represent these symptoms as business rules in a workflow. After the rules have been processed, we provide as a result, that is an alert to the physician for considering diagnosis of lung cancer as well as instructions for urgent Chest X-Ray immediate referral. This result is displayed as an alert in the EHR. Fig. 3 shows a BPMN representation of the guideline.

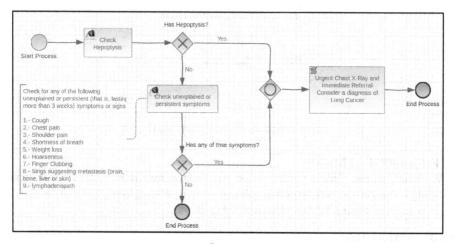

Fig. 3. BPMN Process for Diagnosis of Lung Cancer

2.4   The CDS Service Processing Steps

1. The process initiates as soon as new problems for a patient are entered in the EHR by the physician, and the patient record is modified.
2. The Tolven plugin collects this patient data and transforms it into HL7 vMR format.
3. The vMR is then sent as a CDS request to CDS Service . There is a verification performed against the vMR standard conformance for the incoming request.
4. The problems list encapsulated in the vMR are converted into independent SCA Components. The SCA Composite for Lung cancer guideline is shown in Fig. 4. There are two rules associated with this process. 1) Check Hemoptisis and 2) Check Unexplained or Persistent Symptoms (this includes nine symptoms). These components are wired together to a process called Lung Cancer Clinical Guideline (NICE_Lung_Cancer_Clinical_Guideline). The CDS Rules Service checks if either of these are represented as problems in the vMR. If either of them is true, a message "Urgent Chest X-Ray and Immediate Referral" is generated and sent as a response to Tolven eCHR interface. This message is shown as an alert to the Physician at the point of care. This message is displayed as an alert to the Physician at the point of care as shown in Fig 5.

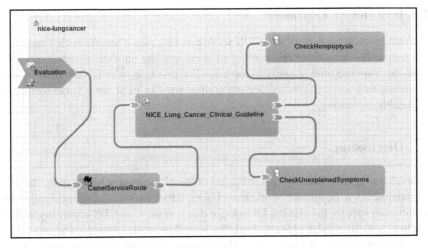

Fig. 4. SCA Composite for Lung Cancer Guideline

Problems		Document		Alerts	
				03/26/2014	CDS Service: Urgent Chest X-Ray and Immediate Referral
03/26/2014	Widespread metastatic malignant neoplastic disease (disorder)	ACTIVE		03/26/2014	CDS Service: Consider Diagnosis for Lung Cancer
03/26/2014	Shoulder pain (finding)	ACTIVE			
03/26/2014	Hemoptysis (disorder)	ACTIVE			
03/26/2014	Lymphadenopathy (disorder)	ACTIVE			
03/26/2014	Finger clubbing (disorder)	ACTIVE			
03/26/2014	Hoarse (finding)	ACTIVE			

Fig. 5. Tolven eCHR user interface showing Alerts

3   Results

3.1   Testing

According to the Clinical Decision Support Consortium, an effective CDS service has to be less than a second [15]. We have used the open source load testing software, LoadUI[7], to measure the results of performance testing. We measured the service response times to test the scalability of the service. The service was tested for 30, 50 and 60 simultaneous users respectively for a period of five minutes. Our results are shown in Table 1.

Table 1. Evaluation testing results for CDS Rules Service

Time (min)	No of Users	No of Requests	Response Time (ms)
05.00	30	881	274
05.00	50	1504	567
05.00	60	1779	987

---

[7] http://www.loadui.org/

3.2   Performance Evaluation

The average response time of our CDS service is less than a second with a maximum of 60 users. If we increase the number of users and the number of simultaneous requests, the response time is likely to increase. For managing a relatively small number of requests, this service is suited for integration with an EHR for a small to medium sized healthcare setting.

4   Discussion

We developed a standardized representation of the clinical rules by mapping the clinical guideline as a healthcare workflow. Using BPMN to model clinical rules in a guideline can specify the clinical knowledge that can serve as CDS capability within a workflow as well as independently from the workflow model. Using standards such as vMR, there is no need for separate EHRs to maintain proprietary structures for messages. Secondly, the java based interface plugin (Tolven Plugin) can validate any incoming patient data against the vMR, hence promoting a standardized data format. Our SCA composite for the Lung Cancer Diagnosis scenario can be exposed as a web service for other clinical diagnosis scenarios. Every component in the composite can act independently of one another and can be wired to other processes, thus allowing reusability. Rule governance is to ensure efficient maintenance of all the processes that are deployed as CDS services. This is achieved through assigning roles and responsibilities to members involved in the clinical scenario. These include rules author, rule analyst, rule administrator, business policies owner. All of these members are responsible for performing their tasks by following the agile business rules development methodology. This ensures monitoring and management of the rules life cycle in an iterative manner. Additionally, it allows updating rules as new evidence base becomes available, provides a scalable solution to CDS.

5   Conclusion

The aim of this research was to provide a mechanism for leveraging a rule-based approach for implementing clinical guidelines to provide robust and flexible clinical decision support. We have demonstrated that BPMN and Rules, can together serve as a CDS Service at the point of care. To address the features of an SOA based solution, we leveraged Service Component Architecture (SCA) infrastructure, that provides reusable CDS rules and processes in the form of an SCA Composite. We have shown that this CDS service can be integrated with a commercial EHR to provide clinical decision support integrated within a healthcare workflow. The proposed architecture successfully automates the processing of symptoms presented by the patient in the EHR application, hence initiating an alert in the Tolven eCHR™ user interface, calling for an urgent chest X-ray and immediate referral to specialist services. Additionally, we demonstrate an important functionality of reusability, by retaining SCA Composite, BPMN and DRL Files, as reusable services. Finally as rules in Clinical

Guidelines are liable to changes over time, we use agile business rules development methodology to monitor and track changes in all the processes that constitute the clinical workflow, thus ensuring rules management and governance over a sustained period of time. The future work involves testing this system using a real-time scenario in a healthcare setting.

References

1. Lewis, S.J., Orland, B.I.: The importance and impact of evidence-based medicine. J. Manag. Care Pharm. 10(5. suppl A), S3–S5 (2004)
2. Sittig, D., Wright, A., Osheroff, J.A., Middletone, B., Jteich, J., Ash, J., et al.: Grand challenges in clinical decision support. J. Biomed. Inform. 41(2), 387–392 (2008)
3. Tierney, W.M., Overhage, J.M., Takesue, B.Y.: Computerizing guidelines to improve care and patient outcomes: The example of heart failure. J. Am. Med. Inform. Assoc. 2, 316–322 (1995)
4. Vissers, M.C., Hasman, A., van der Linden, C.J.: Impact of a protocol processing system (ProtoVIEW) on clinical behaviour of residents and treatment. Int. J. Biomed. Comput. 42, 143–150 (1996)
5. Kawamoto, K., Houlihan, C.A., Balas, E.A., Lobach, D.F.: Improving clinical practice using clinical decision support systems: A systematic review of trials to identify features critical to success. BMJ (2005)
6. Boyer, J., Hafedh, M.: Agile Business Rule Development: Process, Architecture and JRule Examples. Springer, Heidelberg (2011)
7. Service Component Architecture, OASIS Standard, https://www.oasis-open.org/committees/tc_home.php?wg_abbrev=sca-j
8. Tolven eCHR. Tolven Inc. (2014), http://home.tolven.org/
9. JBoss Switchyard, http://www.jboss.org/switchyard
10. Davis, J.: Open Source SOA. Manning Publications Co., Greenwick (2009)
11. OMG, Business Process Model And Notation (BPMN) Version 2.0 (2011)
12. Clinical Decision Support Service (CDSS), http://www.omg.org/spec/CDSS/1.0/
13. HL7 Virtual Medical Record for Clinical Decision Support, http://www.hl7.org/implement/standards/product_brief.cfm?product_id=271
14. National Institute for Health and Care Excellence (The diagnosis and treatment of Lung Cancer) (CG121) NICE, London (2013), http://www.nice.org.uk/CG121
15. Paterno, M.D., Goldberg, H.S., Simonaitis, L., Dixon, B.E., Wright, A., et al.: Using a service oriented architecture approach to clinical decision support: Performance results from two CDS Consortium demonstrations. In: AMIA Annu. Symp. Proc. 2012, pp. 8–690 (2012)

Requirement Compound Mining and Analysis

Juyeon Kang[1,2] and Patrick Saint-Dizier[1]

[1] IRIT - CNRS, Toulouse, France
[2] Prometil, Toulouse, France
j.kang@prometil.com, stdizier@irit.fr

Abstract. In this paper, we motivate and develop the linguistic characteristics of requirement compounds which are major types of business rules. The discourse structures that further refine or elaborate requirements are also analyzed. An implementation is then presented. It is carried out in Dislog on the <TextCoop> platform. Dislog allows high level specifications in logic that allow fast and easy prototyping at a high level of linguistic adequacy. Elements of an indicative evaluation are provided.

1 Motivations

1.1 Requirement Compounds

Business rules in written texts or dialogues seldom come in isolation, as independent statements. They are often embedded into a context that indicates e.g. circumstances, elaborations or purposes. Relations between a business rule and its context may be conceptually complex. Furthermore, such rules often appear in small and closely related groups or clusters. These clusters contain a few rules that often share similar aims, where the first one is complemented, supported, reformulated, contrasted or elaborated by the subsequent ones and by additional statements. These small groups may also include statements in contrastive or concessive configurations. The elements in these units share strong relations: it is somewhat conceptually difficult to split them into isolated and autonomous units.

It is therefore crucial to consider these clusters (group of related rules with context) as a whole, since their different constituents state constraints on their scope and validity or illustrate or reformulate some of their facets for a better understanding.

In terms of language realization, clusters of rules and their related context may be all included into a single sentence via coordination or subordination or may appear as separate sentences. In both cases, the relations between the different elements of a cluster are realized by means of conjunctions, connectors, various forms of references and punctuation. We call such a cluster an **rule compound**. The idea behind this term is that the elements in a compound form a single, possibly complex, unit, which must be considered as a whole from a conceptual point of view. Such a compound consists of a small number of sentences, so that its contents can be easily assimilated.

A. Bikakis et al. (Eds.): RuleML 2014, LNCS 8620, pp. 186–200, 2014.

Technical documents (e.g. procedures, product manuals, specifications) form a linguistic genre with relatively strong linguistic constraints in terms of lexical realizations, including business or domain dependent aspects, grammar, style and overall organization. Technical documents cover a large variety of types of documents: procedures, equipment and product manuals, various notices such as security notices, regulations of various types (security, management), requirements and product or process specifications. These documents are designed to be as efficient and unambiguous as possible. For that purpose, they tend to follow precise and strict authoring principles concerning both their form and contents. Technical documents abound in various types of rules and recommendations.

Regulations and requirements form a specific subgenre in technical documents, a specific class of business rules (as specified in SBVR): they do not describe how to realize a task but the constraints that hold on tasks or products, e.g. the way they must be manufactured, used, stored and maintained (Hull et al. 2011). Requirements can also be process or product specifications describing the properties and the expectations related to a product or a process.

We focus in this paper on requirement mining to identify **requirement compounds**. It is crucial to clearly identify requirements and their contexts since they play important roles in technical documents, e.g. stating constraints or preventing risks. Traceability and coherence are properties that requirements must meet. A typical example[1] is the following requirement compound with two requirements followed by a third sentence which is a concession that applies to the second requirement:

Ex. 1. *The component shall be tested at room temperature. The component shall be mounted to the test stand in a manner equivalent to its engine orientation. However, in agreement with X, the component could be tested following its own definition axes .*

1.2   Related Works

Identifying discourse structures in general is a real challenge since linguistic cues are relatively limited (see e.g. http://www.sfu.ca/rst/). Several approaches, based on corpus analysis with a strong linguistic basis, are of much interest for our approach. Besides the Penn Discourse Treebank, relations have been investigated together with their linguistic markers in e.g. (Delin et al. 1994), (Marcu 1997) and (Miltasaki et al. 2004). (Rossner et al. 1992) and (Saito et al. 2006) developed an extensive study on how markers can be quite systematically acquired. Results are applied in e.g. (Kosseim et al. 2000) for language generation. (Stede 2012) develops a useful typology of markers.

A few systems have been developed such as (Marcu 2000), Boxer (http://svn.ask.it.usyd.edu.au/trac/candc/wiki/boxer), (Feng et al. 2012), or Hilda (Hernault et al. 2010). The first two systems use a kind of logic and produce a discourse graph or a formal representation (DRT for Boxer), the last two systems are based on support vector machines and a set of precise linguistic features.

---

[1] To preserve confidentiality of data, crucial terms have been changed or replaced by a variable such as X.

The TextCoop platform and the Dislog language on which our implementation is based (Saint-Dizier 2014) is an application of logic programming to discourse analysis. It includes a rich language to describe discourse structure identification rules together with reasoning capabilities to resolve ambiguities.

1.3 Overall Structure of Technical Documents

Specification documents are in general not a mere list of organized requirements. They often start with general considerations such as purpose, scope, or context. Then follow definitions, examples, scenarios or schemas. Then come a series of sections that address, via sets of requirements, the different facets of the problem at stake. Each section may include for its own purpose general elements followed by relevant requirements with comments, notes, etc. Each requirement can be associated with e.g. conditions and forms of explanation such as justifications or reformulations. Requirements are often not easy to identify in specification texts, unless a specific typography is developed. It is the reader's conceptual and pragmatic knowledge that allow this identification. Automatically identifying this structure and producing a conceptual representation adequate for subsequent treatments is the major concern of this paper.

The relatively well controlled way requirement documents are written makes it possible to develop a computational model, based on a set of rules and lexical marks, that identifies requirement compounds and their internal articulations with a good accuracy.

Besides extracting or tagging requirements, this work has many applications which are crucial for the industry, among which the creation of requirement repositories, the management of traceability, and the analysis of requirement coherence.

2 Linguistic Analysis

2.1 Corpus Characteristics

In some documents, requirements are identified by typographic marks or by an ID. This makes it possible to design a development corpus without the need of an expert. The main features considered to validate our corpus are the following:

- specifications come form various industrial areas: telecoms, transportations, aeronautics, energy, software, finance, staff management;
- documents are produced by various types of actors and related processes, system, design, and software requirements;
- requirement documents follow various authoring guidelines (e.g. the IEEE ones or imposed by companies);
- requirements correspond to different conceptual levels: functional, non-functional, safety, security.

The diversity in style, structure and contents found in this corpus enables us to capture the main linguistic characteristics of requirements, over domains, styles and target audiences. This guarantees a certain generality to the analysis and the resulting rules.

Our corpus of requirements comes from 3 organizations and 6 companies. Our corpus contains 1,138 pages of text extracted from 22 documents. Our development and test corpora are extracts of this corpus. The test corpus is composed of 64 pages extracted from this corpus. the other 1074 pages have been used for requirement analysis and the construction of rules. About 80 pages of this set of 1074 pages has been used to develop the requirement compound analysis from a manual tagging.

2.2 Requirement Identification

It is first important to identify requirements, and then to identify the structures around them. Requirements are the 'head' of requirement compounds. The automatic identification of requirements taken in isolation has been developed in (Kang et al. 2013). Since requirements follow relatively strict authoring guidelines and are relatively short sentences (between 10 and 30 words), (1) identification rules are quite easy to develop and (2) results are really good. Our system is implemented in Dislog via 12 rules and related lexical resources (about 500 lexical items of various categories). On out test corpus of 64 pages of text (22 058 words), where 215 requirements have been manually annotated, a precision of 97% and a recall of 96% have been reached. Errors result from a few problematic situations of poorly written requirements.

One difficulty we have identified is the linguistic proximity of requirements with warnings. Warnings abound in technical documents where security is crucial. The structure of warnings has been investigated in depth in (Saint-Dizier 2012). It turns out that their structure, although quite close to requirements can be distinguished on the basis of two criteria:

- most warnings (about 95%) are composed of a conclusion and at least one support, whereas this ratio is of about 5% for requirements,
- warnings contain negatively oriented expressions or connectors that express risks or problems (e.g. *damage, injure, under the risk of*), which is not usual in requirements, even those in the negative voice.

To manage the risks of ambiguity, our system first identifies warnings (accuracy of conclusion recognition: 91% and of support: 94%), and then identifies requirements. A constraint in Dislog states that a warning cannot also be identified as a requirement.

In the framework of argumentation (requirements are arguments), the conclusion is the main clause while the support explains the importance of the conclusion by, e.g. outlining potential risks. In requirements, supports are not very frequently realized because they are relatively obvious to the reader.

Finally, in our approach, our aim is to identify requirements without any need of domain knowledge, essentially on the basis of lexical criteria, so that the system is re-usable in many contexts.

2.3   Processing Requirement Compounds

Let us first develop the linguistic structure of requirement compounds. The different subtasks are: (1) delimitation of compounds, (2) identification of requirements taken in isolation, (3) identification of the relations between requirements and (4) identification of the discourse relations that the sentences other than requirements play in the compound. Our approach is to develop identification methods, rules ad resources for each component separately, and then to investigate how they can be bound.

The analysis starts from manually annotated structures by the authors of this paper. A typical tagged example is the following:

Ex. 2. <*ReqCompound*> <*definition*> *Inventory of qualifications refers to norm YY.* < */definition*>
<*mainReq*> *Periodically, an inventory of supplier's qualifications shall be produced.* < */mainReq*>
<*secondaryReq*>*In addition, the supplier's quality department shall periodically conduct a monitoring audit program.*< */secondaryReq*>
<*elaboration*> *At any time, the supplier should be able to provide evidences that EC qualification is maintained.* </*elaboration*> < */ReqCompound*>

Identification and Delimitation of Requirement Compounds. The principle is that all the statements in a compound must be related either by the reference to the same theme or via phrasal connectors. These form a **cohesion link** in the compound. The theme is a nominal construction (object or event, e.g. *inventory of qualifications* in Ex. 2)).

In general, the development of relatedness criteria and measures between a requirement and its support(s) or related discourse structures is complex and a source of ambiguity. Requirement authoring guidelines recommend to produce explicit links between utterances which are related. These links are linguistically realized by the following categories of language constructs in our corpus:

1. the use of the theme in the sentences that follow or precede the main requirement (e.g. *inventory of qualifications* in Ex. 2). This theme can possibly undergo morphological variations, a different determination (e.g. *safety test, all safety tests*) and simple syntactic variations. However, the variation threshold for this latter point is not easy to evaluate. This situation occurs in about 82% of the cases. the theme is the subject of the clause (about 65% of the cases) when the subject is not a human actor or the direct object in the other cases (35%).
2. the use of a more generic term than the theme or a generic part of the theme, used as a simple form of reference, e.g. *this process, this constraint, the plan,* in the utterances that follow the main requirement (about 17% of the cases). We identified 42 such terms.
3. the reference to the parts (or the main ones) of the requirement theme e.g. *the identification system* and the parts: *the ID, the password, the encryption*

key, or a generic form such as *each individual parts*, this is quite infrequent (3%) and requires domain knowledge,

4. the use of discourse connectors to introduce a sentence, e.g. *however, for that purpose, if, if not*, etc., found in about 27%

5. the use of sentence binders such as: *for information, in this case, at any time, in addition, also*, etc. found in 19% of the cases.

Obviously these criteria may overlap, in particular in utterances other than requirements where the theme and a connector can be found. Using pronouns is not recommended and is unusual.

For example in:

Ex. 3. *Endurance tests are defined in regulation H65. Endurance shall be demonstrated by test or analysis. The endurance test or justification shall demonstrate that the equipment meets the performance requirements. Cycle data for endurance analysis are available in the individual equipment specification. A simplified endurance test may be acceptable, provided it is of an equivalent or greater severity. However, in agreement with X, the endurance could be tested ....*

The link is the nominal *endurance test*. The first sentence is a definition. The two sentences that follow are requirements that complement each other. The three last sentences stand in discourse relations with the requirements, respectively as 'localization', and for the last two as 'concessions'. The cohesion between these five sentences is realized via the repetition of the nominal *endurance test* with variations, and the connector *however*.

Relations between Requirements in a Compound. Our observations show that the first requirement is always the main requirement of the compound. The requirements that follow develop some of its facets. In Ex. 3, the second requirement (sentence 3) develops the purpose and the expected result of the endurance test, it is not a support of the main requirement. The identification of the precise functional relations between the main requirement and its associated secondary ones is often based on domain expertise. Secondary requirements essentially develop forms of:

- **contrast**, (Wolf and Gibson 2005) and (Spenader and Lobanova 2007), which is a relation between two requirements that introduce one or more equivalent but alternative solutions, but which refer to a unique situation. Formally, the apparent contradiction that results motivates the use of a defeasible inference logic and semantics to preserve the coherence of the whole structure. Contrast is introduced by *however, although, but* combined, in the utterance, with e.g. adverbs such as *also*, modals or the expression of two different situations.

- **concession** states a general requirement followed by an apparently contradictory requirement that could be admitted as an exception (e.g. sentences 4 and 5 of Ex. 3.). The contradiction with the implicit conclusion which can be drawn from the first requirement is partial (e.g. (Couper-Kuhlen et al. 2000)). Concessions are often categorized as denied phenomenal cause or motivational cause. Typical marks are, e.g.: *however, although, even though, despite,* or modal constructions such as *may be, could be.*

- **specializations** which are subtypes of elaboration relation, develop additional scenarios or constraints.
- **purpose, result** as described below, to express via a requirement the type of expected result.

Contrasts, concessions and specializations are the most frequent relations. In our approach, our aim is to identify them without any need of domain knowledge, so that the system is re-usable in many contexts. The introduction of domain knowledge would be too complex and costly and would probably introduce additional errors. We however observed a kind of continuum between contrasts and concessions. To resolve the ambiguity when it occurs we introduce the *polymorphic relation* 'contrast-concession'. Ambiguities may then be resolved by experts if necessary.

Linguistic Characterization of Discourse Structures in a Compound. Sentences not identified as requirements must be bound to requirements via discourse relations and must be characterized by the function they play. In a large diversity of types of texts, (Grosz et al. 1986) show that discourse markers or equivalent terms are used by human subjects both as cohesive links between adjacent clauses and as connectors between larger textual units. The Penn Discourse Treebank framework[2] (Webber et al. 2012) develops this view in a very accurate manner with tools to identify structures and marks. Our problem is much more restricted and subject to less ambiguous situations since the language of requirements is restricted by guidelines. The structure of the markers and connectors typical of discourse relations found in technical texts are developed in (Saint-Dizier 2014). These have been enhanced and adapted to the requirement context via several sequences of tests on our corpus. The main relations are the following:

- **information and definitions** which always occur before the main requirement. They anticipate and develop notions given in the main requirement which may be complex or insufficiently clear to the reader,
- **elaborations** which always follow a requirement, they develop some facets of the requirement to facilitate its understanding. Since this relation is very large, we consider it as the by-default relation in the compound.
- **result** which specifies the outcome of an action. Its linguistic structure is basically the active-inchoative alternation (i.e. action / result of action) that describes the expected result. For example, it can be formed by the theme of the main requirement combined with (1) the main requirement verb in past participle form, or a quasi-synonym or (2) an aspectual verb denoting completion or quasi-completion. (e.g. *shall maintain a capability* → *capability is reached*).

---

[2] Available at http://www.seas.upenn.edu/pdtb

- **circumstance** which introduces a kind of local frame under which the requirement compound is valid or relevant. Circumstances often appear before the requirement(s) they apply to. Circumstances introduce temporal, spatial or factual contexts or particular events or occasions, in our corpus they are often realized as independent short sentences.
- **purpose** which expresses the underlying motivations of the requirements. It must not be confused with supports. These are introduced by purpose connectors, causal verbs, purpose verbs (e.g. *demonstrate*) or expressions such as *the objective is*.

3   Implementation in Dislog

3.1   TextCoop: A Platform for Discourse Analysis

The TextCoop platform and the Dislog language (for Discourse in Logic) are based on logic programming. They have been primarily designed for argument analysis and discourse processing. The foundations, the methodological elements, and the performances of TextCoop are published in (Saint-Dizier 2014). Very briefly, TextCoop is a platform that includes:

(1) **Dislog**, which is a logic-based language designed to describe by means of rules and in a declarative way discourse structures and the way they can be bound via selective binding rules,

(2) **an engine** associated with a set of processing strategies, basically bottom-up, which is preferable for processing discourse. Dislog rules are processed according to a cascade that specifies their execution order. This engine also offers several mechanisms to deal with ambiguity and **concurrency** when different discourse structures can be recognized on a given text fragment,

(3) **a set of active constraints**, in the sense of Constraint Logic Programming, that check at each step of the proof procedure for the well-formedness of discourse structures (e.g. precedence, dominance, bounding nodes). These constraints can be parameterized by the grammar writer,

(4) simple **input-output facilities** (XML, MS Word, LaTeX), and interfaces with other environments

(5) a set of **lexical resources** which are frequently used in discourse analysis (e.g. connectors),

(6) a set of about 180 **generic rules** that describe 12 frequently encountered discourse structures such as reformulation, illustration, cause, contrast, concession, etc.

3.2   Main Features of Dislog and TextCoop

In Dislog, rules and constraints are specified in an abstract and declarative way which is well adapted to deal with the complexity of discourse processing. This rule system extends the possibilities offered by regular expressions. The main features of Dislog rules are:

- Rules are composed of terminal, preterminal and non-terminal symbols (used to encode grammars specific to a phenomenon: e.g. temporal expressions). Symbols are associated with feature structures,
- Dislog allows 'gap' symbols, which are symbols that stand for finite sequences of words of no interest for the rule: these words must be skipped. Dislog offers the possibility to specify in a gap a list of elements which must not be skipped. When such an element is found before the termination of the gap, then the gap fails.
- Rules may be associated with forms of reasoning e.g. to resolve analysis ambiguities or to elaborate a semantic representation,
- Rules are associated with a pattern to construct a representation based on XML tags or on dependencies.

As an illustration, consider the simple rules for the 'circumstance' structure (that form a *rule cluster*):

Ex. 4. *circumstance* →
conn(circ), gap(G), punctuation. / gap(G), verb(aspectual), eos.
Lexical resources are quite diverse:
conn(circ): when, once, as soon as, after, before, in case of,
verb(aspectual): start, resume, stop

In this simple rule, the circumstance ranges between the marker (conn(circ)) and a punctuation.

3.3   Architecture of the Rule System

In this section we illustrate the linguistic analysis developed above. An indicative evaluation of the performances is provided. Such an evaluation is limited and preliminary, it is designed to indicate improvement directions and difficulties.

Requirement Identification. The set of rules developed to identify requirements is developed in (Kang et al. 2014). Since requirement authoring guidelines are relatively strict, developing a domain independent grammar that recognizes requirements is relatively feasible. For example, requirements composed of a modal, the auxiliary 'be' and an action verb used as a past participle are encoded by the following Dislog rule:
requirement → bos, gap(G1), modal, aux(be), advP,
verb(action, past-participle), gap(G2), eos.
where bos stands for beginning of sentence, and eos for end of sentence, advP is an adverb phrase that is optional, e.g.:
the system XD55 shall be always left active before...

The identification of the relations between the main and the secondary requirements is treated as any discourse relation identification (Saint-Dizier 2014). For example, here are a few simple rules that recognize the contrast relation:

Ex. 5. *Contrast* →
conn(opposition_whe), gap(G), ponct(comma). /
conn(opposition_whe), gap(G), eos. / conn(opposition_how), gap(G), eos.
Resources are essentially: conn(oppositio_whe): *whereas, but whereas, however, although, but, while,*
Typical examples are (the contrast follows the requirement): *The code shall be optimized for a 8-core CPU. However in general it will not be used on such machines.*
A key of type RD shall be used to open the pipe. However, in case of emergency any immediately available key must be used.

Higher-Order Programming for Compound Delimitation. A requirement compound is then identified by its theme and by its boundaries (where it starts and ends) following the criteria given in 2.3.1. Let T_0 be the theme as identified in the main requirement. Let $variant(T_0)$ be the finite set of the n variants which can be generated from T_0 via functions producing morphological variants, generalizations, etc.:

$$variant(T_0) = \{T_i, \ i \in [1, n]\}.$$

Then all the sentences S_j, $j \in [1, k]$, $k < 6$ (assuming that a compound has a maximum of 5 sentences, this is a parameter) in the compound must meet the following constraint, expressed by the following two Dislog rules:

$\forall S_j \ j \in [1, k] \ \exists \ i, i \in [1, n]; \ sentence \rightarrow$
$T_i, \ gap(G), \ eos \ /$
$gap(G1), \ verb, \ T_i, \ gap(G2), \ eos.$

These rules introduce a kind of higher-order programming with a quantification on the form of the theme. The rules state that the theme or its variants must appear in the set of related sentences either in subject or object position.

In more concrete terms, given a theme T and Ti one of its expressions (word or expression), identified from a main argument, related sentences are identified by the following pattern, where P is a compound identifier:

compound_identifier(P) → beginSentence, gap(G1), word(Ti), gap(G2), endSentence.

In order to avoid grouping unrelated compounds, in addition to the number of sentence limit, a constraint is that compounds cannot go over paragraphs.

Discourse Relation Identification. Discourse rules typical of technical documents originate from (Saint-Dizier 2014). The adaptation carried out in this work consists in considering independent sentences or propositions instead of subordinate clauses and tuning the markers and structure w.r.t. guidelines. These rules follow schemas which are relatively regular. Due to space limitations we simply provide here a few simple samples. The whole set of rules is available from the authors under a Creative Commons BY NC license.

Illustration → exp(illus_eg), gap(G), eos. /
[here], auxiliary(be), gap(G1), exp(illus_exa), gap(G2), eos. /
[let,us,take], gap(G), exp(illus_bwe), eos.
With, for example, the following resources:
exp(illus_eg): e.g., including, such as
exp(illus_exa): example, an example, examples etc.
20 rules have been developed to cover the various structures of illustration.
    Purpose →
conn(purpose), verb(action, infinitive), gap(G), ponct(comma). /
conn(purpose), verb(action, infinitive), gap(G), eos.
conn(purpose): to, in order to, so as to.

A typical example is: *To reschedule the process, the following elements shall....*
    These rules for processing discourse structures may seem simple, they indeed are to some extent. However, they turn out to be sufficient for technical texts where the language complexity is strongly controlled. Furthermore, the lexical resources needed for these rules are rather limited, which makes the system re-usable in a large number of contexts. There are obviously ambiguities in the recognition of discourse rules, in particular between the concession and the contrast and between the circumstance and condition relations. However, these ambiguities are also relatively marginal. Obviously, the situation would not be the same for texts with little language control.

Selective Binding Rules. Binding rule allow, under constraints, to bind requirements or to bind a requirement with one or more discourse structures, possibly under constraints. Binding rules are abstract, higher-order schemas. For example, binding the main requirement R1 with the structure G1 (e.g. G1 = definition) that precedes it is represented as follows:

```
<X>, gap(G1), </X> <req status="main"> gap(R) </req> →
<Reqcompound> <X>, G1, </X> <req status="main">, R, </req>
</Reqcompound>.
```

This rule inserts G1 and R into the <Reqcompound> tag. X is a variable that stand for any structure provided that the precedence constraints (see next subsection) are met. Only 5 such rules are necessary for requirement compound analysis. Besides binding structures, these rules double-check that the two sentences share the same cohesion link, as described in the previous subsection.
    The above example is simple and binds two adjacent structures. Selective binding rules can relate adjacent as well as non-adjacent structures. Binding is realized in a bottom-up fashion, it can occur between groups of structures: a set of structures (discourse and arguments) can be bound, and then bound to another group of structures. This allows the construction of subtrees, which is a frequent situation. This requires some form or priority among binding rules. This is a relatively complex and generic investigation that is on-going. In our approach we basically proceed by aggregating structures around the main argument.

Constraints. Constraints mainly encode in this investigation precedence constraints (noted via "<"). In Dislog, they are specified in a very straightforward manner. The TextCoop engine checks that constraints are met at each step of the processing. The following constraints induce a partial ordering of discourse structures in a requirement compound:

information, definition, circumstance < req.:
Information, circumstance and definition occur before any requirement.
reqMain, reqSecondary < result. :
result always follows a requirement.
reqMain < concession, contrast. :
Contrasts and Concessions always follow the main requirement.
reqMain < reqSecondary.
reqMain < elaboration.
contrast <> concession.: contrast and concessions cannot co-occur in a compound.

Finally, a requirement compound must be fully realized within a paragraph, therefore, the node paragraph is a bounding node:
bounding_node([paragraph]).
Precedence constraints in TextCoop are so far checked in a strict manner. However, corpus shows that in some cases precedence should also include overlap since for example circumstances or results can be realized within requirements. This is an evolution of constraints that must be managed with care.

Overall Architecture. TextCoop is used for requirement compound analysis. It allows for a very declarative specification of rules and lexical data, it manages constraints and concurrency. Rule clusters are activated one after the other with an order specified in a cascade. This cascade allows, among others, to specify priorities (a cluster must be fully processed before another one is activated) and to avoid ambiguities. The cascade has the following structure, represented as an ordered list with cluster IDs:

```
cascade([requirement, goal, contrast, concession, illustration,
circumstance, condition]).
```

Indicative Evaluation. Let us now present an indicative evaluation, which is a preliminary evaluation designed to identify improvement directions. The evaluation has been realized on our test corpus, extracted from our main corpus. It is composed of 218 requirement compounds.

The first step, requirement identification, produces very good results since their form is very regular: precision 97%, recall 96%.

The second step, compound identification, produces the following results:

	precision	recall
identification	93%	88%
opening boundary	96%	91%
closing boundary	92%	82%

The identification deals with the identification of a compound from requirements. Given this identification, the next stage is to delimit the compound, characterized by its boundaries. This is evaluated in the next two lines. The closing boundary is more difficult to identify because some terms out of the compound can be interpreted as theme variants. The accuracy of a compound identification could be improved by adding more theme variants, but there is a trade-off to elaborate in order to avoid noise.

Secondary requirements are identified as following the main one which is the first requirement in the compound. The identification of discourse structures in a compound produces the following results. These results have been obtained from the 64 pages of our test corpus. These pages cover several domains, and therefore the results are general. It is clear that there are minor differences between domains and authoring strategies. Discourse structures are however more complex to recognize, even in technical texts. Accuracy is given instead of precision and recall due to the small size of the samples:

relations	nb of rules	nb of annotations	precision	recall
contrast	14	24	84	88
concession	11	44	89	88
specialization	5	37	72	71
information	6	23	86	80
definition	9	69	87	78
elaboration	13	107	84	82
result	14	97	86	80
circumstance	15	102	89	83
purpose	17	93	91	83

Some relations have more elaborated sets of rules because they have been reused and improved from previous experiments. This explains the differences in number of rules. Some sets of rules may need further expansion to produce more accurate results, this is the case for 'specialization' which remains somewhat vague. Information and definition are not necessarily identified on the basis of marks but on their position in the compound, which is also a vague criterion. However, results are good for a discourse processing task.

4 Perspectives

In this paper, we have developed a linguistic model for requirement compounds analysis. This can be considered as **discourse grammar dedicated to requirement compounds**. An important aspect is an analysis of requirement compounds that takes into account the discourse structures that constitute their context. These specific discourse relations are conceptually characterized, with the functions they play. The implementation is carried out in Dislog on the <TextCoop> platform. Dislog allows high level specifications in logic that with relatively fast and easy prototyping.

The role of natural language processing technology for requirement authoring, control and analysis in requirement engineering processes has been developed two decades ago, but the results obtained have not been as useful and important as shown in e.g. the analysis of (Ryan 1993). Language processing has been used more recently in conjunction with requirements for the development of authoring tools (e.g. via boilerplates as developed by RAT-RQA, The Reuse company) and Rubric, or for mining tools to extract attributes from isolated requirements to develop efficient traceability (Dick 2012). Closely related work on business rules is of much interest, e.g. (Guisse 2013), (Cisternino et al. 2009) and from a conceptual analysis perspective, e.g. (Ceravolo et al. 2007). The focus is mainly on the integration of ontological knowledge and controls on the way rules are produced (via conceptual schemas) and maintained. Our contribution could certainly be of much use for these approaches with these works since none of them has the capability to mine arguments.

Another feature of much importance, consistency checking, is developed in (Bagheri et al. 2011) and (Mirbel et al. 2012). These two works remain so far rather theoretical, the need of identifying requirements and representing their semantic contents is outlined via illustrations. This motivates our contribution, which could be paired with these works. (Haley, 2007) develops a model for a logical analysis of security requirements for a system that can validate the satisfiability of security requirements in texts. In this work, the semantic representation of requirements is limited to lists of attributes. In our case, we aim at defining a more conceptual representation based on inference.

References

1. Bagheri, E., Ensan, F.: Consolidating Multiple Requirement Specifcations through Argumentation. In: Proceedings of the 2011 ACM Symposium on Applied Computing, SAC 2011 (2011)
2. Ceravolo, P., Fugazza, C., Leida, M.: Modeling semantics of business rules. In: Digital EcoSystems and Technologies Conference, DEST 2007 (2007)
3. Cisternino, V., Corallo, A., Elia, G., Fugazza, C.: Business rules for semantics-aware business modelling: Overview and open issues. Int. J. Web Eng. Technol. 5 (2009)
4. Couper-Kuhlen, E., Kortmann, B.: Cause, Condition, Concession, Contrast: Cognitive and Discourse Perspectives. In: Topics in English Linguistics, vol. 33. de Gryuter (2000)
5. Delin, J., Hartley, A., Paris, C., Scott, D.: Keith Vander Linden: Expressing Procedural Relationships in Multilingual Instructions. In: Proceedings of the Seventh International Workshop on Natural Language Generation, USA, pp. 61–70 (1994)
6. van Eemeren, F., Grootendorst, R.: Argumentation, communication, and fallacies: A pragma-dialectical perspective. Lawrence Erlbaum Associates (1992)
7. Dick, A.J.J.: Evidence-based development - Coupling structured argumentation with requirements development, System Safety. In: 7th IET International Conference on Incorporating the Cyber Security Conference, UK (2012)
8. Feng, V., Hirst, G.: Text-level discourse parsing with rich linguistic features. In: Proc. 50th ACL Meeting (2012)
9. Grosz, B., Sidner, C.: Attention, intention and the structure of discourse. Computational Linguistics 12(3) (1986)
10. Guissé, A.: Une plateforme d' aide a l' acquisition et á la maintenance des règles metier, PhD dissertation, Paris Nord (2013)

11. Haley, C.B., Mottet, J.D., Laney, R., Nuseibeh, B.: Arguing Security: Validating Security Requirements Using Structured Argumentation. In: Proceedings of the Third Symposium on Requirements Engineering for Information Security, SREIS 2005 (2005)
12. Hernault, H., Prendinger, H., Ishuzuka, M.: HILDA: A discourse parser using support vector machine classification. Diualogue and Discourse 1(3) (2010)
13. Hull, E., Jackson, K., Dick, J.: Requirements Engineering. Springer (2011)
14. Kang, J., Saint-Dizier, P.: Discourse Structure Analysis for Requirement Mining. International Journal of Knowledge Content Development and Technology 3(2) (2013)
15. Kosseim, L., Lapalme, G.: Choosing Rhetorical Structures to Plan Instructional Texts. Computational Intelligence, Blackwell, Boston (2000)
16. Mann, W., Thompson, S.: Rhetorical Structure Theory: Towards a Functional Theory of Text Organisation. TEXT 8(3), 243–281 (1988)
17. Marcu, D.: The Theory and Practice of Discourse Parsing and Summarization. MIT Press (2000)
18. Mich, L.: NL-OOPS: From natural language to object oriented requirements using the natural language processing system LOLITA. Natural Language Engineering 2, 161–187 (1996)
19. Miltasaki, E., Prasad, R., Joshi, A., Webber, B.: Annotating Discourse Connectives and Their Arguments. In: New Frontiers in NLP (2004)
20. Mirbel, I., Villata, S.: Enhancing Goal-based Requirements Consistency: An Argumentation-based Approach. In: Fisher, M., van der Torre, L., Dastani, M., Governatori, G. (eds.) CLIMA XIII 2012. LNCS (LNAI), vol. 7486, pp. 110–127. Springer, Heidelberg (2012)
21. Rosner, D., Stede, M.: Customizing RST for the Automatic Production of Technical Manuals. In: Dale, R., Rösner, D., Stock, O., Hovy, E. (eds.) IWNLG 1992. LNCS, vol. 587, pp. 199–214. Springer, Heidelberg (1992)
22. Ryan, K.: The role of natural language understanding in requirement engineering. In: IEEE Symposium on Requirements, San Diego (1993)
23. Saint-Dizier, P.: Processing natural language arguments with the TextCoop platform. Journal of Argumentation and Computation 3(1) (2012)
24. Saint-Dizier, P.: Challenges of Discourse processing: The case of technical documents. Cambridge Scholars Publising (2014)
25. Saito, M.: Using Phrasal Patterns to Identify Discourse Relations. In: Proceedings ACL 2006 (2006)
26. Spenader, J., Lobanova, A.: Reliable Discourse Markers for Contrast. Eighth International Workshop on Computational Semantics, Tilburg (2007)
27. Stede, M.: Discourse Processing. Morgan and Claypool Publishers (2012)
28. Taboada, M., Mann, W.C.: Rhetorical Structure Theory: Looking back and moving ahead. Discourse Studies 8(3), 423–459 (2006)
29. Villalba, M.G., Saint-Dizier, P.: Some Facets of Argument Mining for Opinion Analysis. In: COMMA. IOS Publising, Vienna (2012)
30. Walton, D., Reed, C., Macagno, F.: Argumentation Schemes. Cambridge University Press (2008)
31. Walton, D.: Argument Mining by Applying Argumentation Schemes. Studies in Logic 4(1) (2011)
32. Webber, B., Joshi, A.: Discourse Structure: Past, Present and Future. In: Proceedings of the ACL 2012 Workshop on Rediscovering 50 Years of Discoveries 2012, pp. 42–54. Republic of Korea, Jeju (2012)
33. Wolf, F., Gibson, E.: Representing Discourse Coherence: A Corpus-Based Study. Computational Linguistics 31(2), 249–288 (2005)

Semi-automated Vocabulary Building
for Structured Legal English

Shashishekar Ramakrishna and Adrian Paschke

Department of Computer Science, Freie Universität Berlin,
Königin-Luise-Str. 24-26,
14195 Berlin, Germany
shashi792@gmail.com, paschke@inf.fu-berlin.de

Abstract. Structured English has been applied as computational independent language for defining business vocabularies and business rules,
e.g., in the context of OMG's Semantics and Business Vocabulary Representation (SBVR). It allows non-technical domain experts to engineer
knowledge in natural language, but with an underlying semi-formal semantics which eases the automation of machine transformation into formal knowledge representations and logic-based machine interpretation.
We adapt this approach to the legal domain in order to support legal domain experts in their task to build legal vocabularies and legal
rules in Structured English from legal texts. In this paper we contribute
with a semi-automated vocabulary and rule development process which
is supported by automated suggestions of legal concepts computed by
a semantic legal text analysis. We implement a proof-of-concept in the
KR4IPLaw tool, which enables legal domain experts to represent their
knowledge in Structured English. We evaluate the proposed approach on
the basis of use cases in the domain of IP and patent law.

Keywords: Controlled Natural Language, SBVR, Structured English,
Legal Norms, LegalRuleML.

1 Introduction

Typically there exists a gap concerning the understanding of the knowledge
from a particular domain between a domain expert and a knowledge engineer
who models such domain knowledge - often in a structured, formal language-
for its use in (semi-)automated reasoning. Such a problem can be easily seen
in the legal domain, wherein, the cost associated with not reducing such gap is
substantially high [1].

Structured English (SE) has be applied as Computational Independent Model
(CIM) language for defining business vocabularies and business rules. For instance, in the context of OMG's Semantics and Business Vocabulary Representation (SBVR), SE provides an efficient solution to the problem [2]. It allows
non-technical domain experts to engineer knowledge (vocabularies and rules) in
natural language, but with an underlying semi-formal semantics defined in the

A. Bikakis et al. (Eds.): RuleML 2014, LNCS 8620, pp. 201–215, 2014.

SBVR standard, which eases the automation of machine transformation into formal knowledge representations (KRs)[1] and logic-based machine interpretation. However, the problem is still, that the manual modelling of the legal vocabularies from legal text is one of the most time consuming parts of the legal knowledge engineering [4]. Non-existence of a global public/privately shared vocabulary, makes the task of building legal vocabulary more tedious and time consuming. In this paper we contribute with a semi-automated vocabulary and rule development process which is supported by automated suggestions of legal concepts computed by a semantic legal text analysis.

The paper is structured as follows. Section 2, introduces and compares a subset of existing controlled natural languages for their use in legal domain. Sections 3 and 4 deal with the the use of SBVR-SE and in Section 5 we illustrate with an example how SBVR-SE could be used as a semi-formal KR format to represent legal information. In Section 6 we compare a subset of existing knowledge extraction tools for their use in legal domain and propose a recommender system to semantically enrich the legal information represented in previous sections. Section 7, deals with the transformation of legal knowledge from a Computational Independent Modelling (CIM) layer to a Platform Independent Modelling (PIM) layer and finally to a Platform Specific Modelling (PIM) layer. Section 8, concludes the paper and presents some future directions.

2   Controlled Natural Language, 'CNL'

Controlled Natural Language (CNL) is a subset of natural language that can be accurately and effectively processed by a computer, because it avoids semantic ambiguity and supports natural language processing with its controlled grammar. Although controlled CNLs are expressive enough to allow natural usage by a non-specialist.

There exists a wide variety of CNL's, amongst them we consider a subset of CNLs to study their applicability to our problem domain of semi-formal knowledge engineering:

- Attempto Controlled English (ACE): ACE is a CNL which includes restricted syntax and a restricted semantics (of base (English) language) described by a small set of construction and interpretation rules [5].
- SBVR Structured English: SBVR-SE is a CNL originally developed for representing business rules. It is more reliable for automatic interpretation due to its high syntax restrictions. It ignores the grammatical structure followed by its peer base language when representing the same rule/statement.
- Drafters Language: Drafters Language is a CNL originally developed for DRAFTER-II system. It works on a conceptual authoring approach which provided a relatively simple pseudo-text to specify a complex configuration of action and object entities and the relations between them [6].

---

[1] E.g., in [3], we define a transformation process with a modal first-order semantics.

- Massachusetts Legislative Drafting Language: Is a CNL developed for describing legal texts (originally for Massachusetts Senate). It provides a uniformity in drafting style by specifying a restricted syntax, restricted semantics and restricted document structure [7].

To compare the efficiency of different CNL's we use the evaluation methodology as proposed by Kuhn [8]. The evaluation is done based on four parameters described below:

- Precision: Shows the degree to which the meaning of text can be directly retrieved from its textual form.
- Expressivity: Describes the range of propositions that a certain language is able to express.
- Naturalness: Describes how close the language is to its base English (base language of considered problem domain) language.
- Simplicity: Describes simplicity/complexity of exact and comprehensive language description.

Fig 1, compares the four CNL's based on the four parameters discussed above. From the Figure we see that two out of four CNL's, i.e. SBVR-SE and ACE seem to fulfill the requirements required to represent our problem domain. Legal practitioners being both the authors and end-users of CNL based systems, we need to add another evaluation parameter 'learning curve'. From a legal practitioners' point of view, the learning curve involved in ACE seemed to be higher than that involved in SBVR-SE.

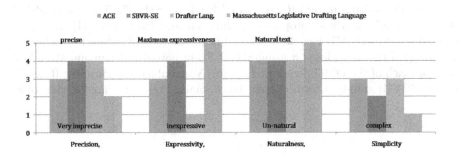

Fig. 1. Comparision of CNL's

3   SBVR Structured English

The OMGs Model Driven Architecture (MDA) [9] provides a basis for representing information on different layers of KR models (CIM, PIM and PSM). Semantic Business Vocabulary and Business Rules, SBVR [2], is an ISO terminological dictionary (vocabulary) for defining business concepts and rules. SBVR works on the Computational Independent Model (CIM) layer of the OMGs MDA. It

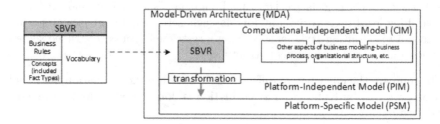

Fig. 2. SBVR position in MDA (adapted from [2])

suggests the use of Structured English (SE), a computational-independent English (natural) with a structured syntax for representing business vocabularies and business rules. SBVR captures the structural and behavioral aspects of business processes, as well as the policies that should guide the business behavior in certain situations. A core idea of business rules formally supported by SBVR is the following: Rules build on facts, and facts build on concepts as expressed by terms. Terms express business concepts; facts make assertions about these concepts; rules constrain and support these facts [2]. Fig 2 depicts the relation of SBVR and OMGs MDA.

4   Semi-formal KR in Legal Domain

The power of SBVR is disclosed by the fact that the SBVR specification itself was formally written in SBVR Structured English, 'SSE' [2]. The use of SBVR in legal domain was first proposed by Johnsen and Berre [10] [11]. In [4] we showed how OMGs MDA could be viewed in the domain of patent law, wherein, we provided the first ideas on using SBVR SE in patent law domain. We adapt the approach of the OMG Semantic Business Vocabulary and Business Rules [2] (OMG SBVR) standard to the patent law domain. Fig 3 gives an overview of it.

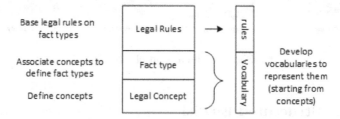

Fig. 3. Building legal vocabulary

SBVR defines the vocabulary and rules for describing the legal semantics using SSE. Even though SSE does not provide all the expressivity required for translating the procedural rules into a formal reasoning, the simple approach of SSE helps the end users (i.e. the domain experts and legal practitioners) to define their legal vocabularies and rules in a more understandable manner, which at the same time can be also interpretable by the computer. Like in SBVR, we define the legal (procedural/substantive) rules in a structured natural language (a Structured English syntax) using predefined **legal vocabularies**, consisting of **legal concepts** (concepts which have a meaning in the legal tradition, e.g. claim construction vocabulary) in template-based **legal rules**.

- **Legal Noun concepts**, which correspond to legal concepts.
- **Legal Verb concepts**, which correspond to relationships between legal concepts.
- **Legal rules**, which constrain these relationships so that they can be used to define consistent and complete arguments.

Legal concepts represented by noun concepts must be explicitly defined with the intended semantics given in an authoritative source or otherwise acknowledge by implicit pragmatic understanding (the ordinary natural language meaning of the term used). Verb concepts can only use such recognized noun concepts as their terms. The legal rules can then be constructed using the "*if ... then ...*", "*at least*", "*each*" as well as definitional alethic and behavioral deontic legal norm modalities ("*obliged*", "*permitted*" ...), etc. The following example in the next section illustrates its use.

5   Example

To illustrate the use of SSE in the legal domain, we consider legal (procedural) rules followed by an examiner in evaluating the essential subject matter requirement as defined in Paragraph ¶ 7.33.01 of United States Patent Law [12] - which states as follows

---

¶ 7.33.01 Rejection, 35 U.S.C. 112, 1st Paragraph, Essential Subject Matter Missing From Claims (Enablement)

Claim [1] rejected under 35 U.S.C. 112, first paragraph, as based on a disclosure which is not enabling. [2] critical or essential to the practice of the invention, but not included in the claim(s) is not enabled by the disclosure.

1. This rejection must be preceded by form paragraph 7.30.01 or 7.103.
2. In bracket 2, recite the subject matter omitted from the claims.

Using SBVR Structured English:

Legal Concepts: *Noun concepts defined in green and individual noun concepts are defined in dark-green starting with capital letters.*

claim	
Definition	Define the invention and are what aspects are legally enforceable
Dictionary basis	patentlaw
Source	USPTOGlossary
General Concept	patent

building on the same lines, we obtain other legal concepts like:
    examiner office_action paragraph statement argument date drawing
    applicant effective_feature invention
    essential_subject_matter_requirement

Paragraph_7_33_01

Legal Facts: *Verb concepts are defined in blue.*
    office_action *includes* paragraph
    claim *is_rejected_under* essential_subject_matter_requirement
    office_action *include* statement
    applicant *conceals* effective_feature
    effective_feature *is_about* the invention
    examiner *applies* **Paragraph_7_33_01**
    examiner *rejects* the claim
    examiner *rejects* the claim

Legal (procedural) rules: *for ¶ 7.33.01.*

1. It is obligatory that examiner *rejects* the claim and office_action *includes* paragraphs **Paragraph_7_33_01** if claim *is_rejected_under* essential_subject_matter_requirement.
2. It is obligatory that office_action *include* statement and argument and date and drawing if office_action *includes* paragraph **Paragraph_7_33_01**.
3. It is obligatory that examiner *applies* **Paragraph_7_33_01** if applicant *conceals* effective_feature and effective_feature *is_about* the invention.

6   Semi-automated Vocabulary Building

In [4], we introduced a proof-of-concept implementation of the tool KR4IPLaw (Knowledge Representation for Intellectual property law). The long term goal of this tool is to provide a user interface, which can be easily handled by legal practitioners and be capable enough to provide all the necessary inputs for a knowledge engineer to model legal rules for (semi-/)automated reasoning thereafter. In this paper, we contribute with an additional conceptual functionality in the architecture of KR4IPLaw, which is provided by a terminology recommender system. Such a system complementary to KR4IPLaw helps to fill the gap between a legal vocabulary/rules built by legal practitioner and all possible concepts/rules which can be identified by the automated system. We strongly believe, that in the legal domain, as an effect of the pragmatics involved, it is rarely possible for a system to fully automate the entire process of building legal rules/vocabularies accurately. Human intervention in confirming the system's automatically generated results is needed in an iterative process during the whole knowledge engineering and formalization process. The recommender system proposed here should provide the required additional context information that can be derived out of the legal context in which a legal vocabulary is built (e.g., case-law, definitions, synonyms etc. pertaining to the section/legal text under consideration). We divide the terminology recommender system into two parts, first one providing legal concepts, i.e., identification of new concepts and semantic enrichment of existing legal concepts. The second one is working on generating the legal facts and building legal rules based on legal facts. In this paper, we mainly concentrate on the first part.

In [4], we already showed how legal practitioners/domain experts either define case based legal vocabularies from scratch or use the preagreed legal vocabulary stored in a central public/privately-shared repositories (such as OntoMaven [13] [14]) and build legal rules based on it as shown before.

For the purpose of legal concept recommendation, we consider a small subset of the available Semantic-Knowledge Extraction (S-KE) tools suitable for its application to our considered legal domain:

- AlchemyAPI: AlchemyAPI [15], is a tool which employs the methods of deep linguistic parsing, statistical natural language processing, and machine learning for named entity extraction, keyword extraction, fact and relation extraction, document categorization, concept tagging and language detection. It builds upon semantic web functionality, AlchemyAPI concepts and entities are linked to DBpedia, Freebase, OpenCyc, GeoNames etc. It is available as a Web application or as a REST service.
- DBpedia Spotlight: A tool for automatically annotating entities in text as DBpedia resources, providing a solution for linking unstructured information sources to the Linked Open Data cloud through DBpedia. It is available as a Web application, as a REST service or as downloadable source [16]. Also language specific versions exist, e.g. DBPedia German[2].
- NERD: NERD [17] proposes a Web framework which unifies numerous named entity extractors using the NERD ontology which provides a rich set of axioms aligning the taxonomies of these tools. Extractors supported by NERD are AlchemyAPI, DBpedia Spotlight, OpenCalais, etc..
- FRED: A tool for automatically producing RDF/OWL ontologies and linked data from natural language sentences. It links the extracted knowledge to both lexical linked data and datasets. It is available as a Web application or as a REST service [18].

Based on [19], a feature based comparison of the considered S-KE tools is as shown in Table 1. Where, NER refers to Named Entity Recognition, DIS refers

---

[2] http://www.corporate-semantic-web.de/dbpedia-deutsch-spotlight.html

Table 1. Feature based comparison of the semantic-knowledge extraction tools for legal concept recommendation (adapted from [19])

	Topic	NER	DIS	TAX	REL	SemRole	Events	Frames
AlchemyAPI	Yes	Yes	Yes	No	Yes	No	No	No
DBpedia Spotlight	No	Yes	Yes	Yes	No	No	No	No
NERD	No	Yes	Yes	No	No	No	No	No
FRED	No	Yes	Yes	Yes	Yes	Yes	Yes	Yes

to the sense disambiguation feature, TAX refers to Taxonomy identification capability and SemRole refers to the identification of semantic roles against an extracted concept.

From Table 1, we can see that FRED offers more features than its considered counterparts. Based on performance evaluation of the S-KE tools as shown in [19], FRED at the time of review provides better results than DBpedia, AlchemyAPI and NERD. For our proof of concept implementation and evaluation we make use of FRED, and adapt it to the legal domain so that it can be used as a legal concept recommender system, working in conjunction with the existing KR4IPLaw tool. FRED considers a legal sections/text given in its base (English) language as an input to produce semantic data and ontologies with a quality closer to what is expected at-least from average linked data-sets and vocabularies by passing through DRS produced by Boxer. It includes Named Entity Resolution (based on Apache Stanbol) and Word Sense Disambiguation

FRED offers several functionalities [20] as required by any legal recommender system. Some functionalities supported by it are as stated below.

- Captures accurate semantic structures,
- Represents complex relations,
- Supports integration of sophisticated lexical reasoners (like OpenNLP, Verb-Net, FrameNet)
- Supports open information extraction,
- Maps natural language to RDF/OWL and
- Links the extracted knowledge to both lexical linked data and datasets (WordNet, DB-pedia and other foundational ontologies)

Fig 4, shows a snippet of the output for a legal text out of the paragraph ¶ 7.30.01.

With the legal text provided as an input, the next step requires the extraction of the required semantic information out of the obtained RDF/OWL ontology. The extracted information is thereafter used to enrich the existing legal vocabulary. The required information is extracted using SPARQL queries and then mapped to legal vocabulary with the help of a mapping scheme as proposed in Table 2.

As a part of the evaluation, we adapt the performance evaluation of NLP tools, proposed by Hirschman and Thompson [21] and its derived methodology proposed in [22]. We assume that a legal practitioner builds a legal vocabulary

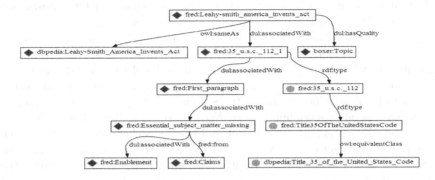

Fig. 4. FRED's output for a legal text

Table 2. Mapping scheme: Parsed legal text to legal (SBVR) vocabulary

RDF class ⟼	Legal (Noun) Concept
rdfs:subClassOf ⟼	General Concept
owl:sameAs ⟼	Synonyms
owl:equivalentClass ⟼	Synonyms
wn:lang ⟼	Language
wn:gloss ⟼	Legal Concept Definition
⟨ boxer⟩: hasModality ⟼	Necessity/Possibility
boxerpos/pennpos: 'v'/'VB' ⟼	Legal (verb) concept
boxerpos/pennpos: 'n'/'NN'/'NNS' ⟼	Legal (Noun) Concept
boxerpos/pennpos: 'np'/'NNP'/'NNPS' ⟼	Legal (Individual Noun) Concept

from scratch to suit, e.g., case-law requirements as an alternative to use/build the existing (pre-agreed) shared vocabulary.

Figure 5, shows a Venn diagram depicting different terms (and its relations) used in this methodology. Building legal arguments (based on legal rules) being the main concern in this evaluation study, a legal practitioner is only interested in the concepts required to build legal rules and rule-based arguments (i.e., $N_{legal(Noun)}$ concepts, $N_{Legal(verb)}$ concept, and $N_{legal(Indv)}$ concepts). In this

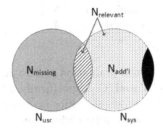

Fig. 5. Venn diagram

evaluation we study to which extent the system is capable of filling/enriching the semantic information attached to each legal concept.

N_{usr} here denotes the inputs from the user in building the legal vocabulary, (where N denotes the number of respective items added). N_{sys} denotes the systems effort in identifying the information/items related to this section of legal text under consideration. $N_{relevant}$ refers to the items that are relevant/meaningful out of the identified items by the system (i.e N_{sys}). The relevance of an item is determined by a domain expert. $N_{missing}$ refers to the difference in number between the items that are relevant and the items that were used/identified by the user/legal practitioner. $N_{add'l}$ refers to the additional relevant items identified by the system which are currently not used by the user. To evaluate the efficiency of such systems, we consider two parameters, $Eff_{sys\ vs.\ relevant}$ and $Eff_{relevant\ vs.\ add'l}$ as shown below:

$$Eff_{sys\ vs.\ relevant} = \frac{N_{relevant}}{N_{sys}} \times 100\% \Rightarrow SystemReliability \qquad (1)$$

$$Eff_{relevant\ vs.\ add'l} = \frac{N_{add'l}}{N_{relevant}} \times 100\% \Rightarrow SystemIntelligence \qquad (2)$$

wherein;

$Eff_{sys\ vs.\ relevant}$ denotes the efficiency of the system in identifying relevant/meaningful items in a given legal passage/text and $Eff_{relevant\ vs.\ add'l}$ refers to the efficiency of the system in providing additional information out of its identified relevant items. We consider the example shown in the last section as an input to the recommender system. Table 3 shows a chart comprising of both inputs from the user as well as from the system. The efficiency of the system is as shown in Figure 6 (i.e. Legal Text A).

Table 3. Recommender system outcome analysis

	N_{usr}	N_{sys}	$N_{relevant}$	$N_{missing}$	$N_{add'l}$
Language (Legal concepts)	0	1	1	0	1
Definitions identified	0	4	4	8	0
General concepts identified	0	14	2	NA	2
Synonyms identified	0	4	2	NA	2
$N_{Legal(Noun)}$concepts identified	12	14	9	8	5
$N_{Legal(Verb)}$concepts identified	6	5	3	5	2
$N_{Legal(Indv)}$concepts identified	1	4	4	0	3

Figure 6 gives the results of the evaluation on two additional legal paragraphs (denoted here as legal texts 'B' and 'C'). Specifically, Fig 6a, shows the efficiency $Eff_{sys\ vs.\ relevant}$ and Fig 6b, shows the efficiency $Eff_{relevant\ vs.\ add'l}$. The second part of the recommender system involving (semi-/)automatized building of legal rules is still an open research question. There have been several works in automatic extraction of SBVR business rules [23] [22] [24] [25]. Adapting it to

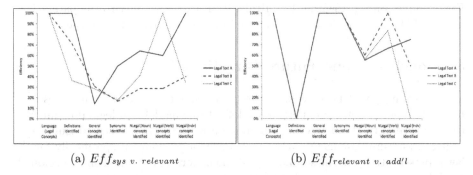

(a) $Eff_{sys\ v.\ relevant}$ (b) $Eff_{relevant\ v.\ add'l}$

Fig. 6. Efficiency evaluation

legal domain has shown high inconsistencies between the actual legal texts to its constructed legal rules. The architecture of FRED is designed to allow the use of domain specific legal lexical resources, which includes the knowledge base (legal vocabulary) built during the semi-formal representation of the procedural legal rules.

7   CIM to PIM to PSM

Moving from computational independent layer (i.e. SBVR-SE) to platform independent layer requires storing the semantically enriched legal vocabulary and rules in a machine oriented format. Legal vocabularies (Legal Concepts and Legal facts) are mapped into an OWL2 ontology. In [26] [27] [28], authors have proposed a possible mapping scheme for such transformations. For interchanging the legal rules in a platform independent way, we propose to translate them into XML using the language family of 'RuleML' [29] as expression language. In particular, we make use of two complementary OASIS standards-OASIS Legal Document Markup Language, 'LegalDocML' [30] and OASIS Legal Rule Markup Language, 'LegalRuleML' [31] [32] in combination with Reaction RuleML [33] [34] for the said transformation. The details of this semantic transformation process are out of scope of this paper. They can be found in [3].

For reasoning with such transformed legal rules using legal knowledge bases, we use Prova [35] [36] [37] [38], as a rule engine. Prova is both a Semantic Web rule language and a high expressive distributed rule engine. It, supports the execution of declarative (legal) rules including scoped reasoning [37] [36] [38], Rule-Based Data Access (RBDA) to external semantic web data via SPARQL, and Ontology-Based Data Access (OBDA) with DL typed reasoning [39]. For the purpose of ontology reasoning on-top of legal knowledge bases (domain ontologies), Prova integrates SPARQL-DL API [40], a subset of SPARQL tailored for ontology-specific requests related to OWL and it is more expressive than existing DL query languages by allowing a mix of TBox, RBox, and ABox queries. It can be regarded as an OBDA interface to any ontology reasoner supporting OWL-API. Reasoning with legal rules in Prova is also out of the scope of this paper.

For examples on representing LegalRuleML in Prova we refer to the patent law use case[3] [41] and the copyright use case[4] of the LegalRuleML tutorials.

8   Conclusion and Future Directions

The paper in its first part explored the use of controlled natural languages as a bridge between a domain expert and a knowledge modeler in legal domain. We then showed with the help of an example on how SBVR Structured English, a controlled natural language, can be used in the legal domain (specifically for IP law representation). In the second part of the paper, we presented an extension of our KR4IPLaw system with a legal concept recommender system which supports the manual vocabulary building process by making automated suggestions. We implemented a proof-of-concept and studied the feasibility of the automation approach of semantically enriching legal vocabularies by means of case study examples. During the course of this studies, we identified some new and re-iterated some known research problems existing in the process of automation in legal domain. The long term goal of this KR4IPLaw project is to build a system which acts as a platform to model, represent, recommend, and reason about legal patent law knowledge.

Acknowledgements. The authors would like to thank the entire Corporate Semantic Web team at the Free University of Berlin for their constructive comments and suggestions. The authors would also like to thank Mr Spurthishekar for assisting in sentence structure and grammatical error corrections.

References

1. Palmirani, M., Contissa, G., Rubino, R.: Fill the gap in the legal knowledge modelling. In: Governatori, G., Hall, J., Paschke, A. (eds.) RuleML 2009. LNCS, vol. 5858, pp. 305–314. Springer, Heidelberg (2009)
2. OMG: Semantics of Business Vocabulary and Business Rules (SBVR)- Version 1.2. Technical Report November, Object Management Group (2013)
3. Ramakrishna, S., Paschke, A.: A Process for Knowledge Transformation and Knowledge Representation of Patent Law. In: RuleML 2014. LNCS, vol. 8620, pp. 308–325. Springer, Heidelberg (2014)
4. Ramakrishna, S., Paschke, A.: Bridging the gap between Legal Practitioners and Knowledge Engineers using semi-formal KR. In: The 8th International Workshop on Value Modeling and Business Ontology, VMBO, Berlin (2014)

---

[3] http://2013.ruleml.org/presentations/
RuleML2013Tutorial_PaschkePatentLaw.pdf
[4] https://lists.oasis-open.org/archives/legalruleml/201208/msg00040/
LegalRuleML-palmirani2012_-RuleML2012v3.pdf, slide 39-54.

5. Fuchs, N.E., Schwitter, R.: Attempto controlled english (ace). arXiv preprint cmp-lg/9603003 (1996)
6. Paris, C., Linden, K.V.: DRAFTER: An Interactive Support Tool for Writing Multilingual Instructions. IEEE Computer, Special Issue on Interactive NLP (July 1996)
7. Sullivan, D.E.: Legislative drafting and legal manual (2003)
8. Kuhn, T.: Controlled Natural Language and Opportunities for Standardization. In: International Workshop on Terminology, Languages, and Content Resources (June 2013)
9. Bézivin, J., Gerbé, O.: Towards a precise definition of the OMG/MDA framework. In: Proceedings of the 16th Annual International Conference on Automated Software Engineering, ASE 2001, pp. 273–280. IEEE (2001)
10. Johnsen, A.S.: Semantisk modellering av juridisk regelverk med bruk av SBVR - en brobygger mellom jus og IT. Master thesis, University of Oslo (2011)
11. Johnsen, A.S., Berre, A.J.R.: A bridge between legislator and technologist - Formalization in SBVR for improved quality and understanding of legal rules. In: International Workshop on Business Models, Business Rules and Ontologies, Bressanone, Brixen, Italy (2010)
12. USC: Title 35 of the United States Code (1952)
13. Paschke, A.: OntoMaven API4KB - A Maven-based API for Knowledge Bases. In: 6th International Semantic Web Applications and Tools for the Life Science (SWAT4LS 2013), Edinburgh, UK, December 10-12 (2013)
14. Paschke, A.: OntoMaven. In: 9th International Workshop on Semantic Web Enabled Software Engineering (SWESE 2013), Berlin, Germany, December 2-5 (2013)
15. Turian, J.: Using AlchemyAPI for Enterprise-Grade Text Analysis. Technical report, AlchemyAPI (August 2013)
16. Mendes, P.N., Jakob, M., García-Silva, A., Bizer, C.: Dbpedia spotlight: Shedding light on the web of documents. In: Proceedings of the 7th International Conference on Semantic Systems. I-Semantics 2011, pp. 1–8. ACM, New York (2011)
17. Van Erp, M., Rizzo, G., Troncy, R.: Learning with the web: Spotting named entities on the intersection of nerd and machine learning. In: Proceedings of the 3rd Workshop on Making Sense of Microposts (# MSM 2013) (2013)
18. Draicchio, F., Gangemi, A., Presutti, V., Nuzzolese, A.G.: FRED: From Natural Language Text to RDF and OWL in One Click. In: Cimiano, P., Fernández, M., Lopez, V., Schlobach, S., Völker, J. (eds.) ESWC 2013. LNCS, vol. 7955, pp. 263–267. Springer, Heidelberg (2013)
19. Gangemi, A.: A comparison of knowledge extraction tools for the semantic web. In: Cimiano, P., Corcho, O., Presutti, V., Hollink, L., Rudolph, S. (eds.) ESWC 2013. LNCS, vol. 7882, pp. 351–366. Springer, Heidelberg (2013)
20. Gangemi, A., Draicchio, F., Presutti, V., Nuzzolese, A.G., Recupero, D.R.: A machine reader for the semantic web. In: International Semantic Web Conference (Posters & Demos), pp. 149–152 (2013)
21. Hirschman, L., Thompson, H.S.: Chapter 13: Overview of Evaluation in Speech and Natural Language Processing. In: Survey of the State of the Art in Human Language Technology, pp. 385–420 (1995)
22. Afreen, H., Bajwa, I.S.: Generating UML Class Models from SBVR Software Requirements Specifications. In: 23rd Benelux Conference on Artificial Intelligence (BNAIC 2011), Gent, Belgium, pp. 23–32 (2011)

23. Bajwa, I., Lee, M., Bordbar, B.: SBVR Business Rules Generation from Natural Language Specification. In: AAAI 2011 Spring Symposium AI for Business Agility, San Francisco, USA, pp. 2–8 (2011)

24. Martínez-Fernández, J.L., González, J.C., Villena, J., Martínez, P.: A preliminary approach to the automatic extraction of business rules from unrestricted text in the banking industry. In: Kapetanios, E., Sugumaran, V., Spiliopoulou, M. (eds.) NLDB 2008. LNCS, vol. 5039, pp. 299–310. Springer, Heidelberg (2008)

25. Chaparro, O., Aponte, J., Ortega, F., Marcus, A.: Towards the Automatic Extraction of Structural Business Rules from Legacy Databases. In: 2012 19th Working Conference on Reverse Engineering (WCRE), pp. 479–488 (October 2012)

26. Elisa, K., Mark, H.L.: Mapping SBVR to OWL2. Technical report, IBM Research Division, New York, NY (2013)

27. Reynares, E., Caliusco, M.A., Galli, M.R.: Automatable Approach for SBVR to OWL2 Mappings. In: XVI Ibero-American Conference on Software Engineering (CIbSE 2013), Montevideo, Uruguay (2013)

28. Karpovic, J., Nemuraite, L.: Transforming SBVR Business Semantics into Web Ontology Language OWL2: Main Concepts. In: In Proc. 17th International Conference on Information and Software Technologies, IT 2011, pp. 231–254 (2011)

29. Boley, H., Paschke, A., Shafiq, O.: RuleML 1.0: The Overarching Specification of Web Rules. In: Dean, M., Hall, J., Rotolo, A., Tabet, S. (eds.) RuleML 2010. LNCS, vol. 6403, pp. 162–178. Springer, Heidelberg (2010)

30. Gordon, T.F.: The Legal Knowledge Interchange Format (LKIF). Technical report, European project for Standardized Transparent Representations in order to Extend LegaL Accessibility Specific Targeted Research or Innovation Project (2008)

31. Palmirani, M., Governatori, G., Rotolo, A., Tabet, S., Boley, H., Paschke, A.: LegalRuleML: XML-Based Rules and Norms. In: Palmirani, M. (ed.) RuleML 2011 - America. LNCS, vol. 7018, pp. 298–312. Springer, Heidelberg (2011)

32. Athan, T., Boley, H., Governatori, G., Palmirani, M., Paschke, A., Wyner, A.: OASIS LegalRuleML. In: Proceedings of 14th International Conference on Artificial Intelligence and Law (ICAIL 2013). ACM (2013)

33. Paschke, A., Boley, H., Zhao, Z., Teymourian, K., Athan, T.: Reaction RuleML 1.0: Standardized Semantic Reaction Rules. In: Bikakis, A., Giurca, A. (eds.) RuleML 2012. LNCS, vol. 7438, pp. 100–119. Springer, Heidelberg (2012)

34. Paschke, A.: Reaction RuleML 1.0 for Rules, Events and Actions in Semantic Complex Event Processing. In: RuleML 2014. LNCS, vol. 8620, pp. 1–18. Springer, Heidelberg (2014)

35. Kozlenkov, A., Paschke, A.: Prova Rule Language Version 3.0 User's Guide (2010), http://prova.ws/index.html

36. Paschke, A.: Rules and logic programming for the web. In: Polleres, A., d'Amato, C., Arenas, M., Handschuh, S., Kroner, P., Ossowski, S., Patel-Schneider, P. (eds.) Reasoning Web 2011. LNCS, vol. 6848, pp. 326–381. Springer, Heidelberg (2011)

37. Paschke, A., Boley, H.: Rule Responder: Rule-Based Agents for the Semantic-Pragmatic Web. International Journal on Artificial Intelligence Tools 20(6), 1043–1081 (2011)

38. Paschke, A.: Rule based service level agreements: RBSLA; knowledge representation for automated e-contract, SLA and policy management. Idea Verlag GmbH (2007)

39. Paschke, A.: A Typed Hybrid Description Logic Programming Language with Polymorphic Order-Sorted DL-Typed Unification for Semantic Web Type Systems. In: Proceedings of the OWLED 2006 Workshop on OWL: Experiences and Directions, Athens, Georgia, USA, November 10-11. CEUR Workshop Proceedings, vol. 216, CEUR-WS.org (2006)
40. Sirin, E., Parsia, B.: SPARQL-DL: SPARQL Query for OWL-DL. In: 3rd OWL Experiences and Directions Workshop, OWLED 2007 (2007)
41. Paschke, A., Ramakrishna, S.: Legal RuleML Tutorial Use Case - LegalRuleML for Legal Reasoning in Patent Law (2013)

Basics for a Grammar Engine to Verbalize Logical Theories in isiZulu

C. Maria Keet[1] and Langa Khumalo[2]

[1] Department of Computer Science, University of Cape Town, South Africa
mkeet@cs.uct.ac.za
[2] Linguistics Program, School of Arts, University of KwaZulu-Natal, South Africa
Khumalol@ukzn.ac.za

Abstract. The language isiZulu is the largest in South Africa by numbers of first language speakers, yet, it is still an underresourced language. In this paper, we approach the grammar piecemeal from a natural language generation approach, and viewed from a potential utility for verbalizing OWL ontologies as a tangible use case. The elaborate rules of the grammar show that a grammar engine and dictionary is essential even for basic verbalizations in OWL 2 EL. This is due to, mainly, the 17 noun classes with embedded semantics and the agglutinative nature of isiZulu. The verbalization of basic constructs requires merging a prefix with a noun and distinguishing an 'and' between a list and linking clauses.

1 Introduction

South Africa has hitherto seen limited investment in human language technologies and computational linguistics, especially for its 9 official African languages. Large companies, such as Google and Microsoft, do pick the low-hanging fruit with localizations of the user interfaces of their software. The South African Department of Science and Technology demands for its potential outputs, notably with its "National Recordal System" (NRS) project by its National Indigenous Knowledge Systems Office. NRS software infrastructure was launched in 2013 and requires not just a standard document system [7] but for full usage, it requires an 'intelligent' one [1] that can handle multilingualism in, among others, document search and annotation, and in model development of the knowledge that is to be stored in the NRS. Systems with relevant functionalities for the NRS exist elsewhere for multiple languages in Europe, e.g., the multilingual and collaborative systems by [2,10], or a CNL-mediated query interface (e.g., [6]). This is to quite an extent thanks to large FP7 projects, such as Monnet [http://www.monnet-project.eu] for foundational aspects and applied projects such as Organic.Lingua [http://www.organic-lingua.eu]. No such resources exist for promoting the 9 official African languages in South Africa, yet such system requirements for, among others, the NRS, demand for both NLP and NLG technologies for those languages. Here, we focus on NLG for isiZulu, which is the first ("home") language for about 23% of the population (±10 million), about

A. Bikakis et al. (Eds.): RuleML 2014, LNCS 8620, pp. 216–225, 2014.

half of the population in South Africa can speak it, and it has several closely related languages, such as isiXhosa.

Unlike for NLP and corpus building [16,18], no NLG results exist for any of the languages in the Nguni language group, of which isiZulu is a member. One could consider Google Translate, which has English–isiZulu since October 2013, but it cannot handle articles and quantification (among other things), and its technology is proprietary and inaccessible. There are mainly old and out-dated grammar books and Doke's seminal work on the general description of the isiZulu morphology [4,5] has remained an important reference for linguistic work not only in isiZulu but in Southern Bantu languages; this makes it challenging to commence defining grammars similar to Kuhn [12]. It will take many years and resources to fill this gap. Here, we start with some basics that should aid both linguists and information systems development. To this end, we take language constructs of a practical logic language with low expressiveness, such as the OWL 2 EL profile [14], as a starting point and extant approaches for other languages and systems. Concerning such practical verbalizations of logical theories, there are verbalization options within English [17], implementations in different systems, such as for the Semantic Web (ACE [8]) and for conceptual data models (e.g., monolingual [3] and multilingual ORM [9]), and we assume that a multilingual ontology is in place, perhaps managed through the *Lemon* model [13]. For isiZulu, it appears that the grammar rules are quite complex, and we summarise those for subsumption, disjointness, existential and universal quantification, and conjunction. There are two particular features of isiZulu that have a major effect on verbalizations, which are that the semantics of the noun (more precisely: the category of the entity it refers to) and the quantifiers in an axiom influence the verbalization patterns.

The remainder of this paper is organised as follows. Section 2 describes some basic aspects of isiZulu, and Section 3 presents the main results on verbalization patterns for simple taxonomic subsumption, disjointness (negation), conjunction, and quantification. We reflect in Section 4 and conclude in Section 5.

2   Some Very Basic Aspects of isiZulu

IsiZulu is a highly agglutinating language with a complex morphology. As is emblematic of Bantu languages, isiZulu has a system of noun classes. Every noun belongs to a noun class. The class is often identifiable from the noun prefix that is attached to the noun, and it governs the agreement of all words that modify the noun, as well as of predicates of which the noun is a subject. Object agreement may also be marked on the predicate.

There is more than one convention for labeling and referring to these classes, most of which are essentially numbering systems. We will use Meinhof's (1948) classification system, which is used in most scholarly works and permits comparison of corresponding classes across Bantu languages, all of which lack at least some of the classes posited for proto-Bantu. Most noun classes are set off into pairs in isiZulu such that most nouns have a singular form in one class and a

Table 1. Zulu noun classes, with examples. The noun class prefix of classes 1 and 3 is conditioned by the morphology of the stem to which it attaches: *-mu-* before monosyllabic stems and *-m-* for other stems. The *n* of the noun prefixes of noun class 9 and 10 fuses with the following consonant forming prenasalized consonants; NC: Noun class, AU: augment, PRE: prefix.

NC	AU	PRE	Stem (example)	Meaning	Example	
1	u-	m(u)-	-fana	humans and other	umfana	boy
2	a-	ba-	-fana	animates	abafana	boys
1a	u-	-	-baba	kinship terms and proper	ubaba	father
2a	o-	-	-baba	names	obaba	fathers
3a	u-	-	-shizi	nonhuman	ushizi	cheese
(2a)	o-	-	-shizi		oshizi	cheeses
3	u-	m(u)-	-fula	trees, plants, non-paired	umfula	river
4	i-	mi-	-fula	body parts	imifula	rivers
5	i-	(li)-	-gama	fruits, paired body parts,	igama	name
6	a-	ma-	-gama	and natural phenomena	amagama	names
7	i-	si-	-hlalo	inanimates and manner/	isihlalo	chair
8	i-	zi-	-hlalo	style	izihlalo	chairs
9a	i-	-	-rabha	nonhuman	irabha	rubber
(6)	a-	ma-	-rabha		amarabha	rubbers
9	i(n)-	-	-ja	animals	inja	dog
10	i-	zi(n)-	-ja		izinja	dogs
11	u-	(lu)-	-thi	inanimates and long thin	uthi	stick
(10)	i-	zi(n)-	-thi	objects	izinthi	sticks
14	u-	bu-	-hle	abstract nouns	ubuhle	beauty
15	u-	ku-	-cula	infinitives	ukucula	to sing
17		ku-		locatives, remote/ general		locative

plural form in another; the classes are summarised in Table 1. The morphological structure of a noun in isiZulu typically takes the shape of the tree structure.

For the most part, the semantics of a noun plays a role in determining what noun class a word falls in; their deeper meanings as well as shift and colloquial use are being investigated (e.g., [15]), and is summarised in column 5 of Table 1. Most noun stems belong to only one noun class pair, but exceptions exist (e.g., *-ntu*). Noun class prefixes can also be used to form new nouns from other noun stems and other stems, like noun class 15 that creates infinitives out of verbal stems. The vast majority of the nouns in noun class 14 is derived as well: the prefix *-bu-* forms abstract nouns from other noun stems and adjective stems. Class 17 is a non-productive locative class with the noun prefix *ku-*. IsiZulu lacks classes 12 and 13, which are found in other Bantu languages.

The complexity of the morphology of isiZulu is compounded by the fact that a number of prefixes have allomorphic forms. This is a consequence of the fact that isiZulu proscribes vowel sequencing, so that a prefix whose canonical form is *nga-* will have an allomorph *ng-* before roots that begin with vowels. Furthermore, many morphemes are homographs, so that the prefix *nga-* could represent either the potential mood morpheme or a form of the negative that occurs in subordinate clauses; and the sequence *ng-* could be the allomorph of either of these, or of a number of homographic morphemes *ngi-*, which represent the first person singular in various moods. Besides these phonologically conditioned allomorphs, there are also morphologically conditioned ones; e.g., the locative prefix *e-* has an allomorph *o-* that occurs in certain morphological circumstances [18] (p1023). Nominal morphology triggers agreement, as is shown in the example:

Abafana abancane bazozithenga izincwadi ezinkulu
aba-fana **aba**-ncane **ba**-   zo- **zi**- thenga **izi**-ncwadi e-**zi**-nkulu
2.boy   **2**.small   **2.SUBJ**-FUT-**10.OBJ**-buy 10.book REL-**10**.big
'The little boys will buy the big books'

The fact that the subject *abafana* ('boys') is of noun class 2 is reflected both in the agreement prefix on the adjective *abancane* ('small') and in the subject agreement on the verb. The noun class 10 feature of the object *izincwadi* ('books') is reflected in the class 10 agreement on the adjective *ezinkulu* ('big') and in the object marker on the verb. A selection of such agreements, called concords, is included in Table 2. The normal word order is Subject Verb Object (SVO) but there is attested variation since post verbal subjects are also common.

It is imperative to further state that isiZulu also has a very complex verbal morphology. The verbs can be conjugated in five different tenses (remote past, recent past, present, immediate future and remote future) as well as for various aspects and moods. The verb usually agrees with the subject and sometimes with the object in person and number (as shown in the example above) and in 3rd person for noun class as well. To account for this, a verb form can consist of many morphemes. Such complex morphology characteristic of most Bantu languages presents a lot of challenges in the attempts to develop computational technologies in isiZulu.

3   Verbalization Patterns and Algorithms

We obviously cannot cover all the grammar rules, and will focus only on the—from a logic viewpoint—seemingly 'simple' constructs, being subsumption, conjunction, negation, and quantification. This fits roughly with the OWL 2 EL profile (plus negation), that has a nice use-case scenario: upon localizing SNOMED CT, the axioms can then be verbalised in isiZulu and be used in healthcare applications. We will take examples from the general domain, however, so as not to complicate matters with medicine, and we assume a suitable multilingual encoding of the ontology, and use the Description Logics notation for conciseness.

Universal Quantification. We consider here only the universal quantification at the start of the concept inclusion axiom, such as for verbalizing taxonomic subsumption for atomic classes and the typical 'forall-some' construction, or, in linguistic terms, the nominal head. In isiZulu, the 'all'/'each' uses *-onke*, which is prefixed with the oral prefix (see AU and PRE in Table 1) of the noun class

Table 2. Zulu noun classes with a selection of 'concords'. NC: Noun class; QC: quantitative concord; NEG SC: negative subject concord, PRON: pronominal; RC: relative concord; EC: enumerative concord; oral: oral prefix (see also AU and PRE in Table 1).

NC	QC (all)		NEG SC	PRON	RC	QC_{dwa}	EC
	$QC_{oral+onke}$	QC_{nke}					
1	u-onke → wonke	wo-	aka-	yena	o-	ye-	mu-
2	ba-onke → bonke	bo-	aba-	bona	aba-	bo-	ba-
1a	u-onke → wonke	wo-	aka-	yena	o-	ye-	mu-
2a	ba-onke → bonke	bo-	aba-	bona	aba-	bo-	ba-
3a	u-onke → wonke	wo-	aka-	wona	o-	ye-	mu-
(2a)	ba-onke → bonke	bo-	aba-	bona	aba-	bo-	ba-
3	u-onke → wonke	wo-	awu-	wona	o-	wo-	mu-
4	i-onke → yonke	yo-	ayi-	yona	e-	yo-	mi-
5	li-onke → lonke	lo-	ali-	lona	eli-	lo-	li-
6	a-onke → onke	o-	awa-	wona	a-	wo-	ma-
7	si-onke → sonke	so-	asi-	sona	esi-	so-	si-
8	zi-onke → zonke	zo-	azi-	zona	ezi	zo-	zi-
9a	i-onke → yonke	yo-	ayi-	yona	e-	yo-	yi-
(6)	a-onke → onke	o-	awa-	wona	a-	wo-	ma-
9	i-onke → yonke	yo-	ayi-	yona	e-	yo-	yi-
10	zi-onke → zonke	zo-	azi-	zona	ezi-	zo-	zi-
11	lu-onke → lonke	lo-	alu-	lona	olu-	lo-	lu-
(10)	zi-onke → zonke	zo-	azi-	zona	ezi-	zo-	zi-
14	ba-onke → bonke	bo-	abu-	bona	obu-	bo-	bu-
15	ku-onke → konke	zo-	aku-	khona	oku-	zo-	ku-

of that first noun—i.e., a named OWL class/DL concept on the left-hand side of ⊑ in the ontology—and modified based on what the prefix was; e.g.:

(U1) Girl ⊑ ...
<u>wonke</u> umfana ...   ('<u>each</u> girl...'; u- + -$onke$)
<u>bonke</u> abafana ...   ('<u>all</u> girls...'; ba- + -$onke$)

This looks laborious, but it can be simplified computationally. The oral prefixes are stable for each noun class, so one can pre-compute the complete list of nominal heads (column 2 in Table 2) and carry out a simple look-up of the term when generating the verbalization. Whether singular or plural should be used depends on the context, and will be addressed below and in Algorithms 1 and 3.

Subsumption. There are different ways of carving up the nouns to determine which rules apply for verbalizing subsumption. One can use either the living/non-living thing distinction into which nouns are grouped, but we postulate that a purely syntactic approach may be feasible, which is easier to implement computationally. The latter requires one to select the right copulative ('is a'), which is based on the first letter of the noun of the superclass, being ng for nouns starting with a-, o-, or u-, or else y. In addition, among generic and determinate verbalization, the generic is chosen. For instance:

(S1) `Giraffes ⊑ Animals`
izindlulamithi yizilwane   ('giraffes <u>are</u> animals'; animals: *izilwane*)
(S2) `MedicinalHerb ⊑ Plant`
ikhambi ngumuthi   (*umuthi*: (medicinal) plant)

The general pattern that emerges is as follows: $<noun1>$ $<ng/y$ *depending on first letter of noun2$><noun2>$. This holds for when the subsumption is not followed by negation. If it is followed by negation, then the verbalization for subsumption and negation are combined into one term and the copulative is omitted. This can be with or without including the quantifiers in the verbalization. For instance:

(SN1) `Cup ⊑ ¬Glass`
zonke izindebe aziyona ingilazi   ('all cups <u>are not a</u> glass')

Here, we address only the negation in the context of the subsumption symbol. The *azi-* is the negative subject concord (NEG SC) for the noun class of the noun (name of the OWL class) on the left-hand side of the subsumption (noun class 10 for *izindebe*), and the *-yona* is the part indicating the pronomial (PRON) for the noun of the class on the right-hand side of the subsumption (*ingilazi* is in noun class 9a), which is then adjusted for each class; see Table 2. Thus, the pattern for simple disjointness is: $<QC$-*all of* $NC_x>$ $<plural\ of\ noun1\ with$ $NC_x>$ $<NEG\ SC\ of\ NC_x><PRON\ of\ NC_y>$ $<noun2\ with\ NC_y>$. The high-level algorithm for simple class subsumption and disjointness for isiZulu is included as Algorithm 1, which is more elaborate compared to the 'is a' and 'is not a' in English verbalization templates. We leave the more complicated cases, like $\forall R.C \sqsubseteq \exists S.(D \sqcap E)$, for future work, as well as negation in other contexts.

Conjunction. The 'and' in the sense of a list of things uses *na*, but this changes into (a + i =) *ne* or (a + u =) *no*, depending on the first letter of the noun that follows it, and this *no* or *ne* is then a prefix to the second noun that drops its first letter (always a vowel); e.g. (C1). Conjunction as connective of clauses uses a different term for 'and', being *kanye* or *futhi*; e.g., (C2).

(C1) `Milk ⊓ Butter`
Ubisi nebhotela   (*Ubisi* + *na* + *Ibhotela*)
(C2) `... ∃has_filling.Cream ⊓ ∃has_Icing.Lemon_flavour ...`
...kune zigcwalisa ukhilimu <u>kanye</u> nezinye uqweqwe olunambitheka_ulamula...

That is, the pattern for the enumerative-and is $<noun1>$ $<na/ne/no\ depending$ *on noun2$><noun2\ minus\ first\ character>$, and for the connective-and it is $<first$ *clause$>$ $<kanye>$ $<second\ clause>$. Algorithm 2 first recognises whether it is a listing of atomic classes or several axioms—check the first element after the ⊓: if it is an OWL object or data property (relationship or attribute), then use the connective-and, else an enumeration-and—and if the former, then it checks the first letter of the second word to choose the *na/ne/no*.

Algorithm 1. Determine the verbalization of simple taxonomic subsumption

---

1: $\mathcal{C}$ set of classes, language $\mathcal{L}$ with $\sqsubseteq$ for subsumption and $\neg$ for negation; variables: A axiom, NC_i nounclass, $c_1, c_2 \in \mathcal{C}$, a_1 term, a_2 letter; functions: $getFirstClass(A)$, $getSecondClass(A)$, $getNC(C)$, $pluralizeNoun(C, NC_i)$, $checkNegation(A)$, $getFirstChar(C)$, $getNSC(NC_i)$, $getPNC(NC_i)$.

Require: axiom A with a $\sqsubseteq$ has been retrieved

2: $c_1 \leftarrow getFirstClass(A)$ {get subclass}
3: $c_2 \leftarrow getSecondClass(A)$ {get superclass}
4: $NC_1 \leftarrow getNC(c_1)$ {determine noun class by augment and prefix or dictionary}
5: $NC_2 \leftarrow getNC(c_2)$ {determine noun class by augment and prefix or dictionary}
6: **if** $checkNegation(A) = true$ **then**
7:      $NC_1' \leftarrow$ lookup plural nounclass of NC_1 {from known list}
8:      $c_1' \leftarrow pluralizeNoun(c_1, NC_1')$
9:      $a_1 \leftarrow$ lookup quantitative concord for NC_1' {from quantitative concord (QC(all)) list}
10:     $n \leftarrow getNSC(NC_1')$ {get negative subject concord for c_1'}
11:     $p \leftarrow getPNC(NC_2)$ {get pronomial for c_2}
12:     RESULT $\leftarrow$ ' a_1 c_1' np c_2. '   {verbalise the disjointness}
13: **else**
14:     $a_2 \leftarrow getFirstChar(c_2)$ {retrieve first letter of c_2}
15:     **select case**
16:         $a_2 = $ 'i' **then**
17:             RESULT $\leftarrow$ ' c_1 yc_2 '   {verbalise as taxonomic subsumption with y}
18:         $a_2 = \{$'a', 'o', 'u'$\}$ **then**
19:             RESULT $\leftarrow$ ' c_1 ngc_2 '   {verbalise as taxonomic subsumption with ng}
20:         $a_2 \notin \{$'a', 'i', 'o', 'u',$\}$ **then**
21:             RESULT $\leftarrow$ 'this is not a well-formed isiZulu noun'
22:     **end select case**
23: **end if**
24: **return** RESULT

Existential Quantification. There are multiple aspects to the verbalization, and we focus here only on the existential quantification, not the verb, due to additioanl complexities of verb tenses and the prepositions that are typically put in the name of the object property in the ontology or conceptual data model. Choices are discussed in [11], and we show here only the final outcome, using the *-dwa* option. For instance:

(E1) Professor $\sqsubseteq \exists$teaches.Module   ('all professors teach <u>at least one</u> module')
bonke oSolwazi bafundisa isifundo <u>esisodwa</u>

The *esisodwa* in (E1) is composed of the relative concord (RC), which is determined by the noun class system, that is attached to the quantitative concord (QC) and then suffixed with the quantitative suffix *-dwa*; e.g.: *esi* (RC7) + *so* (QC7) + *dwa*. The RC and QC for each noun class is fixed, and is included in Table 2. Overall, the following pattern is obtained: $<QC$-all of $NC_x>$ $<$pl. noun1 of $NC_x>$ [conjugated verb] $<$noun2 of $NC_y>$ $<$RC for $NC_y><$QC for $NC_y>$dwa; This is presented in Algorithm 3.

Algorithm 2. Determine the verbalization of conjunction in an axiom

---

1: $\mathcal{R}$ is the set of relationships, $\mathcal{A}$ of attributes, $\mathcal{C}$ of classes, and language $\mathcal{L}$ uses $\sqcap$ to denote conjunction; variables: e_2, c_1 a letter, A axiom; functions: $getNextVocabularyElement(A)$, $getFirstChar(e_2)$.

Require: axiom with a $\sqcap$ has been retrieved and position in string is known

2: $e_2 \leftarrow getNextVocabularyElement(A)$　　　　　　　{retrieve element after the $\sqcap$}

3: **if** $e_2 \in \mathcal{R} \cup \mathcal{A}$ **then**

4: 　　RESULT $\leftarrow$ ' kanye '　　　　　　　　　{verbalise $\sqcap$ as kanye}

5: **else**

6: 　　**if** $e_2 \in \mathcal{C}$ **then**

7: 　　　　$c_1 \leftarrow getFirstChar(e_2)$　　　　　　{retrieve first letter of e_2}

8: 　　　　**select case**

9: 　　　　　　$c_1 =$ 'i' **then**

10: 　　　　　　　$e_2^- \leftarrow$ drop c_1 from e_2

11: 　　　　　　　RESULT $\leftarrow$ ' nee$_2^-$ '　　　　{verbalise $\sqcap$ with ne- prefix}

12: 　　　　　　$c_1 =$ 'u' **then**

13: 　　　　　　　$e_2^- \leftarrow$ drop c_1 from e_2

14: 　　　　　　　RESULT $\leftarrow$ ' noe$_2^-$ '　　　　{verbalise $\sqcap$ with no- prefix}

15: 　　　　　　$c_1 =$ 'a' **then**

16: 　　　　　　　$e_2^- \leftarrow$ drop c_1 from e_2

17: 　　　　　　　RESULT $\leftarrow$ ' nae$_2^-$ '　　　　{verbalise $\sqcap$ with na- prefix}

18: 　　　　　　$c_1 \notin \{$'i', 'u', 'a'$\}$ **then**

19: 　　　　　　　RESULT $\leftarrow$ 'this is not a well-formed isiZulu noun'

20: 　　　　**end select case**

21: 　　**else**

22: 　　　　RESULT $\leftarrow$ 'this is not a well-formed axiom'

23: 　　**end if**

24: **end if**

25: **return** RESULT

---

4   Discussion

For grammatically less complicated languages that have an isolating morphology, such as English, verbalization templates are known to be an effective way to tackle the problem, and may even suffice. This approach breaks down for grammatically richer languages [9], and for isiZulu, we have, so far, not found a single case where a plain template suffices. The insufficiently structured grammar rules in the outdated documentation made it also clear that committing to a comprehensive specification of the isiZulu grammar in such a way as to be computationally useful and correct (e.g., by using the Grammatical Framework [http://www.grammaticalframework.org/]), will take a substantial amount of resources. Such resources are not available at present, yet something has to be done for multilingual knowledge repositories that are adequate in the multilingual society in South Africa. Despite that no software has been presented in this paper, we hope to have provided some motivational use cases for investigation, which is benefiting both isiZulu linguistics and ICT in general, and introduced some interesting new challenges for the verbalization of logical theories in grammatically rich

Algorithm 3. Determine the verbalization of existential quantification with object property (first, basic, version)

1: $\mathcal{C}$ set of classes, language $\mathcal{L}$ with $\sqsubseteq$ for subsumption and $\exists$ for existential quantification; variables: A axiom, NC_i noun class, $c_1, c_2 \in \mathcal{C}$, $o \in \mathcal{R}$, a_1 a term; r_2, q_2 concords; functions: $getFirstClass(A)$, $getSecondClass(A)$, $getNC(C)$, $pluralizeNoun(C, NC_i)$, $getRC(NC_i)$ $getQC(NC_i)$.

Require: axiom A with a $\sqsubseteq$ and a $\exists$ on the rhs of the inclusion has been retrieved

2: $c_1 \leftarrow getFirstClass(A)$ {get subclass}
3: $c_2 \leftarrow getSecondClass(A)$ {get superclass}
4: $o \leftarrow getObjProp(A)$ {get object property}
5: $NC_1 \leftarrow getNC(c_1)$ {determine noun class by augment and prefix or dictionary}
6: $NC_2 \leftarrow getNC(c_2)$ {determine noun class by augment and prefix or dictionary}
7: $NC_1' \leftarrow$ lookup plural nounclass of NC_1 {from known list}
8: $c_1' \leftarrow pluralizeNoun(c_1, NC_1')$
9: $a_1 \leftarrow$ lookup quantitative concord for NC_1' {from quantitative concord (QC(all)) list}
10: $o' \leftarrow AlgoConjugate(o, NC_1)$ {call algorithm $AlgoConjugate$ to conjugate o}
11: $r_2 \leftarrow getRC(NC_2)$ {get relative concord for c_2}
12: $q_2 \leftarrow getQC(NC_2)$ {get quantitative concord for c_2 from the QC$_{dwa}$-list}
13: RESULT $\leftarrow$ ' $a_1\ c_1'\ o'\ c_2\ r_2 q_2$dwa. '   {verbalise the simple axiom}
14: **return** RESULT

languages. We will continue to extend the algorithms, add more, and implement them.

The algorithms may also be of use for machine translation. For instance, Google Translate English-isiZulu translates, e.g., "mix the sugar and milk and butter" as "*hlanganisa ushukela nobisi ibhotela*" (translation d.d. 14-1-2014), which misses the second conjunction in the enumeration, whereas a ushukela$\sqcap$ ubisi $\sqcap$ ibhotela with Algorithm 2 obtains the correct verbalisation/translation (*ushukela nobisi nebhotela*). Similarly, "all giraffes eat twigs" is translated as "*yonke izindlulamithi udle amahlumela*" (translation d.d. 14-1-2014), but *izindlulamithi* is in noun class 10, not 9, so it goes with *zonke* instead, not Google Translate's *yonke*. This can be correctly verbalised following Algorithm 1, line 9.

An aspect of further investigation is the implementability of subsumption with the living/non-living thing distinction compared to the syntax-based shortcut, as it is not clear yet whether a syntax-based criteria holds for other cases when a distinction is made between living and non-living things. Such annotations will be less than assigning noun classes to each term. Also, this means there has to be some way to encode such multilingual information, which may be possible by extending the *Lemon* model [13] or putting it in a designated annotation field.

5   Conclusions

Verbalizing ontologies in isiZulu requires more than a template-based approach for each construct investigated. We provided novel verbalization patterns for simple subsumption, disjoint classes, conjunction, and basic options with quantification. The main features complicating verbalization in isiZulu were the 17 noun classes with embedded semantics in the term, the agglutinative nature of isiZulu, and contextual knowledge about the position of the symbol in the axiom.

There are many avenues for further works on the verbalization rules, with more variations on the basic axioms, more construct, and conjugation. There are also questions concerning how to make the ontology multilingual so that it covers the aspects that need to be recorded to facilitate verbalization.

References

1. Alberts, R., Fogwill, T., Keet, C.M.: Several required OWL features for indigenous knowledge management systems. In: Proc. of OWLED 2012, vol. 849, pp. 27–28. CEUR-WS, Crete (2012)
2. Bosca, A., Dragoni, M., Francescomarino, C.D., Ghidini, C.: Collaborative management of multilingual ontologies. In: Buitelaar, P., Cimiano, P. (eds.) Towards the Multilingual Semantic Web. Springer (in press, 2014)
3. Curland, M., Halpin, T.: Model driven development with NORMA. In: Proc. of HICSS-40, pp. 286a–286a. IEEE Computer Society, Los Alamitos (2007)
4. Doke, C.: Text Book of Zulu Grammar. Witwatersrand University Press (1927)
5. Doke, C.: Bantu Linguistic Terminology. Longman, Green and Co., London (1935)
6. Dongilli, P., Franconi, E.: An Intelligent Query Interface with Natural Language Support. In: Proc. of FLAIRS 2006, Melbourne Beach, Florida, USA (May 2006)
7. Fogwill, T., Viviers, I., Engelbrecht, L., Krause, C., Alberts, R.: A software architecture for an indigenous knowledge management system. In: Indigenous Knowledge Technology Conference 2011, Windhoek, Namibia, November 2-4 (2011)
8. Fuchs, N.E., Kaljurand, K., Kuhn, T.: Discourse Representation Structures for ACE 6.6. Tech. Rep. ifi-2010.0010, Dept of Informatics, University of Zurich, Switzerland (2010)
9. Jarrar, M., Keet, C.M., Dongilli, P.: Multilingual verbalization of ORM conceptual models and axiomatized ontologies. Starlab technical report, Vrije Universiteit Brussel, Belgium (February 2006)
10. Kaljurand, K., Kuhn, T., Canedo, L.: Collaborative multilingual knowledge management based on controlled natural language. Semantic Web J. (2013) (submitted)
11. Keet, C., Khumalo, L.: Toward verbalizing logical theories in isizulu. In: Proc. of CNL 2014, Galway, Ireland, August 20-22. LNCS (LNAI). Springer (accepted, 2014)
12. Kuhn, T.: A principled approach to grammars for controlled natural languages and predictive editors. Journal of Logic, Language and Information 22(1), 33–70 (2013)
13. McCrae, J., et al.: The Lemon cookbook. Tech. rep., Monnet Project (2012)
14. Motik, B., Grau, B.C., Horrocks, I., Wu, Z., Fokoue, A., Lutz, C.: OWL 2 Web Ontology Language Profiles (October 27, 2009)
15. Ngcobo, M.N.: Zulu noun classes revisited: A spoken corpus-based approach. South African Journal of African Languages 1, 11–21 (2010)
16. Pretorius, L., Bosch, S.E.: Enabling computer interaction in the indigenous languages of South Africa: The central role of computational morphology. ACM Interactions 56 (March + April 2003)
17. Schwitter, R., et al.: A comparison of three controlled natural languages for OWL 1.1. In: Proc. of OWLED 2008DC, Washington, DC, USA, April 1-2 (2008)
18. Spiegler, S., van der Spuy, A., Flach, P.A.: Ukwabelana – an open-source morphological Zulu corpus. In: Proc. of COLING 2010, pp. 1020–1028. ACL (2010)

Formal Rule Representation and Verification from Natural Language Requirements Using an Ontology

Driss Sadoun[1,2], Catherine Dubois[3,4], Yacine Ghamri-Doudane[5], and Brigitte Grau[1,3]

[1] LIMSI/CNRS, France
[2] University Paris-Sud, France
[3] ENSIIE, France
[4] CEDRIC/CNAM, France
[5] University of La Rochelle/L3i Lab, France

Abstract. The development of a system is usually based on shared and accepted requirements. Hence, to be largely understood by the stakeholders, requirements are often written in *natural language* (NL). However, checking requirements completeness and consistency requires having them in a formal form. In this article, we focus on user requirements describing a system behaviour, i.e. its behavioural rules. We show how to transform behavioural rules identified from NL requirements and represented within an OWL ontology into the formal specification language Maude. The OWL ontology represents the generic behaviour of a system and allow us to bridge the gap between informal and formal languages and to automate the transformation of NL rules into a Maude specification.

Keywords: Knowledge representation, OWL ontology, NL requirements, formal verification.

1 Introduction

Requirements correspond to a specification of what should be implemented. Among other, they describe how a system should behave. Stakeholders of a system development often use natural language (NL) for a broader understanding, which may lead to various interpretations, as NL texts can contain semantic ambiguities or implicit information and be incoherent. Thus, requirements have to be checked and this requires them to be represented in a formal language. A transformation of NL requirements into formal specifications is usually costly in human and material resources and would benefit of an automatic method. A direct transformation is difficult, if not impossible [5], which leads to the need of an intermediate representation to reduce the gap between the two formalisms. Both works of [5] and [9] propose a first step in the formalization process by transforming NL specifications into SBVR. Similarly, in [7], the authors use SBVR as an intermediate representation to transform NL business rules into semi-formal

A. Bikakis et al. (Eds.): RuleML 2014, LNCS 8620, pp. 226–235, 2014.

models such as UML. The tool NL2Alloy [1] also uses SBVR as a pivot representation to generate Alloy[1] code from NL constraints. To our knowledge, only NL2Alloy proposes a complete chain of transformation from NL to formal specifications, but it does not perform formal verifications on the intermediate representations to validate it. Indeed, verifying extracted information needs formal knowledge representation and inference mechanisms. However, controlled natural languages as SBVR or semi-formal representation models as UML often lack validation mechanisms and inference engines. These shortcomings have led many researchers to explore the transformation of SBVR or UML into languages such as OWL and SWRL [6,10] or as Maude [3].

We propose an OWL-DL ontology based on description logics as an intermediate representation. We use this ontology to guide the automatic identification of behavioural rules from NL requirements analysis and to represent them formally [8]. Behavioural rules are represented in the ontology in order to be transformed into a formal specification language. Indeed, OWL allows us to check the consistency and the completeness of the modelled rules. However, it cannot represent state evolution or sequential rules application. Hence, to simulate and validate the whole system behaviour, we propose to transform the ontology model into a formal specification Maude. In this article, we focus on the ontology conception choices and the transformation process that enable us to automate the production of formal specifications and to maintain the link between NL requirements and their formal representation.

This work has been done in the framework of the project *ENVIE VERTE*[2] which aims to allow a user to configure her own smart space by describing her requirements in natural language. A smart space is a set of communicating objects (sensors, actuators and control processes) that may influence, under well defined conditions, the behaviour of the smart space devices (physical processes). The behavioural rules determine desired component interactions.

2   Ontology of a System Behaviour

2.1   Conceptualisation Choices

An ontology defines concepts ($\mathbb{C}$), properties ($\mathbb{P}$) and individuals ($\mathbb{I}$) of a domain. Concepts and properties of an ontology are defined by terminological axioms ($\mathbb{A}$). We represent an ontology $\mathbb{O}$ as a tuple $< \mathbb{C}, \mathbb{P}, \mathbb{A}, \mathbb{I}, \mathfrak{I}^{\mathbb{C}}, \mathfrak{I}^{\mathbb{P}} >$ where:

- $\mathbb{C}$ is a set of concepts;
- $\mathbb{P}$ is a set of binary properties;
- $\mathbb{A}$ is a set of terminological axioms;
- $\mathbb{I}$ is a set of individuals;
- $\mathfrak{I}^{\mathbb{C}}$ is a function that associates to each concept a set of individuals;
- $\mathfrak{I}^{\mathbb{P}}$ is a function that associates to each property a set of couples of individuals or of couples individual/value.

---

[1] A language and tool for relational model verification.
   http://alloy.mit.edu/alloy/
[2] Funded by *DIGITEO*, projet DIM LSC 2010.

The ontology of a system behaviour has to define the components of the system, their characteristics and the way they behave. In this framework, it is important to highlight a distinction between two kinds of individuals within ontologies: 1) individuals representing entities; 2) individuals representing a type characterizing entities, which lead us to distinguish two sorts of concepts: *individual concepts* and *generic concepts*. This distinction is pertinent for both NL requirement analysis and the automatic ontology translation into the formal language Maude. Based on that, we define two high level concepts to represent a system behaviour: *Component* ($\mathbb{C}_C \subseteq \mathbb{C}$) and *Type* ($\mathbb{C}_T \subseteq \mathbb{C}$) (cf. figure 1).

1. each sub-concept of *Component* is an *individual concept* defining sets of individuals representing entities of the domain (physical components, software components, phenomena, ...);
2. each sub-concept of *Type* is a *generic concept* defining specific types (color, model, brand, ...) of the domain. It extends predefined data types (integer, real, boolean, string, ...), used to characterize the components of the system.

Representing the system behaviour requires taking into account the dynamic aspects of its operation. Thus, we modelled two super-properties in the ontology: 1) *Relation* for describing an interaction between two components of the system; 2) *Attribute* for describing a characteristic of a component, defined as follows:

1. sub-properties of *Relation* are defined exclusively between two sub-concepts of *Component*. Within OWL, each property is defined as an *ObjectProperty*. Formally $\mathbb{P}_R$ is the set of properties P of type *Relation* such that $D \triangleleft P \triangleright R$[3] with $D \subseteq \mathbb{C}_C$ and $R \subseteq \mathbb{C}_C$ et $\mathfrak{I}^{\mathbb{P}}(P) \subseteq \mathfrak{I}^C[\mathbb{C}_C] \times \mathfrak{I}^C[\mathbb{C}_C]$[4].
2. sub-properties of *Attribute* are defined between a sub-concept of *Component* or *Type* and an OWL type. Within OWL, each property is defined as *ObjectProperty* between sub-concepts of *Component* and sub-concepts of *Component* or *Type*, or as a *DataProperty* between *Component* or *Type* and an OWL type. Formally $\mathbb{P}_A$ is the set of properties P of type *Attribute* such that $D \triangleleft P \triangleright R$[3] with $D \subseteq \mathbb{C}_C \cup \mathbb{C}_T$ and $R \subseteq \mathbb{C}_C \cup \mathbb{C}_T \cup T$ and $\mathfrak{I}^{\mathbb{P}}(P) \subseteq (\mathfrak{I}^C[\mathbb{C}_C] \cup \mathfrak{I}^C[\mathbb{C}_T]) \times (\mathfrak{I}^C[\mathbb{C}_C] \cup \mathfrak{I}^C[\mathbb{C}_T] \cup \mathbb{V})$. We also distinguish two types of attributes:
   - *dynamic attribute* whose value may evolve over the time, as the balance of a bank account;
   - *static attribute* whose value is not set to change, such as a bank account ID. This last kind of attribute corresponds to definitional properties of a concept that can be used to identify and distinguish its individuals.

The result of our conceptualisation choices is the ontology illustrated in Figure 1. The ontology is divided in two parts: the upper level ontology models a generic system behaviour and the domain specific ontology models a smart space behaviour. This specific part contains fourteen concepts : seven sub-concepts of

---

[3] We note $D \triangleleft P \triangleright R$ to define for each property P its *domain* D and its *range* R.

[4] $\mathfrak{I}^C[\mathbb{C}_C]$ represents the ranges of all the elements of $\mathbb{C}_C$ by $\mathfrak{I}^C$ ($\mathfrak{I}^C[\mathbb{C}_C] = \bigcup_{c \in C} \mathfrak{I}^C(C)$).

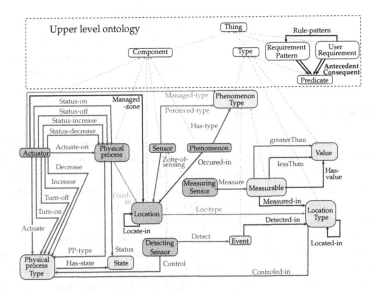

Fig. 1. The ontology of smart space behaviour

Component, and seven sub-concepts of *Type*. The properties are represented by oriented arrows linking concepts of their domain and range. We only figure properties corresponding to *ObjectProperty*, they are thirty one. Dotted Arrows represents subsumption relations.

2.2   Behavioural Rules

As concepts and properties, *Behavioural rules* participate to the domain definition, by modelling its dynamic aspects. They are formed as *antecedent* → *consequent*. The *antecedent* defines conditions under which the rule applies. The *consequent* defines the result of its application. Each of them corresponds to a conjunction of predicates denoting instances of a property $P(i_x, i_y)$ with $(i_x, i_y) \in \mathfrak{I}^{\mathbb{P}}(P)$, since, in our approach, rule identification is guided by property instance identification [8]. Within the ontology, we model a behavioural rule as two sets of predicates $P_k(i_x, i_y)$ with P_k a binary predicate referring to a property instance and i_x an individual, a literal (value of a basic data type) or a variable. We defined a concept *Predicate* as a sub-concept of the concept *Type* (cf. figure 1), associated to the two properties *Antecedent* & *Consequent* (cf. figure 1) on which the behavioural rules are constituted.

We distinguish two types of behavioural rules: 1) rules describing the general behaviour of the system that is independent of the user needs; 2) rules specific to the user requirements. We propose to model within the ontology the two concepts *Requirement-Pattern* and *User-Requirement*. *Requirement-Pattern* is a set of different generic patterns of rules. Its individuals are defined by an expert of the domain to guide the NL requirement analysis. *User-Requirement* is a set of behavioural rules specified by a user. Its individuals are created automatically from NL requirements analysis and linked to their model pattern by the property *Rule-pattern* (cf. figure 1). Within the ontology five requirement patterns have been defined for guiding the identification of behavioural rules of a smart space.

2.3   Population of the Ontology

In [8], we proposed an approach for ontology population based on the identification of property instances in sentences which leads to recognize triples of individuals. Instance property recognition enables to resolve some ambiguities and to infer implicit individuals. The creation of *User-Requirement* individuals exploits these property instances and depends on two verifications based on the use of OWL reasoning and SQWRL queries. First, for each requirement pattern represented in the ontology, we check that all the predicates (i.e. property instances) specializing it have been recognized and do not introduce any inconsistency in the ontology, then, that the resulting rule, i.e. the individual of *User-Requirement* is correctly formed. If this two verifications hold, an instance of the concept *User-Requirement* is created. During the ontology population process, several instances of *User-Requirement* can be associated to an instance of *Requirement-Pattern* via the property Rule-Pattern (cf. Figure 1). Each of them is associated with the sentence number it is extracted from. It enables to keep the link between textual requirements and formal rules.

We collected user requirements of a smart space behaviour configuration via a platform[5] available on the web[5]. We collected about hundred sentences[6] (2171 words). Figure 2 presents an example of an individual of *User-Requirement* that specializes an instance of *Requirement-Pattern*. It was created automatically from the NL requirement analysis and was identified from the sentence number 1 "*When I enter a room the door opens automatically.*" of the analysed user requirements. Right elements in bold are instances identified from user requirements analysis. Elements preceded by a question mark '?' correspond to variables. The left property in bold is a super-property[7] that determines the type of property to identify from user requirements analysis.

Within the hundred sentences, 62 were manually annotated as containing a behavioural rule. From user requirements analysis, a total of 28 rules were completely identified and created in the ontology and 34 rules were partially recognized. During the ontology reasoning, two rules among the 28 were rejected, being inconsistent with two existing rules and 3 were identified as containing an additional (incorrect) predicate. As within the ontology, identified individuals are linked to the sentence they were extracted, a precise feedback is returned to the user, highlighting missing and incorrect information in order to let her correct or complete the concerned requirement. Once all the necessary checks have been performed successfully, the validated rules are transformed into Maude.

---

[5] http://perso.limsi.fr/sadoun/Application/en/SmartHome.php
[6] A rule is extracted from a sentence.
[7] *Actuate* is the super-property of *Turn-on*.

An individual of *Requirement-Pattern* (a generic rule).	R-1 : When I enter a room the door opens automatically.
Detected-in(**t**,**l**)	*Detected-in*(**movement-in**,**room**)
Controlled-in(**p**,**l**)	*Controlled-in*(**door**,**room**)
Has-type(?ph,**t**)	*Has-type*(?s,**movement-in**)
Occurred-in(?ph,?loc)	*Occurred-in*(?s,?I1-445)
Perceived-type(?s,**t**)	*Perceived-type*(?I1-280,**movement-in**)
Zone-of-sensing(?s,?loc)	*Zone-of-sensing*(?I1-280,?I1-445)
Managed-type(?a,**t**)	*Managed-type*(?I1-8,**movement-in**)
Managed-zone(?a,?loc)	*Managed-zone*(?I1-8,?I1-445)
Loc-type(?loc,**l**)	*Loc-type*(?I1-445,**room**)
⇒ **Actuate**(?a,**p**)	⇒ **Turn-on**(?I1-8,**door**)

Fig. 2. A user requirement created from NL requirement analysis

3   From the Ontology to the Maude Formal Specifications

3.1   The Formal Specification Language Maude

Maude[8] enables to describe the dynamic of a system, i.e. its state changes, and provides different tools for checking it. The state space of a system is represented by a signature Σ that defines sorts (i.e. types) of constants and variables manipulated by Maude and operators that will act upon the manipulated data and by a set of equations $\mathcal{E}$ built between terms using the signature. Within Maude, the evolution of the system state is described by *rewriting rules* of the form $R : t \rightarrow t'$, where t and t' are terms formed on the signature. Rewriting rules rewrite each term of the left hand side of the rule into a term of the right hand side. The rewriting mechanism allows for specification animation and verification of certain properties as the reachability or the non-reachability of particular states.

Maude defines an *object-oriented module* that offers an object-oriented syntax which is well adapted for concurrent systems, using sets of objects, and a communication mechanism based on message transmission between objects. We use it as a target module for the transformation of the ontology model.

In an object-oriented module, objects are of the form $<O : C|a_1 : v_1, ..., a_n : v_n>$ with O the object identifier, C the object class, a_i ($i \in 1..n$) its attribute names and v_i ($i \in 1..n$) the corresponding attribute values. Messages represent the dynamic interaction between objects. They have the form *msg Mes : Oid, T_1, ..., T_k → Msg* . with *msg* a keyword, *Mes* the message name, *Oid* the type of the recipient object and T_i ($i \in 1..k$) the types of the message arguments. The state of a system, called configuration, corresponds to a multiset of objects and messages. It is defined using a Maude equation of the form: *eq Conf = Ob_1 ... Ob_m Mes_1 ... Mes_n* . with *eq* a keyword, *Conf* the configuration name, Ob_i and Mes_i the objects and messages of the state system.

We represent a Maude object oriented model as a tuple $<\mathcal{C},\mathcal{M},\Sigma,\mathcal{E},\mathcal{R}>$ with:

- $\mathcal{C}$ is the set of class names with, for each class, its set of pairs (attribute, type);
- $\mathcal{M}$ denotes the set of message names;

---

[8] http://maude.cs.uiuc.edu/

- Σ corresponds to the typing environment. Each element (constant or variable) is associated to its type;
- $\mathcal{E}$ corresponds to the set of equations representing the state of the system (its configuration) with $\mathcal{E} = \mathcal{E}_\mathcal{O} \cup \mathcal{E}_\mathcal{M}$ such that:
  - $\mathcal{E}_\mathcal{O}$: the set of configurations-objects pairs;
  - $\mathcal{E}_\mathcal{M}$: the set of configurations-messages pairs.
  - $\mathcal{R}$ contains the rewriting rules.

3.2 Transformation Approach

In this section, we propose a mapping between the ontological elements and the object-oriented Maude elements for an automatic translation. Ontological elements to translate are those contributing to the representation of the system state evolution. They correspond to *User-Requirement* instances and the elements necessary for their definition: concepts *Component* and *Type*, properties (attributes and relations), individuals and their property values. Figure 3 illustrates this mapping. The set of relations $\mathbb{P}_R$ is represented in Maude by a set of messages $\mathcal{M}$ between two objects as they represent evolving relations. The set of attributes $\mathbb{P}_A$ is translated as object attributes. Finally, instances of *User-requirement* are translated as rewriting rules with an antecedent and a consequent built on objects, messages, attributes, literals (i.e. values of basic types) and variables.

The dynamic evolution of a rewriting rule depends on messages and dynamic attributes (cf. section 2.1). When a rule applies, messages of the antecedent are not rewritten and some new messages may appear in the consequent, also *dynamic attributes* values may change and new attributes may appear in the consequent as in Figure 4, which illustrates a *rewriting rule* created from the user requirement *R-1* (cf. Figure 2) and extracted from the sentence number 1 "*When I enter a room the door opens automatically.*" the dynamic attribute *Turn-on* of the object *Actuator* is created in the consequent part.

3.3 Automatic Translation of the Ontology into Maude Specifications

Following the mapping of Figure 3, we implemented the translation function $Trad_O$ which exploits *getter-functions* (prefixed by *get-*) issued from the *Java*

OWL Ontology	object oriented model Maude
Individual of the concept *Component* ($\in I_C$)	Object ($\in \mathcal{E}$)
Individual of the concept *Type* ($\in I_T$)	Attribute value ($\in \mathcal{E}$)
Sub-concept of the concept *Component* ($\in C_C$)	Class ($\in \mathcal{C}$)
Sub-concept of the concept *Type* ($\in C_T$)	Sort *Oid* ($\in \Sigma$)
Relation ($\in \mathbb{P}_R$)	Message ($\in \mathcal{M}$)
Attribute (static & dynamic) ($\in \mathbb{P}_A$)	Attribute ($\in \Sigma$)
Instance of *User-Requirement* ($\in I_{RU}$)	Rewriting rule ($\in \mathcal{R}$)

Fig. 3. Correspondence between our ontology model and Maude model

rl [R-1] : < **door** : **Physical-process-Type** | Controlled-in : **room** >
< I1-445-8 : **Location** | Loc-type : **room** >
< I1-326-6 : **Phenomenon** | Has-type : movement-in, Occurred-in : I1-445-8 >
< I1-280-7 : **Sensor** | Perceived-type : movement-in, Zone-of-sensing : I1-445-8 >
< **room** : **Location-Type** | >
< smoke : **Event** | Detected-in : **room** >
< I1-8-2 : **Actuator** | Managed-type : movement-in, Managed-zone : I1-445-8 >
$\longrightarrow$
< **door** : **Physical-process-Type** | Controlled-in : **room** >
< I1-445-8 : **Location** | Loc-type : **room** >
< I1-326-6 : **Phenomenon** | Has-type : movement-in, Occurred-in : I1-445-8 >
< I1-280-7 : **Sensor** | Perceived-type : movement-in, Zone-of-sensing : I1-445-8 >
< **room** : **Location-Type** | >
< smoke : **Event** | Detected-in : **room** >
< I1-8-2 : **Actuator** | Managed-type : movement-in, Managed-zone : I1-445-8, **Turn-on** : **door** > .

Fig. 4. A Maude rewriting rule translated from the behavioural rule R-1

APIs OWL and *Jess* or implemented by us to query the ontological elements. $Trad_O$ takes the ontology model $(\mathbb{C}, \mathbb{P}, \mathbb{A}, \mathbb{I}, \mathfrak{I}^C, \mathfrak{I}^{\mathbb{P}})$ as input and calls four translation functions (cf. Algorithm $Trad_O$): $Trad_C$, $Trad_M$, $Trad_E$ and $Trad_R$. Each of these functions takes as input a subset of the ontology model and translates it into a sub-set of the Maude model. In order to generate Maude specifications from the resulting Maude model, we implemented *pretty-printing* functions (prefixed by *pp-*) that generate portions of Maude code. Their application results in the creation of a Maude specification file. The main function *pp-generation-of-code-Maude* takes as input the output result of $Trad_O$ ($<\mathcal{C},\mathcal{M},\Sigma,\mathcal{E},\mathcal{R}>$) and produces a Maude specification file. It calls eight *pretty-printing* functions (cf. Algorithm *pp-generation-of-code-Maude*) that writes each a sub-set of Maude specifications. The operator $\twoheadleftarrow$ denotes the automatic Maude code generation into the specification document *Spec-Maude*.

Input:$\mathbb{C}, \mathbb{P}, \mathbb{A}, \mathbb{I}, \mathfrak{I}^C, \mathfrak{I}^{\mathbb{P}}$;
Output:$< \mathcal{C},\mathcal{M},\Sigma,\mathcal{E},\mathcal{R} >$;
$\mathbb{C}_C \leftarrow get\text{-}ConceptSubClasses(\mathbb{A}, Composant)$;
$\mathbb{C}_T \leftarrow get\text{-}ConceptSubClasses(\mathbb{A}, Type)$;
$\mathbb{C}_{RU} \leftarrow get\text{-}SubConcepts(\mathbb{A}, User\text{-}requirement)$;
$\mathbb{I}_{RU} \leftarrow get\text{-}ConceptIndividuals(\mathbb{C}_{RU}, \mathfrak{I}^C)$;
$\mathbb{P}_R \leftarrow get\text{-}OntologyRelations(\mathbb{A})$;
$\mathcal{C} \leftarrow Trad_C(\mathbb{C}_C, \mathbb{C}_T, \mathbb{A})$;
$\mathcal{M} \leftarrow Trad_M(\mathbb{P}_R)$;
$<\mathcal{E},\Sigma_0> \leftarrow Trad_E(\mathbb{C}_C, \mathbb{P}_R, \mathbb{A}, \mathbb{I}, \mathfrak{I}^C, \mathfrak{I}^{\mathbb{P}})$;
$<\mathcal{R},\Sigma> \leftarrow Trad_R(\mathbb{I}_{RU}, \mathfrak{I}^{\mathbb{P}}, \mathbb{P}_R, \mathbb{A}, \Sigma_0)$;
Algorithm $Trad_O$

Input:$< \mathcal{C},\mathcal{M},\Sigma,\mathcal{E},\mathcal{R} >$,*Spec-Maude*;
Output:*Spec-Maude*;
Spec-Maude $\twoheadleftarrow$ *pp-declareClass($\mathcal{C}$)*;
Spec-Maude $\twoheadleftarrow$ *pp-declareMessage($\mathcal{M}$)*;
Spec-Maude $\twoheadleftarrow$ *pp-declareObject(Σ)*;
Spec-Maude $\twoheadleftarrow$ *pp-declareVariables(Σ)*;
Spec-Maude $\twoheadleftarrow$ *pp-declareObjectConfiguration(Σ)*;
Spec-Maude $\twoheadleftarrow$ *pp-createObjectConfiguration($\mathcal{E}$)*;
Spec-Maude $\twoheadleftarrow$ *pp-createMsgConfiguration($\mathcal{E}$)*;
Spec-Maude $\twoheadleftarrow$ *pp-createRules($\mathcal{R}$)*;
Algorithm *pp-generation-of-code-Maude*

The algorithm 1 details the function $Trad_R$ (cf. Algorithm $Trad_O$) that translates the *user requirements* ($\mathbb{I}_{RU}$) modelled in the ontology into rewriting rules describing the system behaviour within Maude. These rules are formed by binary predicates representing ontology properties. Each predicate may have as argument individuals, literals or variables. Existing objects have been declared in Σ_0 and created in $\mathcal{E}$ within the function $Trad_E$ (cf. Algorithm $Trad_O$). Variables and literals still need to be declared. For each predicate of the properties *Antecedent* and *Consequent*, *getter-functions* are called to get its name (the property to which it refers) and its domain and range values. These values are inputs of the function *updateObjects* that creates objects or updates their values if they already exist. For example, during the creation of the rewriting rule R-1 (cf. Figure 4) the object *Actuator* has been created from the predicate *Managed-type*, then updated by the predicate *Managed-zone* and finally updated in the *consequent* of the rule by the predicate *Turn-on* that represents a dynamic attribute.

3.4   User Requirements Verification in Maude

Maude incorporates a variety of validation and verification tools [2] including a model checker [4]. A model-checker enables the model exploration. From an initial configuration, it explores the possible states of the represented system based on rewriting rules application. The model-checking allows us to check undesirable state reachability as states resulting from the simultaneous application of rules in contradiction i.e. that can be triggered at the same time and contains in their consequents predicates in opposition (as *Turn-on* and *Turn-off*) on the same object. Then we say that the rules are inconsistent. Hence, the rule created from the sentence 88 "*When a sensor detects a hot temperature in any room combined with smoke in this room, close all the doors and windows.*" was identified as inconsistent with the rule number 1. Model checking also allows us to check the completeness of the specified system by checking the reachability of desirable states. For example, in the framework of a smart space, it is necessary to check if all physical processes can reach the states *on* and *off* at least once.

```
Input: $\mathbb{I}_{RU}, \mathbb{J}^{\mathbb{P}}, \mathbb{P}_R, \mathbb{A}, \Sigma_0$
Output: $\mathcal{R}, \Sigma$
$\mathcal{R} \leftarrow \emptyset$; $\Sigma \leftarrow \Sigma_0$; Objs-Antecedent $\leftarrow \emptyset$; Objs-Consequent $\leftarrow \emptyset$;
Msg-Antecedent $\leftarrow \emptyset$; Msg-Consequent $\leftarrow \emptyset$; Class-Attributes-Values $\leftarrow \emptyset$;
for each $i_{RU}$ in $\mathbb{I}_{RU}$ do
    A-predicates $\leftarrow$ get-RangeValue($i_{RU}$, Antecedent, $\mathbb{J}^{\mathbb{P}}$) ;
    C-predicates $\leftarrow$ get-RangeValue($i_{RU}$, Consequent, $\mathbb{J}^{\mathbb{P}}$) ;
    for each a-predicate in A-predicates do   //predicates of the antecedent
    $p \leftarrow$ get-PredicateName(a-predicate) ;
    $v_D \leftarrow$ get-PredicateDomainValue(a-predicate) ;
    $v_R \leftarrow$ get-PredicateRangeValue(a-predicate) ;
    $t_D \leftarrow$ get-Domain(p,$\mathbb{A}$); $t_R \leftarrow$ get-Range(p,$\mathbb{A}$) ;
    if isVariableOrLitteral($v_D$) then
        | $\Sigma \leftarrow \Sigma \cup \{(v_D, t_D)\}$;
    if isVariableOrLitteral($v_R$) then
        | $\Sigma \leftarrow \Sigma \cup \{(v_R, t_R)\}$;
    if $p \in \mathbb{P}_R$ then   //p is a relation
    Msg-Antecedent $\leftarrow$ Msg-Antecedent $\cup \{(p, v_D, v_R)\}$;
    Objs-Antecedent $\leftarrow$ updateObjects(Objs-Antecedent,$\{(v_D, t_D, \emptyset, \emptyset)\}$);
    Objs-Antecedent $\leftarrow$ updateObjects(Objs-Antecedent,$\{(v_R, t_R, \emptyset, \emptyset)\}$);
    else   //p is an attribute
    Objs-Antecedent $\leftarrow$ updateObjects(Objs-Antecedent,$\{(v_D, t_D, p, v_R)\}$);
    Objs-Consequent $\leftarrow$ Objs-Antecedent;
    for each c-predicate in C-predicates do   //predicates of the consequent
    $p \leftarrow$ get-PredicateName(c-predicate) ;
    $v_D \leftarrow$ get-PredicateDomainValue(c-predicate) ;
    $v_R \leftarrow$ get-PredicateRangeValue(c-predicate) ;
    $t_D \leftarrow$ get-Domain(p,$\mathbb{A}$); $t_R \leftarrow$ get-Range(p,$\mathbb{A}$) ;
    if isDynamic(p,$\mathbb{A}$) then   //p is an dynamic attribute
    Objs-Consequent $\leftarrow$ updateObjects(Objs-Consequent,$\{(v_D, t_D, p, v_R)\}$) else
        | if $p \in \mathbb{P}_R$ then   //p is a relation
        | Msg-Consequent $\leftarrow$ Msg-Consequent $\cup \{(p, v_D, v_R)\}$;
    $\mathcal{R} \leftarrow \mathcal{R} \cup \{(Objs\text{-}Antecedent, Objs\text{-}Consequent, Msg\text{-}Antecedent, Msg\text{-}Consequent)\}$;
```
Algorithm 1: Type declaration and rewriting rules creation

Thus, a message can be returned to the user. As it was the case for the lack of a rule that *turns off* the physical process *light-bathroom*.

4 Conclusion

We proposed an approach for behavioural rules representation and formalization from user requirements written in natural language. The core of this approach is an OWL-DL ontology that encompasses the general behaviour of a system. The ontology is used as a pivot representation as it defines a framework for guiding the identification of behavioural rules and allows us to implement an automated transformation of them into a formal specification in Maude. We described an application of our approach on the domain of smart spaces and showed how representing the behaviour of smart space by a Maude specification enabled us to check its consistency and completeness.

References

1. Bajwa, I.S., Bordbar, B., Lee, M., Anastasakis, K.: Nl2alloy: A tool to generate alloy from nl constraints. JDIM 10(6) (2012)
2. Clavel, M., Durán, F., Hendrix, J., Lucas, S., Meseguer, J., Ölveczky, P.C.: The maude formal tool environment. In: Mossakowski, T., Montanari, U., Haveraaen, M. (eds.) CALCO 2007. LNCS, vol. 4624, pp. 173–178. Springer, Heidelberg (2007)
3. Durán, F., Gogolla, M., Roldán, M.: Tracing properties of uml and ocl models with maude. In: AMMSE (2011)
4. Eker, S., Meseguer, J., Sridharanarayanan, A.: The maude {LTL} model checker. ENTCS 71, 162–187 (2004)
5. Guissé, A., Lévy, F., Nazarenko, A.: From regulatory texts to brms: how to guide the acquisition of business rules? In: Bikakis, A., Giurca, A. (eds.) RuleML 2012. LNCS, vol. 7438, pp. 77–91. Springer, Heidelberg (2012)
6. Karpovic, J., Nemuraite, L., Stankeviciene, M.: Requirements for semantic business vocabularies and rules for transforming them into consistent owl2 ontologies. In: Skersys, T., Butleris, R., Butkiene, R. (eds.) ICIST 2012. CCIS, vol. 319, pp. 420–435. Springer, Heidelberg (2012)
7. Njonko, P., El Abed, W.: From natural language business requirements to executable models via sbvr. In: ICSAI (2012)
8. Sadoun, D., Dubois, C., Ghamri-Doudane, Y., Grau, B.: From natural language requirements to formal specification using an ontology. In: ICTAI (2013)
9. Selway, M., Grossmann, G., Mayer, W., Stumptner, M.: Formalising natural language specifications using a cognitive linguistics/configuration based approach. In: EDOC, pp. 59–68 (2013)
10. Sukys, A., Nemuraite, L., Paradauskas, B., Sinkevicius, E.: Transformation framework for sbvr based semantic queries in business information systems. In: BUSTECH, pp. 19–24 (2012)

Learning Business Rules
with Association Rule Classifiers

Tomáš Kliegr[1,4], Jaroslav Kuchař[1,2], Davide Sottara[3], and Stanislav Vojíř[1]

[1] Department of Information and Knowledge Engineering,
Faculty of Informatics and Statistics,
University of Economics, Prague, Czech Republic
first.last@vse.cz
[2] Web Engineering Group, Faculty of Information Technology,
Czech Technical University in Prague, Czech Republic
[3] Biomedical Informatics Department,
Arizona State University, Phoenix, AZ, USA
dsottara@asu.edu
[4] Multimedia and Vision Research Group,
Queen Mary, University of London, UK

Abstract. The main obstacles for a straightforward use of association rules as candidate business rules are the excessive number of rules discovered even on small datasets, and the fact that contradicting rules are generated. This paper shows that Association Rule Classification algorithms, such as CBA, solve both these problems, and provides a practical guide on using discovered rules in the Drools BRMS and on setting the ARC parameters. Experiments performed with modified CBA on several UCI datasets indicate that data coverage rule pruning keeps the number of rules manageable, while not adversely impacting the accuracy. The best results in terms of overall accuracy are obtained using minimum support and confidence thresholds. Disjunction between attribute values seem to provide a desirable balance between accuracy and rule count, while negated literals have not been found beneficial.

Keywords: association rules, rule pruning, business rules, Drools.

1 Introduction

Association rule learning cannot be directly used for learning business rules, due to the excessive number of rules generated even for small datasets, and the lack of a rule conflict resolution strategy. However, if several techniques originally developed for association rule classification (ARC) are adopted, association rules can be used as classification business rules. ARC algorithms contain a rule pruning step, which significantly reduces the number of rules, and define a conflict resolution strategy for cases when one object is matched by multiple rules.

This paper has two focus areas. Due to the limited amount of prior work, in the first part of the paper we evaluate to what degree ARC algorithms meet the requirements of the business rule learning task and demonstrates how the

A. Bikakis et al. (Eds.): RuleML 2014, LNCS 8620, pp. 236–250, 2014.

discovered rules can be used in a Drools Business Rule Management System (BRMS) system. The second part of the paper describes our implementation and experimental evaluation of a business rule learning system. In contrast to mainstream ARC algorithms, the system allows to learn disjunctive and negative rules. We hypothesize that the additional expressiveness could result in a rule set which is smaller, and thus more intelligible for the business user. Another modification is a simplification of the rule pruning phase.

This paper is organized as follows. Section 2 reviews related research. Section 3 presents a set of requirements on business rule learning algorithm and contrasts it with what ARC algorithms provide. Section 4 describes how rules learnt from data can be used in the Drools. Section 5 presents our experimental business rule learning system *brCBA*. Section 6 presents experimental evaluation on several datasets. Finally, Section 7 summarizes our findings, gives limitations of the presented work and outlines viable directions of future research.

2 Related Work

There is a very limited amount of prior work on learning business rules from data. This paper is restricted to what we call *classification* business rules i.e. rules that assign a class (a type) to an object whenever its description matches the conditions contained in the rule's body. This corresponds to what is known in the rule learning literature as *classification rule* or *predictive rule.*

Association rule learning algorithms such as *apriori* [1] or FP-growth [3] can be used to learn conjunctive classification rules from data if the mining setup is constrained so that only the target class values can occur in the consequent of the rules. The GUHA method [7] is an alternative approach to mine association rules, which allows to learn also rules featuring negation and disjunction between attribute values.

The main obstacles for a straightforward use of association rules as candidate business rules are the excessive number of rules discovered even on small datasets, and the fact that contradicting rules are generated. Association Rule Classifier (ARC) algorithms provide an extension over association rule learning algorithms which address exactly these issues. These algorithms contain a rule pruning step, which significantly reduces the number of rules, and define a conflict resolution strategy for cases when one object is matched by multiple rules.

The first ARC algorithm dubbed CBA (Classification based on Associations) was introduced in 1998 by Liu et al. [5]. While there were multiple follow-up algorithms providing incremental improvements in classification performance (e.g. CPAR [15], CMAR [4] and MMAC [10]), the structure of most ARC algorithms follows that of CBA [13]: 1) learn association rules, 2) prune the set of classification rules, 3) classify new objects. Our proposed brCBA algorithm also follows this structure. It differs from CBA and other algorithms by using a GUHA-based algorithm in the "learn association rules" phase, which allows us to explore the effects of disjunction and negation on classification performance. To the best of our knowledge, the impact of the increased expressiveness added by these connectives on ARC performance has not yet been reported.

The output of association rule learning algorithms is determined typically by two parameters: minimum confidence and support thresholds on the training data. The confidence of a rule is defined as $a/(a+b)$, where a is the number of correctly classified objects, i.e. those matching rule antecedent as well rule consequent, and b is the number of misclassified objects, i.e. those matching the antecedent, but not the consequent. The support of a rule is defined as a/n, where n is the number of all objects (relative support), or simply as a (absolute support). The confidence threshold can be used to control the quality of the resulting classifier. While the authors of ARC classifiers report the confidence threshold used in their experimental setups (0.3 [10], 0.4 [9], 0.5 [5]), the impact of varying the value of this threshold on classifier performance has not yet been studied (to the best of our knowledge). To help guide the setting of ARC algorithms, we provide a detailed study of the effect of confidence threshold and support thresholds on the classification accuracy and rule count.

There is also a very limited work on effects of rule pruning. A qualitative review of rule pruning algorithms used in ARC are given e.g. in [13,8]. The effect of pruning on the size of the rule set is reported in [5], which presents evaluation on 26 UCI datasets. The average number of rules per dataset without pruning was 35,140, with pruning the average number of rules was reduced to 69. However, this paper focuses on the evaluation of less commonly employed pessimistic pruning. We focus on evaluation of data coverage pruning, which is the most commonly used pruning algorithm (present, with some modifications, in CBA, CMAR and MMAC).

3   Business Rule Learning Requirements

The business rule learning workflow imposes some specific demands on the selection of a suitable rule learning algorithm. In this section, we discuss the compliance of ARC algorithms with some of the requirements that we have identified.

BRMS Supported Rule Expressiveness. The rules learnt are composed of a conjunction of constraints on attribute values in the antecedent, and a single value for the class attribute in the consequent. The operations performed by later steps in ARC execution, such as pruning or ranking, do not change the internal structure of the rules.

Example 1. Rule learnt on the Iris dataset.

$\ulcorner$petalLength=$\langle 3.95; 4.54\rangle$ ∧ petalWidth=$\langle 1.3; 1.54\rangle$ $\rightarrow_{1,0.14}$ Class=Iris-versicolor$\urcorner$, where 1 is rule confidence and 0.14 (relative) rule support.

Rules, such as the one depicted in Example 1, can be translated into technical rule languages for execution inside a rule engine. In our earlier work [14] we presented the mapping to DRL, the format used by the open source BRMS system Drools.

Small number of output rules. Perhaps the biggest challenge in converting association rules to business rules is the fact that the number of discovered rules is often too large to be presented to a user. The two common strategies to solve this problem are rule grouping and rule pruning.

Rule grouping algorithms cluster the rules according to a predefined distance measure [12]. Most ARC algorithms use rule pruning. The details of the individual types of pruning algorithms is given e.g. in [13,11,8]. The most commonly used method according to these survey papers is *Data Coverage Pruning* (see Subs. 5.2).

Exhaustive set of rules. Most ARC algorithms use an exact association rule learning algorithm, either based on apriori or FP-Growth. These algorithms learn exhaustive set of rules matching predefined minimum confidence and minimum support thresholds [13].

However, some rules are removed in the pruning phase. Since pruning[1] removes only rules which cover objects which are already covered by another higher priority rule, the pruning typically affects only rules that would be viewed by the user as redundant.

Rule conflict resolution. Once association rules are generated and pruned, ARC algorithms use them to classify new objects. There are two fundamental approaches: *single rule* and *multiple rule* classification [13], depending on the number of rules that are involved in assigning a class to an object. The *single rule* classification used in CBA is described in Section 5.3 and subject to experimental evaluation as part of our implementation in Section 6. An overview of possible implementation in the Drools Rule Engine is present in Section 4.

Ability to control rule quality. The rule quality can be controlled by setting the minimum confidence (and support) thresholds. It should be noted that ARC algorithms try to cover every training object with at least one rule, for example, CBA ensures this by adding a default rule to the rule set. The default rule insertion needs to be omitted (ref. to Subs. 5.2) in order to allow the user to control the overall quality of the rule set.

4   Drools-Based Rule Engine

The learning algorithm generates association rules which establish an implication between the antecedent and the consequent. In the case of classification rules, the consequent is the type of an individual object whose features have been matched by the antecedent. So, they can naturally be reinterpreted as business rules with the semantics of production rules. This allows to decouple recognition from decision making, resulting in more robust knowledge bases. Moreover, (production) rule engines can be considered commodity components: in particular, we have used the popular open source business logic platform Drools[2]. Drools is written in Java and relies on an object-oriented rule engine inspired from the RETE algorithm.

---

[1] Referring to the "database coverage" algorithm.

[2] http://drools.jboss.org

Listing 1.2. A Conflict Resolution Meta-Rule in Drools

```
rule 'Block by confidence'  @Direct
  when
    $m1 : Match( associationRole == 'premise', $t : tuple )
    $m2 : Match( this != $m1, associationRole == 'premise', tuple == $t,
                 confidence > $m1.confidence ||
                 confidence == $m1.confidence && support > $m1.support ||
                 antecedent < $m1.antecedent )
  then
    kcontext.cancelMatch( $m1 );
  end
```

In our implementation, we have created a simple, generic data model with two classes to model attributes and inferred types: `DrlObject` and `DrlAR` respectively. This allows to write rules such as the one in Listing 1.1.

Listing 1.1. A Sample Classification Rule in Drools

```
rule "rule_1" @associationRole(premise)
    @antecedent(4) @confidence(1) @support(0.06)
  when
    DrlObj( name == "petalLength", numVal >= 1 && < 1.59 )
    DrlObj( name == "petalWidth",  numVal >= 0.1 && < 0.34 )
    DrlObj( name == "sepalLength",
            numVal >= ( 4.3 && < 4.66 ) || ( >= 4.66 && < 5.02 ) )
    DrlObj( name == "sepalWidth", numVal >= 2.96 && < 3.2) )
  then
    DrlAR $type = new DrlAR( "rule_1", "Iris_Setosa", 4, 1, 0.06 );
    insertLogical( $type );
end
```

The rules are generated automatically from the output of the rule learner. Since the learner produces XML, we have applied an XSLT transformation to generate DRL, the Drools technical rule language. Notice that information such as confidence and support is retained as metadata and modelled using Java-like @annotations.

In order to implement the conflict resolution strategies mentioned in Section 5.2, we have exploited the "declarative agenda" feature of the rule engine. In a production rule engine, whenever one or more facts match the left-hand side of a rule, a rule activation is created and queued into an agenda. Activations are then consumed and the actions in the right-hand side are executed by the engine. Drools' declarative agenda allows to define rules that match and process the activations queued in the agenda itself. Such "meta-rules" are deployed into the same rule base as the standard rules. More specifically, entries in the agenda are instance of the class `Match`, which holds references to the rule that was activated as well as the tuple that caused the activation. Any metadata that is attached to the original rule is exposed by the engine as a virtual property of the activation, so that the meta-rule can constrain their value. Thanks to these capabilities, any conflict resolution strategy can be implemented with a single meta-rule, as shown in Listing 1.2. In our case, the activation of a rule with higher priority will cancel the activation of a rule with a lower priority for the same tuple.

5   brCBA - CBA for Business Rule Learning

In this section, we describe the setup used to perform the experimental evaluation. The implementation comes out of the seminal CBA algorithm. However, there are minor differences in individual steps, which are summarized in Table 1 and explained in the remainder of this section. Most importantly, brCBA uses for rule learning the LISp-Miner system[3], an implementation of the GUHA method, instead of the apriori algorithm.

Table 1. Comparison of CBA and brCBA

stage	CBA [5]	brCBA
learning	conjunctive rules (apriori)	conj. rules, disjunctions between attribute values, negations (GUHA method)
pruning	pessimistic pruning (optional), data coverage, default rule replacement	no pruning, data coverage pruning
classification	complete	partial

5.1   Rule Expressiveness

The mainstream systems for mining association rules employed in ARC, including CBA, output conjunctive association rules. The basic building block of an association rule is a literal.[4]

Definition 1. *(literal) A literal p is an attribute-value pair, taking the form of (A_i, v) in which A_i is an attribute and v a value. An object o satisfies a literal $p = (A_i, v)$ if and only if $o_i = v$, where o_i is the value of the ith attribute of o.*

Definition 2. *(rule) A rule r, which takes the form of "$l_1 \wedge l_2, \wedge \ldots \wedge l_m \rightarrow c$", consists of a conjunction of literals $l_1, l_2, \ldots, l_m$, associated with a class label c. An object satisfies rule r's body if and only if it satisfies every literal in the rule. If object satisfies r's body, r predicts that the object is of class c. If a rule contains zero literal, its body is satisfied by any object.*

In brCBA we extend the original notion of literal present in Def. 1 to allow for disjunction between attribute values (dynamic binning) and negated literals.

Dynamic Binning (disjunctions between attribute values). Typically value binning is performed during the preprocessing step, creating a modified data table which contains a smaller number of merged values. This approach may negatively impact the quality of the rule learning if the bins created are too narrow or too broad. In brCBA we extend the definition of literal to allow for dynamic binning, which merges multiple values during *rule learning* into a value range (an enumeration of values or an interval).

---

[3] http://lispminer.vse.cz

[4] We introduce the definition of literal and an association rule from [15] substituting the machine learning term "tuple" by term "object" common in the BRMS field.

Definition 3. (positive literal) *A positive literal p is an association of an attribute with a value range, taking the form of (A_i, V) in which A_i is an attribute and V is a value range. An object o satisfies a positive literal $p = (A_i, V)$ if and only if $o_i \in V$, where o_i is a value of the ith attribute of object o.*

From the options offered by the LISp-Miner system, we consider two types of dynamic binning: **Subset** binning merges up to a prespecified number of values, while **Sequence** (Interval) binning merges up to a prespecified number of *adjacent* values [7]. Subset binning is typically applied on on nominal attributes, while adjacent value binning on numerical or ordinal attributes.

The maximum number of values to be merged is set by parameter λ (for both methods). The result of dynamic binning on an attribute is a set of literals. Unlike some greedy algorithms (such as the algorithm for grouping values in C4.5 [6]), the dynamic binning operator is exhaustive. For an attribute A_i with n distinct values, assuming that $n \geq \lambda$, sequence binning creates $\sum_{j=1}^{\lambda} n - j + 1$ literals, while subset binning $\sum_{j=1}^{\lambda} \binom{n}{j}$ literals.

Example 2. Binning

The discretization on the petalLength attribute from the Iris dataset was performed by creating equidistant bins during preprocessing[a]: $[1; 1.59)$, $[1.59; 3.95)$, $[3.95; 4.54)$, $[4.54; 5.13)$, $[5.13; 5.72)$. Interval binning set to maximum length $\lambda=2$ will create 9 literals: five literals corresponding the original values plus the following four: $[1; 1.59) \vee [1.59; 3.95)$, $[1.59; 3.95) \vee [3.95; 4.54]$, $[3.95; 4.54) \vee [4.54; 5.13)$, $[4.54; 5.13) \vee [5.13; 5.72)$.

An example rule featuring dynamically binned intervals: ⌜petalLength = $[4.54; 5.13) \vee \langle 5.13; 5.72) \rightarrow_{0.77, 0.33}$ Class=Iris-versicolor⌝,

---
[a] Merging bins with too small support count into one bin.

Negation. Considering negative literals in addition to the positive ones during rule mining produces a richer set of rules. It was previously conjectured that this could benefit the performance of ARC [2].

Definition 4. (negative literal) *A negative literal n is an association of an attribute with a value range, taking the form of (A_i, V) in which A_i is an attribute and V is a value range. An object o satisfies a negative literal $n = (A_i, V)$ if and only if $o_i \notin V$, where o_i is a value of the ith attribute of o.*

Example 3. Rule with a negative literal

⌜¬petalLength=$[1; 1.59) \wedge$ petalWidth $[0.1; 0.34) \rightarrow_{1, 0.05}$ Class=Iris-setosa⌝

5.2   Rule Pruning

CBA and brCBA use the *data coverage* rule pruning algorithm. This algorithm applies to a sorted list of ranked rules. Each rule is matched against the training

---

Algorithm 1. Data Coverage

Require: rules – sorted list of rules, T – set of objects in the training dataset
Ensure: rules – pruned list of rules

    rules := sort rules according to criteria on Fig. 1
    for all *rule* ∈ *rules* **do**
        matches:= set of objects from T that match both rule ant. and conseq.
        if matches==∅ **then**
            remove *rule* from *rules*
        else
            remove *matches* from T
        end if
    end for
    return *rules*

---

data. If a rule does not correctly classify any object, it is discarded. Otherwise, the rule is kept, and the objects correctly classified are removed (ref. to Alg. 1).

The output of rule pruning is a reduced set of rules, where the redundant rules have been removed. If there are two rules matching one training object, the weaker rule (acc. to Fig. 1) will be removed.

1. r_a is ranked higher if confidence of r_a is greater than that of r_b,
2. r_a is ranked higher if confidence of r_a is the same as confidence of r_b, but support of r_a is greater than that of r_b,
3. r_a is ranked higher if r_a has shorter antecedent (fewer conditions) than r_b.

Fig. 1. Rule ranking criteria. Tie-breaking conditions applied if antecedents of two rules r_a and r_b match the same object.

It should be noted that the original CBA classifier contains two additional pruning steps: a) pessimistic pruning and b) replacement of rules performing worse than the majority class baseline with the default rule predicting the majority class. Pessimistic pruning is not featured in our setup, since it was not found to improve performance [5]. The omission of the default rule pruning in brCBA gives the user the control over the quality of the rule set, which can be influenced by the minimum confidence parameter, obtaining a *partial classifier* (not all objects may be labeled).

5.3 Classification and Rule Conflict Handling

If an input object matches exactly one rule, the classification step is very simple – the class contained in the consequent of the rule is assigned to the object. However, the output of association rule learning contains all too often an excessive number of redundant and conflicting rules. Employing rule pruning alleviates the number of conflicts since the number of redundant rules is reduced. Nevertheless pruning does not ensure that rule conflict will not emerge.

Rule conflict occurs if for a given object, there are at least two rules r_a and r_b, whose antecedents match the object. In practical terms, handling rule conflict is of importance if the consequents of these two rules are different, i.e. the rules assign a different class.

Association rules readily come with several scores that could be used to define a priority. These are primarily confidence and support, however additional measures such as chi-square or lift can be computed. The problem is thus to select, or combine these metrics into a total order, which would allow to solve ties between individual rules. brCBA uses the same method as CBA. In the first step, rules are sorted according to confidence, support and rule length – in the same way as in the data coverage pruning (see Fig. 1). The conflict is resolved by selecting the consequent of the top-ranked rule matching the object.

6   Experiments

The purpose of the experimental evaluation was to assess the impact of the following settings of association rule classifiers in the context of partial classification: data coverage rule pruning, dynamic binning, negated literals, and confidence/support thresholds.

6.1   Setup

Datasets. Experiments were performed on Iris, Balance Scale and Glass datasets from the UCI repository[5], which are frequently used for benchmarking classification systems. The use of a smaller number of datasets than in most related work allows us to present a detailed qualitative analysis of the results.

Preprocessing. Numerical attributes were discretized using equidistant binning with custom merging of bins with small support.

Rule Learning. To perform the experiments, we used the LISp-Miner system[6] for learning association rules. LISp-Miner allows to perform learning of negative and disjunctive rules. Disjunctive rules (dynamic binning) are learnt through the setting of the LISp-Miner coefficient feature on individual input attributes to *subset* or, respectively, *sequence* type. The maximum length parameter λ was set to 2.[7]

Rule Pruning. To perform rule pruning we used our Java implementation of the data coverage algorithm. This algorithm does not have any parameters.

Conflict Resolution. We used the conflict resolution according to Fig. 1.

---

[5] http://archive.ics.uci.edu/ml/

[6] http://lispminer.vse.cz

[7] The system allows to enter also the minimum length parameter, which was left set to 1. For experiments involving negative rules, the system was set to consider both positive and negative version for each literal. The remaining parameters of the LISp-Miner system were left at their default values.

6.2   Results

The experimental results achieved on individual datasets are depicted on Table 2-5 in terms of accuracy and rule count. Accuracy is computed as $correct/N$, where $correct$ is the number of correct predictions and N the total number of objects.

Since brCBA is a partial classifier, it may not assign a label to all objects. For this reason, we also provide complementary results using precision, which we compute as $correct/N_{cov}$, where N_{cov} is the number of covered (classified) objects. The plots depicted on Figure 2-5 provide accuracy and precision at minimum confidence levels 0.5, 0.6, 0.7, 0.8, 0.9 and 1.0 along with the average number of unclassified objects $(N - N_{cov})$.

All results are reported using ten fold cross validation with macro averaging.

Table 2. Dataset: Iris, minimum support threshold: 7 objects (5.18%)

| | not pruned | | | | pruned | | | |
| | without binning | | sequence 1-2 | | without binning | | sequence 1-2 | |
confidence	rules	accuracy	rules	accuracy	rules	accuracy	rules	accuracy
0.5	96	0.940	972.2	0.940	20	0.920	17	**0.953**
0.6	87	0.940	903.6	0.940	19	0.920	17	**0.953**
0.7	83	0.940	839.6	0.940	17	0.920	17	**0.953**
0.8	76	0.940	734.7	0.940	17	0.920	15	0.947
0.9	68	0.900	603.2	0.940	15	0.880	14	0.940

Table 3. Dataset: Balance Scale, minimum support threshold: 10 objects (1.78%)

| | not pruned | | | | pruned | | | |
| | without binning | | subset 1-2 | | without binning | | subset 1-2 | |
confidence	rules	accuracy	rules	accuracy	rules	accuracy	rules	accuracy
0.6	124	**0.891**	11947	0.758	78	0.870	153	0.779
0.7	86	0.875	8462	0.826	70	0.864	153	0.779
0.8	50	0.790	4881	0.838	50	0.782	153	0.779
0.9	24	0.547	2193	0.838	24	0.547	153	0.779
1.0	1	0.047	1001	0.811	1	0.047	99	0.758

Minimum Support and Confidence Thresholds. Experimental results show that the lower minimum support threshold is generally associated with improved accuracy. This is demonstrated on Table 5.

For Iris and Balance Scale datasets the precision and accuracy do not react to an increase of minimum confidence within a certain interval (Figure 2-4). This phenomenon is encountered without respect to whether the pruning is turned on or off. This can be explained by the fact that the mining output for a given minimum confidence threshold contains also the higher confidence rules. If these higher confidence rules cover all test objects that are covered by the lower confidence rules, due to the conflict resolution strategy used the lower confidence

Table 4. Dataset: Glass, minimum support threshold: 10 objects (5.18%)

	not pruned				pruned		
	positive only		with negations		positive only		with negations
confidence	rules	accuracy	rules	accuracy	rules	accuracy	rules	accuracy
0.5	58.3	0.529	1418.8	0.492	25.8	**0.534**	44.3	0.519
0.6	31.8	0.464	838.5	0.492	21.1	0.464	42.4	0.492
0.7	10.3	0.290	416.7	0.449	8.4	0.286	29.3	0.444
0.8	2.4	0.117	195.6	0.225	1.8	0.117	11.9	0.225
0.9	0.4	0.010	63.8	0.071	0.2	0.010	1.8	0.071

Table 5. Impact of miminum support treshold. minimum confidence 0.6.

Dataset, task	support	not pruned		pruned	
		rules	accuracy	rules	accuracy
iris	7 (4.7%)	87	0.940	19	0.920
"	2 (1.3%)	168	0.947	21	0.913
"	1 (0.7%)	291	**0.967**	23	0.927
iris, sequence 1-2	7 (4.7%)	904	0.940	17	0.953
"	2 (1.3%)	1661	0.953	19	**0.960**
"	1 (0.7%)	2653	**0.960**	19	**0.960**
glass	10 (4.7%)	32	0.464	21	0.464
"	2 (0.9%)	2374	**0.622**	68	0.608
balance scale	10 (1.7%)	124	**0.891**	78	0.870
"	2 (0.4%)	558	0.841	216	0.714
balance scale, subset 1-2	10 (1.7%)	11947	0.758	153	**0.779**

rules are never applied. The minimum confidence threshold thus starts to have effect once it removes rules which cover objects uncovered by any other higher confidence rule.

A Similar effect can be observed for the minimum support threshold. An optimal support threshold of 1% is reported in [5], [9] gives 2%, while [10] suggests 2% or 3%. Our results indicate that the best results are obtained with support threshold set to 1 object.[8]

Pruning. Experimental results show that pruning is an effective tool for reducing the number of rules without significantly affecting classification accuracy and precision. Without pruning, confidence and support thresholds need to be carefully chosen in order to balance number of rules and performance (Table 2-5). Pruning ensures a manageable number of rules even for low threshold values. For example, the best performing setup on iris dataset achieves accuracy of 0.967 with 291 rules, no test object is left unclassified. Pruning reduces the number of rules to only 23 with a slight drop in accuracy due to an increase in the number of unclassified objects (Fig. 2).

Negation and Dynamic Binning. Experiments performed on the Glass and Iris datasets explore the effect of negation (ref. to Table 4 and Fig. 4). The results

---

[8] This setup is referred to in the literature as "no support" mining.

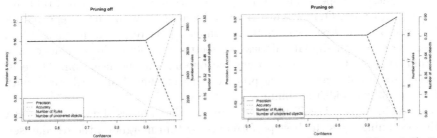

Fig. 2. Effect of pruning. Setting: Iris dataset, minimum support threshold 1.

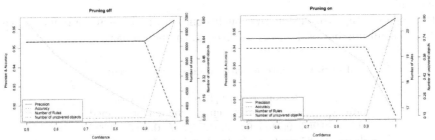

Fig. 3. Effect of dynamic binning on numerical attributes (sequence of length 2). Setting: Iris dataset, minimum support 1, dynamic binning on.

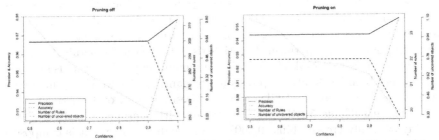

Fig. 4. Effect of including negative literals. Setting: Iris dataset, minimum support threshold 1.

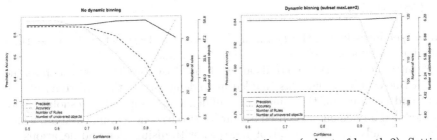

Fig. 5. Effect of dynamic binning on nominal attributes (subset of length 2). Setting: minimum support threshold 10, pruning on, Balance Scale dataset.

show that involving negation in rule learning phase significantly increases the computational demands of the rule learner used, while the results are generally unaffected in terms of accuracy, and inflated in terms of rule count.

Sequence binning was performed on the Iris dataset, which contains only numerical attributes. The results for a higher minimum support thresholds indicate that sequence binning slightly improves performance (Table 2) while simultaneously decreasing rule count. While overall the best accuracy of 0.967 is achieved without binning (Table 5), the result obtained with a pruned set of rules featuring dynamically created bins (0.960) is only slightly worse, but is composed of a much smaller set of rules (19 vs 291). For the Balance Scale dataset, which contains nominal attributes, subset binning was performed. This highly computationally intensive operation did not provide accuracy improvement (Table 3). **Comparison with Other Algorithms.** To compare with earlier reported results for CBA, the first two brCBA columns report results from runs, which were generated with similar rule learning settings of 50% min. confidence and 1% min. support thresholds, no dynamic binning and no negation. There is, however, some difference in data preprocessing of numerical attributes – with brCBA we used equidistant binning (see Example 2).

The results depicted on Table 6 indicate that the in terms of accuracy, brCBA with no pruning gives the best performance by thin margin on the iris dataset, but lags behind significantly on the glass dataset. Comparing runs with pruning, the additional pruning steps in the "full" CBA provide better accuracy. And, according to the comparison with the rule count reported in [5], even smaller rule count.

It should be emphasized that the conclusions drawn above are only indicative due to a small number of datasets involved in the benchmark.

Table 6. Comparison with other systems – accuracy

| dataset | previous results [4,15] | | | | | brCBA | |
	c4.5	ripper	cmar	cpar	cba	not pr.	pruned
iris	0.953	0.940	0.940	0.94.7	0.947	**0.967**	0.927
glass	0.687	0.691	0.701	**0.744**	0.739	0.622	0.612

7 Conclusion

This paper investigated the possibility of learning classification business rules from data using association rule learning algorithms.

We introduced brCBA, a modification of the CBA algorithm, which omits the default rule classification. This enabled us to demonstrate the sensitivity of rule count and accuracy on the minimum confidence and support thresholds. Also, our modified implementation used a more expressive rule learning system, which allowed to study the effect of involving rules with disjunction and negations.

Our experimental evaluation on several UCI datasets lead to the following recommendations for business rule learning with ARC algorithms:

- The lowest confidence and support thresholds produce the best results. Since low threshold values have adverse effect on computational tractability, the setting of these thresholds is constrained by the available computational resources.
- Omission of important rules by pruning is a marginal, if any, issue, since pruned rule set maintains the accuracy of the original rule set on test data. Since pruning was at the same time found to significantly reduce the rule count, it is suitable for a business rule pruning setup.
- Involving higher expressiveness rules is not recommended given the substantial increase in computational demands and a negligible positive effect on accuracy and rule count (as opposed to default run with pruning).

It should be noted that the applicability of these recommendation is limited by the small number of the datasets involved in the experimental evaluation. Additionally, we have shown that the rule ranking algorithm used in CBA can be easily implemented as a rule conflict handling method in the Drools BRMS system, providing a complete workflow from data to actionable business rules.

As a future work, we plan to create an experimental web-based system that would allow to perform business rule learning with ARC algorithms. Also, we would like to further explore the topic of dynamic binning (disjunctions between values of one attribute), which provided promising results. It would be also interesting to perform additional experiments on a larger number of datasets.

Acknowledgment. The authors would like to thank the anonymous reviewers for their insightful comments. This work is supported by the European Union under grant no. FP7-ICT-2011-7 LinkedTV (Television Linked To The Web) and by the University of Economics in Prague by grants no. IGA 20/2013 and institutional support (IP 400040).

References

1. Agrawal, R., Imielinski, T., Swami, A.N.: Mining association rules between sets of items in large databases. In: SIGMOD, pp. 207–216. ACM Press (1993)
2. Antonie, M.-L., Zaïane, O.R.: Mining positive and negative association rules: An approach for confined rules. In: Boulicaut, J.-F., Esposito, F., Giannotti, F., Pedreschi, D. (eds.) PKDD 2004. LNCS (LNAI), vol. 3202, pp. 27–38. Springer, Heidelberg (2004)
3. Han, J., Pei, J., Yin, Y., Mao, R.: Mining frequent patterns without candidate generation: A frequent-pattern tree approach. Data Min. Knowl. Discov. 8(1), 53–87 (2004)
4. Li, W., Han, J., Pei, J.: CMAR: accurate and efficient classification based on multiple class-association rules. In: ICDM 2001, pp. 369–376 (2001)
5. Liu, B., Hsu, W., Ma, Y.: Integrating classification and association rule mining. In: KDD 1998, pp. 80–86 (1998)
6. Ross Quinlan, J.: C4.5: Programs for Machine Learning. Morgan Kaufmann (1993)
7. Rauch, J., Šimůnek, M.: An alternative approach to mining association rules. Foundation of Data Mining and Knowl. Discovery 6, 211–231 (2005)

8. Thabtah, F.: Pruning techniques in associative classification: Survey and comparison. Journal of Digital Information Management 4(3) (2006)
9. Thabtah, F., Cowling, P., Peng, Y.: The impact of rule ranking on the quality of associative classifiers. In: Bramer, M., Coenen, F., Allen, T. (eds.) Research and Development in Intelligent Systems XXII, pp. 277–287. Springer, London (2006)
10. Thabtah, F., Cowling, P., Peng, Y.: Multiple labels associative classification. Knowledge and Information Systems 9(1), 109–129 (2006)
11. Thabtah, F.A.: A review of associative classification mining. Knowledge Eng. Review 22(1), 37–65 (2007)
12. Toivonen, H., Klemettinen, M., Ronkainen, P., Htnen, K., Mannila, H.: Pruning and grouping discovered association rules. In: ECML 1995 Workshop on Statistics, Machine Learning and Knowledge Discovery in Databases, pp. 47–52 (1995)
13. Vanhoof, K., Depaire, B.: Structure of association rule classifiers: a review. In: 2010 International Conference on Intelligent Systems and Knowledge Engineering (ISKE), pp. 9–12 (November 2010)
14. Vojíř, S., Kliegr, T., Hazucha, A., Skrabal, R., Šimunek, M.: Transforming association rules to business rules: Easyminer meets drools. In: Fodor, P., Roman, D., Anicic, D., Wyner, A., Palmirani, M., Sottara, D., Lévy, F. (eds.) RuleML (2). CEUR Workshop Proceedings, vol. 1004. CEUR-WS.org (2013)
15. Yin, X., Han, J.: CPAR: Classification based on predictive association rules. In: Proceedings of the SIAM International Conference on Data Mining, pp. 369–376. SIAM, San Franciso (2003)

Interpreting Web Shop User's Behavioral Patterns as Fictitious Explicit Rating for Preference Learning

Ladislav Peska and Peter Vojtas

Faculty of Mathematics and Physics,
Charles University in Prague,
Malostranske namesti 25, Prague, Czech Republic
{Peska,vojtas}@ksi.mff.cuni.cz

Abstract. We consider applications of user preference rule learning in marketing. We chose rules because of human-understandability. We chose fuzzy logic because it enables to order items for recommendation. In this paper we introduce a rule based system equivalent to the Fagin-Lotem-Naor preference system. We show a multi-user version, introduce induction and compare it to several methods for learning user preference. The methods are based, first, on interpreting e-shop user's behavioral patterns collected by scripts as fictitious explicit rating. After this we use this (fictitious) explicit rating for content based preference learning.

Our main motivation is on recommending for small or medium-sized e-commerce portals. Due to high competition, users of these portals are not too loyal and e.g. refuse to register or provide any/enough explicit feedback. Furthermore, products such as tours, cars or furniture have very low average consumption rate preventing us from tracking unregistered user between two consecutive purchases. Recommending on such domains proves to be very challenging, yet interesting research task. As a test bed, we have conducted several off-line experiments with real user data from travel agency website confirming competitiveness of our method.

Keywords: Recommender Systems, Implicit Feedback, User Preference Rules, E-Commerce.

1   Introduction and Related Work

We face the growth of information on the web with an increasing offer of products, information and services. Automation of web content processing is necessary. Several solutions are available, ranging from search engines to e-shops, aggregation shops and recommender systems. The main problem we are interested in is the personalization of web information processing by user preference mining. Hence, ordering resources/items by user preference. Rules are a type of the most human-understandable knowledge. This is important in e-commerce and marketing. Our main starting point is using fuzzy (many valued) logic rules and interpreting each fuzzy value as a degree

A. Bikakis et al. (Eds.): RuleML 2014, LNCS 8620, pp. 251–265, 2014.
© Springer International Publishing Switzerland 2014

of user preference - higher the fuzzy value, higher the preference (analogically to e.g. one star vs. five stars user rating). So practically, fuzzy sets – facts - induce ordering depending on user preferences on an attribute. Fuzzy rules can describe combination of such preferences.

The e-commerce area can be divided over several axes, laying different constraints for a recommendation task. We focus on the recommendation for rather small e-commerce sites. Moreover we are interested in domains, where an average customer do not purchases an item very often (e.g. once a year). The competition of such sites is usually very high, so the users tend not to be very loyal, visit more sites comparing offers and do not provide any data about themselves (register or rate products). When a new user comes to such a website, he/she usually spends few minutes going through the objects and comparing them. There might be some historical data from his/her previous visits, but usually not too much. Mostly, there are neither registrations information available, nor previous purchases. So it is necessary to deal with personalization and recommendation for a non-registered user based on very little information. Note here, we cannot use NPS – Net Promoter Score - traditional rating used in business industry, because user can not be identified repeatedly. Hence we cannot use action-rules as introduced in [22].

In this paper we combine learning user preference rules with e- commerce area. We have described a quite general model of fuzzy logic programming in [17]. Nevertheless this model is not well suited for induction. Main reason is that we have to learn various connectives of fuzzy logic (and for each user these connectives can be different). In [13] we have shown that FLP^+, a certain generalization of our model is equivalent with GAP^-, a certain restriction of Generalized Annotated Programs [11]. Our GAP^- is much better suited for inductive procedures. In [10] we have studied IGAP (induction of GAP^- programs from ordinal data) and results were promising. One problem of implementation of our method was that we could use only a small finite set of truth values. Induced ordering had usually a large set of items in the best class and hence could not be used for practical recommendation for user.

In [8] authors described data structure and a fuzzy system which aggregates global preference on items from local preferences on attributes. A main result of this paper is an optimal algorithm for find top-k answer without necessity of checking whole database.

Our solution starts from describing the [8] system by a set of fuzzy GAP^- rules. Special database index described in [6] enables to use our rule version of the FLN-algorithm for different users simultaneously. Finally, in [7] we have introduced a hybrid learning system, where learning of local preferences uses regression techniques. Basic assumption of [7] (see also [2]) is that we have user explicit ratings of a small sample of items. Main practical problem with this approach is that users usually do not like to rate items.

Contrary to the explicit feedback, usage of implicit feedback requires no additional effort from the user of the system. Monitoring implicit feedback varies from simple user visit or play counts to more sophisticated ones like scrolling or mouse movement tracking. Due to its effortlessness, data are obtained in much larger quantities for each user. On the other hand, data are inherently noisy, messy and hard to interpret. During early research on implicit feedback, several papers comparing implicit and explicit feedback occurred. We chose to mention Claypool et al. [1] work on implicit interest indicators as it is one of very few studies involving multiple types of implicit feedback and containing idea to combine them in order to achieve better results. We extend this approach. A different approach to implicit user behavior is elaborated in [23] and [24].

In our early work [14-16], we have continued on with this subject and conducted online experiment with real users corroborating that using multiple implicit feedback improves recommendation according to the click-through rate.

The vast majority of e-shops do not force users to register at all, which makes it difficult to track them. Combination of unregistered user and low consumption rate on particular product domains (tours, cars, furniture, specialized sport goods etc.) prevents us in many cases from effectively tracking consecutive purchases of the user. Given the described preconditions, the vast majority of users appear to be new users exacerbating the cold start problem. We cannot hope for tens of ratings as in multimedia portals, but rather need to cope with a few visited pages.

In [4,5,9] we have studied several practical aspects of our systems.

For aggregation several parameterized families of T-conorms were introduced, where level of compensation is determined with a parameter λ. All S-norms used during our experiments are described in detail in [12]. The formula of Sugeno-Weber parametric S-norm is following (parameter λ will be tuned in our inductive methods)

$$S_{sw}(x, y) = \min (1, x + y + \lambda xy)$$

We did not find any reference using methods of inducing fuzzy rule system for recommendation.

Main Contribution

The main contributions of this paper are:

- Designing and using fuzzy rule system for content based recommendation for multiple users with optimal top-k evaluation (based on TA from [8])
- A new method for learning user preference rules from multiple implicit feedbacks.
- Off-line experiments on travel agency dataset.

The rest of the paper is organized as follows: In section 2 we describe our GAP⁻ rule version of the FLN-system and database index enabling efficient rule evaluation algorithm. In section 3 the travel agency dataset and observed user feedback will be described and section 4 presents our model of learning user's preference rules. Section 5 describes conducted experiments and finally section 6 concludes our paper and points to our future work.

2   Rule Systems Describing User Preferences

Main challenge of this paper is to improve recommendation for users of a web shop. We chose rule systems, because rules are a type of the most human-understandable knowledge. Recommendation is per se connected with ordering – best (top-k) recommendations. We represent user preference rules with ordering.

2.1 Preferential Interpretation of Fuzzy Logic

To connect rules and ordering we chose fuzzy (many valued) logic. On a set of items I (we freely switch between using object and item), for a user u, the preference is defined by a fuzzy function $f_u:I \to [0,1]$. An item i_1 is preferred (or bigger in ordering $<_{fu}$ induced by f_u) wrt item i_2 iff $f_u(i_1) > f_u(i_2)$. Note, that our system is comparative, the numeric value of the fuzzy set is not important, what does matter is that $i_2 <_{fu} i_1$). Moreover, we will freely switch between $f(u, i): UxI \to [0,1]$, $f:U \to (I \to [0,1])$ and $f_u:I \to [0,1]$.

It is a generally accepted assumption that user's preference can be described by ideal value (interval) concept (of course ceteris paribus is also an option, see [7]).

Assume we have items with attribute A with a linearly ordered domain $(D_A, <_A)$, a user u with ideal interval $a_2^u < a_3^u$ (and intervals of rejection $min_{<A}D_A < a_1^u (< a_2^u)$ and $(a_3^u <) a_4^u < max_{<A}D_A$). The preference of such a user is described by fuzzy function $f^A_u:D_A \to [0,1]$ defined as follows

$f^A_u(x) = 0$ if $x \in [min_{<A}D_A , a_1^u]$,
$f^A_u(x) = (x- a_1^u)/(a_2^u - a_1^u)$ if $x \in [a_1^u, a_2^u]$,
$f^A_u(x) = 1$ if $x \in [a_2^u, a_3^u]$,
$f^A_u(x) = (a_4^u -x)/(a_4^u - a_3^u)$ if $x \in [a_3^u, a_4^u]$,
$f^A_u(x) = 0$ if $x \in [a_4^u, max_{<A}D_A]$,

with natural extensions for possible equalities and extremes. We do not consider nonlinear behavior of f^A_u, it can be tuned by aggregations. We illustrate examples of such fuzzy sets in Figure 1.

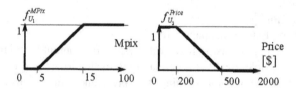

Fig. 1. User's preference represented by fuzzy sets generated be ideal intervals, users u_1 and u_2; attributes Mpix (domain [0, 100]) and Price (domain [0, 2000]); ideal intervals(of rejection) with $a_1^{u1}=5$, $a_2^{u1}=15$ and $a_3^{u1}= max_{<}D_{Mpix}$ ($a_2^{u2}= min_{<}D_{Price}$, $a_3^{u2}=200$ and $a_4^{u2}= 500$).

2.2 Induction of Generalized Annotated Programs

Using fuzzy logic program FLP - rules ([17]) is not very suitable for our purpose, because we have to specify which logic (connectives) we use (and maybe each user has different fuzzy connectives and hence fuzzy logic). In [13] we have shown that (a certain extension of FLP) is equivalent to certain restriction/extension of GAP – Generalized Annotated Programs [11], which are more suitable for learning (GAP rules use classical – two valued conjunction and implication). Our GAP rules have following form:

Annotation range through (generally a lattice L of truth values, here) unit interval $L=[0,1]$ (note that these are degrees of preference and depending on application we can use a finite subset; e.g. for ratings with 0*, ..., 5* we consider $L = \{0, \frac{1}{4}, \frac{1}{2}, \frac{3}{4}, 1\}$. Note that our system is comparative; numerical value of rating is not important, important is ordering defined by it).

An annotation is either an annotation variable or a complex annotation term (built up from both annotation variables and domain variables). In our case, complex annotations are (left continuous) aggregations (see e.g. [12]) or function of type $f^A{}_u$ (also left continuous constant annotations are allowed). Here we differ from [11], which does not have continuous semantics – in [13] we have shown that our semantics is continuous (in the sense of Scott-topology on possible worlds).

If H is an usual atomic formula and α is an annotation, then $H{:}\alpha$ is an annotated atom (by the nature of α it can be variable (v) or term (t) - annotated).

If $H{:}\rho$ is an annotated atom and $B_1{:}\mu_1$ & ... & $B_k{:}\mu_k$ are c- or v-annotated atoms and $C_{k+1}(\_, \mu_{k+1})$ & ... & $C_{k+m}(\_, \mu_{k+m})$ are usual predicate calculus atom and μ_{k+1}, ... μ_{k+m} are domain variables (here our approach also differs from [11]), then

$$H{:}\rho \leftarrow B_1{:}\mu_1 \ \& \ ... \ \& \ B_k{:}\mu_k \ \& \ C_{k+1}(\_, \mu_{k+1}) \ \& \ ... \ \& \ C_{k+m}(\_, \mu_{k+m})$$

is an annotated clause. A GAP⁻ (⁻ means that this is a GAP program in our sense) program is a set of annotated clauses.

Note, that this is a predicate calculus version (which was implemented). We can switch to propositional calculus with all atoms considered ground (nevertheless this approach has complexity problems).

Using our camera example, preference rules can be described by following GAP⁻ program (for each user u there is a possibly different set of rules):

$GoodCameraFor(u,o){:}@_u(x_1; x_2; x_3) \leftarrow GoodPriceFor(u,o){:}x_1 \ \&$
$\qquad\qquad\qquad \& \ GoodDisplayFor(u,o){:}x_2 \ \& \ GoodMPixFor(u,o){:}x_3.$
$\qquad$ and e.g.
$GoodPriceFor(u,o){:}f_u^{Price}(y_1) \leftarrow Price(o, y_1).$

The meaning of these rules is: when price of the item o is y_1 then for user u degree of preference of o is at least $f_u^{Price}(y_1)$. When degrees of preferences on price, display and MPix are at least $x_1; x_2; x_3$ respectively, then the overall preference of o is at least $@_u(x_1; x_2; x_3)$. We developed the theory and methods of IGAP – induction of GA programs in [3-5, 9,10] (implemented only for a small number of preference degrees).

We will deal with preference learning in Chapter 4. Here we mention only induction for GAP briefly. Background knowledge C consists of items data and description of our truth value structure L (L is a small set of truth values); Example set E is a (partial) fuzzy set on the user-item matrix UxI, or with attribute values of items $UxA_1x...xA_n$. Hypothesis $H = \cup H_\alpha$ set are rules learned by classical ILP method separately for each degree $\alpha \in L$ of preference (after certain discretization of domains of attributes). As we will see in evaluation of experiments, this method has a disadvantage, that truth value set has to be limited (because we have to embed it into our knowledge base) and then there are too many items with highest degree of recommendation and we cannot distinguish between item placed on position e.g. 200-400 (or rating 9*).

2.3   The Preference Model of Fagin-Lotem-Naor

In [8] R. Fagin, A. Lotem, and M. Naor presented a preference model which is practically equivalent with the GAP model for a single user.

The model in [8] is described as follows: We assume that each database consists of a finite set of N many objects. Associated with each object R are m fields $x_1^R, ..., x_m^R$; where $x_i^R \in [0, 1]$ for each i: We may refer to x_i^R as the ith field of R: The database can be thought of as consisting of a single relation, where one column corresponds to the object id, and the other columns correspond to m attributes of the object (but we do not go this way). Alternatively, the way we shall think of a database is as consisting of m sorted lists $L_1;...;L_m$; each of length N (there is one entry in each list for each of the N objects). We may refer to L_i as list i. Each entry of L_i is of the form (R; x_i^R); where x_i^R is the ith field of R. These are in fact RDF data. Each list L_i is sorted in descending order by the x_i^R value (this ordering is very important feature of this model). We assume, there is an aggregation $t:[0,1]^m \rightarrow [0,1]$ and rank of the object R is

$$t(R) = t(x_1^R, ..., x_m^R)$$

In [8] authors take this take this view of a database, since this view enables optimal algorithm for finding top-k object according to $t(R)$. Fagin, Lotem and Naor consider two modes of access to data. The first mode of access is sorted (or sequential) access. Here the system obtains the grade of an object in one of the sorted lists by proceeding through the list sequentially from the top. Thus, if object R has the ℓth highest grade in the ith list, then ℓ sorted accesses to the ith list are required to see this grade under sorted access. The second mode of access is random access. Here, the system requests the grade of object R in the ith list, and obtains it in one random access. If there are s sorted accesses and r random accesses, then the sorted access cost is sc_S; the random access cost is rc_R; and the system cost is $sc_S + rc_R$ (the sum of the sorted access cost and the random access cost), for some positive constants c_S and rc_R.

A significant contribution of [8] is the threshold algorithm TA for evaluation of top-k results which has optimal cost with respect to all algorithms correctly evaluating top-k without guessing.

Let us assume that list L_i orders object according to rating of ith attribute. This preference model is then semantically equivalent to GAP program with rules

$A_i(R, y_i) \leftarrow A(R,\_ ,y_i, \_)$. for each $i = 1, ..., m$

$rank(R): t(x_1^R, ..., x_m^R) \leftarrow C_1(R): x_1^R \ \& \ ... \ \& \ C_m(R): x_m^R$. (no annotations in body)

$C_i(R): f^i(R, y_i) \leftarrow A_i(R, y_i)$ putting $f^i(R, y_i) = x_i^R$ for each $i = 1, ..., m$

To make it computationally equivalent, we have to assume that evaluation of this GAP program has all atoms of type $C_i(R): f^i(R, y_i)$ ordered descending by $f^i(R, y_i)$ and random access is enabled. Note that classical evaluation can be also used, but we have to add rules for finding ℓ^{th} entry (or random access). Nevertheless this would enormously increase costs c_S and c_R.

In [8] only a single user model is presented, authors do not consider multiple user challenge or its induction. To transform semantically the above GAP to a multiuser version is easy, we just add an additional attribute for the user $rank(u, R), C_i(u, R), ...$

To transform this preference model computationally to an optimal multiuser model is not so straightforward (although using classical GAP evaluation can be again used with increased costs c_S and rc_R.). Basic assumptions of optimality of the TA algorithm are monotonicity of the aggregation operator t and ordered access to the ordered lists of items. But different users can have different ideal points (ideal intervals) and hence different ordering of lists. Many users lead to idea of having for each user u another list L^u_i. Nevertheless, this idea (of having so many ordered lists as users) is not viable.

In [6] we have presented an index structure (an extension of the B^+ tree where f^{Ai}_u can guide navigation) giving us monotone access for different users. This corresponds to a new evaluation of GAP rule base (with rules for each user u) using this index. This lead us to computational model TA_{GAP}, where classical parts of GAP evaluation (binding variables, substitution, …) are empowered by our index on attributes A_i and a navigation guided by $f_u^{Ai}(R, y_i)$.

How to learn such rule base will be dealt in Chapter 4. Note that our GAP⁻ programs do not use negation; hence the computational model is monotone. Sometimes, we will our GAP⁻ programs call "monotone user preference rules".

3   Data - Users' Behavior and Item Properties

We have collected usage data from one of the major Czech travel agencies. Data were collected from December 2012 to January 2014. Travel agency is typical e-commerce enterprise, where customers buy products only once in a while (most typically once a year). The site does not force users to register and so we can track unique users only with cookies stored in the browser. User typically either land straight on intended object via search engine (less interesting case), or browses or searches through several categories, compares few objects (possibly on more websites) and eventually buys a single object. Buying more than one object at the time when the cookie is still valid is very rare.

We have access to the source data, so we could (after approval) collect user behavior. The captured user behavior is based on implicit indicators introduced by Claypool [1], however some additional indicators were added.

The dataset has a form of:

ImplicitFeedback(UID, OID, PageView, Mouse, Scroll, Open, Time, Purchase),

where UID and *OID* are unique user and object(item) identifiers, the rest will be denoted as $F_1 = PageView$, … $F_5 = Time$, $F_6 = Purchase$ and Table 1 contains full description of feedback types. Note that *UID* is based on cookie stored by browser, so we cannot e.g. distinguish between two persons using the same computer. Table contains approx. 350 000 records with 0.0007% density of $UID \times OID$ matrix and in average 1.6 visited objects per user. For learning the dataset was then restricted to only users with at least one purchased and 4 visited objects leaving over 3500 records from 364 users.

Table 1. Description of the collected implicit feedbacks for user visiting an object

Factor	Description
F_1 PageView	Count(*OnLoad()* event on object page)
F_2 Mouse	Count(*OnMouseOver()* events on object page)
F_3 Scroll	Count(OnScroll() events on object page)
F_4 Open	Count(Item was opened from the list of recommended objects)
F_5 Time	Sum(time spent on object page)
F_6 Purchase	1 IFF user bought the item, 0 else

3.1   Content Based Attributes

As our previous work corroborated [14-16], using purely collaborative filtering methods on such a sparse dataset comes up with poor results, so some content-based algorithms were used in the experiments.

Table 2. Description of content-based attributes of a tour

Attribute	Description
A_1 TourType	Type of the tour (e.g. sightseeing, beach holidays, spa etc.)
A_2 Country	Destination country of the tour (e.g. Spain)
A_3 Destination	More specific destination (e.g. Costa Brava)
A_4 AccomodatType	Quality of the accommodation (e.g. 3*)
A_5 Accommodation	ID of accommodation (hotel) assigned for the tour
A_6 Board	Type of board (e.g. breakfast, half-board)
A_7 Transport	Type of transport (coach, plane...)
A_8 Price	Price per person; integer

The success of content-based or hybrid algorithms are highly dependent on the quality content-based attributes, which varies over domains. The travel agency dataset can be classified somewhere in the middle as there are some informative attributes (Tour type, Country, Price...), but a lot of important information is accessible only through textual description. Table 2 contains description of attributes used in the experiments. In what follows we will denote them $A_1 = TourType, ..., A_8 = Price$ (note, most of them are nominal).

4   Learning User Preference Rules from Behavioral Patterns

In Chapter 2 we have described our user preference rule model. As mentioned earlier, we can solve it by classical tools for ILP, just adding to background knowledge information about truth values $L, <$ (hence L has to be small) and split it to several tasks (example set is split to positive and negative by $\alpha \in L$ and background knowledge is used always all, see [10]). Nevertheless, this has some disadvantages. Using small L does not help to order items (e.g. to compute top-10). Here we decided to use regression to learn real valued preferences. To learn the model in practice the main challenge is sparsity of data in the user-item matrix. Even methods of matrix factorization do not work on our data and moreover we are going beyond RMSE evaluation (see [15]). Second challenge is the choice of preference indicator. In our data, we have only one direct preference indicator – namely purchase. But purchases are even sparsely than collected behavior data. We tested classical recommendation techniques – collaborative, item based – filtering – these did not work. As a base-line we used standard machine learning methods. Nevertheless, these do not provide monotone (with ideal point assumption) user preference rules. Only rule induction method which gave improvement was content based recommendation.

Our strategy is to divide the task into two steps

1. Interpret user behavior patterns (of all users glued together) as fictitious explicit rating (methods will be denoted by subscript 1, e.g. m_1, n_1).
2. Use this fictitious explicit rating in a content based learning we developed e.g. in [7] (see also [2]), (methods will be denoted by subscript 2, e.g. m_2, n_2.

Steps are somewhat similar, in both we have several attributes and an aggregation, in both we tried to optimize through several learning methods. All these methods were implemented, with optimization and necessary cross validation in [21] and [14].

4.1   Interpreting User's Behavioral Patterns as Fictitious Explicit Rating

We adopt business-like point of view and state that user positively prefers the object(s) which he/she has *purchased*.

Gluing Data from All Users Together. For each implicit factor $F_1, \ldots F_5$ we sum up number of all purchases for all users with given value of this factor as in Figure 2

$$g_i(j) = \Sigma\{F_6(u,o): F_i(u,o)=j, u \in UID, o \in OID, \}$$

(relativized to [0,1]). Note, $g_i(j)$ is not good to use for prediction, we have to use a

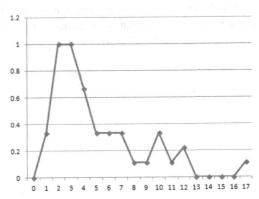

Fig. 2. Relative purchases per F_1 page view – all users together

statistical data mining method m_1 to learn a generalization

$$g_i^{m1}:D_{Fi} \to [0,1]$$

In the experiment section we will report only on best combination of these methods (e.g. m_1 = linear regression).

Using these, we have transformed $\prod_{i=1}^{N} D_{Fi}$ into cube $[0,1]^5$. Second parameter to optimize is aggregation $@_1$ used to map $[0,1]^5$ into $[0,1]$ is learned by method n_1.

Note, that composition $b_{n1}^{ml} = @^{n1}{}_1(g_1^{ml}, \dots g_5^{ml}) : \prod_{i=1}^{5} D_{Fi} \rightarrow [0,1]$ is not dependent on the user. We consider this b_{n1}^{ml} as an interpretation of user behavior patterns and will use to generate user fictitious rating on visited objects as follows:

For an user u and an object (item) o and user behavior on this object described by vector

$$[F_1(u,o), \dots, F_5(u,o)]$$

We generate fictitious explicit rating of this object

$$r_{n1}^{ml}(u,o) = b_{n1}^{ml}(F_1(u,o), \dots, F_5(u,o)) \in [0,1]$$

Only we have to remember is, that this is depending on the choice of method m_1 and n_1 (and not on any user u). Varying over all possible choices we can find best.

4.2 Using Fictitious Explicit Rating for Content Based Preference Learning

We have now Fictitious Explicit Rating from interpretation of (a new) user behavior on a set of visited objects (items). Formally, from the point of view of data representation, we are now in a situation which is same as we would have a true explicit rating of a sample of objects (items) visited by user u. The only difference is that explicit rating would come from a user explicit activity and in our case it comes from interpretation of user's behavior.

Let us assume we have a user u, a set of objects S_u visited by u and rating $r_u: S_u \subseteq I \subseteq \Pi D_{Ai} \rightarrow [0,1]$ (r_u was obtained as some $r_{n1}^{m1}(u,o)$; m_1, n_1 are no more important and we fix u).

Now we would like to induce the GAP rule system equivalent to Fagin-Lotem-Naor preference model for content based learning. Recall, it consist of local preferences $f^{Ai}{}_u : D_{Ai} \rightarrow [0,1]$, $i=1,\dots,8$ and an aggregation $@_{2u}:[0,1]^8 \rightarrow [0,1]$.

First step is, for each i, to project ratings to product $D_{Ai} \times [0,1]$ (see circles in Figure 3) $Proj(r_u, i) = \{(a, r_u(o)): o \in S_u, o.i = a\}$. Then use a regression method m_2 to

Fig. 3. Projection of ratings and Peak regression method

generalize those points. In this paper we have used *Linear*, *Quadratic* and *Peak* regressions in the experiments. The idea of *Peak* regression comes from previous work of our research group [7] using the fact, that users prefer the most a value (ideal point) somewhere in the attribute domain and the preference decreases with distance from this ideal point. More formally the Peak method traverses the values of the domain present in the training set. Each value $a \in D_{Ai}$ is tested as a candidate for the most preferred value - "the peak". The method constructs two linear functions for each candidate a: one is defined on the numbers lower than a and the other is defined on the higher numbers. Then the error on the training set is measured using MAE.

Hence for each i and method $\boldsymbol{m_2}$ we get $f_u^{i,m2}:D_{Ai} \rightarrow [0,1]$ (mostly we omit $\boldsymbol{m_2}$).

Learning / optimizing Global Preferences. We have tested here several methods $\boldsymbol{n_2}$ for learning aggregation $@_{2u}$(recall that this applies to choice of aggregation $@_1$ in the first step when interpreting behavior of users). Combination of $@_{2u}$ with all local preference methods f^{Ai}_u gives a total preference on all objects

$$p_u: I \subseteq \Pi D_{Ai} \rightarrow [0,1]$$

Note, p_u is defined on whole I, and hence it makes sense to calculate the position of purchased object in ordering of all objects considered. This is a preference model in the sense of [8] and gives a monotone rule preference system for each user.

For $\boldsymbol{n_2}$, first is to consider several parametric families of S-norms ([12]). In this case we have to tune parameter, which gives best results (in combination with all other choices we try to optimize together). Best results were achieved with Sugeno-Weber conorm (formula is in the Chapter1).

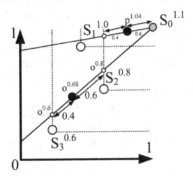

Fig. 4. The geometry method, works on Pareto cube of unit intervals [0,1], point are projections of data point by local preferences, value 1.1 is set heuristically

Second method is the geometric method (see Figure 4). The basic idea is, that when we are in the preference cube $[0,1]^8$, and when local preferences optimally monotonized data (more on this see in Chapter 5), then working with Pareto ordering from the geometrical point of view, we can get a clue for aggregation. Geometric aggregation method is based on a line that connects item o and the ideal point S_0. In Figure 4 - the gray point S_0 is the ideal point (probably not in the domain), and it is assumed to have a rating 1.1. This method evaluates a new object (black) using the objects with known ratings (white) and an ideal object (gray). We examine the intersection of the line and the boundaries of the subspaces dominating the training points

S_i (they have rating from r^u). There are at most two intersections that are closest to o, represented by small white circles. Then the average of objects rating dominated by these two subspaces and weighted by the inverse of the distance, is computed. In our case o gets 0.68. This gives an ordering induced by interval $[0, 1.1]$.

5   Experiments

So far we have described our preference models, data from an e-shop and a variety of models of learning our preference model. In our implementation [21] we have possibility to choose method m_1 for interpretation of user behavior, n_1 for aggregation $@_1$, method m_2 for content based learning of local preferences and n_2 for aggregation $@_{2u}$. See Figure 4 for evaluation of m_1 wrt all combinations with n_1, m_1 and n_2. As baseline, we considered some statistical data mining method in place of combination of m_1 with n_1 and/or of m_2 with n_2. Comparison with our classical IGAP was tested too. Several other methods from [18-19] were tested too.

The challenge now is the metric we will optimize choice of combination of our methods. In this paper we have chosen the average position of purchased object.

5.1   Evaluating Local Preference Methods for Behavioral Data

Given user behavior, local preference methods transforms data cube ΠF_i into the preference cube $[0,1]^5$ with Pareto ordering. We can test quality of this local preference learning independently on optimization of other methods. We can simple compare whether *purchases* and Pareto ordering agree or not.

Hence, for a given user u, objects o_1 and o_2 and known $F_6(o_1) < F_6(o_2)$ we distinguish three situations (and in our data and best methods frequency was promising):

- Correctly ordered preferences i.e. for all i, $g_i^{m1}(u,o_1) < g_i^{m1}(u,o_2)$, it was observed in 59% of cases.
- Incorrectly ordered i.e. for all i, $g_i^{m1}(u,o_1) \geq g_i^{m1}(u,o_2)$ and $\exists i$: the inequality is strict , it was observed in 4% of cases, this is quite surprising for us.
- Incomparable if nothing from the above applies, it was observed in 37% of cases.

Methods seem to be well designed as majority of evaluated pairs are correctly ordered and only less than 5% are ordered incorrectly (this is an unrepairable mistake, as aggregation preserves ordering). Possible disagreement can be even smaller if aggregation correctly orders group of incomparable pairs. Remember that this is checked only on rated objects from S^u and average position metric will evaluate position of purchased object in ordering of all objects.

5.2   Evaluating Global Preference Methods

Now we can move to the evaluation of resulting p_u preferences. In this phase we have also included results of SVM and M5P (we used WEKA implementation of SVM for regression and M5P decision tree) decision tree methods to be compared with our two-step preference model. More than 50 methods varying in local preference method, parametric S-norms, IGAP and geometry methods were evaluated. Table 4 shows results of some representatives.

Table 4. Results of our experiments (average after cross validation)

Experiment results		
From behavioral patterns to fictitious explicit rating	*From fictitious explicit rating to recommendation*	*Average position*
n_1=tuned Sugeno-Weber + m_1=linear	n_2=tuned Sugeno-Weber + m_2=quadratic	163.2
m_1+ n_1=M5P	n_2=Geometry + m_2=peak	181.4
n_1=tuned Sugeno-Weber + m_1=linear	m_2+ n_2=IGAP	200-400 or 9*
m_1+ n_1=M5P	m_2+ n_2=IGAP	200-400 or 9*

Results show that two-step model of user preferences is comparable with standard machine learning methods or even slightly better.

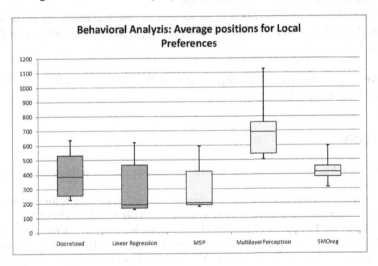

Fig. 5. Quality of local behavioral methods m_1 optimized over all combination of remaining methods (computing @$_1$, @$_{2u}$, local preferences f^i_u)

Last Figure 4 shows quality of learning local preferences with methods m_1 from behavioral data and optimized over all combination of remaining methods (computing @$_1$, @$_{2u}$, local preferences f^{Ai}_u). This is possible because combination of all methods gives ordering on all items and hence it makes sense to ask which methods from m_1 contributed most. Note, that in 5.1 we evaluated m_1 alone because we could not compute position. We could compute only agreement of Pareto ordering of images ordering with purchases.

6   Conclusions and Future Work

In this paper, we have discussed the problem of learning user preference rules using implicit feedback as possible indicators of user preference. The only direct preference indicator we used are purchases. We can confirm this hypothesis. Our system can learn (at least in average position of purchased object) user's preference better than best statistical data mining method.

We have introduced a multiuser rule based system equivalent to the Fagin-Lotem-Naor preference system. Our new methods are based, first, on interpreting e-shop user's behavioral patterns collected by scripts as fictitious explicit rating. After this we use this (fictitious) explicit rating for content based preference learning.

Our main motivation is on recommending for small or medium-sized e-commerce portals. As a test bed, we have conducted several off-line experiments with real user data from travel agency website confirming competitiveness of our methods. So far we are not fully satisfied with our results (AP=163 is probably not practically business relevant). As a future work we plan to collect more detailed data on user behavior and browsing inside the e-shop, improve our methods and then to convince the owner that online testing is worth to test.

Our activity can be understood as an attempt to continue along use-cases designed in W3C Uncertainty Reasoning for the World Wide Web Incubator Group [20], see also [3].

Acknowledgments. This work was supported by Czech grants SVV-2013-267312, P46 and GAUK-126313.

References

1. Claypool, M., Le, P., Wased, M., Brown, D.: Implicit interest indicators. In: IUI 2001, pp. 33–40. ACM, New York (2001)
2. Eckhardt, A.: Similarity of users' (content-based) preference models for Collaborative filtering in few ratings scenario. Expert Syst. Appl. 39(14), 11511–11516 (2012)
3. Eckhardt, A., Horváth, T., Maruščák, D., Novotný, R., Vojtáš, P.: Uncertainty Issues and Algorithms in Automating Process Connecting Web and User. In: da Costa, P.C.G., d'Amato, C., Fanizzi, N., Laskey, K.B., Laskey, K.J., Lukasiewicz, T., Nickles, M., Pool, M. (eds.) URSW 2005 - 2007. LNCS (LNAI), vol. 5327, pp. 207–223. Springer, Heidelberg (2008)
4. Eckhardt, A., Horváth, T., Vojtáš, P.: Learning Different User Profile Annotated Rules for Fuzzy Preference Top-k Querying. In: Prade, H., Subrahmanian, V.S. (eds.) SUM 2007. LNCS (LNAI), vol. 4772, pp. 116–130. Springer, Heidelberg (2007)
5. Eckhardt, A., Horváth, T., Vojtás, P.: PHASES: A User Profile Learning Approach for Web Search. Web Intelligence, 780–783 (2007)
6. Eckhardt, A., Pokorný, J., Vojtás, P.: A System Recommending Top-k Objects for Multiple Users Preferences. In: FUZZ-IEEE, pp. 1–6 (2007)
7. Eckhardt, A., Vojtáš, P.: Learning user preferences for 2cp-regression for a recommender system. In: van Leeuwen, J., Muscholl, A., Peleg, D., Pokorný, J., Rumpe, B. (eds.) SOFSEM 2010. LNCS, vol. 5901, pp. 346–357. Springer, Heidelberg (2010)

8. Fagin, R., Lotem, A., Naor, M.: Optimal aggregation algorithms for middleware. J. Computer System Sciences 66, 614–656 (2003)
9. Horváth, T., Sudzina, F., Vojtás, P.: Mining Rules from Monotone Classification Measuring Impact of Information Systems on Business Competitiveness. In: Camarinha-Matos, L.M. (ed.) Emerging Solutions for Future Manufacturing Systems. IFIP, vol. 159, pp. 451–458. Springer, Boston (2004)
10. Horváth, T., Vojtáš, P.: Induction of Fuzzy and Annotated Logic Programs. In: Muggleton, S.H., Otero, R., Tamaddoni-Nezhad, A. (eds.) ILP 2006. LNCS (LNAI), vol. 4455, pp. 260–274. Springer, Heidelberg (2007)
11. Kifer, M., Subrahmanian, V.S.: Theory of Generalized Annotated Logic Programming and its Applications. J. Log. Program. 12(3&4), 335–367 (1992)
12. Klement, E.P., Mesiar, R., Pap, E.: Triangular Norms. Springer, Netherlands (2000)
13. Krajci, S., Lencses, R., Vojtás, P.: A comparison of fuzzy and annotated logic programming. Fuzzy Sets and Systems 144(1), 173–192 (2004)
14. Peska, L., Eckhardt, A., Vojtás, P.: UPComp - A PHP Component for Recommendation Based on User Behaviour. In: Web Intelligence/IAT Workshops, pp. 306–309 (2011)
15. Peska, L., Vojtas, P.: Evaluating Various Implicit Factors in E-commerce. In: RUE (RecSys) 2012 ACM RecSys Workshop on Recommendation Utility Evaluation: Beyond RMSE, CEUR, vol. 910, pp. 51–55 (2012)
16. Peska, L., Vojtas, P.: Recommending for Disloyal Customers with Low Consumption Rate. In: Geffert, V., Preneel, B., Rovan, B., Štuller, J., Tjoa, A.M. (eds.) SOFSEM 2014. LNCS, vol. 8327, pp. 455–465. Springer, Heidelberg (2014)
17. Vojtás, P.: Fuzzy logic programming. Fuzzy Sets and Systems 124(3), 361–370 (2001)
18. Vojtáš, P., Vomlelová, M.: On models of comparison of multiple monotone classifications. In: IPMU 2006 - Information Processing and management under Uncertainty, pp. 1236–1243. Éditions EDK, Paris (2006) ISBN: 2-84254-112-X
19. Vojtás, P., Vomlelová, M.: Trasformation of deductive and inductive tasks between models of logic programming with imperfect information. In: Bouchon-Meunier, B., et al. (eds.) Proc. IPMU 2004, pp. 839–846. Editrice Universita La Sapienza, Roma (2004)
20. W3C Uncertainty Reasoning for the World Wide Web Incubator Group, http://www.w3.org/2005/Incubator/urw3/XGR-urw3/
21. Eckhardt, A.: Prefwork - A framework for testing of methods for user preference learning, https://code.google.com/p/prefwork/
22. Raś, Z.W., Wieczorkowska, A.A.: Action-rules: how to increase profit of a company. In: Zighed, D.A., Komorowski, J., Żytkow, J.M. (eds.) PKDD 2000. LNCS (LNAI), vol. 1910, pp. 587–592. Springer, Heidelberg (2000)
23. Hu, Y., Koren, Y., Volinsky, C.: Collaborative Filtering for Implicit Feedback Datasets. In: ICDM 2008, pp. 263–272. IEEE Computer Society, Washington, DC (2008)
24. Lee, D.H., Brusilovsky, P.: Reinforcing Recommendation Using Implicit Negative Feedback. In: Houben, G.-J., McCalla, G., Pianesi, F., Zancanaro, M. (eds.) UMAP 2009. LNCS, vol. 5535, pp. 422–427. Springer, Heidelberg (2009)

Learning Association Rules from Data through Domain Knowledge and Automation

Jan Rauch and Milan Šimůnek

Faculty of Informatics and Statistics, University of Economics
nám W. Churchilla 4, 130 67 Prague 3, Czech Republic
{rauch,simunek}@vse.cz

Abstract. An approach to automated data mining with association rules based on domain knowledge is introduced. Association rules are understood as interesting pairs of general Boolean attributes. Items of domain knowledge corresponding to various relations of non-Boolean attributes are used to formulate reasonable analytical questions. Particular items of knowledge are mapped to sets of association rules which can be considered their consequences. The sets of consequences are then used to interpret sets of association rules resulting from a data mining procedure.

1 Introduction

Association rules were introduced in [1] together with apriori algorithm producing them from a given database. The association rule is an expression $X \to Y$ where X,Y are disjoint subsets of a large set I of items. The analysed database is a set of baskets $b_1, \ldots, b_n$ where $b_i \subset I$ for $i = 1, \ldots, n$. Meaning of the rule $X \to Y$ is that market baskets containing set X tend to contain set Y of items. The idea of association rules was generalized to data in the tabular, attribute-value form. The association rule is understood as a relation between conjunctions of attribute-value pairs called antecedent and consequent (i.e. succedent).

However, the concept of association rules was introduced and studied much earlier in the framework of development of the GUHA method of mechanized hypothesis formation [5]. A milestone in the GUHA development was the monograph [6], which introduces the general theory of mechanized hypothesis formation based on mathematical logic and statistics. Association rules defined and studied in [6] are relations between two general Boolean attributes derived from the columns of an analysed data matrix. These relations between Boolean attributes were not called association rules even if the procedure mining for them is called ASSOC [7]. The term *association rules* has been used for patterns mined by the ASSOC procedure since the association rules were introduced in [1].

The 4ft-Miner procedure [21] dealing with the association rules – interesting couples of Boolean attributes has been developed as an implementation of the ASSOC procedure. New theoretical results has been achieved, they can be seen as a logic of association rules [19]. An original approach to use of domain knowledge in mining association rules has been introduced [17] and tested [22]. A formal

A. Bikakis et al. (Eds.): RuleML 2014, LNCS 8620, pp. 266–280, 2014.
© Springer International Publishing Switzerland 2014

framework FOFRADAR making possible to describe formally the process of data mining with domain knowledge and association rules has been developed [19, 20].

The idea is to deal with formalized items of domain knowledge corresponding to more complex patterns than single association rules. The following principles are used:

- Each given item of domain knowledge is mapped to a set of simple association rules in co-operation with a domain expert.
- This set is further expanded using logical deduction to a set of all association rules which can be considered as consequences of the given item of knowledge.
- Resulting sets of rules – consequences of given items of domain knowledge – are then used to interpret results of a data mining procedure.

All necessary steps of dealing with such items of domain knowledge are formally described by FOFRADAR and are supported by the LISp-Miner system, part of which is also the procedure 4ft-Miner [21, 22]. However, theirs applications involves elaborate operations in several modules of the LISp-Miner system. Thus a scripting language LMCL (LISp-Miner Control Language) has been developed [25, 27]. The LMCL makes possible to describe necessary operations and run them automatically by programmable means.

The goal of this paper is to describe first experience with utilization of the LMCL to automate dealing with domain knowledge in the data mining with association rules. We use a medical data set STULONG, however, the goal of the paper is not to get new medical knowledge.

The structure of the paper is as follows. The medical data set STULONG is shortly described in Section 2 together with related domain knowledge. The association rules – relations of general Boolean attributes are introduced in Section 3 as well as relevant results on logic of association rules. Mapping an item of domain knowledge to a set of association rules which can be considered as its consequences is described in Section 4. An example of formulation of an analytical question based on an item of domain knowledge is in Section 5 together with a description of a solution of this question by the LISp-Miner system. An attempt to utilize FOFRADAR and LMCL to automate the process of formulating and solution of such analytical questions is introduced in Section 6. Remarks to related research are in Section 7.1.

2   STULONG Data Set

2.1   Data Matrix Entry

We use data set STULONG concerning *Longitudinal Study of Atherosclerosis Risk Factors* [1]. Data set consists of four data matrices, we deal with data matrix *Entry* only. It concerns 1417 patients – men that have been examined at the beginning of the study. Each row of the data matrix describes one patient. The

---

[1] See http://euromise.vse.cz/challenge2004/, cited March 1, 2014.

data matrix has 64 columns corresponding to particular attributes – characteristics of patients. The attributes can be divided into various groups, We use three groups defined for this paper - *Measures, Personal,* and *Blood pressure.*

Group *Measures* has three attributes - *BMI* i.e. Body Mass Index, *Subsc* i.e. a skinfold above the musculus subscapularis (in mm), and *Tric* i.e. a skinfold above the musculus triceps (in mm). The original values were transformed such that these attributes have the following possible values (i.e. categories):

BMI : ≤ 21, $(21; 22)$, $(22; 23)$, ..., $(31; 32)$, > 32 (13 categories)
Subsc : < 10, $(10; 12)$, $(12; 14)$, ..., $(30; 32)$, $(32; 36)$, > 36 (14 categories)
Tric : ≤ 4, $5, 6, ..., 12, 13 - 14, 15 - 17, \geq 18$ (12 categories).

Group *Personal* has two attributes with 4 categories each, frequencies of particular categories ar e in brackets (there are some missing values, too):

Status: married (1210), *divorced* (104), *single* (95), *widower* (10)
Education: basic (151), *apprentice* (405), *secondary* (444), *university* (397).

Group *Blood pressure* has two attributes - *Diastolic* i.e. Diastolic blood pressure and *Systolic* i.e. Systolic blood pressure The original values were transformed such that these attributes have the following categories:

Diastolic : < 65, $(65; 75)$, $(75; 85)$, ..., $(105; 115)$, ≥ 115 (7 categories)
Systolic : < 105, $(105; 115)$, $(115; 125)$, ..., $(165; 175)$, ≥ 175 (9 categories).

2.2 Domain Knowledge

There are various types of domain knowledge related to STULONG data. Three of them are managed by the LISp-Miner system [22]: *groups of attributes, information on particular attributes* and *mutual influence of attributes.* Examples of groups of attributes are introduced above. Information on particular attributes include information on types of attributes (nominal/ordinal/cardinal). Attribute *Status* is an example of nominal attribute, attributes *Education* and *Diastolic* are examples of ordinal attributes.

There are several types of influences among attributes, most of them are relevant to specified types of attributes. The expression *BMI* ↑↑ *Diastolic* is an example of an item of domain knowledge of the type *mutual influence of attributes.* This expression says that *if body mass index of a patient increases then his/here diastolic blood pressure increases too.*

3   Association Rules and Logic of Association Rules

3.1   Association Rules

The association rule is understood as an expression $\varphi \approx \psi$ where φ and ψ are Boolean attributes. The rule means that the Boolean attributes φ and ψ are associated in a way given by the symbol $\approx$ which is called the *4ft-quantifier.* It corresponds to a condition concerning a contingency table of φ and ψ. The association rule $\varphi \approx \psi$ can be true or false in analysed data matrix $\mathcal{M}$. An example of data matrix is data matrix *Entry* a fragment of which is in Fig. 1.

	attributes			examples of basic Boolean attributes	
patient	Status	BMI	...	Status(*single*)	$BMI(\langle 21; 22\rangle, \langle 22; 23\rangle)$
o_1	*single*	$\langle 16; 21\rangle$	...	1	0
$\vdots$	$\vdots$	$\vdots$	$\ddots$	$\vdots$	$\vdots$
o_{1417}	*married*	$\langle 22; 23\rangle$	...	0	1

Fig. 1. Data matrix *Entry* and examples of Boolean attributes

The Boolean attributes are derived from columns of analysed data matrix $\mathcal{M}$. We assume there is a finite number of possible values (i.e. *categories*) for each column of $\mathcal{M}$. *Basic Boolean attributes* are created first. The basic Boolean attribute is each expression $A(\alpha)$ where $\alpha \subset \{a_1, \ldots a_k\}$ and $\{a_1, \ldots a_k\}$ is the set of all categories of the column A. The basic Boolean attribute $A(\alpha)$ is true in row o of $\mathcal{M}$ if it is $a \in \alpha$ where a is the value of the column A in row o. Set α is called a *coefficient* of $A(\alpha)$. Boolean attributes are derived from basic Boolean attributes using propositional connectives $\vee$, $\wedge$ and $\neg$ in a usual way.

There are two examples of basic Boolean attributes in Fig. 1 - Status(*single*) and $BMI(\langle 21; 22\rangle, \langle 22; 23\rangle)$. Attribute Status(*single*) is true for patient o_1 and false for patient o_{1417}, we write "1" or "0" respectively in corresponding rows and columns. Attribute $BMI(\langle 21; 22\rangle, \langle 22; 23\rangle)$ is false for patient o_1 because $\langle 16; 21\rangle \notin \{\langle 21; 22\rangle, \langle 22; 23\rangle)\}$ and attribute $BMI(\langle 21; 22\rangle, \langle 22; 23\rangle)$ is true for o_{1417} because $\langle 22; 23\rangle \in \{\langle 21; 22\rangle, \langle 22; 23\rangle)\}$. Please note that we should write Status(\{*single*\}) etc. but we will use a more simple form Status(*single*). We will also usually write $BMI\langle 21; 23\rangle$ instead of BMI $(\langle 21; 22\rangle, \langle 22; 23\rangle)$ etc.

Let us emphasize that the procedure 4ft-Miner dealing with rules built from general Boolean attributes $A(\alpha)$ has tools to focus only to really relevant subsets α, see Section 5.2. This way the search space can be substantially limited.

The rule $\varphi \approx \psi$ is *true in data matrix* $\mathcal{M}$ if the condition corresponding to the 4ft-quantifier is satisfied in the contingency table of φ and ψ in $\mathcal{M}$, otherwise $\varphi \approx \psi$ is *false in data matrix* $\mathcal{M}$. The contingency table $4ft(\varphi, \psi, \mathcal{M})$ of φ and ψ in data matrix $\mathcal{M}$ is a quadruple $\langle a, b, c, d\rangle$ where a is the number of rows of $\mathcal{M}$ satisfying both φ and ψ, b is the number of rows of $\mathcal{M}$ satisfying φ and not satisfying ψ etc., see Table 1.

Table 1. 4ft table $4ft(\varphi, \psi, \mathcal{M})$ of φ and ψ in $\mathcal{M}$

$\mathcal{M}$	ψ	$\neg\psi$
φ	a	b
$\neg\varphi$	c	d

There are tens various 4ft-quantifiers, some of them are based on statistical hypothesis tests [6, 19]. We use here 4ft-quantifier $\Rightarrow_{p,B}$ of *founded implication* [6]. It is defined for $0 < p \leq 1$ and $B > 0$ by the condition $\frac{a}{a+b} \geq p \wedge a \geq B$. The association rule $\varphi \Rightarrow_{p,B} \psi$ means that at least $100p$ per cent of rows of $\mathcal{M}$

satisfying φ satisfy also ψ and that there are at least B rows of $\mathcal{M}$ satisfying both φ and ψ. Let us note that 4ft-quantifier $\rightarrow_{p,s}$ is defined for $0 < p \leq 1$ and $0 < s \leq 1$ by the condition $\frac{a}{a+b} \geq p \wedge \frac{a}{a+b+c+d} \geq s$ and thus the rule $\varphi \rightarrow_{p,s} \psi$ is true if its confidence is at least p and its support is at least s.

3.2 Logic of Association Rules

Logical calculi of association rules are introduced and studied in [19]. Formulas of them correspond to association rules informally introduced above. There are various theoretical results related to these calculi. We use here results concerning correctness of deduction rules $\frac{\varphi \Rightarrow_{p,B} \psi}{\varphi' \Rightarrow_{p,B} \psi'}$ where both $\varphi \Rightarrow_{p,B} \psi$ and $\varphi' \Rightarrow_{p,B} \psi'$ are association rules. Deduction rule $\frac{\varphi \Rightarrow_{p,B} \psi}{\varphi' \Rightarrow_{p,B} \psi'}$ is correct if it holds for each data matrix $\mathcal{M}$:

$$\text{If } \varphi \Rightarrow_{p,B} \psi \text{ is true in } \mathcal{M} \text{ then also } \varphi' \Rightarrow_{p,B} \psi' \text{ is true in } \mathcal{M} .$$

Deduction rule $\frac{BMI\langle 21;22\rangle \Rightarrow_{0.9,30} Diastolic\langle 65;75\rangle}{BMI\langle 21;22\rangle \Rightarrow_{0.9,30} Diastolic\langle 65;85\rangle}$ is a very simple example of correct deduction rule, an additional example of a correct deduction rule is

$$\frac{BMI\langle 21;22\rangle \wedge Status(married) \Rightarrow_{0.9,30} Diastolic\langle 65;75\rangle}{BMI\langle 21;22\rangle \Rightarrow_{0.9,30} Diastolic\langle 65;75\rangle \vee \neg Status(married)} .$$

However, the deduction rule $\frac{BMI\langle 21;22\rangle \Rightarrow_{0.9,30} Diastolic\langle 65;75\rangle}{BMI\langle 21;22\rangle \wedge Status(married) \Rightarrow_{0.9,30} Diastolic\langle 65;75\rangle}$ is not correct.

If deduction rule $\frac{\varphi \Rightarrow_{p,Base} \psi}{\varphi' \Rightarrow_{p,Base} \psi'}$ is correct then we say that $\varphi' \Rightarrow_{p,Base} \psi'$ logically follows from $\varphi \Rightarrow_{p,Base} \psi$. There are reasonable criteria making possible to decide if a given deduction rule $\frac{\varphi \Rightarrow_{p,Base} \psi}{\varphi' \Rightarrow_{p,Base} \psi'}$ is correct, there analogous results for additional important 4ft-quantifiers [19].

4   Consequences of Item of Domain Knowledge

4.1 Principles

The core of our approach is to map a given item of domain knowledge of the type *mutual influence of attributes* to a set of simple association rules. This set is further expanded using logical deduction to a set of all association rules which can be considered as consequences of the given item of domain knowledge. A resulting set of rules - consequences of items of domain knowledge is then used to interpret results of data mining for association rules. An example of item of domain knowledge is the expression $BMI \uparrow\uparrow Diastolic$ saying that if body mass index of a patient increases then his/here diastolic blood pressure increases too, see Section 2.2.

We define a set $Cons(\Omega, \Rightarrow_{0.9,30})$ of all association rules $\varphi \Rightarrow_{0.9,30} \psi$ which can be considered as consequences of a given item of domain knowledge Ω of the type *mutual influence of attributes* for 4ft-quantifier $\Rightarrow_{0.9,30}$ used in Sections 5 and 6. The set $Cons(\Omega, \Rightarrow_{0.9,30})$ is defined in cooperation with a domain expert, deduction rules $\frac{\varphi \Rightarrow_{0.9,30} \psi}{\varphi' \Rightarrow_{0.9,30} \psi'}$ introduced in Section 3.2 are used. The set $Cons(\Omega, \Rightarrow_{0.9,30})$ is defined in four steps:

1. A set $AC(\Omega, \Rightarrow_{0.9,30})$ of *atomic consequences of* Ω for $\Rightarrow_{0.9,30}$ is defined as a set of very simple rules $\kappa \Rightarrow_{p,B} \lambda$ which can be, according to the domain expert, considered as direct consequences of Ω. An example is in Section 4.2.
2. A set $AgC(\Omega, \Rightarrow_{0.9,30})$ of *agreed consequences* of Ω for $\Rightarrow_{0.9,30}$ is defined. A rule $\rho \Rightarrow_{p,B} \sigma$ belongs to $AgC(\Omega, \Rightarrow_{0.9,30})$ if the following conditions are satisfied:
   - $\rho \Rightarrow_{p,B} \sigma \notin AC(\Omega, \Rightarrow_{0.9,30})$
   - there is no $\kappa \Rightarrow_{p,B} \lambda \in AC(\Omega, \Rightarrow_{0.9,30})$ such that $\rho \Rightarrow_{p,B} \sigma$ logically follows from $\kappa \Rightarrow_{p,B} \lambda$
   - there is $\kappa \Rightarrow_{p,B} \lambda \in AC(\Omega, \Rightarrow_{0.9,30})$ such that, according to the domain expert, it is possible to agree that $\rho \Rightarrow_{p,B} \sigma$ says nothing new in addition to $\kappa \Rightarrow_{p,B} \lambda$.

   Examples are provided in Section 4.3.
3. A set $LgC(\Omega, \Rightarrow_{0.9,30})$ of *logical consequences* of Ω for $\Rightarrow_{0.9,30}$ is defined. A rule $\varphi \Rightarrow_{p,B} \psi$ belongs to $LgC(\Omega, \Rightarrow_{0.9,30})$ if the following conditions are satisfied:
   - $\varphi \Rightarrow_{p,B} \psi \notin (AC(\Omega, \Rightarrow_{0.9,30}) \cup AgC(\Omega, \Rightarrow_{0.9,30}))$
   - there is $\tau \Rightarrow_{p,B} \omega \in (AC(\Omega, \Rightarrow_{0.9,30}) \cup AgC(\Omega, \Rightarrow_{0.9,30}))$ such that $\varphi \Rightarrow_{p,B} \psi$ logically follows from $\tau \Rightarrow_{p,B} \omega$.
4. $Cons(\Omega, \Rightarrow_{0.9,30}) = AC(\Omega, \Rightarrow_{0.9,30}) \cup AgC(\Omega, \Rightarrow_{0.9,30}) \cup LgC(\Omega, \Rightarrow_{0.9,30})$, see Section 4.4.

In Sections 4.2 – 4.4, there are examples concerning definition of the set $Cons(BMI \uparrow\uparrow Diastolic, \Rightarrow_{0.9,30})$ where $BMI \uparrow\uparrow Diastolic$ is the item of domain knowledge used in examples in Sections 5 and 6.

4.2 Atomic Consequences

We are going to define a set $AC(BMI \uparrow\uparrow Diastolic, \Rightarrow_{0.9,30})$ of atomic consequences of $BMI \uparrow\uparrow Diastolic$ for $\Rightarrow_{0.9,30}$. This will be a set of very simple rules $\kappa \Rightarrow_{p,B} \lambda$ which can be, according to the domain expert, considered as direct consequences of $BMI \uparrow\uparrow Diastolic$.

The idea is to define $AC(BMI \uparrow\uparrow Diastolic, \Rightarrow_{0.9,30})$ as a set of all rules $BMI(\alpha) \Rightarrow_{p,B} Diastolic(\beta)$ where $p \geq 0.9$, $B \geq 30$ and α and β are, according to the domain expert, suitable coefficients for attributes BMI and $Diastolic$. We show a way in which coefficients α and β can be defined. Informally speaking, if $BMI(\alpha)$ and $Diastolic(\beta)$ can be considered as saying "BMI is low" and "$Diastolic$ is low" respectively, then the rule $BMI(\alpha) \Rightarrow_{0.9,30} Diastolic(\beta)$ can be considered as a simple consequence of $BMI \uparrow\uparrow Diastolic$.

Attribute BMI has 13 categories $\leq 21, (21; 22), (22; 23), \ldots, (31; 32), > 32$ and attribute $Diastolic$ has 7 categories $< 65, \langle 65; 75), \ldots, \langle 105; 115), \geq 115$. We can decide in cooperation with a domain expert that each basic Boolean attribute $BMI(\alpha)$ satisfying condition $\alpha \subset Low_{BMI}$ will be considered as saying "BMI is low" if $Low_{BMI} = \{\leq 21, (21;22), \ldots, (24;25)\}$. We can similarly decide that basic Boolean attribute $Diastolic(\beta)$ will be considered as saying "$Diastolic$ is low" if $\beta \subset Low_{Diastolic}$ where $Low_{Diastolic} = \{< 65, \langle 65;75 \rangle, \langle 75;85 \rangle\}$. Thus, we can say that the set of all rules $BMI("is\ low") \Rightarrow_{0.9,30} Diastolic("is\ low")$ is defined by the rectangle

$$Low_{BMI} \times Low_{Diastolic} = \{< 21, (21;22), \ldots, (24;25)\} \times \{< 65, \langle 65;75 \rangle, \langle 75;85 \rangle\} .$$

The LISp-Miner makes possible to define set $AC(BMI \uparrow\uparrow Diastolic, \Rightarrow_{0.9,30})$ by a union $\mathcal{A}_1 \times \mathcal{S}_1 \cup \ldots \cup \mathcal{A}_R \times \mathcal{S}_R$ of R similar, possibly overlapping, rectangles. The set $AC(BMI \uparrow\uparrow Diastolic, \Rightarrow_{0.9,30})$ is then considered as a set of all rules $BMI(\alpha) \Rightarrow_{p,B} Diastolic(\beta)$ satisfying $p \geq 0.9$ and $B \geq 30$ for which there is $i \in \{1, \ldots, R\}$ such that $\alpha \subset \mathcal{A}_i$ and $\beta \subset \mathcal{S}_i$. An example of such a definition is in Fig. 2, three rectangles are used. We can say that $AC(BMI \uparrow\uparrow Diastolic, \Rightarrow_{0.9,30})$ is given by a union

$$Low_{BMI} \times Low_{Diastolic} \cup Medium_{BMI} \times Medium_{Diastolic} \cup High_{BMI} \times High_{Diastolic}$$

defined in Fig. 2.

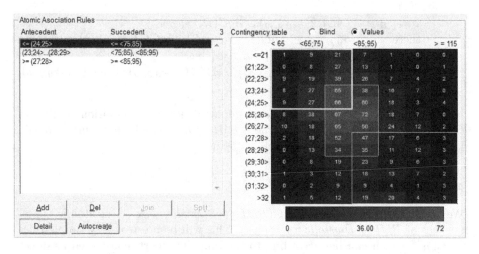

Fig. 2. An example of a definition of detail of $AC(BMI \uparrow\uparrow Diastolic, \Rightarrow_{0.9,30})$

4.3   Agreed Consequences

It is easy to prove that an association rule $A_1(\alpha) \wedge \chi \Rightarrow_{p,B} A_2(\beta)$ does not logically follow from the association rule $A_1(\alpha) \Rightarrow_{p,B} A_2(\beta)$. The core of the proof is the fact that if there are at least B rows of a data matrix $\mathcal{M}$ satisfying $A_1(\alpha) \wedge A_2(\beta)$ then there still can be no row of $\mathcal{M}$ satisfying $A_1(\alpha) \wedge \chi \wedge A_2(\beta)$. However, in *some* cases it can be reasonable from the point of view of a domain expert to agree that $A_1(\alpha) \wedge \chi \Rightarrow_{p,B} A_2(\beta)$ is a consequence of $A(\alpha) \Rightarrow_{p,B} B(\beta)$. In such a case we call the rule $A_1(\alpha) \wedge \chi \Rightarrow_{p,B} A_2(\beta)$ an *agreed consequence* of $A_1(\alpha) \Rightarrow_{p,B} A_2(\beta)$.

The rule $\mathrm{BMI}(\langle 22; 23 \rangle, \langle 23; 24 \rangle) \Rightarrow_{0.9,30} \mathrm{Diastolic}(< 65, \langle 65; 75 \rangle)$ i.e. shortly $\mathrm{BMI}\langle 22; 24 \rangle \Rightarrow_{0.9,30} \mathrm{Diastolic}(< 75)$ belongs to $AC(\mathrm{BMI} \uparrow\uparrow \mathrm{Diastolic}, \Rightarrow_{0.9,30})$, see Fig. 2. The rule $\mathrm{BMI}\langle 22; 24 \rangle \wedge \mathrm{Education}(university) \Rightarrow_{0.9,30} \mathrm{Diastolic}(< 75)$ does not logically follow from the rule $\mathrm{BMI}\langle 21; 24 \rangle \Rightarrow_{0.9,30} \mathrm{Diastolic}(< 75)$. However, this rule says nothing new because the truthfulness of Boolean attribute $\mathrm{Education}(university)$ has no influence on the relation of BMI and $Diastolic$. Thus we can add $\mathrm{BMI}\langle 22; 24 \rangle \wedge \mathrm{Education}(university) \Rightarrow_{0.9,30} \mathrm{Diastolic}(< 75)$ to the set $AgC(\mathrm{BMI} \uparrow\uparrow \mathrm{Diastolic}, \Rightarrow_{0.9,30})$ of agreed consequences of $\mathrm{BMI} \uparrow\uparrow \mathrm{Diastolic}$ for $\Rightarrow_{0.9,30}$.

This way, the set $AgC(\mathrm{BMI} \uparrow\uparrow \mathrm{Diastolic}, \Rightarrow_{0.9,30})$ can be defined. However, cooperation with a domain expert is necessary. Below, we assume that if a rule $\mathrm{BMI}(\alpha) \Rightarrow_{p,B} \mathrm{Diastolic}(\beta)$ belongs to $AC(\mathrm{BMI} \uparrow\uparrow \mathrm{Diastolic}, \Rightarrow_{0.9,30})$ then rules $\mathrm{BMI}(\alpha) \wedge \mathrm{Status}(\gamma) \Rightarrow_{p,B} \mathrm{Diastolic}(\beta)$, $\mathrm{BMI}(\alpha) \wedge \mathrm{Education}(\delta) \Rightarrow_{p,B} \mathrm{Diastolic}(\beta)$, and $\mathrm{BMI}(\alpha) \wedge \mathrm{Status}(\gamma) \wedge \mathrm{Education}(\delta) \Rightarrow_{p,B} \mathrm{Diastolic}(\beta)$ belong to the set $AgC(\mathrm{BMI} \uparrow\uparrow \mathrm{Diastolic}, \Rightarrow_{0.9,30})$.

4.4   Set $Cons(BMI \uparrow\uparrow Diastolic, \Rightarrow_{0.9,30})$

The set $Cons(BMI \uparrow\uparrow Diastolic, \Rightarrow_{0.9,30})$ of consequences of $BMI \uparrow\uparrow Diastolic$ for 4ft-quantifier $\Rightarrow_{0.9,30})$ is defined as

$$AC(BMI \uparrow\uparrow Diastolic, \Rightarrow_{0.9,30}) \ \cup \ AgC(BMI \uparrow\uparrow Diastolic, \Rightarrow_{0.9,30}) \ \cup$$

$$\cup \ LG(BMI \uparrow\uparrow Diastolic, \Rightarrow_{0.9,30})$$

where $LG(BMI \uparrow\uparrow Diastolic, \Rightarrow_{0.9,30})$ is a set of all rules $\varphi \Rightarrow_{p,B} \psi$ satisfying the following conditions:

- $\varphi \Rightarrow_{p,B} \psi \notin (AC(BMI \uparrow\uparrow Diastolic, \Rightarrow_{0.9,30}) \ \cup \ AgC(BMI \uparrow\uparrow Diastolic, \Rightarrow_{0.9,30}))$
- there is
  $\tau \Rightarrow_{p,B} \omega \in (AC(BMI \uparrow\uparrow Diastolic, \Rightarrow_{0.9,30}) \ \cup \ AgC(BMI \uparrow\uparrow Diastolic, \Rightarrow_{0.9,30}))$
  such that $\varphi \Rightarrow_{p,B} \psi$ logically follows from $\tau \Rightarrow_{p,B} \omega$,

see point 3 at the beginning of Section 4.

The rule $\mathrm{BMI}(\leq 22) \wedge \mathrm{Status}(married) \Rightarrow_{0.96,65} \mathrm{Diastolic}(\leq 95)$ is an example of a rule belonging to $LG(BMI \uparrow\uparrow Diastolic, \Rightarrow_{0.9,30})$. This is because of:

- rule $\mathrm{BMI}(\leq 22) \Rightarrow_{0.96,65} \mathrm{Diastolic}(\leq 85)$ belongs to
  $AC(BMI \uparrow\uparrow Diastolic, \Rightarrow_{0.9,30})$, see Section 4.2
- thus the rule $\mathrm{BMI}(\leq 22) \wedge \mathrm{Status}(married) \Rightarrow_{0.96,65} \mathrm{Diastolic}(\leq 85)$ belongs to $AgC(BMI \uparrow\uparrow Diastolic, \Rightarrow_{0.9,30})$, see Section 4.3
- the rule $\mathrm{BMI}(\leq 22) \wedge \mathrm{Status}(married) \Rightarrow_{0.96,65} \mathrm{Diastolic}(\leq 95)$ logically follows from the rule $\mathrm{BMI}(\leq 22) \wedge \mathrm{Status}(married) \Rightarrow_{0.96,65} \mathrm{Diastolic}(\leq 85)$, see below.

Let us denote $\varphi = BMI(\leq 22) \wedge Status(married)$. We have to show that the rule $\varphi \Rightarrow_{0.96,65} Diastolic(\leq 95)$ logically follows from $\varphi \Rightarrow_{0.96,65} Diastolic(\leq 85)$. Let $\mathcal{M}$ be a data matrix, let us denote $4ft(\varphi, Diastolic(\leq 85), \mathcal{M}) = \langle a, b, c, d \rangle$ and $4ft(\varphi, Diastolic(\leq 95), \mathcal{M}) = \langle a', b', c', d' \rangle$, see Fig. 3.

$\mathcal{M}$	$Diastolic(\leq 85)$	$\neg Diastolic(\leq 85)$
φ	a	b
$\neg\varphi$	c	d

$4ft(\varphi, Diastolic(\leq 85), \mathcal{M})$

$\mathcal{M}$	$Diastolic(\leq 95)$	$\neg Diastolic(\leq 95)$
φ	a'	b'
$\neg\varphi$	c'	d'

$4ft(\varphi, Diastolic(\leq 95), \mathcal{M})$

Fig. 3. $4ft(\varphi, Diastolic(\leq 85), \mathcal{M})$ and $4ft(\varphi, Diastolic(\leq 95), \mathcal{M})$

It must be $a + b = a' + b'$ since both $a + b$ and $a' + b'$ are equal to the number of rows of $\mathcal{M}$ satisfying φ. In addition, it must be $a' \geq a$ since each row of $\mathcal{M}$ satisfying $Diastolic(\leq 85)$ satisfies also $Diastolic(\leq 95)$ and $a + b = a' + b'$ together with $a' \geq a$ means $b' \leq b$. We can conclude that if $\frac{a}{a+b} \geq 0.9$ then also $\frac{a'}{a'+b'} \geq \frac{a'}{a'+b} \geq \frac{a}{a+b} \geq 0.9$ and if $a \geq 30$ then also $a' \geq 30$.

This way we can show that also additional rules belong to the set $Cons(BMI \uparrow\uparrow Diastolic, \Rightarrow_{0.9,30})$.

5   Formulating and Solving Analytical Question

5.1   From Domain Knowledge to Analytical Questions

Items of domain knowledge introduced in Section 2.2 makes possible to formulate various analytical questions. An example is the question *Are there any interesting relations between attributes from group* Measures *and attributes from group* Blood pressure *in data matrix* Entry? *Attributes from group* Measures *can be combined with attributes from group* Personal. *Interesting relation is a relation which is strong enough and which is not a consequence of the known dependency* BMI $\uparrow\uparrow$ Diastolic.

We deal with association rules, thus we convert our question to a question concerning association rules. This can be symbolically expressed as

$$[Entry : (BMI \uparrow\uparrow Diastolic) \not\to \mathcal{B}(Measures), \mathcal{B}(Personal) \approx^? \mathcal{B}(Blood\ pressure)].$$

Here $\mathcal{B}(Measures)$ means a set of all Boolean attributes derived from attributes of the group *Measures* we consider relevant to our analytical question, similarly for $\mathcal{B}(Personal)$ and $\mathcal{B}(Blood\ pressure)$. We search for rules $\varphi_M \wedge \varphi_P \approx \psi_B$ which are true in data matrix *Entry*, cannot be understood as consequences of *BMI* $\uparrow\uparrow$ *Diastolic* and $\varphi_M \in \mathcal{B}(Measures)$, $\varphi_P \in \mathcal{B}(Personal)$, and $\psi_B \in \mathcal{B}(Blood\ pressure)$.

5.2   Applying 4ft-Miner

The procedure 4ft-Miner does not use the well known a-priori algorithm. It uses representation of analyzed data by suitable strings of bits [21]. This way 4ft-Miner has fine tools to define sets of relevant association rules. In Fig. 4, there is an example of a definition of a set of association rules relevant to the analytical question introduced in Section 5.1.

ANTECEDENT		QUANTIFIERS		SUCCEDENT	
Measures	Con, 1 - 3	BASE p= 30 Abs.		Blood pressure	Con, 1 - 2
» BMI (seq), 1 - 3	B, pos	FUI p= 0.900		» Diastolic (seq), 1 - 3	B, pos
» Subsc (seq), 1 - 3	B, pos			» Systolic (seq), 1 - 4	B, pos
» Tric (seq), 1 - 3	B, pos				
Personal	Con, 0 - 2				
» Status (subset), 1 - 1	B, pos				
» Education (seq), 1 - 2	B, pos				

Fig. 4. Input parameters of the 4ft-Miner procedure

Set $\mathcal{B}(Measures)$ is defined in row **Measures Conj, 1-3** and in three consecutive rows in column **ANTECEDENT**. Each φ_M is a conjunction of 1 - 3 Boolean attributes derived from particular attributes of the group *Measures*. Set of all Boolean attributes derived from attribute *BMI* is defined by the row **BMI(seq), 1-3 B, pos**. It means that all Boolean attributes $BMI(\alpha)$ where α is a sequence of 1 - 3 consecutive categories are generated. Examples of such Boolean attributes are $BMI(16; 21\rangle$, $BMI(\langle 21; 22\rangle, (22; 23\rangle)$ i.e. $BMI(21; 23\rangle$, and $BMI(\langle 21; 22\rangle, (22; 23\rangle, (23; 24\rangle)$ i.e. $BMI(21; 24\rangle$. Sets of Boolean attributes derived from attributes *Subsc* and *Tric* are defined similarly. An example of $\varphi_M \in \mathcal{B}(Measures)$ is the conjunction $\varphi_M = BMI(21; 24\rangle \wedge Subsc\langle 4; 14\rangle$. Strings "B,pos" in all rows of Fig. 4 are additional parameters, they have no influence in our example, for details see [21].

Each φ_P is a disjunction of 0 - 2 Boolean attributes derived from particular attributes of the group *Personal*. There are four Boolean attributes derived from attribute *Status* – Status(*married*), Status(*divorced*), Status(*single*), Status(*widower*) i.e. subsets of 1 - 1 categories of attribute *Status* defined by the row **Status(subset), 1-1 B, pos**. Set of Boolean attributes derived from attribute *Education* is defined similarly as for attribute *BMI*.

Set $\mathcal{B}(Blood\ pressure)$ is defined in row **Blood pressure Conj, 1-2** and in two consecutive rows of column **SUCCEDENT** in a way similar to that in which set $\mathcal{B}(Measures)$ is defined. The quantifier $\Rightarrow_{0.9,30}$ of founded implication is specified in column **QUANTIFIERS**.

A task of generating all relevant rules $\varphi_M \wedge \varphi_P \Rightarrow_{0.9,30} \psi_B$ and testing them in data matrix *Entry* was solved in 126 seconds (PC with 4GB RAM and Intel Core processor at 2.6 GHz). $12.47 * 10^6$ association rules were generated and tested, 363 rules true were found. The rule

$BMI(\leq 22) \wedge Subsc(< 14) \wedge Education(secondary,\ university) \Rightarrow_{1.0,31} Systolic\langle 105; 145)$

is the strongest one (i.e. with the highest confidence). It means that 31 patients satisfy $BMI(\leq 22) \land Subsc(< 14) \land Education(secondary, university)$ and all of them satisfy also $Syst\langle 105; 145\rangle$.

5.3   Interpreting Results

Let us remember that we are solving the analytical question: *Are there any interesting relations between attributes from group* Measures *and attributes from group* Blood pressure *in data matrix* Entry*? Attributes from group* Measures *can be combined with attributes from group* Personal*. Interesting relation is a relation which is strong enough and which is not a consequence of the known dependency* $BMI \uparrow\uparrow Diastolic$*, see Section 5.1.

We have applied the 4ft-Miner data mining procedure with input parameters defining a set of potentially interesting association rules in a way described in Fig. 4 in Section 5.2. The procedure 4ft-Miner has tools to filter out all rules which can be considered as consequences of $BMI \uparrow\uparrow Diastolic$. Definition of the set of these consequences is given in Section 4. Among 363 output rules, there are 194 rules which can be considered as consequences of $BMI \uparrow\uparrow Diastolic$.

The remaining 169 rules can be understood as answers to the above introduced question. But this is only a small fraction of a possible comprehensive answer we can get by applications of the 4ft-Miner procedure and additional analytical procedures and tools implemented in the LISp-Miner system. However, it requires a long chain of applications of particular procedures and modules with various feedbacks. The only way to do such analysis effectively is to automate the analytical process.

6   Applying LISp-Miner Control Language

The goal of automation of the data mining process with the 4ft-Miner procedure and domain knowledge is to make possible to solve complex tasks which are too hard to be solved manually in an effective way. An example of such a task is outlined in Section 6.1. Principles of automation of its solution are introduced in Section 6.2. Examples of results are in Section 6.3.

6.1   Example of Complex Task

Remember the question

$$[Entry : (BMI \uparrow\uparrow Diastolic) \not\rightarrow \mathcal{B}(Measures), \mathcal{B}(Personal) \approx^? \mathcal{B}(Blood\ pressure)]$$

introduced in Section 5.1. This means that we are interested in association rules $\varphi_M \land \varphi_P \approx \psi_B$ which are true in data matrix *Entry*, cannot be understood as consequences of $BMI \uparrow\uparrow Diastolic$, $\varphi_M \in \mathcal{B}(Measures)$, $\varphi_P \in \mathcal{B}(Personal)$, and $\psi_B \in \mathcal{B}(Blood\ pressure)$.

This question can be extended such that we are interested in relations of a set $\mathcal{T}(Measures, Personal \Rightarrow_{0.9,30} Blood\ pressure; Entry)$ of all association rules

$\varphi_M \wedge \varphi_P \approx \psi_B$ true in data matrix *Entry* to sets of rules which can be considered as consequences of various additional relations of mutual influence between attributes *BMI*, *Subsc* and *Tric* from the group *Measures* and attributes *Diastolic* and *Systolic* from the group *Blood pressure*. We do not consider additional relations as items of domain knowledge, we are only interested if there are true association rules – indicators of such relations of mutual influence.

We found that the set $\mathcal{T}(Measures, Personal \Rightarrow_{0.9,30} Blood pressure; Entry)$ contains 363 rules and that 194 from these rules belong also to the set $Cons(BMI \uparrow\uparrow Diastolic, \Rightarrow_{0.9,30})$, see Section 5. There is a challenge to check the remaining 169 rules for really interesting ones. Examples of really interesting rules are rules which can be considered as exceptions to *BMI* $\uparrow\uparrow$ *Diastolic* or as indications of new, unknown relations of mutual influence between attributes.

This can be understood as an example of the above introduced extended question. We deal with sets $\mathcal{T}(Measures, Personal \Rightarrow_{0.9,30} Blood pressure, Entry)$ and $Cons(BMI \uparrow\uparrow Systolic, \Rightarrow_{0.9,30})$, $Cons(Subsc \uparrow\uparrow Diastolic, \Rightarrow_{0.9,30})$, ..., $Cons(Tric \uparrow\uparrow Systolic, \Rightarrow_{0.9,30})$. We can use also additional relations of mutual influence. An example is the relation *Tric* $\uparrow\downarrow$ *Diastolic* meaning *if the skinfold above the musculus triceps increases then diastolic blood pressure decreases*. Of course, we can use also additional 4ft-quantifiers.

6.2 Principles of Solution

The above introduced complex task can be solved in two main steps. In the first step we define sets $Cons(\Omega, \Rightarrow_{0.9,30})$ of all association rules $\varphi \Rightarrow_{0.9,30} \psi$ which can be considered as consequences of all relations Ω of mutual inference in question (i.e. *BMI* $\uparrow\uparrow$ *Systolic*, ..., *Tric* $\uparrow\downarrow$ *Diastolic*). Using the FOFRADAR formal framework, we can exactly describe the whole process of formulation and solution of the task introduced in Section 6.1, the principles outlined in Section 4 are applied, see also [20]. However, this description is not an executable program.

In the second step we describe the solution in the LMCL language as an executable program and we execute it. It takes just five seconds to pre-create all the possible pairs of mutual influences, to compare them to already mined association rules and to prepare a comparison summary. More details on LMCL language are available in [25, 27].

6.3 Examples of Results

Structured analytical reports are results of solutions of complex tasks. The reports describe resulting sets of association rules together with their relevant characteristics and summarizing explanations. In Fig. 5, there is an example of a part of an analytical report describing solution of the task introduced in Section 6.1.

This part gives an overview of found association rules. For each item of mutual influence mentioned in Section 6.1, there is the number of rules which can be considered as consequences of this item, as well as the number of rules which are interesting from the point of view of further investigation. A rule is interesting

T(Measures, Personal →$_{0.9,30}$ Blood pressure; Entry) -- Mutual Influence Report

Found association rules: 363

Mutual Influence		Number of association rules	
Item of Mutual Influence	Influence type	Consequences of the Item	To be Investigated
BMI ↑↑ Diastolic	Positive influence	169	0
Subsc ↑↑ Diastolic	Positive influence	141	29
Tric ↑↓ Diastolic	Negative influence	109	42
BMI ↑↑ Systolic	Positive influence	97	2
Subsc ↑↑ Systolic	Positive influence	70	18
Tric ↑↑ Systolic	Positive influence	59	8

Fig. 5. Found association rules to mutual influences relationships summary

from the point of view of further investigation if it can be considered as an exception to the relation of the mutual influence in question. A rule is also interesting if it can be considered as an indication of an additional relation of mutual relation. List of such rules are available through the provided link.

There are 109 rules which can be considered as consequences of the relation *Tric ↑↓ Diastolic* and 42 rules which are interesting from the point of view of further investigation. The rule

$$BMI(\leq 22) \wedge Tric(\leq 5) \Rightarrow_{0.92,36} Diastolic\langle 65; 95 \rangle$$

is an example of a rule interesting from the point of view of further investigation. This is because this rule can be seen as an agreed consequence of the rule $Tric(\leq 5) \Rightarrow_{0.92,36} Diastolic\langle 65; 95 \rangle$ which says that if $Tric$ is small then $Diastolic$ is not high and this is in a conflict with the mutual influence *Tric ↑↓ Diastolic*, see also possible values of $Tric$ and $Diastolic$ in Section 2.1, for more details see [20]. Let us note that this approach to exceptions differs from that introduced in [23].

7 Conclusions

7.1 Related Research

There is no similar approach to dealing with domain knowledge in association rules known to the authors. There are various related papers, e.g. [2–4, 12–16, 28, 30]. Their detailed comparison with the presented approach is out of the scope of this paper and it is left as a further work. However, let us note that these approaches do not use the formalization of data mining process based on observational calculi.

Let us also mention the project GUHA80 [8, 10] of automated data analysis. The project was based on applications of the GUHA procedures, however, it was never realised. The principles of the project differ from the approach used here.

7.2   Summary and Further Research

We have introduced an approach to learning association rules from data through domain knowledge and automation. It was shown that it is possible to formalize the process of formulating of reasonable analytical questions using formulas expressing mutual influence of non-Boolean attributes and to use logical deduction in calculus of association rule to deal with consequences of such formulas. The formulas expressing mutual influence of non-Boolean attributes can be used as items of domain knowledge. The whole process of learning rules can be formally described by tools of the FOFRADAR formal frame for data mining. The formal description can be converted to an executable program in LMCL. We have shown an experiment to solve a complex analytical question.

In the next steps we assume to use FOFRADAR and LMCL to solve additional complex analytical questions and to automate the whole data mining process with association rules, see also [27].

References

1. Agrawal, R., Imielinski, T., Swami, A.: Mining Associations between Sets of Items in Large Databases. In: Buneman, P., Jajodia, S. (eds.) Proceedings of the 1993 ACM SIGMOD International Conference on Management of Data, pp. 207–216. ACM Press, Fort Collins (1993)
2. Atzmüller, M., Puppe, F., Buscher, H.P.: Exploiting Background Knowledge for Knowledge-Intensive Subgroup Discovery. In: Kaelbling, L.P., Saffiotti, A. (eds.) Proceedings of the Nineteenth International Joint Conference on Artificial Intelligence, IJCAI 2005, Edinburgh, Scotland, UK, pp. 647–652 (2005)
3. Atzmüller, M., Puppe, F., Buscher, H.P.: A Semi-Automatic Approach for Confounding-Aware Subgroup Discovery. International Journal on Artificial Intelligence Tools 18, 81–98 (2009)
4. Aumann, Y., Lindell, Y.: A Statistical Theory for Quantitative Association Rules. J. Intell. Inf. Syst. 20, 255–283 (2003)
5. Hájek, P., Havel, I., Chytil, M.: The GUHA method of automatic hypothesis determinantion. Computing 1, 293–308 (1966)
6. Hájek, P., Havránek, T.: Mechanising Hypothesis Formation - Mathematical Foundations for a General Theory. Springer, Heidelberg (1978)
7. Hájek, P.: The new version of the GUHA procedure ASSOC. In: Proceedings of COMPSTAT 1984, pp. 360–365 (1984)
8. Hájek, P., Havránek, T.: GUHA 80: An Application of Artificial Intelligence to Data Analysis. Computers and Artificial Intelligence 1, 107–134 (1982)
9. Hájek, P., Holeňa, M., Rauch, J.: The GUHA method and its meaning for data mining. J. Comput. Syst. Sci. 76, 34–48 (2010)
10. Hájek, P., Ivánek, J.: Artificial Intelligence and Data Analysis. In: Caussinus, H., Ettinger, P., Tomassone, R. (eds.) Proceedings COMPSTAT 1982, pp. 54–60. Physica Verlag, Wien (1982)
11. Ierusalimschy, R., Figueiredo, L.H., de Celes, W.: Lua – an extensible extension language. Software: Practice & Experience 26, 635–652 (1996)
12. Jaroszewicz, S., Simovici, D.A.: Interestingness of frequent itemsets using Bayesian networks as background knowledge. In: Kim, W., et al. (eds.) Proceedings of the Tenth ACM SIGKDD International Conference on Knowledge Discovery and Data Mining, Seattle, Washington, USA, pp. 178–186 (2004)

13. Jaroszewicz, S., Scheffer, T., Simovici, D.A.: Scalable pattern mining with Bayesian networks as background knowledge. Data Min. Knowl. Discov. 18, 56–100 (2009)
14. Lavrac, N., et al.: The utility of background knowledge in learning medical diagnostic rules. Applied Artificial Intelligence 7, 273–293 (1993)
15. Mansingh, G., Osei-Bryson, K.-M., Reichgelt, H.: Using ontologies to facilitate post-processing of association rules by domain experts. Information Sciences 181, 419–434 (2011)
16. Phillips, J., Buchanan, B.G.: Ontology guided knowledge discovery in databases. In: Proc. First International Conference on Knowledge Capture, pp. 123–130. ACM, Victoria (2001)
17. Rauch, J.: Considerations on Logical Calculi for Dealing with Knowledge in Data Mining. In: Ras, Z.W., Dardzinska, A. (eds.) Advances in Data Management. SCI, vol. 223, pp. 177–199. Springer, Heidelberg (2009)
18. Rauch, J.: Formalizing Data Mining with Association Rules. In: Proceedings of 2012 IEEE International Conference on Granular Computing (GRC 2012), pp. 406–411. IEEE Computer Society, Los Alamitos (2012)
19. Rauch, J.: Observational Calculi and Association Rules, p. 296. Springer, Berlin (2013)
20. Rauch, J.: Formal Framework for Data Mining with Association Rules and Domain Knowledge – Overview of an Approach Observational Calculi and Association Rules. To appear in Fundamenta Informaticae
21. Rauch, J., Šimůnek, M.: An Alternative Approach to Mining Association Rules. In: Lin, T.Y., et al. (eds.) Data Mining: Foundations, Methods, and Applications. SCI, vol. 6, pp. 211–231. Springer (2005)
22. Rauch, J., Šimůnek, M.: Applying Domain Knowledge in Association Rules Mining Process - First Experience. In: Kryszkiewicz, M., Rybinski, H., Skowron, A., Raś, Z.W., et al. (eds.) ISMIS 2011. LNCS (LNAI), vol. 6804, pp. 113–122. Springer, Heidelberg (2011)
23. Suzuki, E.: Undirected Discovery of Interesting Exception Rules. International Journal of Pattern Recognition and Artificial Intelligence 16(8), 1065–1086 (2002)
24. Šimůnek, M.: Academic KDD Project LISp-Miner. In: Abraham, A., Franke, K., Köppen, M. (eds.) Intelligent Systems Design and Applications. AISC, vol. 23, pp. 263–272. Springer, Heidelberg (2003)
25. Šimůnek, M.: LISp-Miner Control Language – description of scripting language implementation. Journal of System Integration 5(2) (2014), http://www.si-journal.org/index.php/JSI/article/view/193
26. Šimůnek, M., Rauch, J.: EverMiner – Towards Fully Automated KDD Process. In: Funatsu, K., Hasegava, K. (eds.) New Fundamental Technologies in Data Mining, pp. 221–240. InTech, Rijeka (2011)
27. Šimůnek, M., Rauch, J.: EverMiner Prototype using LISp-Miner Control Language. In: Andreasen, T., Christiansen, H., Cubero, J.-C., Raś, Z.W. (eds.) ISMIS 2014. LNCS (LNAI), vol. 8502, pp. 113–122. Springer, Heidelberg (2014), http://isl.ruc.dk/ismis2014/
28. Sharma, S., Osei-Bryson, K.-M.: Toward an integrated knowledge discovery and data mining process model. The Knowledge Engineering Review 25, 49–67 (2010)
29. Tan, P.-N., Kumar, V., Srivastava, J.: Selecting the right objective measure for association analysis. Information Systems 29, 293–313 (2004)
30. Vavpetic, A., Podpecan, V., Lavrac, N.: Semantic subgroup explanations. J. Intell. Inf. Syst. 42, 233–254 (2014)

Using Discriminative Rule Mining to Discover Declarative Process Models with Non-atomic Activities

Mario Luca Bernardi[1], Marta Cimitile[2],
Chiara Di Francescomarino[3], and Fabrizio Maria Maggi[4]

[1] University of Sannio, Benevento, Italy
mlbernar@unisannio.it
[2] Unitelma Sapienza University, Rome, Italy
marta.cimitile@unitelma.it
[3] FBK-IRST, Trento, Italy
dfmchiara@fbk.eu
[4] University of Tartu, Tartu, Estonia
f.m.maggi@ut.ee

Abstract. Process discovery techniques try to generate process models from execution logs. Declarative process modeling languages are more suitable than procedural notations for representing the discovery results deriving from logs of processes working in dynamic and low-predictable environments. However, existing declarative discovery approaches aim at mining declarative specifications considering each activity in a business process as an atomic/instantaneous event. In spite of this, often, in realistic environments, process activities are not instantaneous; rather, their execution spans across a time interval and is characterized by a sequence of states of a transactional lifecycle. In this paper, we investigate how to use discriminative rule mining in the discovery task, to characterize lifecycles that determine constraint violations and lifecycles that ensure constraint fulfillments. The approach has been implemented as a plug-in of the process mining tool ProM and validated on synthetic logs and on a real-life log recorded by an incident and problem management system called VINST in use at Volvo IT Belgium.

Keywords: Process Discovery, Rule Mining, Discriminative Mining, Non-Atomic Activities, Activity lifecycle, Linear Temporal Logic.

1 Introduction

Process discovery techniques are widely considered as critical for successful business process management and monitoring. In particular, the discovery of declarative models can be used in complex environments where process executions involve multiple alternatives and high flexibility is needed [2] [9]. Consider, for example, a business process for handling natural disasters. This type of process is totally unpredictable and should be adapted every time to specific conditions characteristic of specific cases. Using declarative models for describing processes like this, allows analysts to define generic constraints to be followed during the process execution instead of explicitly representing the flows of events allowed. At runtime, anything that does not violate these constraints

A. Bikakis et al. (Eds.): RuleML 2014, LNCS 8620, pp. 281–295, 2014.

is possible. In this way, process participants are free to adapt their tasks to the environment characteristics as long as these general rules are respected. At the same time, models remain under-specified and easy to understand for humans.

Existing process discovery techniques for generating declarative specifications, do not take activity lifecycles and their characteristics into consideration, even if, in many practical cases, activities are non-atomic. In the reality, activities have a duration spanning over time intervals in which transactional states (a.k.a. *event types*) of the activity can occur. The sequences of event types that occur when an activity is executed, characterize the lifecycle of that activity. For example, when an activity a is executed, the lifecycle $\langle a_{assign}, a_{start}, a_{complete} \rangle$ can take place, including event types *assign*, *start*, and *complete*. If available, this information is very relevant to be considered when mining an event log, since it allows analysts to understand not only the constraints between activities but also the ones that relate event types appearing inside the lifecycle of one single activity.

In 2010, the IEEE Task Force on Process Mining has adopted XES (eXtensible Event Stream) [19] as the standard for storing data in event logs. XES supports a specific extension (Lifecycle Extension) to keep track of information related to the lifecycle of an activity in a log. In addition, XES defines a standard transactional model for activity lifecycles in a log through a state machine describing the allowed sequences of event types for an activity.

Starting from this definition, in this paper, we present a novel approach to discover declarative specifications from logs with a strong focus on the activity lifecycles. For describing declarative models, we use Declare, a declarative process modeling language, first introduced in [15], that combines a formal semantics grounded in Linear Temporal Logic (LTL) on finite traces[1] with a graphical representation. Here, we slightly modify the original semantics of Declare constraints to adapt it to the non-atomic case. In addition, the proposed approach relies on the notion of *constraint activation* [5]. For the constraint "every request is eventually acknowledged" each request is an activation. This activation becomes a fulfillment or a violation depending on whether the request is followed by an acknowledgement or not.

In our approach, in a first phase, starting from a log, we try to group together events belonging to the same lifecycle of the same activity (discharging the "malformed" lifecycles according to an input transactional model for activity lifecycles like, e.g., XES). The lifecycle identification can be done using (i) a FIFO-based approach [6], or (ii) event correlations [3]. The FIFO -based approach is a typical "conservative approach" first in-first out, in which if a new upcoming event can be connected to two events occurred in the past and belonging to two different lifecycles, the priority is given to the one that occurred before. With event correlations, events are connected as part of the same lifecycle whenever they share common values for some data attributes. This approach can only be applied if events in the log carry data. In our implemented prototype, we have used the FIFO-based approach, but the tool can be easily extended to support lifecycle identification through event correlations.

In a second phase of our approach, we generate a set of candidate Declare constraints (over non-atomic activities) considering the constraints that are most frequently

---

[1] For compactness, we will use the LTL acronym to denote LTL on finite traces.

activated in the log. In this way, we discover information about the inter-relations between lifecycles of different activities.

In a third phase, we use discriminative rule mining to retrieve characteristics of the lifecycle of an activation of a constraint that discriminate between cases in which that activation is a fulfillment and the cases in which the activation leads to a violation for that constraint. For example, we want to find rules like "if a registration ends with an abortion the user cannot be notified via e-mail", or "if an analysis is suspended more than twice then eventually a check should be executed". Using discriminative rule mining we can discover intra-relations between transactional states inside the lifecycle of a constraint activation that discriminate between cases in which the activation is a fulfillment and cases in which the activation is a violation. In particular, we use a decision tree to learn from contrasting training data discriminative rules related to the lifecycle control flow. Lifecycles are encoded, in the form of Declare constraints, as features of the tree and the resulting decision rules are used to express the lifecycle characteristics able to discriminate between fulfillments and violations.

The approach presented in this paper has been implemented as a plug-in of the ProM[2] process mining toolset. This prototype has been used to validate our technique on both synthetic logs and a real life log recorded by an incident and problem management system called VINST in use at Volvo IT Belgium.

The paper is structured as follows. Section 2 provides a preliminary background about the Declare language, introduces the concepts of non-atomic activities and activity lifecycles and provides an overview on discriminative rule mining. Next, Section 3 illustrates the approach, based on the combination of declarative process mining algorithms (extended to the non-atomic logs) and discriminative mining approaches. In Section 4, the experimentation is discussed. Section 5 reports some conclusion and future work.

2   Background

In this section, we introduce some preliminary knowledge needed to understand the techniques presented in this paper. In particular, in Section 2.1, we give an overview of the Declare language. In Section 2.2, we describe the transactional model for activity lifecycles defined in the XES standard. Finally, in Section 2.3, we give some background about discriminative rule mining.

2.1 Declare: The Language

Declare is a language for describing declarative process models first introduced in [15]. A Declare model consists of a set of constraints applied to (atomic) activities. Constraints, in turn, are based on templates. Templates are abstract parameterized patterns and constraints are their concrete instantiations on real activities. Templates have a user-friendly graphical representation understandable to the user and their semantics can be formalized using different logics [14], the main one being Linear Temporal Logic

---

[2] www.processmining.org

Table 1. Graphical notation and LTL formalization of some Declare templates

TEMPLATE	FORMALIZATION	NOTATION
responded existence(A,B)	$\Diamond A \rightarrow \Diamond B$	A ●—— B
response(A,B)	$\Box(A \rightarrow \Diamond B)$	A ●—▶ B
precedence(A,B)	$\neg B \, \mathcal{W} \, A$	A —▶ B
alternate response(A,B)	$\Box(A \rightarrow \bigcirc(\neg A \, \mathcal{U} \, B))$	A ●═▶ B
alternate precedence(A,B)	$(\neg B \, \mathcal{W} \, A) \wedge \Box(B \rightarrow \bigcirc(\neg B \, \mathcal{W} \, A))$	A ═▶ B
chain response(A,B)	$\Box(A \rightarrow \bigcirc B)$	A ●━▶ B
chain precedence(A,B)	$\Box(\bigcirc B \rightarrow A)$	A ━▶ B
not resp. existence(A,B)	$\Diamond A \rightarrow \neg \Diamond B$	A ●∦ B
not response(A,B)	$\Box(A \rightarrow \neg \Diamond B)$	A ●∦▶ B
not precedence(A,B)	$\Box(A \rightarrow \neg \Diamond B)$	A ∦▶ B
not chain response(A,B)	$\Box(A \rightarrow \neg \bigcirc B)$	A ∦▶ B
not chain precedence(A,B)	$\Box(A \rightarrow \neg \bigcirc B)$	A ∦▶ B

over finite traces, making them verifiable and executable. Each constraint inherits the graphical representation and semantics from its templates. The major benefit of using templates is that analysts do not have to be aware of the underlying logic-based formalization to understand the models. They work with the graphical representation of templates, while the underlying formulas remain hidden. Table 1 summarizes some Declare templates. The reader can refer to [1] for a full description of the language. Here, we indicate template parameters with capital letters (see Table 1) and real activities in their instantiations with lower case letters (e.g., constraint $\Box(a \rightarrow \Diamond b)$).

Consider, for example, the *response* constraint $\Box(a \rightarrow \Diamond b)$. This constraint indicates that if a occurs, b must eventually *follow*. Therefore, this constraint is satisfied for traces such as $\langle a, a, b, c \rangle$, $\langle b, b, c, d \rangle$, and $\langle a, b, c, b \rangle$, but not for $\langle a, b, a, c \rangle$ because, in this case, the second instance of a is not followed by a b. Note that, in trace $\langle b, b, c, d \rangle$, the considered response constraint is satisfied in a trivial way because a never occurs. In this case, we say that the constraint is *vacuously satisfied* [11]. An *activation* of a constraint in a trace is an event whose occurrence imposes, because of that constraint, some obligations on other events in the same trace. For example, a is an activation for the *response* constraint $\Box(a \rightarrow \Diamond b)$, because the execution of a forces b to be executed eventually.

An activation of a constraint can be a *fulfillment* or a *violation* for that constraint. When a trace is perfectly compliant with respect to a constraint, every activation of the constraint in the trace leads to a fulfillment. Consider, again, the response constraint $\Box(a \rightarrow \Diamond b)$. In trace $\langle a, a, b, c \rangle$, the constraint is activated and fulfilled twice, whereas, in trace $\langle a, b, c, b \rangle$, the same constraint is activated and fulfilled only once. On the other hand, when a trace is not compliant with respect to a constraint, an activation of the constraint in the trace can lead to a fulfillment but also to a violation (at least one activation leads to a violation). In trace $\langle a, b, a, c \rangle$, for example, the response constraint $\Box(a \rightarrow \Diamond b)$ is activated twice, but the first activation leads to a fulfillment (eventually b occurs) and the second activation leads to a violation (b does not occur subsequently).

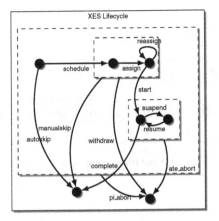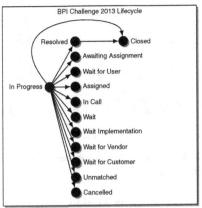

Fig. 1. XES Standard and BPI Challenge 2013 transactional models for activity lifecycles

2.2 Activity Lifecycle

In real business applications, activities cannot be considered as atomic/instantaneous events, but they traverse different states in their lifecycle. Consider, for example, activity *Check*. This activity, during its execution can traverse different transactional states like, e.g., (i) *schedule* ($Check_{schedule}$), meaning that a check has been scheduled, (ii) *start* ($Check_{start}$), indicating that the check activity has started its execution, and (iii) *complete* ($Check_{complete}$), meaning that the check has been completed.

A transactional model for activity lifecycles represents the set of the admissible sequences of states that an activity can assume during its lifecycle. Figure 1 depicts the XES standard transactional model [10], which allows keeping track in the log of information related to activity lifecycles. In particular, the model is provided as a state machine describing the admissible flows of the different states an activity can assume. In addition, using the Lifecycle Extension provided in XES, users can customize the transactional model allowed in an event log.

Figure 2 reports an example that we will use as running example throughout the paper. In the figure, t_0 represents an execution trace containing only atomic activities (a, b, and c). t_1 includes non-atomic activities and different event types assumed by activities a, b and c (based on the XES standard transactional model). Activity a appears with three event types (once with *assign*, and twice with *start* and *complete*) b occurs with two event types (twice with *start* and *complete*), and activity c appears only with event type *start*. From this example, it is clear that we need a mechanism to connect events belonging to the same activity lifecycle together. In this paper, we use a conservative, FIFO-based approach. Using this approach, events at positions 1, 3 and 6 for activity a are grouped together, and, also, events at positions 5 and 7. Events at positions 2 and 4, and positions 8 and 10 for activity b are grouped together. Notice that, executions of activities can overlap. For example, the first lifecycle of activity a in the figure completes after that the first lifecycle of activity b has started. Also notice that some lifecycles are malformed, like the one of activity c that does not have a completion.

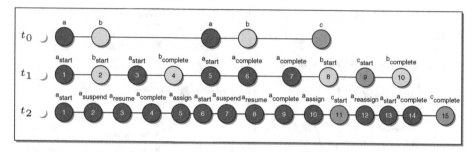

Fig. 2. An example of a trace including atomic activities (t_0) and traces composed of non-atomic activities (t_1 and t_2)

2.3 Discriminative Mining

Discriminative mining aims at extracting, from an existing set of data, patterns that are discriminative with respect to a given criterion. In the literature, several branches of works, differing with each other based on the type of mined patterns (e.g., sequences or rules), fall under this umbrella, like, for example, discriminative pattern mining [8], discriminative sequence mining [12] or classification rule approaches [18]. All these approaches are usually based on supervised or non-supervised learning techniques. In this work, we exploit decision tree supervised learning [7] in order to mine a set of declarative rules that discriminate between fulfillments and violations of a given constraint. Decision trees have been applied in the context of discriminative rule mining (also on top of other techniques) for their capability to construct readable rules [18]. Decision tree learning uses a decision tree as a model to predict the value of a target variable based on input variables (features). Decision trees are built from a set of training dataset. Each internal node of the tree is labeled with an input feature. Arcs stemming from a node labeled with a feature are labeled with possible values or value ranges of the feature. Each leaf of the decision tree is labeled with a class, i.e., a value of the target variable given the values of the input variables represented by the path from the root to the leaf. Moreover, each leaf of the decision tree is associated with a support (*support*) and a probability distribution (*class probability*). Support represents the number of examples in the training dataset that follow the path from the root to the leaf and that are correctly classified; class probability is the percentage of examples correctly classified with respect to all examples following that specific path.

In this work we rely on the Weka J48 implementation of one of the most known decision tree algorithms, the C4.5 algorithm [16], which exploits the normalized information gain to choose, for each node of the tree, the feature to be used for splitting the set of examples.

3   Approach

Figure 3 illustrates our proposed approach. Given a log containing non-atomic activities and a transactional model for activity lifecycles as a reference, it returns as output (i) a set of Declare constraints with non-atomic activities, and (ii) for each constraint, a set of characteristics of the involved activity lifecycles, which are possibly related to the

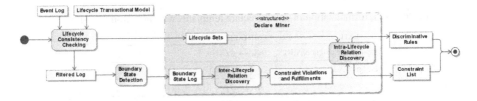

Fig. 3. An overview of the proposed approach

fulfillment or to the violation of the constraint. Roughly speaking, the approach takes into consideration a list of candidate Declare constraints (involving non-atomic activities), and it uses standard discovery techniques [13] for identifying fulfillments and violations for each of them. Then, a discriminative rule mining approach is used to find the characteristics of the lifecycle of an activation of a candidate constraint that allows us to discriminate between cases in which that activation was a fulfillment, and cases in which the activation was a violation for the considered constraint. In the following sections, we describe the main steps of the approach in detail.

3.1 Lifecycle Consistency Checking

The first step of our proposed technique aims at processing the input log to (i) connect together activity states belonging to the same lifecycle, and (ii) remove all the "malformed" lifecycles that are not consistent with the input transactional model. As already mentioned in Section 2, there are two possibilities for grouping event types of an activity belonging to the same lifecycle. One way to do it is by using event correlations as explained in [3]. If the event log contains (event) data attributes, it is possible to connect activity states that share some data values, e.g., an event id. However, this approach is applicable only if attributes that can be used to connect events exist. Therefore, for our experimentation, we decided to implement a conservative approach that is less precise, but applicable also in cases of logs with no data attributes or with data attributes that cannot be used for event correlation. In particular, we use a FIFO-based algorithm. We explain this approach using our running example in Fig. 2, and using the XES standard transactional model for activity lifecycles as reference. Based on this transactional model, events in trace t_1 of the example can be grouped in separate lifecycles in different ways. For example, $a_{complete}$ at position 6 can be connected with a_{start} at position 3, or with a_{start} at position 5. Applying our FIFO-based algorithm, we can disambiguate the correlation using a conservative approach. This means that $a_{complete}$ at position 6 is connected with the a_{start} event that occurred first, i.e., the one at position 3. Following this approach, we can identify, in trace t_1, the following lifecycles:

- $a_1 = \langle a_{assign}(1), a_{start}(3), a_{complete}(6) \rangle$,
- $a_2 = \langle a_{start}(5), a_{complete}(7) \rangle$,
- $b_1 = \langle b_{start}(2), b_{complete}(4) \rangle$,
- $b_2 = \langle b_{start}(8), b_{complete}(10) \rangle$,
- $c_1 = \langle c_{start}(9) \rangle$,

where numbers between brackets indicate the position of the event in the trace.

As already mentioned, when we have all the lifecycles grouped together we can filter out the ones that are inconsistent with respect to the input transactional model. For

Table 2. LTL formalization of some Declare templates with non-atomic activities

TEMPLATE	FORMALIZATION
responded existence(A,B)	$\Diamond A_i \rightarrow \Diamond B_i$
response(A,B)	$\Box(A_f \rightarrow \Diamond B_i)$
precedence(A,B)	$\neg B_i \, \mathcal{W} \, A_f$
alternate response(A,B)	$\Box(A_f \rightarrow O(\neg A_f \, \mathcal{U} \, B_i))$
alternate precedence(A,B)	$(\neg B_i \, \mathcal{W} \, A_f) \wedge \Box(B_i \rightarrow O(\neg B_i \, \mathcal{W} \, A_f))$
chain response(A,B)	$\Box(A_f \rightarrow O B_i)$
chain precedence(A,B)	$\Box(O B_i \rightarrow A_f)$
not responded existence(A,B)	$\Diamond A_i \rightarrow \neg \Diamond B_i$
not response(A,B)	$\Box(A_f \rightarrow \neg \Diamond B_i)$
not precedence(A,B)	$\Box(A_f \rightarrow \neg \Diamond B_i)$
not chain response(A,B)	$\Box(A_f \rightarrow \neg O B_i)$
not chain precedence(A,B)	$\Box(A_f \rightarrow \neg O B_i)$

example, in our case, lifecycle c_1 is not allowed in the XES standard model, since a completion is missing. For this reason, this lifecycle will be filtered out and not considered for further analysis. The outputs of this step of our proposed approach are, respectively, the filtered log and the list of all the activities lifecycles (described by sequences of event types) that are contained in the log.

3.2 Boundary State Detection

The aim of this step is to abstract the activity lifecycles in the log by replacing them with placeholders marking the start and the end of each lifecycle in the log. This transformation is needed to discover Declare constraints with semantics for non-atomic activities described in Table 2. The formulas are straightforward and directly follow by the corresponding formulas in standard Declare. The idea is that, for verifying constraints involving non-atomic activities, it is sufficient to take into account the boundary states of lifecycles (in the table the initial state is indicated with "i" and the final one with "f"), abstracting away from the lifecycle details. For example, for the *response* template, it is enough to verify that the final state of activity A (A_f) is followed by the initial state B (B_i). In general, we consider most of the constraints valid for non-overlapping lifecycles. The only exceptions are the semantics of templates *responded existence* and *not responded existence* that we consider valid also for overlapping lifecycles of parallel activities.

In this step of the approach, we take as input the filtered log obtained by the previous step and produce a new log in which internal states of each lifecycle (i.e., states that are neither initial nor final) are filtered out. Trace $\mathbf{t}_1$ of our running example would be transformed into trace $\langle a_{assign}, b_{start}, b_{complete}, a_{start}, a_{complete}, a_{complete}, b_{start}, b_{complete} \rangle$. Event $a_{start}(3)$ is filtered out because it is not a boundary event in lifecycle $a_1 = (a_{assign}(1), a_{start}(3), a_{complete}(6))$. Events in the log are further transformed by abstracting away from the specific event type that corresponds to the first or the last event of each lifecycle: each starting state will be indicated with "i" and each final state with "f". For instance, t_1 would become $\langle a_i, b_i, b_f, a_i, a_f, a_f, b_i, b_f \rangle$.

3.3   Discovering Inter-Lifecycle Relations

In this step, the boundary state log derived from the previous step is mined using the approach presented in [3] to discover Declare constraints with semantics for non-atomic activities described in Table 2. As shown in the table, this semantics take into consideration only the boundary events of the activity lifecycles. The outcome of this step of the approach is a set of candidate Declare constraints connecting elements of different lifecycles (inter-lifecycle relations). For each candidate, we extract the set of fulfillments and the set of violations in the log. These sets will be input of the supervised learning problem defined in the next step of our proposed technique needed to find intra-lifecycle relations discriminating between lifecycles of constraint activations that eventually lead to a fulfillment and lifecycles of activations that lead to a constraint violation.

3.4   Discovering Intra-Lifecycle Relations

In the previous step of our proposed approach, we extract fulfillments and violations for a list of candidate constraints describing inter-lifecycle relations between activities in the log. For example, in trace t_1 of our running example, $b_{complete}(4)$ is a fulfillment for constraint $\square(b_f \rightarrow \lozenge a_i)$ (in this case b_f is eventually followed by a_i), whereas $b_{complete}(10)$ is a violation for the same constraint. Note that, at this point of our approach, we take again into consideration the entire lifecycles connected to the boundary events in the log and we analyze their control flow characteristics to discriminate between lifecycles of activations that are fulfillments and the ones that are violations for each candidate constraint. These characteristics will be expressed, in turn, using Declare. In this case, the Declare constraints express intra-lifecycle relations between event types of the same activity.

This problem can be reformulated in terms of a supervised learning problem. For each candidate constraint $constr$, defined over a pair (a, b), with a activation of $constr$, the features of the lifecycle of a discriminating with respect to fullfillments/violations of $constr$, are learned from a set L of sequences representing all the lifecycles of a in the log. These sequences are classified in two sets L_{ful} and L_{viol} according to whether the lifecycle corresponds to a fulfillment or to a violation of $constr$.

For example, consider traces t_1 and t_2 in our running example and constraint $\square(a_f \rightarrow \lozenge b_i)$. Lifecycles $a_1 = \langle a_{start}, a_{complete} \rangle$ and $a_2 = \langle a_{assign}, a_{start}, a_{complete} \rangle$ in trace t_1 correspond to fulfillments for the considered constraint since they are followed by an occurrence of b_i. Lifecycles $a_3 = \{ \langle a_{start}, a_{suspend}, a_{resume}, a_{complete} \rangle, a_4 = \langle a_{assign}, a_{start}, a_{suspend}, a_{resume}, a_{complete} \rangle$, and $a_5 = \langle a_{assign}, a_{reassign}, a_{start}, a_{complete} \rangle$ in trace t_2 correspond to violations. Therefore, in this case, we have $L_{ful} = \{ \langle a_{start}, a_{complete} \rangle, \langle a_{assign}, a_{start}, a_{complete} \rangle \}$ and $L_{viol} = \{ \langle a_{start}, a_{suspend}, a_{resume}, a_{complete} \rangle, \langle a_{assign}, a_{start}, a_{suspend}, a_{resume}, a_{complete} \rangle, \langle a_{assign}, a_{reassign}, a_{start}, a_{complete} \rangle \}$.

From these sets, we could learn, for example, that it is likely that $\square(a_f \rightarrow \lozenge b_i)$ is verified when a_{start} is immediately followed by $a_{complete}$ but is not immediately preceded by $a_{reassign}$ in the lifecycle of a. In particular, we exploit decision tree learning in order to identify the conditions (*decision rules*) on the lifecycle of an activation given the training sets L_{ful} and L_{viol}.

Each lifecycle of an activation a is encoded in terms of a set of Declare constraints (over the states of the lifecycle). In particular, each lifecycle is encoded as a vector of (boolean) values representing whether all these (intra-lifecycle) constraints are satisfied or not on that lifecycle. The decision tree is trained using the intra-lifecycle conditions as features and the classification of the lifecycle as part of L_{ful} or L_{viol}. The analysis of the tree allows us to retrieve the set of conditions on the features which possibly make the constraint under consideration fulfilled or violated. Figure 4 shows a possible decision tree generated over the lifecycle of the running example described above. In order to have the inter-lifecycle constraint $\Box(a_f \rightarrow \Diamond b_i)$ fulfilled, the intra-lifecycle conditions $\Box(a_{start} \rightarrow \bigcirc a_{complete})$ (chain response between a_{start} and $a_{complete}$) and $\neg\Box(\bigcirc a_{reassign} \rightarrow a_{start})$ (chain precedence between $a_{reassign}$ and a_{start}) should hold. In summary, the result of the decision tree learning will be a set of Declare constraints over the states of the lifecycles of a which would bring to fulfillments or to violations for $\Box(a_f \rightarrow \Diamond b_i)$.

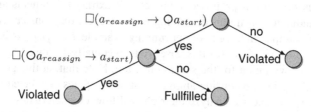

Fig. 4. A decision tree generated over the lifecycle of the running example

4   Experiments

In order to evaluate the proposed approach, we have implemented it as a plug-in of the process mining tool ProM. Then, the implemented plug-in has been applied to (i) a set of execution logs synthetically generated (to verify its capability to capture known discriminating behaviors); (ii) a real-life log (to check the scalability and the applicability of the approach to real-life settings). All the experiments have been conducted on a machine with an Intel i7 processor (limiting the execution to just one core), 8 GB of RAM and the Oracle Java virtual machine installed on a GNU/Linux Ubuntu operating system and are discussed in this section.

4.1   Synthetic Log Analysis

The purpose of the synthetic log analysis is to verify whether the discriminative rules discovered reflect the actual discriminating behaviors (with respect to constraint fulfillments/violations) of the execution logs under examination. To this aim, four synthetic logs have been generated, taking inspiration from the insurance claim process presented in [4]. The process describes the handling of health insurance claims in a travel agency, starting from the registration up to the claim archiving. The approach has been applied to each synthetic log and discriminative rules have been extracted. In the following subsections, we illustrate how we have generated the logs and the results obtained.

Synthetic Log 1. Synthetic Log 1 contains 1000 traces in which $Register$ occurs with one of the following possible lifecycles:

- $\langle\, Register_{start},\, Register_{complete}\, \rangle$
- $\langle\, Register_{abort}\, \rangle$
- $\langle\, Register_{assign},\, Register_{start},\, Register_{complete}\, \rangle$
- $\langle\, Register_{start},\, Register_{abort}\, \rangle$
- $\langle\, Register_{start},\, Register_{suspend},\, Register_{abort}\, \rangle$

Whenever $Register$ is aborted (see second, fourth and fifth lifecycle in the list), the claimer is notified via phone; on the other hand, if the registration completes normally (see first and third lifecycle in the list), the e-mail notification is required. Therefore, in the log, whenever $Register$ is aborted, the response constraint $\Box(Register \rightarrow \Diamond Notify\_by\_phone)$ is verified, otherwise this constraint does not hold.

Synthetic Log 2. Synthetic Log 2 contains 1000 traces in which the non-atomic activity $Send\_questionnaire$ occurs with one of the following possible lifecycles:

- $\langle\, Send\_questionnaire_{start},\, Send\_questionnaire_{complete}\rangle$
- $\langle\, Send\_questionnaire_{withdraw}\, \rangle$
- $\langle\, Send\_questionnaire_{assign},\, Send\_questionnaire_{withdraw}\, \rangle$
- $\langle\, Send\_questionnaire_{start},\, Send\_questionnaire_{suspend},\, Send\_questionnaire_{abort}\, \rangle$
- $\langle\, Send\_questionnaire_{complete}\, \rangle$

When $Send\_questionnaire$ is withdrawn or aborted (see second, third and fourth lifecycle in the list), $Skip\_response$ for skipping the response is executed. On the other hand, whenever $Send\_questionnaire$ completes normally (see first and fifth lifecycle in the list), $Skip\_response$ is not executed. Therefore, in the log, the response constraint $\Box(Send\_questionnaire \rightarrow \Diamond(Skip\_response))$ is verified only if $Send\_questionnaire$ does not complete normally (i.e., with withdraw or abort).

Synthetic Log 3. Synthetic Log 3 contains 1000 traces in which the non-atomic activity $High\_medical\_history\_check$ occurs with one of the following possible lifecycles:

- $\langle\, High\_medical\_history\_check_{withdraw}\, \rangle$
- $\langle\, High\_medical\_history\_check_{start},\, High\_medical\_history\_check_{complete}\rangle$
- $\langle\, High\_medical\_history\_check_{start},\, High\_medical\_history\_check_{abort}\rangle$
- $\langle\, High\_medical\_history\_check_{assign},\, High\_medical\_history\_check_{autoskip}\rangle$
- $\langle\, High\_medical\_history\_check_{assign},\, High\_medical\_history\_check_{start},$
  $High\_medical\_history\_check_{complete}\, \rangle$

When $High\_medical\_history\_check$ does not complete normally (see first, third and fourth in the list), $Contact\_hospital$ is executed eventually. On the other hand, in cases in which the verification procedure completes normally (see second and fifth lifecycle in the list), there is no need to contact the hospital. Therefore, in the log, the response constraint $\Box(High\_medical\_history\_check \rightarrow \Diamond Contact\_hospital)$ holds if and only if $High\_medical\_history\_check$ fails.

Table 3. Synthetic Log Results

LOG	INTER-LIFECYCLE RELATION	INTRA-LIFECYCLE RELATION
1	response($Register, Notify\_by\_phone$)	exactly $(1, Register_{abort})$
2	response ($Send\_questionnaire, Skip\_response$)	exclusive choice ($Send\_questionnaire_{abort}$, $Send\_questionnaire_{withdraw}$)
3	response ($High\_medical\_history\_check, Contact\_hospital$)	$\neg$ alternate response ($High\_medical\_history\_check_{start}$, $High\_medical\_history\_check_{complete}$)
4	response($Register, Notify\_by\_email$)	alternate succession ($Register_{resume}, Register_{complete}$)

Synthetic Log 4. Synthetic Log 4 contains 1000 traces in which the non-atomic activity *Register* occurs with one of the following possible lifecycles:

- $\langle\ Register_{start},\ Register_{suspend},\ Register_{resume},\ Register_{complete}\ \rangle$
- $\langle\ Register_{start},\ Register_{suspend},\ Register_{abort}\ \rangle$
- $\langle\ Register_{start},\ Register_{suspend},\ Register_{resume},\ Register_{suspend},\ Register_{resume},$ $Register_{complete}\rangle$
- $\langle\ Register_{start},\ Register_{suspend},\ Register_{resume},\ Register_{suspend},\ Register_{withdraw}\ \rangle$

When *Register* is suspended and ends with an abort or a withdraw (see second and fourth lifecycle in the list), or *Register* is suspended (and resumed) more than once (see third lifecycle in the list), the claimer has to be notified via phone; if there is only one suspension correctly resumed, i.e., a single cycle suspend/resume and, eventually, a normal completion (see first lifecycle in the list), the claimer can be notified via e-mail. Therefore, in the log, whenever *Register* is suspended and not resumed, or suspended more than once, the response constraint $\Box(Register \rightarrow \Diamond Notify\_by\_phone)$ is verified, otherwise this constraint does not hold.

Discussion of the Results. Table 3 shows some of the constraints discovered. For Synthetic Log 1 and the response constraint between *Register* and *Notify_by_phone* the discriminative rule discovered is exactly(1, $Register_{abort}$). Whenever $Register_{abort}$ occurs (exactly once, since it cannot occur more than once based on the XES transactional model), the claimer has to be notified via phone. This result confirms the rationale behind the construction of Synthetic Log 1: whenever a registration is aborted, the claimer has to be notified via phone, otherwise *Notify_by_phone* is not executed.

Concerning Synthetic Log 2 and the response constraint between *Send_questionnaire* and *Skip_response*, the exclusive choice between $Send\_questionnaire_{abort}$ and $Send\_questionnaire_{withdraw}$ is discovered as discriminative rule. If and only if the lifecycle of *Send_questionnaire* contains either $Send\_questionnaire_{abort}$ or $Send\_questionnaire_{withdraw}$, the questionnaire response is skipped. This perfectly fits with the behavior characterizing the log: whenever *Send_questionnaire* cannot complete normally, the questionnaire response is skipped.

The response constraint between *High_medical_history_check* and *Contact_hospital* in Synthetic Log 3 is valid when the intra-lifecycle relation $\neg$ alternate response between $High\_medical\_history\_check_{start}$ and $High\_medical\_history\_check_{complete}$ holds. If and only if $High\_medical\_history\_check_{start}$ is not followed by

Table 4. BPI 2013 Results

	INTER-LIFECYCLE RELATION	INTRA-LIFECYCLE RELATION	CLASS PROB.	SUPPORT
(1)	precedence ($Accepted,Completed$)	not responded existence $(Completed_{Cancelled},Completed_{Closed})$	0.65	3711
(2)	precedence ($Queued,Accepted$)	init($Accepted_{Assigned}$) $\vee$ init ($Accepted_{Wait\_implementation}$)	0.75	92
(3)	precedence ($Queued, Completed$)	co-existence $(Completed_{In\_call},Completed_{Cancelled})$	0.8	4551
(4)	response ($Completed, Queued$)	$\neg$ responded existence $(Completed_{Resolved},Completed_{Closed})$	0.98	7570
(5)	responded existence ($Completed, Accepted$)	not responded existence $(Completed_{Cancelled},Completed_{Closed})$	0.66	3771
(6)	responded existence ($Completed, Queued$)	co-existence $(Completed_{In\_call},Completed_{Cancelled})$	0.8	4595

$High\_medical\_history\_check_{complete}$, the hospital has to be contacted. The result is in line with what described in Synthetic Log 3: whenever, in the lifecycle of $High\_medical\_history\_check$, there is a $High\_medical\_history\_check_{start}$ that is not followed by $High\_medical\_history\_check_{complete}$, the hospital has to be contacted.

Finally, for Synthetic Log 4 and the response constraint between $Register$ and $Notify\_by\_email$, the discriminative rule discovered for the verification of this constraint is the alternate succession between $Register_{resume}$ and $Register_{complete}$. If and only if $Register_{resume}$ is followed by $Register_{complete}$ and not more than one $Register_{resume}$ is executed before $Register_{complete}$ (at most one suspend/resume cycle occurs), then the response constraint between $Register$ and $Notify\_by\_email$ is verified. This result is in line with the behavior injected into Synthetic Log 4: whenever $Register$ is suspended and and correctly resumed at most once, the customer is notified via e-mail.

4.2 BPI Challenge 2013

The proposed approach has also been applied to a real-life log. The log, which was provided for the BPI Challenge 2013 [17], has been taken from an incident and problem management system called VINST. The VINST system includes the activities required to diagnose the root causes of incidents and to secure the resolution of those problems ensuring high levels of service quality and availability of services operated by Volvo IT. The log contains 7,554 cases and 65,533 events and is characterized by four different activities ($Accepted, Completed, Queued$ and $Unmatched$) and 14 event types like $In\_Call, Assigned, Cancelled, Resolved$ and $Closed$. The transactional model for activity lifecycles followed in the log is reported in Figure 1 on the right hand side.

Table 4 shows a list of discovered constraints and, for each of them, the (intralifecycle) rules to discriminate between fulfillments and violations. The last two columns of the table also report class probability and support associated to each discovered discriminative rule.

The first row of the table (1) suggests that a possible discriminating behavior for which $Completed$ is preceded by $Accepted$ is that either $Completed_{Cancelled}$ or $Completed_{Closed}$ occurs in the lifecycle of $Completed$. The same rule is also discriminating for fulfillments/violations of the responded existence between *Completed* and *Accepted* (i.e., the constraint assessing that whenever *Completed* occurs, then, *Accepted* has to occur in the future or has already occurred before). In the second row of Table 4 (2), we can see that whenever the lifecycle of *Accepted* starts with $Accepted_{Assigned}$ or with $Accepted_{Wait\_Implementation}$, *Accepted* is preceded by *Queued*. These results are the ones with the lowest class probability and support. For example, the class probability of the rule in (1) (0.65) indicates that only in 65% of the cases in which the constraint is actually verified, the corresponding discriminative rule also holds. Similarly, the support of (2) indicates that the cases in which the constraint and the corresponding discovered discriminative rule are both verified are 92.

On the other hand, the remaining rules present both a reasonable class probability (> 0.8) and a good support (> 4500). In particular, the co-occurrence of $Completed_{In\_Call}$ and $Completed_{Cancelled}$ discriminates both on the precedence (3) and on the responded existence (6) between *Queued* and *Completed*, i.e., whenever both *In_Call* and *Cancelled* occur in the lifecycle of *Completed*, it means that *Completed* is preceded by *Queued* or, more in general (with a slightly higher support), that *Queued* occurs at least once before or after *Completed*.

Finally, the discovered discriminating behavior with the highest class probability (almost 1) and support (more than 7000) is the one related to the response constraint between *Completed* and *Queued* (6): *Queued* eventually follows *Completed* if and only if only one among $Completed_{Resolved}$ and $Completed_{Closed}$ occurs in the lifecycle of *Completed*.

5   Conclusion and Future Work

This paper presents a novel approach for the discovery of declarative process models from logs containing non-atomic activities. Discriminative rule mining is used to characterize the lifecycle of each constraint activation and discriminate between lifecycles that ensure that the activation is a fulfillment and lifecycles that correspond to violations of the constraint under examination.

In order to assess the applicability of the proposed approach, we applied it to four synthetic logs and a real-life log recorded by an incident and problem management system in use at Volvo IT Belgium. Our experiments show the effectiveness of the approach and its applicability in real-life scenarios. As future work, we will conduct a wider experimentation of the proposed framework on several case studies in real-life scenarios and different transactional models for activity lifecycles. In addition, we will implement the identifications of lifecycles through event correlations and compare this approach with the FIFO-based approach presented in this paper.

Acknowledgment. This research has been carried out with the valuable comments and support of Andrea Burattin from University of Padua.

References

1. Van der Aalst, W., Pesic, M., Schonenberg, H.: Declarative Workflows: Balancing Between Flexibility and Support. Computer Science - R&D, 99–113 (2009)

2. Bernardi, M.L., Cimitile, M., Lucca, G.A.D., Maggi, F.M.: Using declarative workflow languages to develop process-centric web applications. In: 16th IEEE International Enterprise Distributed Object Computing Conference Workshops, EDOC Workshops, Beijing, China, September 10-14, pp. 56–65 (2012)
3. Bose, R.P.J.C., Maggi, F.M., van der Aalst, W.M.P.: Enhancing declare maps based on event correlations. In: Daniel, F., Wang, J., Weber, B. (eds.) BPM 2013. LNCS, vol. 8094, pp. 97–112. Springer, Heidelberg (2013),
   http://dx.doi.org/10.1007/978-3-642-40176-3_9
4. Bose, R.J.C.: Process Mining in the Large: Preprocessing, Discovery, and Diagnostics. Ph.D. thesis, Eindhoven University of Technology (2012)
5. Burattin, A., Maggi, F., van der Aalst, W., Sperduti, A.: Techniques for a Posteriori Analysis of Declarative Processes. In: EDOC, pp. 41–50 (2012)
6. Burattin, A., Sperduti, A.: Heuristics Miner for Time Intervals. In: European Symposium on Artificial Neural Networks (ESANN), Bruges, Belgium (2010)
7. Caruana, R., Niculescu-Mizil, A.: An empirical comparison of supervised learning algorithms. In: Proceedings of the 23rd International Conference on Machine Learning, ICML 2006, pp. 161–168. ACM, New York (2006),
   http://doi.acm.org/10.1145/1143844.1143865
8. Cheng, H., Yan, X., Han, J., Yu, P.S.: Direct discriminative pattern mining for effective classification. In: Proceedings of the 2008 IEEE 24th International Conference on Data Engineering, ICDE 2008, pp. 169–178. IEEE Computer Society, Washington, DC (2008),
   http://dx.doi.org/10.1109/ICDE.2008.4497425
9. Chesani, F., Lamma, E., Mello, P., Montali, M., Riguzzi, F., Storari, S.: Exploiting inductive logic programming techniques for declarative process mining. Transactions on Petri Nets and Other Models of Concurrency II, Special Issue on Concurrency in Process-Aware Information Systems 2, 278–295 (2009)
10. Günther, C.W.: XES Standard Definition (2009), www.xes-standard.org, http://www.xes-standard.org/_media/xes/xes_standard_proposal.pdf
11. Kupferman, O., Vardi, M.: Vacuity Detection in Temporal Model Checking. Int. Journal on Software Tools for Technology Transfer, 224–233 (2003)
12. Lo, D., Cheng, H.: Lucia: Mining closed discriminative dyadic sequential patterns. In: Proc. of the International Conference on Extending Database Technology (EDBT), pp. 21–32. Springer (2011)
13. Maggi, F.M., Bose, R.P.J.C., van der Aalst, W.M.P.: Efficient discovery of understandable declarative models from event logs. In: Ralyté, J., Franch, X., Brinkkemper, S., Wrycza, S. (eds.) CAiSE 2012. LNCS, vol. 7328, pp. 270–285. Springer, Heidelberg (2012)
14. Montali, M., Pesic, M., van der Aalst, W.M.P., Chesani, F., Mello, P., Storari, S.: Declarative Specification and Verification of Service Choreographies. ACM Transactions on the Web 4(1) (2010)
15. Pesic, M., Schonenberg, M.H., van der Aalst, W.M.P.: Declare: Full support for loosely-structured processes. In: EDOC, pp. 287–300 (2007)
16. Quinlan, J.R.: C4.5: Programs for Machine Learning. M. Kaufmann Publishers Inc. (1993)
17. Steeman, W.: Bpi challenge 2013, incidents (2013), http://dx.doi.org/10.4121/uuid:500573e6-accc-4b0c-9576-aa5468b10cee
18. Sun, C., Du, J., Chen, N., Khoo, S.C., Yang, Y.: Mining explicit rules for software process evaluation. In: Proceedings of the 2013 International Conference on Software and System Process, ICSSP 2013, pp. 118–125. ACM, New York (2013),
   http://doi.acm.org/10.1145/2486046.2486067
19. Verbeek, E.H.M.W., Buijs, J., van Dongen, B., van der Aalst, W.M.P.: ProM 6: The Process Mining Toolkit. In: BPM 2010 Demo, pp. 34–39 (2010)

Modeling Obligations with Event-Calculus*

Mustafa Hashmi[1,2], Guido Governatori[1,2], and Moe Thandar Wynn[2,1]

[1] NICTA, Queensland Research Laboratory, 2 George St. Brisbane Australia
{mustafa.hashmi,guido.governatori}@nicta.com.au
[2] Queensland University of Technology (QUT) Brisbane, Australia
m.wynn@qut.edu.au

Abstract. Time plays an important role in norms. In this paper we start from our previously proposed classification of obligations, and point out some shortcomings of Event Calculus (EC) to represent obligations. We propose an extension of EC that avoids such shortcomings and we show how to use it to model the various types of obligations.

Keywords: Legal norms, Event Calculus, Temporal aspect, Compliance.

1 Introduction

Time plays an essential role in norms, legal reasoning and in areas governed by norms. For example many of the normative requirements in the area of business process compliance concern the temporal aspects of norms. Suppose you have a contract specifying that one party has thirty days to pay for an invoice, and that goods cannot be delivered without payment. Thus you have an obligation to pay after receiving an invoice, which, in turn, requires that the payment *must be made before* the time of delivery. Receiving the invoice triggers (enforces) the obligation to make a payment to complete the transaction. Accordingly we have conditions that must be fulfilled in a determined time interval or within a given deadline, and other conditions that must happen before or after specific events. Moreover, some obligations may include conditions that *must persist over an interval of time* e.g., continuous monitoring of the patient's blood pressure and ECG during a surgical operation. Regardless of the type, validity and nature of the legal effect(s) that an obligation represents, the temporal aspect of an obligation revolves around the following generic aspects [17]: (i) *the time when an obligation is in force*, (ii) *the time when an obligation is fulfilled*, and (iii) *the time of application*. Accordingly, when a business process is subject to norms, it is particularly important that the process complies with the obligations imposed by the norms for the whole duration of its validity and meets the deadlines, and follows constraints for maintaining and delaying actions.

Capturing the real meaning of norms is paramount for modelling and reasoning about compliance checking of business processes, and, in general, for legal reasoning. It is also important that the chosen language supports the highest degree of abstraction to model the real meaning of the norms and the obligations they define: this means it

* NICTA is funded by the Australian Government through the Department of Communication and the Australian Research Council through the ICT Center of Excellence Program.

A. Bikakis et al. (Eds.): RuleML 2014, LNCS 8620, pp. 296–310, 2014.
© Springer International Publishing Switzerland 2014

should be able to model states of affairs, actions as well as (temporal) relationships between activities. Many studies have been conducted for modelling obligations, and various classifications of obligations have been identified in these studies, in particular in the context of business process compliance where *time* is the key concept of such classifications, see among others [13,10,8]. For example, [19] classifies obligations from the legal viewpoint while [13] classifies obligations along the temporal structure and the temporal distribution of the obligations. [8] characterises the types of obligations based on deadlines, and [3] classifies obligations types as existence, choice, relation, and negative constraints. These classifications do not encompass various types of obligations based on the time, effects of an obligation on other obligations and obligations arising from the violations. In [7,12] we provided a classification of obligations along temporal dimensions. The key aspects of the classification are: what constitutes the violation in terms of the temporal validity of an obligation, and whether violated obligations can be compensated for or not. In the classification, along the temporal dimension, for each type of obligations we specified when an obligation comes into force and until when it remains in force or it is violated at a particular time point. Unlike other classifications, our proposed classification encompasses the generic temporal model about the validity and persistence effects of obligations after violations. Given our new classification, the natural question is *how to model each element of the classification of obligations for business process compliance checking.*

The families of Deontic Logics (DL), Temporal Logics (TL), and EventCalculus (EC) are widely used formalisms for modeling norms. Each of these formalisms has a reasonable degree of expressiveness to model different types of obligations yet they have limitations. Our starting point to model norms, in particular the new classes of obligations, is the classical EC [14] because it provides a logical framework for representing and modeling the effects of events and the current state of affairs in terms of fluents. Also, it has the ability to model the time when fluents come to existence and cease to hold dynamically [5]. One may argue that modeling the deontic notions with EC is rather well developed as several variants of EC already exist (see, [16,18] for further listing of EC variants), and widely used for reasoning and representing the legal knowledge (see, Section 6 for a detailed discussion on some such approaches), but we believe that the EC has some major issues for reasoning about legal norms. One of such issues is related to the basic predicate of EC $Initiates(E,X,T)$. Its meaning is that event E at time T initiates the fluent X, and the fluent holds from the next instant of time (see Section 3 and Axiom A1 below for the details). This effectively means that the norm enters into force at the next instant. However, for legal norms, this might not be the case. There are cases where the norm enters into force at the same instant as the triggering event happens e.g., the obligation to remove shoes when one enters in a mosque or the norms is in force after a delay e.g., a complaint cannot be acknowledged until all details pertaining is issue have been received.[1]

In the context of business process compliance checking, the aim of this paper is to explore whether or not the different obligation classes defined in our classification model can be faithfully represented using the discrete event driven formalism the EC.

---

[1] In addition it is possible to have that a norm enters in force retroactively. Thus the fluent holds before the event that initiates it. We blatantly ignore this aspect in this paper.

The paper is structured as follows: in Section 2 we revisit the classification of normative requirements proposed elsewhere ([7,12]) and provide formal definitions of the concepts. Section 3 provides a terse background of the EC and introduces new predicates for modeling the legal norms followed by the modeling of various obligation types using the new predicates in Section 4. The proof sketch of the provided axioms is given in Section 5 followed by a short discussion on related studies in the problem domain in Section 6. Section 7 concludes the paper with some final remarks.

2   Normative Requirements Revisited

The purpose of this section is to provide a summary of the notions and the classes of obligations defined in our classificatory model. For more detailed discussions and concrete examples of the various types of obligations taken from real legal acts, see [7,12]. The definitions below also provide precise semantics of these notions and they will be used to evaluate our proposed extension to EC.

Norms regulate the behaviour of their subjects and produce normative effects when applied. From a business process compliance perspective the normative effects of interest are the deontic effects. The three basic deontic effects –from which other deontic effects can be derived (see, [19])– are: *obligation*, *prohibition*, and *permission*.

An *Obligation*[2] is a situation, act or a course of actions one is legally bound to and if it is not achieved or performed results in a violation; whereas for *prohibition*, one should avoid a certain course of actions to avoid a violation. *Obligations* and *prohibitions* are constraints that limit the behaviour of a business process; and both types can be violated. Notice that a prohibition is a negative obligation (i.e., obligation not), thus, when we speak of obligations we include prohibitions as well. *Permissions*, on the other hand, are constraints that cannot be violated thus they do not play a direct role in compliance. Instead, they can be used to determine that there are no obligations or prohibitions to the contrary.

Compliance means to identify whether a business process violated a set of obligations. Thus the first step is to determine *whether* and *when* an obligation is in force. Essentially, a norm can specify when an obligation is in force at a particular time point only (*non-persistent obligations*), or more often, a norm indicates when an obligation enters into force. An obligation remains in force until it is terminated or removed (*persistent obligations*).

Non-Persistent obligations are also called *punctual obligations*: the obligation contents are immediately achieved otherwise a violation is triggered. In contrast, a *persistent obligation* which is to be obeyed for all time instances within the interval it is in force is a *maintenance obligation*. If achieving the contents of an obligation at least once is enough, then it is an *achievement obligation*. For an achievement obligation, if the obligation could be fulfilled even before it is actually in force, we speak of a *preemptive* obligation; otherwise it is a *non-preemptive* obligation.

An important aspect of obligations that differentiates them from other types of constraints is that an obligation can be violated. However, the violation of an obligation

---

[2] The definition is taken from the glossary created by the OASIS LegalRuleML workgroup http://www.oasis-open.org/apps/org/workgroup/legalruleml

does not necessarily mean the termination of interaction of a business process because some violations can be compensated for while keeping the underlying process still compliant [9,11]. However, not all violations are compensable, and an uncompensated violation would mean the process is non-complaint. If an obligation persists after being violated, it is a *perdurant obligation* if not then we have a *non-perdurant obligation*.

Next we formally define the meanings of the obligations, all we need is the concept of timeline, i.e., a (possibly infinite[3]) totally ordered discrete set of time points. Also, we assume that the timeline has a minimum. In what follows, we assume the existence of a logical language $\mathfrak{L}$ (can be a set of atomic propositions) on which the formulas are written to model obligations and the representation of the environment.

Definition 1 (State). *Given a timeline, we define a function* $State: \mathbb{N} \mapsto 2^{\mathfrak{L}}$.

The meaning of the function *State* is to identify what formulas are evaluated as true at the n-th time instant of a timeline.

Definition 2 (Obligation in Force). *Given a timeline, we define a function* $Force: \mathbb{N} \mapsto 2^{\mathfrak{L}}$.

The meaning of the function *Force* is to identify the obligations in force at the n-th instant of time in a given timeline.

Definition 3 (Punctual Obligation). *Given a timeline, an obligation o is a punctual obligation if and only if:*

$$\exists n \in \mathbb{N} : o \notin Force(n-1), o \notin Force(n+1), o \in Force(n)$$

A punctual obligation is violated at n if and only if $o \notin State(n)$.

The conditions of a *punctual obligation* must be fulfilled immediately otherwise we have a violation i.e., o is violated at time n if o is not true at n (or at the n-th instant of time in the timeline).

Definition 4 (Persistent Obligation). *Given a timeline, an obligation o is a persistent obligation if and only if:*

$$\exists n, m \in \mathbb{N} : n < m, o \notin Force(n-1), o \notin Force(m+1),$$
$$\forall k : n \leq k \leq m, o \in Force(k)$$

The obligation o is in force *between n and m.*

A *persistent obligation* is an obligation in force in an interval time, and can be further classified as: (a) *achievement*, and (b) *maintenance* obligation. The violation conditions for a persistent obligation can be derived from the violation conditions of these subclasses.

Definition 5 (Achievement Obligation). *Given a timeline, an obligation o is an achievement obligation if and only if $\exists n, m \in \mathbb{N}$, $n < m$ such that o is a persistent obligation in force between n and m.*

An achievement obligation o in force between n and m is violated if and only if:

---

[3] Notice an infinite timeline is isomorphic to the set of natural numbers (and we can restrict to a finite set of natural numbers in case of a finite timeline).

- o is preemptive and $\forall k : k \leq m, o \notin State(k)$;
- o is non-preemptive and $\forall k : n \leq k \leq m, o \notin State(k)$.

An *achievement obligation* is in force in an interval in the timeline, and can be further classified as: *preemptive* and *non-preemptive*. A preemptive achievement obligation o is an obligation that can be fulfilled even before the obligation is actually in force. In contrast, a non-preemptive achievement obligation can be discharged only after it enters in force. The violation of an achievement obligation depends on whether we have a preemptive or non-preemptive obligation. Notice that the violation of an achievement obligation can only be asserted after the deadline.

Definition 6 (Maintenance Obligation). *Given a timeline, an obligation o is a maintenance obligation if and only if $\exists n, m \in \mathbb{N}, n < m$ such that o is a persistent obligation in force between n and m.*

A maintenance obligation o in force between n and m is violated if and only if

$$\exists k : n \leq k \leq m, o \notin State(k).$$

Unlike achievement obligations, a *maintenance obligation* must be complied with for all the instances between the interval otherwise we have a violation. Also, no deadline is required for a maintenance obligation insofar we do not need it to detect a violation. The deadline signal that after that instant the obligation is no longer in force. Furthermore it is possible to define maintenance obligation without a deadline, meaning the that the obligation remains in force forever after its activation; for this case, one has to drop the reference to instant m in the above definition.

The next three definitions capture the notion of compensation of a violation. A compensation is a set of obligations that are in force after a violation of an obligation, and fulfilling them makes amend for the violation.

Definition 7 (Compensation). *A compensation is a function Comp: $\mathcal{L} \mapsto 2^{\mathcal{L}}$.*

The intuition behind the function *Comp* is that it associates to each formula a set of formulas, meaning that if a formula corresponds to an obligation, and the obligation is violated, then the violation is compensated (or excused) by the formulas associated to the obligation. This is formalised by the next definition.

Definition 8 (Compensable). *Given a timeline, an obligation o is compensable if and only if $Comp(o) \neq \emptyset$ and $\forall o' \in Comp(o), \exists n \in \mathbb{N} : o' \in Force(n)$.*

Notice that we have two requirements for an obligation to be compensable: the first is that there are ways to make amend i.e., that $Comp \neq \emptyset$, and the second is that the actions that compensate are recognised as such (they are obligations in force) or they are not forbidden. Finally, in the most general form, there are no temporal requirements on when the compensation happens.[4]

Since the compensations are obligations themselves they can be further violated, accordingly they can be compensated for the violations as well, thus a recursive definition of a compensated obligation is required.

---

[4] In vast majority of cases, it is expected that the compensatory obligations are in force after the violation. However, the definition above does not exclude retroactive compensations.

Definition 9 (Compensated Obligation). *Given a timeline, an obligation o is compensated if and only if it is violated and for every $o' \in Comp(o)$ either: 1. o' is not violated; 2. o' is compensated.*

For a stricter notion, i.e., a compensated compensation does not amend the violation the compensation was meant to compensate, we can simply remove the recursive call, thus removing 2 from the above condition.

The last type of obligation is that of *perdurant obligation*. The idea is that when an obligation is violated, the violated obligation is not terminated yet remains in force. Given the conditions of primary obligation an obligation may perdure no matter how many times the obligation has been violated. The violation of a perdurant obligation results in penalty for which one has to consider the original obligation as well as penalties associated with the violation.

Definition 10 (Perdurant). *Given a timeline, an obligation o is a perdurant obligation with a deadline d if and only if o is in force between n and m, and $n < d < m$.*

A perdurant obligation o with a deadline d in force between n and m is violated if and only if

$$\forall j, j \leq d, o \notin State(j)$$

3 Event Calculus

The Event Calculus [14] is a well known event based formalism for reasoning about '*events and change*' and the '*effects of change*' resulting from the occurrence of events over time. EC provides a set of rich axioms for capturing the behaviour of dynamic occurrences of both domain dependent and domain independent events. Hence the formalism is particularly suitable to model the behaviour of a variety of dynamic systems. It is based on the idea of the state that time-varying properties of the world, called fluents hold at particular time-points initiated by some event at an earlier time, and not terminated by some other event between that time period. Accordingly, a fluent does not hold at some time if it was previously terminated and not resumed during that time [15]. In contrast, domain dependent axioms illustrate the situations under which an event initiates and terminates. In this paper, we make use of the predicates and axioms depicted in Table 1 from [16]. The language provides predicates expressing the various states of an event occurrence, e.g., *Happens* (occurrence of an event at a time point), *Initiates* (an event triggers the property of the system), *Terminates* (an event terminates the property of the system), and *HoldsAt* (that the property of the system holds at a point of time). In addition, some auxiliary predicates to express premature termination (*Clipped*) and resumption (*Declipped*) of a fluent at a particular point of time between the time interval are given. The *InitiallyTrue* and *InitiallyFalse* allow for the modeling of system's state where only partial information about the domain is available. In contrast, the domain independent axioms describe the states when a fluent holds or does not hold at particular point of time.

For example, consider the following axioms [16]:

$$HoldsAt(P,T_2) \leftarrow Happens(P,T_1) \wedge Initiates(X,P,T_1) \wedge$$
$$\neg Clipped(T_1,P,T_2) \wedge (T_1 < T_2) \tag{A1}$$

Table 1. Predicates and Axioms of the EC and meanings

Basic Predicates	
$InitiallyTrue(P)$	The fluent P is true from the beginning of time.
$InitiallyFalse(P)$	The fluent P is false from the beginning of time.
$Happens(X,T)$	Event X occurs at time T.
$Initiates(X,P,T)$	Event X initiates the variable (fluent) P at time T.
$HoldsAt(P,T)$	The variable (fluent) P holds at time T.
$Terminates(X,P,T)$	Event X terminates the variable (fluent) P at time T
Auxiliary Predicates	
▮▮▮▮▮▮▮▮▮▮	The variable (fluent) P is interrupted sometime between T_1 and T_2.
$Declipped(T_1,P,T_2)$	The variable (fluent) P is resumed/initiated sometime between T_1 and T_2.
Domain Independent Axioms	
▮▮▮▮▮▮▮▮▮▮	$HoldsAt(P,T_1) \wedge (T_1 < T_2) \wedge \neg Clipped(T_1,P,T_2)$
$HoldsAt(P,T_2) \leftarrow$	$Happens(P,T_1) \wedge Initiates(X,P,T_1) \wedge$ $\neg Clipped(T_1,P,T_2) \wedge (T_1 < T_2)$
$\neg HoldsAt(P,T_2) \leftarrow$	$Happens(X,T_1) \wedge Terminates(X,P,T_1) \wedge$ $(T_1 < T_2) \wedge \neg Declipped(T_1,P,T_2)$
$\neg HoldsAt(P,T_2) \leftarrow$	$\neg HoldsAt(P,T_1) \wedge (T_1 < T_2) \wedge \neg Declipped(T_1,P,T_2)$
$Clipped(T_1,P,T_2) \equiv$	$\exists X,T : Happens(X,T) \wedge (T_1 \leq T < T_2) \wedge$ $Terminates(X,P,T)$
$Declipped(T_1,P,T_2) \equiv$	$\exists X,T : Happens(X,T) \wedge (T_1 \leq T < T_2) \wedge$ $Initiates(X,P,T)$

The (Axiom A1) states that the fluent P continues to hold until an event that terminates it occurs, provided that there was an event that happened at some previous time which was a trigger for the fluent.

$$\neg HoldsAt(P,T_2) \leftarrow Happens(X,T_1) \wedge Terminates(X,P,T_1) \wedge \\ (T_1 < T_2) \wedge \neg Declipped(T_1,P,T_2) \tag{A2}$$

Whereas (Axiom A2) states that fluent P that has been terminated by the event X continues not to hold until it is resumed by some other event occurrence.

The above axiomatisation can be used to model the non-deterministic behaviour of a system thus EC is suitable for modeling obligations that can be effected by unpredictable situations. However, as was noted earlier in Section 1, an obligation might not enter into force immediately after the occurrence of an event rather after some time delay. A second problem is that the base predicate *Initiates* does not gurantee that the fluent in its arguments is actually *initiated* by the event. Suppose that the domain dependent axioms specify that both the events E_1 and E_2 individually initiate the fluent P, and event E_1 happens at time 10 and event E_2 at time 20, P does not holds initially and no other event initiates or terminates fluent P between 0 and 30. This means that P starts to hold from 11 and continues to hold up to 30, and event E_2 is irrelevant to determine the status of P. Also, there are cases where an obligation enters in force at the same time of initiating an event (and not the next time instant).

4   Modeling Obligations with Event Calculus

In this section we propose a set of axioms to extend the EC to model the various obligation classes of the classification model described in Section 2.

As we have seen at the end of the previous section, the standard *Initiates* and *HoldsAt* predicates of EC present some shortcomings for modelling obligations. To obviate these problems, we introduce a new 'deontically holds at' predicate $DHoldsAt(P,T)$ meaning that the 'deontic fluent', i.e., a particular type of obligation, P holds at time T. The main difference with the standard EC *HoldsAt* predicate is on the conditions of *initiation*. Each obligation has its own specific triggering events, and the happening of one of those triggering events initiates the obligation. In addition, there could be a delay (which could be null) between the time the triggering event happens and the time obligation enters in to force. A triggering event for an obligation is represented by $trigger(O^{x,T}X,N)$, where $O^{x,T}X$ is a deontic fluent, and N the delay. $O^{x,T}$ [5] represents the type of the obligation (see Section 2) and the time when the obligation enters in force T, X is a variable attached to the obligation representing the contents of the obligation, which can be either an event or a fluent, and N is the delay. As we said above the purpose of the triggering event is to initiate the obligation. For a trigger to be effective, one has to specify the conditions defining the trigger for an obligation. Also, the delay must be specified because the delay determines the difference in time from when the triggering event occurs and when the obligation enters into force.

For the termination of deontic fluents we introduce the new predicate $DTerminates(E,P,N,T_{ter})$ meaning that an event E deontically terminates the fluent P, with some delay N, at time T_{ter}. The delay N define the time distance from when the terminating event happens and the actual termination of the deontic fluent. After a deontic termination an obligation has no legal effects on the execution of the process from the time it is terminated. Also for specifying the deadlines for obligations, in the same say, we define a special deadline-triggering event $deadline(O^{x,T}X,T_d)$, where $O^{x,T}$ and X are the arguments for deadline event and serve as triggering events and T_d represents the time of the deadline event occurrence. The purpose of the deadline event is to signal the time (deadline) until when the obligation conditions must be fulfilled, a violation of the obligation conditions is triggered otherwise.

We provide generic axioms that we need to model the obligations. These axioms provide the conditions for no legal effects (not deontically Holds) after the termination of an obligation (Axiom A3) and the conditions when no fluent deontically holds (Axiom A4).

$$\neg DHoldsAt(X,T+1) \leftarrow \exists E : DTerminates(E,X,N,T) \tag{A3}$$

$$\neg DHoldsAt(X,T_k) \leftarrow \neg DHoldsAt(X,T) \wedge \neg Happens(trigger(X,N),T_j) \wedge \atop (T \leq T_k) \wedge (T \leq T_j + N \leq T_k) \tag{A4}$$

In what follows we will have several cases where the trigger for an obligation does not only trigger the initiation for the obligation but also the termination. This means that we have to write expression with the following form

$$DTerminates(trigger(P,N),P,N,T) \tag{1}$$

---

[5] Notice $O^{x,T}$ has only one time stamp because one can be certain that an obligation holds after deontically initiated but one cannot be certain when it is going to be terminated.

where we have to repeat twice the parameters P and N. To ease readability we will use the convention of dropping the P and N from the arguments *DTerminates*, using thus

$$DTerminates(trigger(P,N),T) \tag{2}$$

The reader should keep in mind that (2) is a shorthand for (1).

4.1 Punctual Obligation

The axioms describing when a punctual obligation holds are the following:

$$DHoldsAt(O^{p,T_s}X, T_s) \leftarrow$$
$$\exists T_t, N : Happens(trigger(O^{p,T_s}X, N), T_t) \wedge \tag{A5}$$
$$(T_s = T_t + N) \wedge N \geq 0$$

$$DTerminates(trigger(O^{p,T_s}X, N), T_s) \leftarrow$$
$$\exists T_t, N : Happens(trigger(O^{p,T_s}X, N), T_t) \wedge \tag{A6}$$
$$(T_s = T_t + N) \wedge N \geq 0$$

Let us examine in details the above axioms. An obligation is represented as a fluent; specifically the (punctual) obligation of X is represented by the fluent $O^{p,T_s}X$ where O^{p,T_s} is an obligation modality (a specific type of the obligation) and time when the obligation enters into force (T_s), and X is a variable referring the contents of obligation. In addition, we create a special event $trigger(O^xY, N)$ whose meaning is to initiate the obligation. In this way, all one has to do is to specify when an obligation enters in force by defining the conditions for the trigger. Axiom (A6) specifies that the same event that triggers the obligation, terminates the obligation, and obligation terminates in the same time instant when it is initiated. Thus in combination with (Axiom (A3)) we have a punctual obligation is in force for only one time instant. The axiom specifying when a punctual obligation is violated is:

$$Happens(violation(O^{p,T_s}X), T_v) \leftarrow$$
$$DHoldsAt(O^{p,T_s}X, T_s) \wedge \tag{A7}$$
$$\neg Happens(X, T_s) \wedge \neg HoldsAt(X, T_s) \wedge (T_v = T_s)$$

The violation of a punctual obligation happens when we do not have the content of the obligation at the right time. This can happen in two cases: (a) *the content is a fluent and it does not hold at the time*; or (b) *it is an event and it does not happens at the time.*[6]

Notice that we introduce a violation event $(violation(O^{p,T_v}X))$.

Example 1. Australian Telecommunications Consumers Protection Code 2012 (TCPC 2012). Article 8.2.1.

A Supplier must take the following actions to enable this outcome:

(a) **Demonstrate fairness, courtesy, objectivity and efficiency:** Suppliers must demonstrate, fairness and courtesy, objectivity, and efficiency by:

    (i) Acknowledging a Complaint:

---

[6] To capture that nothing is both and event and a fluent we add the axiom $\bot \leftarrow Happens(X,T) \wedge HoldsAt(X,T')$.

    A. immediately where the Complaint is made in person or by telephone;

    B. within 2 Working Days of receipt where the Complaint is made by email;

    ....

Consider the clause (A) of the Article 8.2.1 where the obligation must be fulfilled immediately. This can be modeled as:

$$Happens(trigger(O^{p,T}Acknowledge,0),T) \leftarrow$$
$$Happens(Complaint,T) \wedge \qquad\qquad (3)$$
$$(HoldsAt(inPerson,T) \vee HoldsAt(byPhone,T))$$

Suppose there is an event *Complaint* at time T and the fluent *byPhone* holds at the same time. Then from the domain Axiom (3), we derive $trigger(O^{p,T}Acknowledge,0),T)$, and then from Axioms: (A5), (A6) and (A3) we obtain $DHoldsAt(O^{p,T}Acknowledge,T)$ and $\neg DHoldsAt(O^{p,T}Acknowledge,T+1)$. Meaning that the obligation to acknowledge the complaint on reception of it. Moreover, suppose that we model the acknowledgement as an event, and we have $Happens(Acknowledge,T)$, then the conditions for having a violation do not hold. Suppose now that $Happens(Acknowledge,T)$ is not true, i.e., the complaint is not acknolwedged, thus $\neg Happens(Acknowledge,T)$ is true. In addition, given that *Acknowledge* is an event, if we have $\neg HoldsAt(Acknowledge,T)$, then, we can use Axiom (A7) to conclude that the obligation to acknowledge a complaint by phone on the spot has been violated.

4.2 Persistent Obligation

The following axiom describes a persistent obligation with a natural deadline when the fluent holds in interval:[7]

$$DHoldsAt(O^{per,T_s}X,T_k) \leftarrow$$
$$\exists T_t,N : Happens(trigger(O^{per,T_s}X,N),T_t) \wedge$$
$$\neg DClipped(T_s,O^{per,T_s}X,T_k) \wedge \qquad\qquad (A8)$$
$$DTerminates(trigger(O^{per,T_s}X,N),T_e) \wedge$$
$$(T_s = T_t + N) \wedge (T_e > T_s) \wedge (T_s \leq T_k \leq T_e) \wedge N \geq 0$$

By '*natural deadline*' we mean that if no other (relevant) event happens the obligation is in force from the T_s and T_e, and that T_e is determined by the same event that triggers the (persistent) obligation.

Achievement Obligation. An achievement obligation is a special case of a persistent obligation where there might not be a natural deadline for the obligation. Hence there are two cases for achievement obligations:

(i) *when the obligation has no termination point*, i.e., initiation of achievement obligation.

$$DHoldsAt(O^{a,T_s}X,T_s) \leftarrow$$
$$\exists T_t,N : Happens(trigger(O^{a,T_s}X,N),T_t) \wedge (T_s = T_t + N) \wedge N \geq 0 \qquad (A9)$$

---

[7] The defintion of *DClipped* is the same as that for *Clipped* where *Terminates* is replaced by *DTerminates*.

(ii) *The obligation Holds at a particular time point deontically initiated and not clipped between the interval*, i.e., start time and the point until it holds.

$$
\begin{aligned}
&DHoldsAt(O^{a,T_s}X,T_k) \leftarrow \\
&\quad DHoldsAt(O^{a,T_s}X,T_s) \wedge \neg DClipped(T_s,O^{a,T_s}X,T_k) \wedge (T_s \leq T_k)
\end{aligned} \quad \text{(A10)}
$$

There are two cases of the termination of an achievement obligation:

1. An arbitrary event terminates the obligation when the obligation conditions are fulfilled before the deadline of obligation.

$$
\begin{aligned}
&DTerminates(\_,O^{a,T_s}X,N,T_k) \leftarrow \\
&\quad Happens(\_,T_k) \wedge DHoldsAt(O^{a,T_s}X,T_k) \wedge \\
&\quad (Happens(X,T_k) \vee HoldsAt(X,T_k)) \wedge \\
&\quad FulfillTerminable(O^{a,T_s}X) \wedge (T_s \leq T_k)
\end{aligned} \quad \text{(A11)}
$$

The symbol '$\_$' represents an arbitrary event, which can be anything, e.g., a new obligation, an activity or even a deadline etc., that terminates the obligation.

2. Where the deadline itself terminates the obligation.

$$
\begin{aligned}
&DTerminates(deadline(O^{a,T_s}X,T_d),T_d) \leftarrow \\
&\quad Happens(deadline(O^{a,T_s}X),T_d) \wedge (T_s \leq T_d)
\end{aligned} \quad \text{(A12)}
$$

The axiom for the termination of a preemptive obligation is:

$$
\begin{aligned}
&DTerminates(\_,O^{a,T_s}X,N,T_e) \leftarrow \\
&\quad Happens(\_,T_e) \wedge DHoldsAt(O^{a,T_s}X,T_s) \wedge \\
&\quad \exists T' : (Happens(X,T') \vee HoldsAt(X,T')) \wedge \\
&\quad FulfillTerminable(O^{a,T_s}X) \wedge \\
&\quad (T_e = T_s + 1) \wedge (T' < T_s)
\end{aligned} \quad \text{(A13)}
$$

The predicate '*FulfillTerminable*' is a boolean switch that allows for checking whether or not the obligation can be terminated upon fulfillment. This leave us to determine the conditions under which we have a violation of an achievement obligation. To this end we need a special event $deadline(O^{a,T_s}X)$ signaling the deadline after which a violation occurs if the achievement is not fulfilled by that time/event.

$$
\begin{aligned}
&Happens(violation(O^{a,T_s}X),T_v) \leftarrow \\
&\quad DHoldsAt(O^{a,T_s}X,T_e) \wedge \\
&\quad Happens(deadline(O^{a,T_s}X),T_e) \wedge \\
&\quad (\neg Happens(X,T_e) \wedge \neg HoldsAt(X,T_e)) \wedge \\
&\quad FulfillTerminable(O^{a,T_s}X) \wedge (T_v = T_e)
\end{aligned} \quad \text{(A14)}
$$

Maintenance Obligation. Maintenance is another case of persistent obligation where it is different from achievement in the sense that the obligation conditions must be fulfilled for every instance of the interval the obligation is in force. The (Axiom A8) can represent the maintenance obligation. Contrary to achievement obligation, a maintenance obligation is violated if the obligation contents are not fulfilled for all the instances.

$$Happens(violation(O^{m,T_s}X),T_k) \leftarrow$$
$$DHoldsAt(O^{m,T_s}X,T_k) \land \tag{A15}$$
$$\neg Happens(X,T_k) \land \neg HoldsAt(X,T_k) \land (T_s \leq T_k)$$

The violation of a maintenance obligation may terminate the obligation if the obligation is *'ViolationTerminable'* which is again a boolean switch for checking whether a maintenance obligation can be terminated upon violation. The conditions for termination after the violation are:

$$DTerminates(O^{m,T_s}X,T_v) \leftarrow$$
$$Happens(violation(O^{m,T_s}X),T_v) \land \tag{A16}$$
$$ViolationTerminable(O^{m,T_s}X)$$

For a non-perdurant maintenance obligation the violation of the obligation itself terminates the obligation.

$$DTerminates(violation(O^{m,T_v}X),T_v) \leftarrow$$
$$DHoldsAt(O^{m,T_v}X,t_v) \land ViolationTerminable(O^{m,T_s}X) \land \tag{A17}$$
$$Happens(violation(O^{m,T_s}X),T_v) \land (T_s \leq T_v)$$

4.3   Compensation Obligation

A compensation is an obligation itself. The event triggering a compensation is the violation of a norm compensation compensates. Thus, we have domain specific axioms for the two case of compensation:

– *Compensation of the violation by a single obligation*:

$$Happens(compensation(O^{x,T_s}P),T_{s_c}) \leftarrow$$
$$\exists O^{y,T_{s_c}}Q : (Compensates(O^{y,T_{s_c}}Q,O^{x,T_s}P),T_{s_c}) \land$$
$$Happens(violation(O^{x,T_s}P),T_v) \land \tag{A18}$$
$$DHoldsAt(O^{y,T_{s_c}}Q,T_{s_c}) \land$$
$$(Happens(Q,T_{s_c}) \lor HoldsAt(Q,T_{s_c})) \land (T_s \leq T_v \leq T_{s_c})$$

– *Recursive compensation when a compensation obligation itself is violated*:

$$Happens(compensation(O^{x,T_s}P),T_{s_c}) \leftarrow$$
$$Compensates(O^{y,T_{s_c}}Q,O^{x,T_s}P) \land$$
$$Happens(violation(O^{y,T_{s_c}}Q),T_v) \land \tag{A19}$$
$$Happens(compensation(O^{y,T_{s_c}}Q),T_z) \land$$
$$RecursivelyCompensable(O^{x,T_s}P) \land (T_s \leq T_{s_c} \leq T_z) \land (T_v \leq T_z)$$

For the two axioms above we have to introduce the special event *compensation*, indicating that a (violated) deontic fluent has been compensated for, and the binary predicate *Compensates* where the two arguments are two deontic fluents. The meaning of *Compensates* is that fulfilling the first deontic fluent make amend to the violation of the second deontic fluents and implements the *Comp* function introduced in Section 2, Definition 7. Again the predicate *RecursivelyCompensable* is a boolean switch meant to capture the intuition given by condition 2 of Definition 9.

5   Proof Sketches of Correctness

The aim of this section is to show how to prove the correctness of our formalisation of norms in EC and the classificatory conditions of Section 2. For space reasons we provide only the proof sketch of the axioms for punctual obligation. The proofs for the remaining axioms are essentially similar.

First we introduce some base conditions relating to the basic predicates of EC and the functions *Force* and *State* providing thus the basic bridge between the axiomatisation in Section 4 and the conditions in Section 2.

C1. $HoldsAt(X,T)$ if and only if $X \in State(T)$,
C2. $Happens(X,T)$ if and only if $X \in State(T)$,
C3. $DHoldsAt(X,T)$ if and only if $X \in Force(T)$.

Lemma 1 (Punctual Obligation). *If $DHoldsAt(O^{p,T_s}X,T_s)$ is true, then X is a punctual obligation in Force at time T_s, $X \in Force(T_s)$*

Proof (Sketch). By Definition 3 the semantics of a punctual obligation is given by (A) $o \in Force(n)$, (B) $o \notin Force(n-1)$, (C) $o \notin Force(n+1)$. Suppose, we have the right hand side of Axiom A5, from this we obtain $DHoldsAt(O^{p,T_s}X,T_s)$, then from condition $C3$ we have $DHoldsAt(X,T)$ if and only if $X \in Force(T)$ which is equivalent to $X \in Force(T_s)$, and then $\exists n$ such that $X \in Force(n)$. This satisfies (A).

For (B), we assume that $\neg DHoldsAt(O^{p,T_s}X,0)$, where 0 is the initial time instant. By Axiom A4 this guarantees that the fluent $O^{p,T_s}X$ is not in *Force* function before the time, i.e., T_s. This means that $X \notin Force(t)$, for $0 \le t < T_s$; hence $X \notin Force(T_s-1)$. This satisfies condition (B).

Given that the right hand side of Axiom A6 is the same as that of Axiom A5, we have $DTerminates(trigger(O^{p,T_s}X,N),T_s)$. From Axiom A3 we conclude $\neg DHoldsAt(O^{p,T_s}X,T_s+1)$. From condition C3 above we get $X \notin Force(T_s+1)$, which satisfies conditions (C).

Lemma 2 (Violation of Punctual Obligation). *If $Happens(violation(O^{p,T_s}X),T_s)$ is true, then X is a punctual obligation in force at time T_s, and $X \notin State(T_s)$.*

Proof (Sketch). To have a violation of a punctual obligation o, conditions (A), (B), (C) of Lemma 1 have to be satisfied and the additional condition (D) $o \notin State(n)$. That $Happens(violation(O^{p,T_s}X),T_s)$ is true means that also the right hand side of Axiom A7 is true. Thus we have $DHoldsAt(O^{p,T_s}X,T_s)$, from which we conclude the $X \in Force(T_s)$ by Lemma 1 above. In addition we have $\neg HoldsAt(X,T_s)$ and $\neg Happens(X,T_s)$ from which by conditions C1 and C2 above we conclude $X \notin State(T_s)$. This satisfies condition (D).

6   Related Work

In [6], EC is used to express temporal rules about the obligations and permissions in a business process interaction. Rich axioms that translate the temporal properties of deontic assignments and capture the effects of activities of obligations and permissions on the agents have been proposed. The study is limited in scope because it only covers obligations and permissions while other obligations types have been left out. Also, the temporal validity of an obligation and its effects on the violation, as presented in our work, has not been considered. Such parameters and ability to faithfully model obligations, and capture the effects of violations is imperative from a business process compliance checking perspective. [4] provides formal specifications of commitments and precommitments, instutionalised power and context using EC. The formal representation of norms is limited to obligations and permissions only as in [6]. No explicit distinction between the different types of obligations and effects of the violation on obligations has been made, as made in this work, although the notion of sanctions has been formally presented in the study.

[2] translates both the policies and system behaviour specifications into formal specifications using EC. The proposed formal specifications are expressive enough to efficiently model the systems using various types of policies representing obligations. These formal specifications can be used, together with abductive reasoning, for detecting and representing the conflicts between the policy specifications (particularly those related to the authorisation and permissions). These specifications are useful in the sense that a priori knowledge about the event and/or fluent's state can be used to simplify the representation of preemptive obligations but we do not consider the a priori knowledge of events/fluents instead we use the notion of preemptiveness to distinguish different cases of the violation of an achievement obligation and model it in EC. [1] proposes a norms representation approach using EC enabling the agents to use norms in their practical reasoning. The work considers only two classes of norms: *obligations* and *prohibitions* for which authors introduced three fluents i.e., *fPun* and *oPun* referring obligation norm violation and prohibition norm violation respectively, and *oRew* for obligation fulfillment. The scope of this work is limited because it only considers obligations and ignores the obligations modalities as we do. Also, the Anderson's reduction view of norm which suggests that every violation of a norm is followed by a sanction [20] has been used. We argue that initially not in every case sanctions are/can be directly imposed as under a sub-ideal situation processes can still be compliant [11]. The notions of compensation and obligations perduring after the violation as defined in our work are the norms types that strengthen this argument.

7 Final Remarks

In this paper we formally modeled the various types of obligations using classical EC. We used these obligations types from our previously proposed classification model, and introduced a triggering event (*trigger*) with some time delay replacing the *Initiates*, base predicate of the EC. The aim of the triggering event is to capture the deontic effects of obligations from when they enter into force not from when the event is triggered, which in our view is not possible with the existing variants of EC. The new predicates extend the expressive power of the EC and make it possible to model all types of legal norms. We are currently working on an implementation to validate the computational efficiency of the proposed extension to EC. Accordingly, we plan to continue this work and check the expressive power of various formalisms e.g., temporal logic, first-order-logic and defeasible and deontic logic. Also, we will look at the *state of affairs* in the formal modeling of the legal knowledge and what is lacking in this direction.

References

1. Alrawagfeh, W.: Norm Representation and Reasoning: A Formalization in Event Calculus. In: Boella, G., Elkind, E., Savarimuthu, B.T.R., Dignum, F., Purvis, M.K. (eds.) PRIMA 2013. LNCS (LNAI), vol. 8291, pp. 5–20. Springer, Heidelberg (2013)
2. Bandara, A., Lupu, E., Russo, A.: Using Event Calculus to Formalise Policy Specification and Analysis. In: POLICY 2003, pp. 26–39 (2003)
3. DECLARE. Declarative Process Models, http://www.win.tue.nl/declare/
4. Fornara, N., Colombetti, M.: Specifying artificial institutions in the event calculus. In: Handbook of Research on Multi-Agent Systems: Sematnics and Dynamics of Organisational Models, pp. 335–366. IGI Global (2009)
5. Goedertier, S., Vanthienen, J.: Business Rules for Compliant Business Process Models. In: BIS 2006. LNI, vol. P-85, pp. 558–579. Gesellschaft für Informatik (2006)
6. Goedertier, S., Vanthienen, J.: Designing Compliant Business Processes with Obligations and Permissions. In: Eder, J., Dustdar, S. (eds.) BPM Workshops 2006. LNCS, vol. 4103, pp. 5–14. Springer, Heidelberg (2006)
7. Governatori, G.: Business Process Compliance: An Abstract Normative Framework. It-Information Technoloby 55(6), 231–238 (2013)
8. Governatori, G., Hulstijn, J., Riveret, R., Rotolo, A.: Characterising Deadlines in Temporal Modal Defeasible Logic. In: Orgun, M.A., Thornton, J. (eds.) AI 2007. LNCS (LNAI), vol. 4830, pp. 486–496. Springer, Heidelberg (2007)
9. Governatori, G., Milosevic, Z.: Dealing with Contract Violations: Formalism and Domain Specific Language. In: EDOC 2005, pp. 46–57. IEEE Computer Society (2005)
10. Governatori, G., Rotolo, A., Sartor, G.: Temporalised Normative Positions in Defeasible Logic. In: ICAIL 2005, pp. 25–34. ACM (2005)
11. Governatori, G., Sadiq, S.: The Journey to Business Process Compliance. In: Handbook of Research on Business Process Management, pp. 426–454. IGI Global (2009)
12. Hashmi, M., Governatori, G., Wynn, M.T.: Normative Requirements for Business Process Compliance. In: Davis, J.G., Demirkan, H., Motahari-Nezhad, H.R. (eds.) ASSRI 2013. LNBIP, vol. 177, pp. 100–116. Springer, Heidelberg (2013)
13. Hilty, M., Basin, D., Pretschner, A.: On Obligations. In: de Capitani di Vimercati, S., Syverson, P., Gollmann, D. (eds.) ESORICS 2005. LNCS, vol. 3679, pp. 98–117. Springer, Heidelberg (2005)
14. Kowalski, R., Sergot, M.: A Logic-Based Calculus of Events. In: Schmidt, J., Thanos, C. (eds.) Foundations of Knowledge Base Management. Topics in Information Systems, pp. 23–55. Springer (1989)
15. Miller, R., Shanahan, M.: The Event Calculus in Classical Logic - Alternative Axiomatisations. Electron. Trans. Artif. Intell. 3(A), 77–105 (1999)
16. Miller, R., Shanahan, M.: Some Alternative Formulations of the Event-Calculus. In: Kakas, A.C., Sadri, F. (eds.) Computat. Logic (Kowalski Festschrift). LNCS (LNAI), vol. 2408, pp. 452–490. Springer, Heidelberg (2002)
17. Palmirani, M., Governatori, G., Contissa, G.: Modelling Temporal Legal Rules. In: ICAIL, pp. 131–135 (2011)
18. Sadri, F., Kowalski, R.: Variants of the Event Calculus. In: Sterling, L. (ed.) Proceedings of the Twelth International Conference on Logic Programming. MIT, Cambridge (1995)
19. Sartor, G.: Legal Reasoning: A Cognitive Approach to the Law. Springer (2005)
20. Soeteman, A.: Pluralism and Law. In: Proceedings of the 20th IVR World Congress of the Int'l Association of Philosophy of Law and Social Philosophy, vol. 4, p. 104 (2001)

A Process for Knowledge Transformation and Knowledge Representation of Patent Law

Shashishekar Ramakrishna and Adrian Paschke

Department of Computer Science Freie Universität Berlin,
Königin-Luise-Str. 24-26, 14195 Berlin, Germany
shashi792@gmail.com, paschke@inf.fu-berlin.de

Abstract. Automated support to model and reason based on such modeled legal norms using expert systems, for its use scenarios such as court-fillings or argumentation has increasingly become a subject of interest in last few decades. The core problem in all such automation is removing the vagueness embedded within legal texts/sections and this vagueness is due to the pragmatics involved. As of today, we believe, it is impossible for a system to handle any such problems dealing with legal pragmatics. This work proposes a process which acts a bridge between a legal practitioner can and a knowledge modeler wherein, a legal practitioner provides the legal information pertaining to a section in a simpler form as required by the modeler. We also propose several knowledge representation formats to represent the information at each layer of the proposed process. Additionally during the course of the paper, we propose a mapping scheme from legal norms in natural language format to Controlled Natural Language (CNL) format and finally to a platform independent rule representation format.

Keywords: Elementary Pragmatics, LegalDocML, SBVR, Structured English, Legal Norms, LegalRuleML.

1 Introduction

In general, laws are designed to be vague. Their vagueness is to accommodate different possible scenarios under which a law can be applied. Pragmatics is an important aspect in the legal domain. It explains the context in which such laws are being applied. Pragmatics within law/legal texts is both boon and bane. The use of pragmatics in applying the laws to different scenarios is good, when viewed from a legal practitioner perspective and the same pragmatics is hard to deal with for a legal knowledge engineer who needs to model it in a precise Knowledge Representation (KR) for (semi/-)automated legal reasoning systems.

The negative aspects of pragmatics is due to the difficulty involved in separating their concerns. In this paper, we propose a process which deals with the disaggregation of a law and their legal sections into elementary norms with Elementary Pragmatics (EP). The process provides the required degree of separation (i.e. separation into elementary concern) sufficient enough to minimize

A. Bikakis et al. (Eds.): RuleML 2014, LNCS 8620, pp. 311–328, 2014.

the vagueness and thereby making the legal language simple. The different steps of this process require adequate knowledge representation formats which we contribute in this paper.

As a direct contribution this process minimizes the vagueness, which results in a legal language which is simpler than before. Thereby, providing enough information in an elementary form which can be easier represented using rule representation formats, enabling further automated processing down the line (e.g., automated legal argumentation).

The paper is structured as follows: Section 2, discusses the related work. We introduce a running example in Section 4. Sections 5, 6 and 7, deal with annotation, disaggregation and representation of the legal section/example introduced in Section 4 in a computational independent language. We then map such semi-formally represented legal norms to a platform independent legal norm representation format in Section 8. Section 11, provides the conclusion and future directions to this work.

2   Related Work

In [1], we introduced the concept of *Elementary Pragmatics* (EP) in the patent law domain. For the purpose of understanding, we re-iterate only the definitional part of an EP. EPs are considered as disclosures about an 'object' (e.g. patents-norms/precedents/guidelines) of law, with its pragmatics referring to the context in which such an 'object' is understood and applied by a 'reasonable man'[1] [3].

Several methods have been proposed for annotating law/legal documents. Amongst them are EnAct [4], EUR-Lex FORMEX [5], MetaLex [6], Akoma Ntoso [7] etc. We make use of the OASIS LegalDocML standard (which is based on Akomo Ntoso) due to its expressiveness in terms of metadata annotations and its direct compatibility with our further layers of legal knowledge representations using OASIS LegalRuleML. LegalDocML is an standardization under OASIS. It supports the long-term preservation of legal documents (i.e. evolution of laws over time) with their intended meanings, by creating common data and metadata models.

The OMG's Model Driven Architecture (MDA) [8] provides a basis for representing information on different layers of (knowledge) representation models, namely Computation Independent Models (CIM), Platform-Independent Models (PIM) and Platform-Specific Model (PSM). Semantic Business Vocabulary and Business Rules, 'SBVR' [9], is an ISO terminological dictionary (vocabulary) based representation standard for defining business concepts and business rules. SBVR suggests the use of Structured English (SE), a computational-independent English (natural) language having the syntax of a structured declarative programming language for representing business vocabularies and business rules. The adaption of SBVR to the legal domain was proposed by Johnsen and Berre in [10]. In [11] we showed how OMG's MDA layering could be applied in the domain of Intellectual Property (IP) law (with focus in patent law), with a

---

[1] A 'reasonable man' is also a Person Having Ordinary Skill In The Art, '*PHOSITA*' [2].

layered knowledge representation using SBVR-SE on its CIM layer. As a proof-of-concept implementation we presented our KR4IPLaw tool, which enables legal domain experts to represent their knowledge in Structured English. In [12], we further extended KPI4Law with a semi-automated vocabulary recommender functionality which gives automated suggestions for legal concepts computed by a semantic legal text analysis.

LegalRuleML [13], is a standardization under OASIS of a XML-based rule language representation format for legal norm representation on the PIM layer. It integrates into the overarching RuleML language family[2][14] and supports Deliberation RuleML and Reaction RuleML 1.0^3[15,16]. It supports multiple semantic annotations, wherein each legal annotation can represent a different pragmatic context involved with it such as a particular jurisdiction context, temporal context etc. LegalRuleML enables temporal life cycle management of rules. As a part of provenance context, LegalRuleML provides the necessary information for identifying (N:M) relationships between the formalized legal rules to its original sources (textual provisions) and between the original authors and the engineers of the legal KR.

3   Generalized Process

Figure 1 shows the abstract generalized process which we propose for the disaggregation of patent norms and their pragmatics and for the legal knowledge annotation, representation and transformation leading to a formal representation as required for automated reasoning and argumentation. In this section we give an overview on the layers, tools and technologies. The process is general, such that, the input to the process may be any legal text, e.g., a legal section from any National Patent System (NPS), and the output from the process is a formal KR reasoning step, producing conclusions (+ justification proofs), which can be input to existing formal legal argumentation systems.

For our purpose, a legal section from any NPS, e.g., § 112 of US patent law or § 69 of EPC etc., is an input to the process model. Such legal sections are then annotated (manually or with semi-automated annotation support) in step 1 using a legal document markup standards. In addition to the annotation, additional information pertaining to the considered legal section in the form of judgments, opinions, amicus briefs, etc., are annotated. Such additional information provide the necessary additional pragmatic/context information needed to understand the considered legal section. They do not change the legal section itself. Legal sections are changed only through regulations or acts. The core and additional annotations form the metadata of the legal KR. Identification of all associated metadata through an annotation step helps in the structuring and life-cycle management of legal information.

The next step in the process is to deal with the disaggregation of a law/legal sections. For the purpose of this disaggregation, legal sections are converted

---

[2] http://www.ruleml.org
[3] http://reaction.ruleml.org

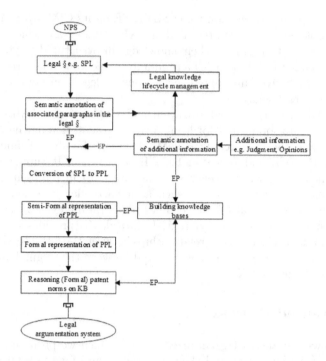

Fig. 1. Generalized process for obtaining elementary norms with EP's

form their substantive form (Substantive Patent Law (SPL)) into a procedural form (Procedural Patent Law (PPL)) using legal decision models, which are procedural decision structures based on the elementary concerns derived from the statutory. These decision models can be represented, e.g., as decision trees or flow-chart-based process models. This provides the required degree of separation (i.e., separation of elementary concerns from complex statutory legal norms) sufficient enough to minimize the vagueness and thereby making the legal language clearer and easier (to enforce).

The next step is to transform such elementary legal norms into a semi-formal knowledge representation format. For this step, we propose a semantic vocabulary-based Controlled Natural Language (CNL), approach for the semi-formal representation on the 'CIM' layer, which acts as a "bridge" between the legal domain experts and the legal knowledge engineers. Continuing the process, the CNL based patent norms are then further transformed and formalized in a rule representation format using the additional metadata from the annotation step. On this PIM layer, we propose using established XML-based knowledge representation standards for the legal data, metadata and legal rules, in order to provide the necessary semi-structuring for machine processing, modularization (e.g., modular publication on the Web), and standardized platform-independent interchange of legal knowledge for re-use in other contexts. Parallel to this transformation steps, a Knowledge Base (KB) with the semantic legal vocabulary and elementary pragmatic knowledge is built and maintained based on the elementary pragmatics obtained during each step of annotation and transformation. Finally for the purpose of reasoning, the formalized elementary patent norms (XML-based) are transformed into a PSM format to allow (semi-)automatic reasoning in the context of the elementary patent pragmatics using the legal knowledge base. The conclusions and proof-justifications derived from the reasoning step can be further used as an input to other existing formal legal reasoning systems, e.g., legal argumentation systems.

In the following sections we will instantiate the proposed process of obtaining and formally representing elementary norms in the context of elementary pragmatics by means of a running example, which is Paragraph 1 of Section 112, of the United States patent law, dealing with the patent enablement.

4 Example

---

35 U.S. Code § 112 - Specification

(a) In General –The specification shall contain a written description of the invention, and of the manner and process of making and using it, in such full, clear, concise, and exact terms as to enable any person skilled in the art to which it pertains, or with which it is most nearly connected, to make and use the same, and shall set forth the best mode contemplated by the inventor or joint inventor of carrying out the invention.

---

5 Annotation

Legal Document Markup Language (LegalDocML) is an standardization under OASIS for managing legal documents. We use LegalDocML, to annotate the legal section described above. We split the annotation into two parts, the context and the content. The context comprises meta-data dealing with the context information of the legal section and the content deals with the actually legal paragraph itself.

The XML listing 1.1 and 1.2, shows the annotation of Section 112 1st Paragraph[4].

```
<akomaNtoso xmlns:xsi="http://www.w3.org/2001/XMLSchema-instance">
    <act contains="singleVersion">...</act>
    <meta>
    <!-- Metadata describing the source, author, country etc.. of the legal section-->
        <identification source="#LII">
            <FRBRWork>
                <FRBRthis value="/us/codes;us/main"/>
                <FRBRdate date="1946" name="creation"/>
                <FRBRcountry value="us"/>
            </FRBRWork>
            <FRBRExpression>
                <FRBRdate value="2014-03-26" name="Generation"/>
                <FRBRauthor href="#LII" as="editor"/>
            </FRBRExpression>
```

---

[4] Due to space restrictions, some XML data has been curtailed.

```
        <FRBRManifestation>   </FRBRManifestation>
    </identification>
<!-- Metadata describing the lifecycle (generation, amendment etc..) of the legal section-->
    <lifecycle source="#FUB">
        <eventRef source="#ref1" id="e1" type="generation" date="1946"/>
        <eventRef source="#ref7" id="e7" type="ammendment" date="2011-09-16"/>
    </lifecycle>
    <temporalData source="#FUB">
        <temporalGroup is="#t8">
            <temporalInterval refersto="#inforce" start="e8"/>
            <temporalInterval refersto="#efficacy" start="e8"/>
        </temporalGroup>
    </temporalData>
<!-- Metadata describing the references used (Role, Organization etc..) of the legal section-->
    <references source="#FUB">
        <original href="/us/codes;us/patentlaw/#title35" showAs=" Title 35, US Code"id="ref1"/>
        <TLCOrganization id="LII" href="/ontology/organizations/LII/"showAs="Cornell University"/>
        <TLCPerson id="FUB" href="/ontology/person/editors/FUB"showAs="Free University of Berlin"/>
    </references>
<!-- Metadata describing the addtional information in the form of notes for the legal section-->
    <notes source="#FUB">
    <note id="#n1"><p> Leahy-Smith America Invents Act: First to file policy.</p></note>
    </notes>
</meta>
```

Listing 1.1. Context annotation of first paragraph of § 112

```
    <preface>
        <block name="preface"><docTitle id="title">United States Code </docTitle></block>
    </preface>
    <body>
      <title id="tit35">
        <num>Title 35</num>
        <heading>PATENTS</heading>
        <section id="tit35-112" period="#t4">
          <num> &#xA7; 112 </num>
          <heading>Specification</heading>
        </section>
        <clause id="112-a">
          <num>(a)</num>
          <noteRef href="#n1"/>
          <heading>In General.</heading>
          <list id="tit35-sec112-par1">
              <content>
                <p> -The specification shall contain a written description of the invention, ..., and shall
                      set forth the best mode contemplated by the inventor ...of carrying out the
                      invention. - </p>
              </content>
          </list>
        </clause>
      </title>
    </body>
</akomaNtoso>
```

Listing 1.2. Content annotation of first paragraph of § 112

Wherein, **<documenttype>** defines the type of document under consideration. The **<preface>**, **<preamble>**, **<body> and <conclusion>** defines the content of the legal section under consideration. The context information concerning the legal section/document under consideration is described through the **<meta>**. The meta information is further subdivided into several classes (Only those relevant to our example are considered here):

- **<identification>**: In our case it is the source of the document #LII
- **<lifecycle>**: Defines the lifecycle of the legal section under consideration. In our example, the legal section was first written in 1946 and the latest ammendment was done in the year 2011.
- **<temporaldata>**: Defines a temporal information. In our considered example, the temporal block t8, defines the #inforce (i.e. 2011-09-16) and #efficacy (i.e. 2012-09-16) of the legal section.
- **<FRBRWork>, <FRBRExpression> and <FRBRManifestation>**: Defines the work/legal section, the specific form of that work and physical embodiments of an expression of work respectively.

- **\<notes\>**: Additional information relating to a legal document. In our example, the latest amendment to this act is also known as 'First to File Policy'.

We also annotate the landmark decisions such as, *In re Ruschig Fed Cir and Pfizer Inc. v. Teva Pharmaceuticals Inc* pertaining to this legal section. These additionally annotations capture the pragmatic context in which such a law section has to be applied. I.o.w, it defines new pragmatics, in terms of understanding and commitment, encompassing the legal section.

6 Disaggregation

The disaggregation extracts elementary concerns from the compound concerns of the statutory and transforms them from their vague SPL semantics into a concrete PPL semantics, i.e., a legal norm representation (syntax) which has a concrete meaning (semantics) in PPL is understood and evaluated (pragmatics) within the context of case law. In the US patent law, the United States Patent and Trademark Office, 'USPTO', uses a standard patent evaluation procedure provided in the Manual for Patent Examination Procedure, 'MPEP'. We transform such procedures into legal decision models, wherein, each decision point is a single procedure or a set of procedures to be carried out.

The landmark decisions (*In re Ruschig Fed Cir and Pfizer Inc. v. Teva Pharmaceuticals Inc*) are also represented as procedural decision models and are integrated into the decision model generated for the specific legal section. Thus forming a generic decision model for a specific legal section. This allows capturing the different interpretations of the same section in different case laws. The context information for the legal section and its related judgments, which have been annotated before, are added as meta information to the decision model. Figure 2[5], depicts a generalized decision model for the considered legal section.

Further, we use the easy to understand decision models as basis for writing the legal norms and their elementary concerns in terms of constitutive vocabulary definitions and prescriptive behavioural legal rules in SBVR's Structured English. We can classify the mapping relationships as 1:1- wherein each decision is mapped into a single SBVR rule, 1:M- where, a single decision is mapped into many SBVR rules or an M:M relationship. Legal domain experts and trained formal knowledge engineers can work together in this formalization process using Structured English as common computational independent knowledge representation language.

7 Semi-formal Representation

In [11] and [12], we showed in detail, the use of SBVR Structured English (SSE), as a semi-formal representation format for representing legal (procedural) norms. The core idea of SBVR adapted to the legal domain is: **legal rules** build on legal

---

[5] The textual content inside the decision model is left out on purpose to handle the space restrictions.

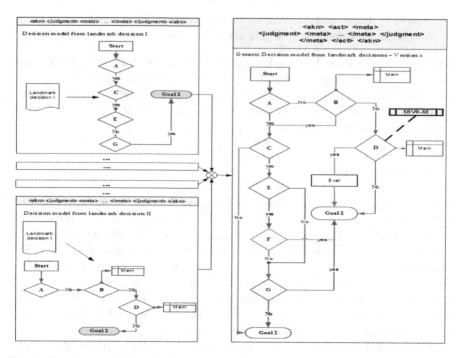

Fig. 2. Decision model with the <meta> information about legal section as overhead(adapted from [1])

facts, and **legal facts** build on **legal concepts** which are expressed by **legal terms**. Terms express legal concepts; facts make assertions about these concepts; rules constrain and support these facts. Using the resulting semi-formal legal vocabulary and rules the decision models can be semantically enriched, giving them an underlying formal semantics.

To illustrate the use of SSE as a semi-formal representation format, A decision point 'D' is chosen from the decision model (i.e. from Figure 2). Decision 'D' comprises of a procedural rule as stated below:

Essential Subject Matter Missing From Claims

"A claim rejected under 35 U.S.C. 112, first paragraph, as based on a disclosure which is not enabling, critical or essential to the practice of the invention, but not included in the claim(s) is not enabled by the disclosure"

SBVR Structured English, SSE:

Legal Concepts: *Noun concepts defined in green and individual noun concepts are defined in dark-green starting with capital letters.*

claim	
Definition	Define the invention and are what aspects are legally enforceable
Dictionary basis	patentlaw
Source	based on USPTOGlossary
General Concept	patent

building on the same lines, we obtain other legal concepts like:
examiner office_action paragraph argument applicant patent_application
invention essential_subject_matter_requirement **Paragraph_7_33_01 US**

Legal Facts: *Verb concepts are defined in blue.*
office_action *includes* **Paragraph_7_33_01**
claim *is_rejected_under* essential_subject_matter_requirement
patent_application *is_filed_in* **US**
patent_application *includes* at least 1 claim
examiner *rejects* the claim

Legal (procedural) rules: *for ¶7.33.01.*

1. It is obligatory that examiner *rejects* the claim and
   office_action *includes* **Paragraph_7_33_01**,
   if claim *is_rejected_under* essential_subject_matter_requirement.

2. It is necessary that a patent_application *includes* at least 1 claim,
   if patent_application *is_filed_in* **US**

8 Formal Representation

Legal norms in their elementary form as represented in semi-formal SSE are translated into a formal representation language. Although a direct translation into a platform-specific language of a logic reasoner is possible, for the purpose of machine processing, reusability, interchange and structured Web publication, we propose to use OASIS LegalRuleML as a standardize XML-based expression language on the PIM layer first. LegalRuleML, supports the modeling of both constitutive (legal concept definitions) and prescriptive (behavioural) rules. Among other expressiveness, it supports the representation of legal meta-data, penalty, reparation and specific deontic operators. Like LegalDocML, LegalRuleML also provides the capability to manage multiple semantic annotations through annotation blocks as internal or external metadata. By that it manages the temporal issues such as, provisions, provenance references, application of rules and their histories in a unambiguous manner. Furthermore, with its flexibility to separate the logical layer and the context layer, it seamlessly integrates into the the overarching RuleML language family[6][14] and supports reuse of Deliberation RuleML and Reaction RuleML 1.0[7][15,16], in particular for the inner rule's norm representation.

---

[6] http://www.ruleml.org
[7] http://reaction.ruleml.org

Continuing our example, the representation is split into two parts. Firstly, defining the context information in terms of its LegalRuleML meta-data and secondly, describing the rules content, i.e., the inner legal norms on the logical layer in terms of reaction rules [15].

```
<!-- Defines the source of the legal text-->
  <lrml:LegalSources>
      <lrml:LegalSource key="ref1" sameAS="http://mpep.patentbargroup.com/html/0700_706_03_c.htm"/>
  </lrml:LegalSources>
  <lrml:References>
      <lrml:Reference refersTo="ref2" refID="us/codes;us/patentlaw/main#title35/"
          refIDSystemName="AkomaNtoso3.0"/>
  </lrml:References>
  <lrml:Authorities>
      <lrml:Authority key="USPTO" sameAS="/ontology/organizations/PatentOffice/USPTO"/>
      <lrml:type iri="&lrmlv;PatentOffice"/>
  </lrml:Authorities>
  <lrml:Agents>
      <lrml:Agent key="examiner"
          sameAS="/ontology/organizations/PatentOffice/USPTO/Person#Examiner"/>
  </lrml:Agents>
  <lrml:TimeInstants>
      <ruleml:Time Key="#t7"><ruleml:Data Type="xs:Date">2011-09-16</ruleml:Data></ruleml:Time>
      <ruleml:Time key="#t8"><ruleml:Data Type="xs:Date">2012-09-16</ruleml:Data></ruleml:Time>
  </lrml:TimeInstants>
<!-- Temporal characterstics of the rule -->
  <lrml:TemporalCharacterstic key="tblock1">
      <lrml:forRuleStatus iri="&lrmlv;#Efficacious"/>
      <lrml:hasStatusDevelopment iri="&lrmlv;#End"/>
      <lrml:atTimeInstant keyref="#t8"/>
  </lrml:TemporalCharacterstic>
<!-- Rule Qualification/Override Principle -->
  <lrml:hasQualification><lrml:Overrides over="#ps1" under="#ps2"/></lrml:hasQualification>
<!-- Jurisdictions of the rule -->
  <lrml:hasJurisdciton><lrml:Jurisdictions key="#jurisdiction1"/></lrml:hasJurisdciton>
<!-- Context Information-->
  <lrml:hasContext>
      <lrml:appliesSelection keyref="#r1"/>
      <lrml:toStatement keyref="#ps1"/>
      <lrml:appliesjurisdiction keyref="#jurisdiction1" iri="&jurisdictions;us"/>
  </lrml:hasContext>
```

Wherein, <**LegalSource**> is used for describing the source of a legal norm under consideration i.e. MPEP, as in our case. <**Authority**> and <**Jurisdiction**>, defines the authority responsible for drafting a given legal norm and the jurisdiction where such a legal norm is applicable respectively. The authority responsible for making changes to MPEP is the USPTO and the jurisdiction defined in our example is limited to US. The <**TemporalCharacterstic**> and <**TimeInstants**> defines temporal aspects and captures the changes to a considered norm respectively. <**Qualification**> defined the importance/priority of a rule to another rule. In our example, Rule 2 overrides Rule 1.

Figure 3, shows the representation of the logical part of the norm in LegalRuleML and Reaction RuleML format. Wherein, the SBVR constraints are translated into prescriptive constraint statements. Figure 3(a) and 3(b) exemplifies the representation of deontic obligations and alethic necessity. The SBVR legal vocabulary is translated into an OWL2 ontology with the help of mapping schemas provided in [17] [18]. The IRI's obtained from the OWL2 ontologies of the SBVR legal vocabulary are used to type the logical parts of the norm represented using RuleML's typing approach (@type attribute)[14]. While we illustrated the transformation and syntactic representation of SBVR Structured English in LegalRuleML and Reaction RuleML in this section, we will define a semantic-preserving translation from SSE to RuleML in the next section.

```
<lrml: PrescriptiveStatement key="#ps1">
   <lrml:hasTemplate>
      <rrml:Rule key="#r1">
         <lrml:hasParaphrase> It is obligatory that examiner rejects
                 the claim and office_action includes
                 Paragarph_7_33_01 if claim is_rejected_under
                 essential_subject_matter_requirement
         </lrml:hasParaphrase>
         <rrml:if>
            <rrml:Atom key="sbvrfact1">
         <rrml:Rel iri="&voc; is_rejected_under"/>
         <rrml: Var type="&voc;claim"/>
         <rrml: Var type="&voc; essential_subject_matter_
                            -requirement"/>
            </rrml:Atom>
         </rrml:if>
         <rrml:then>
            <lrml:Obligation>
               <rrml:And>
                  <rrml:Atom key="sbvrfact2">
         <rrml:Rel per="modal" type="&voc; rejects "/>
         <rrml:Var type="&voc; examiner"/>
         <rrml:Var type="&voc; claim"/>
                  </rrml:Atom>
                  <rrml:Atom key="sbvrfact3">
         <rrml:Rel per="modal" type="&voc; includes" />
         <rrml:Var type="&voc; office_action"/>
         <rrml:Ind type="&voc;Paragarph_7_33_01"/>
                  </rrml:Atom>
               </rrml:And>
            </lrml:Obligation>
         </rrml:then>
      </rrml:Rule>
   </lrml:hasTemplate>
</lrml: PrescriptiveStatement>

                  (a)
```

```
<lrml:ConstitutiveStatement key="#ps2">
   <lrml:hasTemplate>
      <rrml:Rule key="#r2">
         <lrml:hasParaphrase>It is necessary that a
                 patent_application includes at least 1 claim
                 if patent_application is_filed_in US
         </lrml:hasParaphrase>
         <rrml:if>
            <rrml:Atom key="sbvrfact4">
         <rrml:Rel type="&voc; is_filed_in "/>
         <rrml:Var type="&voc;patent_application "/>
         <rrml: Ind iri="&voc:US"/>
            </rrml:Atom>
         </rrml:if>
      <rrml:then>
      <rrml:Operator type="rrml:AlethicOperator"
      iri="rrml:Necessary">
         <rrml:Atom key="sbvrfact5">
            <rrml:quantification>
               <rrml:Exists>
                  <rrml:Var type="&voc; claim">claim</rrml:Var>
               </rrml:Exists>
            </rrml:quantification>
            <rrml:Rel per="modal" iri="&voc; includes"/>
            <rrml:Var type="&voc; patent_application"/>
            <rrml:Var type="&voc; claim">claim</rrml:Var>
         </rrml:Atom>
      </rrml:Operator>
      </rrml:then>
      </rrml:Operator>
      </rrml:Rule>
   </lrml:hasTemplate>
</lrml:ConstitutiveStatement>

                  (b)
```

Fig. 3. Legal norms on PIM layer. (a) Representation of deontic legal using the existing LegalRuleML deontic operators. (b) Representation of alethic legal by extending LegalRuleML to accommodate alethic operators.

9 Semantic Transformation and Reasoning

To map from SBVR Structured English into LegalRuleML (which includes Reaction RuleML) we define a semantics preserving translation of both into a First-Order Deontic-Alethic Logic (FODAL) [19]. FODAL is a multi-modal first order extension combining quantified Standard Deontic Logic and the quantified Alethic Modal Logic S4. It is used as the underlying formal semantics for both of our patent law representation languages, i.e. SBVR and LegalRuleML. This semantics also forms the basis for further transformations from restricted subsets of FODAL into logics for practical reasoning, namely description logics (the DL $ALCQI$) and logic programming (quantified extended horn logic). This enables us to map the legal vocabularies, represented in SBVR, into OWL2 ontologies, and the SBVR respectively LegalRuleML rules into Prova rule bases, on which efficient reasoning can be done.

In the following subsections, we first give a compact description of the FO-DAL language, its semantics and combined axiomatic system, and then define a translation function for the mapping between SBVR and LegalRuleML via the FODAL semantics. The complete definition can be found in the corresponding FODAL Semantic Profile[8], which has been defined for Reaction RuleML.

```
<evaluation>
    <Profile type="FirstOrderDeonticAlethicLogicProfile"/>
</evaluation>
```

Using Reaction RuleML's Semantic Profile mechanism[16], the FODAL semantics can be specified as intended semantics for the interpretation of Legal Reaction RuleML representations and for further transformations.

9.1   Syntax

Definition 1. *(**Alphabet**) The alphabet Σ consists of the following class of symbols:*

- *A signature $S = \langle \overline{P}, \overline{F}, arity, \overline{c} \rangle$, with*
  - *$\overline{P}$ an infinite set of predicate symbols $\langle P_1, .., P_n \rangle$.*
  - *$\overline{F}$ a infinite set of function symbols $\langle F_1, .., F_m \rangle$*
  - *For each P_i respectively each F_j, $arity(P_i)$ resp. $arity(F_j)$ is a non-zero natural number denoting the arity of P_i resp. F_i.*
  - *$\overline{c} = \langle c1, .., c_o \rangle$ is a finite or infinite sequence of constant symbols.*
- *A collection of variables V which will be denoted by identifiers starting with a capital letter like U,V,X*
- *Logical connectives / operators: $\neg$ (negation), $\wedge$ (conjunction), $\vee$ (disjunction), $\rightarrow$ (implication), $\leftrightarrow$ (iff) and $\equiv$ (equivalent).*
- *Modal connectives / operators: $\square$ (alethic necessity), $\diamond$ (alethic possibility), O (deontic obligation), P (deontic permission), F (deontic forbidden).*
- *Quantifier: $\forall$ (forall), $\exists$ (exists).*
- *Parentheses symbols: "(", ")".*

A formula ϕ is defined as in FOL with the extension of a set of modal formulas ϕ^{Mod} ($\square\phi$, $\diamond\phi$, $O\phi$, $P\phi$, $F\phi$) with the additional modal operators ($\diamond$, P, F) definable in terms of the others:

- $\diamond\phi$ (possibly ϕ) $\equiv \neg\square\neg\phi$ (not necessarily not ϕ")
- $P\phi$ (permitted ϕ) $\equiv \neg O\neg\phi$ (not obligatory that not ϕ)
- $F\phi$ (forbidden ϕ) $\equiv O\neg\phi$ (obligatory that not ϕ)

---

[8] FODAL Semantic Profile http://reaction.ruleml.org/
1.0/profiles/FirstOrderDeonticAlethicLogicProfile.pdf

9.2   Semantics

The semantics is defined by a two layered Kripke semantics with augmented bimodal frames consisting of two accessibility relations, R_O and $R_\Box$ between possible worlds.

Definition 2. *(Augmented frame) A varying domain augmented bimodal frame $A = \langle W, R_O, R_\Box, d \rangle$ consists of a non-empty set, W, whose members are possible worlds, two binary accessibility relations, R_O and $R_\Box$, that hold (or not) between the possible worlds of W, a domain function d mapping possible worlds w to a non-empty set P such that if $d(w, P)$, then P is true at w.*

As in S4 the alethic accessibility relation is reflexive and transitive [20] and the deontic accessibility relation is serial as in KD [21]. The FODAL semantics additionally defines the bi-modal FODAL frame with the modal formula for the interaction between alethic and deontic logic.

– $\Box\phi \rightarrow O\phi$ (Everything which is necessary is also obligatory)

Definition 3. *(Interpretation and model) An interpretation I in an augmented frame A is an interpretation function which assigns to each possible world w and each predicate symbol p some n-ary relation to the domain $D(w)$ of that world. A model M is an interpretation of an augmented FODAL frame A, if A is true wrt to I.*

The satisfiability relation between FODAL models and formulae is then defined in the usual way: ϕ is a FODAL formula and σ is an assignment to the interpretation I, then the relation $I \models \phi[\sigma]$ means that ϕ is true in I when there is a substitute for each free variable V of ϕ with the value of $\sigma(V)$. We omit the definition of the inductive requirements of "$\models$" here and refer to [19]. Accordingly, a formula ϕ is satisfied by an interpretation I ($I \models \phi$) iff $I \models_\sigma \phi$ for all variable assignments σ.

9.3   Axiomatization

Following [22] the formalization is given as an axiomatic system in the typical way for a normal modal logic. The FODAL axiomatization is obtained by combining the axiom systems of S4 and KD and extending it with the additional axioms defining the relations between alethic and deontic modalities.

Definition 4. *(Axioms)*

– *All S4 and KD tautologies and axioms*
– *All instances of the Kripke schema: $\Box(A \rightarrow B) \rightarrow (\Box A \rightarrow \Box B)$ and $O(A \rightarrow B) \rightarrow (OA \rightarrow OB)$*
– *(Vacuous $\forall$) $\forall x\phi \equiv \phi$ with x not being free in ϕ*
– *($\forall$ Distributivity) $\forall x(\phi \rightarrow \psi) \rightarrow (\forall x\phi \rightarrow \forall x\psi)$*
– *($\forall$ Permutation) $\forall x\forall y\phi \rightarrow \forall y\forall x\phi$*

- (∀ Elimination) $\forall y(\forall x \phi(x) \rightarrow \phi(y))$
- (Necessary O) $\Box \phi \rightarrow O\phi$

and additionally inference rules

- (Detachment) $\frac{\phi \rightarrow \psi}{\psi}$
- (Necessiation) $\frac{\phi}{\Box \phi}$ and $\frac{\phi}{(O)\phi}$
- (∀ Generalization) $\frac{\phi}{\forall x \phi}$

For proof of soundness and completeness see [19]. It also gives a consistency proof based on satisfiability reduction in the case of only atomic mono-modal sentences.

9.4   Translation from SBVR to LegalRuleML

For the translation from SBVR into FODAL, the following translation $\tau_{SBVR}(\cdot)$ from elements of $SBVR$ to closed formulas in first-order deontic-alethic logic is used:

- for each noun concept N from $SBVR$, $\tau_{SBVR}(N)$ is an unary predicate in FODAL.
- fore each n-ary verb concept V from $SBVR$, $\tau_{SBVR}(V)$ is a n-ary predicate in FODAL.
- for each rule R from $SBVR$, $\tau_{SBVR}(R)$ is defined inductively as follows:
  - $\tau_{SBVR}(\hat{R}) = \phi_{\hat{R}}$, where $\hat{R}$ is a non-modal SBVR expression and $\phi_{\hat{R}}$ is its non-modal first-order logic translation,
  - $\tau_{SBVR}(\neg R) = \neg \tau_{SBVR}(R)$,
  - $\tau_{SBVR}(R_1 \circ R_2) = \tau_{SBVR}(R_1) \circ \tau_{SBVR}(R_2)$, where R_1 and R_2 are SBVR rules and $\circ \in \{\wedge, \vee, \rightarrow, \leftrightarrow\}$.
  - $\tau_{SBVR}(\Box \hat{R}) = \Box \tau_{SBVR}(\hat{R})$ and $\tau_{SBVR}(O\hat{R}) = O\tau_{SBVR}(\hat{R})$

For the translation into LegalRuleML we normalize the FODAL sentences to atomic modal sentences using the typical axioms of normal modal logic, as defined in the previous subsection. Furthermore, we restrict the expressiveness to only mono-modal closed formula, i.e., the original SBVR rules are allowed to contain only one modality[9]. We define the translation as the inverse translation function $\tau_{LRML}(\cdot)^{-1}$ from normalized mono-modal FODAL formulas to LRML as follows:

- for each constant c (i.e.m an individual object/thing in SBVR), $\tau_{LRML}^{-1}(c)$ maps it
  - to a data term $< Data >$ in $LRML$ if the constant has an interpretation as a data type in the the XML Schema data types.

---

[9] Since our patent law constraints in SBVR only have one modality as well as Legal-RuleML statements are mono-modal, mono-modal FODAL provides enough expressiveness.

- to an individual term $< Ind >$ in $LRML$ otherwise.
- for each variable v, $\tau_{LRML}^{-1}(v)$ maps it to a variable $< Var >$ in $LRML$.
- for each unary predicate p in $FODAL$, $\tau_{LRML}^{-1}(p)$ maps its only argument term (a constant or a variable) into a term in $LRML$ and assigns the predicate relation p_r as type attribute to the $LRML$ term $@type = "p_r"$ [10].
- for each n-ary predicate p in $FODAL$, $\tau_{LRML}^{-1}(p)$ maps it into an n-ary atom $< Atom >$ in $LRML$ using the predicate relation as relation $< Rel >$ [11] for the atom and each argument term in the $FODAL$ predicate p is mapped into a typed term in the $LRML$ atom, where the type is coming from the previous mapping of a unary predicate which gives the type of the term.
- for each formula R in $FODAL$, $\tau_{LRML}^{-1}(R)$ is defined inductively as follows:
  - $\tau_{LRML}^{-1}(\hat{R})$ maps into a corresponding $LRML$ formula $< formula >$, where $\hat{R}$ is a non-modal first-order logic formula and the $LRML$ formula is its non-modal LRML translation. In particular:
    * if $\hat{R}$ is a conjunction it is mapped into $< And >$.
    * if $\hat{R}$ is a disjunction it is mapped into $< Or >$.
    * if $\hat{R}$ is an implication (or a formula which logically corresponds to an implication) it is mapped into $< Rule >$.
    * if $\hat{R}$ is a universal quantifier or existential quantifier it is mapped into a quantifier $< Forall >$ (might be left implicit if no further constraints are defined on the quantifier) or $< Exists >$, with the declared variables being typed $@type$ with their type (see unary predicate mapping) and additional quantifier constraints defined in the $LRML$ quantifier ("such that" $< formula >$ and guard constraints $< guard >$).
  - $\tau_{LRML}^{-1}(\neg R)$ maps into a $LRML$ negation $< Neg >$ with $\tau_{LRML}^{-1}(R)$ being the corresponding $LRML$ formula which is negated.
  - $\tau_{LRML}^{-1}(R_1 \circ R_2)$, where R_1 and R_2 are FODAL formulas and $\circ \in \{\wedge, \vee, \to, \leftrightarrow\}$ maps into $\tau_{LRML}^{-1}(R_1)\tau_{LRML}^{-1}(\circ)\tau_{LRML}^{-1}(R_2)$, with $\tau_{LRML}^{-1}(\circ) = \{\wedge =< And >, \vee =< Or >, \to< Rule >, \leftrightarrow =< Equivalent >\}$.
  - $\tau_{LRML}^{-1}(\Box\hat{R})$ maps into a (definition) constitutive statement $< ConstitutiveStatement >$ in $LRML$ with the alethic necessary operator $\Box$ mapped into $< rrml : Operatortype = "rrml : AlethicOperator"iri = "rrml : Necessary" >$ and $\tau_{LRML}^{-1}(\hat{R})$ mapped into its corresponding $LRML$ formula and $\tau_{LRML}^{-1}(O\hat{R})$ maps into a (behavioural) prescriptive statement $< PrescriptiveStatement >$ with the deontic obligation operator O mapped into the obligation $< Obligation >$ in $LRML$ and $\tau_{LRML}^{-1}(\hat{R})$ mapped into its corresponding $LRML$ formula. [12] For the other alethic and deontic operators τ_{LRML}^{-1} gives a similar mapping.

---

[10] We use webized types coming from the SBVR Web vocabulary respectively translated OWL2 ontology, i.e., we use the IRIs of the vocabulary/ontology as sort symbol names.

[11] We use the IRI from the SBVR vocabulary or its translated OWL2 ontology.

[12] The transformation might additionally denormalize the formulas and map into a $LRML$ templates $hasTemplate$ using the original SBVR expressions.

An SSE expression R $=$"It is $necessary$ $that$ a $patent\_application$ $includes$ at $least$ 1 $claim$" becomes translated by $\tau_{SBVR}(R)$ into a FODAL sentence $F = \forall X \exists Y (Patent\_Application(X) \wedge Claim(Y) \wedge includes(X,Y))$ and by $\tau_{LRML}^{-1}(F)$ into an $LRML$ formula which corresponds to the alethic necessity conclusion of the "ConstitutiveStatement" rule shown in Figure 3b. The SSE expression "It is $obligatory$ $that$ $examiner$ $rejects$ the $claim$ and $office\_action$ $includes$ $Paragraph\_7\_33\_01$" becomes the FODAL formula $\mathbf{O}(\forall X, Y, Z (Examiner(X) \wedge Claim(Y) \wedge rejects(X,Y) \wedge Office\_Action(Z) \wedge includes(Z,"Paragraph\_7\_33\_01")))$, which corresponds to the deontic obligation conclusion of the "PrescriptiveStatement" rule shown in Figure 3(a).

10 KR4IPLaw

Figure 4, shows the overview of our proof-of-concept system, called 'KR4IPLaw' (Knowledge Representation for Intellectual Property Law) [11]. KR4IPLaw is a system built to support the process described in this paper. The system comprises of a Language Independent Markup Editor, 'LIME' [23] for the purpose of legal document annotation, An Unified Markup Language (UML)s' activity diagram tool to graphical represent the procedural norms into decision models and SBeaVeR [24] based KR4IPLaw tool, for semi-formal representation of a decision point or set of decision points using SBVR-SE. The system also integrates a recommender system, which (semi-)automatically translates the procedural legal texts from the decision models into semantically enriched legal concepts, which thereafter is used to build semi-formal legal norms. Semantically enriched legal vocabularies are mapped onto an OWL2 ontology as a part of the KB (as described in section 3).

For reasoning, the platform independent legal rules (represented by Legal-RuleML) are transformed into platform specific elementary legal rules. We use Prova [25], a rule language and rule engine for legal rule representation (platform specific) and for reasoning such rules on top of legal knowledge bases. Prova is both a Semantic Web rule language and a high expressive distributed rule engine.

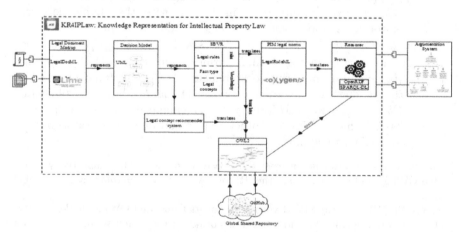

Fig. 4. KR4IPLaw - proof-of-concept implementation

It supports, the execution of declarative (decision) legal rules [26], access to external semantic web data via SPARQL, ontology reasoners and supports scoped reasoning. The EP's represented as meta-data acts for a considered legal rule act as explicit scope for constructive queries on the knowledge base. In addition to scopes, we make use of the *guards* functionality provided by Prova. *Guards*, act as additional pre-condition constraints (e.g. reasoning only those rules from trusted authors). The long term goal of this system is to act as an interface, which can be easily handled by legal practitioners and at the same time still be capable enough to provide all the necessary tools for a knowledge engineer.

11   Conclusion and Future Directions

In this paper we presented a process which enables a legal practitioner to move from a natural language legal norm/section to a machine readable rule representation format. We presented several knowledge representation formats involved in each step of this process. We then showed, how piggybacking the meta information during the disaggregation process helps in retaining the original pragmatics in a mode modular form resulting in a elementary norm with elementary pragmatics. This paper also argued on the use of semi-formal approach like SBVR-SE as an intermediate step in transforming the legal norms in natural text to a format sufficient enough for reasoning using existing reasoners. We proposed several mapping schemes useful for transforming a SBVR-rule (in its modal form) to a PIM layer rule representation format like LegalRuleML using ReactionRuleML. The future research of this work aims to study this approach on an interface level and how to manage the interdependency factor that arises with a rich information flow between systems/layers. Another future work includes the study of paradoxes that are attached with the modal logics under consideration.

References

1. Ramakrishna, S.: First Approaches on Knowledge Representation of Elementary (Patent) Pragmatics. In: Proceedings of the 7th International Rule Challenge, the Special Track on Human Language Technology and the 3rd RuleML Doctoral Consortium (2013)
2. KSR Intl Co. v. Teleflex Inc: U.S. 550 U.S. 398 (2007)
3. Balkin, J.M.: Understanding legal understanding: The legal subject and the problem of legal coherence. Yale Law Journal, 105–176 (1993)
4. Arnold-Moore, T., Clemes, J.: Connected to the Law: Tasmanian Legislation Using EnAct. Journal of Information, Law and Technology (1) (2000)
5. Dell, P.: Eur-lex :the access to european union law, Slides of a talk given on December 3 2010. Zagreb University (2010)
6. Boer, A., Hoekstra, R., Winkels, R.: MetaLex: Legislation in XML (2002)
7. Palmirani, M., Vitali, F.: Akoma-Ntoso for Legal Documents. In: Legislative XML for the Semantic Web. Law, Governance and Technology Series, vol. 4, pp. 75–100. Springer, Netherlands (2011)

8. Bézivin, J., Gerbé, O.: Towards a precise definition of the OMG/MDA framework. In: Proceedings of the 16th Annual International Conference on Automated Software Engineering, ASE 2001, pp. 273–280. IEEE (2001)
9. OMG: Semantics of Business Vocabulary and Business Rules (SBVR). Technical Report November, O M G Document (2013)
10. Johnsen, A.S., Berre, A.J.R.: A bridge between legislator and technologist - Formalization in SBVR for improved quality and understanding of legal rules. In: International Workshop on Business Models, Business Rules and Ontologies, Bressanone, Brixen, Italy (2010)
11. Ramakrishna, S., Paschke, A.: Bridging the gap between Legal Practitioners and Knowledge Engineers using semi-formal KR. In: The 8th International Workshop on Value Modeling and Business Ontology, VMBO, Berlin (2014)
12. Ramakrishna, S., Paschke, A.: Semi-Automated Vocabulary Building for Structured Legal English. In: RuleML 2014. LNCS, vol. 8620, Springer, Heidelberg (2014)
13. Palmirani, M., Governatori, G., Rotolo, A., Tabet, S., Boley, H., Paschke, A.: LegalRuleML: XML-Based Rules and Norms. In: Olken, F., Palmirani, M., Sottara, D. (eds.) RuleML 2011 - America 2011. LNCS, vol. 7018, pp. 298–312. Springer, Heidelberg (2011)
14. Boley, H., Paschke, A., Shafiq, O.: Ruleml 1.0: The overarching specification of web rules. In: Dean, M., Hall, J., Rotolo, A., Tabet, S. (eds.) RuleML 2010. LNCS, vol. 6403, pp. 162–178. Springer, Heidelberg (2010)
15. Paschke, A., Boley, H., Zhao, Z., Teymourian, K., Athan, T.: Reaction RuleML 1.0: Standardized Semantic Reaction Rules. In: Bikakis, A., Giurca, A. (eds.) RuleML 2012. LNCS, vol. 7438, pp. 100–119. Springer, Heidelberg (2012)
16. Paschke, A.: Reaction RuleML 1.0 for Rules, Events and Actions in Semantic Complex Event Processing. In: RuleML 2014. LNCS, vol. 8620, pp. 1–18. Springer, Heidelberg (2014)
17. Elisa, K., Mark, H.L.: Mapping SBVR to OWL2. Technical report, IBM Research Division, New York, NY (2013)
18. Karpovic, J., Nemuraite, L.: Transforming SBVR Business Semantics into Web Ontology Language OWL2: Main Concepts. In: Proc. 17th International Conference on Information and Software Technologies, IT 2011, pp. 231–254 (2011)
19. Solomakhin, D., Franconi, E., Mosca, A.: Logic-based reasoning support for SBVR. In: Proceedings of the 26th Italian Conference on Computational Logic (CILC 2011), Pescara, Italy, August 31-September 2, pp. 311–325 (2011)
20. Blackburn, P., de Rijke, M., Venema, Y.: Modal Logic. Cambridge Tracts in Theoretical Computer Science, vol. 53. Cambridge University Press (2001)
21. McNamara, P.: Deontic logic. In: Zalta, E.N. (ed.) The Stanford Encyclopedia of Philosophy, Fall 2010 edn. Stanford University (September 2010)
22. Fitting, M., Mendelsohn, R.L.: First-order Modal Logic. Kluwer Academic Publishers, Norwell (1999)
23. Palmirani, M., Vitali, F., Cervone, L.: LIME: The Language Independent Markup Editor. University of Bologna
24. De Tommasi, M., Corallo, A.: SBEAVER: A Tool for Modeling Business Vocabularies and Business Rules. In: Gabrys, B., Howlett, R.J., Jain, L.C. (eds.) KES 2006, Part III. LNCS (LNAI), vol. 4253, pp. 1083–1091. Springer, Heidelberg (2006)
25. Kozlenkov, A.: Prova Rule Language Version 3.0 User's Guide (2010), http://prova.ws/index.html
26. Paschke, A., Ramakrishna, S.: Legal RuleML Tutorial Use Case - LegalRuleML for Legal Reasoning in Patent Law (2013)

Legal Responsibility for the Acts of Others:
A Logical Analysis

Clara Smith[1], Erica Calardo[2], Antonino Rotolo[2], and Giovanni Sartor[3]

[1] Faculty of Informatics and Faculty of Law, University of La Plata, Argentina
[2] CIRSFID, University of Bologna, Italy
[3] European University Institute, Florence, Italy / CIRSFID, University of Bologna, Italy

Abstract. This paper offers a logical analysis of two cases where legal responsibility may emerge for the acts of others: (a) reflex responsibility, and (b) responsibility in the *negotiorum gestio* doctrine. The current contribution works within a fresh multi-modal system where the new operators are introduced for denoting intentions and actions in the interest of other agents, and the objectively ideal sets of actions for agents.

Keywords: Legal Responsibility, Vicarious Liability, Multi-modal logics.

1   Introduction

An adequate analysis of the idea of legal responsibility is essential for developing a comprehensive model for reasoning about legal rules. A crucial question concerns what effects the cooperation between agents may have with regard to third parties. In this paper we study legal scenarios where *responsibility* emerges between a principal agent and a helper agent. The idea of responsibility we are going to formalize seems closely aligned with various legal concepts: consider, for instance, the provisions settled by Italian and Argentinean provisions for *persons* (e.g. art. 1113 of the Argentinean Civil Code and art. 1228 of the Italian Civil Code). In particular, we examine two cases: (*a*) responsibility having its origin in occasional, non-contractual courtesy relations—also called *reflex responsibility* [25]—and (*b*) responsibility in the *negotiorum gestio* doctrine (see, e.g., art. 2288 of the Argentinean Civil Code and art. 2028 of the Italian Civil Code). So far, no logical reconstruction of these cases has been offered, except [25]: the current paper extends the research started in [25] by (*i*) working out a more general definition of reflex responsibility, (*ii*) integrating the logical framework with two modal operators for agent's ability and for expressing objectively ideal states of affairs, and (*iii*) handling *negotiorum gestio*.

We work on a wide range of situations where normally an agent *h*, the *helper*, accomplishes a task in order to satisfy the interests of another agent *p*, the *principal*, with the explicit or implicit agreement of the principal itself. This form of agent-based coordination has an impact also with regard to third parties: in the case of reflex responsibility a damaged third party often has the right to obtain a compensation also—or only—from the principal agent; in the case of *negotiorum gestio* the principal becomes bond to the third party through the obligation taken by the helper.

A. Bikakis et al. (Eds.): RuleML 2014, LNCS 8620, pp. 329–338, 2014.

Notice that we do not consider here contractual situations, neat employer/employee relationships, mandates, and any conferral of a power of representation accompanied by an obligation of representation in certain ways (e.g., a cheque is a mandate from the customer to her bank to pay the sum in question). In contractual scenarios, usually responsibilities and sanctions are clearly pre-settled. We will neither address cases where one is *legally responsible* for another agent's behaviour which is totally independent from one's goals and intentions (i.e., parents are legally responsible for damages caused to third parties by their underage children). We are rather interested in situations where trust, altruism, friendship and courtesy are at the basis of the cooperation between the agents. Our plan is thus to model *occasional* cooperative links that may occur between two agents, and from which the attribution of responsibility can come. The business may be initially of any kind and of course may have legal effects such as paying the debts of another, or when a shop manager asks a friend to take temporarily her place since she has an urgent business to do, or when a person asks a colleague to manage her blog for some time, or when one participates in an auction and buys an object for another. In these cases, the entrusted helper is expected to behave according to some standards: when the helper damages a third party, while acting in the interest of the principal, the obligation to compensate should fall primarily upon the principal, as long as the damage pertains to the helper's performance on the principal's interest. And when a helper enters into a contract on behalf of the principal, the principal must respond for the obligations in that contract.

The paper is organized as follows. Section 2 presents the definition of dependence we use for defining reflex responsibility, and the legal concept of *negotiorum gestio*. Section 3 introduces the proposed logical framework and introduces the notions of intention in the interest of another agent, action in the interest of another agent, the objectively ideal set of actions for an agent, dependence, *negotiorum gestio*. A formalization of related forms of responsibility is given in Section 4. Section 5 offers a conceptual discussion of the proposed formalization of reflex responsibility.

2   The Legal Background

The Notion of Dependence. The common-law doctrine focuses on the idea of vicarious responsibility, which acknowledges that one agent be liable for the torts committed by another agent [26]. Vicarious liability comes to break the notion of one agent responding only for the harm she made and extends the original principle that says that one is liable in tort law for her own acts. Although the employer/employee relationship is assumed in [26] to be the basis of vicarious liability, we can relax this assumption and identify these components in responsibility in cooperative relations:

  i) a *harmful act* carried out by a helper agent, upon the condition that
  ii) an *occasional dependence relation* between principal and helper occurs.

The harmful act is at the core of any responsibility model, it is its trigger. If there is no harmful act, no one is to be liable.

We next unpack the black-boxed idea of occasional dependence and make some of its internal structure explicit. For dependence to exist, the following two constitutive elements are required:

i) the principal meant that the helper carries out a *function* in the principal's interest, and

ii) the helper *counts as* a subordinate of the principal only w.r.t. the performance of such function, i.e. she acts in the interest of the principal and she believes that this is what the principal wants.

The principal must have the intention that the helper performs that sole task, while the helper is aware of this intention. The helper will somehow be "activated" not only by the belief that the principal intends that she (the helper) does the task but also with her (the helper's) own intention (in the interest of *p*) to carry out the task. The task is meant to be understood as a unity (e.g. 'purchase') and not as a continuity of small tasks (e.g. the robbery of a pearls' necklace by robbing one pearl a day).

Agency and *Negotiorum Gestio*. The concept of 'agency' is similar in common-law systems to vicarious liability: it also renders one person liable for the torts of another within the scope of his authority, be it real or apparent [26, p. 109]. There is a tendency of courts to use 'agency' to mean 'the fiduciary relationship which exists between two persons, one of whom expressly or impliedly manifests assent that the other should act on his behalf so as to affect his relations with third parties and the other of whom manifests assent so to act or so acts pursuant to that manifestation'.

Two categories of claims merge vicarious liability with agency: motor vehicles and un-delegable duties. Regarding motor vehicles, one of the earlier 19th century principles seems to keep the master liable concerning horse accidents. Nowadays, this argument is kept: the principal remains liable (as she is the one who keeps control because she is the owner of the vehicle); but a second element is added: the insurance issue. The car owner is usually understood to be more able to pay for damages, according to the principles of loss distribution and victim compensation. Regarding non-delegable duties, the arguments appear to be straightforward: if such a duty is cast personally to an agent (e.g. to an artisan), she could not get rid of the task by delegating the performance to a third person.

In civil law the intervention in other's affairs, without mandate, falls under the doctrine of *negotiorium gestio,* this last being a type of spontaneous agency or interference of one person in the business of another person; the underlying principle is intended as an act of generosity and friendship and not to allow the *gestor* to profit from her agency [27]. It is clear that this agency cannot properly be said to originate in a contract, one agent has come forward and managed the business of another without mandate for doing so, and the latter is laid under obligations even though she knows nothing of what has taken place.

The *gestor* is only entitled to reimbursement for expenses and not to remuneration. For the recovery of expenses it is not necessary that the agent should have had in mind the particular principal in whose interest the business is being carried out (e.g the *gestor* thought A was the principal, but it was indeed B.) Whether there is a need of a subsequent ratification of the gestor's acts, so as to preclude the *negotiorum gestio,* the positions are contradictory. This seems not necessary, as the principal may die and, the *negotiorum gestio* is not to be extinct, differently from what conceptually happens with a mandate[1]. The act must have been advantageous to the principal. The mere fact that it failed to result in ultimate benefit to the principal would not deprive the *gestor* of her right to reimbursement, provided she has been diligent. The business must have been beneficial to the principal from an objective point of view.

Modern civil codes such as the Argentinean and the Italian have a form of reflex responsibility of the principal in the sense that the principal remains committed by those obligations that the *gestor* entered on his behalf (Argentinean Civil Code art. 2289, Italian Civil Code art. 2031). Nonetheless, the responsibility w.r.t. third parties remains on the *gestor* (Argentinean Civil Code arts. 2291 and 2292.)

Example 1 (Letellier vs Derode [Cassation, France, 1872] [27]). Letellier, a merchant in Paris, bought from Derode, a merchant from Havre, 25,000 bags of American wheat. Derode left Havre with the wheat, without receiving further instructions from Letellier. Letellier had many debts in Paris, and had no place available where to store the wheat. When in Paris, Derode stored the wheat at Letellier's expense. The Court said Derode acted as a *negotiorum gestor* in the interest of Letellier. Letellier had to pay for the contract of storage Derode entered for the custody of Letellier's wheat.

3   The Logical Framework

Our logical framework is a combination of normal and non-normal modal logics [3,25]. We have a finite set of agents $A = \{x, y, z...\}$ and a countable set of atomic propositions $P = \{p, q, r, ...\}$. In the language of [3] complex expressions (denoted by $A, B, C...$) are formed from the above elements, plus the following unary modalities:

- $Goal_x A$, where Goal is a K_n operator, means that "agent x has the goal that A", where A is a proposition [4,20].
- $Int_x A$, where Int is KD_n operator, stands for "agent x has the intention to make A true".
- $Bel_x A$, where Bel is a $KD45_n$ operator, represents that "agent x has the belief that A".
- O and O^x are KD and KD_n operators representing, respectively, generic obligations, meaning "it is obligatory that" and directed obligations, meaning "it is obligatory in the interest of x that" [5,11,13].
- $Does_x A$ represents successful agency in the sense given by [6], i.e. agent x indeed brings about A. We assume that in expressions like $Does_x A$, A denotes behavioral actions concerning only single conducts of agents. For the sake of simplicity, we assume that no other modal operator can occur within the scope of Does.

We adopt for Does the axiomatization of [7]. Since Does captures successful actions, we validate the schema $Does_x A \rightarrow A$. The language is enriched with the following new operators:

- $Int^p_h A$ which stands for "agent h intends A to become true in the interest of agent p" [8]. This expression is to be interpreted subjectively, i.e. h intends A as being in the interest of p.

---

[1] Though, some codes, such as the Argentinean and the Italian ones, collapse *negotiorum gestio* to mandate.

- Does^P_h $\mathcal{A}$, which stands for "agent h brings it about that $\mathcal{A}$ in the interest of agent p", and is meant to capture directed material performance by h, but on account and in the interest of p.
- Able$_x$ $\mathcal{A}$ represents ability in the sense given by [6,7], i.e. agent x has the capacity to do $\mathcal{A}$. Considering agency as the exercise of the agent's ability to act, ability is implied by agency. For the sake of simplicity, we assume that no other modal operator can occur within the scope of Able.
- I^P $\mathcal{A}$, which stands for "$\mathcal{A}$ is objectively ideal (or 'good') for agent p".

By Int^P_h $\mathcal{A}$ we mean a directed and coordinated relation triangulating p, h, and $\mathcal{A}$. We aim to use Int^P_h $\mathcal{A}$ for capturing courtesy behavior i.e. h may be an altruistic agent not expecting any reward, merely intending to fulfill p's expectations, even occasionally. It captures an intention reflecting the interest of another w.r.t. $\mathcal{A}$ (nonetheless we later impose a precondition for altruistic intention to hold, namely $\neg$O^P_h $\mathcal{A}$, to assure that h is not obliged to do $\mathcal{A}$ in the interest of p through, e.g., a contract) Directed agency is a basic type of event and reflects a similar intuition behind directed intentions.

The semantics for I$^P\mathcal{A}$ is the one for **KD$_n$**: I$^P\mathcal{A}$ at a world w means $\mathcal{A}$ holds in all of w's ideal versions. The Able operator has a classical semantics [6,7]. We also assume the bridge schema Does$_x$ $\mathcal{A} \rightarrow$ Able$_x$ $\mathcal{A}$. Axiomatics and semantics for Int^P_h and Does^P_h $\mathcal{A}$ are essentially the same as those for Int$_h$ and Does$_h$. However, three new schemata are provided:

$$\text{Does}^P_h\,\mathcal{A} \rightarrow \text{Does}_h\,\mathcal{A} \qquad\qquad \text{(DDirDInd)}$$
$$\text{Int}^P_h\,\mathcal{A} \rightarrow \text{Int}_h\,\mathcal{A} \qquad\qquad \text{(IDirIInd)}$$
$$\text{Int}^P_h\,\text{Does}_h\,\mathcal{A} \leftrightarrow \text{Int}_h\,\text{Does}^P_h\,\mathcal{A} \qquad\qquad \text{(IntDoesEq)}$$

While if an agent h does or intends something in the interest of another agent p, this implies that the agent h does or intends this something, the converse does not hold, because generic actions and intentions can also be not in the interest of anyone.

We also include the following schemata:

$$\text{Int}^P_h\,\mathcal{A} \rightarrow \text{Bel}_h(\text{I}^P\,\mathcal{A}) \qquad\qquad \text{(Int}^P_h\text{ Introspection)}$$
$$\text{Does}^P_h\,\mathcal{A} \rightarrow \text{Bel}_h(\text{I}^P\,\mathcal{A}) \qquad\qquad \text{(Does}^P_h\text{ Introspection)}$$
$$\text{Does}^P_h\,\mathcal{A} \rightarrow \text{Int}^P_h\,\mathcal{A} \qquad\qquad \text{(IntentionalAgency)}$$
$$\text{O}^P\,\mathcal{A} \rightarrow \text{I}^P\,\mathcal{A} \qquad\qquad \text{(OI)}$$

The first two capture a form of introspection, meaning that if one intends/carries out something in the interest of another is because one believes that such something is ideal (i.e. objectively good) for that other. The third one captures a specific notion of intentional action meaning that if one carries out a task in the interest of other agent is because one intends to do the task in the interest of this other agent. The fourth one reflects the idea that obligations in the interest of p are a subset of what it is objectively ideal for p.[2]

---

[2] Space reasons prevent us from presenting here a suitable semantics, which, in fact, only requires a simple extension of the one in [25].

4   A Formal Analysis of Responsibility in Cooperative Relations

Reflex responsibility is at the core of the common law's concept of vicarious liability and agency, of the Romanic concept of liability in the interest of others, and of *negotiorum gestio*. From a representational point of view our approach is thus different from e.g. the notion of *functional responsibility* given by [17]. There, the operational aspect of an obligation is modeled: the fact that the obligated agent is actually expected to perform a task herself is expressed by $FR(a;P;b;x)$ meaning that a has the functional responsibility, for which it is accountable to b, to ensure P, *and that this responsibility comes from normative source x*. This is why, in that framework, functional responsibility is formally equivalent to an obligation.

We must consider as a precondition, given p principal, h helper and action $\mathcal{A}$, that $\neg O^p_h \mathcal{A}$ holds, i.e. that there exists no obligation that h carries out $\mathcal{A}$ in the interest of p. This because, if $O^p_h \mathcal{A}$ holds, then this fact induces the existence of a mandate or a contract, which weakens the idea of intention in the interest of another.

We model dependence as a *coordination relation*, as follows:

$$Dep^p_h \mathcal{A} \equiv Goal_p \mathcal{A} \wedge Int_p(Does^p_h \mathcal{A}) \wedge (Bel_h(Int_p(Does^p_h \mathcal{A})) \wedge Int^p_h \mathcal{A} \tag{1}$$

meaning that h is dependent from p with regard to the performance of $\mathcal{A}$ if $\mathcal{A}$ is one of p's goals, p intends that h carries out $\mathcal{A}$ in his (p's) interest, h is aware of that, and intends to achieve $\mathcal{A}$ in the interest of p. Note that for the employer/employee relationship we would use $O^p_h \mathcal{A}$, which is to be used to refer to a lawful bond.

Let us focus on the concepts of agency, insurances and non-delegable duties:

i)   Cases of agency where helpers act in the scope of an authority are to collapse under vicarious liability and are somehow covered by (1).

ii)   Cases of agency where principals ratify the helper's wrongful performance are vicarious: this fact will be represented the propositional constant Ratify.

iii) In the case of insurances (typically car insurances) we may not have that the act is intended by the principal nor that the helper intends to drive the car in the interest of the principal, e.g. that $Int_p \mathcal{A}$ nor $Int^p_h \mathcal{A}$ hold; we may nor even have that driving the car is one of the principal's goal ($Goal_p \mathcal{A}$) nor he intends his car driven by his helper ($Int_p(Does^p_h \mathcal{A})$) nor even that his helper believes so (($Bel_h(Int_p(Does^p_h \mathcal{A}))$)). Indeed, we must have that $\neg O^p_h \mathcal{A}$, and $Does_h \mathcal{A}$, and $Does_h$Damage hold. And we must have that the principal has an insurance regarding $\mathcal{A}$ (let us represent it by the propositional constant Insurance).

Cases of non-delegable duties are identifiable with a previous specific contract involving principal and helper; therefore liability arises under ordinary principles.

Now for the formalization of reflex responsibility, conditioned to the fact that

i)   the helper h is not obliged to do $\mathcal{A}$ in the interest of p, and

ii)   by doing $\mathcal{A}$, h causes a damage (if this does not hold, h's action that brings $\mathcal{A}$ about is irrelevant to the allocation of responsibility).

A principal p is reflexively responsible for h who does $\mathcal{A}$ iff there is the dependence described in (1), or p is insured w.r.t. $\mathcal{A}$, or p ratifies h's wrongful performance:

$$[\neg O^P_h \, \mathcal{A} \wedge (\text{Does}_h \, \mathcal{A} \rightarrow \text{Does}_h\text{Damage})] \rightarrow$$
$$[(\neg\text{Does}_p \, \mathcal{A} \; \wedge (\text{Dep}^P_h \, \mathcal{A} \wedge \text{Does}^P_h \, \mathcal{A}) \vee \text{Insurance} \vee \text{Ratify}) \leftrightarrow \text{Reflex}^P_h \, \mathcal{A}] \tag{2}$$

Recall that the dependence relation is insufficient to create any contractual relation or an employer/employee relationship.

Typically, being reflexively responsible for the principal for an action performed by the helper generates either an obligation compensate it:

$$\text{Reflex}^P_h \, \mathcal{A} \rightarrow \text{ODoes}_p \, \text{Compensate} \tag{3}$$

or a directed obligation to compensate in the interest of the damaged third party t:

$$\text{Reflex}^P_h \, \mathcal{A} \rightarrow \text{O}_t\text{Does}_p \, \text{Compensate} \tag{3'}$$

Example 2. Let us assume the next sentences:

$$\text{Goal}_p \, \text{Mb} \tag{4}$$
$$\text{Int}_p(\text{Does}^P_h \, \text{Mb}) \tag{5}$$
$$\text{Bel}_h(\text{Int}_p(\text{Does}^P_h \, \text{Mb}) \tag{6}$$
$$\text{Does}^P_h \, \text{Mb} \tag{7}$$
$$\neg\text{Does}_p \, \text{Mb} \tag{8}$$
$$\text{Does}_h \, \mathcal{A} \rightarrow \text{Does}_h\text{Damage} \tag{9}$$

where Mb means "the helper h managed the principal p's blog". We can infer from 4, 5, and 6 that there is a relation of dependence between h and p with regard to Mb: Dep^P_h Mb. According to rule 2 above and premises 7, 8 and 9, this entails the following: Reflex^P_h Mb. According to schema 3, we can infer: ODoes_p Compensate. Notice that premise 7 implies, through schema (DDirDInt), that $\text{Does}_h \, \mathcal{A}$ holds, thus leading to $\text{Does}_h\text{Damage}$. In other words, reflex responsibility occurs when the action of h causes a damage, which in fact justifies the obligation to compensate derived via schema 3.

In turn, one possible definition for *negotiorum gestio* is the following:

$$\text{Ges}^P_h \, \mathcal{A} \equiv \text{Int}^P_h \, \mathcal{A} \wedge \text{Int}_p \, \mathcal{A} \wedge \neg\text{Able}_p \, \mathcal{A} \wedge \text{Does}^P_h \, \mathcal{A} \tag{10}$$

which means that the helper agent h has the intention of carrying out $\mathcal{A}$ by herself but in the interest of p, p intends to obtain $\mathcal{A}$ but she not able to do so, and h carries out $\mathcal{A}$ in the interest of p. Then we get a form of reflex responsibility in the next setting:

$$\text{Ges}^P_h \, \mathcal{A} \rightarrow (\text{O}^t_h \, \mathcal{A} \rightarrow \text{O}^t_p \, \mathcal{A}) \tag{10'}$$

meaning that if h is a *gestor* of p, if h becomes obliged to a third party t w.r.t. action $\mathcal{A}$, then p is obliged to t w.r.t. $\mathcal{A}$. (A.C.C. art. 2289), where t is the third party.

Example 3 (Negotiorum Gestio). First scenario (general rule of responsibility applicable to the *gestor*'s acts). John left home unexpectedly for some time, leaving the house unattended. Frank thinks keeping John's garden tidy will help John, so he cuts the garden's grass. John is unaware of this. One day, on cutting the grass, Frank hurts Jane's Chihuahua. The general rule of liability is applicable, independently of the *negotiorum gestio* relationship between John and Frank. Frank is liable.

Example 4 (Negotiorum Gestio). Second Scenario (principal attached to contracts entered by the *gestor*). John left home unexpectedly for some time, leaving his Chihuahua outside. Frank passes by and sees the dog sad, hungry and unattended in John's garden. Frank agrees with Jane, John's neighbour, that she will take care of John's Chihuahua while he is away. Although unaware of the agreement between Frank and Jane, John should return Jane the dog's expenses when he is back.

5   Discussion

The core at the notion of responsibility for the acts of others is reflex responsibility, which refers to complex relations between actions and intentions, and their results. In the versions presented here however, this notion does not remain abstract because the individual actions are not hidden. Reflex responsibility is not modeled as a primitive operator and its occurrence can be established by detecting more elementary components. A different approach is offered in [17], where a similar type of responsibility is represented by a suitable operator.

In some legal systems (e.g. Argentina), reflex responsibility of the principal with regard to the helper's performance may be inexcusable (i.e. *iuris et de iure*), that is, it cannot be avoided because of the principal's *absence of guilt*. To get rid of reflex responsibility, the principal must prove the lack of one of its requisites. Reflex responsibility, as in (3), belongs to the category of *accountability* responsibility [17] since the principal has a particular connection to the harm so that she may have to give an explanation (an account) of why the harm happened, and, of course, she may possibly be sued. According to [2], p is legally liable for the harmful event because all conditions for connecting the harm to p are realized: there is dependence, and the directed action connects p through d to the harmful act $Does^p_h \, \mathcal{A}$.

Clearly, (3) does not include cases of responsibility for the principal's own wrongdoing. However, notice that reflex responsibility as defined in (3) does not necessarily cover the category of *blameworthiness* responsibility [21,17], which refers to principals who failed to comply with moral or legal demands. In fact, and regarding occasional dependence, the principal intended that the action of the helper was performed, but she may not have anticipated the damaging effects of that action, or the anticipation of the possibility of such effect may have been an acceptable risk.

Reflex responsibility implies that $\mathcal{A}$ is the case. In the 'occasional dependence' part of (3) the principal p has contributed, in some way, to the fact that $\mathcal{A}$ is true, because there is a link between h's performance and h's intention and p's intention. (It is likely that h would not have brought about $\mathcal{A}$ is in case she had not been aware that p intended that: agent p made another agent or organization h do something—by no means of an obligation—which made p responsible for the fact.)

We cannot conceive a case where the principal is responsible but the dependent is not[3]. In particular we can obtain that, when the action of the helper does not cause any damage there is no reflex liability. Indeed, whenever $Does_h\mathcal{A}$ is true but $Does_h Damage$

---

[3] This simplifies the analysis of agentive responsibility of h, i.e., the causal link between $\mathcal{A}$ and the action of this agent. Interesting discussions on this issue can be found, e.g., in [14,15,16,17].

is false, then the antecedent of (2), too, is false, thus the antecedent of (3) cannot be realized. In other words, we get that $\neg(\text{Does}_h \text{ Damage}) \rightarrow \neg\text{Reflex}^P_h \, \mathcal{A}$.

A consequence of reflex responsibility in some legal systems is the helper's obligation to reimburse the principal of what she has given as a compensation to the third (damaged) agent: $(\text{Reflex}^P_h \, \mathcal{A} \wedge \text{Does}_p \text{ Compensate}) \rightarrow O^P(\text{Does}_h \text{ Reimburse})$.

The interesting basis of this reimbursement is the type of relation between principal and helper. Recall that if their relation is contractual the dependent's wrongdoing implies she has not fulfilled his obligations with regard to the principal, and the reimbursement is possibly pre-settled (for contractual electronic bindings, see e.g. [23,24]).

If the relationship is factual, then the basis of this reimbursement lays on the circumstance that the principal is an indirect victim of the helper's wrongdoing. This distinction between types of dependence relations is crucial for determining, e.g., the amount of the compensations. An interesting and high level of sophistication in the outline of the lawful support of a system can be achieved with the aid of the notion of reflex responsibility.

Example 5 (Reflex responsibility and trust deception). Paul lends to me his user name and password, so as I can use the wireless connection at his university, which I am visiting. I made wrong use of some contents, got a database damaged, and I— under Paul's user name—got blacklisted. He is reflexively responsible for my misuse. As a consequence of this, and given that I have violated the trust he put on me, Paul may radically change any intention regarding myself doing anything on his behalf: $\text{Reflex}^P_h \, \mathcal{A} \rightarrow \neg\text{Int}^P_h \, \mathcal{B}$.

6   Summary

This paper offered a logical analysis of two cases where legal responsibility emerges between a principal agent and a helper agent: (*a*) responsibility having its origin in occasional, non-contractual courtesy relations—also called *reflex responsibility*—and (*b*) responsibility in the *negotiorum gestio* doctrine. The current paper extends the research in [25] by (*i*) working out a more general definition of reflex responsibility, (*ii*) integrating the logical framework with two modal operators for agent's ability and for expressing objectively ideal states of affairs, and (*iii*) handling the case *negotiorum gestio*. Legal systems make persons responsible for damages caused by others also in different cases (e.g, when damages result from unintentional activities): how to generalize the current analysis to that is left to future research.

References

[1]   Chopra, S., White, L.: Artificial Agents – Personhood in Law and Philosophy. In: Proc. ECAI (2004)
[2]   Sartor, G., et al.: Framework for addressing the introduction of automated technologies in socio-technical systems, in particular with regard to legal liability. E.02.13-ALIAS-D1.1. EUI (2011)
[3]   Smith, C., Rotolo, A.: Collective trust and normative agents. Logic Journal of IGPL 18, 195–213 (2010)

[4]   Dunin-Keplicz, B., Verbrugge, R.: Collective intentions. Fundamenta Informaticae, 271–295 (2002)

[5]   Jones, A., Sergot, M.: A logical framework. In: Open Agent Societies (2007)

[6]   Elgesem, D.: The modal logic of agency. Nordic Journal of Philosophical Logic 2, 1–46 (1997)

[7]   Governatori, G., Rotolo, A.: On the Axiomatization of Elgesem's Logic of Agency and Ability. Journal of Philosophical Logic 34, 403–431 (2005)

[8]   Smith, C.: Principal and Helper: Notes on Reflex Responsibility in MAS. In: Proc. RDA2 (2012)

[9]   Broersen, J., Dignum, F.P.M., Dignum, V., Meyer, J.-J.C.: Designing a Deontic Logic of Deadlines. In: Lomuscio, A., Nute, D. (eds.) DEON 2004. LNCS (LNAI), vol. 3065, pp. 43–56. Springer, Heidelberg (2004)

[10] Smith, C., Rotolo, A., Sartor, G.: Representations of time within normative MAS. In: Proc. JURIX (2010)

[11] Herrestad, H., Krogh, C.: Obligations Directed from Bearers and Counterparties. In: Proc. ICAIL (1995)

[12] Smith, C., Ambrossio, A., Mendoza, L., Rotolo, A.: Combinations of normal and non-normal modal logics for modeling collective trust in normative MAS. In: Palmirani, M., Pagallo, U., Casanovas, P., Sartor, G. (eds.) AICOL WorkshopS 2011. LNCS (LNAI), vol. 7639, pp. 189–203. Springer, Heidelberg (2012)

[13] Sartor, G.: Legal Reasoning: A Cognitive Approach to the Law. Springer, Dordrecht (2005)

[14] Cholvy, L., Cuppens, F., Saurel, C.: Towards a Logical Formalization of Responsibility. In: Proc. ICAIL (1997)

[15] Sergot, M.J.: Action and Agency in Norm-Governed Multi-agent Systems. In: Artikis, A., O'Hare, G.M.P., Stathis, K., Vouros, G.A. (eds.) ESAW 2007. LNCS (LNAI), vol. 4995, pp. 1–54. Springer, Heidelberg (2008)

[16] Sergot, M.: Norms, action and agency in multi-agent systems. In: Governatori, G., Sartor, G. (eds.) DEON 2010. LNCS (LNAI), vol. 6181, p. 2. Springer, Heidelberg (2010)

[17] Ben Ghorbel-Talbi, M., Cuppens, F., Cuppens-Boulahia, N., Le Métayer, D., Piolle, G.: Delegation of Obligations and Responsibility. In: Camenisch, J., Fischer-Hübner, S., Murayama, Y., Portmann, A., Rieder, C. (eds.) SEC 2011. IFIP AICT, vol. 354, pp. 197–209. Springer, Heidelberg (2011)

[18] Grossi, D., Jones, A.: Constitutive Norms and Counts-as Conditionals. In: Handbook of Deontic Logic and Normative Systems. College Publications (2013)

[19] Fajardo, R., Finger, M.: Non-normal modalisation. In: Proc. AiML (2002)

[20] Fagin, R., Halpern, J.Y., Moses, Y., Vardi, M.Y.: Reasoning about Knowledge. MIT Press (1995)

[21] Hart, H.L.A.: Punishment and Responsibility. Oxford University Press (1968)

[22] Gabbay, D.: Fibring Logics. Oxford University Press (1999)

[23] Weitzenböck, E.M.: Good faith and fair dealing in contracts formed and performed by electronic agents. Artificial Intelligence and Law 12, 83–110 (2004)

[24] Sartor, G.: Cognitive automata and the law: electronic contracting and the intentionality of software agents. Artificial Intelligence and Law 17, 253–290 (2009)

[25] Smith, C., Rotolo, A., Sartor, G.: Reflex Responsibility of Agents. In: Proc. JURIX (2013)

[26] Giliker, P.: Liability in Tort Law. A Comparative Perspective. In: CUP (2010)

[27] Lorenzen, E.G.: Negotiorum Gestio. In: Roman and Modern Civil Law. Faculty Scholarship Series. Paper 4576 (1928),
      http://digitalcommons.law.yale.edu/fss_papers/4576

Author Index